# ACCOUNTING PRINCIPLES

## THIRD CANADIAN EDITION

# ACCOUNTING PRINCIPLES

▶ **JERRY J. WEYGANDT** *Ph.D., C.P.A.*

Arthur Andersen Alumni Professor of Accounting
University of Wisconsin—Madison

▶ **DONALD E. KIESO** *Ph.D., C.P.A.*

KPMG Emeritus Professor of Accountancy
Northern Illinois University

▶ **PAUL D. KIMMEL** *Ph.D., C.P.A.*

University of Wisconsin—Milwaukee

▶ **BARBARA TRENHOLM** *M.B.A., F.C.A.*

University of New Brunswick—Fredericton

**John Wiley & Sons Canada, Ltd.**

# To our students — past, present, and future

## National Library of Canadian Cataloguing in Publication Data

Jerry J. Weygandt
    Accounting principles

3rd Canadian ed.

Includes index.
ISBN 0-470-83375-0 (pt. 1)

    1. Accounting.  I. Weygandt, Jerry J

HF5635.A3778  2003      657'.044      C2003-905260-5

## Production Credits

Publisher:  John Horne
Publishing Services Director:  Karen Bryan
Editorial Manager:  Karen Staudinger
Developmental Editor: Zoë Craig
Senior Marketing Manager:  Janine Daoust
Manager, Business and Online Marketing: Carolyn J. Wells
New Media Editor: Elsa Passera
Editorial Assistant: Gail Brown
Design & Typesetting:  Appleby Color Lab
Cover Design:  Interrobang Graphic Design
CD Design & Programming: Ian Koo/Tia Seifert
Printing & Binding:  Tri-Graphic Printing Limited

Printed and bound in Canada
10 9 8 7 6 5 4 3 2 1

John Wiley & Sons Canada, Ltd.
22 Worcester Road
Etobicoke, Ontario  M9W 1L1
Visit our website at: www.wiley.com/canada

# Second Canadian Edition

**Barbara Trenholm, MBA, FCA,** is a professor of accounting at the University of New Brunswick. Her teaching and educational leadership is renowned. She is a recipient of the National Post/Pricewaterhouse Coopers Leaders in Management Education Award, the Global Teaching Excellence Award, and the University of New Brunswick's Merit Award and Dr. Allan P. Stuart Award for Excellence in Teaching. A recent edition of the *Maclean's Guide to Canadian Universities and Colleges* named her as one of the University of New Brunswick's most popular professors. In 2003, she was named a Teaching Fellow of the University of New Brunswick.

Her experience and involvement in professional accounting education is widely recognized throughout Canada. She is a past-president of the New Brunswick Institute of Chartered Accountants. She has served as chair of the Canadian Institute of Chartered Accountants Academic Research Committee, Interprovincial Education Committee, and Canadian Institute of Chartered Accountants/Canadian Academic Accounting Association Liaison Committee. She has served as a member of the Canadian Institute of Chartered Accountants Qualification Committee, International Qualifications Appraisal Board, Education Reeingineering Task Force, and the American Accounting Association's Globalization Initiatives Task Force. She has chaired and been a member of numerous other education committees at both the national and provincial levels of the profession.

Professor Trenholm is a member of the boards of many organizations, including Atomic Energy of Canada and the Canadian Institute of Chartered Accountants. She is co-chair of the University of New Brunswick Pension Board of Trustees. She has also served as a member of the Atlantic School of Chartered Accountancy Board of Governors.

In addition to her involvement with her profession, she has an extensive record of service in leadership roles in the university and community. She has served as acting dean of the Faculty of Administration and as a member of the University Senate, in addition to chairing and serving on many university and faculty committees.

She has published widely in the field of accounting standard-setting and explored various director and auditor liability issues in journals including *Accounting Horizons, International Journal of Production Economics, CAmagazine, CGA Magazine*, and *CMA Magazine*. She is on the editorial board of the *Journal of Academy of Business Administration* and on the board of reviewers for the *Journal of Business Education*. She is also the Canadian author of the Kimmel, Weygandt, Kieso, Trenholm, *Financial Accounting: Tools for Business Decision Making*, published by John Wiley & Sons Canada, Ltd.

## About The Collaborator

The end-of-chapter material was prepared in collaboration with Valerie Kinnear of Mount Royal College. Both the text and the end-of-chapter material have benefited significantly from Valerie's insights and perspective. Her contributions were exceptional and are gratefully acknowledged.

**Valerie A. Kinnear, BSW, MSc (Bus. Admin.), CA** is an instructor of accounting at the Bissett School of Business, Mount Royal College, in Calgary, Alberta. She has public accounting experience with PricewaterhouseCoopers, Farvolden and Company, and Kinnear & Smistad, where she was a partner in her own public practice.

Valerie has a wide range of teaching experience, both at the College and in the Faculty of Management at the University of Calgary where she taught prior to joining Mount Royal College in 1989. She has taught introductory, intermediate, and advanced financial accounting as well as introductory management accounting and finance courses. She has been nominated for the Distinguished Faculty Award at Mount Royal College for her teaching expertise.

Valerie has served on numerous faculty and college committees and held a variety of administrative positions at Mount Royal College, including acting dean of the School of Business, acting director of Business Education and Training in the Faculty of Continuing Education and Extension, and chair of the Accounting and Insurance programs, amongst others.

She has also been active in professional accounting education. She has participated in the Institute of Chartered Accountants of Alberta student education program in a variety of roles, including as an instructor, marker, author, and member of the Institute's Examinations Committee. Valerie has also served as a member of the Professional Services Policy Board of the Canadian Institute of Chartered Accountants and has served as treasurer for many volunteer community organizations in Calgary.

# U.S. Edition

**Jerry J. Weygandt, PhD, CPA**, is the Arthur Andersen Alumni Professor of Accounting at the University of Wisconsin—Madison. He holds a PhD in accounting from the University of Illinois. Articles by Professor Weygandt have appeared in *Accounting Review*, *Journal of Accounting Research*, *Accounting Horizons*, *Journal of Accountancy*, and other academic and professional journals. These articles have examined such financial reporting issues as accounting for price-level adjustments, pensions, convertible securities, stock option contracts, and interim reports. Professor Weygandt is the author of other accounting and financial reporting books and is a member of the American Accounting Association, the American Institute of Certified Public Accountants, and the Wisconsin Society of Certified Public Accountants. He has served on numerous committees of the American Accounting Association and as a member of the editorial board of *Accounting Review*; he also has served as President and Secretary-Treasurer of the American Accounting Association. In addition, he has been actively involved with the American Institute of Certified Public Accountants and has been a member of the Accounting Standards Executive Committee (AcSEC) of that organization. He has served on the FASB task force that examined the reporting issues related to accounting for income taxes and is presently a trustee of the Financial Accounting Foundation. Professor Weygandt has received the Chancellor's Award for Excellence in Teaching and the Beta Gamma Sigma Dean's Teaching Award. He is on the board of directors of M&I Bank of Southern Wisconsin and the Dean Foundation. He is the recipient of the Wisconsin Institute of CPA's Outstanding Educator's Award and the Lifetime Achievement Award. In 2001 he received the American Accounting Association's Outstanding Accounting Educator Award.

**Donald E. Kieso, PhD, CPA**, received his bachelor's degree from Aurora University and his doctorate in accounting from the University of Illinois. He has served as chairman of the Department of Accountancy and is currently the KPMG Emeritus Professor of Accounting at Northern Illinois University. He has public accounting experience with Price Waterhouse & Co. (San Francisco and Chicago) and Arthur Andersen & Co. (Chicago) and research experience with the Research Division of the American Institute of Certified Public Accountants (New York). He has done post-doctoral work as a Visiting Scholar at the University of California at Berkeley and is a recipient of NIU's Teaching Excellence Award and four Golden Apple Teaching Awards. Professor Kieso is the author of other accounting and business books and is a member of the American Accounting Association, the American Institute of Certified Public Accountants, and the Illinois CPA Society. He has served as a member of the Board of Directors of the Illinois CPA Society, the AACSB's Accounting Accreditation Committees, the State of Illinois Comptroller's Commission, as Secretary-Treasurer of the Federation of Schools of Accountancy, and as Secretary-Treasurer of the American Accounting Association. Professor Kieso is currently serving on the Board of Trustees and Executive Committee of Aurora University, as a member of the Board of Directors of Castle Banc-Group Inc., and as Treasurer and Director of Valley West Community Hospital. He served as a charter member of the national Accounting Education Change Commission. He is the recipient of the Outstanding Accounting Educator Award from the Illinois CPA Society, the FSA's Joseph A. Silvoso Award of Merit, the NIU Foundation's Humanitarian Award for Service to Higher Education, the Distinguished Service Award from the Illinois CPA Society, and the Community Citizen of the Year Award from Rotary International.

**Paul D. Kimmel, PhD, CPA**, received his bachelor's degree from the University of Minnesota and his doctorate in accounting from the University of Wisconsin. He is an Associate Professor at the University of Wisconsin—Milwaukee, and has public accounting experience with Deloitte & Touche (Minneapolis). He was the recipient of the UWM School of Business Advisory Council Teaching Award and the Reggie Taite Excellence in Teaching Award, and is a three-time winner of the Outstanding Teaching Assistant Award at the University of Wisconsin. He is also a recipient of the Elijah Watts Sells Award for Honorary Distinction for his results on the CPA exam. He is a member of the American Accounting Association and has published articles in *Accounting Review*, *Accounting Horizons*, *Advances in Management Accounting*, *Managerial Finance*, *Issues in Accounting Education*, and *Journal of Accounting Education*, as well as other journals. His research interests include accounting for financial instruments and innovation in accounting education. He has published papers and given numerous talks on incorporating critical thinking into accounting education, and helped prepare a catalogue of critical thinking resources for the Federated Schools of Accountancy.

# Student letter to students

Student,

I am a student of accounting who had no previous background in the subject before my studies began. I believe that whether you are pursuing degree or diploma studies, planning to be a professional accountant, or using the concepts on a personal level, you will discover that a basic knowledge of accounting is vital.

At the end of your studies, using this text, *Accounting Principles*, you will have gained a strong understanding of the fundamentals of accounting and a good foundation for all your remaining accounting and/or business courses. I also used the *Study Guide* that accompanies this text since English is my second language and I found the summaries and extra practice useful. Here are some successful tips I used which should be helpful to you:

- Take time to **read the chapter before class** to get a general understanding of the concepts and procedures being introduced.
- Make use of the textbook study aids. The list of **Study Objectives** and **Chapter Preview** will help you understand what the chapter is all about. The **Before You Go On** exercises will tell you whether you have understood the material in each section. The **Accounting Equation Analyses** beside each journal entry will help you understand the impact of the transaction. The **Glossary** will introduce to new accounting terms. The **Demonstration Problem** will help you to understand the core requirement of a problem and how it is solved. The **Navigator** provides a useful checklist to make sure you haven't missed anything important. The **Interactive Student Navigator CD** that comes with the textbook offers additional practice opportunities and tutorial assistance.
- **Do your homework!!** This is the time to pick up on the relevant information and practise what you have learned.
- **Read Accounting in Action.** These will give you a good understanding of how accounting is used in the "real world".
- **Stay current.** Each lesson in accounting builds on the previous lesson. If you fall behind you will have difficulty in grasping new lessons. **Avoid the struggle.** Stay on top of your homework and reading.

I have had a successful introduction to accounting. Energetic professors facilitated my experience, but I had to do the work myself. I hope your experience will be as successful as mine as together we pursue further accounting studies.

A.Kajidi,
Centennial College

# How to use the study aids in this book

**Concepts for Review**, listed at the beginning of each chapter, are the accounting concepts you learned in previous chapters that you will need to know in order to understand the topics you are about to cover. Page references are provided if you need to review before reading the chapter.

The **Feature Story** helps you picture how the chapter topic relates to the real world of accounting and business. Throughout the chapter, references to the Feature Story will help you put new ideas in context, organize them, and remember them.

chapter | 2

## concepts for review >>

Before studying this chapter, you should understand or, if necessary, review:
a. Why assets equal liabilities plus owner's equity. (Ch. 1, p. 10)
b. What assets, liabilities, owner's capital, drawings, revenues, and expenses are. (Ch. 1, pp. 10–12)
c. What transactions are, and how they affect the basic accounting equation. (Ch. 1, pp. 13–18)

### A Taste for Business

BURNABY, BC—Who can resist the aroma of fresh-baked cookies? Ask anyone in line at the Sweet Factory/Monsieur Félix and Mr. Norton store at the Metrotown Shopping Centre and chances are they'll tell you it's easier said than done.

Store owner Pak Chuen Chan bought his first Sweet Factory franchise in 1996, selling bulk candy, chocolate, and other treats. He later opened a second outlet in the same mall and combined it with a counter selling Félix and Norton cookies—a Montreal-based gourmet cookie line that

*Felix and Norton: www.felixandnorton.com*

...remises," he says. ...people in the two ...ore alone, where ...sales.

...success depends ...ich are the right ...ess also depends

...he end of every ...eport from each ...—that shows net ...ber of customers. ... time sheets, plus ...ry and store sup- ...es, rent, utilities, ...ver to my accoun-

...tant, who takes care of everything else for me," he explains.

"Everything else" includes recording transactions, looking after payroll, filing sales tax reports, and preparing financial statements, in this case all done using Simply Accounting software. That's a lot to do when you've got two stores to run and cookies to bake—and why Mr. Chan leaves most of the work to an accounting professional.

What does he like best about his business? Mr. Chan says he enjoys talking to the people from all walks of life who come into his stores. And of course, he confesses to having a bit of a sweet tooth himself. "After all," he says, "it's important to enjoy your job!"

## the navigator

- Understand *Concepts for Review*
- Read *Feature Story*
- Scan *Study Objectives*
- Read *Chapter Preview*
- Read text and answer *Before You Go On*
- Work *Demonstration Problem*
- Review *Summary of Study Objectives*
- Answer *Self-Study Questions*
- Complete assignments

chapter | 2

chapter 2

## The Recording Process

## study objectives >>

After studying this chapter, you should be able to:
1. Explain what an account is and how it helps in the recording process.
2. Define debits and credits and illustrate how they are used to record business transactions.
3. Describe the basic steps in the recording process.
4. Explain what a journal is and how it helps in the recording process, and journalize business transactions.
5. Explain what a ledger is and how it helps in the recording process.
6. Explain what posting is and how it helps in the recording process.
7. Explain the purpose of a trial balance, and prepare one.

49

**The Navigator** is a learning system designed to help guide you through each chapter and help you succeed in learning the material. It consists of (1) a checklist at the beginning of each chapter, which outlines text features and study skills you will need, and (2) a series of check boxes that prompts you to use the learning aids in the chapter and set priorities as you study.

**Study Objectives** at the beginning of each chapter provide you with a framework for learning the specific concepts and procedures covered in the chapter. Each study objective reappears at the point within the chapter where the concept is discussed. You can review all the study objectives in the **Summary** at the end of the chapter.

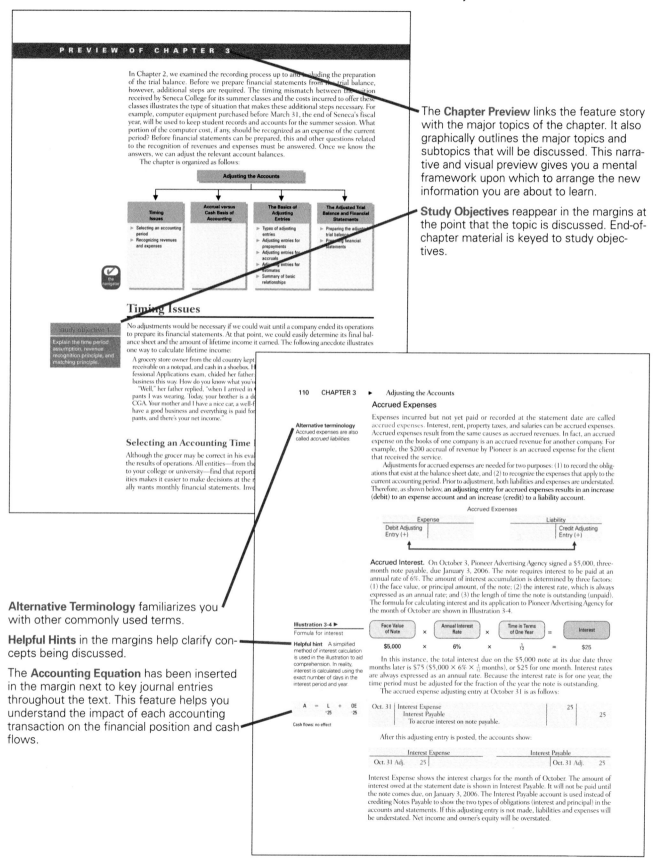

The **Chapter Preview** links the feature story with the major topics of the chapter. It also graphically outlines the major topics and subtopics that will be discussed. This narrative and visual preview gives you a mental framework upon which to arrange the new information you are about to learn.

**Study Objectives** reappear in the margins at the point that the topic is discussed. End-of-chapter material is keyed to study objectives.

**Alternative Terminology** familiarizes you with other commonly used terms.

**Helpful Hints** in the margins help clarify concepts being discussed.

The **Accounting Equation** has been inserted in the margin next to key journal entries throughout the text. This feature helps you understand the impact of each accounting transaction on the financial position and cash flows.

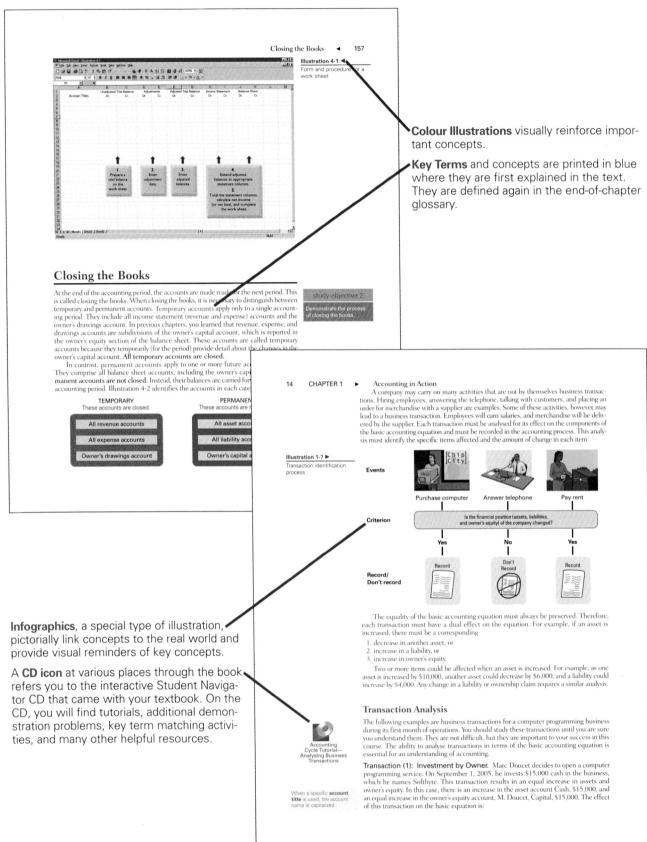

**Colour Illustrations** visually reinforce important concepts.

**Key Terms** and concepts are printed in blue where they are first explained in the text. They are defined again in the end-of-chapter glossary.

**Infographics**, a special type of illustration, pictorially link concepts to the real world and provide visual reminders of key concepts.

A **CD icon** at various places through the book refers you to the interactive Student Navigator CD that came with your textbook. On the CD, you will find tutorials, additional demonstration problems, key term matching activities, and many other helpful resources.

**Before You Go On** sections follow each key topic. *Review It* questions prompt you to stop and review the key points you have just studied. If you cannot answer these questions, you should go back and read the section again.

*Review It* questions about The Forzani Group ask you to find information in Forzani's financial statements, which are featured in Appendix A at the end of the text.

Brief *Do It* exercises ask you to put your newly acquired knowledge to work. They outline an *Action Plan* necessary to complete the exercise, and the accompanying *Solution* helps you see how the problem should be solved. (The Before You Go On section is keyed to similar brief exercises and exercises.)

---

290   CHAPTER 6   ►   Inventory Costing

Whichever cost flow assumption is chosen by a company, it should be used from one period to the next. Consistency makes financial statements comparable over successive time periods. Using FIFO in one year and average cost in the next year would make it difficult to compare the net incomes for the two years.

Although consistency is preferred, a company may change its cost flow assumption. Such a change and its effects on net income should be disclosed in the financial statements. This conforms with the full disclosure principle, which requires all relevant information to be disclosed. The full disclosure principle is discussed further in Chapter 11.

**BEFORE YOU GO ON . . .**

**► Review It**

1. How do the cost, matching, and full disclosure principles apply to inventory costs?
2. How are the three cost flow assumptions applied in allocating cost of goods available for sale?
3. Which inventory cost flow assumption produces the highest net income in a period of rising prices? The highest balance sheet valuation? The highest cash flow?
4. What factors should be considered by management when choosing an inventory cost flow assumption?
5. Which inventory cost flow assumption does The Forzani Group Ltd. use? The answer to this question is provided at the end of this chapter.

**► Do It**

The accounting records of the Cookie Cutters Company show the following data:

|  |  |
|---|---|
| Beginning inventory | 4,000 units at $3 |
| Purchases | 6,000 units at $4 |
| Sales | 8,000 units at $8 |

Determine the cost of goods sold and ending inventory under a periodic inventory system using (a) FIFO, (b) average cost, and (c) LIFO.

**Action Plan**

- Ignore selling price in allocating cost.
- Allocate costs between goods sold and goods on hand for each cost flow assumption.
- For FIFO, allocate the earliest costs to the goods sold and the latest costs to the goods on hand.
- For average cost, determine the weighted average unit cost (cost of goods available for sale ÷ number of units available for sale). Multiply this cost by the number of units sold and the number of units on hand.
- For LIFO, allocate the latest costs to the goods sold and the earliest costs to the goods on hand.
- Prove your work: cost of goods sold + ending inventory = cost of goods available for sale.

**Solution**

(a) Ending inventory = 4,000 + 6,000 − 8,000 = 2,000 units
   FIFO cost of goods sold: (4,000 × $3) + (4,000 × $4) = $28,000
   FIFO ending inventory: 2,000 × $4 = $8,000
   Proof: $28,000 + $8,000 = $36,000
(b) Weighted average unit cost: [(4,000 × $3) + (6,000 × $4)] ÷ 10,000 = $3.60
   Average cost of goods sold: 8,000 × $3.60 = $28,800
   Average ending inventory: 2,000 × $3.60 = $7,200
   Proof: $28,800 + $7,200 = $36,000
(c) LIFO cost of goods sold: (6,000 × $4) + (2,000 × $3) = $30,000
   LIFO ending inventory: 2,000 × $3 = $6,000
   Proof: $30,000 + $6,000 = $36,000

the navigator

*Related exercise material:* BE6–3, BE6–4, BE6–5, BE6–6, E6–3, E6–4, E6–5, and E6–6.

---

### Taking a Physical Inventory

You will recall from Chapter 5 that merchandisers account for their inventory by using either a perpetual or a periodic inventory system. In a **perpetual system**, the accounting records continuously—perpetually—show the quantity that should be on hand. A physical count is done at some point in the accuracy of the accounting records. The College of the North Atlantic Drive Campus Bookstore, described in the feature story, takes a physical a year to be sure that the actual quantities on hand agree with the accounting records.

In a **periodic inventory system**, inventory quantities are not maintained on a continuous basis. Instead they are determined at the end of each reporting ical count. Whether inventory quantities are maintained by the perpetual inventory system, a physical inventory count is necessary to determine the or to confirm their accuracy.

Taking a physical inventory involves actually counting, weighing, or measuring each kind of inventory on hand. Taking an inventory can be a formidable task for many companies, especially if they have thousands of inventory items, like the Prince Philip Drive Campus Bookstore. An inventory count is generally more accurate when goods are not being sold or received during the counting. This is why companies often count their inventory when the business is closed or when business is slow.

To minimize errors in taking the inventory, a company should ensure that it has a good system of internal control in place. **Internal control** consists of policies and procedures to optimize resources, prevent and detect errors, safeguard assets, and enhance the accuracy and reliability of accounting records. Some internal control procedures for counting inventory include the following:

1. The counting should be done by employees who do not have custodial or record-keeping responsibility for the inventory.
2. Each counter should establish the authenticity of each inventory item. For example, does each box contain a television set? Does each storage tank contain gasoline?
3. There should be a second count by another employee or auditor. Counting should take place in teams of two.
4. Prenumbered inventory tags should be used. All inventory tags should be accounted for.
5. At the end of the count, a designated supervisor should check that all inventory items are tagged and that no items have more than one tag.

We will learn more about internal controls in Chapter 7.

After the physical inventory is taken, the quantity of each kind of inventory is listed on inventory summary sheets. To ensure accuracy, the listing should be verified by a second employee, or auditor.

Unit costs are then applied to the quantities in order to determine the total cost of the inventory—this will be explained later in the chapter. To estimate the cost of inventory when a physical count cannot be taken (if the inventory is destroyed, for example, or when it is inconvenient (during interim periods), estimating methods are applied. These methods (the gross profit and retail inventory methods) are discussed in Appendix 6B.

**ACCOUNTING IN ACTION ► Ethics Insight**

Over the years, inventory has played a role in many fraud cases. A classic one involved salad oil. Management filled storage tanks mostly with water, and since oil rises to the top, the auditors thought the tanks were full of oil. In this instance, management also said the company had more tanks than it really did—numbers were repainted on the tanks to confuse the auditors.

In recent years, the management of women's apparel maker The Leslie Fay Company was convicted of falsifying inventory records to boost net earnings and management bonuses. In another case, Frost Fence was forced into bankruptcy after it was discovered that $17 million in inventory was on the company's books but not in its storage yard.

**Accounting in Action** boxes give you more glimpses into the real world of accounting by discussing actual challenges faced by accountants. Each type of issue—business, **e**-business, international or ethics—is identified by its own icon.

**Ethics Notes** help sensitize you to the real-world ethical dilemmas of accounting.

**PIONEER ADVERTISING AGENCY**
**Trial Balance**
**October 31, 2005**

|  | Debit | Credit |
|---|---|---|
| Cash | $15,200 | |
| Accounts receivable | 0 | |
| Advertising supplies | 2,500 | |
| Prepaid insurance | 600 | |
| Office equipment | 5,000 | |
| Notes payable | | $ 5,000 |
| Accounts payable | | 2,500 |
| Unearned revenue | | 1,200 |
| C. R. Byrd, capital | | 10,000 |
| C. R. Byrd, drawings | 500 | |
| Service revenue | | 10,000 |
| Salaries expense | 4,000 | |
| Rent expense | 900 | |
| Totals | $28,700 | $28,700 |

Note that the total debits of $28,700 equal the total credits of $28,700. Accounts with zero balances, such as Accounts Receivable, are often omitted from the trial balance. Account numbers are sometimes shown to the left of the account titles in the trial balance.

### Limitations of a Trial Balance

Although a trial balance reveals many types of errors which can be made in the book-keeping process, **a trial balance does not prove that all transactions have been recorded or that the ledger is correct.** Many errors may exist even though the trial balance columns agree. For example, the trial balance may balance in the following cases: (1) a transaction is not journalized, (2) a correct journal entry is not posted, (3) a journal entry is posted twice, (4) incorrect accounts are used in journalizing or posting, or (5) offsetting errors are made in recording the amount of a transaction. In other words, as long as equal debits and credits are posted, even to the wrong account or in the wrong amount, the total debits will equal the total credits when the trial balance is prepared.

### Locating Errors

**▶ Ethics note**

Auditors see errors and irregularities differently when evaluating the accounting system. An error is the result of an unintentional mistake. As such, it is neither ethical nor unethical. An irregularity, on the other hand, is an intentional misstatement, which is generally viewed as unethical.

The procedure for preparing a trial balance is relatively simple. However, if the trial balance does not balance, locating an error in a manual accounting system can be time-consuming, tedious, and frustrating. Errors generally result from mathematical mistakes, incorrect postings, or simply transcribing data incorrectly. Errors in a computerized system usually involve the initial recording rather than some software error in the posting or preparation of a trial balance.

What do you do if you are faced with a manual trial balance that does not balance? First determine the amount of the difference between the two columns of the trial balance. After this amount is known, the following steps are often helpful:
1. If the error is an amount such as $1, $100, or $1,000, re-add the trial balance columns. Recalculate the account balances.
2. If the error is divisible by two, scan the trial balance to see if a balance equal to half the error has been entered in the wrong column.

fashion. On the other hand, low inventory lev[...] disgruntled customers.

Inventory is a significant component of th[...] introduced in Chapter 4. In Chapter 5, we i[...] helps determine the profitability of the cost of [...] liquidity ratio that is commonly used to evalua[...] ratio. We also present a related measure, the a[...]

### Inventory Turnover

The inventory turnover ratio measures the [...] sold during the period. It is calculated by dividi[...]

Whenever a ratio compares a balance sheet [...] ment figure (e.g., cost of goods sold), the balan[...] balance sheet figures are determined by adding beginning and ending balances together and dividing by two. Averages are used to ensure that the balance sheet figures (which represent end-of-period amounts) cover the same period of time as the income statement figures (which represent amounts for the entire period). Illustration 6-12 shows the formula for calculating the inventory turnover ratio for The Forzani Group for fiscal 2003 (dollar amounts in thousands).

**Illustration 6-12 ▶**
Inventory turnover

$$\$603,326 \div \frac{\$268,519 + \$229,270}{2} = 2.4 \text{ times}$$

Generally, the greater the number of times per year the inventory turns over, the more efficiently sales are being made.

### Days Sales in Inventory

It is informative to convert the inventory turnover ratio into a period of time, describing the age of the inventory. This ratio, called days sales in inventory, is calculated by dividing 365 days by the inventory turnover, as in Illustration 6-13.

**Illustration 6-13 ▶**
Days sales in inventory

| Days in year | ÷ | Inventory turnover | = | Days sales in inventory |
|---|---|---|---|---|
| 365 days | ÷ | 2.4 | = | 152 days |

This means that Forzani's inventory, on average, is in stock for 152 days. One has to be careful in interpreting this ratio: it should be compared to the company's ratio in prior years, and to the industry average. However, you must recognize that this average will differ for each type of inventory item (e.g., sneakers vs. bicycles). What we see here is a total average only.

### BEFORE YOU GO ON . . .

**▶ Review It**

1. When is it appropriate to report inventory at the lower of cost and market?
2. What inventory information should be disclosed in the financial statements?
3. How can you tell if a company has too much or too little inventory on hand?

*Related exercise material:* BE6–9, BE6–10, BE6–11, E6–9, and E6–10.

One technique for determining the meaning of the information on financial statements is **ratio analysis**. Throughout this text, you will analyse key financial ratios using data from Forzani's financial statements. Chapter 18 addresses the topic of financial analysis in detail.

ing illustration. Note that except for land (which has an unlimited useful life), all other property, plant, and equipment items are amortized. This includes leasehold improvements, which are long-lived additions or renovations made to leased property.

**Illustration 4-9 ◀**
Property, plant, and equipment section

### LA SENZA CORPORATION
### Notes to the Financial Statements (partial)
### February 1, 2003
### (in thousands)

**6. Fixed assets**

| | Cost | Accumulated Amortization | Net Carrying Amount |
|---|---|---|---|
| Land | $ 1,307 | $ — | $ 1,307 |
| Building | 4,540 | 885 | 3,655 |
| Furniture and fixtures | 23,267 | 13,536 | 9,731 |
| Furniture and fixtures under capital lease | 7,468 | 1,649 | 5,819 |
| Leasehold improvements | 69,157 | 44,414 | 24,743 |
| Leasehold improvements under capital lease | 32,327 | 7,829 | 24,498 |
| Computer equipment | 15,308 | 7,648 | 7,660 |
| Computer equipment under capital lease | 935 | 60 | 875 |
| | $154,309 | $76,021 | $78,288 |

### Intangible Assets

Intangible assets are noncurrent resources that do not have physical substance. They include goodwill, patents, copyrights, trademarks, trade names, and licences that give the company exclusive right of use. Similar to buildings and equipment, intangible assets with estimated useful lives are amortized. Similar to land, intangible assets with indefinite lives are not amortized.

Illustration 4-10 shows how Shaw Communications reported intangible assets in its balance sheet. All of Shaw Communications' intangible assets have indefinite lives so no amortization was deducted from these.

**Illustration 4-10 ◀**
Intangible assets section

### SHAW COMMUNICATIONS INC.
### Balance Sheet (partial)
### August 31, 2002
### (in thousands)

| | |
|---|---|
| | $4,877,256 |
| | 145,865 |
| | 5,023,121 |

liabilities and owner's equity section of the balance that are expected to be paid within the coming the creation of other current liabilities. Current lia payable, salaries payable, interest payable, sales of long-term liabilities (payments to be made within

---

**Financial statements** appear throughout the book. Those from real companies are often identified by a logo. Numbers or categories are frequently highlighted in coloured type to draw your attention to key information.

---

**Additional Demonstration Problems**

## Demonstration Problem

Nge Aung opened the Campus Laundromat on September 1, 2005. During the first month of operations, the following transactions occurred:

Sept. 1 Invested $20,000 cash in the business.
2 Paid $1,000 cash for store rent for the month of September.
3 Purchased washers and dryers for $25,000, paying $10,000 in cash and signing a $15,000, six-month, 5% note payable.
6 Paid $1,200 for a one-year insurance policy.
10 Received bill from *The Daily News* for advertising the opening of the laundromat, $200.
20 Withdrew $700 cash for personal use.
30 Cash receipts for laundry services performed for the month were $6,200.
30 Laundry services performed on account for a nearby restaurant totalled $500. The account is due on October 25.

The chart of accounts for the company is the same as the one for Pioneer Advertising Agency in Illustration 2-7 except for the following: No. 153 Laundry Equipment and No. 610 Advertising Expense.

*Instructions*

(a) Journalize the September transactions.
(b) Open ledger accounts and post the September transactions.
(c) Prepare a trial balance at September 30, 2005.
(d) Prepare an income statement, statement of owner's equity, and balance sheet for Campus Laundromat.

*Solution to Demonstration Problem*

(a)

| | GENERAL JOURNAL | | | J1 |
|---|---|---|---|---|
| Date | Account Titles and Explanation | Ref. | Debit | Credit |
| 2005 | | | | |
| Sept. 1 | Cash | 101 | 20,000 | |
| | Nge Aung, Capital | 301 | | 20,000 |
| | Invested cash in business. | | | |
| 2 | Rent Expense | 729 | 1,000 | |
| | Cash | 101 | | 1,000 |
| | Paid September rent. | | | |
| 3 | Laundry Equipment | 153 | 25,000 | |
| | Cash | 101 | | 10,000 |
| | Notes Payable | 200 | | 15,000 |
| | Purchased laundry equipment for cash and 6-month, 5% note payable. | | | |
| 6 | Prepaid Insurance | 130 | 1,200 | |
| | Cash | 101 | | 1,200 |
| | Paid one-year insurance policy. | | | |
| 10 | Advertising Expense | 610 | 200 | |
| | Accounts Payable | 201 | | 200 |
| | Received bill from *The Daily News* for advertising. | | | |
| 20 | Nge Aung, Drawings | 306 | 700 | |
| | Cash | 101 | | 700 |
| | Withdrew cash for personal use. | | | |
| 30 | Cash | 101 | 6,200 | |
| | Service Revenue | 400 | | 6,200 |
| | Received cash for laundry services. | | | |
| 30 | Accounts Receivable | 112 | 500 | |
| | Service Revenue | 400 | | 500 |
| | Performed laundry services on account. | | | |

**Action Plan**
- Separate journal entries are made for each transaction.
- In journalizing, make sure debits equal credits.
- In journalizing, use specific account titles taken from the chart of accounts.
- Provide an appropriate description of each journal entry.
- Arrange the ledger in statement order, beginning with the balance sheet accounts.
- Post in chronological order.
- Numbers in the reference column indicate the amount has been posted.
- The trial balance lists accounts in the order in which they appear in the ledger.
- Debit balances are listed in the left column of the trial balance, credit balances in the right column.

---

**Demonstration Problems** review the chapter material. These sample problems provide you with *Action Plans* that list the strategies needed to solve the problem and *Solutions*. The *CD icon* tells you there are additional demonstration problems you can work through on the Student Navigator CD that came with your textbook.

76    CHAPTER 2    ►    The Recording Process

## Summary of Study Objectives

1. *Explain what an account is and how it helps in the recording process.* An account is an individual accounting record of increases and decreases in a specific asset, liability, or owner's equity item.

2. *Define debits and credits and illustrate how they are used to record business transactions.* Assets, drawings, and expenses are increased by debits (left-hand side of the account) and decreased by credits (right-hand side of the account). Liabilities, owner's capital, and revenues are increased by credits (right-hand side of the account) and decreased by debits (left-hand side of the account).

3. *Describe the basic steps in the recording process.* The basic steps in the recording process are as follows: (a) analyse each transaction in terms of its effect on the accounts, (b) enter the transaction information in a journal, and (c) transfer the journal information to the appropriate accounts in the ledger.

4. *Explain what a journal is and how it helps in the recording process, and journalize business transactions.* The first accounting record of a transaction is entered in a journal, and the data are later transferred to the general ledger. A journal (a) discloses in one place the complete

effect of a transaction, (b) provides a chronological record of transactions, (c) prevents and helps locate errors because the debit and credit amounts for each entry can be easily compared, and (d) provides an explanation of the transaction and reference to the source document, where applicable.

5. *Explain what a ledger is and how it helps in the recording process.* The entire group of accounts maintained by a company is called the ledger. The ledger keeps in one place all the information about changes in each of the specific account balances.

6. *Explain what posting is and how it helps in the recording process.* Posting is the procedure of transferring journal entries to the ledger accounts. This phase of the recording process accumulates the effects of journalized transactions in the individual accounts.

7. *Explain the purpose of a trial balance, and prepare one.* A trial balance is a list of accounts and their balances at a specific time. Its primary purpose is to prove the equality of debits and credits after posting. A trial balance also uncovers certain types of errors in journalizing and posting, and is useful in preparing financial statements.

## Glossary

 Key Term Matching Activity

**Account** A record of increases and decreases in a specific asset, liability, or owner's equity item. (p. 50)

**Chart of accounts** A list of accounts and the account numbers which identify their location in the ledger. (p. 60)

**Compound entry** An entry that involves three or more accounts. (p. 57)

**Credit** The right side of an account. (p. 51)

**Debit** The left side of an account. (p. 51)

**Double-entry system** A system that records the dual effect of each transaction in appropriate accounts. (p. 51)

**General journal** The book of original entry in which transactions are recorded when they are not recorded in other specialized journals. (p. 55)

**General ledger** A ledger that contains accounts for all assets, liabilities, equities, revenues, and expenses. (p. 58)

**Journal** An accounting record in which transactions are recorded in chronological (date) order. (p. 55)

**Journalizing** The entering of transaction data in the journal. (p. 55)

**Ledger** A book that contains all accounts for the company or specialized accounts supporting other ledgers. (p. 58)

**Posting** The procedure of transferring journal entries to the ledger accounts.

**T account** with the title to the left of t

**Trial balance** a specific time period. (p. 69)

---

The **Summary of Study Objectives** relates the study objectives to the key points in the chapter. It gives you another opportunity to review as well as to see how all the key topics within the chapter are related.

The **Glossary** defines all the terms and concepts introduced in the chapter. Page references help you find any terms you need to study further. The *CD icon* tells you that there is a Key Term Matching Activity on the Student Navigator CD that came with your textbook that will help you master the terms and concepts.

---

Questions    ◄    77

## Self-Study Questions

 Chapter 2 Self-Test

Answers are at the end of the chapter.

(SO 1) K  1. Which of the following statements about an account is true?
   (a) The left side of an account is the credit or decrease side.
   (b) An account is an individual accounting record of increases and decreases in specific asset, liability, and owner's equity items.
   (c) There are separate accounts for specific assets and liabilities but only one account for owner's equity items.
   (d) In its simplest form, an account consists of two parts.

(SO 2) K  2. Debits:
   (a) increase both assets and liabilities.
   (b) decrease both assets and liabilities.
   (c) increase assets and decrease liabilities.
   (d) decrease assets and increase liabilities.

(SO 2) K  3. A revenue account:
   (a) is increased by debits.
   (b) is decreased by credits.
   (c) has a normal balance of a debit.
   (d) is increased by credits.

(SO 2) K  4. Accounts that normally have debit balances are:
   (a) assets, expenses, and revenues.
   (b) assets, expenses, and owner's capital.
   (c) assets, liabilities, and drawings.
   (d) assets, drawings, and expenses.

(SO 3) K  5. Which of the following is not part of the recording process?
   (a) Analysing transactions
   (b) Preparing a trial balance
   (c) Entering transactions in a journal
   (d) Posting transactions

6. Which of the following statements about a journal    (SO 4) K
is false?
   (a) It is not a book of original entry.
   (b) It provides a chronological record of transactions.
   (c) It helps to locate errors because the debit and credit amounts for each entry can be readily compared.
   (d) It discloses in one place the complete effect of a transaction.

7. A ledger:    (SO 5) K
   (a) contains only asset and liability accounts.
   (b) should show accounts in alphabetical order.
   (c) is a collection of the entire group of accounts maintained by a company.
   (d) is a book of original entry.

8. Posting:    (SO 6) K
   (a) normally occurs before journalizing.
   (b) transfers ledger transaction data to the journal.
   (c) is an optional step in the recording process.
   (d) transfers journal entries to ledger accounts.

9. A trial balance:    (SO 7) K
   (a) is a list of accounts with their balances at a specific time.
   (b) proves the accuracy of journalized transactions.
   (c) will not balance if a correct journal entry is posted twice.
   (d) proves that all transactions have been recorded.

10. A trial balance will not balance if:    (SO 7) C
   (a) a correct journal entry is posted twice.
   (b) the purchase of supplies on account is debited to Supplies and credited to Cash.
   (c) a $100 cash drawing by the owner is debited to Drawings for $1,000 and credited to Cash for $100.
   (d) a $450 payment on account is debited to Accounts Payable for $45 and credited to Cash for $45.

## Questions

(SO 2) C  1. Should the balance in total owner's equity equal the balance in the Cash account? Explain why or why not.

(SO 2) C  2. Jos Arcelus, a fellow student, says that the double-entry system means each transaction must be recorded twice. Is Jos correct? Explain.

(SO 2) C  3. Kim Nguyen, a beginning accounting student, believes debit balances are favourable and credit balances are unfavourable. Is Kim correct? Discuss.

(SO 2) K  4. State the rules of debit and credit and identify the normal balance for (a) asset accounts, (b) liability accounts, and (c) owner's equity accounts: (1) capital, (2) drawings, (3) revenue, and (4) expense.

5. What is the normal balance for each of the following accounts?    (SO 2) K
   (a) Accounts Receivable    (e) Service Revenue
   (b) Cash    (f) Salaries Expense
   (c) Drawings    (g) Owner's Capital
   (d) Accounts Payable    (h) Prepaid Insurance

6. Decide whether each of the following accounts is an    (SO 2) K
asset, a liability, or an owner's equity account and whether it would have a normal debit or credit balance:
   (a) Accounts Receivable    (d) Drawings
   (b) Accounts Payable    (e) Supplies
   (c) Equipment    (f) Unearned Revenue

---

**Self-Study Questions** are a practice test, keyed to Study Objectives, that give you an opportunity to check your knowledge of important topics. Answers appear on the last page of the chapter. (Keyed to Study Objectives and Bloom's Taxonomy.)

The level of cognitive skill required to solve the question, exercise, or problem has been classified with a letter code following Bloom's Taxonomy. You will find more information about Bloom's and this coding system on page XIX this Preface.

The **web icon** tells you that there is an additional Self-Test on the Weygandt website <www.wiley.com/canada/weygandt>.

**Questions** allow you to explain your understanding of concepts and relationships covered in the chapter. (Keyed to Study Objectives and Bloom's Taxonomy.)

**Brief Exercises** help you focus on one Study Objective at a time. They help you build confidence in your basic skills and knowledge. (Keyed to Study Objectives and Bloom's Taxonomy.)

(SO 6) C 17. What is a contra account? Why do we use a contra account to record accumulated amortization instead of directly reducing the long-lived asset?

(SO 6) AP 18. Cheung Company purchased equipment for $12,000. Annual amortization expense is $4,000. Show the presentation of the equipment and the accumulated amortization on the balance sheet at the end of the first and second fiscal years.

(SO 4, 5, 6) C 19. For each of the following items before adjustment, indicate the type of adjusting entry (prepaid expense, unearned revenue, accrued revenue, accrued expense, estimate) that is needed to correct the misstatement. If an item could result in more than one type of adjusting entry, indicate each of the types.
(a) Assets are understated.
(b) Liabilities are overstated.
(c) Liabilities are understated.
(d) Expenses are understated.
(e) Assets are overstated.
(f) Revenue is understated.

(SO 4, 5, 6) K 20. One half of the adjusting entry is given below. Indicate the account title for the other half of the entry.

(a) Salaries Expense is debited.
(b) Amortization Expense is debited.
(c) Interest Payable is credited.
(d) Supplies is credited.
(e) Accounts Receivable is debited.
(f) Unearned Revenue is debited.

(SO 4, 5, 6) C 21. "An adjusting entry may affect more than one balance sheet or income statement account." Do you agree? Why or why not?

(SO 7) C 22. What is the purpose of preparing an adjusted trial balance? What is it used for?

(SO 7) C 23. Net income is shown on the income statement and the statement of owner's equity. It is also indirectly included on the balance sheet. Do you agree or disagree? Why?

(SO 8) C *24. Some companies debit an expense account at the time the expense is prepaid instead of debiting an asset account. Will this result in a different net income or different amount of total assets on the balance sheet than if they had instead debited an asset account at the time the amount was paid?

## Brief Exercises

BE3–1 Calculate the missing information in each of the following independent situations:

| | A Co. | B Co. | C Co. | D Co. |
|---|---|---|---|---|
| Supplies on hand, May 31, 2004 | $ 475 | $ 875 | $ 640 | $ ? |
| Supplies purchased during the year | 1,695 | ? | 2,865 | 2,970 |
| Supplies on hand, May 31, 2005 | 250 | 1,295 | ? | 1,190 |
| Supplies used during the year | ? | 2,810 | 2,715 | 3,295 |

Calculate missing data for supplies.
(SO 4) AP

BE3–2 Spahn Cleaning Company had $745 of cleaning supplies on hand on January 1, 2005. During 2005 it purchased additional cleaning supplies for $3,680 on credit. On December 31, 2005, there were $830 of cleaning supplies on hand.
(a) Prepare the journal entry to record the purchase of supplies during the year.
... plies used during the year.
... quired at December 31, 2005.
...2005, balance in Cleaning Supplies and Cleaning Supplies, and indicate the adjusted balance in each account.

Prepare and post transaction and adjusting entries for supplies.
(SO 4) AP

...$9,780 for a one-year insurance policy. Bere Co. has ...
...nth and the number of months remaining in the pol-
...at expired during 2004 and the unexpired cost as at
...ber 31, 2004.
...tries and indicate the adjusted balance in each account.

Prepare and post transaction and adjusting entries for insurance.
(SO 4) AP

---

BE7–8 Referring to BE7–7, indicate (a) the items that will result in an adjustment to the company's records, and (b) why the other items do not require adjustment.

Identify reconciling items that require journal entries.
(SO 7) C

BE7–9 In the month of November, Johal Company wrote and recorded cheques in the amount of $9,520. In December, it wrote and recorded cheques in the amount of $12,617. Of these cheques, $8,687 were presented to the bank for payment in November, and $10,989 in December. What is the amount for outstanding cheques at the end of November? At the end of December?

Analyse outstanding cheques.
(SO 7) AP

BE7–10 On July 31, Manuliak Company had an unadjusted cash balance of $9,100. An examination of the July bank statement shows a balance of $7,920 on July 31; bank service charges $35; deposits in transit $2,152; interest earned $25; outstanding cheques $1,144; and an NSF cheque of $162. Prepare a bank reconciliation at July 31.

Prepare bank reconciliation.
(SO 7) AP

BE7–11 Refer to the bank reconciliation prepared in BE7–10. Prepare the adjusting journal entries for Manuliak Company on July 31.

Prepare entries from bank reconciliation.
(SO 7) AP

BE7–12 Dupré Company has the following cash balances: Cash in Bank $17,540; Payroll Bank Account $6,000; and Plant Expansion Fund Cash $25,000. Dupré maintains a $5,000 compensating bank balance in a separate account. Explain how each balance should be reported on the balance sheet.

Explain statement presentation of cash balances.
(SO 8) C

## Exercises

E7–1 Per Paasche is the owner of Luna's Pizza. Luna's is operated strictly on a carry-out basis. Customers pick up their orders at a counter where a clerk exchanges the pizzas for cash. While at the counter, the customer can see other employees making the pizzas and the large ovens in which the pizzas are baked.

Identify principles of internal control.
(SO 2, 3) C

*Instructions*
Identify the principles of internal control and give an example of each principle that you might observe when picking up your pizza. (*Note:* It may not be possible to observe all of the principles in action.)

E7–2 The following control procedures are used in the Sheridan Company for over-the-counter cash receipts.
1. Cashiers are experienced, so they are not bonded.
2. All over-the-counter receipts are received by one of three clerks who share a cash register with a single cash drawer.
3. To minimize the risk of robbery, cash in excess of $100 is stored in an unlocked desk drawer in a back room until it is deposited in the bank.
4. At the end of each day, the total receipts are counted by the cashier on duty and reconciled to the cash register total.
5. The company accountant makes the bank deposit and then records the day's receipts.
6. If a customer has exact change and does not want a receipt, the sale is not rung through the cash register.

Identify weaknesses in internal control over cash receipts, and suggest improvements.
(SO 2, 3) AN

*Instructions*
(a) For each procedure, explain the weakness in internal control and identify the control principle that is violated.
(b) For each weakness, suggest a change in procedure that will result in better internal control.

E7–3 In the Abekah Company, cheques are not prenumbered. Both the purchasing agent and the comptroller are authorized to issue cheques. Each signer has access to unissued cheques kept in an unlocked file cabinet. The purchasing agent pays all bills for goods purchased for resale. Before making a payment, the purchasing agent determines that the goods have been received and verifies the mathematical accuracy of the vendor's invoice. After payment, the invoice is filed by the vendor, and the purchasing agent records the payment in the cash payments journal. The comptroller pays all other bills after receiving approval from authorized employees. After payment, the comptroller stamps all bills PAID, files them by payment date, and records the cheques in the cash payments journal. Abekah Company maintains one chequing account that is reconciled by the comptroller.

Identify weaknesses in internal control over cash disbursements, and suggest improvements.
(SO 2, 4) S

**Exercises** help you continue to build your confidence. (Keyed to Study Objectives and Bloom's Taxonomy.)
Certain exercises or problems marked with an icon help you practise business *writing skills*.

Each **Problem** helps you pull together and apply several concepts of the chapter.

Two sets of problems—*Set A* and *Set B*—are usually keyed to the same study objectives and cognitive level. These provide additional opportunities to apply concepts learned in the chapter.

An **Interactive Homework** icon tells you that you can practise certain Exercises interactively on the web.

---

Problems: Set A    ◀    83

## Problems: Set A

P2–1A  Yee Company has the following accounts:

|  | (1) Type of Account | (2) Financial Statement | (3) Normal Balance | (4) Increase | (5) Decrease |
|---|---|---|---|---|---|
| Account | | | | | |
| 1. Cash | Asset | Balance sheet | Debit | Debit | Credit |
| 2. A. Yee, Drawings | | | | | |
| 3. Accounts Receivable | | | | | |
| 4. Consulting Fees Earned | | | | | |
| 5. Interest Expense | | | | | |
| 6. Land | | | | | |
| 7. Notes Payable | | | | | |
| 8. Office Supplies | | | | | |
| 9. Office Supplies Expense | | | | | |
| 10. Salary Expense | | | | | |

*Instructions*

Complete the table by identifying (1) the type of account (e.g., asset, liability, owner's capital, drawings, revenue, expense), (2) what financial statement it is presented on, (3) the normal balance of the account, (4) whether the account is increased by a debit or credit, and (5) whether the account is decreased by a debit or credit. The first one is done for you as an example.

P2–2A  The Bucket Club Miniature Golf and Driving Range was opened on May 1 by Jamil Mawani. The following selected events and transactions occurred during May:

May  1 Invested $65,000 cash in the business.
    3 Purchased Lee's Golf Land for $188,000. The price consists of land, $97,000; building, $53,000; and equipment, $38,000. Paid $38,000 cash and signed a note payable for the balance.
    5 Advertised the opening of the driving range and miniature golf course, paying advertising expenses of $2,300.
    6 Paid $2,736 cash for a one-year insurance policy.
    10 Purchased golf clubs and other equipment for $16,000 from Woods Company, payable in 30 days.
    18 Received golf fees of $5,800 in cash.
    19 Sold 100 coupon books for $35 each. Each book contains 10 coupons that entitle the holder to one round of miniature golf or to hit one bucket of golf balls.
    25 Withdrew $2,750 cash for personal use.
    30 Paid salaries of $2,975.
    30 Paid Woods Company in full.

Identify increases, decreases, normal balances, and types of accounts. (SO 2) K

Interactive Homework

Journalize transactions. (SO 2, 4) AP

...e payable.
...; Prepaid Insurance; Land; Buildings; Equipment; ...Notes Payable; Jamil Mawani, Capital; Jamil Mawani, ...xpense; Salaries Expense; and Interest Expense.

...formed a company called Rojas Designs. During the ...he following events and transactions occurred:
...00 of office equipment.
...t a salary of $1,200 monthly.
...$950.
...s on account from Halo Company, $1,700.
...ort for G. Fellows and billed him $900 for services.
...om R. Welk for the design of a new home.

Journalize transactions, post, and prepare trial balance. (SO 4, 6, 7) AP

---

206    CHAPTER 4    ▶    Completion of the Accounting Cycle

## Continuing Cookie Chronicle

(Note: The Continuing Cookie Chronicle was started in Chapter 1 and continued in Chapters 2 and 3. From the information gathered through Chapter 3, follow the instructions below using the general ledger accounts you have already prepared.)

Natalie is gearing up for the Christmas season. During the month of December, the following transactions happen:

Dec.  1 Natalie hires an assistant to help with cookie making and to do some administrative duties. Natalie and her assistant agree on an hourly rate of $8.
    4 Natalie teaches the class that was booked on November 25 and receives the balance outstanding.
    8 She collects the amount due from the neighbourhood school that was accrued at the end of November, 2004.
    10 She receives $625 in advance from the local school board for five classes that are to be given during December and January.
    15 She pays for the cellphone bill accrued in the adjusting journal entries in November 2004.
    16 Natalie issues a cheque to her brother for payment of the website he set up in November 2004.
    18 She receives a deposit of $50 on a cookie class that is scheduled for early January.
    24 Natalie adds up all of the additional revenue for the classes taught during the month. She has not had time to account for each class individually. She determines that during the period December 1 to 24 she taught $3,500 worth of cookie-making classes. For these classes, she has collected $3,000 in cash and sent out invoices for $500. (This is in addition to the December 4 and the December 10 transactions.)
    24 Natalie adds up all of the sugar, flour, and chocolate chips she purchased during the month. In total she paid $1,250 for these baking supplies.
    24 Natalie issues a cheque to her assistant for $800. Her assistant worked approximately 100 hours from the time she started working for Natalie until December 24.
    24 Because Natalie has had such a busy December doing school work and giving lessons, she decides to take the rest of the month off. She also withdraws $500 in cash to make a personal car loan payment.

As at December 31, the following adjusting entry data is available:

1. A count reveals that $50 of brochures and posters remain at the end of December.
2. Another month's worth of amortization needs to be recorded on the baking equipment purchased in November. (Recall that the baking equipment has a useful life of five years or 60 months.)
3. One month's worth of amortization needs to be recorded for the website. (Recall that the website has a useful life of two years or 24 months.)
4. An additional month's worth of interest on her grandmother's loan needs to be accrued. (Recall that the interest rate is 6%.)
5. One month's worth of insurance has expired.
6. Natalie is unexpectedly telephoned on December 28 to give a cookie class at the neighbourhood community centre. In January, she invoices the centre for $375 and the manager of the centre tells Natalie that the invoice will be paid sometime in early January.
7. A count on December 31 reveals that $1,000 of baking supplies were used during December.
8. Natalie receives her cellphone bill, $75. The bill is for services provided during the month of December and is due January 15. (Recall that the cellphone is only used for business.)
9. Because the cookie-making class on December 28 is for such a large group of children, Natalie's assistant helps out. Her assistant works seven hours at a rate of $8 per hour.
10. An analysis of the unearned revenue account reveals that two of the five classes paid for by the local school board on December 10 have still not been taught by the end of December. The $50 deposit received on December 18 for another class also remains unearned.

---

The **Continuing Cookie Chronicle** is a serial problem found in each chapter that collectively reinforce topical concepts.

In selected chapters, a **Cumulative Coverage Problem** follows the A and B problem sets. The cumulative coverage problem pulls together, and uses, topics you have learned over several chapters.

---

*Instructions*

Using the information that you have gathered through Chapter 3, and the new information above, do the following:

(a) Prepare and post the December 2004 transactions. (Use the general ledger accounts that you prepared in Chapter 3.)
(b) Prepare a trial balance as at December 31, 2004.
(c) Prepare and post adjusting journal entries for the month of December.
(d) Prepare an adjusted trial balance as at December 31, 2004.
(e) Prepare an income statement and a statement of owner's equity for the two months ended December 31, 2004, and a classified balance sheet as at December 31, 2004.
(f) Natalie has decided that her year end will be December 31, 2004. Prepare and post closing entries as at December 31, 2004.
(g) Prepare a post-closing trial balance.

## Cumulative Coverage—Chapters 2 to 4

Lee Chan opened Lee's Window Washing on July 1, 2005. During July, the following transactions were completed:

July   1   Invested $14,000 cash in the business.
      1   Purchased a used truck for $26,000, paying $4,000 cash and the balance on account.
      1   Paid $500 rent for the month.
      3   Purchased cleaning supplies for $800 on account.
      5   Paid $1,800 on a one-year insurance policy, effective July 1.
    12   Billed customers $3,800 for cleaning services.
    18   Paid $3,000 of amount owed on truck, and $400 of amount owed on cleaning supplies.
    20   Paid $1,600 for employee salaries.
    21   Collected $1,400 from customers billed on July 12.
    25   Billed customers $3,000 for cleaning services.
    31   Paid gas and oil for the month on the truck, $250.
    31   Withdrew $1,600 cash for personal use.

*Instructions*

(a) Journalize and post the July transactions.
(b) Prepare a trial balance at July 31.
(c) Journalize and post the following adjustments:
    1. Earned but unbilled fees at July 31 were $1,500.
    2. Amortization on truck for the month was $700.
    3. One-twelfth of the insurance expired.
       cleaning supplies on hand at July 31.
       ries were $400.
       atement of owner's equity for July, and a classified
       , and complete the closing process.
       July 31.

---

*Instructions*

(a) Enter the September 1 balances in general ledger accounts.
(b) Journalize the September transactions.
(c) Post to the ledger accounts.
(d) Prepare a trial balance at September 30.
(e) Journalize and post adjusting entries.
(f) Prepare an adjusted trial balance.
(g) Prepare an income statement and a statement of owner's equity for September, and a balance sheet at September 30, 2004.

## BROADENING YOUR PERSPECTIVE

## Financial Reporting and Analysis

 Practice Tools

### Financial Reporting Problem

BYP3–1   The financial statements of The Forzani Group are presented in Appendix A at the end of this textbook.

*Instructions*

(a) What title does Forzani use for its income statement?
(b) What different types of revenues were reported by Forzani (see note 12)?
(c) Does Forzani report any prepayments on its balance sheet? If so, identify each item that is a prepaid expense or unearned (deferred) revenue. Indicate what other account title would likely be used in preparing adjusting entries for these accounts.
(d) Does Forzani report any accruals on its balance sheet? If so, identify each item that is an accrued revenue or accrued expense. Indicate what other account title would likely be used in preparing adjusting entries for these accounts.
(e) What are the cost, accumulated amortization, and net book value of Forzani's capital assets at February 2, 2003 (see note 3)?

### Interpreting Financial Statements

BYP3–2   Rogers Cable Inc. is Canada's largest cable television service provider. Rogers is also a leading North American provider of high-speed Internet service. Rogers' balance sheet included a current liability of $35,256,000 at December 31, 2002, called Unearned Revenue. An excerpt from the notes to the financial statements follows:

---

The **Broadening Your Perspective** section helps you pull together various concepts covered in the chapter and apply them to real-life business decisions.

The **CD icon** tells you there are additional tools on the Student Navigator CD that came with your textbook to help you master the material.

**Financial Reporting Problems** familiarize you with the format, content, and uses of financial statements prepared by The Forzani Group Ltd., which are presented in Appendix A at the end of the text.

**Interpreting Financial Statements** asks you to apply the concepts you have learned to specific situations faced by actual companies.

Critical Thinking   ◄   325

sold. Comment on whether Indigo's inventory management improved or deteriorated in 2003.
(c) Indigo uses the retail inventory method to value its inventories. Indigo's main competitor, Amazon.Com, Inc., uses the FIFO cost flow assumption to value its inventories. Is one of these two methods more accurate than the other? Explain.
(d) Which company would have the better balance sheet valuation? Explain.
(e) Why would a company use the retail inventory method to value its inventory?

## Accounting on the Web

**BYP6–3** This problem uses an annual report to identify the inventory cost flow assumption and to calculate inventory ratios.

*Instructions*
Specific requirements of this Internet case are available on the Weygandt website.

## Critical Thinking

### Collaborative Learning Activity

**BYP6–4** Just-in-Time (JIT) Auto Parts manufactures auto parts. The company's inventories reported on its balance sheet at July 31, 2005, total $1,094.7 million. Assume that the following transactions occurred during July and August:
1. Office supplies were shipped to JIT Auto Parts by Office Maxx, FOB destination. The goods were shipped July 31 and received August 3.
2. JIT Auto Parts purchased specialty plastic from DuPont Canada for use in the manufacture of door mouldings. The goods were shipped FOB shipping point July 31 and received August 3.
3. Ford Motor Company of Canada, Limited, purchased 3,000 rear liftgate assemblies from JIT to be used in the manufacture of the Ford Windstar. They were shipped FOB shipping point July 29, and were received by Ford August 1.
4. Nadeau Furniture shipped office furniture to JIT Auto Parts, FOB destination, on July 27. The furniture was received August 3.
5. Inland Specialty Chemical shipped JIT Auto Parts chemicals that JIT uses in the manufacture of door mouldings and other items. The goods were sent FOB shipping point July 30 and received August 3.
6. JIT Auto Parts purchased new Cadillac Sevilles for its executives to [...] shipped FOB destination July 30 and received August 5.
7. JIT Auto Parts purchased steel, to be used in expanding its manuf[...] IPSCO, FOB Regina (shipping point). The steel was shipped July 3[...] August 2, and at JIT Auto Parts' plant in Aurora on August 3.
8. JIT Auto Parts shipped instrument panels to Jaguar, FOB destinat[...] shipped July 15 and arrived at Jaguar's headquarters in England Aug[...]

*Instructions*
With the class divided into groups, answer the following:
(a) Determine which of the above transactions affect JIT Auto Parts' in[...] each item that has an effect, would the transaction result in an incr[...] the inventory account at July 31, 2005?
(b) For each transaction that does not affect JIT Auto Parts' inventory a[...] owns the relevant items and how they should be reported.

Critical Thinking   ◄   97

### Communication Activity

**BYP2–5** White Glove Company offers home cleaning services. Two common transactions for the company are billing customers for services performed and paying employee salaries. For example, on March 15, bills that totalled $6,000 were sent to customers, and $2,000 in salaries was paid to employees.

*Instructions*
Write a memo to your instructor that lists the steps in the recording process and applies these steps to each of the March 15 transactions.

### Ethics Case

**BYP2–6** Vu Hung is the assistant chief accountant at Lim Company, a manufacturer of computer chips and cellular phones. The company presently has total sales of $20 million. It is the end of the first quarter. Vu is hurriedly trying to prepare a general ledger trial balance so that quarterly financial statements can be prepared and released to management and regulatory agencies. The total credits on the trial balance exceed the debits by $1,000.
In order to meet the 4 p.m. deadline, Vu decides to force the debits and credits into balance by adding the amount of the difference to the Equipment account. She chose Equipment because it is one of the larger account balances. Proportionally, it will be the least misstated. She believes that the difference will not affect anyone's decisions. She wishes that she had more time to find the error, but realizes that the financial statements are already late.

*Instructions*
(a) Who are the stakeholders in this situation?
(b) What are the ethical issues involved?
(c) What are Vu's alternatives?

### Answers to Self-Study Questions
1. b   2. c   3. d   4. d   5. b   6. a   7. c   8. d   9. a   10. c

### Answer to Forzani Review It Question 4
Normal balances: Accounts Receivable (asset)—debit; Accounts Payable and Accrued Liabilities (liability)—credit; Corporate Revenue (revenue)—credit; and Store Operating Expense (expense)—debit.

Remember to go back to the Navigator Box at the beginning of the chapter to check off your completed work.

---

**Accounting on the Web** cases ask you to visit websites where you can find and analyse information related to the chapter topic. Case details are found on the Weygandt website <www.wiley.com/canada/weygandt>.
At the book's website, you will also find many other valuable resources and activities, including interactive quizzes, a Checklist of Key Figures, PowerPoint presentations, demonstration problems, and web cases.

**Collaborative Learning Activities** prepare you for the business world, where you will be working with many people, by giving you practice in solving problems with colleagues.

**Communication Activities** ask you to engage in real-life business situations using your writing, speaking, or presentation skills.

Through **Ethics Cases**, you will reflect on ethical situations an accountant typically confronts.

**Answers to Self-Study Questions** provide feedback on your understanding of concepts.

**Answers to *Review It* Questions** based on The Forzani Group's financial statements can be found here.

After you complete your assignments, it's a good idea to go back to **The Navigator** checklist at the start of the chapter to see if you have used all the study aids of the chapter.

# The Use of Bloom's Taxonomy

Bloom's Taxonomy is a classification framework that you can use to develop your skills from the most basic to the most advanced competence levels: Knowledge, comprehension, application, analysis, synthesis, and evaluation. These levels are hierarchical in nature in that performance at each level requires mastery of all prior levels.

Questions, exercises, and problems at the end of each chapter of this text have been classified by the knowledge level required in answering each one. Below you will learn what your role is in each of the six skill levels and how you can demonstrate mastery at each level. Key word clues will help you recognize the skill level required for a particular question. You will also find an example from the text which will help illustrate each skill level.

## (K) Knowledge (Remembering)

**Student's role:** "I read, listen, watch or observe, I take notes and am able to recall information, ask and respond to questions."
**Student demonstrates knowledge by:** stating who, what, when, why, and how in the same form in which they learned it.
**Key words clues:** define, identify, label, name, etc.
**Example from** *Accounting Principles*: "What is the basic accounting equation?"

## (C) Comprehension (Understanding)

**Student's role:** "I understand the information or skill. I can recognize it in other forms and I can explain it to others and make use of it."
**Student demonstrates comprehension by:** giving an original example of how the information would be used.
**Key words clues:** describe, distinguish, give example, compare, differentiate, explain, etc.
**Example from** *Accounting Principles*: "Indicate whether each of the following items is an asset (A), liability (L) or part of owner's equity (OE)."

## (AP) Application (Solving the Problem)

**Student's role:** "I can apply my prior knowledge and understanding to new situations."
**Student demonstrates knowledge by:** solving problems independently. Recognizing when the information or skill is needed and uses it to solve new problems or complete tasks.
**Key word clues:** calculate, illustrate, prepare, complete, use, produce, etc.
**Example from** *Accounting Principles*: "The liabilities of Cai Company are $90,000. Meiyu Cai's capital account is $150,000; drawings are $40,000; revenues, $450,000; and expenses, $320,000. What is the amount of Cai Company's total assets?"

## (AN) Analysis (Detecting)

**Student's role:** "I can break down the information into simpler parts and understand how these parts are related."
**Student demonstrates knowledge by:** recognizing patterns and hidden meanings, filling in missing information, correcting errors, identifying components and effects
**Key word clues:** analyse, breakdown, compare, contrast, deduce, differentiate, etc.
**Example from** *Accounting Principles*: "Indicate the effect and amount of the error—understatement (U), overstatement (O), or no effect (NE)—on the income statement and balance sheet components."

## (S) Synthesis (Creating)

**Student's role:** "I use all knowledge, understanding, and skills to create alternatives. I can convey this information to others effectively."
**Student demonstrates knowledge by:** acting as a guide to others, designing, creating.
**Key word clues:** relate, tell, write, categorize, devise, formulate, generalize, create, design.
**Example from** *Accounting Principles*: "Write a memo discussing whether you believe cash-based income is a more reliable performance measure than accrual-based net income."

## (E) Evaluation (Appraisal)

**Student's role:** "I am open to and appreciative of the value of ideas, procedures, and methods and can make well-supported judgements, backed up by knowledge, understanding, and skills."
**Student demonstrates knowledge by:** formulating and presenting well-supported judgement, displaying consideration of others, examining personal options, making wise choices.
**Key word clues:** appraise, assess, criticize, critique, decide, evaluate, judge, justify, recommend.
**Example from** *Accounting Principles*: "Evaluate the effect of the revenue recognition principle on recorded revenues, expenses, and net income for the period in question."

# How Do You Learn Best?

This questionnaire aims to find out something about your preferences for the way you work with information. You will have a preferred learning style. One part of that learning style is your preference for the intake and the output of ideas and information. Circle the letter of the answer that best explains your preference. Circle more than one if a single answer does not match your perception. Leave blank any question that does not apply.

1. You are about to give directions to a person who is staying with you. She is staying in a hotel in town and wants to visit your house later. She has a rental car. Would you
   V) draw a map on paper?
   R) write down the directions (without a map)?
   A) tell her the directions?
   K) pick her up at the hotel in your car?

2. You are staying in a hotel and have a rental car. You would like to visit friends whose address you do not know. Would you like them to
   V) draw you a map on paper?
   R) write down the directions (without a map)?
   A) tell you the directions by phone?
   K) pick you up at the hotel in their car?

3. You have just received a copy of your itinerary for a world trip. This is of interest to a friend. Would you
   A) call her immediately and tell her about it?
   R) send her a copy of the printed itinerary?
   V) show her on a map of the world?
   K) share what you plan to do at each place you visit?

4. You are going to cook something as a special treat for your family. Do you
   K) cook something familiar without need for instructions?
   V) thumb through the cookbook looking for ideas from the pictures?
   R) refer to a specific cookbook where there is a good recipe?
   A) ask for advice from others?

5. A group of tourists has been assigned to you to find out about national parks. Would you
   K) drive them to a national park?
   R) give them pamphlets or a book on national parks?
   V) show them slides and photographs?
   A) give them a talk on national parks?

6. You are about to purchase a new CD player. Other than price, what would most influence your decision?
   A) The salesperson telling you what you want to know.
   K) Listening to it.
   R) Reading the details about it.
   V) Its distinctive, upscale appearance.

7. Recall a time in your life when you learned how to do something like playing a new board game. (Try to avoid choosing a very physical skill, e.g., riding a bike.) How did you learn best? By
   V) visual clues—pictures, diagrams, charts?
   A) listening to somebody explaining it?
   R) written instructions?
   K) doing it?

8. You have an eye problem. Would you prefer that the doctor
   A) tell you what is wrong?
   V) show you a diagram of what is wrong?
   K) use a model to show what is wrong?

9. You are about to learn to use a new program on a computer. Would you
   K) sit down at the keyboard and begin to experiment with the program's features?
   R) read the manual that comes with the program?
   A) telephone a friend and ask questions about it?

10. You are not sure whether a word should be spelled "dependent" or "dependant." Do you
    R) look it up in the dictionary or check the grammar software?
    V) see the word in your mind and choose the best way it looks?
    A) sound it out in your mind?
    K) write both versions down?

11. Apart from price, what would most influence your decision to buy a particular book?
    K) You have used a copy before.
    R) Quickly reading parts of it.
    A) A friend talking about it.
    V) The way it looks is appealing.

12. A new movie has arrived in town. What would most influence your decision to go or not to go?
    A) You heard a radio review of it.
    R) You read a review of it.
    V) You saw a preview of it.

13. Do you prefer an instructor who likes to use
    R) textbook, handouts, readings?
    V) flow diagrams, charts, graphics?
    K) field trips, labs, practical sessions?
    A) discussion, guest speakers?

Count your choices:    ☐    ☐    ☐    ☐
                        V    A    R    K

Now match the letter or letters you have recorded most to the same letter or letters in the Learning Styles Chart on the following page. You may have more than one learning style preference—many people do. Next to each letter in the Chart are suggestions that will refer you to different learning aids throughout this text.

# Learning Styles Chart

 Visual

| WHAT TO DO IN CLASS | WHAT TO DO WHEN STUDYING | TEXT FEATURES THAT MAY HELP YOU | WHAT TO DO PRIOR TO EXAMS |
|---|---|---|---|
| • Pay close attention to charts, drawings, and handouts your instructor uses.<br>• Underline and highlight.<br>• Use different colours.<br>• Use symbols, flow charts, graphs, different arrangements on the page, white space. | Convert your lecture notes into "page pictures." To do this:<br>• Use the "What to do in class" strategies.<br>• Reconstruct images in different ways.<br>• Redraw pages from memory.<br>• Replace words with symbols and initials.<br>• Look at your pages. | • The Navigator<br>• Feature Story<br>• Preview<br>• Infographics/Illustrations<br>• Photos<br>• Accounting in Action<br>• Accounting Equation Analyses in margins<br>• Key Terms in blue<br>• Words in bold<br>• Demonstration Problem/Action Plan<br>• Questions/Exercises/Problems<br>• Financial Reporting and Analysis | • Recall your "page pictures."<br>• Draw diagrams where appropriate.<br>• Practise turning your visuals back into words. |

 Aural

| WHAT TO DO IN CLASS | WHAT TO DO WHEN STUDYING | TEXT FEATURES THAT MAY HELP YOU | WHAT TO DO PRIOR TO EXAMS |
|---|---|---|---|
| • Attend lectures and tutorials.<br>• Discuss topics with students and instructors.<br>• Explain new ideas to other people.<br>• Use a tape recorder.<br>• Leave spaces in your lecture notes for later recall.<br>• Describe overheads, pictures, and visuals to somebody who was not in class. | You may take poor notes because you prefer to listen. Therefore:<br>• Expand your notes by talking with others and with information from your textbook.<br>• Tape record summarized notes and listen.<br>• Read summarized notes out loud.<br>• Explain your notes to another "aural" person. | • Preview<br>• Infographics/Illustrations<br>• Accounting in Action<br>• Review It/Do It/Action Plan<br>• Summary of Study Objectives<br>• Glossary<br>• Demonstration Problem/Action Plan<br>• Self-Study Questions<br>• Questions/Exercises/Problems<br>• Financial Reporting and Analysis<br>• Critical Thinking | • Talk with the instructor.<br>• Spend time in quiet places recalling the ideas.<br>• Practise writing answers to old exam questions.<br>• Say your answers out loud. |

# Reading/Writing

| WHAT TO DO IN CLASS | WHAT TO DO WHEN STUDYING | TEXT FEATURES THAT MAY HELP YOU | WHAT TO DO PRIOR TO EXAMS |
|---|---|---|---|
| • Use lists and headings.<br>• Use dictionaries, glossaries, and definitions.<br>• Read handouts, textbooks, and supplemental library readings.<br>• Use lecture notes. | • Write out words again and again.<br>• Reread notes silently.<br>• Rewrite ideas and principles into other words.<br>• Turn charts, diagrams, and other illustrations into statements. | • The Navigator<br>• Feature Story<br>• Study Objectives<br>• Preview<br>• Accounting Equation Analysis in margins<br>• Review It/Do It/Action Plan<br>• Summary of Study Objectives<br>• Glossary<br>• Self-Study Questions<br>• Questions/Exercises/Problems<br>• Writing Problems<br>• Financial Reporting and Analysis<br>• Critical Thinking | • Write exam answers.<br>• Practise with multiple choice questions.<br>• Write paragraphs, beginnings and endings.<br>• Write your lists in outline form.<br>• Arrange your words into hierarchies and points. |

# Kinesthetic

| WHAT TO DO IN CLASS | WHAT TO DO WHEN STUDYING | TEXT FEATURES THAT MAY HELP YOU | WHAT TO DO PRIOR TO EXAMS |
|---|---|---|---|
| • Use all your senses.<br>• Go to labs, take field trips.<br>• Listen to real-life examples.<br>• Pay attention to applications.<br>• Use hands-on approaches.<br>• Use trial-and-error methods. | You may take poor notes because topics do not seem concrete or relevant. Therefore:<br>• Put examples in your summaries.<br>• Use case studies and applications to help with principles and abstract concepts.<br>• Talk about your notes with another "kinesthetic" person.<br>• Use pictures and photographs that illustrate an idea. | • The Navigator<br>• Feature Story<br>• Preview<br>• Infographics/Illustrations<br>• Review It/Do It/Action Plan<br>• Summary of Study Objectives<br>• Demonstration Problem/Action Plan<br>• Self-Study Questions<br>• Questions/Exercises/Problems<br>• Financial Reporting and Analysis<br>• Critical Thinking | • Write practice answers.<br>• Role-play the exam situation. |

 For all learning styles: Be sure to use the Student Navigator CD to enhance your understanding of the concepts and procedures of the text. In particular, use the writing handbook, interactive navigator, animated tutorials and videos, additional demonstration problems, key term matching activities, and interpreting financial statement cases.

# Special Student Supplements That Help You Get The Best Grade You Can

## Student Navigator CD

Included with this text is an interactive CD packed with a learning styles assessment, animated tutorials and videos, demonstration problems complete with action plans and solutions, key term matching exercises, a working with Annual Reports section, a writing handbook, a working in groups handbook, career information, and much more.

## The Accounting Principles Website <www.wiley.com/canada/weygandt>

This resource and learning tool serves as a launching pad to numerous activities, resources, and related sites. On the website, you'll find learning styles charts designed to help you discover how you learn best, study skills and tools, interactive quizzing, an on-line glossary, accounting on the web cases, additional demonstration problems, and other useful references. In addition, there are links to companies discussed in the text and items available for downloading such as a checklist of key figures and PowerPoint presentations.

This website also contains the Interactive Homework Exercises marked in the text. These exercises allow students to work on selected end-of-chapter exercises in an online environment at their own pace, and get feedback and solutions. Many contain an algorithmic function which provides you with limitless practice possibilities and immediate feedback.

## EGrade Plus

If your instructor has adopted eGrade Plus, additional resources are available on-line to help you develop your conceptual understanding of the class material and increase your ability to solve problems. eGrade Plus features:

**Study and Practice** resources that can include select interactive, end-of-chapter problems linked directly to text content, allowing you to review the text while you study. Additional resources can include web-based tutorials, videos, PowerPoint presentations, and lecture outlines, as well as other problem-solving resources that build confidence and understanding.

An **Assignment** area that helps you stay "on task" by containing all homework assignments in one location. These assignments will be graded automatically so you benefit by receiving immediate feedback on your work, allowing you to determine right away how well you understand the course material. Many homework problems contain a link to the relevant sections of the ebook, providing you with context-sensitive help that allows you to conquer problem-solving obstacles. Also, the majority are generated algorithmically so that each time you access a problem the variables will be different, thus providing unlimited opportunities for practice.

A **Personal Gradebook** will allow you to view your results from past assignments at any time.

## A Reader's Guide to Accounting Principles: Strategies for Successful Reading and Supplemental Glossary

Reading strategies for increased comprehension and retention include a number of techniques for handling, understanding, and remembering difficult vocabulary. A supplemental dictionary of commonly used business terms and idioms complements the accounting terms defined in the end-of-chapter glossaries.

## Student Study Guide

The Student Study Guide is a comprehensive review of accounting and a powerful tool for student use. Each chapter includes a preview of the chapter, study objectives, and a summary of key points in the chapter. A demonstration problem is included, in addition to other opportunities for students to practise their knowledge and skills through true/false, multiple-choice, matching questions related to key terms, and exercises linked to study objectives. Solutions to these questions, exercises, and problems explain the hows and whys so you get immediate feedback.

## Working Papers

Working Papers are partially completed accounting forms for all end-of-chapter questions, brief exercises, exercises, problems, and cases. Journals, ledgers, T accounts, and other required working papers have been predetermined and included for each textbook assignment, so that you can redirect limited time to important accounting concepts rather than formatting. The Working Papers are available in hard copy and in an electronic format on a CD. The CD version has been prepared using Excel—a leading spreadsheet and analysis software package. Students who purchase the CD have the option of completing assignments using the computer and gaining experience in applying those features of Excel that are important to business users: formatting, organizing, and working with data.

## Mark's Music Practice Set

This practice set exposes you to a real world simulation of maintaining a complete set of accounting records for a business. Business papers add a realistic dimension by enabling you to handle documents, cheques, invoices, and receipts that you would encounter in a small proprietorship. This practice set reinforces key concepts from Chapters 1 through 4 and allows you to apply the information you have learned. It is an excellent way to see how these concepts are all brought together to generate the accounting information that is essential in assessing the financial position and operating results of a company.

# To The Instructor

In the previous editions of *Accounting Principles*, we sought to create a book about business that made the subject clear and fascinating to students. And that is still our passion: to provide a link between accounting principles, student learning, and the real world.

## Developmental Research

In our effort to create an even more effective text, we surveyed the market and held extensive consultations with instructors and students. Over 50 instructors across the country took part in telephone surveys, workshops with the author, or reviews, culminating in an unprecedented text revision that is the result of intensive feedback.

We listened very carefully to everything we were told, and we believe we have responded effectively to both instructors' and students' concerns. Our overriding goal continues to be to help instructors teach and students learn by giving students the tools and the motivation they need to succeed in their accounting courses and their future careers.

## Goals and Features of the Third Canadian Edition

This revision of *Accounting Principles* provided us with an opportunity to improve a textbook that had already set high standards for quality. The consultations held with instructors and students gave us valuable insight that helped shape this edition to better meet their needs. We added topical coverage as suggested and significantly increased the breadth and depth of the end-of-chapter material. In addition, we increased the number and type of interactive learning aids for students and enhanced the technological features of the text to help both instructors and students.

More specifically, we gathered the following messages from our consultations and developmental research.

## Pedagogical Effectiveness

We confirmed that our texts are leaders in pedagogical effectiveness. We were the first accounting textbook to apply a pedagogical framework to accounting principles. *The Navigator*, our guide to the learning process, and the use of Bloom's Taxonomy, which categorizes material progressively to aid learning in a stepwise fashion, were rated as incredibly effective learning aids by both instructors and students.

The third edition places increased emphasis, throughout the text, on the processes students go through as they learn. Our Learning Styles model, introduced in previous editions, is incorporated throughout the text to enable students with different learning approaches to help them better understand the material. In addition, more summaries were added throughout the chapter to help students stop and assimilate the material they just learned. Stepped-out pedagogy was used to break down complex topics, making the material more manageable for students. Before You Go On feedback sections at the end of each major study objective and Demonstration Problems were augmented in both number and content coverage to facilitate student understanding.

We also expanded the use of our accounting equation analyses. Given the increasing focus on cash flow, accounting equations (presented in the margins next to journal entries) were supplemented to show the cash flow effect of the transaction. This will also help students better understand the impact of transactions on the financial position of a company and better distinguish between cash and accruals.

## Simplified Presentation

We made design enhancements in response to comments made by instructors and students. These include a crisper, cleaner look along with more open margin space, which will aid readability and understanding. The text material has been thoroughly reviewed by an instructor of English as a Second Language to ensure that *Accounting Principles* continues to provide an unprecedented level of clarity and readability.

We continue to believe that infographics help visual learners quickly assimilate difficult concepts. Many of these graphics were redesigned to be even more student-oriented.

## Flexible Solutions

During our Weygandt Workshops, instructors spoke in detail about their courses. We learned many things during these discussions but most of all we learned that no two courses are the same! In response to this reality, we made it our goal to provide you with the flexibility to tailor your course materials—text, technology, and supplements—to your course needs. We reviewed course outlines from across the country to determine where to split the text in order to meet the needs of the widest possible range of courses. Whether you teach accounting major, business major, general students, or a mix, the new splits will allow you to create a course package that gives your students precisely what they need. We have developed a rich selection of technology supplements that can not only be used as is, but also customized for the way you teach. You can add a little technology to your lectures, you can adapt our on-line material specifically for your course and track your students' grades on one of our sites, or you can do something in between—the choice is yours. Finally, we offer a full range of supplements with identical flexibility allowing you to tailor all materials to your specific needs.

## Student Empowerment

Previous editions were also rated highly by instructors and students for the involvement of students in the learning process.

Our Student Navigator CD, integrated throughout the text, empowers students to succeed by teaching them how to study, what to study, and why they study. This CD continues to provide the widest range of supplementary material available anywhere to help students learn.

We received strong, recurring messages from students, asking for more tutorial assistance on certain accounting topics. In addition to the accounting cycle tutorial and worksheet walkthrough, new animated tutorials for inventory cost flow assumptions, bad debts, amortization, and annual reports have been added.

Students also asked for more solved, problem material. In addition to a new tutorial on how to solve problems, students now have twice as many demonstration problems—nearly 50 in total—complete with problem-solving strategies and Excel worksheets. Tutorials also feature a significantly increased number of multiple choice questions and solutions. For example, the accounting cycle tutorial alone has 45 new multiple choice questions.

In addition, the end-of-chapter material now includes a selection of Interactive Homework exercises. These exercises, derived from Exercises in the end-of-chapter section of the text, provide students with immediate feedback on their work. Many of the exercises contain an algorithmic function that allows students to work through the same exercise with different data every time the exercise file is opened. Students can keep practising until they reach the level of success they desire.

Wiley eGradePlus—web-based software that automates the assigning, delivering, grading, and routing of homework, quizzes, and exams—is also available for instructors.

## Spotlight on Ethics

We found that ethics are of increasing concern to both instructors and students. Recent financial scandals and accounting misdeeds have been addressed in feature stories, Accounting in Action insights, and throughout the chapter material as appropriate. Chapter 1, which previously included material on how to solve ethical dilemmas, now includes a new section defending the importance of accounting and its contributions to our economy. Ethical insights and cases in the end-of-chapter material have been thoroughly revised to inform students of the consequences of various actions on financial reporting.

In addition, the Student Navigator CD provides an expanded discussion of ethics and ethical issues as they relate to the accounting and the financial reporting environment. A framework for analysis of ethical issues along with some sample ethics cases (with suggested solutions) are also available on the CD, as are links to additional resources on ethics.

## Relevance to Users

This edition continues, and expands, the inclusion of user-oriented material to demonstrate the relevance of accounting to all students, no matter their area of study. To give the students the opportunity to follow a new, extended real-world example, we have replaced Second Cup as our feature company with The

Forzani Group—the largest sporting goods retailer in Canada. References to Forzani have been included throughout the chapter, including Review It questions, ratio analysis, end-of-chapter assignments, and the inclusion of Forzani's financial statements in Appendix A at the end of the textbook.

This edition was also subject to a comprehensive updating to ensure that it is relevant and fresh. Updating involved replacing a significant number of the chapter-opening feature stories, Accounting in Action boxes, and real-world examples cited in the text.

## Expanded Topical Coverage

Additional topical coverage was requested by instructors to help them better prepare students for the complexities of today's world of accounting. These topics had to pass a strict test to warrant their inclusion: they were added only if they represented a major concept, issue, or procedure that a beginning student should understand. Some of the more significant additions include the following:

- The impact of transaction analysis on the financial position of the company was expanded to include each separate component of owner's equity in Chapter 1: Accounting in Action.
- The Income Summary account was reintroduced into the closing process in Chapter 4: Completion of the Accounting Cycle.
- A new appendix on sales and purchase discounts was added to Chapter 5: Accounting for Merchandising Operations.
- Additional information was added in Chapter 7: Internal Control and Cash about how debit and credit cards work. New sections have been added about electronic receipts and payments. The cheque clearing process is explained, and further detail has been added about internal control over cheques and electronic payments.
- Accounting for asset exchanges was expanded in Chapter 9: Long-Lived Assets. Explanations about amortization for partial periods were extended. Additional information was added regarding impairment losses. This chapter was thoroughly revised for new *CICA Handbook* changes in terminology, amortization practices, and treatment of restoration costs. The effect of extracted natural resources on inventory was also added to this chapter.
- The liabilities in Chapter 10: Current Liabilities were revised and clarified where appropriate. A new estimated liability, for promotions and coupons, was added to help students understand the accounting that has become an everyday occurrence in our shopping experience.
- Chapter 11: Accounting Principles was updated for recent changes to the conceptual framework. A section about revisions of estimates in the percentage of completion method of revenue recognition was added. In addition, Appendix 10A, Payroll Accounting, now illustrates the preparation of a payroll register.
- Chapter 12: Accounting for Partnerships expands upon the discussion of liability. The allocation of net income to partners was clarified, and the impact the death of a partner has on the partnership was added.

- Chapter 13: Corporations: Organization and Share Capital Transactions now includes an introduction to stock compensation plans and a detailed explanation on how to account for the reacquisition of shares.
- Chapter 14: Corporations: Dividends, Retained Earnings and Income Reporting expands upon the discussion of earnings per share to include weighted average calculations.
- Chapter 15: Long-Term Liabilities increase emphasis on notes payable. New sections discussing the conversion of bonds into shares and off-balance sheet financing were added.
- Chapter 17: The Cash Flow Statement now includes a discussion of EBITDA and free cash flow.
- Chapter 18: Financial Statement Analysis now includes a discussion about sustainable earnings. A new section on the quality of earnings was also added, including a discussion of pro forma earnings and improper recognition of revenue and expense.
- Chapter 20: Cost-Volume-Profit Relationships contains new coverage on the CVP income statement.

## Organizational Changes

Organizational changes were made to simplify chapters or to provide instructors with greater flexibility of coverage. Some of the areas most affected are as follows:

- The presentation of journal entries for periodic inventory systems was moved from Chapter 6: Inventory Costing to an appendix to Chapter 5: Accounting for Merchandising Operations to even out coverage and difficulty. Instructors generally felt that the coverage of journal entries—whether perpetual or periodic—should be combined in one chapter. The discussion of the periodic inventory system was expanded in Chapter 5 and now includes a conceptual discussion of how to calculate cost of goods sold.

  In addition, the format of the perpetual inventory records was simplified to make them even more understandable to students. Calculation of the gross profit margin and profit margins were added to Chapter 5, and inventory turnover ratios were moved to Chapter 6.
- The appendix on sales taxes (Appendix 5A in the second edition) was expanded to include services as well as goods. It was moved to an end-of-textbook appendix to allow instructors to position coverage of this topic wherever they feel it best meets their course objectives. Some instructors expressed preferences to cover this material in Chapter 2, some in Chapter 5, some in Chapter 10, and some not at all.
- Some of the material related to subsidiary ledgers and special journals previously found in the second edition's Chapter 7: Accounting Information Systems has been integrated into the chapter material where appropriate. An end-of-text appendix provides further detail to support the application of this topic to multiple chapters.
- Chapter 8: Accounting for Receivables was substantially reorganized to facilitate students' understanding of the allowance method.
- Discontinued operations, extraordinary items, and changes in accounting principles were moved from Chapter 14: Corporations: Dividends, Retained Earnings, and Income Reporting

to Chapter 18: Financial Statement Analysis, where they are now part of the discussion about sustainable earnings.
- In Chapter 15: Long-Term Liabilities, the section on bonds payable was simplified, and the coverage of the effective-interest and straight-line amortization methods were moved to end-of-chapter appendices.
- Chapter 18: Financial Statement Analysis summarizes ratio analysis in the chapter, but the detailed ratio calculations were moved to an appendix.
- Appendix B: Present Value Concepts was integrated in Chapter 15: Long-Term Liabilities as appropriate and moved to the Student Navigator CD, where coverage was expanded to include present value concepts related to notes payable.

## Deleted Material

We condensed or deleted concepts and procedures that are little used or are better suited to advanced courses.

- Chapter 10: Current Liabilities, internal controls over payroll were deleted from Appendix 10A because this topic was adequately covered in Chapter 7.
- Par and stated values were deleted from Chapter 12: Corporations: Organization and Share Capital Transactions.
- In Chapter 15: Long-Term Liabilities, coverage of issuing bonds between interest dates was deleted to help simplify this normally difficult chapter.
- Chapter 17: The Cash Flow Statement was rewritten and streamlined by covering all cash flow activities and transactions in a one-year extended illustration rather than over two years.
- Chapter 20: Managerial Accounting simplified the coverage of manufacturing costs by deleting prime costs and conversion costs.
- We have changed the sequence and reduced the quantity of ratios to enhance usefulness for analysis.

## Unparalleled End-of-Chapter Material

The second Canadian edition had more end-of-chapter material than any other textbook. This material guides students through the basic levels of cognitive understanding—knowledge, comprehension, application, analysis, synthesis, and evaluation—in a step-by-step process, starting first with questions, followed by brief exercises, exercises, problems, and finally, integrative cases.

Instructors told us they wanted more breadth and depth within each of these groupings to give them more flexibility in assigning end-of-chapter material. Using Bloom's Taxonomy of Learning, all of the end-of-chapter material was carefully reviewed. Topical gaps were identified and additional material added as required to facilitate progressive learning. Existing material was expanded, where relevant, to include additional transactions. Added complexities were added to selected end-of-chapter material to increase the range and difficulty level of material available to test critical problems solving skills.

As well, more cumulative coverage problems were added and an exciting new serial problem, the Continuing Cookie Chronicle, was introduced. The Continuing Cookie Chronicle begins in Part 1 with a student who organizes a service business and incurs transactions concurrent with the chapter topics. The business later expands to include a merchandising aspect and incorporates inventory transactions. In Part 2, the business deals with other issues related to accounts receivable, long-lived assets, and current liabilities. In Part 3, the business considers transforming itself into a partnership but chooses instead to reorganize as a corporation. Topical material relevant to each chapter continues to be applied as appropriate.

The Continuing Cookie Chronicle provides students with an opportunity to apply accounting concepts from each chapter to a familiar, recurring business situation. This type of serial problem, threaded through each chapter, is unique to introductory accounting textbooks and supplements the cumulative coverage problems, which cover several chapters. The Continuing Cookie Chronicle is a complimentary pedagogical feature, consistent with the Bloom's focus of the text, which carefully layers material in a building block format to foster student success.

# Acknowledgements

During the course of development of Accounting Principles, Third Canadian Edition, the authors benefited greatly from the feedback from instructors and students of accounting principles courses throughout the country, including many users of the previous editions of this text. The constructive suggestions and innovative ideas helped focus this revision on the needs of the students. In addition, the input and advice of the reviewers and ancillary authors and the throughnessthoroughness and accuracy of the proofers provided valuable feedback throughout the development of this revision.

## Survey Participants

Richard Boyack, *Southern Alberta Institute of Technology*
Alice Cleveland, *Nova Scotia Community College*
John S. Daye, *New Brunswick Community College*
Michael Douglas, *Seneca College of Applied Arts and & Technology*
Andrew Dykstra, *Georgian College of Applied Arts and & Technology*
David Eliason, *Southern Alberta Institute of Technology*
Bernard Finn, *St. Lawrence College*
Mary Hamm, *British Columbia Institute of Technology*
Ross Holmes, *Niagara College of Applied Arts & Technology*
David Hummel, *Conestoga College*
Alice Jardine, *New Brunswick Community College*
Connie Johl, *Douglas College*
JoAnn Lamore, *Mohawk College*
Paul J. Levie, *Camosun College*
Michael Malkoun, *St. Clair College*
Stephen Martin, *John Abbott College*
Muriel McKenna, *Seneca College of Applied Arts and & Technology*
Tony McNeil, *Sir Sandford Fleming College*
Jan Nyholt, *Southern Alberta Institute of Technology*
Penny Parker, *Fanshawe College of Applied Arts & Technology*
Ann Paterson, *Humber Institute of Technology and Advanced Learning*
Joe Pidutti, *Durham College*

Sharon Ramstad, *Grant MacEwan Community College*
Peter Richter, *John Abbott College*
Doug Ringrose, *Grant MacEwan Community College*
Carmel Robbins, *Southern Alberta Institute of Technology*
David J. Sale, *Kwantlen University College*
Pina Salvaggio, *Dawson College*
Agatha Thalheimer, *Camosun College*
John Vermeer, *Humber Institute of Technology and Advanced Learning*
Kathy Vincent, *Fanshawe College of Applied Arts & Technology*
John Western, *Kwantlen University College*
Julie Wong, *Dawson College*
Al Woodward, *Seneca College of Applied Arts and & Technology*
Barrie Yackness, *British Columbia Institute of Technology*

## Workshop Participants

Cécile Ashman, *Algonquin College*
Maria Bélanger, *Algonquin College*
Carole Reid Clyne, *Centennial College*
Chaman Doma, *Centennial College*
David Eliason, *Southern Alberta Institute of Technology*
Henry Funk, *Red River College*
Connie Johl, *Douglas College*
Rob Harvey, *Algonquin College*
Elizabeth Hicks, *Douglas College*
Valerie A. Kinnear, *Mount Royal College*
Douglas A. Leatherdale, *Georgian College of Applied Arts & Technology*
Joe Pidutti, *Durham College*
Carmel Robbins, *Southern Alberta Institute of Technology*
David J. Sale, *Kwantlen University College*
Pina Salvaggio, *Dawson College*
Marie Sinnott, *College of New Caledonia*
Nancy Tait, *Sir Sandford Fleming College*
Denise Terry, *Saskatchewan Institute of Applied Science and Technology*
Julie Wong, *Dawson College*

## Reviewers

David Fleming, *George Brown College*
Jeremy Frape, *Humber Institute of Technology and Advanced Learning*
Sharon Hatten, *British Columbia Institute of Technology*
Nadine Lancaster, *British Columbia Institute of Technology*
Michael Malkoun, *St. Clair College*
Keri Norrie, *Camosun College*

## Ancillary Authors, Contributors, and Proofers

Sally Anderson, *Mount Royal College*—Problem Material contributor and Solutions Manual checker
Cécile Ashman, *Algonquin College*—Sales Tax Appendix and Practice Set author
Hilary Becker, *Carleton University*—Student Navigator CD contributor
Maria Bélanger, *Algonquin College*—Student Navigator CD contributor
Tashia Batstone, *Memorial University of Newfoundland*—Solutions Manual and Test Bank author and, Student Navigator CD contributor
Susan Cohlmeyer, *Memorial University of Newfoundland*—Solutions Manual author and Student Navigator CD contributor
Carole Reid Clyne, *Centennial College*—Study Guide author
Elizabeth d'Anjou—Student Navigator CD contributor
Ian Farmer—Solutions Manual checker
Françoise Giovannangeli—Feature Story author
Ruth Heathcoate—Student Navigator CD contributor
Joanne Hinton, *University of New Brunswick*—Problem Material contributor and Solutions Manual checker
James Hughes, *British Columbia Institute of Technology*—Student Navigator CD contributor
Zofia Laubitz—proofreader
Robert Maher, *University of New Brunswick*—Student Navigator CD contributor
Michael Malkoun, *St. Clair College*—Website contributor
Keri Norrie, *Camosun College*—PowerPoint Slides author
David Schwinghamer—copyeditor and Reader's Guide author
Marie Sinnott, *College of New Caledonia*—Instructor's Manual author
Enola Stoyle, *University of Toronto*—Solutions Manual checker

## Accuracy

We have made every effort to ensure that this text is error-free. Accounting Principles has been extensively reviewed and proofed at three different production stages prior to publication. In addition, the ancillary authors read the draft text and provided valuable feedback. As well, the end-of-chapter material has been independently solved by at least three individuals, in addition to the authors. We would like to express our sincere gratitude to every one who spent countless hours ensuring the accuracy of this text and the solutions to the end-of-chapter material.

## Publications

We would like to thank The Forzani Group Ltd., for allowing us to reproduce its 2003 financial statements in Appendix A. We would also like to acknowledge the co-operation of many Canadian and international companies that allowed us to include extracts from their financial statements in the text and end-of-chapter material.

## A Final Note of Thanks

I consider myself privileged to be able to work with Valerie Kinnear and the US author team of Jerry Weygandt, Don Kieso, and Paul Kimmel. They have been generous in sharing their extensive teaching and writing experiences with me.

I appreciate the exemplary support and professional commitment given me by the talented team in the Wiley Canada higher education division. I wish to also thank Wiley's dedicated sales representatives who work tirelessly to service your needs.

It would not have been possible to write this text without the understanding of my employer, colleagues, students, family, and friends. Together, they provided a creative and supportive environment for my work.

Suggestions and comments from all users—instructors and students alike—of this textbook are encouraged and appreciated.

Barbara Trenholm
trenholm@unb.ca
Fredericton, New Brunswick
November 2003

---

## Chapter 6 ▶ Inventory Costing    276
*Minding the Books on Campus*

## Chapter 7 ▶ Internal Control and Cash    330
*Keeping Track of the Cash*

---

## concepts for review >>

Before studying this chapter, you should understand or, if necessary, review:

a. How to use the study aids in this book. (Student Owner's Manual, pp. viii–xviii)

b. What the Bloom's Taxonomy classifications (K, C, AP, AN, S, and E) mean. (Student Owner's Manual, p. xix)

c. How you learn best. (Student Owner's Manual, pp. xx–xxii)

d. The student supplements that accompany this text. (Student Owner's Manual, p. xxiii)

# Making the Right Moves

*The Forzani Group: www.forzanigroup.com*

CALGARY, Alta.—When it comes to football, everyone knows you need to "keep your eye on the ball" if you want to stay in the game. In business, as in sports, an organization needs to keep a careful eye on its financial accounting information if it wants to succeed and thrive. Consider the story of Calgary-based Forzani Group Ltd., Canada's largest retailer of sporting goods.

The company kicked off in 1974 when Calgary Stampeder John Forzani and three of his teammates launched Forzani's Locker Room, a small retail operation that sold athletic footwear. Gradually, the business expanded to include clothing and sports equipment. In 1988, it launched RnR, its Relaxed and Rugged banner, specializing in leisure and recreational apparel.

A series of acquisitions over the next decade resulted in further expansion. Meanwhile, in 1993, the company went public and its shares began trading on the Toronto Stock Exchange.

Today, The Forzani Group operates 376 corporate and franchise stores across Canada under the names Sport Chek, Sports Experts, Coast Mountain Sports, Sport Mart, Intersport, RnR, Econosports, and Atmosphere, as well as two e-commerce websites, Sportcheck.ca and Sportmart.ca. For its fiscal year ending February 2, 2003, the company scored sales of more than $1 billion and net income of $30.5 million.

That's pretty impressive for a company that started out as a single retail outlet! In fact, this spectacular growth is the result of countless decisions made all along the way. Does a particular acquisition make sense financially? Should the company operate its stores under separate banners? Is e-commerce worth pursuing? While many factors have no doubt contributed to The Forzani Group's success, one thing is certain: to make these strategic decisions and others, the company's management relied on accounting information.

They're not the only ones. Over the years, The Forzani Group's financial information has been used by other parties too. Its shareholders and potential investors have used it to make investment decisions, and its creditors have analysed it in determining whether to issue loans or other forms of credit.

In short, sound accounting information lets The Forzani Group and all interested parties know exactly how the business is doing at all times—an essential part of any winning strategy!

**The Navigator** learning system encourages you to use the learning aids in the chapter and set priorities as you study.

## the navigator ✔

- Understand *Concepts for Review*
- Read *Feature Story*
- Scan *Study Objectives*
- Read *Chapter Preview*
- Read text and answer *Before You Go On*
- Work *Demonstration Problem*
- Review *Summary of Study Objectives*
- Answer *Self-Study Questions*
- Complete assignments

# chapter 1
# Accounting in Action

**Study Objectives** give you a framework for learning the specific concepts presented in the chapter.

## study objectives >>

After studying this chapter, you should be able to:

1. Explain what accounting is.
2. Identify the users and explain the uses of accounting.
3. Demonstrate an understanding of why ethics is a fundamental business concept.
4. Explain generally accepted accounting principles and assumptions.
5. State and utilize the basic accounting equation and explain the meaning of assets, liabilities, and owner's equity.
6. Calculate the effect of business transactions on the basic accounting equation.
7. Understand what the four financial statements are and how they are prepared.

The opening story about The Forzani Group highlights the importance of having good financial information to make effective business decisions. Regardless of one's pursuits, the need for financial information is inescapable. You cannot earn a living, spend money, buy on credit, make an investment, or pay taxes without receiving, using, or giving financial information. Good decision-making depends on good information.

This chapter shows you that accounting is the system used to provide useful financial information. The chapter is organized as follows:

The **Preview** outlines the major topics and subtopics you will see in the chapter.

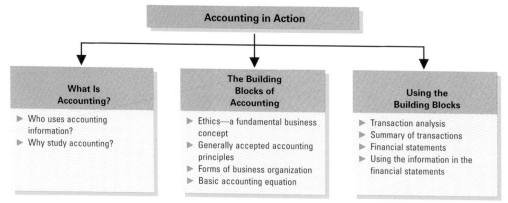

# What Is Accounting?

study objective 1

Explain what accounting is.

**Essential terms** are printed in blue when they first appear, and are defined in the end-of-chapter glossary.

Accounting is an information system that identifies, records, and communicates the economic events of an organization to interested users. Economic events are activities related to the production and distribution of goods and services in an organization. Let's take a closer look at these activities:

1. **Identifying economic activities** involves selecting those events that are evidence of economic activity by a particular organization. The sale of sporting goods by Forzani, the delivery of telephone services by Bell Canada, and the payment of salaries by major league sports teams are examples of economic events.

2. Once identified, economic events are recorded to provide a history of the organization's financial activities. Recording consists of keeping a **systematic chronological diary of events measured in dollars and cents**. In recording, economic events are also **classified** and **summarized**.

3. This identification and recording of activities is only useful if the information is **communicated** to interested users. The information is communicated through accounting reports, the most common of which are called **financial statements**. To make the financial information meaningful, accountants report the recorded data in a standardized way. Information resulting from similar transactions is accumulated and totalled. Because the transactions are grouped together, they are said to be reported in aggregate.

For example, all sales transactions of The Forzani Group are accumulated over a certain period of time and reported as one amount in its financial statements. By presenting the recorded data in aggregate, the accounting process simplifies a multitude of transactions and makes a series of activities understandable and meaningful. This simplification can result in a loss of detail, however. The Forzani Group's financial statements are highly condensed and some critics would argue that the presentation is too simple. Still, Forzani is not alone in this reporting practice. Most companies report condensed information for simplicity, but also to avoid revealing significant details to their competitors.

A vital part of communicating economic events is the accountant's ability and responsibility to **analyse** and **interpret** the reported information. Analysis involves the use of ratios, percentages, graphs, and charts to highlight significant financial trends and relationships. Interpretation involves explaining the uses, meaning, and limitations of reported data.

The accounting process may be summarized as follows:

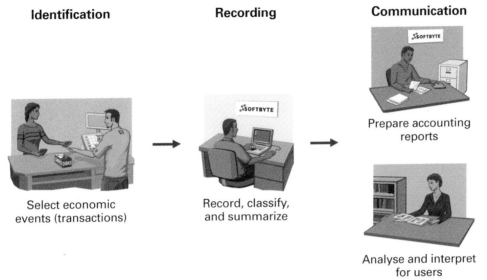

| Identification | Recording | Communication |
|---|---|---|
| Select economic events (transactions) | Record, classify, and summarize | Prepare accounting reports |
| | | Analyse and interpret for users |

**Illustration 1-1 ◄**
Accounting process

Accounting must consider the needs of the users of financial information. Therefore, accountants need to know who these users are and something about their needs for information.

## Who Uses Accounting Information?

Because it communicates financial information, accounting is often called the language of business. The information a user of financial information needs depends upon the kinds of decisions that user makes. The differences in the decisions divide the users of financial information into two broad groups: internal users and external users.

**study objective 2**

Identify the users and explain the uses of accounting.

### Internal Users

Internal users of accounting information are those who plan, organize, and run a business. These include **marketing managers, production supervisors, finance directors, and company officers**. In running a business, internal users must answer many important questions, as shown in Illustration 1-2.

**Illustration 1-2 ▶**

Questions asked by internal
users

## Questions Asked by Internal Users

Is cash sufficient to pay bills?

What is the cost of manufacturing each
unit of product?

Can we afford to give employee
pay raises this year?

Which product line is the
most profitable?

To answer these and other questions, users need detailed information on a timely basis. For internal users, accounting provides internal reports. Examples are financial comparisons of operating alternatives, projections of earnings from new sales campaigns, and forecasts of cash needs for the next year.

## External Users

External users are those who work for other organizations but who have an interest in and need for information about the company's financial position and performance. There are several types of external users of accounting information. **Investors** (owners) use accounting information to make decisions to buy, hold, or sell their ownership interest. **Creditors**, such as suppliers and bankers, use accounting information to evaluate the risks of granting credit or lending money. Some questions that investors and creditors may ask about a company are shown in Illustration 1-3.

**Illustration 1-3 ▶**

Questions asked by
external users

## Questions Asked by External Users

Is the company earning
satisfactory income?

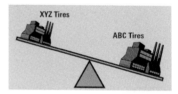

How does the company
compare in size and profitability
with competitors?

Will the company be able to pay
its debts as they come due?

The information needs and questions of other external users vary considerably. **Taxing authorities**, such as the Canada Customs and Revenue Agency, want to know whether the company respects the tax laws. **Regulatory agencies**, such as provincial securities commissions, want to know whether the company is operating within established rules. **Customers** are interested in whether a company will continue to honour product warranties and support its product lines. **Labour unions** want to know whether the owners can pay increased wages and benefits. **Economic planners** use accounting information to forecast economic activity.

---

**ACCOUNTING IN ACTION ► International Insight**

Concern over the quality and honesty of financial reporting isn't limited to North America. Recently, the Chinese Ministry of Finance reprimanded a large accounting firm for preparing false financial reports for several publicly traded companies. Afterward, the state-run news agency noted that investors and analysts actually felt that the punishment of the firm was not adequate. In fact, a survey of investors in China found that less than 10% had full confidence in companies' annual reports. As a result of these concerns, the Chinese Institute of Certified Public Accountants promised to strengthen its policing of its members.

**Accounting in Action** insights provide examples of accounting situations from various perspectives—international, e-business, business, and ethics.

## Why Study Accounting?

In the early 2000s, Canada saw the collapse of the high-tech industry, a falling stock market, employee layoffs, and the bankruptcy of several well-known companies. Corporate scandals made headlines on a weekly basis. The impact was staggering and was felt around the world. For example, when the global communications company WorldCom lowered its stated income by US$3.8 billion, this restatement contributed to investor losses of US$179.3 billion and 17,000 job losses. Energy trader Enron's schemes that falsely increased its income by US$568 million, leading to financial restatements and bankruptcy, caused investor losses of US$66.4 billion and 6,100 job losses. These are only two of the many high-profile companies that, in a matter of a few years, were investigated in more than one country for accusations of accounting misstatements, bogus securities trading, or misleading investors.

Proposals to improve business practices, corporate governance, public oversight, and accountability have come from regulators, the investment community, and the accounting profession. As a result, new requirements now guide business behaviour as well as accounting and auditing practices.

One thing is very evident from all these embarrassing, illegal, and unethical business events—**accounting is important**. Good accounting is essential to sound business and investing decisions. Bad accounting will not be tolerated. If there is the slightest hint that a company's accounting practices cannot be trusted, investors sell their holdings and the company's share price falls dramatically.

The world's economic systems are dependent upon highly transparent, reliable, and accurate financial reporting. Accounting has long been labelled "the language of business." That language must be understandable, useful, and truthful to be of any value.

Recent events such as these reinforce the worth of studying, understanding, and using accounting information. This textbook is your introduction to accounting as a valuable tool of business record keeping, communication, and analysis. Make the most of this course—it will serve you for a lifetime in ways you cannot now imagine.

On the Student Navigator CD that accompanies this text, more information is available about why accounting is important, potential career paths, and profiles of business people who use accounting information.

This **CD Icon** informs you of additional resources available on the Student Navigator CD that came with your text.

Career Paths

## BEFORE YOU GO ON . . .

**Before You Go On** questions at the end of major text sections offer an opportunity to stop and re-examine the key points you have studied. Related exercise material directs you to Brief Exercises (BE) and Exercises (E) with similar study objectives.

▶**Review It**

1. What is accounting?
2. What is meant by analysis and interpretation?
3. Who uses accounting information? Identify specific internal and external users of accounting information.
4. How can the study of accounting benefit you?

*Related exercise material:* BE1–1.

# The Building Blocks of Accounting

Every profession develops a body of theory that consists of principles and assumptions. Accounting is no exception. Just as a doctor follows certain standards to treat a patient's illness, an accountant follows certain standards to report financial information. For these standards to work, a fundamental business concept is followed—ethical behaviour.

## Ethics—A Fundamental Business Concept

The corporate scandals of the early 2000s made it very clear that certain actions can have a huge impact on other people and organizations. These actions are the strongest argument in favour of the importance of ethics.

The standards of conduct by which one's actions are judged as right or wrong, honest or dishonest, fair or not fair, are **ethics**. We have seen what happens when we cannot depend on the honesty of the individuals we deal with. If managers, customers, investors, employees, and creditors act dishonestly, effective communication and economic activity decline, and information lacks credibility.

Fortunately, most individuals in business are ethical. Their actions are both legal and responsible. They consider the organization's interests when they make decisions. Accounting and other professionals have extensive rules of conduct to guide their behaviour with each other and the public. Many companies today have also adopted codes of conduct that outline their commitment to ethical behaviour in internal and external relationships.

To make you more aware of ethical situations and to give you practice at solving ethical dilemmas, we have included three types of ethics materials: (1) **marginal notes** that provide helpful hints for developing ethical sensitivity, (2) **ethics in accounting boxes** that highlight ethical situations and issues, and (3) in the end-of-chapter material, an **ethics case** that simulates a business situation. When you analyse these ethical situations, you should apply the steps outlined in Illustration 1-4.

**Illustration 1-4** ▼

Steps used to analyse ethical dilemmas

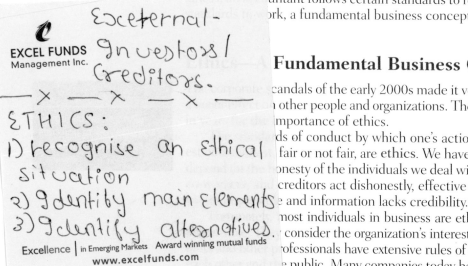

| 1. Recognize an ethical situation and the ethical issues involved. | 2. Identify and analyse the main elements in the situation. | 3. Identify the alternatives, and weigh the impact of each alternative on various stakeholders. |
|---|---|---|
| Use your personal ethics or an organization's code of ethics to identify ethical situations and issues. | Identify the *stakeholders*—persons or groups who may be harmed or benefited. Ask the question: What are the responsibilities and obligations of the parties involved? | Select the most ethical alternative, considering all the consequences. Sometimes there will be one right answer. Other situations involve more than one possible solution. These situations require an evaluation of each alternative and the selection of the best one. |

# Generally Accepted Accounting Principles

The accounting profession has developed a set of standards that are generally accepted and universally practised. This common set of standards is called **generally accepted accounting principles (GAAP)**. These standards—developed over time in response to tradition, experience, and user needs—recommend how to report economic events.

The Canadian Institute of Chartered Accountants (CICA)—through an Accounting Standards Board (AcSB)—has the main responsibility for the development of generally accepted accounting principles in Canada. The AcSB's most important criterion is that accounting principles should generate the most useful financial information for making business decisions. In other words, **the basic objective of financial reporting is to communicate information that is useful to investors, creditors, and other users when they make decisions**.

To meet this objective, the AcSB creates generally accepted accounting principles after a long process of consultation with organizations and individuals that are interested in, or affected by, the standards. Its work is supervised by an independent Accounting Oversight Council. This council protects the public's interests and makes sure that the AcSB takes care of the needs, and considers the viewpoints, of the entire business community, not just the public accounting profession.

GAAP, published in the *CICA Handbook*, has legal status for companies that follow the regulations of the *Canada Business Corporations Act* and the provincial securities commissions. It is important to understand that standards are not static. They should and do change over time to ensure that their main purpose—providing information that is relevant to decision-making—continues to be met.

Internationally, accounting standards can vary from country to country. Most countries have their own standard-setting body. One group, the International Accounting Standards Board, has been working to reduce the differences in accounting practices across countries. This, in turn, improves the ability of investors, creditors, and others to make informed decisions about policies and where to place their resources.

> **study objective 4**
>
> Explain generally accepted accounting principles and assumptions.

---

**ACCOUNTING IN ACTION ▶ International Insight**

Canada is teeming with foreign culture and products—Microsoft, Samsung, Wal-Mart, The Gap, McDonald's, NIKE, and Toyota, just to name a few. Foreign-controlled companies—mostly American, some from Britain and Japan—accounted for 31.5% of the $1.3 trillion in corporate revenue generated in Canada in a recent year.

Canadians have also become more global. More than 220 Canadian companies are listed on at least one stock exchange outside of Canada. Canadian companies are expanding foreign operations, selling to foreign interests, and merging with companies located in other countries. Their goal is to better compete in the global marketplace.

What does this mean to the users of financial information? One must understand not only the differences in reporting requirements, but also important economic, legal, political, and cultural issues before one can make well-informed business decisions.

---

We need to have a good understanding of generally accepted accounting principles in order to prepare and understand accounting information. Many generally accepted accounting principles will be introduced as you progress through the text. In this chapter, we learn about the cost principle. In later chapters, we will introduce the revenue recognition principle (Chapter 3), the matching principle (Chapter 3), and the full disclosure principle (Chapter 11). Chapter 11 explores these principles, and the underlying assumptions and constraints of accounting, in greater detail.

One of the basic principles is the **cost principle**. This principle states that assets should be recorded at their original historical cost. **Cost is the value exchanged at the time something is acquired.** If you buy a house today, the cost is the amount you pay for it, say $125,000. If the house is appraised in two years at $150,000, the appraised amount is its fair market value—the value determined by the market for homes at that time. At the time of acquisition, cost and fair market value are the same. In later periods, cost and fair market value may vary, but the cost amount continues to be used.

To see the importance of the cost principle, consider the following example. At one time, Greyhound had 128 bus stations throughout North America with a cost of approximately $200 million. The current market value of the stations is approximately $1 billion. Under the cost principle, the bus stations are recorded and reported at $200 million, not $1 billion. Until the bus stations are actually sold, estimates of market values are considered to be too subjective.

As the Greyhound example indicates, cost has an important advantage over other valuations. It is reliable. Cost is definite and verifiable. The values exchanged at the time something is acquired can be objectively measured. Users can rely on the information supplied as they know it is based on fact. However, critics argue that cost is often not relevant. They believe market values provide more useful information. Despite its shortcomings, cost continues to be used in financial statements because of its reliability.

When generally accepted accounting principles are developed, certain basic assumptions are guide. These assumptions provide a foundation for the accounting process. One assumption is the cost principle is the **going concern assumption**. Two other important are the **monetary unit assumption** and the **economic entity assumption**.

assumption. A major factor in the decision to record Greyhound's ... , rather than at market, is the **going concern assumption**. Going he firm will continue to operate in the foreseeable future. In spite ess failures, companies have a fairly high continuance rate (they r after year).

s the most appropriate value at which to record assets such as Grey- because the stations were acquired for use in the business, rather than relevance to the company is the amount it gave up to acquire these te of their current worth. The going concern assumption presumes that erate long enough to use its assets for their intended purpose and to fulfill the company's commitments. The going concern assumption and cost principle are modified if the company is expected to discontinue operations. In such cases, the lower of the cost and estimated market value is used as the most relevant value for decision-makers.

### Monetary Unit Assumption.

The **monetary unit assumption** requires that only transaction data that can be expressed in terms of money be included in the accounting records. This assumption enables accounting to quantify (measure) economic events. In Canada, we use the dollar to record these transactions. In Europe, the euro is used. In Japan, the yen is used.

This assumption does prevent some relevant information from being included in the accounting records. For example, the health of the owner, the quality of service, and the morale of employees would not be included, because they cannot be quantified in terms of money.

An important part of the monetary unit assumption is the added assumption that the unit of measure remains sufficiently constant over time. In other words, inflation (a rise in prices) or deflation (a drop in prices) is ignored when adding, subtracting, or comparing dollars of different years. Assume a company purchases land in 1965 for $100,000 and that the same amount of land in a similar location costs $400,000 in 2005, 40 years later. If a second lot of land were purchased in 2005, the land account for the company would show a total cost of land of $500,000. The fact that these dollars had different value (or purchasing power) throughout the years is overlooked. Although inflation was once a significant accounting issue, for the last 75 years inflation has averaged only 3%. Inflation is considered a non-issue for accounting purposes in Canada.

---

**Helpful hints** help clarify concepts or items being discussed.

**Helpful hint** Principles and assumptions will be discussed throughout the text. Those discussed so far are shown in bold:

Principles
**Cost**
Revenue recognition
Matching
Full disclosure

Assumptions
**Going concern**
**Monetary unit**
**Economic entity**
Time period

Economic Entity Assumption. An economic entity can be any organization or unit in society. It may be a business enterprise (such as Bombardier), a governmental unit (such as the Province of Alberta), a municipality (such as the City of Toronto), a native band council (such as the Kingsclear Indian Band), a school board (such as the Burnaby School Board), a curling championship event (such as the Nokia Brier), or a club (such as the Hamilton Rotary Club). The **economic entity assumption** requires that the activities of the entity be kept separate and distinct from the activities of its owner, and all other economic entities.

To illustrate, if Ellen Gélinas, owner of Ellen's Boutique, charges any of her personal living costs as expenses of the Boutique, then the economic entity assumption is violated. Similarly, the economic entity assumption assumes that the activities of Sports Experts and Sport Chek, both owned by Forzani, can be separated into two distinct economic entities for accounting purposes.

## Forms of Business Organization

The economic entity assumption is generally discussed regarding a business enterprise, which may be organized as a proprietorship, partnership, or corporation.

### Proprietorship

A business owned by one person is a **proprietorship**. The owner is usually the operator of the business. Small service businesses (hair stylists, service stations, and bookkeepers), farms, and small retail stores (antique shops, corner grocery stores, and book stores) are often proprietorships. Usually only a relatively small amount of money (capital) is necessary to start in business as a proprietorship. The owner (the proprietor) receives any profits, suffers any losses, and is personally liable (responsible) for all debts of the business. There is no legal distinction between the business as an economic unit and the owner. However, the records of the business activities are kept separate from the personal records and activities of the owner, in accordance with the economic entity assumption.

Proprietorships represent the largest number of businesses in Canada, yet they are typically the smallest in size.

### Partnership

A business owned by two or more persons associated as partners is a **partnership**. In most aspects, a partnership is similar to a proprietorship, except that more than one owner is involved. Typically, a partnership agreement (written or oral) defines such terms as initial investments, duties of each partner, division of net income (or net loss), and settlement to be made upon death or withdrawal of a partner. Each partner generally has unlimited personal liability for all debts of the partnership, regardless of which partner created the debt. Similar to an owner in a proprietorship, a partner's personal assets may be sold to repay the partnership debt. **Like a proprietorship, the partnership activities must be kept separate from the personal activities of the partners for accounting purposes.** Partnerships are often used to organize service-type businesses, including professional practices (lawyers, doctors, architects, and accountants).

### Corporation

A business that is organized as a separate legal entity under federal or provincial corporation law is a **corporation**. Its ownership is divided into transferable shares. The owners of the shares (shareholders) enjoy **limited liability**. They are not personally liable for the debts of the corporate entity. Shareholders **may sell all or part of their shares to other investors at any time.** Easy changes of ownership add to the attractiveness of investing in a corporation. Because ownership can be transferred without dissolving the corporation, the corporation enjoys an **unlimited life**.

Although the combined number of proprietorships and partnerships in Canada is more than the number of corporations, the revenue produced by corporations is far greater. Most of the largest enterprises in Canada—for example, Bell Canada, EnCana, Imperial Oil, Magna, George Weston, and Loblaw—are corporations. The annual revenue of each of these corporations ranges from $10 billion to $25 billion. These corporations are publicly traded. That is, their shares are listed on Canadian stock exchanges. Public corporations commonly distribute their financial statements to shareholders, creditors, other interested parties, and the general public upon request. Forzani is a public corporation. You can access its financial statements on its website, which is given in our feature story, as well as in Appendix A at the back of this textbook.

Other companies are private corporations, which do not issue publicly traded shares. Some of the largest private companies in Canada include McCain Foods, Irving Oil, the West Edmonton Mall, and Palliser Furniture. Like proprietorships and partnerships, these companies seldom distribute their financial statements publicly.

## Basic Accounting Equation

**study objective 5**

State and utilize the basic accounting equation and explain the meaning of assets, liabilities, and owner's equity.

Other essential building blocks of accounting are the categories into which economic events are classified. The two basic elements of a business are what it owns and what it owes. **Assets** are the resources owned by a business. Forzani has total assets of $506.8 million. Liabilities and owner's equity are the rights or claims against these resources. Claims of those to whom money or other obligations are owed (creditors) are called **liabilities**. Claims of owners are called **owner's equity**. Forzani has liabilities of $303.1 million and owner's equity of $203.7 million. This relationship of assets, liabilities, and owner's equity can be expressed as an equation as follows:

**Illustration 1-5 ▶**

The basic accounting equation

| Assets | = | Liabilities | + | Owner's Equity |
|---|---|---|---|---|
| $506.8 million | = | $303.1 million | + | $203.7 million |

This equation is referred to as the basic accounting equation. Assets must equal the sum of liabilities and owner's equity. Because creditors' claims are paid before ownership claims if a business is liquidated, liabilities are shown before owner's equity in the basic accounting equation.

The accounting equation applies to all **economic entities** regardless of size, nature of business, or form of business organization. It applies to a small proprietorship such as a corner grocery store as much as it does to a large corporation such as The Forzani Group. The equation provides the underlying framework for recording and summarizing the economic events of a business enterprise.

Let's look at the categories in the basic accounting equation in more detail.

### Assets

As noted earlier, assets are the resources owned by a business. They are used to carry out activities such as the production and distribution of merchandise. Every asset has the capacity to provide future services or benefits. In a business enterprise, that service potential or future economic benefit eventually results in cash inflows (receipts) to the enterprise.

For example, Campus Pizza owns a delivery truck that provides economic benefits because it is used to deliver pizzas. Other assets of Campus Pizza are tables, chairs, a CD player, a cash register, an oven, dishes, silverware, inventory, supplies, and, of course, cash.

## Liabilities

**Liabilities** are claims against assets. That is, **liabilities are existing debts and obligations**. For example, businesses of all sizes usually borrow money and purchase merchandise inventory and supplies on credit. Campus Pizza, for instance, purchases pizza ingredients and beverages on credit from suppliers. These obligations are called accounts payable. Campus Pizza also has a note payable to the Bank of Montreal for the money borrowed to purchase its delivery truck. Campus Pizza may also have wages payable to employees, GST payable and PST payable to the federal and provincial governments, and property taxes payable to the municipality. All of these persons or entities to which Campus Pizza owes money are called its **creditors**.

A creditor who is not paid may legally force the liquidation of a business. In that case, the law requires that creditor claims be paid before ownership claims.

## Owner's Equity

The ownership claim on total assets is known as **owner's equity**. It is equal to total assets minus total liabilities. To find out what belongs to owners, we subtract creditors' claims (the liabilities) from assets. The remainder—owner's equity—is the owner's claim on the assets of the business. Since the claims of creditors must be paid before ownership claims, the owner's equity is often called residual equity. If the equity is negative—that is, if total liabilities exceed total assets—the term **owner's deficiency** (or deficit) describes the shortage.

In a proprietorship, owner's equity is increased by investments made by the owner and decreased by withdrawals made by the owner. However, the primary purpose of most companies is to generate net income from business activities, which also increases the owner's equity.

**Investments.** **Investments by owner** are the assets the owner puts into the business into what is known as the owner's capital account. Investments may be in the form of cash or other assets (e.g., vehicle, computer) that are contributed by the owner.

**Drawings.** An owner may withdraw cash (or other assets) for personal use. These withdrawals could be recorded as a direct decrease of owner's equity. It is generally considered better to use a separate classification called **drawings** so the total withdrawals for the accounting period can be determined.

**Net Income.** Revenues increase owner's equity and expenses decrease owner's equity. **Net income** results when revenues exceed expenses, and owner's equity will correspondingly increase. Conversely, if expenses exceed revenues, a **net loss** will result and owner's equity will decrease.

***Revenues.*** **Revenues** result from business activities performed to earn income. Generally, revenues result from the sale of merchandise inventory, the performance of services, the rental of property, and the lending of money.

Revenues normally result in an increase in an asset and an increase in owner's equity. They may arise from different sources and are identified by various names, depending on the nature of the business. Campus Pizza, for instance, has two categories of revenues—pizza sales and beverage sales. Common sources of revenue include sales, fees, services, commissions, and rent.

***Expenses.*** **Expenses** are the costs of assets consumed or services used in order to earn revenue. They are decreases in owner's equity that result from operating the business. Like revenues, expenses take many forms and are identified by various names, depending on the type of asset consumed or service used. For example, Campus Pizza recognizes (records) the following expenses: cost of ingredients (meat, flour, cheese, tomato paste, mushrooms, etc.), cost of beverages, wages expense, utility expense (electric, gas, and water expense), telephone expense, delivery expense (gasoline, repairs, licences, etc.), supplies expense (napkins, detergents, aprons, etc.), rent expense, insurance expense, interest expense, and property tax expense.

In summary, the principal sources (increases) of owner's equity are (1) investments by the owner, and (2) net income (revenues − expenses). Decreases in owner's equity result from (1) withdrawals of assets by the owner and (2) net losses. These relationships are shown in Illustration 1-6.

**Illustration 1-6 ▶**

Increases and decreases in owner's equity

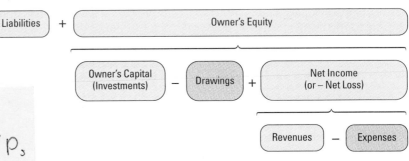

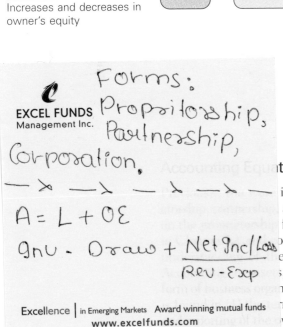

### Accounting Equation Distinctions by Type of Business Organization

You were introduced to the three forms of business organizations—proprietorship, partnership, and corporation. In the early chapters of this text, we focus mostly on the proprietorship form of organization. Partnerships will be discussed in more detail and corporations in Chapter 13. Until that time, you need only a general understanding of the accounting distinctions between these types of organization. Accounting for assets, liabilities, revenues, and expenses is the same, regardless of the form of business organization. The primary distinction between the forms of organizations is (1) the terminology used to name the equity section, and (2) the accounting for the reporting of the owner's investments and withdrawals.

In a proprietorship, the company is owned by one person and the equity is termed **owner's equity**. In a partnership, because there are two or more owners the equity is termed **partners' equity**. In the corporate form of business organization, the owners are the shareholders and the equity is called **shareholders' equity**. In Illustration 1-5, when the assets, liabilities, and equity were reported for The Forzani Group, the equity was identified as owner's equity for simplicity. Technically, since Forzani is a corporation, this equity should have been called *shareholders'* equity.

You have learned that in a proprietorship, owner's equity is increased by owner's investments and net income, and decreased by owner's drawings (and net losses, if they exist). In a partnership, each partner's equity is similarly increased by the investments of the partners and each partner's proportionate share of partnership income, and decreased by the drawings of each partner (and proportionate share of partnership losses, if they exist). In both proprietorships and partnerships, equity is summarized and reported for each owner in a one-line capital account.

It is not practical to do this for a corporation, where thousands of owners may exist. In a corporation, the investments by the shareholders (owners) are made by purchasing shares. These investments are grouped together and called **share capital**. They are the first portion of shareholders' equity. The second portion of shareholders' equity is reported as **retained earnings**. Retained earnings represent the accumulated earnings of the company that have been retained (i.e., not paid out to shareholders). Payments to the shareholders are called **dividends**. Equity is reported for each different type of business organization as follows:

| Proprietorship | | Partnership | | Corporation | |
|---|---|---|---|---|---|
| Owner's equity: | | Partners' equity: | | Shareholders' equity: | |
| V. Buré, capital | $50,000 | M. Wu, capital | $ 75,000 | Share capital | $500,000 |
| | | A. Scholten, capital | 75,000 | Retained earnings | 350,000 |
| | | Total partners' equity | $150,000 | Total shareholders' equity | $850,000 |

## BEFORE YOU GO ON . . .

### ► Review It

1. Why is ethics a fundamental business concept?
2. What are generally accepted accounting principles? Give an example.
3. Explain the going concern, monetary unit, and economic entity assumptions.
4. What is the basic accounting equation?
5. What are assets, liabilities, and owner's equity?
6. Distinguish the types of equity for each form of business organization.

### ► Do It

Classify the following items as investments by owner (I), owner's drawings (D), revenues (R), or expenses (E), and indicate whether these items increase or decrease owner's equity: (1) rent expense, (2) service revenue, (3) drawings, and (4) salaries expense.

#### Action Plan

- Review the rules for changes in owner's equity: Investments and revenues increase owner's equity. Drawings and expenses decrease owner's equity.
- Understand the sources of revenue: the sale of merchandise, performance of services, rental of property, and lending of money.
- Understand what causes expenses: the consumption or use of assets or services.
- Recognize that drawings are withdrawals of cash or other assets from the business for personal use.

#### Solution

1. Rent expense is classified as an expense (E). It decreases net income and ultimately owner's equity.
2. Service revenue is classified as revenue (R). It increases net income and ultimately owner's equity.
3. Drawings are classified as owner's drawings (D). They decrease owner's equity.
4. Salaries expense is classified as an expense (E). It decreases net income and ultimately owner's equity.

*Related exercise material:* BE1–2, BE1–3, BE1–4, BE1–5, E1–1, E1–2, and E1–3.

the
navigator

> Sometimes **Review It** questions stand alone; other times they are accompanied by practice exercises.
> The **Do It** exercises, like the one here, ask you to put newly acquired knowledge to work. They outline the **Action Plan** necessary to complete the exercise and show a **Solution**.

# Using the Building Blocks

Transactions are the economic events of a business that are recorded. Transactions may be external or internal. External transactions are economic events between the company and some outside party. For example, the purchase of cooking equipment by Campus Pizza from a supplier, the payment of monthly rent to the landlord, and the sale of pizzas to customers are all external transactions. Internal transactions are economic events that occur entirely within one company. The use of cooking and cleaning supplies is an internal transaction for Campus Pizza.

**study objective 6**

Calculate the effect of business transactions on the basic accounting equation.

A company may carry on many activities that are not by themselves business transactions. Hiring employees, answering the telephone, talking with customers, and placing an order for merchandise with a supplier are examples. Some of these activities, however, may lead to a business transaction. Employees will earn salaries, and merchandise will be delivered by the supplier. Each transaction must be analysed for its effect on the components of the basic accounting equation and must be recorded in the accounting process. This analysis must identify the specific items affected and the amount of change in each item.

**Illustration 1-7 ▶**

Transaction identification process

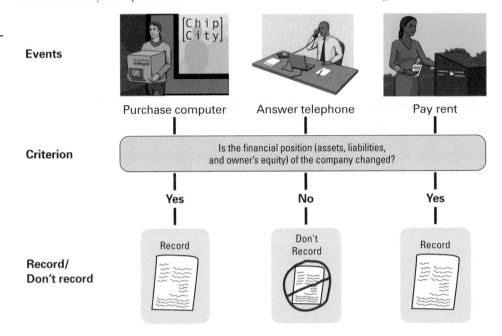

| Events | Purchase computer | Answer telephone | Pay rent |

**Criterion** — Is the financial position (assets, liabilities, and owner's equity) of the company changed?

Yes — No — Yes

**Record/Don't record** — Record / Don't Record / Record

The equality of the basic accounting equation must always be preserved. Therefore, each transaction must have a dual effect on the equation. For example, if an asset is increased, there must be a corresponding

1. decrease in another asset, or
2. increase in a liability, or
3. increase in owner's equity.

Two or more items could be affected when an asset is increased. For example, as one asset is increased by $10,000, another asset could decrease by $6,000, and a liability could increase by $4,000. Any change in a liability or ownership claim requires a similar analysis.

## Transaction Analysis

Accounting Cycle Tutorial— Analysing Business Transactions

The following examples are business transactions for a computer programming business during its first month of operations. You should study these transactions until you are sure you understand them. They are not difficult, but they are important to your success in this course. The ability to analyse transactions in terms of the basic accounting equation is essential for an understanding of accounting.

**Transaction (1): Investment by Owner.** Marc Doucet decides to open a computer programming service. On September 1, 2005, he invests $15,000 cash in the business, which he names Softbyte. This transaction results in an equal increase in assets and owner's equity. In this case, there is an increase in the asset account Cash, $15,000, and an equal increase in the owner's equity account, M. Doucet, Capital, $15,000. The effect of this transaction on the basic equation is:

When a specific **account title** is used, the account name is capitalized.

|  | Assets | = | Liabilities | + | Owner's Equity |
|---|---|---|---|---|---|
|  |  |  |  |  | M. Doucet, |
|  | Cash | = |  |  | Capital |
| (1) | +$15,000 | = |  |  | +$15,000 |

Observe that the two sides of the basic equation remain equal. Note that investments by the owner are not revenues. They are excluded when determining net income. Therefore, it is necessary to make clear that the increase is an investment in the owner's capital account rather than revenue from operations.

**Transaction (2): Purchase of Equipment for Cash.** Softbyte purchases computer equipment for $7,000 cash. This transaction results in an equal increase and decrease in total assets, though the composition of assets changes. Cash is decreased by $7,000, and the asset account Equipment is increased by $7,000. The specific effect of this transaction and the cumulative effect of the first two transactions are:

|  |  | Assets |  |  | = | Liabilities | + | Owner's Equity |
|---|---|---|---|---|---|---|---|---|
|  |  |  |  |  |  |  |  | M. Doucet, |
|  | Balance | Cash | + | Equipment | = |  |  | Capital |
|  | Beginning | $15,000 |  |  |  |  |  | $15,000 |
| (2) |  | −7,000 |  | +$7,000 |  |  |  |  |
|  | Ending | $ 8,000 | + | $7,000 | = |  |  | $15,000 |
|  |  |  | $15,000 |  |  |  | $15,000 |  |

Observe that total assets are still $15,000, and that Doucet's equity also remains at $15,000, the amount of his original investment.

**Transaction (3): Purchase of Supplies on Credit.** Softbyte purchases $1,600 of computer paper and other supplies expected to last several months from the Chuah Supply Company. Chuah Supply agrees to allow Softbyte to pay this bill next month (in October). This transaction is referred to as a purchase on account, or a credit purchase. Assets are increased because of the expected future benefits of using the paper and supplies. Liabilities are increased by the amount due to Chuah Supply Company. The asset Supplies is increased by $1,600, and the liability Accounts Payable is increased by the same amount. The effect on the equation is:

|  |  | Assets |  |  |  |  | = | Liabilities | + | Owner's Equity |
|---|---|---|---|---|---|---|---|---|---|---|
|  |  |  |  |  |  |  |  | Accounts |  | M. Doucet, |
|  | Balance | Cash | + | Supplies | + | Equipment | = | Payable | + | Capital |
|  | Beginning | $8,000 |  |  |  | $7,000 |  |  |  | $15,000 |
| (3) |  |  |  | +$1,600 |  |  |  | +$1,600 |  |  |
|  | Ending | $8,000 | + | $1,600 | + | $7,000 | = | $1,600 | + | $15,000 |
|  |  |  | $16,600 |  |  |  |  | $16,600 |  |  |

Total assets are now $16,600. This total is matched by a $1,600 creditor's claim and a $15,000 ownership claim.

**Transaction (4): Services Provided for Cash.** Softbyte receives $1,200 cash from customers for programming services it has provided. This transaction represents Softbyte's principal revenue-producing activity. Remember that revenue increases net income, which in turn increases owner's equity. Cash is increased by $1,200, and Service Revenue is increased by $1,200. We don't have room to give details for each individual revenue and expense account in this illustration, so revenues (and expenses when we get to them) are summarized under one column heading for Revenues and one for Expenses. However, it is important to keep track of the account titles affected (e.g., Service Revenue) as they will be needed when financial statements are prepared in the next section. The new balances in the equation are:

|  |  | Assets | | | = | Liabilities | + | Owner's Equity | | |
|---|---|---|---|---|---|---|---|---|---|---|
|  |  |  |  |  |  | Accounts | | M. Doucet, | | |
|  | Balance | Cash | + Supplies | + Equipment | = | Payable | + | Capital | + | Revenues |
|  | Beginning | $8,000 | $1,600 | $7,000 | | $1,600 | | $15,000 | | |
| (4) |  | +1,200 | | | | | | | | +$1,200 |
|  | Ending | $9,200 + | $1,600 + | $7,000 | = | $1,600 | + | $15,000 | + | $1,200 |
|  |  | | $17,800 | | | | | $17,800 | | |

The two sides of the equation balance at $17,800.

**Transaction (5): Purchase of Advertising on Credit.** Softbyte receives a bill for $250 from the *National Post* for advertising the opening of its business. It postpones payment of the bill until a later date. This transaction results in an increase in liabilities and a decrease in owner's equity (because the cost of the advertising is an expense). The cost of advertising is an expense, as opposed to an asset, because the benefits have already been used. This expense is included in determining net income. The specific accounts involved are Accounts Payable and Advertising Expense. The effect on the accounting equation is:

|  |  | Assets | | | = | Liabilities | + | Owner's Equity | | | |
|---|---|---|---|---|---|---|---|---|---|---|---|
|  |  |  |  |  |  | Accounts | | M. Doucet, | | | |
|  | Balance | Cash | + Supplies | + Equipment | = | Payable | + | Capital | + | Revenues | − Expenses |
|  | Beginning | $9,200 | $1,600 | $7,000 | | $1,600 | | $15,000 | | $1,200 | |
| (5) |  | | | | | +250 | | | | | −$250 |
|  | Ending | $9,200 + | $1,600 + | $7,000 | = | $1,850 | + | $15,000 | + | $1,200 | − $250 |
|  |  | | $17,800 | | | | | $17,800 | | | |

The two sides of the equation still balance at $17,800.

Expenses do not have to be paid in cash at the time they are incurred. When payment is made at a later date, the liability Accounts Payable will be decreased and the asset Cash will also be decreased [see transaction (8)].

**Transaction (6): Services Provided for Cash and Credit.** Softbyte provides $3,500 of programming services for customers. Cash of $1,500 is received from customers, and the balance of $2,000 is billed to customers on account. This transaction results in an equal increase in assets and owner's equity. Three specific items are affected: Cash is increased by $1,500, Accounts Receivable is increased by $2,000, and Service Revenue is increased by $3,500. The new balances are as follows:

|  |  | Assets | | | | = | Liabilities | + | Owner's Equity | | | |
|---|---|---|---|---|---|---|---|---|---|---|---|---|
|  |  |  | Accounts |  |  |  | Accounts | | M. Doucet, | | | |
|  | Balance | Cash | + Receivable | + Supplies | + Equipment | = | Payable | + | Capital | + | Revenues | − Expenses |
|  | Beginning | $ 9,200 | | $1,600 | $7,000 | | $1,850 | | $15,000 | | $1,200 | $250 |
| (6) |  | +1,500 | +$2,000 | | | | | | | | +3,500 | |
|  | Ending | $10,700 + | $2,000 + | $1,600 + | $7,000 | = | $1,850 | + | $15,000 | + | $4,700 | − $250 |
|  |  | | $21,300 | | | | | | $21,300 | | | |

Why increase owner's equity by $3,500 when only $1,500 has been collected? The reason is that the assets resulting from the earning of revenues do not have to be in the form of cash. Owner's equity is increased when revenues are earned. In Softbyte's case, revenues are earned when the service is provided. When collections on account are received at a later date, Cash will be increased and Accounts Receivable will be decreased [see transaction (9)].

**Transaction (7): Payment of Expenses.** Expenses paid in cash for September are store rent, $600, salaries of employees, $900, and utilities, $200. These payments result in an equal decrease in assets and owner's equity. Cash is decreased by $1,700 in total ($600 + $900 + $200) and expense accounts are increased by the same amount, which, in turn decreases owner's equity. The effect of these payments on the equation is:

|  | | Assets | | | | = | Liabilities | + | | Owner's Equity | | |
|---|---|---|---|---|---|---|---|---|---|---|---|---|
|  | | | Accounts | | | | Accounts | | M. Doucet, | | | |
|  | Balance | Cash | + Receivable | + Supplies | + Equipment | = | Payable | + | Capital | + Revenues | − Expenses |
|  | Beginning | $10,700 | $2,000 | $1,600 | $7,000 | | $1,850 | | $15,000 | $4,700 | $ 250 |
| (7) | | −600 | | | | | | | | | −600 |
|  | | −900 | | | | | | | | | −900 |
|  | | −200 | | | | | | | | | −200 |
|  | Ending | $ 9,000 + | $2,000 + | $1,600 + | $7,000 | = | $1,850 + | | $15,000 + | $4,700 − | $1,950 |

$19,600                                          $19,600

The two sides of the equation now balance at $19,600. Three lines are required in the analysis to indicate the different types of expenses that have been paid.

**Transaction (8): Payment of Accounts Payable.** Softbyte pays its $250 *National Post* advertising bill in cash. Remember that the bill was previously recorded in transaction (5) as an increase in Accounts Payable and a decrease in owner's equity. This payment on account decreases the asset Cash by $250 and also decreases the liability Accounts Payable. The effect of this transaction on the equation is:

|  | | Assets | | | | = | Liabilities | + | | Owner's Equity | | |
|---|---|---|---|---|---|---|---|---|---|---|---|---|
|  | | | Accounts | | | | Accounts | | M. Doucet, | | | |
|  | Balance | Cash | + Receivable | + Supplies | + Equipment | = | Payable | + | Capital | + Revenues | − Expenses |
|  | Beginning | $9,000 | $2,000 | $1,600 | $7,000 | | $1,850 | | $15,000 | $4,700 | $1,950 |
| (8) | | −250 | | | | | −250 | | | | |
|  | Ending | $8,750 + | $2,000 + | $1,600 + | $7,000 | = | $1,600 + | | $15,000 + | $4,700 − | $1,950 |

$19,350                                          $19,350

Observe that the payment of a liability related to an expense that has previously been recorded does not affect owner's equity. This expense was recorded in transaction (5) and should not be recorded again.

**Transaction (9): Receipt of Cash on Account.** The sum of $600 in cash is received from a few of the customers who have previously been billed for services in transaction (6). This transaction does not change total assets, but it does change the composition of those assets. Cash is increased by $600, and Accounts Receivable is decreased by $600. The new balances are:

|  | | Assets | | | | = | Liabilities | + | | Owner's Equity | | |
|---|---|---|---|---|---|---|---|---|---|---|---|---|
|  | | | Accounts | | | | Accounts | | M. Doucet, | | | |
|  | Balance | Cash | + Receivable | + Supplies | + Equipment | = | Payable | + | Capital | + Revenues | − Expenses |
|  | Beginning | $8,750 | $2,000 | $1,600 | $7,000 | | $1,600 | | $15,000 | $4,700 | $1,950 |
| (9) | | +600 | −600 | | | | | | | | |
|  | Ending | $9,350 + | $1,400 + | $1,600 + | $7,000 | = | $1,600 + | | $15,000 + | $4,700 − | $1,950 |

$19,350                                          $19,350

Note that a collection on account for services previously billed and recorded does not affect owner's equity. Revenue was already recorded in transaction (6) and must not be recorded again.

**Transaction (10): Withdrawal of Cash by Owner.** Marc Doucet withdraws $1,300 in cash from the business for his personal use. This transaction results in an equal decrease in assets and owner's equity. The asset Cash is decreased by $1,300, and Drawings is increased by $1,300, which in turn decreases owner's equity, as shown below:

| | Assets | | | | = Liabilities + | | Owner's Equity | | | |
|---|---|---|---|---|---|---|---|---|---|---|
| Balance | Cash | + Accounts Receivable | + Supplies | + Equipment = | Accounts Payable | + M. Doucet, Capital | − M. Doucet, Drawings | + Revenues | − Expenses |
| Beginning | $9,350 | $1,400 | $1,600 | $7,000 | $1,600 | $15,000 | | $4,700 | $1,950 |
| (10) | −1,300 | | | | | | −$1,300 | | |
| Ending | $8,050 + | $1,400 + | $1,600 + | $7,000 = | $1,600 + | $15,000 − | $1,300 + | $4,700 − | $1,950 |

$18,050

$18,050

Observe that the effect of a cash withdrawal by the owner is the opposite of the effect of an investment by the owner. Also note that **owner's drawings are not expenses**. Expenses are incurred for the purpose of earning revenue. Drawings do not generate revenue. They are a *disinvestment*. Like owner's investments, drawings are excluded in determining net income.

## Summary of Transactions

**Illustration 1-8 ▼**

Tabular summary of Softbyte transactions

Softbyte's transactions are summarized in Illustration 1-8 to show their cumulative effect on the basic accounting equation. The transaction number and the specific effects of the transaction are indicated.

| | Assets | | | | = Liabilities + | | Owner's Equity | | | |
|---|---|---|---|---|---|---|---|---|---|---|
| | Cash | + Accounts Receivable | + Supplies | + Equipment = | Accounts Payable | + M. Doucet, Capital | − M. Doucet, Drawings | + Revenues | − Expenses |
| (1) | +$15,000 | | | | | +$15,000 | | | |
| (2) | −7,000 | | | +$7,000 | | | | | |
| (3) | | | +$1,600 | | +$1,600 | | | | |
| (4) | +1,200 | | | | | | | +$1,200 | |
| (5) | | | | | +250 | | | | −$250 |
| (6) | +1,500 | +$2,000 | | | | | | +3,500 | |
| (7) | −600 | | | | | | | | −600 |
| | −900 | | | | | | | | −900 |
| | −200 | | | | | | | | −200 |
| (8) | −250 | | | | −250 | | | | |
| (9) | +600 | −600 | | | | | | | |
| (10) | −1,300 | | | | | | −$1,300 | | |
| | $ 8,050 + | $1,400 + | $1,600 + | $7,000 = | $1,600 + | $15,000 − | $1,300 + | $4,700 − | $1,950 |

$18,050

$18,050

The illustration demonstrates some significant facts:
1. Each transaction must be analysed in terms of its effect on:
   (a) the three components (assets, liabilities, and owner's equity) of the basic accounting equation, and
   (b) specific items within each component.
2. The two sides of the equation must always be equal.

There! You made it through transaction analysis. If you feel a bit shaky on any of the transactions, it might be a good idea to get up, take a short break, and come back again for a 10- to 15-minute review of the transactions. Make sure you understand them before moving on to the next section.

## BEFORE YOU GO ON . . .

### ►Review It

1. Give an example of an external transaction. Give an example of an internal transaction.
2. If an asset increases, what are the three possible effects on the basic accounting equation? What are the possible effects if a liability increases?

### ►Do It

Transactions made by Virmari & Co., a public accounting firm, for the month of August are shown below. Prepare a tabular analysis which shows the effects of these transactions on the basic accounting equation, similar to that shown in Illustration 1-8.

1. The owner invested $25,000 of cash in the business.
2. The company purchased $7,000 of office equipment on credit.
3. The company received $8,000 of cash in exchange for services performed.
4. The company paid $850 for this month's rent.
5. The owner withdrew $1,000 of cash for personal use.

### Action Plan

- Analyse the effects of each transaction on the accounting equation.
- Use appropriate account names (not descriptions).
- Keep the accounting equation in balance.

### Solution

|  | Assets | | = | Liabilities | + | Owner's Equity | | | | |
|---|---|---|---|---|---|---|---|---|---|---|
|  | Cash | + Office Equipment | = | Accounts Payable | + | A. Virmari, Capital | − A. Virmari, Drawings | + Revenues | − Expenses |
| 1. | +$25,000 |  |  |  |  | +$25,000 |  |  |  |
| 2. |  | +$7,000 |  | +$7,000 |  |  |  |  |  |
| 3. | +$8,000 |  |  |  |  |  |  | +$8,000 |  |
| 4. | −850 |  |  |  |  |  |  |  | −$850 |
| 5. | −1,000 |  |  |  |  |  | −$1,000 |  |  |
|  | $31,150 + | $7,000 | = | $7,000 | + | $25,000 | − $1,000 | + $8,000 | − $850 |

$38,150

$38,150

the navigator

*Related exercise material:* BE1–6, BE1–7, E1–4, E1–5, and E1–6.

## Financial Statements

After transactions are identified, recorded, and summarized, four financial statements are prepared from the summarized accounting data:

study objective 7

Understand what the four financial statements are and how they are prepared.

1. An **income statement** presents the revenues and expenses and resulting net income or net loss for a specific period of time.
2. A **statement of owner's equity** summarizes the changes in owner's equity for a specific period of time.
3. A **balance sheet** reports the assets, liabilities, and owner's equity at a specific date.
4. A **cash flow statement** summarizes information about the cash inflows (receipts) and outflows (payments) for a specific period of time.

Each statement provides management, owners, and other interested parties with relevant financial data.

The financial statements of Softbyte and their relationships to each other are shown in Illustration 1-9. The statements are interrelated: (1) **Net income of $2,750 shown on the income statement is added to the beginning balance of owner's capital in the statement of owner's equity. (2) Owner's capital of $16,450 at the end of the reporting period shown in the statement of owner's equity is reported on the balance sheet. (3) Cash of $8,050 on the balance sheet is reported on the cash flow statement.**

For simplicity we have not included cents in the dollar figures we recorded in the Softbyte illustration. In reality, it is important to understand that cents should be and are used in recording transactions in a company's internal accounting records. In contrast, for financial reporting purposes, financial statement amounts are normally rounded to the nearest dollar, thousand dollars, or million dollars, depending on the size of the company. External reporting condenses and simplifies information so that it is easier for the reader to understand.

The essential features of Softbyte's four financial statements are briefly described in the following sections.

## Income Statement

Softbyte's income statement reports the revenues and expenses for a specific period of time. The income statement is prepared from the data appearing in the owner's equity columns (specifically the Revenues and Expenses columns) of Illustration 1-8. The heading of the statement identifies the company, the type of statement, and the time period covered by the statement. The primary focus of the income statement is reporting the profitability of the company's operations over a specified period of time (a month, a quarter, a year). To indicate that it applies to a period of time, the income statement is dated **Month Ended September 30, 2005.**

On the income statement, revenues are listed first, followed by expenses. Finally, net income (or net loss) is determined. Note that investment and withdrawal transactions between the owner and the business are not included in the measurement of net income.

## Statement of Owner's Equity

Softbyte's statement of owner's equity reports the changes in owner's equity for a specific period of time. Data for the preparation of the statement of owner's equity are obtained from the owner's equity columns (specifically the Capital and Drawings columns) of the tabular summary (Illustration 1-8) and from the income statement. The heading of this statement identifies the company, the type of statement, and the time period covered by the statement. The time period is the same as that covered by the income statement. It is therefore dated **Month Ended September 30, 2005.** The beginning owner's equity amount is shown on the first line of the statement. Normally, we don't show zero balances. We have included one here because, except for the first period of operations, companies normally have a beginning balance. Then the owner's investments, the net income, and the drawings are identified. The information in this statement indicates the reasons why owner's equity has increased or decreased during the period.

What if Softbyte reported a net loss in its first month? The loss would reduce owner's capital. There would be no addition of net income, and the loss would be reported as a deduction, along with drawings.

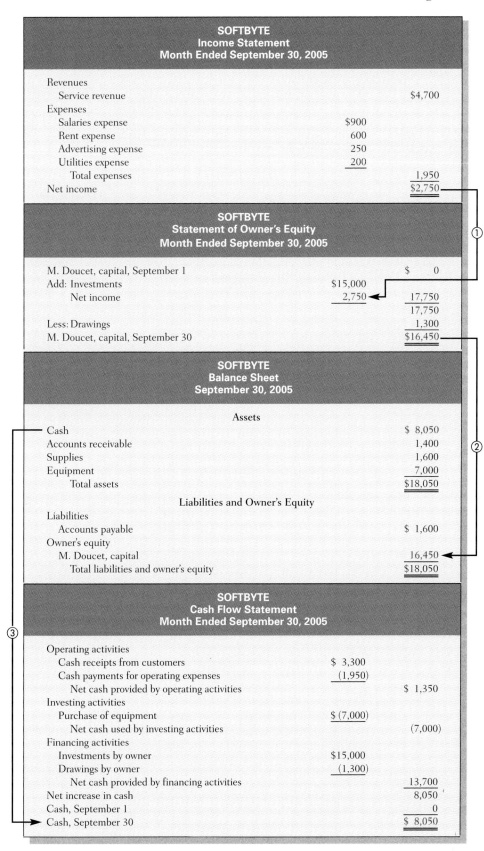

**Illustration 1-9** ◀

Financial statements and their interrelationships

**Helpful hint** Net income is calculated first and is needed to determine the ending balance in owner's equity. The ending balance in owner's equity is needed in preparing the balance sheet. The cash shown on the balance sheet is needed in preparing the cash flow statement.

## Balance Sheet

Softbyte's balance sheet reports the assets, liabilities, and owner's equity at a specific date. The balance sheet is prepared from the Asset and Liability column headings and the month-end data shown in the last line of the tabular summary (Illustration 1-8). The heading of a balance sheet must identify the company, the statement, and the date. The balance sheet is like a snapshot of the company's financial condition at a specific moment in time (usually the end of a quarter or year). To indicate that the balance sheet is at a specific point in time, it is dated **September 30, 2005**. Sometimes, the words "as at" precede the balance sheet date. Observe that the assets are listed at the top, followed by liabilities and owner's equity. Total assets must equal total liabilities and owner's equity. In the Softbyte balance sheet, only one liability, accounts payable, is reported. In most cases, there will be more than one liability.

## Cash Flow Statement

Softbyte's cash flow statement provides information about the cash receipts and cash payments for a specific period of time. To aid investors, creditors, and others in their analysis of cash, the cash flow statement reports the following: (1) the cash effects of a company's operations during a period, (2) the cash inflows and outflows from investing transactions (e.g., the purchase and sale of property, plant, and equipment), (3) the cash inflows and outflows from financing transactions (e.g., borrowing and repayment of debt and investments and withdrawals of equity), (4) the net increase or decrease in cash during the period, and (5) the cash amount at the end of the period.

Reporting the sources, uses, and change in cash is useful because investors, creditors, and others want to know what is happening to a company's most liquid resource, its money. The cash flow statement provides answers to the following simple but important questions:

1. Where did the cash come from during the period?
2. What was the cash used for during the period?
3. What was the change in the cash balance during the period?

Softbyte's cash flow statement, provided in Illustration 1-9, covers the same period of time as the income statement. Note that the positive numbers indicate cash inflows. Numbers in parentheses indicate cash outflows. Parentheses are often used in financial statements to indicate negative, or opposite, directions of numbers. As shown in the statement, cash increased by $8,050 during the month. Net cash flow from operating activities increased cash by $1,350. Cash flow from investing activities decreased cash by $7,000. Cash flow from financing activities increased cash by $13,700. At this time, you do not need to know how these amounts are determined. Chapter 17 will examine the cash flow statement in detail.

# Using the Information in the Financial Statements

Illustration 1-9 introduced the financial statements for Softbyte. Every set of financial statements is accompanied by explanatory notes and supporting schedules that are an essential part of the statements. Public corporations issue their financial statements and supplementary materials in an annual report. The **annual report** is a document that includes useful non-financial information about the company, as well as financial information.

Non-financial information may include a management discussion of the company's mission, goals and objectives, market position, and people involved in the company. Financial information may include a review of current operations and a summary of historical key financial figures and ratios, in addition to comparative financial statements. Public company financial statements are usually audited and have the auditors' report attached to them. A statement of management responsibility for the statements is also attached.

A vital element in communicating economic events is the ability to analyse and interpret the reported information. Analysis involves the use of ratios, percentages, graphs, and charts to highlight significant financial trends and relationships. Interpretation involves explaining the uses, meaning, and limitations of reported data.

Included in Appendix A at the end of this textbook are The Forzani Group Ltd.'s financial statements, extracted from its annual report. Carefully examine the format and content of each financial statement outlined earlier in Illustration 1-9. What similarities can you find between the financial statements in Illustration 1-9 and the more complicated financial statements for Forzani? We will continue to refer to Forzani's financial statements to illustrate selected topics. By the end of this course, you'll be surprised at how much you understand about these and other financial statements.

**Annual Report Walkthrough**

## ACCOUNTING IN ACTION ► Business Insight

Companies preparing their annual reports are piling on the paper in order to ease Enron-type worries on the part of investors. In 2002, U.S.-based natural gas producer Williams Companies, Inc. turned out an eye-glazing annual report 1,234 pages long. Here in Canada, Nortel Networks Corporation added an extra two dozen pages to its annual report. Other companies have done the same.

The trend to fuller disclosure has been a long time coming, observers say. But they caution that more paper does not necessarily mean more information that the average investor will understand. In addition, it is important to remember that annual reports are just one piece of the puzzle of information presented to decision-makers.

*Source:* Elizabeth Church, "No Item Too Small as Firms Cave to Enron Disclosure Craze," *Globe and Mail*, April 1, 2002, B1.

## BEFORE YOU GO ON . . .

### ►Review It

1. What are the income statement, statement of owner's equity, balance sheet, and cash flow statement?
2. Explain how Forzani's financial statements are interrelated: identify specific accounts and amounts. The answer to this question is provided at the end of the chapter.
3. What information is normally found in an annual report?

*Related exercise material:* BE1–8, BE1–9, BE1–10, BE1–11, BE1–12, E1–7, E1–8, E1–9, E1–10, E1–11, E1–12, E1–13, E1–14, E1–15, and E1–16.

For **Review It** questions about The Forzani Group, you need to use Forzani's financial statements presented in Appendix A, at the end of this textbook.

the navigator

# Demonstration Problem

Raman Balakrishnan opens his own law office on July 1, 2005. During the first month of operations, the following transactions occur:

1. Invests $11,000 in cash in the law practice.
2. Pays $800 for July rent on office space.
3. Purchases office equipment on account, $3,000.
4. Provides legal services to clients for cash, $1,500.
5. Borrows $700 cash from a bank on a note payable.
6. Provides legal services to a client on account, $2,000.
7. Pays monthly expenses: salaries, $500; utilities, $300; and telephone, $100.
8. Withdraws $1,000 cash for personal use.

The **Demonstration Problem** is a final review before you work on the assignment material. The problem-solving strategies in the margins give you tips about how to approach the problem. The solutions show both the form and the content of complete answers.

**Additional Demonstration Problems**

### Instructions

(a) Prepare a tabular analysis of the transactions.

(b) Prepare the income statement, statement of owner's equity, and balance sheet at July 31 for Raman Balakrishnan, Barrister & Solicitor.

### Solution to Demonstration Problem

(a)

| Trans-action | Cash | + | Accounts Receivable | + | Equipment | = | Note Payable | + | Accounts Payable | + | Balakrishnan, Capital | − | Balakrishnan, Drawings | + | Revenues | − | Expenses |
|---|---|---|---|---|---|---|---|---|---|---|---|---|---|---|---|---|---|
| (1) | +$11,000 | | | | | = | | | | | +$11,000 | | | | | | |
| (2) | −800 | | | | | | | | | | | | | | | | −$800 |
| (3) | | | | | +$3,000 | = | | | +$3,000 | | | | | | | | |
| (4) | +1,500 | | | | | | | | | | | | | | +$1,500 | | |
| (5) | +700 | | | | | | +$700 | | | | | | | | | | |
| (6) | | | +$2,000 | | | | | | | | | | | | +2,000 | | |
| (7) | −500 | | | | | | | | | | | | | | | | −500 |
| | −300 | | | | | | | | | | | | | | | | −300 |
| | −100 | | | | | | | | | | | | | | | | −100 |
| (8) | −1,000 | | | | | | | | | | | | −$1,000 | | | | |
| | $10,500 | + | $2,000 | + | $3,000 | = | $700 | + | $3,000 | + | $11,000 | − | $1,000 | + | $3,500 | − | $1,700 |

$15,500                     $15,500

(b)

### Action Plan

• Make sure that assets equal liabilities plus owner's equity after each transaction.

• Investments and revenues increase owner's equity. Withdrawals and expenses decrease owner's equity.

• Prepare the financial statements in the order listed.

• The income statement shows revenues and expenses for a period of time.

• The statement of owner's equity shows the changes in owner's equity for the same period of time as the income statement.

• The balance sheet reports assets, liabilities, and owner's equity at a specific date.

**RAMAN BALAKRISHNAN, BARRISTER & SOLICITOR**
**Income Statement**
**Month Ended July 31, 2005**

| | | |
|---|---|---|
| Revenues | | |
| Fees earned | | $3,500 |
| Expenses | | |
| Rent expense | $800 | |
| Salaries expense | 500 | |
| Utilities expense | 300 | |
| Telephone expense | 100 | |
| Total expenses | | 1,700 |
| Net income | | $1,800 |

**RAMAN BALAKRISHNAN, BARRISTER & SOLICITOR**
**Statement of Owner's Equity**
**Month Ended July 31, 2005**

| | | |
|---|---|---|
| Raman Balakrishnan, capital, July 1 | | $      0 |
| Add:   Investments | $11,000 | |
| Net income | 1,800 | 12,800 |
| | | 12,800 |
| Less:  Drawings | | 1,000 |
| Raman Balakrishnan, capital, July 31 | | $11,800 |

**RAMAN BALAKRISHNAN, BARRISTER & SOLICITOR**
**Balance Sheet**
**July 31, 2005**

### Assets

| | |
|---|---:|
| Cash | $10,500 |
| Accounts receivable | 2,000 |
| Equipment | 3,000 |
| Total assets | $15,500 |

### Liabilities and Owner's Equity

| | | |
|---|---:|---:|
| Liabilities | | |
| Note payable | $ 700 | |
| Accounts payable | 3,000 | |
| Total liabilities | | 3,700 |
| Owner's equity | | |
| Raman Balakrishnan, capital | | 11,800 |
| Total liabilities and owner's equity | | $15,500 |

# Summary of Study Objectives

1. *Explain what accounting is.* Accounting identifies, records, and communicates the economic events of an organization to interested users.

2. *Identify the users and explain the uses of accounting.* The major users and uses of accounting are as follows: (a) Internal users, such as management, use accounting information to plan, control, and evaluate business operations. (b) External users include investors and creditors, among others. Investors (owners) decide whether to buy, hold, or sell their financial interests on the basis of accounting data. Creditors (suppliers and bankers) evaluate the risks of granting credit or lending money on the basis of accounting information. Other groups that use accounting information are taxing authorities, regulatory agencies, customers, labour unions, and economic planners.

3. *Demonstrate an understanding of why ethics is a fundamental business concept.* Ethics are the standards of conduct by which one's actions are judged as right or wrong. If you cannot depend on the honesty of the individuals you deal with, effective communication and economic activity will be impossible and information will have no credibility.

4. *Explain generally accepted accounting principles and assumptions.* Generally accepted accounting principles and assumptions are a common set of guidelines used to prepare and report accounting information. The cost principle states that assets should be recorded at their historical (original) cost. The going concern assumption presumes that a business will continue operations for enough time to use its assets for their intended purpose and to fulfill its commitments. The monetary unit assumption requires that only transaction data that can be expressed in terms of money be included in the accounting records. The economic entity assumption requires that the activities of each economic entity be kept separate from the activities of its owner and other economic entities.

5. *State and utilize the basic accounting equation and explain the meaning of assets, liabilities, and owner's equity.* The basic accounting equation is:

Assets = Liabilities + Owner's Equity

Assets are resources owned by a business. Liabilities are creditorship claims on total assets. Owner's equity is the ownership claim on total assets.

6. *Calculate the effect of business transactions on the basic accounting equation.* Each business transaction must have a dual effect on the accounting equation. For example, if an individual asset is increased, there must be a corresponding (1) decrease in another asset, (2) increase in a liability, and/or (3) increase in owner's equity.

7. *Understand what the four financial statements are and how they are prepared.* An income statement presents the revenues and expenses of a company for a specific period of time. A statement of owner's equity summarizes the changes in owner's equity that have occurred for a specific period of time. A balance sheet reports the assets, liabilities, and owner's equity of a business at a specific date. A cash flow statement summarizes information about the cash inflows (receipts) and outflows (payments) for a specific period of time.

# Glossary

 Key Term Matching Activity

**Accounting** The process of identifying, recording, and communicating the economic events of an organization to interested users of the information. (p. 2)

**Accounting equation** Assets = Liabilities + Owner's Equity. (p. 10)

**Annual report** Information provided annually by a company to its shareholders and other interested parties about its operations and financial position. It includes the financial statements and auditors' report, in addition to information and reports by management. (p. 22)

**Assets** Resources owned by a business. (p. 10)

**Assumptions** Basic assumptions (going concern, monetary unit, and economic entity) that underlie the financial accounting structure. (p. 8)

**Balance sheet** A financial statement that reports the assets, liabilities, and owner's equity at a specific date. (p. 19)

**Cash flow statement** A financial statement that provides information about the cash inflows (receipts) and cash outflows (payments) for a specific period of time. (p. 19)

**Corporation** A business organized as a separate legal entity under corporation law, with ownership divided into transferable shares. (p. 9)

**Cost principle** An accounting principle which states that assets should be recorded at their historical (original) cost. (p. 7)

**Drawings** Withdrawals of cash or other assets from an unincorporated business for the personal use of the owner. (p. 11)

**Economic entity assumption** An assumption that economic events can be identified with a particular unit of accountability. (p. 8)

**Economic events** Activities related to the production and distribution of goods and services in an organization. (p. 2)

**Ethics** The standards of conduct by which one's actions are judged as right or wrong, honest or dishonest, fair or unfair. (p. 6)

**Expenses** The cost of assets consumed or services used in the process of earning revenue. (p. 11)

**Generally accepted accounting principles (GAAP)** An accepted set of standards that indicate how to report economic events. (p. 7)

**Going concern assumption** An assumption which states that the entity will continue operations for enough time to use its assets for their intended purpose and to fulfill its obligations. (p. 8)

**Income statement** A financial statement that presents the revenues and expenses and resulting net income (or net loss) for a specific period of time. (p. 19)

**Investments by owner** The assets put into the business by the owner. (p. 11)

**Liabilities** Creditorship claims on total assets. (p. 11)

**Monetary unit assumption** An assumption which states that only transaction data that can be expressed in terms of money may be included in the accounting records. (p. 8)

**Net income** The amount by which revenues exceed expenses. (p. 11)

**Net loss** The amount by which expenses exceed revenues. (p. 11)

**Owner's equity** The ownership claim on total assets. (p. 11)

**Partnership** An association of two or more persons to carry on as co-owners of a business for profit. (p. 9)

**Private corporation** A limited company whose shares are not listed on a stock exchange and are not available to a public investor. (p. 10)

**Proprietorship** A small business owned by one person. (p. 9)

**Public corporation** A limited company whose shares are publicly traded and available for purchase by the general public. (p. 10)

**Revenues** The increase in owner's equity that results from business activities performed to earn income. (p. 11)

**Statement of owner's equity** A financial statement that summarizes the changes in owner's equity for a specific period of time. (p. 19)

**Transactions** The economic events of the business recorded by accountants. (p. 13)

# Self-Study Questions

Answers are at the end of the chapter.

(SO 1) C  1. The accounting process does not include:
(a) identification.     (c) recording.
(b) verification.     (d) communication.

(SO 2) C  2. One of the following statements about users of accounting information is incorrect. The incorrect statement is:
(a) Management is an internal user.
(b) Taxing authorities are external users.
(c) Creditors are external users.
(d) Regulatory authorities are internal users.

(SO 3) K  3. Ethics are the standards of conduct by which one's actions are judged to be:
(a) decent or indecent.
(b) successful or unsuccessful.
(c) profitable or unprofitable.
(d) right or wrong.

(SO 4) K  4. The basic objective of financial reporting is to communicate information that is useful in:
(a) helping investors, creditors, and other users make decisions.
(b) minimizing income taxes.
(c) assessing management's performance.
(d) determining what the company is worth.

(SO 4) K  5. The cost principle states that:
(a) assets should be recorded at cost and adjusted when their market value changes.
(b) activities of an entity should be kept separate and distinct from those of its owner.
(c) assets should be recorded at their historical (original) cost.
(d) only transaction data capable of being expressed in terms of money should be included in the accounting records.

(SO 4) C  6. Which of the following statements about basic assumptions is incorrect?
(a) The going concern assumption assumes that a company ends its operations once a year for reporting purposes.

(b) The economic entity assumption states that there should be a particular unit of accountability.
(c) The monetary unit assumption enables accounting to measure economic events.
(d) An important part of the monetary unit assumption is the stable monetary unit assumption.

7. As at December 31, Stoneland Company has assets of   (SO 5) AP
$3,500 and owner's equity of $2,000. What are the liabilities for Stoneland Company as at December 31?
(a) $1,000.          (c) $2,000.
(b) $1,500.          (d) $2,500.

8. Net income will result during a time period when:   (SO 5) C
(a) assets exceed liabilities.
(b) assets exceed revenues.
(c) expenses exceed revenues.
(d) revenues exceed expenses.

9. The effects on the basic accounting equation of per-   (SO 6) AP
forming services on account are:
(a) increased assets and decreased owner's equity.
(b) increased assets and increased owner's equity.
(c) increased assets and increased liabilities.
(d) increased liabilities and increased owner's equity.

10. Genesis Company buys a $10,000 machine on   (SO 6) AP
credit. This transaction will affect the:
(a) income statement only.
(b) balance sheet only.
(c) income statement and statement of owner's equity only.
(d) income statement, statement of owner's equity, and balance sheet.

11. The financial statement that reports assets, liabili-   (SO 7) K
ties, and owner's equity is the:
(a) income statement.
(b) statement of owner's equity.
(c) balance sheet.
(d) cash flow statement.

the navigator

# Questions

(SO 1) C  1. "Accounting is ingrained in our society and it is vital to our economic system." Do you agree? Explain.

(SO 1) C  2. Identify and describe the steps in the accounting process.

(SO 2) C  3. (a) Who are the internal users of accounting data?
(b) How does accounting provide relevant data for these users?

4. What do the following external users use account-   (SO 2) C
ing information for: (a) investors and (b) creditors?

5. Improper accounting practices can result in stock   (SO 2) C
market losses and employee layoffs. Do you agree? Explain.

6. Why are ethics important to the accounting profession?   (SO 3) AN

(SO 4) AP    7. Ouellette Travel Agency purchased land for $75,000 cash on December 10, 2005. At December 31, 2005, the land's value had increased to $95,000. What amount should be reported for land on Ouellette's balance sheet at December 31, 2005? Would your answer differ if the land value declined to $65,000? Explain.

(SO 4) C    8. What is the monetary unit assumption? What impact does inflation (rising prices) have on the monetary unit assumption?

(SO 4) K    9. What is the economic entity assumption?

(SO 4) C    10. How does the going concern assumption support the cost principle?

(SO 4) C    11. Martha Ross is the owner of a successful printing shop. Recently, her business has been increasing, and Martha has been thinking about changing the organization of her business from a proprietorship to a corporation. Explain the differences in accounting for the business if it is a corporation instead of a proprietorship.

(SO 4) E    12. Down in the Luck Company began operations six months ago. Based on its most recent balance sheet, the company has $50,000 in assets and $300,000 in liabilities. If you were the owner of Down in the Luck, would it matter to you what form of business organization the company was? Support your position. Would your answer change if you were a creditor instead of the owner?

(SO 5) K    13. What is the basic accounting equation?

(SO 5) C    14. (a) Define assets, liabilities, and owner's equity.
(b) What items affect owner's equity?

(SO 5) K    15. Which of the following items are liabilities of Gilt Jewellery Store?
(a) Cash          (e) Equipment
(b) Accounts payable    (f) Salaries payable
(c) Drawings      (g) Service revenue
(d) Accounts receivable  (h) Rent expense

(SO 5) AP    16. Can a business enter into a transaction in which only the left side of the basic accounting equation is affected? If yes, give an example.

17. Are the following events recorded in the accounting records? Explain your answer in each case.    (SO 6) C
(a) The owner of the company dies.
(b) Supplies are purchased on account.
(c) An employee is terminated.
(d) The owner of the business withdraws cash from the business for personal use.

18. Indicate how the following business transactions affect the basic accounting equation:    (SO 6) AP
(a) Paid cash for janitorial services.
(b) Purchased equipment for cash.
(c) Invested cash in the business.
(d) Paid an account payable in full.

19. In February 2005, Paul Dumas invested an additional $10,000 in his business, Dumas's Pharmacy, which is organized as a proprietorship. Dumas's accountant, Donna Wortham, recorded this receipt as an increase in cash and revenues. Is this treatment appropriate? Why or why not?    (SO 6) AP

20. A company's net income appears directly on the income statement and the statement of owner's equity. It is also included indirectly in the company's balance sheet. Do you agree? Explain.    (SO 7) AP

21. Below are some items found in the financial statements of Kaustev Sen, M.D. Indicate in which financial statement(s) the items would appear.    (SO 7) C
(a) Service revenue
(b) Equipment
(c) Advertising expense
(d) Accounts receivable
(e) Kaustev Sen, Capital (ending balance)
(f) Wages payable

22. Forzani's year end is not a fixed date; rather it can vary slightly from one year to the next. What possible problem does this pose for financial statement users?    (SO 7) S

# Brief Exercises

**BE1–1** Match each of the following five decisions with the most appropriate decision-maker listed in (a) to (e):

1. Decide whether the company complied with income tax regulations.
2. Decide whether the company can pay its obligations.
3. Decide whether a marketing proposal will be cost-effective.
4. Decide whether the company's net income will result in an increase in drawings.
5. Decide how the company should finance its operations.

(a) _____ Owner
(b) _____ Marketing manager
(c) _____ Creditors
(d) _____ Chief Financial Officer
(e) _____ Canada Customs and Revenue Agency

*Identify users of accounting information. (SO 2) K*

**BE1–2** Match each of the following forms of business organization with a set of characteristics: proprietorship (P), partnership (PP), corporation (C).

(a) _____ Simple to set up; founder retains control
(b) _____ Shared control; increased skills and resources
(c) _____ Easier to transfer ownership and raise funds; no personal liability

*Describe forms of business organization. (SO 4) AP*

**BE1–3** Presented below is the basic accounting equation. Determine the missing amounts:

|     | Assets | = | Liabilities | + | Owner's Equity |
|-----|--------|---|-------------|---|----------------|
| (a) | $80,000 | | $50,000 | | ? |
| (b) | ? | | $45,000 | | $60,000 |
| (c) | $94,000 | | ? | | $52,000 |

*Solve basic accounting equation. (SO 5) AP*

**BE1–4** Use the accounting equation to answer each of the following questions:

(a) The liabilities of Cai Company are $90,000. Meiyu Cai's capital account is $150,000; drawings are $40,000; revenues, $450,000; and expenses, $320,000. What is the amount of Cai Company's total assets? $A = L + OE$

(b) The total assets of Pereira Company are $57,000. Karen Pereira's capital account is $25,000; drawings are $7,000; revenues, $50,000; and expenses, $35,000. What is the amount of the company's total liabilities?

(c) The total assets of Yap Co. are $600,000 and its liabilities are equal to two-thirds of its total assets. What is the amount of Yap Co.'s owner's equity?

*Solve basic accounting equation. (SO 5) AP*

**BE1–5** At the beginning of the year, Lam Company had total assets of $700,000 and total liabilities of $500,000. Answer the following questions:

(a) If total assets increased by $150,000 during the year and total liabilities decreased by $80,000, what is the amount of owner's equity at the end of the year?

(b) During the year, total liabilities increased by $100,000. The company incurred a net loss of $80,000. Lifei Lam made an additional investment of $10,000 and made no withdrawals. What was the amount of total assets at the end of the year?

(c) Total assets decreased by $90,000 during the year. Net income was $120,000. There were no additional owner's investments or drawings. What is the amount of total liabilities at the end of the year?

*Solve basic accounting equation. (SO 5) AP*

**BE1–6** Presented below are six business transactions. List the letters (a) through (f), with columns for assets, liabilities, and owner's equity. For each column, indicate whether the transactions increased (+), decreased (–), or had no effect (NE) on assets, liabilities, and owner's equity:

(a) Purchased supplies on account.
(b) Received cash for providing a service.
(c) Paid expenses in cash.
(d) Invested cash in the business.
(e) Owner withdrew cash.
(f) Received cash from a customer who had been billed previously for services provided.

*Determine effect of transactions on basic accounting equation. (SO 6) AP*

**Determine effect of transactions on owner's equity.**
(SO 6) AP

**BE1–7** Classify each of the following items as owner's investments (I), drawings (D), revenue (R), expenses (E), or as having no effect on owner's equity (NE):

(a) _____ Costs incurred for advertising    (f) _____ Services performed
(b) _____ Commission earnings    (g) _____ Rent received
(c) _____ Insurance paid    (h) _____ Utilities incurred
(d) _____ Amounts paid to employees    (i) _____ Cash distributed to owner
(e) _____ Cash paid to purchase equipment    (j) _____ Collection of an account receivable

**Identify balance sheet elements.**
(SO 7) C

**BE1–8** Indicate whether each of the following items is an asset (A), liability (L), or part of owner's equity (OE):

(a) _____ Accounts receivable    (e) _____ Capital invested
(b) _____ Salaries payable    (f) _____ Notes payable
(c) _____ Equipment    (g) _____ Drawings
(d) _____ Office supplies    (h) _____ Service revenue

**Identify elements of financial statements.**
(SO 7) AP

**BE1–9** Indicate whether the following items would appear on the income statement (IS), balance sheet (BS), and/or statement of owner's equity (OE):

(a) _____ Notes payable    (f) _____ Interest receivable
(b) _____ Advertising expense    (g) _____ Service revenue
(c) _____ Harrison, capital (ending balance)    (h) _____ Harrison, drawings
(d) _____ Cash    (i) _____ Investments by owner
(e) _____ Fees earned    (j) _____ Net income

**Identify elements of financial statements.**
(SO 7) AP

The financial results of **real companies** included in the end of chapter material are indicated by the company name being shown in red.

**BE1–10** The **Calgary Exhibition and Stampede Limited** has the following selected accounts included in its financial statements. In each case, identify whether the item would appear on the balance sheet (BS) or income statement (IS).

(a) _____ Accounts receivable    (g) _____ Horse racing revenue
(b) _____ Inventories    (h) _____ Accounts payable and accrued
(c) _____ Amortization expense          liabilities
(d) _____ Share capital    (i) _____ Cash and short-term deposits
(e) _____ Building    (j) _____ Administration, marketing, and
(f) _____ Stampede revenue          park services expenses

**Calculate net income.**
(SO 7) AP

**BE1–11** Schwinghamer Enterprises had a capital balance of $168,000 at the beginning of the period. At the end of the accounting period, the capital balance was $198,000.

(a) If there were no additional investments or withdrawals, what is the net income for the period?
(b) Assuming there was an additional investment of $18,000 but no withdrawals, what is the net income for the period?
(c) Assuming there was an additional investment of $25,000 and a withdrawal of $11,000, what is the net income for the period?

**Calculate income statement amounts.**
(SO 7) AP

**BE1–12** Summarized operations for the King Co. for the month of July are as follows:

Revenues earned: for cash, $35,000; on account, $70,000.
Expenses incurred: for cash, $26,000; on account, $40,000.
Owner's investment: $10,000 cash.
Owner's drawings: $7,500 cash.

Indicate the following for King Co.: (a) total revenues, (b) total expenses, and (c) net income for the month of July.

# Exercises

**E1–1** Presented below are the assumptions and principles discussed in this chapter:

1. Cost principle
2. Monetary unit assumption
3. Going concern assumption
4. Economic entity assumption

Identify accounting assumptions and principles.
(SO 4) C

Interactive Homework

*Instructions*

Identify by number the accounting assumption or principle that is described below. Do not use a number more than once.

(a) _____ It is the reason why property, plant, and equipment are not reported at liquidation value. (*Note:* Do not use the cost principle.)
(b) _____ It indicates that personal and business record-keeping should be kept separate.
(c) _____ It assumes that the dollar is the "measuring stick" used to report on financial performance.
(d) _____ It indicates that market value changes after a purchase are not recorded in the accounts.

**E1–2** Marietta Company had three major business transactions during 2005:

(a) Land with a cost of $208,000 is reported at its market value of $260,000.
(b) Marietta paid for the rental of an apartment for the owner's personal use and charged it to Rent Expense.
(c) Marietta wanted to make its 2005 net income look worse than it really was, so it reported its figures in inflation-adjusted dollars, rather than actual dollars.

Identify assumption or principle that has been violated.
(SO 4) C

*Instructions*

In each situation, identify the assumption or principle that has been violated, if any, and state what should have been done.

**E1–3** The following items were taken from the balance sheet of **NIKE, Inc.** NIKE is the world's #1 shoe company, selling its products in 110 countries.

Classify items as assets, liabilities, and shareholders' equity, and prepare accounting equation.
(SO 5) AP

*Instructions*

(a) Classify each of these items as an asset (A), liability (L), or owner's (shareholders') equity (OE) item (all items are in US millions).

| | | | | | |
|---|---|---|---|---|---|
| _____ Cash | $ 575.5 | | _____ Income taxes payable | $ 83.0 | |
| _____ Accounts receivable | 1,807.1 | | _____ Property, plant, and | | |
| _____ Share capital | 536.4 | | equipment | 1,614.5 | |
| _____ Notes payable | 425.2 | | _____ Retained earnings | 3,302.6 | |
| _____ Other assets | 811.6 | | _____ Accounts payable and | | |
| _____ Other liabilities | 823.1 | | accrued liabilities | 1,272.7 | |
| _____ Inventories | 1,373.8 | | _____ Prepaid expenses | 260.5 | |

(b) Determine NIKE's accounting equation by calculating the value of total assets, total liabilities, and total shareholders' equity.

**E1–4** For each of the following, provide an example of a transaction that causes the described effect on the accounting equation:

Describe the effect of transactions on the accounting equation.
(SO 6) C

1. Increases an asset and increases a liability.
2. Increases an asset and increases owner's equity.
3. Decreases an asset and decreases a liability.
4. Decreases an asset and decreases owner's equity.
5. Increases a liability and decreases owner's equity.
6. Increases one asset and decreases another asset.

**E1–5** Selected transactions for Lush Lawn Care Company are listed below:

Analyse effect of transactions.
(SO 6) AP

1. Made cash investment to start business.
2. Paid monthly rent.
3. Purchased equipment on account.
4. Billed customers for services performed.
5. Withdrew cash for owner's personal use.
6. Received cash from customers billed in transaction 4.

Interactive Homework

7. Incurred advertising expense on account.
8. Purchased additional equipment for cash.
9. Received cash from customers when service was performed.
10. Paid cash for equipment purchased in transaction 3.

*Instructions*

Prepare a schedule as shown below and indicate the effect each of the transactions listed above has on assets, liabilities, and the following owner's equity accounts: owner's capital, drawings, revenues, and expenses. Use "+" for increase, "−" for decrease, and "NE" for no effect. The first transaction is done for you as an example.

| | | | | Owner's Equity | | | |
|---|---|---|---|---|---|---|---|
| Trans-action | Assets | Liabilities | Owner's Capital | Drawings | Revenues | Expenses |
| 1. | + | NE | + | NE | NE | NE |

**Analyse transactions.**
**(SO 6) AN**

**E1–6** Lau Computer Company entered into the following transactions during May 2005:

1. Purchased computer terminals for $19,000 from Digital Equipment, on account.
2. Paid $4,000 cash for May rent of storage space.
3. Received $15,000 cash from customers for contracts billed in April.
4. Provided computer services to Brieske Construction Company for $3,000 cash.
5. Paid NB Power $11,000 cash for energy usage in May.
6. Mr. Lau invested an additional $32,000 in the business.
7. Paid Digital Equipment for the terminals purchased in transaction 1 above.
8. Incurred advertising expense for May of $1,000, on account.

*Instructions*

Prepare a tabular analysis of the above transactions, as shown in Illustration 1-8 in the text.

**Analyse transactions and calculate net income.**
**(SO 6, 7) AP**

**E1–7** An analysis of the transactions made by Bourque & Co., a public accounting firm, for the month of August 2005 is shown below:

| | Cash | + | Accounts Receivable | + | Supplies | + | Office Equipment | = | Accounts Payable | + | B. Bourque, Capital | − | B. Bourque, Drawings | + | Revenues | − | Expenses | |
|---|---|---|---|---|---|---|---|---|---|---|---|---|---|---|---|---|---|---|
| 1. | +$10,000 | | | | | | | | | | +$10,000 | | | | | | | |
| 2. | −2,000 | | | | | | +$5,000 | | +$3,000 | | | | | | | | | |
| 3. | −750 | | | | +$750 | | | | | | | | | | | | | |
| 4. | +2,700 | | +$3,400 | | | | | | | | | | | | +6,100 | | | |
| 5. | −1,500 | | | | | | | | −1,500 | | | | | | | | | |
| 6. | −2,000 | | | | | | | | | | | | −2,000 | | | | | |
| 7. | −750 | | | | | | | | | | | | | | | | −750 | Rent |
| 8. | +450 | | −450 | | | | | | | | | | | | | | | |
| 9. | −2,900 | | | | | | | | | | | | | | | | −2,900 | Salaries |
| 10. | | | | | | | | | +550 | | | | | | | | −550 | Utilities |

*Instructions*

(a) Describe each transaction that occurred in the month.
(b) Determine how much owner's equity increased for the month.
(c) Calculate the amount of net income for the month.

**Match words with descriptions.**
**(SO 3, 4, 5, 7) K**

✓ **E1–8** Here is a list of words or phrases discussed in this chapter:

1. Accounts payable
2. Creditor
3. Balance sheet
4. Proprietorship
5. Corporation
6. Ethics
7. Accounts receivable

*Instructions*

Match each word or phrase with the best description below:

(a) _____ A business enterprise that raises money by issuing shares
(b) _____ Standards of conduct by which one's actions are judged as right or wrong
(c) _____ Obligations to suppliers of goods
(d) _____ Amounts due from customers
(e) _____ A party a business owes money to
(f) _____ A financial statement that reports assets, liabilities, and owner's equity at a specific date
(g) _____ A business in which the owner is personally liable for all debts of the business

**E1–9** The summaries of 2005 of balance sheet and income statement data for three proprietorships are presented below. Two items are missing from each summary.

Analyse financial statement items.
(SO 5, 7) AN

Interactive Homework

| | Wyatt Company | Maxim Enterprises | Distasi Services |
|---|---|---|---|
| Beginning of year: | | | |
| Total assets | $ 95,000 | $125,000 | $60,000 |
| Total liabilities | 80,000 | (c) | 25,000 |
| Total owner's equity | (a) | 95,000 | 35,000 |
| End of year: | | | |
| Total assets | 160,000 | 180,000 | (e) |
| Total liabilities | 120,000 | 50,000 | 65,000 |
| Total owner's equity | 40,000 | 130,000 | 15,000 |
| Changes during year in owner's equity: | | | |
| Investments | (b) | 25,000 | 4,000 |
| Drawings | 24,000 | (d) | 30,000 |
| Total revenues | 215,000 | 100,000 | (f) |
| Total expenses | 175,000 | 85,000 | 40,000 |

*Instructions*

Determine the missing amounts.

**E1–10** The Depeau Company had the following assets and liabilities on the dates indicated:

Determine net income (or loss).
(SO 5, 7) AP

| December 31 | Total Assets | Total Liabilities |
|---|---|---|
| 2004 | $400,000 | $250,000 |
| 2005 | 460,000 | 320,000 |
| 2006 | 590,000 | 400,000 |

Depeau began business on January 1, 2004, with an investment of $100,000.

*Instructions*

From an analysis of the accounting equation and the change in owner's equity during the year, calculate the net income (or loss) for:

(a) 2004, assuming Depeau's drawings were $15,000 for the year.
(b) 2005, assuming Depeau made an additional investment of $50,000 and had no drawings in 2005.
(c) 2006, assuming Depeau made an additional investment of $10,000 and had drawings of $20,000 in 2006.

**E1–11** An analysis of transactions for Bourque & Co. is presented in E1–7.

Prepare financial statements.
(SO 7) AP

Interactive Homework

*Instructions*

Prepare an income statement and statement of owner's equity for August, and a balance sheet at August 31, 2005.

**Prepare income statement and statement of owner's equity.**
(SO 7) AP

**E1–12** The following information relates to Serg Co. for the year ended December 31, 2005:

| | | | |
|---|---|---|---|
| A. Serg, capital, January 1, 2005 | $48,000 | A. Serg, drawings | $15,000 |
| Service revenue | 55,000 | Salaries expense | 28,000 |
| Rent expense | 10,400 | Utilities expense | 3,100 |
| Interest expense | 1,700 | Advertising expense | 1,800 |
| Investments by owner in 2005 | 3,000 | | |

*Instructions*

Prepare an income statement and a statement of owner's equity for the year ended December 31, 2005.

**Correct incorrectly prepared balance sheet.**
(SO 7) AN

**E1–13** Clare Gardner is the bookkeeper for Otago Company. Clare has prepared the balance sheet of Otago Company, as follows:

**OTAGO COMPANY**
**Balance Sheet**
**December 31, 2005**

| Assets | | Liabilities | |
|---|---|---|---|
| Cash | $18,500 | Accounts payable | $20,000 |
| Supplies | 8,000 | Accounts receivable | (10,000) |
| Operating expenses | 5,000 | Service revenue | 8,000 |
| Equipment | 46,000 | Otago, capital | 64,500 |
| Otago, drawings | 5,000 | Total liabilities and | |
| Total assets | $82,500 | owner's equity | $82,500 |

*Instructions*

Prepare a correct balance sheet.

**Calculate net income and prepare balance sheet.**
(SO 7) AP

**E1–14** Judy Cumby is the sole owner of Deer Park, a public camping ground near Gros Morne National Park. Judy has compiled the following financial information as at December 31, 2005:

| | | | |
|---|---|---|---|
| Revenues during 2005, | | Revenues during 2005, | |
| camping fees | $160,000 | general store | $ 40,000 |
| Expenses during 2005 | 150,000 | Cash on hand | 10,000 |
| Supplies on hand | 2,500 | Original cost of equipment | 115,500 |
| Market value of equipment | 140,000 | Notes payable | 70,000 |
| Accounts payable | 11,000 | J. Cumby, capital, January 1, 2005 | 17,000 |
| | | J. Cumby, drawings during 2005 | 20,000 |

*Instructions*

(a) Determine Judy's net income from Deer Park for the year ended December 31, 2005.
(b) Prepare a balance sheet for Deer Park as at December 31, 2005.

**Prepare income statement.**
(SO 7) AP

**E1–15** Financial information for the October 2005 operations of the Atlantic Cruise Company is presented below:

| | | | |
|---|---|---|---|
| Maintenance expense | $ 80,000 | Advertising expense | 3,500 |
| Property tax expense | | Ticket revenue | 325,000 |
| (on dock facilities) | 10,000 | Food, fuel, and other | |
| Salaries expense | 142,000 | operating expenses | 20,500 |
| Drawings | 49,000 | | |

*Instructions*

Prepare the income statement for the month of October 2005 for the Atlantic Cruise Company.

**Prepare statement of owner's equity.**
(SO 7) AP

**E1–16** Information for the proprietorship of Lorraine Ring, lawyer, for the year ended January 31, 2005, is presented below:

| | | | |
|---|---|---|---|
| Legal fees earned | $360,000 | Assets, January 31, 2005 | 168,000 |
| Total expenses | 205,000 | Liabilities, January 31, 2005 | 70,000 |
| Assets, February 1, 2004 | 85,000 | L. Ring, drawings | ? |
| Liabilities, February 1, 2004 | 62,000 | | |

*Instructions*

Prepare the statement of owner's equity for Lorraine Ring's legal practice for the year ended January 31, 2005, after determining the missing amount for drawings.

# Problems: Set A

**P1–1A** Financial decisions often depend more on one type of financial statement than others. Consider each of the following hypothetical situations independently:

1. The North Face Inc. is considering extending credit to a new customer. The terms of the credit would require the customer to pay within 30 days of receipt of the goods.
2. An investor is considering investing in WestJet Airlines. The investor plans on holding the investment for at least five years.
3. Caisse d'Économie Base Montréal is thinking about extending a loan to a small company. The company would be required to make interest payments at the end of each year for five years, and to repay the loan at the end of the fifth year.

*Instructions*

In each situation, state whether the individual making the decision would depend mostly on the information in the income statement, the balance sheet, or the cash flow statement. Briefly justify your choice.

*Identify users and uses of financial statements. (SO 2) AP*

**P1–2A** A number of accounting reporting situations are described below:

1. Dot.com Company believes its people are its most significant asset. It estimates and records their value on its balance sheet.
2. Barton Co. is carrying inventory at its current market value of $100,000. The inventory had an original cost of $75,000.
3. Steph Wolfson, president of the Classic CD Company, bought a computer for her personal use. She paid for the computer with company funds and debited the Computers account.

*Instructions*

For each of the above situations, list any assumption or principle that has been violated and explain why the situation violates this assumption or principle.

*Identify assumption or principle violated. (SO 4) AN*

**P1–3A** Presented below are four independent situations:

(a) Dawn Addington, a student looking for summer employment, opened a vegetable stand along a busy local highway. She buys produce from local farmers each morning and then sells it in the afternoon as people return home from work.
(b) Joseph Counsell and Sabra Surkis each own a bike shop. They have decided to combine their businesses and try to expand their operations to include skis and snowboards. They expect that in the coming year they will need significant funds to expand their operations.
(c) Three chemistry professors have formed a business which uses bacteria to clean up toxic waste sites. Each has contributed an equal amount of cash and knowledge to the venture. The use of bacteria in this situation is experimental, and legal obligations could result.
(d) Mary Emery and Richard Goedde recently graduated with graduate degrees in economics. They have decided to start a consulting business focused on teaching the basics of international economics to small business owners interested in international trade.

*Instructions*

In each case, explain what form of organization the business is likely to take: proprietorship, partnership, or corporation. Give reasons for your choice.

*Determine forms of business organization. (SO 4) C*

**P1–4A** On April 1, Angela Loken established the Loken Travel Agency. The following transactions were completed during the month:

Apr. 1 Deposited $12,000 cash in the Canadian Imperial Bank of Commerce, in the name of the agency.
2 Paid $600 cash for April office rent.
2 Purchased office equipment for $5,500, paying $2,000 cash and signing a note payable for the balance.

*Analyse transactions and calculate owner's equity. (SO 5, 6) AN*

Apr.   7  Incurred $300 of advertising costs, on account.
       8  Paid $725 cash for office supplies.
      11  Earned $9,000 for services provided: cash of $1,000 is received from customers, and the balance of $8,000 is billed to customers on account.
      15  Withdrew $200 cash for personal use.
      25  Paid the amount due in the April 7 transaction.
      30  Paid employees' salaries, $2,200.
      30  Received $6,000 in cash from customers who were billed in the April 11 transaction.

*Instructions*

(a) Prepare a tabular analysis of the effect of each of the above transactions on the accounting equation.
(b) From an analysis of the owner's equity columns, calculate the balance in Angela Loken, Capital on April 30.

Analyse transactions and prepare balance sheet.
(SO 6, 7) AN

**P1–5A**  The following events relate to Anita LeTourneau, a Manitoba law school graduate:

1. On March 4, 2005, she spent $10 on a Lucky Seven Lottery ticket.
2. On March 7, she won $240,000 in the lottery and immediately quit her job as a legal assistant.
3. On March 10, she decided to open her own law practice, and deposited $40,000 of her winnings in a business chequing account.
4. On March 14, she purchased a new condominium with a down payment of $100,000 from her personal funds plus a home mortgage of $200,000.
5. On March 16, Ms. LeTourneau signed a rental agreement for her law office space, commencing on April 1, 2005. She had to pay a $2,000 cash damage deposit (from her business cash). It will be fully refundable when she vacates the premises, provided they are in good condition. (*Hint*: This deposit should be treated as a company asset.) The monthly rental payments are to be made in advance on the first business day of each month. The first payment of $1,000 is due April 1.
6. On March 20, she hired a receptionist.  He will be paid $500 per week and will report to work on April 1.
7. On March 25, she purchased a computer and related equipment for her law practice for $2,000 cash plus a $4,500 note payable due in six months.
8. On March 27, she purchased  $1,500 of office supplies on account (to be paid in one month).
9. On March 31, she purchased office furniture for her law practice from a company that had just declared bankruptcy. The furniture was worth at least $12,000 but Anita was able to buy it for only $8,000 cash.

*Instructions*

(a) Use the accounting equation to analyse the effects of the transactions on Anita LeTourneau's law practice.
(b) Prepare a balance sheet for Anita LeTourneau's law practice as at March 31, 2005.

Analyse transactions and prepare financial statements.
(SO 6, 7) AN

**P1–6A**  Tony Tiberio operates a law office under the name Tony Tiberio, Barrister & Solicitor. On July 31, 2005, the balance sheet showed Cash $4,000; Accounts Receivable $1,500; Supplies $500; Office Equipment $5,000; Accounts Payable $4,100; and Tony Tiberio, Capital $6,900. During August the following transactions occurred:

Aug.   4  Collected $1,200 of accounts receivable.
       7  Paid $2,700 cash on accounts payable.
       8  Earned fees of $6,500, of which $3,000 is collected in cash.
      12  Purchased additional office equipment for $1,200, paying $400 in cash and the balance on account.
      15  Paid salaries, $2,500; rent for August, $900; and advertising expenses, $375.
      18  Collected the balance of the fees earned on August 8.
      20  Withdrew $550 in cash for personal use.
      26  Received $2,000 from the Bank of Montreal—money borrowed on a note payable.
      28  Signed a contract to provide legal services to a client in September for $4,500. Client will pay the amount owing after the work has been completed.
      29  Incurred utility expenses for the month on account, $275.
      30  Billed a client $1,000 for services rendered.

## Instructions

(a) Beginning with the July 31 balances, prepare a tabular analysis of the effect of the August transactions on the accounting equation. The column headings should be as follows: Cash + Accounts Receivable + Supplies + Office Equipment = Notes Payable + Accounts Payable + Tony Tiberio, Capital − Tony Tiberio, Drawings + Revenues − Expenses.

(b) Prepare an income statement for August, a statement of owner's equity for August, and a balance sheet at August 31, 2005.

**P1–7A** The following selected data from the 2004 financial statements for Jaroslawsky Trading Company are in random order:

Use financial statement relationships to determine missing amounts.
(SO 5, 7) AN

| | |
|---|---:|
| Liabilities at the end of the year | $470,000 |
| Investments by the owner during the year | 11,000 |
| Assets at the beginning of the year | 617,000 |
| Drawings by the owner during the year | 64,000 |
| Net income for the year | 72,000 |
| Capital at the beginning of the year | 250,000 |
| Total revenue for the year | 348,000 |

## Instructions

Determine the amount of each of the following items:

(a) Liabilities at the beginning of the year
(b) Total expenses for the year
(c) Capital at the end of the year
(d) Assets at the end of the year

**P1–8A** On June 1, Sue Ng started Natural Cosmetics Co., a company that provides individual skin care treatment to clients at their residences. She invested $27,200 cash in the business. Listed below, in alphabetical order, are the assets and liabilities of the company at June 30, and the revenues and expenses for the month of June:

Prepare financial statements.
(SO 6, 7) AP

| | | | |
|---|---:|---|---:|
| Accounts payable | $ 1,200 | Gas and oil expense | $ 800 |
| Accounts receivable | 3,500 | Notes payable | 11,500 |
| Advertising expense | 1,500 | Service revenue | 7,500 |
| Cash | 5,800 | Supplies expense | 1,200 |
| Cosmetic supplies on hand | 2,400 | Utilities expense | 300 |
| Equipment | 30,000 | | |

Sue made no additional investment in June, but withdrew $1,900 in cash for personal use during the month.

## Instructions

Prepare an income statement and statement of owner's equity for the month of June and a balance sheet at June 30, 2005.

**P1–9A** Financial statement information for four different companies follows:

Determine financial statement amounts; prepare statement of owner's equity, and comment.
(SO 6, 7) AN

| | Pine Lake Company | Come By Chance Company | James Bay Company | Lethbridge Company |
|---|---:|---:|---:|---:|
| **January 1, 2004:** | | | | |
| Assets | $ 80,000 | $ 95,000 | (g) | $135,000 |
| Liabilities | 50,000 | (d) | $ 80,000 | (j) |
| Owner's equity | (a) | 60,000 | 45,000 | 90,000 |
| **December 31, 2004:** | | | | |
| Assets | (b) | 124,000 | 190,000 | (k) |
| Liabilities | 65,000 | 68,000 | (h) | 60,000 |
| Owner's equity | 45,000 | (e) | 115,000 | 130,000 |
| **Owner's equity changes in year:** | | | | |
| Investments | (c) | 8,000 | 10,000 | 5,000 |
| Drawings | 10,000 | (f) | 25,000 | 30,000 |
| Total revenues | 350,000 | 400,000 | (i) | 505,000 |
| Total expenses | 365,000 | 380,000 | 360,000 | (l) |

*Instructions*

(a) Determine the missing amounts.
(b) Prepare the statement of owner's equity for Pine Lake Company.
(c) Write a memorandum explaining (1) the sequence for preparing financial statements, and (2) the interrelationships of the statement of owner's equity, income statement, and balance sheet.

Analyse transactions and prepare balance sheet.
(SO 6, 7) AP

**P1–10A**  Plato's Book Shop's balance sheet at April 29, 2005, consisted of the following items (listed here in alphabetical order):

| | | | |
|---|---|---|---|
| Accounts payable | $ 12,000 | Furnishings (store) | $32,000 |
| Accounts receivable | 7,000 | Land | 36,000 |
| Building | 110,000 | Long-term debt payable | 97,000 |
| C. Cai, capital | 91,000 | Notes payable | 22,000 |
| Cash | 8,000 | Office and store supplies | 4,000 |
| Equipment (office) | 25,000 | | |

On the following day, April 30, these transactions and events occurred:

1. Paid $3,000 of the amount owed on accounts payable.
2. Purchased equipment for $18,000. Paid $2,000 in cash and signed a short-term note for the balance.
3. A professional real estate appraiser estimated the value of the land at $50,000.
4. Sold some surplus office equipment for $5,000 in cash, which was the same as the original acquisition cost of the equipment.
5. Made a payment of $7,000 on the long-term debt.

*Instructions*

Prepare a balance sheet in good form for Plato's Book Shop, as at April 30, 2005. Show your calculations for all new amounts.

Prepare financial statements.
(SO 7) AP

**P1–11A**  Bennett's Home Renovations was started in 1999 by Jim Bennett. Jim initially invested $15,000 but the business has grown since then. Jim operates the business from an office in his home but uses the truck for business purposes only. Listed below are the assets and liabilities of the company as at December 31, 2005, and the revenues, expenses, and drawings for the year ended December 31, 2005:

| | | | |
|---|---|---|---|
| Accounts payable | $ 6,600 | Note payable | $ 12,000 |
| Accounts receivable | 7,200 | Office supplies expense | 2,125 |
| Cash | 5,500 | Office supplies on hand | 425 |
| Furniture and equipment | 11,000 | Renovation fee revenue | 110,500 |
| Interest expense | 850 | Truck | 30,000 |
| Jim Bennett, drawings | 62,000 | Truck operating expenses | 3,960 |
| Liability insurance expense | 2,410 | Wages expense | 42,450 |

Jim's capital at the beginning of 2005 was $38,820. He made no investments during 2005.

*Instructions*

Prepare an income statement and statement of owner's equity for 2005 and a balance sheet at December 31, 2005.

# Problems: Set B

Identify users and uses of financial statements.
(SO 2) AP

**P1–1B**  Financial decisions often depend more on one type of financial statement than on others. Consider each of the following hypothetical situations independently:

(a) An Ontario investor is considering investing in Bally Total Fitness Company, which operates 13 fitness centres in the Toronto area. The investor plans on holding the investment for at least three years.
(b) Comeau Ltée is considering extending credit to a new customer. The company would require the customer to pay within 60 days of receipt of the goods.

(c) The Laurentian Bank is considering extending a loan to a small company. The company would be required to make interest payments at the end of each month for five years, and to repay the loan at the end of the fifth year.

**Instructions**

In each situation, state whether the individual making the decision would depend mostly on the information in the income statement, balance sheet, or cash flow statement. Briefly justify your choice.

**P1–2B** A number of accounting reporting situations are described below:

*Identify assumption or principle violated. (SO 4) AN*

1. In preparing its financial statements, Karim Corporation tried to estimate and record the impact of the recent death of its president.
2. Paradis Company recently purchased a power boat. It plans on inviting clients for outings occasionally, so the boat was paid for with company funds and recorded in the company's records. Marc Paradis's family will use the boat whenever it is not being used to entertain clients. It is estimated that the boat will be used by the family about 75 percent of the time.
3. Because of a "flood sale," equipment worth $300,000 was purchased by Montigny Company for only $200,000. The equipment was recorded at $300,000 on the company's books.

**Instructions**

For each of the above situations, list any assumption or principle that has been violated. Explain why the situation violates the assumption or principle.

**P1–3B** Presented below are five independent situations:

*Determine forms of business organization. (SO 4) C*

(a) Three physics professors have formed a business to improve the speed of information transfer over the Internet for stock exchange transactions. Each has contributed an equal amount of cash and knowledge to the venture. While their approach looks promising, they are concerned about the legal liabilities that their business might confront.
(b) Joseph LeBlanc, a student looking for summer employment, opened a bait shop in a small shed on a local fishing dock.
(c) Robert Steven and Tom Cheng each own a shoe manufacturing business. They have decided to combine their businesses. They expect that in the coming year they will need significant funds to expand their operations.
(d) Darcy Becker, Ellen Sweet, and Meg Dwyer recently graduated with marketing degrees. Friends since childhood, they have decided to start a consulting business focused on marketing sporting goods over the Internet.

**Instructions**

In each case, explain what form of organization the business is likely to take: proprietorship, partnership, or corporation. Give reasons for your choice.

**P1–4B** Verma's Repair Shop was started on May 1 by A. Verma. A summary of the May transactions follows:

*Analyse transactions and calculate owner's equity. (SO 5, 6) AN*

May 1 Invested $14,000 to start the repair shop.
2 Purchased equipment for $8,000, paying $2,000 cash and signing a note payable for the balance.
5 Paid $840 cash for May office rent.
7 Purchased $550 of supplies on account.
9 Received $2,100 in cash from customers for repair services.
15 Withdrew $1,500 cash for personal use.
16 Provided repair services on account to customers, $800.
26 Collected cash of $500 for services billed on May 16.
27 Paid for supplies purchased on May 7.
28 Paid $420 cash for advertising.
31 Received the May telephone bill of $200.
31 Paid part-time employee salaries, $1,200.
31 Billed a customer $350 for repair services.

**Instructions**

(a) Prepare a tabular analysis of the effect of the above transactions on the accounting equation.
(b) From an analysis of the owner's equity columns, calculate A. Verma, Capital as at May 31.

Analyse transactions and prepare income statement and balance sheet.
(SO 6, 7) AP

**P1–5B** Lynn Barry started her own consulting firm, Barry Consulting, on June 1, 2005. The following transactions occurred during the month of June:

June  1  Barry sold her shares in WestJet Airlines for $5,000 cash, which she deposited in her personal bank account.
  1  Barry transferred $4,000 cash from her personal account to a business account in the name of Barry Consulting.
  2  Paid $800 for office rent for the month.
  3  Purchased $625 of supplies on account.
  5  Paid $50 to advertise in the *County News*.
  9  Received $1,175 cash for services provided.
  12  Withdrew $800 cash for personal reasons.
  15  Performed $3,000 of services on account.
  17  Paid $2,500 for employee salaries.
  20  Paid for the supplies purchased on account on May 3.
  23  Received a cash payment of $2,000 for services provided on account on May 15.
  25  Signed a contract to provide consulting services to a client for $5,500. Services are to be performed and paid for in July.
  26  Borrowed $5,000 from the bank on a note payable.
  29  Purchased office equipment for $2,900.
  30  Paid $150 for utilities.

*Instructions*

(a) Use the accounting equation to analyse the effects of each transaction.
(b) Prepare an income statement for the month of June.
(c) Prepare a balance sheet at June 30, 2005.

Analyse transactions and prepare financial statements.
(SO 6, 7) AP

**P1–6B** Brian Fraser opened Fraser Veterinary Clinic in Regina on August 1, 2005. On August 31, the balance sheet showed Cash $4,500; Accounts Receivable $1,800; Supplies $350; Office Equipment $6,500; Accounts Payable $3,200; and B. Fraser, Capital $9,950. During September the following transactions occurred:

Sept.  1  Paid $2,800 of the accounts payable.
  1  Paid $1,200 rent for September.
  4  Collected $1,450 of the accounts receivable.
  5  Hired a part-time office assistant at $50 per day to start work the following week.
  8  Purchased additional office equipment for $2,050, paying $700 in cash and the balance on account.
  14  Charged $500 for veterinary services.
  15  Paid $300 for advertising expenses.
  18  Received cash for services performed on September 14.
  20  Paid $200 for Brian's daughter and friends to go horseback riding on her birthday.
  25  Received $7,500 from the Western Bank—money borrowed on a note payable.
  26  Sent a statement reminding a customer that he still owed the company money from August.
  28  Earned revenue of $4,300, of which $2,900 was paid in cash and the balance is due in October.
  29  Paid part-time office assistant $450 for working nine days in September.
  30  Incurred utility expenses for the month on account, $175.
  30  Withdrew $2,500 cash for personal expenses.

*Instructions*

(a) Prepare a tabular analysis of the effect of the September transactions on the accounting equation beginning with the August 31 balances.
(b) Prepare an income statement and statement of owner's equity for September and a balance sheet at September 30, 2005.

Use financial statement relationships to determine missing amounts.
(SO 5, 7) AN

**P1–7B** The following selected data from the 2005 financial statements for the Siksika Trading Company are in random order:

| | |
|---|---:|
| Liabilities at the end of the year | $510,000 |
| Investments by the owner during the year | 15,000 |
| Assets at the beginning of the year | 665,000 |

| | |
|---|---:|
| Drawings by the owner during the year | $ 76,000 |
| Net income for the year | 84,000 |
| Capital at the beginning of the year | 285,000 |
| Total revenue for the year | 387,000 |

*Instructions*

Determine the amount of each of the following items:

(a) Liabilities at the beginning of the year    (c) Capital at the end of the year
(b) Total expenses for the year    (d) Assets at the end of the year

**P1–8B**  On September 1, Emily Shimbashi started Specialty Cosmetics Co. by investing $9,500 cash in the business. The alphabetical list below shows the assets and liabilities of the company at September 30 and the revenues and expenses for the month of September:

*Prepare financial statements.*
*(SO 6, 7) AP*

| | | | |
|---|---:|---|---:|
| Accounts payable | $2,300 | Equipment | $18,000 |
| Accounts receivable | 3,900 | Notes payable | 12,000 |
| Advertising expense | 900 | Service revenue | 4,600 |
| Cash | 4,600 | Supplies expense | 1,500 |
| Cosmetic supplies | 2,700 | Utilities expense | 200 |

Emily invested an additional $5,000 on September 20, and withdrew $1,600 in cash for personal use during the month.

*Instructions*

(a) Prepare an income statement and statement of owner's equity for the month of September and a balance sheet at September 30, 2005.
(b) Indicate how the financial statements in (a) would be affected by the following additional data: (1) Service revenue of $900 was earned but not billed or collected at September 30. (2) Gas and oil expense of $250 was incurred but not recorded or paid.

**P1–9B**  Here are incomplete financial statements for Baxter Company:

*Determine financial statement amounts, and comment.*
*(SO 6, 7) AP*

**BAXTER COMPANY**
**Balance Sheet**
**November 30, 2004**

| Assets | | Liabilities and Owner's Equity | |
|---|---:|---|---:|
| Cash | $ 5,000 | Liabilities | |
| Accounts receivable | 10,000 | Notes payable | $ 69,600 |
| Land | (a) | Accounts payable | (c) |
| Building | 45,000 | Total liabilities | 76,500 |
| Total assets | $ (b) | Owner's equity | |
| | | B. Baxter, capital | (d) |
| | | Total liabilities and | |
| | | owner's equity | $110,000 |

**BAXTER COMPANY**
**Income Statement**
**Year Ended November 30, 2004**

| | | |
|---|---:|---:|
| Revenues | | |
| Fees earned | | $80,000 |
| Expenses | | |
| Rent expense | $ (e) | |
| Salaries expense | 35,000 | |
| Supplies expense | 7,000 | |
| Total expenses | | 60,000 |
| Net income | | $ (f) |

**BAXTER COMPANY**
**Statement of Owner's Equity**
**Year Ended November 30, 2004**

| | |
|---|---:|
| B. Baxter, capital, December 1, 2003 | $18,000 |
| Add:  Investments | 2,500 |
| Net income | (g) |
| | 40,500 |
| Less:  Drawings | (h) |
| B. Baxter, capital, November 30, 2004 | $    (i) |

*Instructions*

(a) Calculate the missing amounts (a) to (i).
(b) Write a memo explaining (1) the sequence for preparing the financial statements and (2) the interrelationships between the balance sheet, income statement, and statement of owner's equity.

*Comment on proper account treatment and prepare corrected balance sheet.*
*(SO 4, 7) E*

**P1–10B**   GG Company was formed on January 1, 2004. On December 31, 2004, Guy Gélinas, the proprietor, decided to prepare a balance sheet, which appeared as follows:

**GG COMPANY**
**Balance Sheet**
**December 31, 2004**

| Assets | | Liabilities and Owner's Equity | |
|---|---:|---|---:|
| Cash | $20,000 | Accounts payable | $40,000 |
| Accounts receivable | 55,000 | Notes payable | 15,000 |
| Inventory | 30,000 | Boat loan | 10,000 |
| Boat | 18,000 | Guy Gélinas, capital | 50,000 |

Guy willingly admits that he is not an accountant by training. He is concerned that his balance sheet might not be correct. He has provided you with the following additional information:

1. The boat actually belongs to Guy Gélinas, not to GG Company. However, because he thinks he might take customers out on the boat occasionally, he decided to list it as an asset of the company. To be consistent, he also listed as a liability of the company his personal loan that he took out at the bank to buy the boat.
2. The inventory was originally purchased for $15,000, but due to a surge in demand Guy now thinks he could sell it for $30,000. He thought it would be best to record it at $30,000.
3. Included in the accounts receivable balance is $10,000 that Guy Gélinas loaned to his brother two years ago. Guy included this in the receivables of GG Company so he would remember that his brother owes him money.

Instructions

(a) Comment on the proper accounting treatment of the three items above.
(b) Provide a corrected balance sheet for GG Company. (*Hint:* To get the balance sheet to balance, adjust owner's equity.)

*Prepare financial statements.*
*(SO 7) AP*

**P1–11B**   Judy Johansen operates an interior design business, Johansen Designs. She rents office space and uses her car regularly for business purposes. The company pays for the business portion of her car expenses. Listed below are the assets and liabilities of the company as at December 31, 2005, and the revenues, expenses, and drawings for the year ended December 31, 2005:

| | | | |
|---|---:|---|---:|
| Accounts payable | $ 4,170 | Judy Johansen, drawings | $57,500 |
| Accounts receivable | 5,460 | Note payable | 4,250 |
| Cash | 7,420 | Office supplies expense | 1,875 |
| Computer equipment | 5,750 | Office supplies on hand | 375 |
| Design fee revenue | 87,425 | Salaries expense | 27,400 |
| Furniture | 8,380 | Telephone expense | 1,175 |
| Interest expense | 225 | Vehicle operating expenses | 3,675 |

Judy's capital at the beginning of 2005 was $23,390. She made no investments during 2005.

*Instructions*

Prepare an income statement and statement of owner's equity for 2005 and a balance sheet at December 31, 2005.

# Continuing Cookie Chronicle

Natalie Koebel spent much of her childhood learning the art of cookie-making from her grandmother. They passed many happy hours mastering every type of cookie imaginable and later devising new recipes that were both healthy and delicious. Now at the start of her second year in college, Natalie is investigating various possibilities for starting her own business as part of the requirements of the Entrepreneurship program she is taking. A long-time friend insists that Natalie has to somehow include cookies in her business plan and, after a series of brainstorming sessions, Natalie settles on the idea of operating a cookie-making school. She will start on a part-time basis and offer her services in peoples' homes. Now that she has started thinking about it, the possibilities seem endless. During the fall she will concentrate on Christmas cookies. She will offer group sessions (which will probably be more entertainment than education for the participants) and individual lessons. Natalie also decides to include children in her target market. The first difficult decision is coming up with the perfect name for her business. In the end she settles on "Cookie Creations" and then moves on to more important issues.

*Instructions*

(a) What form of business organization—proprietorship, partnership, or corporation—do you recommend that Natalie use for her business? Discuss the benefits and weaknesses of each form that Natalie might consider and give your reasons for choosing the form of business organization you are recommending.

(b) Will Natalie need accounting information? If yes, what information will she need and why? How often will she need this information?

(c) Identify specific asset, liability, and equity accounts that Cookie Creations will likely use to record its business transactions.

(d) Should Natalie open a separate bank account for the business? Why or why not?

(e) Natalie expects she will have to use her car to drive to people's homes and to pick up supplies, but she also needs to use her car for personal reasons. She recalls from her first-year accounting course something about keeping business and personal assets separate. She wonders what she should do for accounting purposes. What do you recommend?

# Financial Reporting and Analysis

Practice
Tools

## Financial Reporting Problem

**BYP1–1**  The Forzani Group Ltd.'s financial statements for 2003 have been reproduced in Appendix A at the back of the textbook.

*Instructions*
(a) How many notes to the financial statements are presented for The Forzani Group? How many pages of the financial statement package do these notes occupy? How many pages do the financial statements themselves occupy?
(b) Notice that the dates on the financial statements are February 2, 2003, and January 27, 2002. (The company's 2001 financial statements were dated January 28.) What is The Forzani Group's fiscal year end?
(c) What were The Forzani Group's total assets as at February 2, 2003? January 27, 2002?
(d) What is the amount of change in The Forzani Group's net income (Forzani refers to this figure as net earnings) from 2002 to 2003?
(e) What amount of cash did The Forzani Group have on February 2, 2003? January 27, 2002?

## Interpreting Financial Statements

**BYP1–2**  Corel Corporation is an innovative software company headquartered in Ottawa. In the assets section of its 2002 balance sheet, the following data were presented:

| COREL CORPORATION<br>Balance Sheet (partial)<br>November 30, 2002<br>(in U.S. thousands) | | |
|---|---|---|
| | 2002 | 2001 |
| Current assets | | |
| Cash and cash equivalents | $ 20,432 | $ 44,291 |
| Accounts receivable | 20,208 | 19,961 |
| Inventory | 191 | 799 |
| Prepaid expenses | 2,786 | 1,779 |
| Investments | 65,542 | 87,962 |
| Capital assets | 21,768 | 43,123 |
| Goodwill | | 37,534 |
| Other assets | | 250 |
| Total assets | $130,927 | $235,699 |

*Instructions*
(a) For a software development company such as Corel, what do you think its most important economic resources (assets) would be? Where would these be recorded on the balance sheet? At what value (if any) should they be shown?
(b) Does the balance sheet tell you what Corel Corporation is worth? What information does the balance sheet give you regarding the value of the company?

(c) Why do you think a Canadian company such as Corel would prepare its financial statements in U.S. dollars?

## Accounting on the Web

**BYP1–3** This case views the websites of professional accounting organizations and firms, among others, to learn about career opportunities.

*Instructions*
Specific requirements of this Internet case are available on the Weygandt website.

# Critical Thinking

## Collaborative Learning Activity

**BYP1–4** Patsy and Perry Ross, local golf stars, opened the Chip-Shot Driving Range on May 1, 2005, by investing $20,000 of their cash savings in the business. A caddy shack was constructed for cash at a cost of $6,000, and $800 was spent on golf balls and golf clubs. The Rosses leased five acres of land at a cost of $1,000 per month and paid the first month's rent. During the first month, advertising costs totalled $750, of which $150 was unpaid at May 31. Members of the high school golf team were paid $400 for retrieving golf balls. All fees from customers were deposited in the company's bank account. On May 15, Patsy and Perry withdrew $800 in cash for personal living expenses. A $100 utility bill was received on May 31, but it was not paid. On May 31, the balance in the company's bank account was $15,100.

Patsy and Perry weren't sure how they did in their first month of operations. Their estimates of profitability ranged from a loss of $4,900 to net income of $1,650.

*Instructions*
With the class divided into groups, answer the following:
(a) How could the Rosses have concluded that the business operated at a loss of $4,900? Was this a valid way to determine net income?
(b) How could the Rosses have concluded that the business generated a net income of $1,650? (*Hint:* Prepare a balance sheet at May 31.) Was this a valid way to determine net income?
(c) Without preparing an income statement, determine the actual net income for May.
(d) What were the fees earned in May? (*Hint:* You can determine this either by (1) preparing an income statement, and using your answer from part (c) and the information about expenses to calculate the missing amount for fees earned [revenue], or (2) analysing the changes in cash and inserting the missing amount for fees [cash receipts].)

## Communication Activity

**BYP1–5** Robert Joote is the owner of Peak Company. Robert has prepared the following balance sheet:

**PEAK COMPANY**
**Balance Sheet**
**Month Ended December 31, 2005**

### Assets

| | |
|---|---:|
| Equipment | $20,500 |
| Cash | 10,500 |
| Supplies | 2,000 |
| Accounts payable | (5,000) |
| Total assets | $28,000 |

### Liabilities and Owner's Equity

| | |
|---|---:|
| Joote, capital | $21,000 |
| Accounts receivable | (3,000) |
| Joote, drawings | (2,000) |
| Notes payable | 12,000 |
| Total liabilities and owner's equity | $28,000 |

*Instructions*

In a memo, explain to Robert (a) the purpose of a balance sheet, (b) why his balance sheet is incorrect, and (c) what he should do to correct it.

## Ethics Case

**BYP1–6**  After many campus interviews, Stephane Pelli, a graduating student at the University of New Brunswick, Fredericton, received interview offers from two large firms located in Saint John, New Brunswick. Both firms offered to cover his out-of-pocket expenses (travel, hotel, and meals). He scheduled the interviews for both firms on the same day, one in the morning and one in the afternoon.

At the conclusion of each interview, Stephane submitted to each firm his total out-of-pocket expenses for the trip: use of private vehicle $70 (280 kilometres at $0.25), hotel $120, meals $36, plus parking and tips $18, for a total of $244. He believes this approach is appropriate. If he had made two trips, his cost would have been two times $244. He is also certain that neither firm knew he had visited the other on that same trip.

Within a few days, Stephane received two cheques in the mail, each for $244.

*Instructions*

(a) Who are the stakeholders (affected parties) in this situation?
(b) What are the ethical issues in this case?
(c) What would you do in this situation?

*Answers to Self-Study Questions*
1. b   2. d   3. d   4. a   5. c   6. a   7. b   8. d   9. b   10. b   11. c

*Answer to Forzani Review It Question 2*

The net earnings of $30,531,000 (also known as net income) on the statement of operations (also known as the income statement) are included on the statement of retained earnings to determine the ending balance of retained earnings of $78,857,000. Note that Forzani combines its income statement and statement of retained earnings for presentation purposes, rather than providing two separate financial statements. A statement of retained earnings is prepared by corporations, and is similar to the statement of owner's equity prepared by proprietorships.

The ending retained earnings balance of $78,857,000 shown on Forzani's combined statement of operations and retained earnings is also reported on the balance sheet. Finally, the $523,000 ending cash balance reported as an asset on the balance sheet is explained on the cash flow statement (also known as the statement of cash flows), which ends with this same ending cash balance.

Remember to go back to the Navigator Box at the beginning of the chapter to check off your completed work.

Before studying this chapter, you should understand or, if necessary, review:

    a. Why assets equal liabilities plus owner's equity. (Ch. 1, p. 10)

    b. What assets, liabilities, owner's capital, drawings, revenues, and expenses are. (Ch. 1, pp. 10–12)

    c. What transactions are, and how they affect the basic accounting equation. (Ch. 1, pp. 13–18)

# A Taste for Business

*Felix and Norton: www.felixandnorton.com*

BURNABY, BC—Who can resist the aroma of fresh-baked cookies? Ask anyone in line at the Sweet Factory/Monsieur Félix and Mr. Norton store at the Metrotown Shopping Centre and chances are they'll tell you it's easier said than done.

Store owner Pak Chuen Chan bought his first Sweet Factory franchise in 1996, selling bulk candy, chocolate, and other treats. He later opened a second outlet in the same mall and combined it with a counter selling Félix and Norton cookies—a Montreal-based gourmet cookie line that features 13 different flavours.

"We bake them right here on the premises," he says. Today, Mr. Chan employs a total of 17 people in the two outlets, including 12 in his "combo" store alone, where cookies now account for 15% of total sales.

Like any good recipe, a business's success depends on good ingredients—not least of which are the right products and a great location. But success also depends on good accounting.

Every day after closing, and at the end of every month, Mr. Chan prints out a sales report from each cash register—he has one in each store—that shows net sales, sales by category, and total number of customers.

"I collect monthly sales reports, staff time sheets, plus all my invoices for things like inventory and store supplies, office and administration expenses, rent, utilities, promotion and royalties, and hand them over to my accoun-

tant, who takes care of everything else for me," he explains.

"Everything else" includes recording transactions, looking after payroll, filing sales tax reports, and preparing financial statements, in this case all done using Simply Accounting software. That's a lot to do when you've got two stores to run and cookies to bake—and why Mr. Chan leaves most of the work to an accounting professional.

What does he like best about his business? Mr. Chan says he enjoys talking to the people from all walks of life who come into his stores. And of course, he confesses to having a bit of a sweet tooth himself. "After all," he says, "it's important to enjoy your job!"

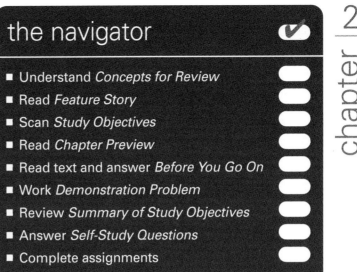

**the navigator** ✓

- Understand *Concepts for Review*
- Read *Feature Story*
- Scan *Study Objectives*
- Read *Chapter Preview*
- Read text and answer *Before You Go On*
- Work *Demonstration Problem*
- Review *Summary of Study Objectives*
- Answer *Self-Study Questions*
- Complete assignments

# chapter 2
# The Recording Process

## study objectives >>

After studying this chapter, you should be able to:

1. Explain what an account is and how it helps in the recording process.
2. Define debits and credits and illustrate how they are used to record business transactions.
3. Describe the basic steps in the recording process.
4. Explain what a journal is and how it helps in the recording process, and journalize business transactions.
5. Explain what a ledger is and how it helps in the recording process.
6. Explain what posting is and how it helps in the recording process.
7. Explain the purpose of a trial balance, and prepare one.

In Chapter 1, we used the accounting equation to analyse business transactions. The cumulative effects of these transactions were presented in tabular equation form. This method could work for small companies like Softbyte (the fictitious company discussed in Chapter 1) because it has relatively few transactions. But imagine Mr. Chan's company in the feature story using the same tabular format as Softbyte. In a single day the cookie company has more than 200 business transactions. To record each transaction this way would be impractical. Instead, a set of procedures and records are used to keep track of transaction data more easily.

This chapter introduces and illustrates the basic procedures and records. The chapter is organized as follows:

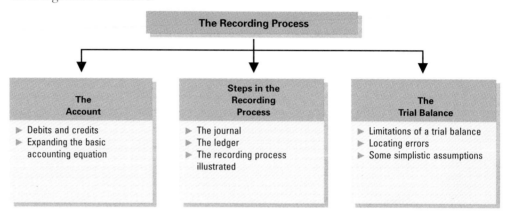

**The Recording Process**

| The Account | Steps in the Recording Process | The Trial Balance |
|---|---|---|
| ▶ Debits and credits<br>▶ Expanding the basic accounting equation | ▶ The journal<br>▶ The ledger<br>▶ The recording process illustrated | ▶ Limitations of a trial balance<br>▶ Locating errors<br>▶ Some simplistic assumptions |

# The Account

**study objective 1**

Explain what an account is and how it helps in the recording process.

An account is an individual accounting record of increases and decreases in a specific asset, liability, or owner's equity item. For example, Softbyte has separate accounts called Cash, Accounts Receivable, Accounts Payable, Service Revenue, Salaries Expense, and so on. In its simplest form, an account consists of three parts: (1) the title of the account, (2) a debit side on the left, and (3) a credit side on the right. Because the positioning of these parts of an account resembles the letter T, it is called a T account. The basic form of an account is shown in Illustration 2-1.

**Illustration 2-1 ▶**

Basic form of T account

Title of Account

| Debit (left) side | Credit (right) side |

Accounting Cycle Tutorial—Recording Business Transactions

This form of account will be used throughout the book to explain basic accounting relationships.

# Debits and Credits

study objective 2

Define debits and credits and illustrate how they are used to record business transactions.

The term debit indicates left. The term credit indicates right. They are commonly abbreviated Dr. for debit and Cr. for credit. These terms come from Latin words that originally meant debtor and creditor. Today they are directional signals. They indicate which side of a T account to record on. Entering an amount on the left side of an account is called **debiting** the account. Making an entry on the right side is called **crediting** the account.

The custom of having debits on the left side of an account and credits on the right side (like the custom of driving on the right-hand side of the road) is simply an accounting custom, or rule. This rule applies to all accounts. When the totals of the two sides are compared, an account will have a **debit balance** if the total of the debit amounts exceeds the credits. Conversely, an account will have a **credit balance** if the credit amounts exceed the debits.

The recording of debits and credits in an account is shown in Illustration 2-2 for Softbyte's cash transactions. The data are taken from the Cash column of the tabular summary in Illustration 1-8.

| Tabular Summary | | | Account Form | | | |
|---|---|---|---|---|---|---|
| **Cash** | | (Debits) | | Cash | (Credits) | |
| +$15,000 | | | 15,000 | | 7,000 | |
| −7,000 | | | 1,200 | | 600 | |
| +1,200 | | | 1,500 | | 900 | |
| +1,500 | | | 600 | | 200 | |
| −600 | | | | | 250 | |
| −900 | | | | | 1,300 | |
| −200 | | Balance | 8,050 | | | |
| −250 | | | | | | |
| +600 | | | | | | |
| −1,300 | | | | | | |
| $ 8,050 | | | | | | |

**Illustration 2-2 ◄**

Tabular summary compared to account form

In the tabular summary, every positive item represents a receipt of cash. Every negative amount represents a payment of cash. Notice that in the account form the increases in cash are recorded as debits, and the decreases in cash are recorded as credits. Having increases on one side and decreases on the other helps in determining the totals of each side of the account, as well as the balance in the account. The account balance, a debit of $8,050, indicates that Softbyte has $8,050 more increases than decreases in cash.

## Debit and Credit Procedure

**Helpful hint** Debits must equal credits for each transaction.

In Chapter 1, you learned the effect of a transaction on the basic accounting equation. Remember that each transaction must affect two or more accounts to keep the basic accounting equation in balance. In other words, for each transaction, **debits must equal credits** in the accounts. The equality of debits and credits is the basis for the double-entry system of recording transactions.

Under the double-entry system, the dual (two-sided) effect of each transaction is recorded in appropriate accounts. This universally used system provides a logical method for recording transactions. It also offers a way of proving the accuracy of the recorded amounts. If every transaction is recorded with equal debits and credits, then the sum of all the debits to the accounts must equal the sum of all the credits.

### Assets and Liabilities.
In the Softbyte illustration, increases in Cash—an asset account—were entered on the left side, and decreases in Cash were entered on the right side. We know that both sides of the basic equation (assets = liabilities + owner's equity) must

be equal. To maintain this equality, increases and decreases have to be recorded opposite each other. Thus, increases in assets must be entered on the left or debit side, and decreases in assets must be entered on the right or credit side. Increases in liabilities must be entered on the right or credit side, and decreases in liabilities must be entered on the left or debit side.

Debits to a specific asset account should exceed the credits to that account. Credits to a liability account should exceed debits to that account. Thus, asset accounts normally show debit balances, and liability accounts normally show credit balances.

The effects that debits and credits have on assets and liabilities and the normal balances are as follows:

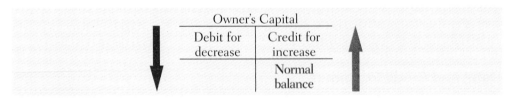

| | Assets | | | | | Liabilities | |
|---|---|---|---|---|---|---|---|
| | Debit for increase | Credit for decrease | | | Debit for decrease | Credit for increase | |
| | Normal balance | | | | | Normal balance | |

**Helpful hint** The normal balance for an account is always on the increase side.

Knowing the normal balance in an account may help you trace errors. In automated systems, the computer is programmed to find these normal balance exceptions and to print out error or exception reports. In manual systems, careful visual inspection of the accounts is required to detect variations from normal balances. For example, a credit balance in an asset account such as Land or a debit balance in a liability account such as Wages Payable would likely indicate recording errors. Occasionally, an abnormal balance may be correct. The Cash account, for example, will have a credit balance when a company has overdrawn its bank balance.

**Owner's Equity.** As indicated in Chapter 1, owner's equity is increased by owner's investments and revenues. It is decreased by owner's drawings and expenses. Separate accounts are kept for each of these types of transactions.

***Owner's Capital.*** Investments by owners are credited to the owner's capital account. Like liability accounts, the owner's capital account is increased by credits and decreased by debits. For example, when cash is invested in the business, the Cash account is debited and Owner's Capital is credited.

The rules of debit and credit for the owner's capital account and the normal balance in this account are as follows:

| | Owner's Capital | |
|---|---|---|
| | Debit for decrease | Credit for increase |
| | | Normal balance |

As liabilities and owner's equity are on the same side of the accounting equation, the rules of debit and credit are the same for these two types of accounts.

***Owner's Drawings.*** An owner may withdraw cash or other assets for personal use. Withdrawals could be debited directly to Owner's Capital to indicate a decrease in owner's equity. However, it is preferable to establish a separate account, called Drawings, as we did in Chapter 1. The separate account makes it easier to determine the total withdrawals for the accounting period and to prepare the statement of owner's equity. The drawings account decreases owner's equity. Owner's drawings are recorded by debits and the account has a normal debit balance. Credits to an owner's drawings account are unusual, but might be used to correct a withdrawal recorded in error, for example.

The rules of debit and credit for the Drawings account and the normal balance are as follows:

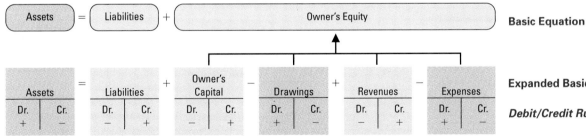

|  | Drawings |  |
|---|---|---|
| ↑ | Debit for increase | Credit for decrease |
|  | Normal balance |  | ↓ |

**Net Income.** Net income results when revenues exceed expenses. Remember that the main reason for earning revenues is to benefit the owner of the business. When revenues are earned, owner's equity is increased. Accordingly, the effect of debits and credits on revenue accounts is identical to their effect on owner's capital. Revenue accounts are increased by credits and decreased by debits.

Expenses have the opposite effect: expenses decrease owner's equity. As a result, expenses are recorded as debits. Since expenses are the negative factor in calculating net income, and revenues are the positive factor, it is logical that the increase and decrease sides of expense accounts should be the reverse of revenue accounts. Thus, expense accounts are increased by debits and decreased by credits.

Credits to revenue accounts should exceed the debits. Debits to expense accounts should exceed credits. Thus, revenue accounts normally show credit balances. Expense accounts normally show debit balances.

The effect of debits and credits on revenues and expenses and the normal balances are as follows:

|  | Revenues |  |  |  | Expenses |  |  |
|---|---|---|---|---|---|---|---|
| ↓ | Debit for decrease | Credit for increase | ↑ | ↑ | Debit for increase | Credit for decrease | ↓ |
|  |  | Normal balance |  |  | Normal balance |  |  |

## Expanding the Basic Accounting Equation

You have already learned the basic accounting equation. Illustration 2-3 expands this equation to show the accounts that form owner's equity. In addition, the debit/credit rules and effects on each type of account are illustrated. Study this diagram carefully. It will help you to understand the fundamentals of the double-entry system. Like the basic equation, the expanded basic equation must always be in balance (total debits must equal total credits).

**Illustration 2-3 ▼**

Expanded basic equation and debit/credit rules and effects

**Basic Equation**

| Assets | = | Liabilities | + | Owner's Equity |
|---|---|---|---|---|

**Expanded Basic Equation**

**Debit/Credit Rules**

| Assets | = | Liabilities | + | Owner's Capital | − | Drawings | + | Revenues | − | Expenses |
|---|---|---|---|---|---|---|---|---|---|---|
| Dr. + | Cr. − | | Dr. − | Cr. + | | Dr. − | Cr. + | | Dr. + | Cr. − | | Dr. − | Cr. + | | Dr. + | Cr. − |

The normal balance of each account is on its increase side. So assets, drawings, and expense accounts have a normal debit balance, while liabilities, owner's capital, and revenue accounts have a normal credit balance.

## BEFORE YOU GO ON . . .

### ▶Review It

1. What do the terms "debit" and "credit" mean?
2. What are the debit and credit effects on the asset, liability, and owner's equity accounts?
3. What are the debit and credit effects on the revenue, expense, and drawings accounts?
4. What are the normal balances for Forzani's Accounts Receivable, Accounts Payable and Accrued Liabilities, Corporate Revenue, and Store Operating Expense accounts? The answer to this question is at the end of this chapter.

### ▶Do It

Eszter Schwenke has just rented space in a shopping mall in which she will open and operate a beauty salon called Hair It Is. Long before opening day and before purchasing equipment, hiring employees, and remodelling the space, Eszter is advised to set up a double-entry set of accounting records to record all of her business transactions.

Name the balance sheet accounts that Eszter will need for recording the transactions that open her business. Indicate whether the normal balance of each account is a debit or a credit.

#### Action Plan

- Determine the types of accounts needed. Eszter will need asset accounts for each different type of asset she invests in the business, and liability accounts for any debts she has.
- Understand the types of owner's equity accounts: Only owner's capital will be needed when Eszter begins the business. Other owner's equity accounts will be added later.

#### Solution

Eszter would likely need the following accounts to record the transactions that prepare her beauty salon for opening day: Cash (debit balance), Supplies (debit balance), Equipment (debit balance), Accounts Payable (credit balance), Notes Payable (credit balance) if she borrows money, and E. Schwenke, Capital (credit balance).

*Related exercise material:* BE2–1, BE2–2, BE2–3, BE2–4, E2–1, and E2–2.

# Steps in the Recording Process

study objective 3

Describe the basic steps in the recording process.

The basic steps in the recording process are:

1. Analyse each transaction in terms of its effects on the accounts.
2. Enter the transaction information in a journal (book of original entry).
3. Transfer the journal information to the appropriate accounts in the ledger (book of accounts).

Although transaction information can be entered directly into the accounts without using a journal or ledger, few businesses do so.

The sequence of events in the recording process begins with the transaction. Evidence is provided by a business document such as a sales slip, cheque, bill, or cash register tape. Mr. Chan's Sweet Factory/Monsieur Félix and Mr. Norton store in the feature story uses sales reports, staff time sheets, and invoices to begin its recording process. This evidence is analysed to determine the effects of the transaction on specific accounts. The transaction is then entered in the journal. Finally, the journal entry is transferred to the correct accounts in the ledger. The sequence of events in the recording process is shown in Illustration 2-4:

**Illustration 2-4** ◀

The recording process

Analyse each transaction

Enter transaction in a journal

Transfer journal information to ledger accounts

The basic steps in the recording process occur repeatedly in every business, whether a computerized or manual accounting system is used. However, the first step—the analysis of each transaction—must be done by people even when a computerized system is used. Determining what to record is the most critical point, and for most businesses the most expensive step, in the accounting process. There are more examples of this step in this and later chapters.

The basic difference between a computerized and a manual accounting system is in the next two steps in the recording process—entering and transferring information. In computerized systems, the information is input and processed through file merging and report generation. These steps occur invisibly. To understand how computerized systems do this, we need to understand manual approaches to processing accounting data.

## The Journal

Transactions are first recorded in chronological (date) order in a journal before being transferred to the accounts. For this reason, the journal is referred to as the book of original entry. For each transaction, the journal shows the debit and credit effects on specific accounts. Companies may use various kinds of journals, but every company has the most basic form of journal, a general journal. Whenever we use the term "journal" in this textbook without a modifying adjective, we mean the general journal.

> **study objective 4**
>
> Explain what a journal is and how it helps in the recording process, and journalize business trans-

The journal makes several significant contributions to the recording process:

- It discloses, in one place, the complete effect of a transaction.
- It provides a chronological record of transactions.
- It helps to prevent and locate errors, because the debit and credit amounts for each entry can easily be compared.
- It provides an explanation of the transaction and, where applicable, identifies the source document.

In a computerized system, "journals" are kept as files, and "accounts" are recorded in computer databases.

### Journalizing

Entering transaction data in the journal is known as journalizing. Separate journal entries are made for each transaction. A complete entry consists of the following: (1) the date of the transaction, (2) the accounts and amounts to be debited and credited, and (3) a brief explanation of the transaction.

To illustrate the technique of journalizing, let's look at the first two transactions of Softbyte. These transactions were (1) September 1, Marc Doucet invested $15,000 cash in the business, and (2) on the same date, computer equipment was purchased for $7,000 cash. In tabular form, these transactions appeared in Chapter 1 as follows:

|  | Assets | = Liabilities + | Owners's Equity |
|---|---|---|---|
|  | Cash + Equipment |  | M. Doucet, Capital |
| (1) | +$15,000 |  | +$15,000 |
| (2) | −7,000 +$7,000 |  |  |

In the margins next to key journal entries are **Equation Analyses**. They summarize the effects of the transactions on the accounting equation (A=L+OE) and cash flows.

| A | = | L | + | OE |
|---|---|---|---|---|
| +15,000 |  |  |  | +15,000 |

⬆ Cash flows: +15,000

| A | = | L | + | OE |
|---|---|---|---|---|
| +7,000 |  |  |  |  |
| −7,000 |  |  |  |  |

⬇ Cash flows: −7,000

Typically, a general journal has spaces for dates, account titles and explanations, references, and two money columns (debit and credit). Since the illustration shows the first page of Softbyte's general journal, it is numbered J1. In journal form, the entries would appear as shown below.

| GENERAL JOURNAL | | | | | J1 |
|---|---|---|---|---|---|
| Date | Account Titles and Explanation | Ref. | Debit | Credit |  |
| 2005 Sept. 1 | Cash | | 15,000 | | |
| | M. Doucet, Capital | | | 15,000 | |
| | Invested cash in business. | | | | |
| 1 | Equipment | | 7,000 | | |
| | Cash | | | 7,000 | |
| | Purchased equipment for cash. | | | | |

The standard form and content of journal entries are as follows:

1. The date of the transaction is entered in the Date column. The date recorded should include the year, month, and day of the transaction.
2. The debit account title (the account to debit) is entered first at the left margin of the column headed Account Titles and Explanation. The credit account title (the account to credit) is entered on the next line, indented from the left margin. The indentation decreases the possibility of confusing the debit and credit amounts.
3. The amounts for the debits are recorded in the Debit (left) column and the amounts for the credits are recorded in the Credit (right) column.
4. A brief explanation of the transaction is given on the line below the credit account title. This explanation also provides an important reference to the source document (invoice number, cheque number, etc.), if applicable. For clearer teaching and assignments in this textbook, journal entry explanations are often left out (after all, you would just be recopying the information you are given). Remember, however, that in real life, explanations are essential for every journal entry.
5. A space is left between journal entries. The blank space separates individual journal entries and makes the entire journal easier to read.
6. The column titled Ref. (which stands for "reference") is left blank when the journal entry is made. This column is used later, when the journal entries are transferred to the ledger accounts. At that time, the ledger account number is placed in the Reference column to indicate where the amount in the journal entry was transferred to.

Computerized journals and manual journals serve the same purpose. The format of the computerized journal may differ slightly from the format described above, but the content is almost always the same. Computerized systems, such as Simply Accounting used by Mr. Chan's company in the feature story, often need an account number rather than an account name to be entered. The account name is automatically inserted for you by the computer. We will discuss account numbers in more detail later in this chapter. Automatic error checks by the software ensure that only correct account numbers are used and that debits and credits balance for each transaction.

**It is important to use correct and specific account titles in journalizing.** Since the accounts appear later in the financial statements, inaccurate account titles lead to incorrect financial statements. There is some flexibility when an account title is first chosen. The main criterion is that each title accurately describe the content of the account. For example, the account title used for the computer equipment purchased by Softbyte may be Equipment, Computer Equipment, Computers, or Office Equipment. However, once a company chooses the specific title to use, all transactions for the account should be recorded under that account title.

In assignments, when specific account titles are given, they should be used. When account titles are not given, you may select account titles that identify the nature and content of each account. The account titles used in journalizing should not contain explanations (such as Cash Paid or Cash Received).

If an entry involves only two accounts, one debit and one credit, it is considered a simple journal entry. Some transactions, however, use more than two accounts in journalizing. When three or more accounts are required in one journal entry, the entry is called a **compound entry**. To illustrate, recall from Chapter 1 that Softbyte provided $3,500 of programming services to customers on September 9. $1,500 cash was received from customers in payment of these services. The balance, $2,000, is owed on account. The compound entry to record this transaction (6) is as follows:

| GENERAL JOURNAL | | | | J1 |
|---|---|---|---|---|
| Date | Account Titles and Explanation | Ref. | Debit | Credit |
| 2005<br>Sept. 9 | Cash | | 1,500 | |
| | Accounts Receivable | | 2,000 | |
| |    Service Revenue | | | 3,500 |
| |      Performed services for cash and credit. | | | |

A = L + OE
+1,500       +3,500
+2,000

↑ Cash flows: +1,500

In a compound entry, the total debit and credit amounts must equal. Also, the standard format requires that all debits be listed before the credits are listed.

## BEFORE YOU GO ON . . .

### ►Review It

1. What is the sequence of steps in the recording process?
2. What contribution does the journal make to the recording process?
3. What is the standard form and content of a journal entry made in the general journal?
4. How does a manual journal entry differ from a computerized journal entry?

### ►Do It

In establishing her beauty salon, Hair It Is, Eszter Schwenke did the following:

May 1 Opened a bank account in the name of Hair It Is and deposited $20,000 of her own money in this account as her initial investment.
    3 Purchased equipment on account (to be paid in 30 days), for a total cost of $4,800.
    5 Interviewed three persons for the position of stylist.

(a) In what form (type of record) should Eszter record these three activities?
(b) Prepare the entries to record the transactions.

#### Action Plan

- Understand which activities need to be recorded and which do not. The ones that have economic effects should be recorded in a journal.
- Analyse the effects of the transactions on asset, liability, and owner's equity accounts.
- Record the transactions in the general journal, which provides a chronological record of the transactions.

**Solution**

(a) Each transaction that is recorded is entered in the general journal.

(b)

| | May | 1 | Cash | 20,000 | |
|---|---|---|---|---|---|
| | | |    E. Schwenke, Capital | | 20,000 |
| | | |       Invested cash in the business. | | |
| | | 3 | Equipment | 4,800 | |
| | | |    Accounts Payable | | 4,800 |
| | | |       Purchased equipment on account. | | |
| | | 5 | No entry because no transaction has occurred. | | |

*Related exercise material:* BE2–5, BE2–6, BE2–7, E2–3, E2–4, and E2–5.

# The Ledger

study objective 5

Explain what a ledger is and how it helps in the recording process.

The entire group of accounts maintained by a company is called the ledger. The ledger keeps in one place all the information about changes in each account.

Companies may use various kinds of ledgers, but every company has a general ledger. A general ledger contains all the assets, liabilities, and owner's equity accounts. Selected accounts are shown in Illustration 2-5. A business can use a looseleaf binder or card file for the ledger. Each account is kept on a separate sheet or card if a manual accounting system is used. In a computerized accounting system, each account is kept in a separate file. Whenever we use the term "ledger" in this textbook without a modifying adjective, we mean the general ledger.

**Illustration 2-5 ▶**

The general ledger

The ledger should be arranged in the order in which accounts are presented in the financial statements, beginning with the balance sheet accounts. The asset accounts come first, followed by liability accounts, owner's capital, drawings, revenues, and expenses. Of course, in a computerized system, the accounts can easily be rearranged in any order desired. Each account is numbered for easier identification.

The ledger provides the balance in each account. For example, the Cash account shows the amount of cash that is available to meet current objectives. Amounts due from customers can be found by examining Accounts Receivable. Amounts owed to creditors can be found by examining Accounts Payable.

## Standard Form of Account

The simple T account form used in accounting textbooks is often very useful for illustrations. However, in reality the account forms used in ledgers are much more structured. A form widely used in both manual and electronic systems is shown below, using data from Softbyte's Cash account:

| GENERAL LEDGER | | | | | |
|---|---|---|---|---|---|
| Cash | | | | | |
| Date | Explanation | Ref. | Debit | Credit | Balance |
| 2005 | | | | | |
| Sept. 1 | | | 15,000 | | 15,000 |
| 1 | | | | 7,000 | 8,000 |
| 3 | | | 1,200 | | 9,200 |
| 9 | | | 1,500 | | 10,700 |
| 17 | | | | 600 | 10,100 |
| 17 | | | | 900 | 9,200 |
| 17 | | | | 200 | 9,000 |
| 20 | | | | 250 | 8,750 |
| 25 | | | 600 | | 9,350 |
| 30 | | | | 1,300 | 8,050 |

This form is often called the three-column form of account because it has three money columns—debit, credit, and balance. The balance in the account is determined after each transaction. Note that the explanation space and reference columns make it possible to provide information about the transaction.

## Posting

The procedure of transferring journal entries to the ledger accounts is called posting. Posting involves the following steps:

1. **General Ledger.** In the ledger, enter the following in the appropriate columns of each affected account: the date, journal page, and debit or credit amount shown in the journal.
2. **General Journal.** In the reference column of the journal, write the account numbers to which the debit and credit amounts were posted.

These steps are shown in Illustration 2-6 on the following page using Softbyte's first journal entry.

The reference column in the journal serves several purposes. The numbers in this column indicate the entries that have been posted. After the last entry has been posted, this column should be looked at carefully to see that all postings have been made. The references also show the account numbers to which the amounts have been posted.

The reference column of a ledger account indicates the journal page from which the transaction was posted. The explanation space of the ledger account is rarely used, because an explanation already appears in the journal. It is used only when detailed analysis of account activity is required.

Posting should be performed in chronological order. That is, all the debits and credits of one journal entry should be posted before proceeding to the next journal entry. Postings should be made on a timely basis—normally monthly—to ensure that the ledger is up to date.

In a computerized accounting system, posting usually occurs simultaneously after each journal entry is prepared. Obvious errors in the recording process (e.g., unbalanced entries or the use of non-existent accounts) are detected by the system and are not processed until corrected. Because the initial entry is so important, many systems search for more subtle errors, such as unreasonable dollar amounts or account balances for specific accounts (e.g., a debit balance when the account has a normal credit balance).

study objective 6

Explain what posting is and how it helps in the recording process.

**Illustration 2-6 ▶**

Posting a journal entry

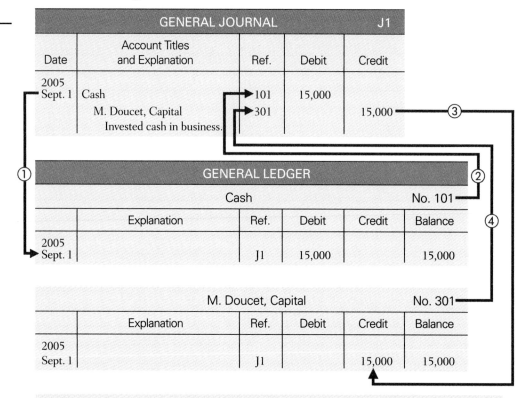

① Post to debit account: enter date, journal page number, and amount.
② Enter debit account number in journal reference column.
③ Post to credit account: enter date, journal page number, and amount.
④ Enter credit account number in journal reference column.

## Chart of Accounts

The number and type of accounts used differ for each enterprise. The number of accounts depends on the amount of detail management wants. The management of one company may want one account for all types of utility expense. Another may keep separate expense accounts for each type of utility expenditure, such as gas, electricity, and water. Similarly, a sole proprietorship like Softbyte has fewer accounts than a corporation like The Forzani Group. Softbyte may be able to manage and report its activities in 20 to 30 accounts, while The Forzani Group requires hundreds of accounts to keep track of its activities.

The first step in designing an accounting system—whether computerized or manual—is to create a chart of accounts. The chart of accounts gives the framework for the entire database of accounting information. The chart of accounts lists the accounts and the account numbers which identify their location in the ledger. The numbering system used to identify the accounts usually starts with the balance sheet accounts and follows with the income statement accounts.

The numbering system used to identify accounts can be quite sophisticated or relatively simple. For example, at Goodyear (a tire and rubber company) an 18-digit system is used. The first three digits identify the division or plant. The second set of three-digit numbers contains the following account classifications:

| | | | |
|---|---|---|---|
| 100–199 | Assets | 300–399 | Revenues |
| 200–299 | Liabilities and Owner's Equity | 400–599 | Expenses |

Other digits describe the location of a specific plant, product line, region of the country, and so on.

In this and the next two chapters, we will explain the accounting for a proprietorship named Pioneer Advertising Agency (a service company). Accounts 100–199 indicate asset accounts, 200–299 indicate liabilities, 300–399 indicate owner's equity accounts, 400–499, revenues, and 600–999, expenses. The chart of accounts for Pioneer Advertising Agency (C. R. Byrd, owner) is shown in Illustration 2-7. Accounts shown in red are used in this chapter; accounts shown in black are explained in later chapters.

**Pioneer Advertising Agency**
**Chart of Accounts**

| Assets | | Owner's Equity | |
|---|---|---|---|
| 101. | Cash | 301. | C. R. Byrd, Capital |
| 112. | Accounts Receivable | 306. | C. R. Byrd, Drawings |
| 129. | Advertising Supplies | 350. | Income Summary |
| 130. | Prepaid Insurance | | |
| 151. | Office Equipment | **Revenues** | |
| 152. | Accumulated Amortization— | 400. | Service Revenue |
| | Office Equipment | | |
| | | **Expenses** | |
| **Liabilities** | | 611. | Advertising Supplies Expense |
| 200. | Notes Payable | 711. | Amortization Expense |
| 201. | Accounts Payable | 722. | Insurance Expense |
| 209. | Unearned Revenue | 726. | Salaries Expense |
| 212. | Salaries Payable | 729. | Rent Expense |
| 230. | Interest Payable | 905. | Interest Expense |

**Illustration 2-7** ◄

Chart of accounts

You will notice that there are gaps in the numbering system of the chart of accounts for Pioneer Advertising. Gaps make it possible to insert new accounts as needed during the life of the business.

A master chart of accounts for a sample company is included in the Study Aids section of the Navigator CD that accompanies this text.

Study
Aids

## The Recording Process Illustrated

Illustrations 2-8 through 2-18 show the basic steps in the recording process, using the October 2005 transactions of the Pioneer Advertising Agency. The agency's accounting period is one month. A basic analysis and a debit/credit analysis precede the journalizing and posting of each transaction. For simplicity, the T account form is used in the illustrations instead of the standard account form. Study these transaction analyses carefully. The purpose of transaction analysis is first to identify the type of account involved, and then to determine whether a debit or a credit to the account is required. You should always do this type of analysis before preparing a journal entry. It will help you understand the journal entries discussed in this chapter, as well as more complex journal entries to be described in later chapters.

Keep in mind that every journal entry affects one or more of the following items: assets, liabilities, owner's capital, revenues, expenses, or drawings. By becoming skilled at transaction analysis, you will be able to quickly recognize the impact of any transaction on these items.

**Illustration 2-8 ▶**

Investment of cash by owner

**Illustration 2-9 ▶**

Purchase of office equipment

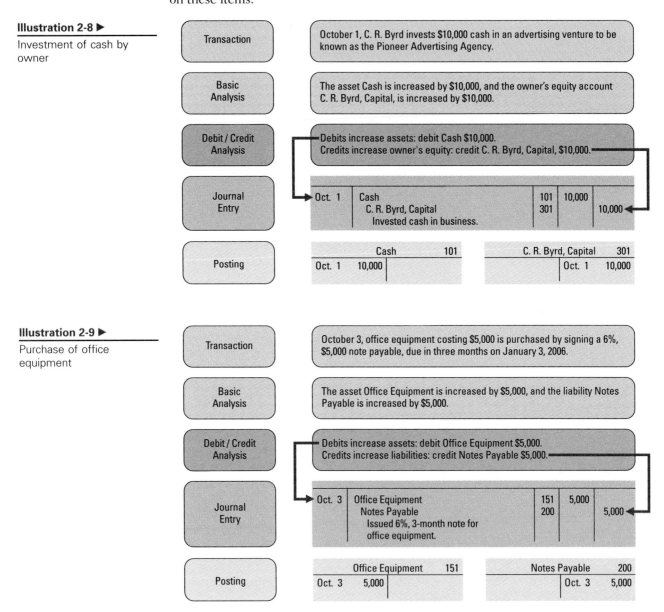

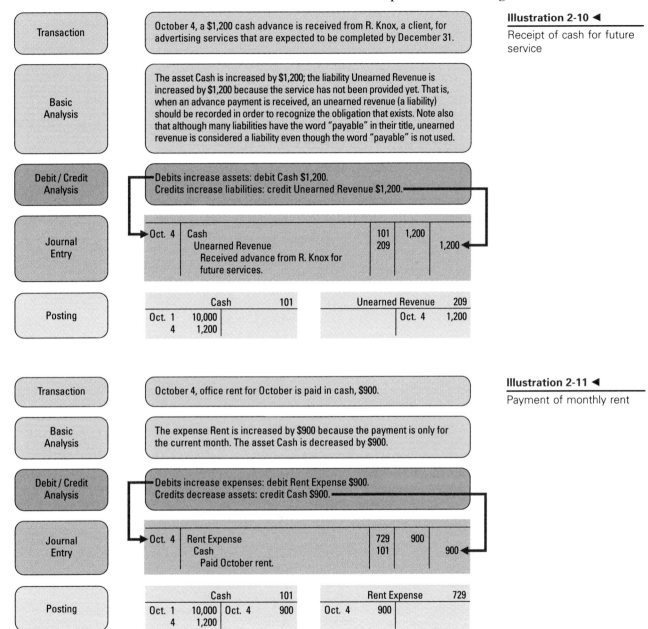

**Illustration 2-10** ◄

Receipt of cash for future service

| Transaction | October 4, a $1,200 cash advance is received from R. Knox, a client, for advertising services that are expected to be completed by December 31. |

| Basic Analysis | The asset Cash is increased by $1,200; the liability Unearned Revenue is increased by $1,200 because the service has not been provided yet. That is, when an advance payment is received, an unearned revenue (a liability) should be recorded in order to recognize the obligation that exists. Note also that although many liabilities have the word "payable" in their title, unearned revenue is considered a liability even though the word "payable" is not used. |

| Debit / Credit Analysis | Debits increase assets: debit Cash $1,200. Credits increase liabilities: credit Unearned Revenue $1,200. |

Journal Entry

| Oct. 4 | Cash | 101 | 1,200 | |
| | Unearned Revenue | 209 | | 1,200 |
| | Received advance from R. Knox for future services. | | | |

Posting

| | Cash | 101 |
|---|---|---|
| Oct. 1 | 10,000 | |
| 4 | 1,200 | |

| | Unearned Revenue | 209 |
|---|---|---|
| | Oct. 4 | 1,200 |

**Illustration 2-11** ◄

Payment of monthly rent

| Transaction | October 4, office rent for October is paid in cash, $900. |

| Basic Analysis | The expense Rent is increased by $900 because the payment is only for the current month. The asset Cash is decreased by $900. |

| Debit / Credit Analysis | Debits increase expenses: debit Rent Expense $900. Credits decrease assets: credit Cash $900. |

Journal Entry

| Oct. 4 | Rent Expense | 729 | 900 | |
| | Cash | 101 | | 900 |
| | Paid October rent. | | | |

Posting

| | Cash | 101 | | |
|---|---|---|---|---|
| Oct. 1 | 10,000 | Oct. 4 | 900 |
| 4 | 1,200 | | |

| | Rent Expense | 729 |
|---|---|---|
| Oct. 4 | 900 | |

**Illustration 2-12** ►

Payment for insurance

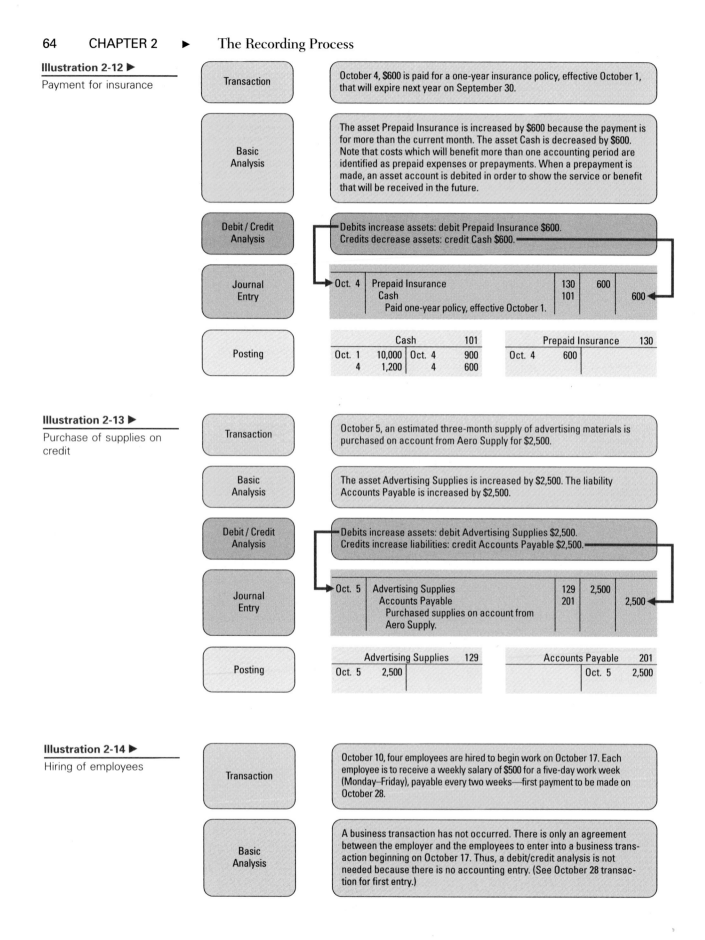

**Illustration 2-13** ►

Purchase of supplies on credit

**Illustration 2-14** ►

Hiring of employees

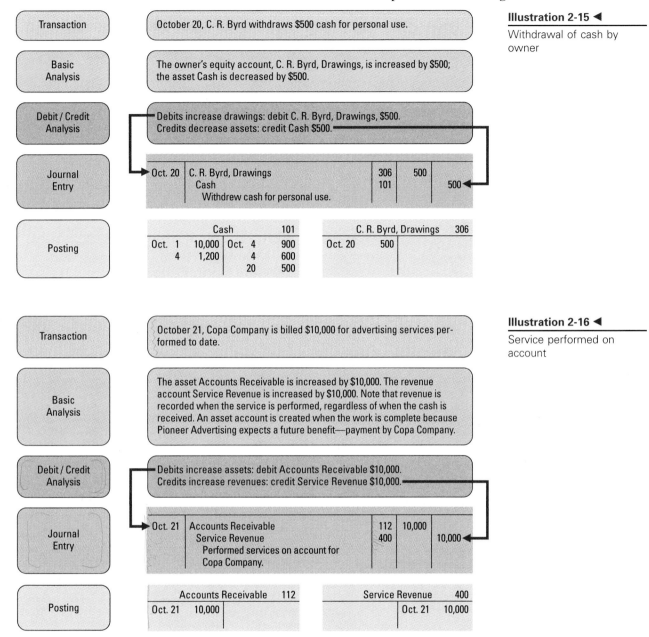

**Illustration 2-15** ◄

Withdrawal of cash by owner

| Transaction | October 20, C. R. Byrd withdraws $500 cash for personal use. |
|---|---|
| Basic Analysis | The owner's equity account, C. R. Byrd, Drawings, is increased by $500; the asset Cash is decreased by $500. |
| Debit / Credit Analysis | Debits increase drawings: debit C. R. Byrd, Drawings, $500. Credits decrease assets: credit Cash $500. |

Journal Entry

| Oct. 20 | C. R. Byrd, Drawings | 306 | 500 | |
|---|---|---|---|---|
| | Cash | 101 | | 500 |
| | Withdrew cash for personal use. | | | |

Posting

|  | Cash | | | 101 |  |
|---|---|---|---|---|---|
| Oct. 1 | 10,000 | Oct. 4 | 900 | | |
| 4 | 1,200 | 4 | 600 | | |
| | | 20 | 500 | | |

|  | C. R. Byrd, Drawings | 306 |
|---|---|---|
| Oct. 20 | 500 | |

**Illustration 2-16** ◄

Service performed on account

| Transaction | October 21, Copa Company is billed $10,000 for advertising services performed to date. |
|---|---|
| Basic Analysis | The asset Accounts Receivable is increased by $10,000. The revenue account Service Revenue is increased by $10,000. Note that revenue is recorded when the service is performed, regardless of when the cash is received. An asset account is created when the work is complete because Pioneer Advertising expects a future benefit—payment by Copa Company. |
| Debit / Credit Analysis | Debits increase assets: debit Accounts Receivable $10,000. Credits increase revenues: credit Service Revenue $10,000. |

Journal Entry

| Oct. 21 | Accounts Receivable | 112 | 10,000 | |
|---|---|---|---|---|
| | Service Revenue | 400 | | 10,000 |
| | Performed services on account for Copa Company. | | | |

Posting

|  | Accounts Receivable | 112 |
|---|---|---|
| Oct. 21 | 10,000 | |

|  | Service Revenue | | 400 |
|---|---|---|---|
| | Oct. 21 | 10,000 | |

**Illustration 2-17 ►**

Payment of salaries

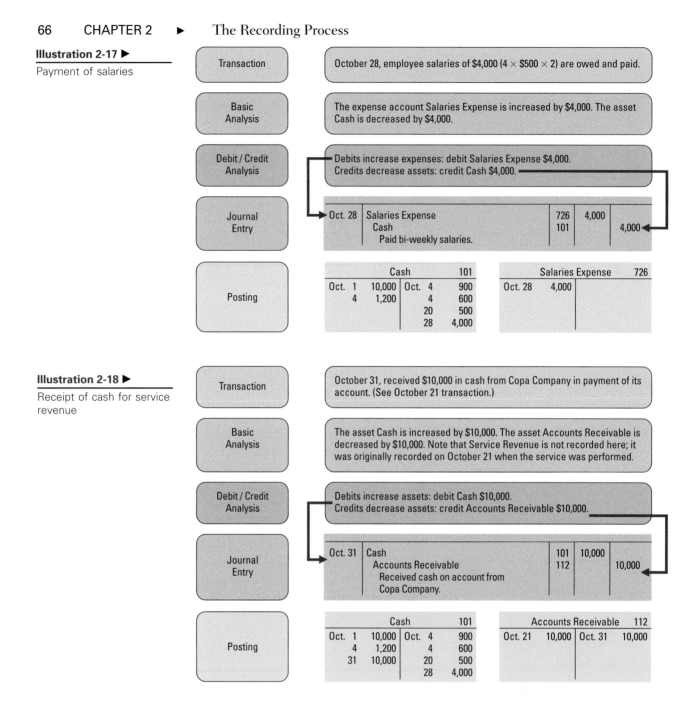

**Illustration 2-18 ►**

Receipt of cash for service revenue

## Summary Illustration of Journalizing and Posting

The general journal and general ledger for Pioneer Advertising Agency for October follows:

| GENERAL JOURNAL | | | | J1 |
|---|---|---|---|---|
| Date | Account Titles and Explanation | Ref. | Debit | Credit |
| 2005 | | | | |
| Oct. 1 | Cash | 101 | 10,000 | |
| | C. R. Byrd, Capital | 301 | | 10,000 |
| | Invested cash in business. | | | |
| 3 | Office Equipment | 151 | 5,000 | |
| | Notes Payable | 200 | | 5,000 |
| | Issued 6%, 3-month note for office equipment. | | | |
| 4 | Cash | 101 | 1,200 | |
| | Unearned Revenue | 209 | | 1,200 |
| | Received advance from R. Knox for future services. | | | |
| 4 | Rent Expense | 729 | 900 | |
| | Cash | 101 | | 900 |
| | Paid October rent. | | | |
| 4 | Prepaid Insurance | 130 | 600 | |
| | Cash | 101 | | 600 |
| | Paid one-year policy, effective October 1. | | | |
| 5 | Advertising Supplies | 129 | 2,500 | |
| | Accounts Payable | 201 | | 2,500 |
| | Purchased supplies on account from Aero Supply. | | | |
| 20 | C. R. Byrd, Drawings | 306 | 500 | |
| | Cash | 101 | | 500 |
| | Withdrew cash for personal use. | | | |
| 21 | Accounts Receivable | 112 | 10,000 | |
| | Service Revenue | 400 | | 10,000 |
| | Performed services on account for Copa Company. | | | |
| 28 | Salaries Expense | 726 | 4,000 | |
| | Cash | 101 | | 4,000 |
| | Paid bi-weekly salaries. | | | |
| 31 | Cash | 101 | 10,000 | |
| | Accounts Receivable | 112 | | 10,000 |
| | Received cash on account from Copa Company. | | | |

## GENERAL LEDGER

### Cash — No. 101

| Date | Explanation | Ref. | Debit | Credit | Balance |
|------|-------------|------|-------|--------|---------|
| 2005 | | | | | |
| Oct. 1 | | J1 | 10,000 | | 10,000 |
| 4 | | J1 | 1,200 | | 11,200 |
| 4 | | J1 | | 900 | 10,300 |
| 4 | | J1 | | 600 | 9,700 |
| 20 | | J1 | | 500 | 9,200 |
| 28 | | J1 | | 4,000 | 5,200 |
| 31 | | J1 | 10,000 | | 15,200 |

### Accounts Receivable — No. 112

| Date | Explanation | Ref. | Debit | Credit | Balance |
|------|-------------|------|-------|--------|---------|
| 2005 | | | | | |
| Oct. 21 | | J1 | 10,000 | | 10,000 |
| 31 | | J1 | | 10,000 | 0 |

### Advertising Supplies — No. 129

| Date | Explanation | Ref. | Debit | Credit | Balance |
|------|-------------|------|-------|--------|---------|
| 2005 | | | | | |
| Oct. 5 | | J1 | 2,500 | | 2,500 |

### Prepaid Insurance — No. 130

| Date | Explanation | Ref. | Debit | Credit | Balance |
|------|-------------|------|-------|--------|---------|
| 2005 | | | | | |
| Oct. 4 | | J1 | 600 | | 600 |

### Office Equipment — No. 151

| Date | Explanation | Ref. | Debit | Credit | Balance |
|------|-------------|------|-------|--------|---------|
| 2005 | | | | | |
| Oct. 3 | | J1 | 5,000 | | 5,000 |

### Notes Payable — No. 200

| Date | Explanation | Ref. | Debit | Credit | Balance |
|------|-------------|------|-------|--------|---------|
| 2005 | | | | | |
| Oct. 3 | | J1 | | 5,000 | 5,000 |

### Accounts Payable — No. 201

| Date | Explanation | Ref. | Debit | Credit | Balance |
|------|-------------|------|-------|--------|---------|
| 2005 | | | | | |
| Oct. 5 | | J1 | | 2,500 | 2,500 |

### Unearned Revenue — No. 209

| Date | Explanation | Ref. | Debit | Credit | Balance |
|------|-------------|------|-------|--------|---------|
| 2005 | | | | | |
| Oct. 4 | | J1 | | 1,200 | 1,200 |

### C. R. Byrd, Capital — No. 301

| Date | Explanation | Ref. | Debit | Credit | Balance |
|------|-------------|------|-------|--------|---------|
| 2005 | | | | | |
| Oct. 1 | | J1 | | 10,000 | 10,000 |

### C. R. Byrd, Drawings — No. 306

| Date | Explanation | Ref. | Debit | Credit | Balance |
|------|-------------|------|-------|--------|---------|
| 2005 | | | | | |
| Oct. 20 | | J1 | 500 | | 500 |

### Service Revenue — No. 400

| Date | Explanation | Ref. | Debit | Credit | Balance |
|------|-------------|------|-------|--------|---------|
| 2005 | | | | | |
| Oct. 21 | | J1 | | 10,000 | 10,000 |

### Salaries Expense — No. 726

| Date | Explanation | Ref. | Debit | Credit | Balance |
|------|-------------|------|-------|--------|---------|
| 2005 | | | | | |
| Oct. 28 | | J1 | 4,000 | | 4,000 |

### Rent Expense — No. 729

| Date | Explanation | Ref. | Debit | Credit | Balance |
|------|-------------|------|-------|--------|---------|
| 2005 | | | | | |
| Oct. 4 | | J1 | 900 | | 900 |

## BEFORE YOU GO ON . . .

### ▶ Review It

1. How does journalizing differ from posting in a manual system? In a computerized system?
2. What is the purpose of (a) the ledger, and (b) a chart of accounts?

### ▶ Do It

In the week of May that followed her successful grand opening of Hair It Is, Eszter Schwenke performed hairstyling services for $1,280 ($1,000 was collected in cash and $280 was on account). In addition, Eszter paid $400 in wages and $92 for utilities. The opening balance in the Cash account was $20,000. Eszter recorded these transactions in a general journal and posted the entries to the general ledger. Record and post these transactions.

### Action Plan

• Analyse the transactions. Determine the accounts affected and whether the transaction increases or decreases the account.
• Record the transaction in the general journal using debits and credits. Remember that credits are indented slightly and shown to the right.

- Posting involves transferring the journalized debits and credits to specific accounts in the ledger.
- Determine the ending balances by netting (calculating the difference between) the total debits and credits.

**Solution**

| May | Cash | 1,000 | |
| | Accounts Receivable | 280 | |
| |    Hairstyling Service Revenue | | 1,280 |
| |       Performed services for cash and on account. | | |
| | Wages Expense | 400 | |
| | Utilities Expense | 92 | |
| |    Cash | | 492 |
| |       Paid cash for services. | | |

| Cash | | Accounts Receivable | | Hairstyling Service Revenue | | Wages Expense | | Utilities Expense | |
|---|---|---|---|---|---|---|---|---|---|
| 20,000 | 492 | 280 | | | 1,280 | 400 | | 92 | |
| 1,000 | | | | | | | | | |
| 20,508 | | | | | | | | | |

*Related exercise material:* BE2–8 and E2–6.

# The Trial Balance

study objective 7

Explain the purpose of a trial balance, and prepare one.

A trial balance is a list of accounts and their balances at a specific time. A trial balance is normally prepared monthly, and at least at the end of each accounting period. The accounts are listed in the order in which they appear in the ledger, with debit balances listed in the left column and credit balances in the right column.

The primary purpose of a trial balance is to prove (check) that the debits equal the credits after posting. If the debits and credits do not agree, the trial balance can uncover errors in journalizing and posting. In addition, it is useful for preparing the financial statements, as will be explained in the next two chapters.

To prepare a trial balance:

1. List the account titles and their balances, using separate columns for debits and credits.
2. Total the debit and credit columns.
3. Ensure that the two columns are equal.

The trial balance prepared from the ledger of Pioneer Advertising Agency follows:

**PIONEER ADVERTISING AGENCY**
**Trial Balance**
**October 31, 2005**

|  | Debit | Credit |
|---|---|---|
| Cash | $15,200 | |
| Accounts receivable | 0 | |
| Advertising supplies | 2,500 | |
| Prepaid insurance | 600 | |
| Office equipment | 5,000 | |
| Notes payable | | $ 5,000 |
| Accounts payable | | 2,500 |
| Unearned revenue | | 1,200 |
| C. R. Byrd, capital | | 10,000 |
| C. R. Byrd, drawings | 500 | |
| Service revenue | | 10,000 |
| Salaries expense | 4,000 | |
| Rent expense | 900 | |
| Totals | $28,700 | $28,700 |

Note that the total debits of $28,700 equal the total credits of $28,700. Accounts with zero balances, such as Accounts Receivable, are often omitted from the trial balance. Account numbers are sometimes shown to the left of the account titles in the trial balance.

## Limitations of a Trial Balance

Although a trial balance reveals many types of errors which can be made in the book-keeping process, **a trial balance does not prove that all transactions have been recorded or that the ledger is correct**. Many errors may exist even though the trial balance columns agree. For example, the trial balance may balance in the following cases: (1) a transaction is not journalized, (2) a correct journal entry is not posted, (3) a journal entry is posted twice, (4) incorrect accounts are used in journalizing or posting, or (5) offsetting errors are made in recording the amount of a transaction. In other words, as long as equal debits and credits are posted, even to the wrong account or in the wrong amount, the total debits will equal the total credits when the trial balance is prepared.

## Locating Errors

▶ **Ethics note**

Auditors see errors and irregularities differently when evaluating the accounting system. An error is the result of an unintentional mistake. As such, it is neither ethical nor unethical. An irregularity, on the other hand, is an intentional misstatement, which is generally viewed as unethical.

The procedure for preparing a trial balance is relatively simple. However, if the trial balance does not balance, locating an error in a manual accounting system can be time-consuming, tedious, and frustrating. Errors generally result from mathematical mistakes, incorrect postings, or simply transcribing data incorrectly. Errors in a computerized system usually involve the initial recording rather than some software error in the posting or preparation of a trial balance.

What do you do if you are faced with a manual trial balance that does not balance? First determine the amount of the difference between the two columns of the trial balance. After this amount is known, the following steps are often helpful:

1. If the error is an amount such as $1, $100, or $1,000, re-add the trial balance columns. Recalculate the account balances.
2. If the error is divisible by two, scan the trial balance to see if a balance equal to half the error has been entered in the wrong column.

3. If the error is divisible by nine, retrace the account balances on the trial balance to see whether they are incorrectly copied from the ledger. For example, if a balance was $12 but was listed as $21, a $9 error has been made. Reversing the order of numbers is called a transposition error.

4. If the error is not divisible by two or nine, scan the ledger to see whether an account balance in the amount of the error has been omitted from the trial balance. Scan the journal to see whether a posting in the amount of the error has been omitted. Check your additions.

Of course, if there is more than one error, these steps may not work.

---

### ACCOUNTING IN ACTION ► Business Insight

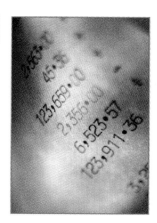

If you've ever made an arithmetic error, you may take some comfort from an accountant's mistake at Fidelity Investments, the world's largest mutual fund investment company. The accountant failed to include a minus sign while doing a tax calculation, which made a $1.3-billion loss look like a $1.3-billion gain. No one expects that kind of mistake at a firm like Fidelity, with sophisticated computer systems and top investment managers.

In explaining the mistake to shareholders, Fidelity's manager, J. Gary Burkhead, wrote: "Some people have asked how, in this age of technology, such a mistake could be made. While many of our processes are computerized, the requirements of the tax code are complex and dictate that some steps must be handled manually by our tax managers and accountants, and people can make mistakes." Evidently so. That's why it pays to do a "reasonableness check." Someone at Fidelity must have had a sense that the year's results shouldn't have been as rosy as the accounting numbers first indicated.

---

## Some Simplistic Assumptions

To keep things simple, we have made a number of assumptions in the material presented to date and in subsequent chapters. These include the omission of cents and sales taxes from the transaction data.

### Use of Dollars and Cents

We have not included cents in the dollar figures we record in journal entries, general ledger accounts, and trial balances. Avoiding cents in entries will save you time and effort and you will still understand the accounting process. In reality, it is important to remember that cents should be, and are, used in the formal accounting records. Cents are important, and quickly add up to dollars!

Dollar signs do not appear in the journals or ledgers. Dollar signs are used only in the trial balance and the financial statements. Generally, a dollar sign is shown only for the first item in the column, and for the total of that column. A single line is placed under the column of figures to be added or subtracted. The total amount is double-underlined to indicate the final sum.

### Sales Taxes

Sales taxes in Canada include the Goods and Services Tax (GST) and the Provincial Sales Tax (PST). In the Atlantic Provinces (except for PEI), GST and PST have been combined into one tax, called the Harmonized Sales Tax (HST).

In general, sales taxes are paid by a company on the goods and services it purchases, and collected on the goods that it sells and the services it provides. However, accounting for sales taxes is complicated and there are many exceptions. For example, not only do provincial sales tax rates vary across the country, but the method of calculating this tax can also vary. In addition, not all companies and their goods are taxable.

Although sales taxes are an important part of business, accounting transactions are presented in this textbook without the added complexity of these taxes. For those students who wish to advance their understanding of this topic, sales taxes are discussed in more detail in Appendix B at the end of this textbook.

## BEFORE YOU GO ON . . .

### ▶Review It

1. What is a trial balance, and what is its primary purpose?
2. How is a trial balance prepared?
3. What are the limitations of a trial balance?

### ▶Do It

Koizumi Kollections has the following alphabetical list of accounts and balances at July 31, 2005:

| Account | Amount | Account | Amount |
|---|---|---|---|
| Accounts payable | $33,700 | Land | $ 51,000 |
| Accounts receivable | 71,200 | Machinery and equipment | 35,700 |
| Building | 86,500 | Notes payable | 49,500 |
| Cash | 3,200 | Operating expenses | 105,100 |
| J. Koizumi, capital | 99,400 | Service revenue | 174,100 |
| J. Koizumi, drawings | 4,000 | | |

Each of the above accounts has a normal balance. Prepare a trial balance, rearranging the accounts in normal ledger (financial statement) order.

### Action Plan

- Reorder the accounts as they would normally appear in the general ledger—balance sheet accounts are listed first (assets, liabilities, and equity) followed by income statement accounts (revenues and expenses).
- Determine whether each account has a normal debit or credit balance.
- List the amounts in the appropriate debit or credit column.
- Total the trial balance columns. Total debits must equal total credits or a mistake has been made.

### Solution

**KOIZUMI KOLLECTIONS**
**Trial Balance**
**July 31, 2005**

| | Debit | Credit |
|---|---|---|
| Cash | $ 3,200 | |
| Accounts receivable | 71,200 | |
| Land | 51,000 | |
| Building | 86,500 | |
| Machinery and equipment | 35,700 | |
| Accounts payable | | $ 33,700 |
| Notes payable | | 49,500 |
| J. Koizumi, drawings | 4,000 | |
| J. Koizumi, capital | | 99,400 |
| Service revenue | | 174,100 |
| Operating expenses | 105,100 | |
| Totals | $356,700 | $356,700 |

*Related exercise material:* BE2–9, BE2–10, E2–7, E2–8, E2–9, and E2–10.

# Demonstration Problem

Nge Aung opened the Campus Laundromat on September 1, 2005. During the first month of operations, the following transactions occurred:

Sept.  1 Invested $20,000 cash in the business.
      2 Paid $1,000 cash for store rent for the month of September.
      3 Purchased washers and dryers for $25,000, paying $10,000 in cash and signing a $15,000, six-month, 5% note payable.
      6 Paid $1,200 for a one-year insurance policy.
     10 Received bill from *The Daily News* for advertising the opening of the laundromat, $200.
     20 Withdrew $700 cash for personal use.
     30 Cash receipts for laundry services performed for the month were $6,200.
     30 Laundry services performed on account for a nearby restaurant totalled $500. The account is due on October 25.

The chart of accounts for the company is the same as the one for Pioneer Advertising Agency in Illustration 2-7 except for the following: No. 153 Laundry Equipment and No. 610 Advertising Expense.

### Instructions

(a) Journalize the September transactions.
(b) Open ledger accounts and post the September transactions.
(c) Prepare a trial balance at September 30, 2005.
(d) Prepare an income statement, statement of owner's equity, and balance sheet for Campus Laundromat.

Additional Demonstration Problems

## Solution to Demonstration Problem

(a)

| | GENERAL JOURNAL | | | J1 |
|---|---|---|---|---|
| Date | Account Titles and Explanation | Ref. | Debit | Credit |
| 2005 | | | | |
| Sept. 1 | Cash | 101 | 20,000 | |
| |    Nge Aung, Capital | 301 | | 20,000 |
| |      Invested cash in business. | | | |
| 2 | Rent Expense | 729 | 1,000 | |
| |    Cash | 101 | | 1,000 |
| |      Paid September rent. | | | |
| 3 | Laundry Equipment | 153 | 25,000 | |
| |    Cash | 101 | | 10,000 |
| |    Notes Payable | 200 | | 15,000 |
| |      Purchased laundry equipment for cash and 6-month, 5% note payable. | | | |
| 6 | Prepaid Insurance | 130 | 1,200 | |
| |    Cash | 101 | | 1,200 |
| |      Paid one-year insurance policy. | | | |
| 10 | Advertising Expense | 610 | 200 | |
| |    Accounts Payable | 201 | | 200 |
| |      Received bill from *The Daily News* for advertising. | | | |
| 20 | Nge Aung, Drawings | 306 | 700 | |
| |    Cash | 101 | | 700 |
| |      Withdrew cash for personal use. | | | |
| 30 | Cash | 101 | 6,200 | |
| |    Service Revenue | 400 | | 6,200 |
| |      Received cash for laundry services. | | | |
| 30 | Accounts Receivable | 112 | 500 | |
| |    Service Revenue | 400 | | 500 |
| |      Performed laundry services on account. | | | |

### Action Plan

- Separate journal entries are made for each transaction.
- In journalizing, make sure debits equal credits.
- In journalizing, use specific account titles taken from the chart of accounts.
- Provide an appropriate description of each journal entry.
- Arrange the ledger in statement order, beginning with the balance sheet accounts.
- Post in chronological order.
- Numbers in the reference column indicate the amount has been posted.
- The trial balance lists accounts in the order in which they appear in the ledger.
- Debit balances are listed in the left column of the trial balance, credit balances in the right column.

(b)

## GENERAL LEDGER

| | | | Cash | | No. 101 |
|---|---|---|---|---|---|
| Date | Explanation | Ref. | Debit | Credit | Balance |
| 2005 | | | | | |
| Sept. 1 | | J1 | 20,000 | | 20,000 |
| 2 | | J1 | | 1,000 | 19,000 |
| 3 | | J1 | | 10,000 | 9,000 |
| 6 | | J1 | | 1,200 | 7,800 |
| 20 | | J1 | | 700 | 7,100 |
| 30 | | J1 | 6,200 | | 13,300 |

| | | Accounts Receivable | | | No. 112 |
|---|---|---|---|---|---|
| Date | Explanation | Ref. | Debit | Credit | Balance |
| 2005 | | | | | |
| Sept.30 | | J1 | 500 | | 500 |

| | | Prepaid Insurance | | | No. 130 |
|---|---|---|---|---|---|
| Date | Explanation | Ref. | Debit | Credit | Balance |
| 2005 | | | | | |
| Sept. 6 | | J1 | 1,200 | | 1,200 |

| | | Laundry Equipment | | | No. 153 |
|---|---|---|---|---|---|
| Date | Explanation | Ref. | Debit | Credit | Balance |
| 2005 | | | | | |
| Sept. 3 | | J1 | 25,000 | | 25,000 |

| | | Notes Payable | | | No. 200 |
|---|---|---|---|---|---|
| Date | Explanation | Ref. | Debit | Credit | Balance |
| 2005 | | | | | |
| Sept. 3 | | J1 | | 15,000 | 15,000 |

| | | Accounts Payable | | | No. 201 |
|---|---|---|---|---|---|
| Date | Explanation | Ref. | Debit | Credit | Balance |
| 2005 | | | | | |
| Sept.10 | | J1 | | 200 | 200 |

| | | Nge Aung, Capital | | | No. 301 |
|---|---|---|---|---|---|
| Date | Explanation | Ref. | Debit | Credit | Balance |
| 2005 | | | | | |
| Sept. 1 | | J1 | | 20,000 | 20,000 |

| | | Nge Aung, Drawings | | | No. 306 |
|---|---|---|---|---|---|
| Date | Explanation | Ref. | Debit | Credit | Balance |
| 2005 | | | | | |
| Sept.20 | | J1 | 700 | | 700 |

| | | Service Revenue | | | No. 400 |
|---|---|---|---|---|---|
| Date | Explanation | Ref. | Debit | Credit | Balance |
| 2005 | | | | | |
| Sept.30 | | J1 | | 6,200 | 6,200 |
| 30 | | J1 | | 500 | 6,700 |

| | | Advertising Expense | | | No. 610 |
|---|---|---|---|---|---|
| Date | Explanation | Ref. | Debit | Credit | Balance |
| 2005 | | | | | |
| Sept.10 | | J1 | 200 | | 200 |

| | | Rent Expense | | | No. 729 |
|---|---|---|---|---|---|
| Date | Explanation | Ref. | Debit | Credit | Balance |
| 2005 | | | | | |
| Sept. 2 | | J1 | 1,000 | | 1,000 |

(c)

## CAMPUS LAUNDROMAT
### Trial Balance
### September 30, 2005

| | Debit | Credit |
|---|---|---|
| Cash | $13,300 | |
| Accounts receivable | 500 | |
| Prepaid insurance | 1,200 | |
| Laundry equipment | 25,000 | |
| Notes payable | | $15,000 |
| Accounts payable | | 200 |
| Nge Aung, capital | | 20,000 |
| Nge Aung, drawings | 700 | |
| Service revenue | | 6,700 |
| Advertising expense | 200 | |
| Rent expense | 1,000 | |
| Totals | $41,900 | $41,900 |

(d)

### CAMPUS LAUNDROMAT
### Income Statement
### Month Ended September 30, 2005

| | | |
|---|---:|---:|
| Revenues | | |
| Service revenue | | $6,700 |
| Expenses | | |
| Rent expense | $1,000 | |
| Advertising expense | 200 | 1,200 |
| Net income | | $5,500 |

### CAMPUS LAUNDROMAT
### Statement of Owner's Equity
### Month Ended September 30, 2005

| | | |
|---|---:|---:|
| Nge Aung, capital, September 1 | | $     0 |
| Add:  Investments | $20,000 | |
| Net income | 5,500 | 25,500 |
| Less:  Drawings | | 700 |
| Nge Aung, capital, September 30 | | $24,800 |

### CAMPUS LAUNDROMAT
### Balance Sheet
### September 30, 2005

| Assets | | |
|---|---:|---:|
| Cash | | $13,300 |
| Accounts receivable | | 500 |
| Prepaid insurance | | 1,200 |
| Laundry equipment | | 25,000 |
| Total assets | | $40,000 |

| Liabilities and Owner's Equity | | |
|---|---:|---:|
| Liabilities | | |
| Notes payable | $15,000 | |
| Accounts payable | 200 | $15,200 |
| Owner's equity | | |
| Nge Aung, capital | | 24,800 |
| Total liabilities and owner's equity | | $40,000 |

the navigator

# Summary of Study Objectives

1. *Explain what an account is and how it helps in the recording process.* An account is an individual accounting record of increases and decreases in a specific asset, liability, or owner's equity item.

2. *Define debits and credits and illustrate how they are used to record business transactions.* Assets, drawings, and expenses are increased by debits (left-hand side of the account) and decreased by credits (right-hand side of the account). Liabilities, owner's capital, and revenues are increased by credits (right-hand side of the account) and decreased by debits (left-hand side of the account).

3. *Describe the basic steps in the recording process.* The basic steps in the recording process are as follows: (a) analyse each transaction in terms of its effect on the accounts, (b) enter the transaction information in a journal, and (c) transfer the journal information to the appropriate accounts in the ledger.

4. *Explain what a journal is and how it helps in the recording process, and journalize business transactions.* The first accounting record of a transaction is entered in a journal, and the data are later transferred to the general ledger. A journal (a) discloses in one place the complete

effect of a transaction, (b) provides a chronological record of transactions, (c) prevents and helps locate errors because the debit and credit amounts for each entry can be easily compared, and (d) provides an explanation of the transaction and reference to the source document, where applicable.

5. *Explain what a ledger is and how it helps in the recording process.* The entire group of accounts maintained by a company is called the ledger. The ledger keeps in one place all the information about changes in each of the specific account balances.

6. *Explain what posting is and how it helps in the recording process.* Posting is the procedure of transferring journal entries to the ledger accounts. This phase of the recording process accumulates the effects of journalized transactions in the individual accounts.

7. *Explain the purpose of a trial balance, and prepare one.* A trial balance is a list of accounts and their balances at a specific time. Its primary purpose is to prove the equality of debits and credits after posting. A trial balance also uncovers certain types of errors in journalizing and posting, and is useful in preparing financial statements.

# Glossary

Key Term Matching Activity

**Account** A record of increases and decreases in a specific asset, liability, or owner's equity item. (p. 50)

**Chart of accounts** A list of accounts and the account numbers which identify their location in the ledger. (p. 60)

**Compound entry** An entry that involves three or more accounts. (p. 57)

**Credit** The right side of an account. (p. 51)

**Debit** The left side of an account. (p. 51)

**Double-entry system** A system that records the dual effect of each transaction in appropriate accounts. (p. 51)

**General journal** The book of original entry in which transactions are recorded when they are not recorded in other specialized journals. (p. 55)

**General ledger** A ledger that contains accounts for all assets, liabilities, equities, revenues, and expenses. (p. 58)

**Journal** An accounting record in which transactions are recorded in chronological (date) order. (p. 55)

**Journalizing** The entering of transaction data in the journal. (p. 55)

**Ledger** A book that contains all accounts for the company or specialized accounts supporting other ledgers. (p. 58)

**Posting** The procedure of transferring journal entries to the ledger accounts. (p. 59)

**T account** A form of account resembling the letter T with the title above the horizontal line. Debits are shown to the left of the vertical line, credits to the right. (p. 50)

**Trial balance** A list of accounts and their balances at a specific time, usually at the end of the accounting period. (p. 69)

# Self-Study Questions

 Chapter 2 Self-Test

Answers are at the end of the chapter.

(SO 1) K  1. Which of the following statements about an account is true?
  (a) The left side of an account is the credit or decrease side.
  (b) An account is an individual accounting record of increases and decreases in specific asset, liability, and owner's equity items.
  (c) There are separate accounts for specific assets and liabilities but only one account for owner's equity items.
  (d) In its simplest form, an account consists of two parts.

(SO 2) K  2. Debits:
  (a) increase both assets and liabilities.
  (b) decrease both assets and liabilities.
  (c) increase assets and decrease liabilities.
  (d) decrease assets and increase liabilities.

(SO 2) K  3. A revenue account:
  (a) is increased by debits.
  (b) is decreased by credits.
  (c) has a normal balance of a debit.
  (d) is increased by credits.

(SO 2) K  4. Accounts that normally have debit balances are:
  (a) assets, expenses, and revenues.
  (b) assets, expenses, and owner's capital.
  (c) assets, liabilities, and drawings.
  (d) assets, drawings, and expenses.

(SO 3) K  5. Which of the following is not part of the recording process?
  (a) Analysing transactions
  (b) Preparing a trial balance
  (c) Entering transactions in a journal
  (d) Posting transactions

(SO 4) K  6. Which of the following statements about a journal is false?
  (a) It is not a book of original entry.
  (b) It provides a chronological record of transactions.
  (c) It helps to locate errors because the debit and credit amounts for each entry can be readily compared.
  (d) It discloses in one place the complete effect of a transaction.

(SO 5) K  7. A ledger:
  (a) contains only asset and liability accounts.
  (b) should show accounts in alphabetical order.
  (c) is a collection of the entire group of accounts maintained by a company.
  (d) is a book of original entry.

(SO 6) K  8. Posting:
  (a) normally occurs before journalizing.
  (b) transfers ledger transaction data to the journal.
  (c) is an optional step in the recording process.
  (d) transfers journal entries to ledger accounts.

(SO 7) K  9. A trial balance:
  (a) is a list of accounts with their balances at a specific time.
  (b) proves the accuracy of journalized transactions.
  (c) will not balance if a correct journal entry is posted twice.
  (d) proves that all transactions have been recorded.

(SO 7) C  10. A trial balance will not balance if:
  (a) a correct journal entry is posted twice.
  (b) the purchase of supplies on account is debited to Supplies and credited to Cash.
  (c) a $100 cash drawing by the owner is debited to Drawings for $1,000 and credited to Cash for $100.
  (d) a $450 payment on account is debited to Accounts Payable for $45 and credited to Cash for $45.

 the navigator

# Questions

(SO 2) C  1. Should the balance in total owner's equity equal the balance in the Cash account? Explain why or why not.

(SO 2) C  2. Jos Arcelus, a fellow student, says that the double-entry system means each transaction must be recorded twice. Is Jos correct? Explain.

(SO 2) C  3. Kim Nguyen, a beginning accounting student, believes debit balances are favourable and credit balances are unfavourable. Is Kim correct? Discuss.

(SO 2) K  4. State the rules of debit and credit and identify the normal balance for (a) asset accounts, (b) liability accounts, and (c) owner's equity accounts: (1) capital, (2) drawings, (3) revenue, and (4) expense.

(SO 2) K  5. What is the normal balance for each of the following accounts?
  (a) Accounts Receivable   (e) Service Revenue
  (b) Cash                  (f) Salaries Expense
  (c) Drawings              (g) Owner's Capital
  (d) Accounts Payable      (h) Prepaid Insurance

(SO 2) K  6. Decide whether each of the following accounts is an asset, a liability, or an owner's equity account and whether it would have a normal debit or credit balance:
  (a) Accounts Receivable   (d) Drawings
  (b) Accounts Payable      (e) Supplies
  (c) Equipment             (f) Unearned Revenue

 wileyplus.com

(SO 2) C    7. For the following transactions, indicate the account debited and the account credited:
(a) Supplies are purchased on account.
(b) Cash is received on signing a note payable.
(c) Employees are paid salaries in cash.

(SO 2) C    8. Indicate whether the following accounts generally will have (a) debit entries only, (b) credit entries only, or (c) both debit and credit entries:
1. Accounts Payable        4. Drawings
2. Accounts Receivable    5. Salaries Expense
3. Cash                          6. Service Revenue

(SO 3) C    9. Ben Benoit, a fellow student, is unclear about the basic steps in the recording process. Briefly explain the steps in the order in which they occur.

(SO 3) K   10. Which of the following items are likely to serve as source documents for journal entries?
(a) Cheque                    (e) Balance sheet
(b) Income statement      (f) Cash register tape
(c) Utility bill                 (g) Trial balance
(d) Invoice from supplier  (h) Sales slip

(SO 4) C   11. The Cookie Cutter Company has an account with the Princess Printing Company. During the month, Princess Printing performs services for Cookie Cutter, printing flyers and other materials. At the end of the month, Princess Printing sends Cookie Cutter a statement and Cookie Cutter pays cash for the full amount owing. How do each of these three transactions (performing printing services, issuing the monthly statement, and collecting amounts due) affect Princess Printing Company's (a) total assets and (b) cash.

(SO 4) K   12. What is the difference between Accounts Payable and Notes Payable? Between Accounts Payable and Accounts Receivable?

(SO 4) C   13. A company receives cash from a customer. What are the three possible accounts that could be credited for this transaction? Describe the circumstances where you would use each of these three accounts.

(SO 4, 5) AP   14. (a) Can business transaction debits and credits be recorded directly in the ledger accounts?
(b) What are the advantages of first recording transactions in the journal, and then posting to the ledger?

(SO 5, 6) AP   15. (a) What is a ledger?
(b) What is a chart of accounts, and why is it important?

(SO 7) AP   16. What is a trial balance? What are its purposes?

(SO 3, 4, 5, 6, 7) AP   17. Kap Shin is confused about how accounting information flows through the accounting system. He believes the flow of information is as follows:
1. Debits and credits are posted to the ledger.
2. The business transaction occurs.
3. Information is entered in the journal.
4. Financial statements are prepared.
5. A trial balance is prepared.
Show Kap the proper flow of information.

(SO 7) S   18. Two students are discussing the use of a trial balance. They wonder if the following errors would prevent the trial balance from balancing. Consider each error separately.
(a) The bookkeeper debited Cash for $600 and credited Wages Expense for $600 for payment of wages.
(b) Cash collected on account was debited to Cash for $900 and credited to Service Revenue for $90.
What would you tell them?

(SO 7) C   19. A company has a December 31 year end and is contemplating whether to use the heading on its trial balance, "Year Ended December 31," or just "December 31." Discuss which one is correct and explain why.

# Brief Exercises

Indicate debit and credit effects and normal balance.
(SO 2) K

**BE2–1**  For each of the following accounts indicate (a) the effect of a debit or credit on the account, and (b) the normal balance:
1. Accounts Payable
2. Advertising Expense
3. Service Revenue
4. Accounts Receivable
5. J. Takamoto, Capital
6. J. Takamoto, Drawings
7. Prepaid Insurance
8. Office Equipment
9. Rent Expense
10. Unearned Revenue
11. Advertising Supplies
12. Notes Payable

Indicate when to use debits and credits.
(SO 2) K

**BE2–2**  Indicate whether you would use a debit or credit to record the following changes:
1. Increase Accounts Payable
2. Decrease Cash
3. Increase Prepaid Insurance
4. Increase Salaries Expense
5. Increase Drawings
6. Decrease Notes Payable
7. Decrease Accounts Receivable
8. Increase Service Revenue

Identify accounts to be debited and credited.
(SO 2) K

**BE2–3**  Transactions for the Ing Company for the month of June are presented below. Identify the accounts to be debited and credited for each transaction.

*[handwritten: P→ gns Dr, Cash cr.]*
*[handwritten: 4 Pays 800 $ for one year ins policy.]*

June 1 D. Ing invests $2,000 cash in a small welding business. *[handwritten: Cap Dr, owweled byp cr]*
2 Buys equipment on account for $1,000. *[handwritten: Equ Dr, A.Pay cr.]*
3 Pays $500 to landlord for June rent. *[handwritten: Rent Dr, cash cr.]*
12 Bills T. Sargeant $300 for welding work done. *[handwritten: Ac's Rect Dr, Serv Rev cr.]*
22 Receives $300 cash from T. Sargeant for worked billed on June 12. *[handwritten: Cash Dr, Ac's Rec cr]*
25 Hires an employee to start work on July 2. *[handwritten: NE]*
29 Pays for equipment purchased on June 2. *[handwritten: A.P Dr, Cash cr]*

✓ **BE2–4** A. Fisher has the following transactions during August of the current year. Indicate (a) the basic analysis, and (b) the debit/credit analysis, as illustrated in the chapter.

Indicate basic and debit/credit analysis.
(SO 2) K

Aug. 1 Opens an office as a financial advisor, investing $6,000 in cash. *[handwritten: cash Dr, cap cr.]*
4 Pays insurance in advance for six months, $1,800. *[handwritten: Pers Dr, cash cr.]*
16 Receives $900 from clients for services provided. *[handwritten: Cash Dr, cSc cr]*
27 Pays secretary $500 salary. *[handwritten: Salary to cash]*
29 Withdraws $400 cash for personal use. *[handwritten: Draw Dr, cash cr.]*

**BE2–5** M. Therriault, a fellow student, is unclear about the steps in the recording process. Identify and briefly explain the steps in the order in which they occur.

Identify and explain steps in recording process.
(SO 3) C

**BE2–6** Using the data in BE2–3 for Ing Company, journalize the transactions.

Journalize transactions.
(SO 4) AP

**BE2–7** Using the data in BE2–4 for A. Fisher, journalize the transactions.

Journalize transactions.
(SO 4) AP

**BE2–8** Selected transactions are presented in journal entry form below. Post the transactions to T accounts.

Post journal entries.
(SO 6) AP

### GENERAL JOURNAL

| Date | Account Titles and Explanation | Ref. | Debit | Credit |
|---|---|---|---|---|
| May 5 | Accounts Receivable | | 3,200 | |
| | Service Revenue | | | 3,200 |
| 12 | Cash | | 2,400 | |
| | Accounts Receivable | | | 2,400 |
| 15 | Cash | | 2,000 | |
| | Service Revenue | | | 2,000 |
| 17 | Salaries Expense | | 750 | |
| | Cash | | | 750 |

**BE2–9** From the ledger balances given below, prepare a trial balance for the Beirsdorf Company at June 30, 2005. All account balances are normal.

Prepare trial balance.
(SO 7) AP

| | | | |
|---|---|---|---|
| Accounts Payable | $ 4,000 | Notes Payable | $5,000 |
| Accounts Receivable | 3,000 | Rent Expense | 1,000 |
| B. Beirsdorf, Capital | 16,100 | Salaries Expense | 4,000 |
| B. Beirsdorf, Drawings | 1,200 | Service Revenue | 6,600 |
| Cash | 8,400 | Supplies | 650 |
| Equipment | 13,600 | Unearned Revenue | 150 |

**BE2–10** An inexperienced bookkeeper prepared the following trial balance, which does not balance. Prepare a correct trial balance, assuming all account balances are normal.

Prepare correct trial balance.
(SO 7) AP

**BOURQUE COMPANY**
**Trial Balance**
**December 31, 2004**

|  | Debit | Credit |
|---|---|---|
| Cash | $15,000 |  |
| Accounts receivable |  | $ 1,800 |
| Prepaid insurance |  | 3,500 |
| Accounts payable |  | 3,000 |
| Unearned revenue | 2,200 |  |
| Lea Bourque, capital |  | 15,000 |
| Lea Bourque, drawings |  | 4,500 |
| Service revenue |  | 25,600 |
| Salaries expense | 18,600 |  |
| Rent expense |  | 2,400 |
| Totals | $35,800 | $55,800 |

# Exercises

Identify debits and credits and their effects on normal balances, and classify accounts.
(SO 2) K

**E2–1** Selected accounts for Poitras Company follow:

1. Accounts Payable
2. Accounts Receivable
3. Cash
4. H. Poitras, Drawings
5. Interest Revenue
6. Office Equipment
7. Prepaid Insurance
8. Rent Expense
9. Supplies
10. Supplies Expense

*Instructions*

(a) Indicate the normal balance of each of the above accounts.
(b) Identify whether a debit or credit is necessary to decrease the normal balance of each of the above accounts.
(c) Indicate the financial statement in which each account appears.

Identify accounts, debits, credits, and normal balances.
(SO 2) K

**Interactive Homework**

**E2–2** Selected transactions for L. Visser, an interior decorator, in her first month of business are as follows:

Mar.  3 Invested $9,000 cash in the business.
    6 Purchased used car for $6,000 cash, for use in the business.
    7 Purchased supplies on account for $500.
    12 Billed customers $1,800 for services performed.
    21 Paid $225 cash for advertising the launch of the business.
    25 Received $700 cash from customers billed on March 12.
    28 Paid creditor $300 cash on account.
    31 Withdrew $500 cash for owner's personal use.
    31 Received $600 cash from a customer for services to be performed in April.

*Instructions*

For each transaction indicate:

(a) The basic type of account debited and credited (asset, liability, owner's equity)
(b) The specific account debited and credited (Cash, Rent Expense, Service Revenue, etc.)
(c) The normal balance of the specific account
(d) Whether the specific account is increased or decreased

Use the following format, in which transaction 1 is given as an example:

| | Account Debited | | | | Account Credited | | | |
|---|---|---|---|---|---|---|---|---|
| | (a) | (b) | (c) | (d) | (a) | (b) | (c) | (d) |
| Trans-action | Basic Type | Specific Account | Normal Balance | Effect | Basic Type | Specific Account | Normal Balance | Effect |
| Mar. 3 | Asset | Cash | Debit | Increase | Owner's Equity | L. Visser, Capital | Credit | Increase |

**E2–3** The information below is for Lynn Gardiner of Gardiner Real Estate Agency:

Journalize transactions. (SO 4) AP

Oct. 1 Begins business as a real estate agent with a cash investment of $15,000. *Cap Dr to Cash*

2 Hires an administrative assistant at an annual salary of $24,000. *NE*

3 Buys office furniture for $1,900, paying $500 cash and the balance on account. *Fur Dr 1900, Cash 500 Cr, Note & Pay 1900.5*

6 Sells a house and lot to B. Rollins. Commission due from Rollins is $5,400 (not paid by Rollins at this time). *Ac Rec Dr to SR Cr 5400*

10 Receives cash of $140 as fee for renting an apartment. *Cash Dr to Rent Cr*

27 Pays $700 on account for the office furniture purchased on October 3. *A P Dr to cash 700*

30 Pays the administrative assistant $2,000 in salary for October. *Salary to cash.*

31 Receives cash of $5,400 from B. Rollins owed from October 6. *Cas Dr to Ac 5400*

*Instructions*

Prepare the debit/credit analysis for each transaction, as illustrated in the chapter.

**E2–4** Data for L. Visser, interior decorator, are presented in E2–2.

Journalize transactions. (SO 4) AP

*Instructions*

Journalize the transactions.

**E2–5** Transaction data for Gardiner Real Estate Agency are presented in E2–3.

Journalize transactions. (SO 4) AP

*Instructions*

Journalize the transactions.

 **Interactive Homework**

**E2–6** Journal entries for Gardiner Real Estate Agency transaction data were prepared in E2–5.

Post journal entries. (SO 6) AP

*Instructions*

Post the journal entries to the general ledger, using T account format.

 **Interactive Homework**

**E2–7** The ledger for Fortin Co. is presented below:

Journalize transactions and prepare trial balance. (SO 4, 7) AP

| | | Cash | | | |
|---|---|---|---|---|---|
| Oct. | 1 | 1,000 | Oct. | 4 | 400 |
| | 10 | 650 | | 12 | 1,500 |
| | 15 | 5,000 | | 30 | 300 |
| | 20 | 500 | | 31 | 250 |
| | 25 | 2,000 | | 31 | 500 |

| | | Accounts Receivable | | | |
|---|---|---|---|---|---|
| Oct. | 6 | 800 | Oct. | 20 | 500 |
| | 20 | 940 | | | |

| | | Supplies | |
|---|---|---|---|
| Oct. | 4 | 400 | |

| | | Furniture | |
|---|---|---|---|
| Oct. | 3 | 2,000 | |

| | Notes Payable | | |
|---|---|---|---|
| | | Oct. 15 | 5,000 |

| | | Accounts Payable | | |
|---|---|---|---|---|
| Oct. 12 | 1,500 | Oct. | 3 | 2,000 |
| | | | 28 | 400 |

| | A. Fortin, Capital | | |
|---|---|---|---|
| | | Oct. 1 | 1,000 |
| | | 25 | 2,000 |

| | | A. Fortin, Drawings | |
|---|---|---|---|
| Oct. 30 | 300 | |

| | Service Revenue | | |
|---|---|---|---|
| | | Oct. 6 | 800 |
| | | 10 | 650 |
| | | 20 | 940 |

| | | Advertising Expense | |
|---|---|---|---|
| Oct. 28 | 400 | |

| | | Store Wages Expense | |
|---|---|---|---|
| Oct. 31 | 500 | |

| | | Rent Expense | |
|---|---|---|---|
| Oct. 31 | 250 | |

*Instructions*

(a) Write the journal entries for the transactions for the month of October, and provide explanations for each entry.

(b) Determine the October 31 balance for each account. Prepare a trial balance at October 31, 2005.

Post journal entries and prepare trial balance.
(SO 6, 7) AP

**E2–8** Selected transactions from the journal of L. Meche, investment broker, are presented below:

**GENERAL JOURNAL**

| Date | Account Titles and Explanation | Ref. | Debit | Credit |
|---|---|---|---|---|
| 2005 | | | | |
| Aug. 1 | Cash | | 2,400 | |
| | L. Meche, Capital | | | 2,400 |
| 10 | Cash | | 1,800 | |
| | Service Revenue | | | 1,800 |
| 12 | Office Equipment | | 4,000 | |
| | Cash | | | 1,000 |
| | Notes Payable | | | 3,000 |
| 25 | Accounts Receivable | | 1,450 | |
| | Service Revenue | | | 1,450 |
| 31 | Cash | | 700 | |
| | Accounts Receivable | | | 700 |

*Instructions*

(a) Post the transactions to T accounts.

(b) Prepare a trial balance at August 31, 2005.

Answer questions about trial balance error.
(SO 7) AN

**E2–9** As the accountant for Smistad Company, you are disappointed to learn that the column totals of the December 31, 2004, trial balance do not balance. The Machinery account has a debit balance of $31,200. In your analysis of transactions, you have determined that a correctly recorded purchase of a machine for $7,000 was posted with a $7,000 debit to the Machinery account and a $7,000 debit to Accounts Payable.

*Instructions*

(a) Is the balance of the Machinery account overstated, understated, or correctly stated?

(b) Is the balance of the Accounts Payable account overstated, understated, or correctly stated?

(c) Is the debit column total of the trial balance overstated, understated, or correctly stated?

(d) Is the credit column total of the trial balance overstated, understated, or correctly stated?

(e) If the credit column total of the trial balance is $360,000 before correcting the error, what is the total of the debit column?

Prepare trial balance and financial statements.
(SO 7) AP

**Interactive Homework**

**E2–10** The accounts in the ledger of Express Delivery Service contain the following balances on July 31, 2005:

| | | | |
|---|---|---|---|
| Accounts Payable | $ 3,632 | Prepaid Insurance | $ 411 |
| Accounts Receivable | 7,396 | Repair Expense | 961 |
| Cash | ? | Salaries Expense | 24,780 |
| Delivery Equipment | 44,980 | Salaries Payable | 815 |
| Gas and Oil Expense | 2,971 | Service Revenue | 30,635 |
| Insurance Expense | 1,644 | Supplies | 492 |
| Interest Expense | 957 | T. Weld, Capital | 44,636 |
| Long-Term Investment | 2,650 | T. Weld, Drawings | 8,400 |
| Notes Payable | 18,450 | Unearned Revenue | 150 |

*Instructions*

(a) Prepare a trial balance, with the accounts arranged in ledger (financial statement) order as illustrated in the chapter, and determine the missing amount for Cash.

(b) Prepare an income statement and statement of owner's equity for the year ended July 31, 2005, and a balance sheet at July 31, 2005.

# Problems: Set A

**P2–1A** Yee Company has the following accounts:

Identify increases, decreases, normal balances, and types of accounts. (SO 2) K

| Account | (1) Type of Account | (2) Financial Statement | (3) Normal Balance | (4) Increase | (5) Decrease |
|---|---|---|---|---|---|
| 1. Cash | Asset | Balance sheet | Debit | Debit | Credit |
| 2. A. Yee, Drawings | | | | | |
| 3. Accounts Receivable | | | | | |
| 4. Consulting Fees Earned | | | | | |
| 5. Interest Expense | | | | | |
| 6. Land | | | | | |
| 7. Notes Payable | | | | | |
| 8. Office Supplies | | | | | |
| 9. Office Supplies Expense | | | | | |
| 10. Salary Expense | | | | | |

*Instructions*

Complete the table by identifying (1) the type of account (e.g., asset, liability, owner's capital, drawings, revenue, expense), (2) what financial statement it is presented on, (3) the normal balance of the account, (4) whether the account is increased by a debit or credit, and (5) whether the account is decreased by a debit or credit. The first one is done for you as an example.

**P2–2A** The Bucket Club Miniature Golf and Driving Range was opened on May 1 by Jamil Mawani. The following selected events and transactions occurred during May:

Journalize transactions. (SO 2, 4) AP

May 1 Invested $65,000 cash in the business.
3 Purchased Lee's Golf Land for $188,000. The price consists of land, $97,000; building, $53,000; and equipment, $38,000. Paid $38,000 cash and signed a note payable for the balance.
5 Advertised the opening of the driving range and miniature golf course, paying advertising expenses of $2,300.
6 Paid $2,736 cash for a one-year insurance policy.
10 Purchased golf clubs and other equipment for $16,000 from Woods Company, payable in 30 days.
18 Received golf fees of $5,800 in cash.
19 Sold 100 coupon books for $35 each. Each book contains 10 coupons that entitle the holder to one round of miniature golf or to hit one bucket of golf balls.
25 Withdrew $2,750 cash for personal use.
30 Paid salaries of $2,975.
30 Paid Woods Company in full.
31 Received $4,550 of fees in cash.
31 Paid $950 of interest on the note payable.

Jamil uses the following accounts: Cash; Prepaid Insurance; Land; Buildings; Equipment; Accounts Payable; Unearned Golf Fees; Notes Payable; Jamil Mawani, Capital; Jamil Mawani, Drawings; Golf Fees Earned; Advertising Expense; Salaries Expense; and Interest Expense.

*Instructions*

Journalize the May transactions.

**P2–3A** Estella Rojas, a licensed architect, formed a company called Rojas Designs. During the first month of operation of her business, the following events and transactions occurred:

Journalize transactions, post, and prepare trial balance. (SO 4, 6, 7) AP

Apr. 1 Invested $15,000 cash and $8,000 of office equipment.
1 Hired a secretary-receptionist at a salary of $1,200 monthly.
2 Paid office rent for the month, $950.
3 Purchased architectural supplies on account from Halo Company, $1,700.
10 Completed blueprints on a carport for G. Fellows and billed him $900 for services.
11 Received $500 cash advance from R. Welk for the design of a new home.

Apr. 20  Received $1,500 cash for services completed and delivered to P. Donahue.
    21  Received $800 from G. Fellows for work completed on April 10.
    30  Paid secretary-receptionist for the month, $1,200.
    30  Paid $900 to Halo Company on account.

Estella uses the following chart of accounts: No. 101 Cash, No. 112 Accounts Receivable, No. 126 Supplies, No. 151 Office Equipment, No. 201 Accounts Payable, No. 209 Unearned Revenue, No. 301 Estella Rojas, Capital, No. 400 Service Revenue, No. 726 Salaries Expense, and No. 729 Rent Expense.

*Instructions*

(a) Journalize the transactions.
(b) Post to the ledger accounts.
(c) Prepare a trial balance as at April 30, 2005.

*Journalize transactions, post, and prepare trial balance.*
*(SO 4, 6, 7) AP*

**P2–4A** Collegiate Laundry has a December 31 fiscal year end. Shown below is the company's trial balance on November 30, 2005:

**COLLEGIATE LAUNDRY**
**Trial Balance**
**November 30, 2005**

|  | Debit | Credit |
|---|---|---|
| Cash | $ 6,300 | |
| Accounts receivable | 1,800 | |
| Supplies | 1,100 | |
| Equipment | 16,000 | |
| Accounts payable | | $ 5,250 |
| Unearned revenue | | 1,300 |
| Jane Cochrane, capital | | 14,500 |
| Jane Cochrane, drawings | 33,000 | |
| Laundry revenue | | 64,900 |
| Salaries expense | 11,525 | |
| Rent expense | 9,350 | |
| Utilities expense | 6,875 | |
| | $85,950 | $85,950 |

The December transactions were as follows:

Dec.  5  Received $1,050 cash from customers in payment of their accounts.
   10  Performed $600 of services for customers who paid in advance in November.
   11  Received $1,350 cash from customers for services provided.
   12  Paid $2,900 to creditors on account.
   15  Purchased $400 of supplies on account.
   20  Billed customers $5,500 for services provided.
   22  Paid employee salaries of $1,400 (includes an end-of-year bonus of $300).
   24  Owner withdrew $2,800 for personal use.
   29  Received $425 cash from a customer for services to be provided in January.
   30  Purchased a used pressing machine for $600 cash from another company. The machine was probably worth $750, but the other company was anxious to sell it prior to the end of the year.
   31  Received the bill for December utilities, $615; will pay it in January.

*Instructions*

(a) Enter the opening balances in the ledger accounts as at December 1.
(b) Journalize the transactions.
(c) Post to the ledger accounts.
(d) Prepare a trial balance as at December 31, 2005.

*Journalize transactions, post, and prepare trial balance.*
*(SO 4, 6, 7) AP*

**P2–5A** The Starlite Theatre, owned by Lee Baroni, is unique as it shows only triple features of sequential theme movies. As at February 28, 2005, the ledger of Starlite showed the following: No. 101 Cash, $15,000; No. 140 Land, $42,000; No. 145 Buildings (concession stand, projection room, ticket booth, and screen), $56,000; No. 157 Equipment, $14,000; No. 201

Accounts Payable, $12,000; No. 275 Mortgage Payable, $65,000; and No. 301 L. Baroni, Capital, $50,000. During the month of March, the following events and transactions occurred:

Mar. 2 Acquired the three *Lord of the Rings* movies to be shown in the first three weeks of March. The film rental was $27,000. Of that amount, $9,000 was paid in cash and $18,000 will be paid on March 10.

3 Ordered the first three *Scream* movies to be shown the last 10 days of March. The film rental fee will cost $300 per night.

9 Received $16,200 cash from admissions.

10 Paid balance due on *Lord of the Rings* movies rental and $3,000 on February 28 accounts payable.

11 Starlite Theatre contracted with Brewer Company to operate the concession stand in the future. Brewer is to pay 16% of gross concession receipts (payable on the last day of each month) for the right to operate the concession stand.

12 Paid advertising expenses, $950.

20 Received $16,600 cash from admissions.

21 Received the *Scream* movies and paid the rental fee of $3,000 ($300 × 10 nights).

30 Sold gift certificates totalling $350.

31 Paid salaries of $4,200.

31 Received statement from Brewer showing gross receipts from concessions of $8,500 and the balance due to Starlite Theatre of $1,360 ($8,500 x 16%) for March. Brewer paid one-half the balance due and will pay the remainder on April 5.

31 Received $18,400 cash from admissions.

31 Paid $900 mortgage payment, which included $425 of interest.

In addition to the accounts identified above, the chart of accounts shows the following: No. 112 Accounts Receivable, No. 210 Unearned Revenues, No. 405 Admission Revenue, No. 406 Concession Revenue, No. 610 Advertising Expense, No. 632 Film Rental Expense, No. 726 Salaries Expense, and No. 750 Interest Expense.

*Instructions*

(a) Enter the beginning balances in the ledger as at March 1.

(b) Journalize the March transactions.

(c) Post the March journal entries to the ledger. Assume that all entries are posted from page 2 of the journal.

(d) Prepare a trial balance as at March 31, 2005.

**P2–6A** Bablad Brokerage Services was formed on May 1, 2005. The following transactions took place during its first month:

Journalize transactions, post, and prepare trial balance and financial statements.
(SO 4, 6, 7) AP

May 1 Jacob Bablad invested $90,000 cash and $25,000 worth of office equipment in the company.

1 Hired two employees to work in the warehouse. They will each be paid a salary of $2,000 per month.

5 Signed a two-year rental agreement on a warehouse and paid $9,000 cash. Half of this was for May 2005 rent and the other half was for the final month's rent. (*Hint*: The portion relating to the final month is considered a deposit.)

8 Purchased warehouse equipment costing $70,000. A cash payment of $20,000 was made immediately. Signed a note payable for the balance.

9 Paid $3,000 cash for a one-year insurance policy on the equipment. (*Hint*: The portion of the cost related to May 2005 is an expense for this month.)

12 Purchased supplies for $1,000 cash.

15 Purchased more supplies for $2,000 on account.

20 Total revenues earned to date were $11,000, consisting of $3,000 cash and $8,000 on account.

22 Paid $800 to suppliers on account.

25 Collected $1,500 from a customer as an advance payment for brokerage services to be provided in June 2005.

26 Withdrew $2,200 cash for personal use.

27 Signed a contract with an advertising agency for a promotion in June. The total cost of $9,000 will be paid in three equal instalments on June 2, 16, and 30.

28 Collected $2,500 from customers on account.

May 30 Received utility bills in the amount of $500, to be paid next month.
   31 Paid the monthly salaries of the two employees, totalling $4,000.

### Instructions

(a) Prepare journal entries to record each of the events listed.
(b) Post the journal entries to ledger accounts.
(c) Prepare a trial balance as at May 31, 2005.
(d) Prepare an income statement and a statement of owner's equity for Bablad Brokerage Services for the month ended May 31, 2005, and a balance sheet as at May 31, 2005.

*Journalize transactions, post, prepare trial balance, and determine elements of financial statements.*
*(SO 4, 6, 7) AP*

**P2–7A** Leo Mataruka owns and manages a computer repair service which had the following trial balance on December 31, 2004 (the end of its fiscal year):

**CYBERDYNE REPAIR SERVICE**
**Trial Balance**
**December 31, 2004**

|  | Debit | Credit |
|---|---|---|
| Cash | $ 2,000 | |
| Accounts receivable | 15,000 | |
| Repair parts inventory | 13,000 | |
| Prepaid rent | 2,800 | |
| Shop equipment | 24,000 | |
| Accounts payable | | $19,000 |
| Leo Mataruka, capital | | 37,800 |
| Totals | $56,800 | $56,800 |

Summarized transactions for January 2005 were as follows:

1. Leo invested $4,000 of additional cash in the business.
2. Advertising costs, paid in cash, $600.
3. Additional repair parts inventory acquired on account, $5,200.
4. Miscellaneous expenses, paid in cash, $1,800.
5. Cash collected from customers on account, $7,000.
6. Cash paid to creditors on account, $5,000.
7. Repair parts used during January, $4,500. (*Hint*: Debit this to Repair Parts Expense.)
8. Repair services performed during January: for cash, $3,000; on account, $12,000.
9. Wages for January, paid in cash, $2,900.
10. Rent expense for the month of January recorded. However, no cash was paid. A rent payment had been made for three months, in advance, on December 1, 2004, in the amount of $4,200.
11. Purchased additional equipment for $5,000 cash.

### Instructions

(a) Explain why the December 31, 2004, balance in the Prepaid Rent account is $2,800. (Refer to the Trial Balance and item 10.)
(b) Open ledger accounts for each of the accounts listed in the trial balance, and enter the opening balances for 2005.
(c) Prepare journal entries to record each of the January transactions.
(d) Post the journal entries to the accounts in the ledger.
(e) Prepare a trial balance as at January 31, 2005.
(f) Determine the total assets as at January 31, 2005. (It is not necessary to prepare a balance sheet. Simply list the relevant amounts from the trial balance and calculate the total.)
(g) Determine the net income or loss for the month of January 2005. (It is not necessary to prepare an income statement. Simply list the relevant amounts from the trial balance and calculate the amount of the net income or loss.)

*Prepare financial statements.*
*(SO 7) AN*

**P2–8A** Refer to the trial balance prepared in part (e) of P2–7A for Cyberdyne Repair Service.

### Instructions

Based upon the data in P2–7A, do the following:

(a) Prepare an income statement for Cyberdyne Repair Service for the month ended January 31, 2005.
(b) Prepare a statement of owner's equity for the month ended January 31, 2005.

(c) Prepare a balance sheet as at January 31, 2005.
(d) Leo can't understand (1) why even though his business is profitable, he still has to invest additional cash, and (2) why he is unable to make any drawings. Based on your review of the financial statements, what explanations can you give Leo?

**P2–9A** A first year co-op student working for Insidz.com recorded the company's transactions for the month. He wasn't exactly sure about the recording process, but he did the best he could. He had a few questions about the following transactions:

*Analyse errors and effects on trial balance. (SO 7) AN*

1. Cash received from a customer on account was recorded as a debit to Cash of $560 and a credit to Accounts Receivable of $650, instead of $560.
2. A service provided for cash was posted as a debit to Cash of $2,000 and a credit to Accounts Receivable of $2,000.
3. A credit of $750 for interest earned was neither recorded nor posted. The debit was recorded and posted correctly.
4. The debit to record $1,000 of drawings was posted to the Salary Expense account. The credit was posted correctly.
5. The purchase, on account, of supplies that cost $2,500 was recorded as a debit to Supplies and a debit to Accounts Payable.
6. Insidz.com received advances of $500 from customers for work to be performed next month. The student debited Cash for $500 but didn't credit anything as he wasn't sure what to credit.
7. A cash payment of $495 for salaries was recorded as a debit to Salaries Expense and a credit to Salaries Payable.
8. Payment of rent for the month was debited to Rent Expense and credited to Cash, $850.

*Instructions*

(a) Indicate which of the above transactions are correct and which are incorrect.
(b) For each error identified in (a), answer the following:
    1. Will the trial balance balance?
    2. Which account(s) will be incorrectly stated because of the error?
    3. State whether each of the incorrect account(s) you identified in (2) will be overstated or understated. By how much?
    4. Is the debit column total of the trial balance overstated or understated? If yes, by how much?
    5. Is the credit column total of the trial balance overstated or understated? If yes, by how much?

**P2–10A** The trial balance of Winau Co. shown below does not balance:

*Prepare correct trial balance. (SO 5, 7) AN*

**WINAU CO.**
**Trial Balance**
**June 30, 2005**

|  | Debit | Credit |
|---|---|---|
| Cash |  | $ 2,840 |
| Accounts receivable | $ 3,231 |  |
| Supplies | 800 |  |
| Equipment | 3,900 |  |
| Accounts payable |  | 3,008 |
| Unearned fees | 1,200 |  |
| T. Winau, capital |  | 9,090 |
| T. Winau, drawings | 800 |  |
| Fees earned |  | 2,380 |
| Salaries expense | 3,200 |  |
| Office expense | 1,110 |  |
|  | $14,241 | $17,318 |

Each of the listed accounts has a normal balance in the general ledger. An examination of the ledger and journal reveals the following errors:

1. Cash received from a customer on account was debited to Cash for $750 and Accounts Receivable was credited for the same amount. The actual collection was for $570.
2. The purchase of a computer printer on account for $360 was recorded as a debit to Supplies for $360 and a credit to Accounts Payable for $360.

3. Services worth $890 were performed on account for a client. Accounts Receivable was debited for $890 and Fees Earned was credited for $89.
4. A debit posting to Salaries Expense of $600 was omitted.
5. A payment on account for $206 was credited to Cash for $206 and credited to Accounts Payable for $602.
6. The withdrawal of $400 cash for Winau's personal use was debited to Salaries Expense for $400 and credited to Cash for $400.
7. A transposition error was made when copying the balance in the capital account to the trial balance. The correct balance as recorded in the account was $9,900.

*Instructions*
Prepare a correct trial balance. Show calculations for each new amount.

# Problems: Set B

Identify increases, decreases, normal balances, and types of accounts.
(SO 2) K

**P2–1B** Kobayashi Company has the following accounts:

| Account | (1) Type of Account | (2) Financial Statement | (3) Normal Balance | (4) Increase | (5) Decrease |
|---|---|---|---|---|---|
| 1. Cash | Asset | Balance sheet | Debit | Debit | Credit |
| 2. M. Kobayashi, Capital | | | | | |
| 3. Accounts Payable | | | | | |
| 4. Building | | | | | |
| 5. Consulting Fee Revenue | | | | | |
| 6. Insurance Expense | | | | | |
| 7. Interest Earned | | | | | |
| 8. Notes Receivable | | | | | |
| 9. Prepaid Insurance | | | | | |
| 10. Rent Expense | | | | | |
| 11. Unearned Consulting Fees | | | | | |

*Instructions*
Complete the table by identifying (1) the type of account (e.g., asset, liability, owner's capital, drawings, revenue, expense), (2) what financial statement it is presented on, (3) the normal balance of the account, (4) whether the account is increased by a debit or credit, and (5) whether the account is decreased by a debit or credit. The first one is done for you as an example.

Journalize transactions.
(SO 2, 4) AP

**P2–2B** The Adventure Biking Park was started on April 1 by Al Rossy. The following selected events and transactions occurred during April:

Apr.  1  Rossy invested $50,000 cash in the business.
     4  Purchased an old ski hill for $206,000, paying $30,000 cash and signing a note payable for the balance. (Price consisted of land, $108,000; building, $62,000; and equipment, $36,000.)
     8  Incurred advertising expenses of $2,800 on account.
    11  Paid salaries to employees, $1,500.
    12  Hired park manager at a salary of $4,000 per month, effective May 1.
    13  Paid $4,500 cash for a one-year insurance policy.
    17  Withdrew $600 cash for personal use.
    20  Received $2,700 in cash for admission fees.
    25  Sold 100 coupon books for $45 each. Each book contains 10 coupons that entitle the holder to one admission to the park.
    30  Received $5,900 in cash for admission fees.
    30  Paid $700 on account for advertising expenses incurred on April 8.
    30  Paid $2,250 interest expense on the note payable.
    30  Counted the coupons that had been redeemed since April 25. Found that 50 coupons had been used in exchange for admission to the park.

Al Rossy uses the following accounts: Cash; Prepaid Insurance; Land; Building; Equipment; Accounts Payable; Unearned Admissions Revenue; Notes Payable; Al Rossy, Capital; Al Rossy, Drawings; Admissions Revenue; Advertising Expense; Salaries Expense; and Interest Expense.

*Instructions*

Journalize the April transactions.

**P2–3B** Carla Liu is a CGA. During the first month of operation of her accounting practice, the following events and transactions occurred:

*Journalize transactions, post, and prepare trial balance.*
*(SO 4, 6, 7) AP*

May   1  Carla invested $18,000 cash and office equipment worth $8,500 in the business.
       2  Hired a secretary-receptionist at a salary of $1,900 per month.
       3  Purchased $1,400 of supplies on account from Read Supply Company.
       7  Paid office rent of $900 cash for the month.
    11  Completed a tax assignment for H. Kwan and billed her $1,175 for services rendered.
    12  Received a $3,500 advance on a management consulting engagement.
    17  Received cash of $1,200 for services completed for Arnold Co.
    21  H. Kwan paid $900 for work completed on May 11.
    31  Paid secretary-receptionist $1,900 salary for the month.
    31  Paid 60% of balance due to Read Supply Company.
    31  Received a $275 telephone bill for May, to be paid next month.

Carla uses the following chart of accounts: No. 101 Cash; No. 112 Accounts Receivable; No. 126 Supplies; No. 151 Office Equipment; No. 201 Accounts Payable; No. 209 Unearned Revenue; No. 301 Carla Liu, Capital; No. 400 Service Revenue; No. 726 Salaries Expense; No. 729 Rent Expense; and No. 737 Telephone Expense.

*Instructions*

(a) Journalize the transactions.
(b) Post to the ledger accounts.
(c) Prepare a trial balance at May 31, 2005.

**P2–4B** Brisebois Dry Cleaners has a July 31 fiscal year end. Shown below is the company's trial balance on June 30, 2005:

*Journalize transactions, post, and prepare trial balance.*
*(SO 4, 6, 7) AP*

**BRISEBOIS DRY CLEANERS**
**Trial Balance**
**June 30, 2005**

|  | Debit | Credit |
|---|---|---|
| Cash | $ 11,636 | |
| Note receivable | 4,000 | |
| Accounts receivable | 5,845 | |
| Supplies | 3,974 | |
| Equipment | 26,480 | |
| Accounts payable | | $ 13,066 |
| Unearned revenue | | 1,920 |
| E. Brisebois, capital | | 51,920 |
| E. Brisebois, drawings | 39,050 | |
| Dry cleaning revenue | | 109,461 |
| Salaries expense | 57,750 | |
| Rent expense | 11,385 | |
| Repair expense | 1,727 | |
| Utilities expense | 14,520 | |
| Totals | $176,367 | $176,367 |

The July transactions were as follows:

July   3  Collected $3,285 in cash on the June 30 accounts receivable.
     9  Paid employee salaries of $2,230.
   10  Performed $1,160 of services for customers who paid in advance in June.
   11  Received $4,730 cash from customers for services performed.
   13  Paid $9,742 to creditors on account.
   14  Purchased supplies on account, at a cost of $494.

July  24  Billed customers $5,950 for services performed.
      25  Collected the $4,000 note receivable plus interest of $320.
      26  Signed a contract with a nursing home to provide cleaning services at a rate of $1,800 per month starting in August. The first payment will be on August 1.
      27  Received $640 cash from a customer for services to be provided in August.
      28  Paid employee salaries of $3,440, and utilities of $1,272.
      30  Purchased a new machine with a catalogue price of $4,600. After extensive negotiating, paid $1,600 cash and signed a note payable for $2,500.
      31  Withdrew $3,750 for personal use.

### Instructions

(a) Enter the opening balances in the ledger accounts as at July 1. You may need to add additional accounts as a result of July transactions.
(b) Journalize the transactions.
(c) Post to the ledger accounts.
(d) Prepare a trial balance at July 31, 2005.

*Journalize transactions, post, and prepare trial balance.*
*(SO 4, 6, 7) AP*

**P2–5B**  The Grand Theatre is owned by Fran Goresht. At March 31, the ledger showed the following: Cash, $6,000; Land, $40,000; Buildings (concession stands, projection room, ticket booth, and screen), $60,000; Equipment, $16,000; Accounts Payable, $4,000; Mortgage Payable, $80,000; and Fran Goresht, Capital, ?. During April, the following events and transactions occurred:

Apr.  2  Paid film rental of $800 on first movie.
      3  Ordered two additional films at $750 each.
      9  Received $1,800 cash from admissions.
      10  Made $2,000 payment on mortgage of which $525 is interest.
      10  Paid $2,600 of the accounts payable.
      11  Grand Theatre contracted with Thoms Company to operate the concession stand in the future. Thoms is to pay 17% of gross concession receipts (payable monthly) for the right to operate the concession stand.
      12  Paid advertising expenses, $620.
      15  Sold gift certificates totalling $400 cash.
      20  Received one of the films ordered on April 3 and was billed $750. The film will be shown in April.
      25  Received $5,300 cash from admissions.
      28  People used $100 of the gift certificates sold on April 15.
      29  Paid salaries, $1,900.
      30  Received statement from Thoms showing gross concession receipts of $2,600 and a balance due to the The Grand Theatre of $442 ($2,600 × 17%) for April. Thoms paid one-half of the balance due and will pay the remainder on May 5.
      30  Prepaid $700 rental on special film to be run in May.

### Instructions

(a) Enter the beginning balances in the ledger as at April 1. Calculate the correct balance in Fran Goresht, Capital as at April 1.
(b) Journalize the April transactions.
(c) Post the April journal entries to the ledger.
(d) Prepare a trial balance at April 30, 2005.

*Journalize transactions, post, and prepare trial balance and financial statements.*
*(SO 4, 6, 7) AP*

**P2–6B**  Rowland Brokerage Services was formed on September 1, 2005. The owner, Rick Rowland, sold all of his personal investments and received $125,000 cash. Rick transferred $100,000 to a bank account in the name of Rowland Brokerage Services. During the month of September, the following transactions took place:

Sept.  2  Hired two employees to work in the warehouse. They will each be paid a monthly salary of $2,500.
       3  Signed a three-year contract for the lease of a warehouse at a monthly rate of $5,500. Paid the first and last month's rent in cash. (*Hint*: The payment for the final month's rent should be considered an asset, Prepaid Rent.)
       4  Moved office equipment and furniture that Rick had previously used at home to the warehouse for use in the business. The original cost of these items was $25,000 but their current value was $15,000.

Sept. 5 Purchased warehouse equipment for $68,000 and a forklift for $13,000. Paid $22,000 cash and signed a note payable for the balance.

6 Purchased an annual insurance policy for $8,700 to be paid in monthly instalments on the sixth day of each month. Paid the first month's premium.

7 Purchased supplies for $1,050 cash.

16 Purchased additional supplies for $2,100 on account.

21 Total revenues earned to date were $16,000 ($7,000 cash and $9,000 on account).

26 Paid $1,150 to suppliers on account

27 Collected $1,800 from a customer for services to be provided in October.

28 Collected $4,800 from customers on account.

30 Received utility bills for the month of September in the amount of $575, to be paid in October.

30 Paid employee salaries, $5,000.

30 Paid property taxes of $2,250 for Rick's home.

30 Withdrew $2,500 cash for Rick's personal use.

### Instructions

(a) Prepare journal entries to record each of the events.
(b) Post the journal entries to ledger accounts.
(c) Prepare a trial balance as at September 30, 2005.
(d) Prepare an income statement and a statement of owner's equity for Rowland Brokerage Services for the month ended September 30, 2005, and a balance sheet as at September 30, 2005.

**P2–7B** Gary Hobson owns and manages a computer repair service which had the following trial balance at March 31, 2005 (the end of its fiscal year):

Journalize transactions, post, prepare trial balance, and determine elements of financial statements. (SO 4, 6, 7) AP

**SOFT-Q REPAIR SERVICE**
**Trial Balance**
**March 31, 2005**

|  | Debit | Credit |
|---|---|---|
| Cash | $ 1,500 | |
| Accounts receivable | 14,000 | |
| Repair parts inventory | 15,500 | |
| Prepaid rent | 3,300 | |
| Shop equipment | 23,000 | |
| Accounts payable | | $21,000 |
| Gary Hobson, capital | | 36,300 |
| Totals | $57,300 | $57,300 |

Summarized transactions for April 2005 were as follows:

1. Gary invested $3,000 of his own cash in the business.
2. Advertising costs, paid in cash, $800.
3. Additional repair parts inventory acquired on account, $4,200.
4. Borrowed $10,000 from the bank for the business. Signed a note payable in the company name.
5. Miscellaneous expenses, paid in cash, $2,150.
6. Cash collected from customers on account, $6,000.
7. Cash paid to creditors on account, $12,000.
8. Repair parts used during April, $3,075. (*Hint*: Debit this to Repair Parts Expense.)
9. Repair services performed during April: for cash, $3,000, on account, $7,000.
10. Wages for April, paid in cash, $4,500.
11. Recorded the rent expense for the month of April. However, no cash was paid. A rent payment had been made for three months, in advance, on March 1, 2005, in the amount of $4,950.
12. Gary's drawings during April were $1,000.
13. Paid $75 interest on the note payable.

*Instructions*

(a) Explain why the March 31, 2005, balance in the Prepaid Rent account is $3,300. (Refer to the Trial Balance and item 11 above.)
(b) Open ledger accounts for each of the accounts listed in the trial balance, and enter the opening balances for April 1, 2005.
(c) Prepare journal entries to record each of the April transactions.
(d) Post the journal entries to the accounts in the ledger.
(e) Prepare a trial balance as at April 30, 2005.
(f) Determine the total assets as at April 30, 2005. (It is not necessary to prepare a balance sheet. Simply list the relevant amounts from the trial balance and calculate the total.)
(g) Determine the net income or loss for the month of April 2005. (It is not necessary to prepare an income statement. Simply list the relevant amounts from the trial balance and calculate the net income or loss.)

Prepare financial statements.
(SO 7) AN

**P2–8B** Refer to the trial balance prepared in part (e) of P2–7B for Soft-Q Repair Service.

*Instructions*

Based on the data in P2–7B, do the following:

(a) Prepare an income statement for Soft-Q Repair Service for the month ended April 30, 2005.
(b) Prepare a statement of owner's equity for the month ended April 30, 2005.
(c) Prepare a balance sheet as at April 30, 2005.
(d) Gary is considering selling the business. Based on your review of the financial statements, would you be interested in buying the business or do you have concerns? Discuss.

Analyse errors and effects on trial balance.
(SO 7) AN

**P2–9B** The bookkeeper for Shigeru's Dance Studio did the following in journalizing and posting:

1. A debit posting to Supplies of $600 was omitted.
2. A debit posting of $300 to Accounts Payable was inadvertently debited to Accounts Receivable.
3. A purchase of supplies on account of $540 was debited to Supplies for $540 and credited to Accounts Payable for $540.
4. A credit to Wages Payable for $1,200 was credited to Wages Expense.
5. A debit posting of $250 to Cash was posted twice.
6. A debit posting for $1,200 of drawings was inadvertently posted to Wages Expense.
7. A credit to Service Revenue for $400 was inadvertently posted as a credit to Unearned Service Revenue.
8. A credit to Accounts Receivable of $250 was posted as a debit to Accounts Receivable.

*Instructions*

(a) Indicate which of the above transactions are correct and which are incorrect.
(b) For each error identified in (a), answer the following:
   1. Will the trial balance balance?
   2. Which account(s) will be incorrectly stated because of the error?
   3. State whether each of the incorrect account(s) you identified in (2) will be overstated or understated. By how much?
   4. Is the debit column total of the trial balance overstated or understated? If yes, by how much?
   5. Is the credit column total of the trial balance overstated or understated? If yes, by how much?

**P2–10B** The trial balance of the Shawnee Company shown below does not balance:

Prepare correct trial
balance.
(SO 5, 7) AN

**SHAWNEE COMPANY**
Trial Balance
May 31, 2005

| | Debit | Credit |
|---|---|---|
| Cash | $ 5,818 | |
| Accounts receivable | | $ 2,750 |
| Prepaid insurance | 600 | |
| Equipment | 9,200 | |
| Accounts payable | | 4,600 |
| Property taxes payable | 560 | |
| M. Flynn, capital | | 12,900 |
| Service revenue | 6,690 | |
| Salaries expense | 4,150 | |
| Advertising expense | | 1,132 |
| Property tax expense | 1,100 | |
| Totals | $28,118 | $21,382 |

Your review of the ledger reveals that each account has a normal balance. You also discover the following errors:

1. Prepaid Insurance, Accounts Payable, and Property Tax Expense were each understated by $200.
2. A transposition error was made in Service Revenue. Based on postings made, the correct balance was $6,960.
3. A debit posting to Salaries Expense of $250 was omitted.
4. A $750 cash withdrawal by the owner was debited to M. Flynn, Capital, for $750 and credited to Cash for $750.
5. A $630 purchase of supplies on account was debited to Equipment for $630 and credited to Cash for $630.
6. A cash payment of $320 for advertising was debited to Advertising Expense for $32 and credited to Cash for $32.
7. A $120 collection from a customer was debited to Cash for $120 and credited to Accounts Payable for $120.
8. A cash collection on account for $90 was recorded as a $90 debit to Cash and a $90 debit to Accounts Receivable.
9. A $2,000 note payable was issued in exchange for the purchase of equipment. The transaction was neither journalized nor posted.

*Instructions*
Prepare a correct trial balance. (*Note*: Additional accounts may be required.)

# Continuing Cookie Chronicle

(*Note*: The Continuing Cookie Chronicle was started in Chapter 1 and will continue in each chapter.)

After researching the different forms of business organization, Natalie Koebel decides to operate "Cookie Creations" as a proprietorship. She then starts the process of getting the business running. In November 2004, the following activities happen:

Nov. 8 Natalie cashes her Canada Savings Bonds and receives $520, which she deposits in her personal bank account.

8 She opens a bank account under the name "Cookie Creations" and transfers $500 from her personal account to the new account.

9 She creates promotional materials: a brochure and a poster for advertising the company and the services available.

11 Natalie pays $95 to have the brochures and posters printed. She plans to distribute these as opportunities arise.

Nov. 13  She buys baking supplies, such as flour, sugar, butter, and chocolate chips, for $125 cash.

14  Natalie starts to gather some baking equipment to take with her when teaching the cookie classes. She has an excellent top-of-the-line food processor and mixer that originally cost her $550. Natalie decides to start using it only in her new business. She estimates that the equipment is currently worth $300.

16  Natalie starts realizing that her initial cash investment is not enough. Her grandmother lends her $2,000 cash, for which Natalie signs a note payable in the name of the business. Natalie deposits the money in the business bank account.

17  She buys more baking equipment for $900 cash.

20  She books her first class for November 29 for $100. One of her mother's friends needed a novel idea for her young daughter's birthday party.

25  Natalie books a second class for December 4 for $125. She receives $25 cash in advance as a down payment.

29  She teaches her first class, booked on November 20, and collects the $100 cash.

30  Natalie's brother designs a website for Cookie Creations that will be used for advertising. She agrees to pay her brother $600 for his work, payable at the end of December. (Because the website is expected to have a useful life of two years before upgrades are needed, it should be treated as an asset.)

30  Natalie pays $1,200 for a one-year insurance policy that will expire on December 1, 2005.

*Instructions*

(a) Prepare journal entries to record the November transactions.
(b) Post the journal entries to general ledger accounts.
(c) Prepare a trial balance at November 30, 2004.

## BROADENING YOUR PERSPECTIVE

# Financial Reporting and Analysis

Practice Tools

## Financial Reporting Problem

**BYP2–1**  The financial statements of **The Forzani Group** for 2003, in Appendix A at the back of this textbook, show the following selected accounts (stated in thousands of dollars):

| | |
|---|---:|
| Accounts Payable and Accrued Liabilities | $209,873 |
| Accounts Receivable | 38,275 |
| Capital Assets | 142,236 |
| Franchise Revenue | 208,792 |
| Inventory | 268,519 |
| Interest Expense | 4,354 |
| Prepaid and Other Expenses | 11,123 |

*Instructions*

(a) Answer the following questions:
  1. What is the increase side (i.e., debit or credit) and decrease side for each of the above accounts?
  2. What is the normal balance for each of these accounts?

(b) Identify the other account probably involved in the transaction, and the effect on that account, when:

  1. Accounts Receivable are decreased.    4. Inventory is increased.
  2. Capital Assets are increased.    5. Interest Expense is increased.
  3. Franchise Revenue is increased.    6. Prepaid and Other Expenses are increased.

## Interpreting Financial Statements

BYP2–2  Agricore United is one of Canada's leading agri-businesses. The following list of accounts and amounts was taken from Agricore United's 2002 financial statements:

| AGRICORE UNITED<br>Trial Balance<br>October 31, 2002<br>(in thousands) | |
| --- | ---: |
| Accounts receivable and prepaid expenses | $  212,454 |
| Accounts payable and accrued expenses | 344,836 |
| Bank and other payables | 388,722 |
| Cash and cash equivalents | 39,117 |
| Cost of goods sold expense | 3,669,961 |
| Depreciation and amortization expense | 82,958 |
| Dividends payable | 4,728 |
| Gain on disposal of assets | 17,221 |
| Income tax recovery | 17,075 |
| Interest expense | 48,408 |
| Inventories | 469,172 |
| Long-term debt | 338,342 |
| Operating, general, and administrative expenses | 382,420 |
| Other assets | 138,305 |
| Other expenses | 4,236 |
| Property, plant, and equipment | 724,926 |
| Sales and revenue from services | 4,130,154 |
| Shareholders' (owner's) equity, November 1, 2001 | 530,879 |

### Instructions

(a) Prepare a trial balance for Agricore United, with accounts reorganized in financial statement order.

(b) Present Agricore United's accounts and amounts in the form of the accounting equation: Assets = Liabilities + Shareholders' (Owner's) Equity.

## Accounting on the Web

BYP2–3  Business ethics provide the necessary foundation for good corporate behaviour. This case explores topical ethical issues facing businesses today and applies the ethical framework introduced in Chapter 1 to these issues.

### Instructions

Specific requirements of this Internet case are available on the Weygandt website.

# Critical Thinking

## Collaborative Learning Activity

BYP2–4  Andrée Boudreau operates the Boudreau Riding Academy. The academy's primary sources of revenue are riding fees and lesson fees, which are provided on a cash basis. Andrée also boards horses for owners, who are billed monthly for boarding fees. In some cases, boarders pay in advance.

The academy owns 10 horses, a stable, a riding corral, riding equipment, and office equipment. It employs stable helpers and an office employee, each of whom receives a weekly salary. At the end of each month, the mail brings bills for advertising, utilities, and veterinary services. Other expenses include feed for the horses and insurance.

Andrée Boudreau's only source of income is the academy. She makes periodic withdrawals of cash for her personal living expenses.

During the first month of operations, an inexperienced bookkeeper was employed. Andrée asks you to review the following nine journal entries (of the 50 entries made during the month). In each case, the explanation for the entry is correct.

| | | | | |
|---|---|---|---|---|
| May | 1 | Cash | 15,000 | |
| | |    A. Boudreau, Capital | | 15,000 |
| | |       Invested $15,000 cash in business. | | |
| | 5 | Cash | 250 | |
| | |    Riding Fees Earned | | 250 |
| | |       Received $250 cash for lesson fees. | | |
| | 7 | Cash | 1,500 | |
| | |    Boarding Fees Earned | | 1,500 |
| | |       Received $1,500 for boarding of horses, beginning June 1. | | |
| | 9 | Hay and Feed Supplies | 1,200 | |
| | |    Cash | | 1,200 |
| | |       Purchased estimated two months' supply of hay and feed for $1,200 on account. | | |
| | 14 | Riding Equipment | 80 | |
| | |    Cash | | 800 |
| | |       Purchased desk and other office equipment for $800 cash. | | |
| | 15 | Salaries Expense | 400 | |
| | |    Cash | | 400 |
| | |       Issued cheque to Andrée Boudreau for personal use. | | |
| | 20 | Cash | 145 | |
| | |    Riding Fees Earned | | 154 |
| | |       Received $154 cash for riding fees. | | |
| | 31 | Veterinary Expense | 75 | |
| | |    Accounts Payable | | 75 |
| | |       Received bill of $75 from veterinarian for services provided. | | |
| | 31 | Hay and Feed Supplies | 700 | |
| | |    Cash | | 700 |
| | |       During month, used $700 worth of the hay and feed purchased on May 9. | | |

*Instructions*

With the class divided into groups, answer the following:

(a) Identify each journal entry that is correct. For each journal entry that is incorrect, prepare the entry that should have been made by the bookkeeper.
(b) Which of the incorrect entries would prevent the trial balance from balancing?
(c) What was the correct net income for May, assuming the bookkeeper reported net income of $4,500 after posting all 50 entries?
(d) What was the correct cash balance at May 31, assuming the bookkeeper reported a balance of $12,475 after posting all 50 entries?

# Communication Activity

**BYP2–5** White Glove Company offers home cleaning services. Two common transactions for the company are billing customers for services performed and paying employee salaries. For example, on March 15, bills that totalled $6,000 were sent to customers, and $2,000 in salaries was paid to employees.

*Instructions*

Write a memo to your instructor that lists the steps in the recording process and applies these steps to each of the March 15 transactions.

# Ethics Case

**BYP2–6** Vu Hung is the assistant chief accountant at Lim Company, a manufacturer of computer chips and cellular phones. The company presently has total sales of $20 million. It is the end of the first quarter. Vu is hurriedly trying to prepare a general ledger trial balance so that quarterly financial statements can be prepared and released to management and regulatory agencies. The total credits on the trial balance exceed the debits by $1,000.

In order to meet the 4 p.m. deadline, Vu decides to force the debits and credits into balance by adding the amount of the difference to the Equipment account. She chose Equipment because it is one of the larger account balances. Proportionally, it will be the least misstated. She believes that the difference will not affect anyone's decisions. She wishes that she had more time to find the error, but realizes that the financial statements are already late.

*Instructions*

(a) Who are the stakeholders in this situation?
(b) What are the ethical issues involved?
(c) What are Vu's alternatives?

---

*Answers to Self-Study Questions*

1. b  2. c  3. d  4. d  5. b  6. a  7. c  8. d  9. a  10. c

*Answer to Forzani Review It Question 4*

Normal balances: Accounts Receivable (asset)—debit; Accounts Payable and Accrued Liabilities (liability)—credit; Corporate Revenue (revenue)—credit; and Store Operating Expense (expense)—debit.

Remember to go back to the Navigator Box at the beginning of the chapter to check off your completed work.

# concepts for review >>

Before studying this chapter, you should understand or, if necessary, review:

a. The double-entry system. (Ch. 2, pp. 51–53)
b. How to increase and decrease assets, liabilities, and owner's equity accounts using debit and credit procedures. (Ch. 2, pp. 51–53)
c. How to journalize transactions. (Ch. 2, pp. 55–57)
d. How to post transactions to the general ledger. (Ch. 2, pp. 59–60)
e. How to prepare a trial balance. (Ch. 2, pp. 69–70)

# Fiscal Year Ends, but Classes Move On

*Seneca College: www.senecac.on.ca*

TORONTO, Ont.—In accounting, as in comedy, timing is everything. An organization's fiscal year end is like a punch line—everything leads up to it. Once it's gone, you start all over.

At Seneca College's dozen campuses in the northern half of Toronto and neighbouring York region, as at most schools, the bulk of students arrive in September and leave in April or May. But the college's books close on March 31, when its fiscal year ends.

"The reason goes back to 1967 and the provincial act establishing community colleges in Ontario," explains Ron Currie, Vice-President of Finance and Administration for Seneca. "That's the government's year end."

No matter what date is selected for Seneca's fiscal year end, the college has to apply revenues in the year in which the service is performed. This is necessary to satisfy the revenue recognition and matching principles. For example, Seneca might collect tuition for the summer term in one accounting period, but provide teaching services in the next accounting period. "Typically," says Mr. Currie, "students pay in March for a summer semester course, so those prepayments get deferred on our balance sheet. Same with the student activity fees."

Seneca also teaches courses that are funded by grant money from the government, private industry, and trade and professional associations. The same principles apply. "Let's say XYZ Corporation came along and gave us $30,000 to run a program in March, April, and May," Mr. Currie elaborates, "We would defer two-thirds of it to the next year."

Expenses, too, must be recorded in the year in which they were incurred. "Our utility bills and invoices for legal fees for the last month or two of the fiscal year tend to come in after our year end," Mr. Currie continues. "In order to match the expenses to the proper year, we accrue them based on an estimate."

For things like course study guides, which are usually prepared by staff in one fiscal year but sold to students the following year, it's the other way around. "In that case we take the costs associated with developing the materials and categorize them as a prepaid expense in one fiscal year and match it with the corresponding revenue in the next fiscal year."

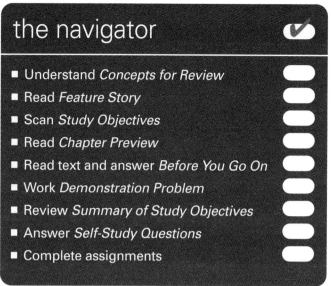

## the navigator

- Understand *Concepts for Review*
- Read *Feature Story*
- Scan *Study Objectives*
- Read *Chapter Preview*
- Read text and answer *Before You Go On*
- Work *Demonstration Problem*
- Review *Summary of Study Objectives*
- Answer *Self-Study Questions*
- Complete assignments

chapter | 3

# c h a p t e r  3
# Adjusting the Accounts

## study objectives >>

the navigator

After studying this chapter, you should be able to:

1. Explain the time period assumption, revenue recognition principle, and matching principle.
2. Explain the accrual basis of accounting.
3. Explain why adjusting entries are needed and identify the major types of adjusting entries.
4. Identify and prepare adjusting entries for prepayments.
5. Identify and prepare adjusting entries for accruals.
6. Identify and prepare the adjusting entry for amortization.
7. Describe the nature and purpose of an adjusted trial balance and prepare one.
8. Identify and prepare adjusting entries for the alternative treatment of prepayments (Appendix 3A).

In Chapter 2, we examined the recording process up to and including the preparation of the trial balance. Before we prepare financial statements from the trial balance, however, additional steps are required. The timing mismatch between the tuition received by Seneca College for its summer classes and the costs incurred to offer these classes illustrates the type of situation that makes these additional steps necessary. For example, computer equipment purchased before March 31, the end of Seneca's fiscal year, will be used to keep student records and accounts for the summer session. What portion of the computer cost, if any, should be recognized as an expense of the current period? Before financial statements can be prepared, this and other questions related to the recognition of revenues and expenses must be answered. Once we know the answers, we can adjust the relevant account balances.

The chapter is organized as follows:

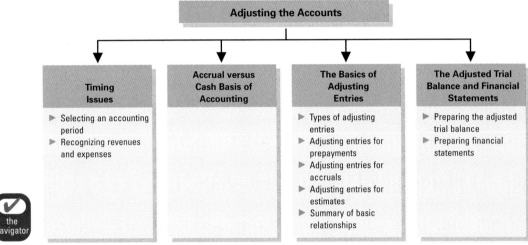

# Timing Issues

study objective 1

Explain the time period assumption, revenue recognition principle, and matching principle.

No adjustments would be necessary if we could wait until a company ended its operations to prepare its financial statements. At that point, we could easily determine its final balance sheet and the amount of lifetime income it earned. The following anecdote illustrates one way to calculate lifetime income:

> A grocery store owner from the old country kept his accounts payable on a spindle, accounts receivable on a notepad, and cash in a shoebox. His daughter, having just passed the CGA Professional Applications exam, chided her father: "I don't understand how you can run your business this way. How do you know what you've earned?"
>
> "Well," her father replied, "when I arrived in Canada 40 years ago, I had nothing but the pants I was wearing. Today, your brother is a doctor, your sister is a teacher, and you are a CGA. Your mother and I have a nice car, a well-furnished house, and a home by the lake. We have a good business and everything is paid for. So, you add all that together, subtract the pants, and there's your net income."

## Selecting an Accounting Time Period

Although the grocer may be correct in his evaluation, it is impractical to wait so long for the results of operations. All entities—from the corner grocery, to a company like Forzani, to your college or university—find that reporting frequently on the results of their activities makes it easier to make decisions at the right time. For example, management usually wants monthly financial statements. Investors want to view the results of publicly traded companies at least quarterly. The Canada Customs and Revenue Agency wants financial statements filed with annual income tax returns. To meet these needs, **accountants make the assumption that the economic life of a business can be divided into artificial time periods**. This assumption is referred to as the time period assumption.

**Accounting time periods are generally one month, one quarter, or one year.** Time periods of less than one year are called **interim periods**. Most large companies are required to report both quarterly and annually.

An accounting time period that is one year in length is referred to as a **fiscal year**. The accounting period used by many businesses is the same as the calendar year (January 1 to December 31). However, this need not be the case. Companies whose fiscal year differs from the calendar year include Sun Ice (January 31), Cara Operations (Sunday closest to March 31), Andrés Wines (March 31), Second Cup (last Saturday in June), United Grain Growers (July 31), and CIBC (October 31). Seneca College's fiscal year is April 1 through March 31, which is typical of many colleges, universities, and governments.

Many business transactions affect more than one of these accounting time periods. For example, the computer equipment purchased by Seneca College last year, the milking machine bought by Farmer Li two years ago, and the airplanes purchased by Air Canada five years ago are still in use today. We must therefore determine the relevance of each business transaction to specific accounting periods. This may involve subjective judgements and estimates.

## Recognizing Revenues and Expenses

Determining the amount of revenues and expenses to report in a specific accounting period can be difficult. To help in this task, accountants have developed two generally accepted accounting principles: (1) the revenue recognition principle, and (2) the matching principle.

The **revenue recognition principle** states that **revenue must be recognized in the accounting period in which it is earned**. In a service company, revenue is considered earned at the time the service is performed. To illustrate, assume that a dry-cleaning business cleans clothing on June 30, and customers do not claim and pay for their clothes until the first week of July. Under the revenue recognition principle, revenue is earned in June when the service is performed, rather than in July when the cash is received. So at June 30, the dry cleaner would report a receivable on its balance sheet and revenue on its income statement for the service performed.

Accountants follow the approach of "let the expenses follow the revenues." That is, expense recognition depends on revenue recognition. In the preceding example, this principle means that the salary expense for the cleaning on June 30 should be reported in the income statement for the same period in which the service revenue is recognized.

The critical issue in expense recognition is the period when efforts are made to generate revenues. This may or may not be the same period in which the expense is paid. If the salary incurred on June 30 is not paid until July, the dry cleaner would still report a salary expense on its June income statement and salaries payable on its June 30 balance sheet. The practice of expense recognition is called the **matching principle** because it **matches efforts (expenses) with accomplishments (revenues)**.

Once the economic life of a business has been divided into artificial time periods, the revenue recognition and matching principles can be applied. The time period assumption and revenue recognition and matching principles provide guidelines for when to report revenues and expenses. These relationships are shown in Illustration 3-1.

**Illustration 3-1 ▶**

GAAP relationships in revenue and expense recognition

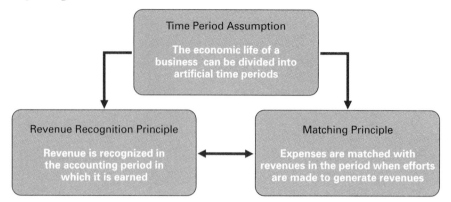

### ACCOUNTING IN ACTION ▶ Business Insight

Suppose you are a filmmaker like David Heyman and spend US$125 million to produce a film such as *Harry Potter and the Philosopher's Stone*. Over what period should the cost be expensed? It should be expensed over the economic life of the film. But what is its economic life? The filmmaker must estimate how much revenue will be earned from box office sales, video sales, television, and games and toys—a period that could be less than a year or many years. This situation illustrates the difficulty Warner Bros. has in properly matching expenses to revenues for its highly successful *Harry Potter* movies, which continue to break box office and product sales records.

# Accrual versus Cash Basis of Accounting

**study objective 2**

Explain the accrual basis of accounting.

If you follow the revenue recognition and matching principles, you are using the **accrual basis of accounting**. Under the accrual basis, transactions that change a company's financial statements are recorded in the periods in which the events occur. For example, service revenue is recognized when it is earned, rather than when the cash is received. The critical event is the performance of the service, not the collection of cash. Expenses are recognized when services (e.g., salaries) or goods (e.g., supplies) are used or consumed, rather than when the cash is paid. As a result, revenues that have been earned are matched with the expenses incurred to earn these same revenues. Thanks to this practice, financial statements are more meaningful for decision-making.

An alternative to the accrual basis of accounting is the cash basis. Under the **cash basis of accounting**, revenue is recorded when cash is received, and expenses are recorded when cash is paid. The cash basis often leads to misleading financial statements. It fails to record revenue which has been earned if the cash has not been received. This violates the revenue recognition principle. In addition, expenses are not matched with revenues, which violates the matching principle. **The cash basis of accounting is not in accordance with generally accepted accounting principles.**

Although most companies use the accrual basis of accounting, some small companies use the cash basis of accounting. Farmers and fishermen also tend to use the cash basis of accounting. The cash basis of accounting is justified for these types of businesses because they have few receivables and payables. Accountants are sometimes asked to convert cash basis records to the accrual basis. As you might expect, extensive journal entries are required for this task.

Using a simple example, Illustration 3-2 shows the relationship between accrual-based numbers and cash-based numbers. Suppose you own a painting company and you paint a large building during year 1. In year 1, you have total expenses of $50,000, which includes the cost of the paint and your employees' salaries. Now assume that you bill your customer $80,000 at the end of year 1, but you aren't paid until year 2. On an accrual basis, you report the revenue during the period when it is earned—year 1. The expenses are then recorded (matched) in the period in which the revenues are earned. Thus your net income for year 1 is $30,000. No revenue or expense from this project is reported in year 2. The $30,000 of income reported for year 1 provides a useful indication of profitability and of your efforts during that period.

If, instead, you were reporting on a cash basis, you would report expenses of $50,000 in year 1 and revenues of $80,000 in year 2. For year 1, you would report a loss of $50,000. For year 2, you would report net income of $80,000. Cash basis measures are not very informative about the results of your efforts during year 1 or year 2.

Note that total net income for all years added together is the same for both the accrual and cash bases ($30,000). However, the timing of when revenue and expense is recognized under each basis differs significantly.

| | Year 1 | | Year 2 | |
|---|---|---|---|---|
| Activity | Purchased paint, painted building, paid employees | | Received payment for work done in year 1 | |
| Accrual basis | Revenue | $80,000 | Revenue | $ 0 |
| | Expense | 50,000 | Expense | 0 |
| | Net income | $30,000 | Net income | $ 0 |
| Cash basis | Revenue | $ 0 | Revenue | $80,000 |
| | Expense | 50,000 | Expense | 0 |
| | Net loss | $(50,000) | Net income | $80,000 |

**Illustration 3-2 ◀**

Accrual versus cash basis accounting

---

## BEFORE YOU GO ON . . .

▶ **Review It**

1. Why do we need to have a time period assumption?
2. What are the revenue recognition and matching principles?
3. What are the differences between the cash and accrual bases of accounting?

*Related exercise material:* E3–1 and E3–2.

---

# The Basics of Adjusting Entries

For revenues to be recorded in the period in which they are earned, and for expenses to be matched with the revenues they generate, adjusting entries are made at the end of the accounting period. In short, **under the accrual basis of accounting, adjusting entries are needed because of the time period assumption and to ensure that the revenue recognition and matching principles are followed.**

Adjusting entries make it possible to report the appropriate assets, liabilities, and owner's equity on the balance sheet. They also make it possible to report the proper revenues and expenses on the income statement for the period. However, the unadjusted trial bal-

study objective 3

Explain why adjusting entries are needed and identify the major types of adjusting entries.

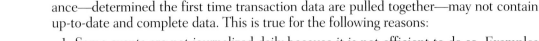

Accounting Cycle
Tutorial—Making
Adjusting Entries

ance—determined the first time transaction data are pulled together—may not contain up-to-date and complete data. This is true for the following reasons:

1. Some events are not journalized daily because it is not efficient to do so. Examples are the consumption of supplies and the earning of wages by employees.
2. Some costs are not journalized during the accounting period because they expire with the passage of time rather than through daily transactions. Examples are rent, insurance, and amortization.
3. Some items may be unrecorded. An example is a utility service bill that will not be received until the next accounting period. The bill, however, covers services delivered in the preceding accounting period.

Adjusting entries are needed every time financial statements are prepared. We first analyse each account in the trial balance to see if it is complete and up to date. The analysis requires a thorough understanding of the company's operations and the interrelationship of accounts. Preparing adjusting entries is often a long process. For example, to accumulate the adjustment data, a company may need to count its remaining supplies. It may also need to prepare supporting schedules of insurance policies, rental agreements, and other contractual commitments.

Adjustment data are often not available until after the end of the period in question. For example, telephone and other bills will not be received until after the month end or year end. In such cases, the data are gathered as soon as possible after the end of the period and adjusting entries are made but still dated as at the balance sheet date.

## Types of Adjusting Entries

Adjusting entries can be classified as prepayments, accruals, or estimates, as shown below:

| Prepayments | Accruals | Estimates |
|---|---|---|
| 1. Prepaid Expenses<br>Expenses paid in cash and recorded as assets before they are used or consumed. | 1. Accrued Expenses<br>Expenses incurred but not yet paid in cash or recorded. | 1. Amortization<br>Allocation of the cost of long-lived assets to expense over their useful lives. |
| 2. Unearned Revenues<br>Cash received and recorded as a liability before revenue is earned. | 2. Accrued Revenues<br>Revenues earned but not yet received in cash or recorded. | |

Specific examples and explanations of each type of adjustment are given on the following pages. Each example is based on the October 31 trial balance of Pioneer Advertising Agency from Chapter 2, reproduced in Illustration 3-3 on the following page. We assume that Pioneer Advertising uses an accounting period of one month. Thus, monthly adjusting entries will be made. The entries will be dated October 31.

## Adjusting Entries for Prepayments

study objective 4

Identify and prepare adjusting entries for pre-payments.

Prepayments are either prepaid expenses or unearned revenues. Adjusting entries are used to record the portion of the prepayment that is for the expense incurred or the revenue earned in the current accounting period. This means that for prepaid expenses, the adjusting entry records the expense which applies to the current period and reduces the asset account where the prepaid expense was originally recorded. This type of adjustment is necessary because the prepayment no longer has future benefit and so stops being an asset; it has been used. For unearned revenues, the adjusting entry records the revenue

Illustration 3-3 ◄

Trial balance

**PIONEER ADVERTISING AGENCY**
**Trial Balance**
**October 31, 2005**

| | Debit | Credit |
|---|---|---|
| Cash | $15,200 | |
| Accounts receivable | 0 | |
| Advertising supplies | 2,500 | |
| Prepaid insurance | 600 | |
| Office equipment | 5,000 | |
| Notes payable | | $ 5,000 |
| Accounts payable | | 2,500 |
| Unearned revenue | | 1,200 |
| C. R. Byrd, capital | | 10,000 |
| C. R. Byrd, drawings | 500 | |
| Service revenue | | 10,000 |
| Salaries expense | 4,000 | |
| Rent expense | 900 | |
| Totals | $28,700 | $28,700 |

earned in the current period and reduces the liability account where the unearned revenue was originally recorded. This type of adjustment is necessary because the unearned revenue is no longer owed and so stops being a liability, because the service has been provided and the revenue earned.

Let's look at each type of adjusting entry for prepayments—prepaid expenses and unearned revenues—in more detail now.

## Prepaid Expenses

Costs paid in cash and recorded as assets before they are used or consumed are called prepaid expenses. When a cost is incurred, an asset account is debited to show the service or benefit that will be received in the future. Prepayments often occur for insurance, supplies, advertising, and rent.

**Alternative terminology**
Prepaid expenses are also called *deferred expenses* or *future expenses*.

Prepaid expenses expire either with the passage of time (e.g., rent and insurance) or through use. It is not necessary (or practical) to record the expiration of these costs on a daily basis. Instead, these expirations are recorded when financial statements are prepared. At each statement date, adjusting entries are made for two purposes: (1) to record the expenses (expired costs) that apply to the current accounting period, and (2) to show the unexpired costs in the asset accounts.

Prior to adjusting prepaid expenses, assets are overstated and expenses are understated. Therefore, as shown below, **an adjusting entry for prepaid expenses results in an increase (debit) to an expense account and a decrease (credit) to an asset account.**

Prepaid Expenses

| Asset | | Expense | |
|---|---|---|---|
| Unadjusted Balance | Credit Adjusting Entry (−) | Debit Adjusting Entry (+) | |

**Supplies.** Businesses use various types of supplies. For example, an accounting firm will have office supplies such as pens, pencils, paper, and envelopes. An advertising firm will have advertising supplies such as graph paper, video film, and poster paper. Supplies are generally debited to an asset account when they are bought. During the course of operations, supplies are depleted. However, the amount of supplies used is only recorded during the adjustment process. At that point, a physical inventory (count) of supplies is taken. The difference between the balance in the supplies (asset) account and the cost of supplies actually remaining gives the supplies used (expense) for the period.

Pioneer Advertising Agency purchased advertising supplies costing $2,500 on October 5. A debit (increase) was made to the asset account Advertising Supplies. This account shows a balance of $2,500 in the October 31 trial balance. An inventory count at the close of business on October 31 reveals that only $1,000 of supplies is still on hand. Thus, the cost of supplies used is $1,500 ($2,500 − $1,000), and the following adjusting entry is made:

A = L + OE
−1,500      −1,500

Cash flows: no effect

| Oct. 31 | Advertising Supplies Expense | 1,500 | |
| | Advertising Supplies | | 1,500 |
| | To record supplies used. | | |

After the adjusting entry is posted, the two advertising supplies accounts show the following:

| Advertising Supplies | | | | Advertising Supplies Expense | |
|---|---|---|---|---|---|
| Oct. 5 | 2,500 | Oct. 31 Adj. | 1,500 | Oct. 31 Adj. | 1,500 |
| Oct. 31 Bal. | 1,000 | | | | |

The asset account Advertising Supplies now shows a balance of $1,000, which is the cost of supplies remaining at the statement date. In addition, Advertising Supplies Expense shows a balance of $1,500, which is the cost of supplies used in October. If the adjusting entry is not made, October expenses will be understated and net income overstated by $1,500. Also, both assets and owner's equity will be overstated by $1,500 on the October 31 balance sheet.

**Insurance.** Most companies have fire and theft insurance for merchandise and equipment, liability insurance for accidents suffered by customers on the company's premises, and automobile insurance for company cars and trucks. The term of coverage is usually one year. Insurance premiums (the cost of the insurance policy) are normally charged to the asset account Prepaid Insurance when they are paid. At the financial statement date, it is necessary to make an adjustment to debit (increase) Insurance Expense and credit (decrease) Prepaid Insurance for the cost that has expired during the period.

On October 4, Pioneer Advertising Agency paid $600 for a one-year fire insurance policy. The effective date of coverage was October 1. The premium was charged to Prepaid Insurance when it was paid. This account shows a balance of $600 in the October 31 trial balance. An analysis of the policy reveals that $50 ($600 ÷ 12) of insurance expires each month. Thus, the following adjusting entry is made:

A = L + OE
−50      −50

Cash flows: no effect

| Oct. 31 | Insurance Expense | 50 | |
| | Prepaid Insurance | | 50 |
| | To record insurance expired. | | |

After the adjusting entry is posted, the accounts show the following:

| Prepaid Insurance | | | | Insurance Expense | |
|---|---|---|---|---|---|
| Oct. 4 | 600 | Oct. 31 Adj. | 50 | Oct. 31 Adj. | 50 |
| Oct. 31 Bal. | 550 | | | | |

The asset Prepaid Insurance shows a balance of $550. This amount represents the unexpired cost for the remaining 11 months of coverage (11 × $50). The $50 balance in Insurance Expense is equal to the insurance cost that has expired in October. If this adjustment is not made, October expenses will be understated by $50 and net income overstated by $50. Also, both assets and owner's equity will be overstated by $50 on the October 31 balance sheet.

als will increase both a balance sheet and an income statement account. We now look at each type of adjusting entry for accruals—accrued revenues and accrued expenses—in more detail.

## Accrued Revenues

Revenues earned but not yet received in cash or recorded at the statement date are **accrued revenues**. Accrued revenues may accumulate (accrue) with the passage of time, as in the case of interest revenue and rent revenue. Or they may result from services that have been performed but for which payment has not been collected, as in the case of commissions and fees. The former are unrecorded because the earning of interest and rent does not involve daily transactions. The latter may be unrecorded because only a portion of the total service has been provided or the bill has not been prepared.

**Alternative terminology**
Accrued revenues are also called *accrued receivables*.

An adjusting entry is required for two purposes: (1) to show the receivable that exists at the balance sheet date, and (2) to record the revenue that has been earned during the period. Prior to adjustment, both assets and revenues are understated. Accordingly, as shown below, **an adjusting entry for accrued revenues results in an increase (debit) to an asset account and an increase (credit) to a revenue account.**

### Accrued Revenues

| Asset | | Revenue | |
|---|---|---|---|
| Debit Adjusting Entry (+) | | | Credit Adjusting Entry (+) |

In October, Pioneer Advertising Agency earned $200 in fees for advertising services that were not billed to clients until November. Because these services have not been billed, they have not been recorded. The following adjusting entry is made on October 31:

| Oct. 31 | Accounts Receivable | 200 | |
| | Service Revenue | | 200 |
| | To accrue revenue earned but not billed or collected. | | |

A = L + OE
+200 +200

Cash flows: no effect

After the adjusting entry is posted, the accounts show the following:

| Accounts Receivable | | | | Service Revenue | | |
|---|---|---|---|---|---|---|
| Oct. 21 | 10,000 | Oct. 31 | 10,000 | | Oct. 21 | 10,000 |
| 31 Adj. | 200 | | | | 31 Adj. | 400 |
| Oct. 31 Bal. | 200 | | | | 31 Adj. | 200 |
| | | | | | Oct. 31 Adj. | 10,600 |

The asset Accounts Receivable shows that $200 is owed by clients at the balance sheet date. The balance of $10,600 in Service Revenue represents the total revenue earned during the month. If the adjusting entry is not made, assets and owner's equity on the balance sheet, and revenues and net income on the income statement, will all be understated.

On November 10, Pioneer receives cash of $200 for the services performed in October. The following entry is made:

| Nov. 10 | Cash | 200 | |
| | Accounts Receivable | | 200 |
| | To record cash collected on account. | | |

A = L + OE
+200
−200

Cash flows: +200

## Accrued Expenses

**Alternative terminology**
Accrued expenses are also
called *accrued liabilities*.

Expenses incurred but not yet paid or recorded at the statement date are called **accrued expenses**. Interest, rent, property taxes, and salaries can be accrued expenses. Accrued expenses result from the same causes as accrued revenues. In fact, an accrued expense on the books of one company is an accrued revenue for another company. For example, the $200 accrual of revenue by Pioneer is an accrued expense for the client that received the service.

Adjustments for accrued expenses are needed for two purposes: (1) to record the obligations that exist at the balance sheet date, and (2) to recognize the expenses that apply to the current accounting period. Prior to adjustment, both liabilities and expenses are understated. Therefore, as shown below, **an adjusting entry for accrued expenses results in an increase (debit) to an expense account and an increase (credit) to a liability account.**

Accrued Expenses

**Accrued Interest.** On October 3, Pioneer Advertising Agency signed a $5,000, three-month note payable, due January 3, 2006. The note requires interest to be paid at an annual rate of 6%. The amount of interest accumulation is determined by three factors: (1) the face value, or principal amount, of the note; (2) the interest rate, which is always expressed as an annual rate; and (3) the length of time the note is outstanding (unpaid). The formula for calculating interest and its application to Pioneer Advertising Agency for the month of October are shown in Illustration 3-4.

**Illustration 3-4 ▶**

Formula for interest

**Helpful hint** A simplified method of interest calculation is used in the illustration to aid comprehension. In reality, interest is calculated using the exact number of days in the interest period and year.

In this instance, the total interest due on the $5,000 note at its due date three months later is $75 ($5,000 × 6% × $\frac{3}{12}$ months), or $25 for one month. Interest rates are always expressed as an annual rate. Because the interest rate is for one year, the time period must be adjusted for the fraction of the year the note is outstanding.

The accrued expense adjusting entry at October 31 is as follows:

| A | = | L | + | OE |
|---|---|---|---|---|
| | | +25 | | −25 |

Cash flows: no effect

| Oct. 31 | Interest Expense | 25 | |
|---|---|---|---|
| | Interest Payable | | 25 |
| | To accrue interest on note payable. | | |

After this adjusting entry is posted, the accounts show:

| Interest Expense | | Interest Payable | |
|---|---|---|---|
| Oct. 31 Adj.    25 | | | Oct. 31 Adj.    25 |

Interest Expense shows the interest charges for the month of October. The amount of interest owed at the statement date is shown in Interest Payable. It will not be paid until the note comes due, on January 3, 2006. The Interest Payable account is used instead of crediting Notes Payable to show the two types of obligations (interest and principal) in the accounts and statements. If this adjusting entry is not made, liabilities and expenses will be understated. Net income and owner's equity will be overstated.

**Accrued Salaries.** Some types of expenses, such as employee salaries and commissions, are paid after the work has been performed. At Pioneer Advertising, employees began work on October 17. They were last paid on October 28. The next payment of salaries will not occur until November 11. As shown in the calendar, one working day remains in October (October 31).

**Helpful hint** Recognition of an accrued expense does not mean that a company is slow or bad at paying its debts. The accrued liability may not be payable until after the balance sheet date.

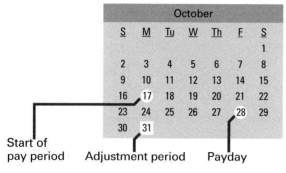

Start of pay period · Adjustment period · Payday · Payday

At October 31, the salaries for the last day (Monday) represent an accrued expense and a liability to Pioneer Advertising. The four employees each earn a salary of $500 for a five-day work week, or $100 per day. Thus, accrued salaries for Pioneer Advertising at October 31 are $400 ($100 × 1 day × 4 employees). The adjusting entry is as follows:

| Oct. 31 | Salaries Expense | 400 | |
| | Salaries Payable | | 400 |
| | To record accrued salaries. | | |

A = L + OE
+400 −400

Cash flows: no effect

After this adjusting entry is posted, the accounts show the following:

| Salaries Expense | | Salaries Payable | |
|---|---|---|---|
| Oct. 28  4,000 | | | Oct. 31 Adj.  400 |
| 31 Adj.  400 | | | |
| Oct. 31 Bal.  4,400 | | | |

After this adjustment, the balance in Salaries Expense of $4,400 ($100 × 11 days × 4 employees) is the actual salary expense for October (the employees started work on October 17). The balance in Salaries Payable of $400 is the amount of the liability for salaries owed as at October 31. If the $400 adjustment for salaries is not recorded, Pioneer's expenses and liabilities will be understated by $400. Net income and owner's equity will be overstated by $400.

At Pioneer Advertising, salaries are payable every two weeks. The next payday is November 11, when total salaries of $4,000 will again be paid. The payment consists of $400 of salaries payable at October 31 plus $3,600 of salaries expense for November ($100 × 9 working days [for the period November 1–11] × 4 employees). The following entry is made on November 11:

| Nov. 11 | Salaries Payable | 400 | |
| | Salaries Expense | 3,600 | |
| | Cash | | 4,000 |
| | To record November 11 payroll. | | |

A = L + OE
−4,000 −400 −3,600

Cash flows: −4,000

This entry does two things: (1) It eliminates the liability for Salaries Payable that was recorded in the October 31 adjusting entry; (2) it records the proper amount of Salaries Expense for the period between November 1 and November 11.

## BEFORE YOU GO ON . . .

### ►Review It

1. If an accrued revenue adjusting entry is not made, what is the effect on assets, owner's equity, revenues, and net income?
2. If an accrued expense adjusting entry is not made, what is the effect on liabilities, owner's equity, expenses, and net income?

### ►Do It

Calvin and Hobbs are the new owners of Micro Computer Services. At the end of August 2005, their first month of ownership, Calvin and Hobbs are trying to prepare monthly financial statements. The following information relates to August:

1. At August 31, Calvin and Hobbs owed their employees $800 in salaries that will be paid on September 2.
2. On August 1, Calvin and Hobbs borrowed $30,000 from a local bank on a five-year term loan. The annual interest rate is 5%.
3. Service revenue earned but not yet billed for August totalled $1,100.

Prepare the adjusting entries needed at August 31, 2005.

#### Action Plan

- Make adjusting entries at the end of the period for revenues earned and expenses incurred to generate these revenues in the period.
- Remember that accruals are entries that were not previously recorded; therefore, the adjustment pattern is different from that for prepayments.
- Adjusting entries for accrued revenues require a debit to a receivable account and a credit to a revenue account.
- Adjusting entries for accrued expenses require a debit to an expense account and a credit to a liability account.

#### Solution

| | | | | |
|---|---|---|---|---|
| 1. Aug. 31 | Salaries Expense | | 800 | |
| |     Salaries Payable | | | 800 |
| |         To record accrued salaries. | | | |
| 2.     31 | Interest Expense | | 125 | |
| |     Interest Payable | | | 125 |
| |         To record accrued interest: $30,000 \times 5\% \times \frac{1}{12}$ = $125 | | | |
| 3. Aug. 31 | Accounts Receivable | | 1,100 | |
| |     Service Revenue | | | 1,100 |
| |         To accrue revenue earned but not billed or collected. | | | |

the navigator

*Related exercise material:* BE3–5, BE3–6, BE3–7, E3–4, E3–5, E3–6, and E3–7.

## Adjusting Entries for Estimates

study objective 6

Identify and prepare the adjusting entry for amortization.

Estimates are required in accounting because we do not always know what will happen in the future. If the current period will be affected by these future events, subjective estimates must be made. Throughout this text, we discuss many estimates found in accounting (e.g., uncollectible accounts receivable, which are discussed in Chapter 8). One important estimate introduced in this chapter is the allocation of the cost of long-lived assets over their estimated future useful lives. This allocation is known as amortization.

## Amortization

A business usually owns productive facilities such as land, buildings, equipment, and vehicles. Each is recorded as an asset, rather than as an expense, in the year it is acquired because these long-lived assets provide a service for a number of years. The time of service is referred to as the useful life.

According to the matching principle, a portion of the cost of long-lived assets such as property, plant, and equipment should be reported as an expense during each period of the asset's useful life. Amortization is the allocation of the cost of these types of assets to expense over their useful lives. Land is an exception. Land is not amortized as it has an unlimited useful life.

**Alternative terminology**
Amortization is also called *depreciation.*

### Need for Amortization Adjustment.

From an accounting perspective, acquiring productive facilities is basically a long-term prepayment for services. The procedure for periodic adjusting entries for amortization is similar to the adjustment procedure for prepaid expenses: recognize the cost that has expired (become an expense) during the period, and report the unexpired cost (which is still an asset) at the end of the period.

At the time an asset is acquired, its useful life is not known with certainty. The asset may be useful for a longer or shorter time than expected, depending on such factors as actual use, deterioration due to weather and other elements, or obsolescence. Thus, it is important to recognize that **amortization is an estimate** rather than a factual measurement of the cost that has expired.

A common procedure for calculating amortization expense is to divide the cost of the asset by its useful life. For example, if the cost of an asset is $5,000 and its useful life is expected to be five years, annual amortization is $1,000. This is known as the **straight-line amortization method**. In its simplest form, the formula to calculate annual amortization is as follows:

| Cost | ÷ | Useful Life (in years) | = | Annual Amortization Expense |
|------|---|------------------------|---|-----------------------------|

**Illustration 3-5 ◄**
Formula for amortization

Of course, if you are calculating amortization for partial periods, the annual expense amount must be adjusted for the relevant portion of the year. For example, if we wish to determine the amortization for the quarter, we would multiply the annual result by $\frac{3}{12}$ months. Calculating amortization is examined in more detail in Chapter 9, including how amortization is affected by any remaining value recovered through disposal (e.g., sale) of the asset at the end of its useful life.

For Pioneer Advertising, amortization on the office equipment is estimated to be $1,000 a year, or $83 per month. Accordingly, amortization for the month of October is recognized by the following adjusting entry:

| Oct. 31 | Amortization Expense | 83 | |
|---------|----------------------|-----|-----|
| | Accumulated Amortization—Office Equipment | | 83 |
| | To record monthly amortization. | | |

| A | = | L | + | OE |
|-----|---|---|---|-----|
| -83 | | | | -83 |

Cash flows: no effect

The following shows the accounts after the adjusting entry has been posted:

| Office Equipment | | Amortization Expense | |
|------------------|--|----------------------|--|
| Oct. 3   5,000 | | Oct. 31 Adj.   83 | |

| Accumulated Amortization—Office Equipment | |
|-------------------------------------------|--|
| | Oct. 31 Adj.   83 |

The balance in the Accumulated Amortization account will increase by $83 each month. After journalizing and posting the adjusting entry at November 30, the balance of the accumulated amortization will be $166. At December 31, the balance of the accumulated amortization will be $249, and so on.

**Statement Presentation.** A **contra account** is an account that is offset against (deducted from) a related account on the income statement or balance sheet. On the balance sheet, it can be a contra asset account (offset against an asset) or a contra liability account (offset against a liability). We will discuss contra income statement accounts in Chapter 5.

Accumulated Amortization—Office Equipment is a contra asset account that is related to the asset account Office Equipment. Its normal balance is a credit—the opposite of the normal debit balance of its related account, Office Equipment. The Accumulated Amortization account is used instead of crediting (decreasing) the Office Equipment account directly in order to **show both the original cost of the equipment and the portion of the cost that has been allocated to expense to date.** In the balance sheet, Accumulated Amortization—Office Equipment is deducted from the related asset account as follows:

| | |
|---|---:|
| Office equipment | $5,000 |
| Less: Accumulated amortization—office equipment | 83 |
| Net book value | $4,917 |

The difference between the cost of any amortizable asset and its accumulated amortization is called the **net book value** (or simply **book value**) of that asset. In the above illustration, the book value of the equipment at the balance sheet date is $4,917. You should realize that the book value and the market value (the price at which it could be sold in the marketplace) of the asset are usually different. The reason the two are different is that amortization is a method of **cost allocation**, not a kind of valuation. That is, amortization does not attempt to show what an asset is worth. It shows only its unallocated cost.

Amortization expense identifies the portion of the asset's cost that has expired in October. As in the case of other adjustments for prepaid expenses, if this adjusting entry is not made, total assets, owner's equity, and net income will be overstated and amortization expense will be understated.

If the company owns additional equipment, such as delivery or store equipment, or if it has a building, amortization expense is recorded on each of these items. Related accumulated amortization accounts are also created, such as Accumulated Amortization—Delivery Equipment, Accumulated Amortization—Store Equipment, and Accumulated Amortization—Building.

## Summary of Basic Relationships

The three basic types of adjusting entries are summarized on the next page. Take some time to study and analyse the adjusting entries shown in the summary. Be sure to note that **each adjusting entry affects one balance sheet account and one income statement account.**

| | Type of Adjustment | Reason for Adjustment | Accounts before Adjustment | Adjusting Entry |
|---|---|---|---|---|
| Prepayments | Prepaid expenses | Prepaid expenses, originally recorded in asset accounts, have been used. | Assets overstated; expenses understated | Dr. Expense Cr. Asset |
| | Unearned revenues | Unearned revenues, initially recorded in liability accounts, have been earned. | Liabilities overstated; revenues understated | Dr. Liability Cr. Revenue |
| Accruals | Accrued revenues | Revenues have been earned but not yet received in cash or recorded. | Assets understated; revenues understated | Dr. Asset Cr. Revenue |
| | Accrued expenses | Expenses have been incurred but not yet paid. | Expenses understated; liabilities understated | Dr. Expense Cr. Liability |
| Estimates | Amortization | Cost of asset must be allocated to expense over useful life. | Assets overstated; expenses understated | Dr. Amortization Expense Cr. Accumulated Amortization |

It is important to understand that **adjusting entries never involve the Cash account** (except for bank reconciliations, which we will study in Chapter 7). In the case of prepayments, cash has already been received or paid, and recorded in the original journal entry. The adjusting entry simply reallocates or adjusts amounts between a balance sheet account (e.g., prepaid assets or unearned revenues) and a statement of earnings account (e.g., expenses or revenues). In the case of accruals, cash will be received or paid in the future and recorded then. The adjusting entry simply records the receivable or payable and the related asset or expense.

The journalizing and posting of adjusting entries for Pioneer Advertising Agency on October 31 are shown below and on the following two pages. All adjustments are identified in the ledger by the reference J2 because they have been journalized on page 2 of the general journal. A centre caption entitled "Adjusting Entries" may be inserted between the last transaction entry and the first adjusting entry to identify these entries. When reviewing the general ledger, note that the adjustments are highlighted in colour.

| GENERAL JOURNAL | | | | J2 |
|---|---|---|---|---|
| Date | Account Titles and Explanation | Ref. | Debit | Credit |
| 2005 | *Adjusting Entries* | | | |
| Oct. 31 | Advertising Supplies Expense | 611 | 1,500 | |
| |     Advertising Supplies | 129 | | 1,500 |
| |     To record supplies used. | | | |
| 31 | Insurance Expense | 722 | 50 | |
| |     Prepaid Insurance | 130 | | 50 |
| |     To record insurance expired. | | | |
| 31 | Unearned Revenue | 209 | 400 | |
| |     Service Revenue | 400 | | 400 |
| |     To record revenue for services provided. | | | |
| 31 | Accounts Receivable | 112 | 200 | |
| |     Service Revenue | 400 | | 200 |
| |     To accrue revenue earned but not billed or collected. | | | |

| Date | Account Titles and Explanation | Ref. | Debit | Credit |
|---|---|---|---|---|
| 2005 | Adjusting Entries | | | |
| Oct. 31 | Interest Expense | 905 | 25 | |
| | Interest Payable | 230 | | 25 |
| | To accrue interest on note payable. | | | |
| 31 | Salaries Expense | 726 | 400 | |
| | Salaries Payable | 212 | | 400 |
| | To record accrued salaries. | | | |
| 31 | Amortization Expense | 711 | 83 | |
| | Accumulated Amortization—Office Equipment | 152 | | 83 |
| | To record monthly amortization. | | | |

## GENERAL LEDGER

### Cash    No. 101

| Date | Explanation | Ref. | Debit | Credit | Balance |
|---|---|---|---|---|---|
| 2005 | | | | | |
| Oct. 1 | | J1 | 10,000 | | 10,000 |
| 4 | | J1 | 1,200 | | 11,200 |
| 4 | | J1 | | 900 | 10,300 |
| 4 | | J1 | | 600 | 9,700 |
| 20 | | J1 | | 500 | 9,200 |
| 28 | | J1 | | 4,000 | 5,200 |
| 31 | | J1 | 10,000 | | 15,200 |

### Accounts Receivable    No. 112

| Date | Explanation | Ref. | Debit | Credit | Balance |
|---|---|---|---|---|---|
| 2005 | | | | | |
| Oct. 21 | | J1 | 10,000 | | 10,000 |
| 31 | | J1 | | 10,000 | 0 |
| 31 | Adj. Entry | J2 | 200 | | 200 |

### Advertising Supplies    No. 129

| Date | Explanation | Ref. | Debit | Credit | Balance |
|---|---|---|---|---|---|
| 2005 | | | | | |
| Oct. 5 | | J1 | 2,500 | | 2,500 |
| 31 | Adj. Entry | J2 | | 1,500 | 1,000 |

### Prepaid Insurance    No. 130

| Date | Explanation | Ref. | Debit | Credit | Balance |
|---|---|---|---|---|---|
| 2005 | | | | | |
| Oct. 4 | | J1 | 600 | | 600 |
| 31 | Adj. Entry | J2 | | 50 | 550 |

### Office Equipment    No. 151

| Date | Explanation | Ref. | Debit | Credit | Balance |
|---|---|---|---|---|---|
| 2005 | | | | | |
| Oct. 3 | | J1 | 5,000 | | 5,000 |

### Accumulated Amortization— Office Equipment    No. 152

| Date | Explanation | Ref. | Debit | Credit | Balance |
|---|---|---|---|---|---|
| 2005 | | | | | |
| Oct. 31 | Adj. Entry | J2 | | 83 | 83 |

### Notes Payable    No. 200

| Date | Explanation | Ref. | Debit | Credit | Balance |
|---|---|---|---|---|---|
| 2005 | | | | | |
| Oct. 3 | | J1 | | 5,000 | 5,000 |

### Accounts Payable    No. 201

| Date | Explanation | Ref. | Debit | Credit | Balance |
|---|---|---|---|---|---|
| 2005 | | | | | |
| Oct. 5 | | J1 | | 2,500 | 2,500 |

### Unearned Revenue    No. 209

| Date | Explanation | Ref. | Debit | Credit | Balance |
|---|---|---|---|---|---|
| 2005 | | | | | |
| Oct. 4 | | J1 | | 1,200 | 1,200 |
| 31 | Adj. Entry | J2 | 400 | | 800 |

### Salaries Payable    No. 212

| Date | Explanation | Ref. | Debit | Credit | Balance |
|---|---|---|---|---|---|
| 2005 | | | | | |
| Oct. 31 | Adj. Entry | J2 | | 400 | 400 |

### Interest Payable    No. 230

| Date | Explanation | Ref. | Debit | Credit | Balance |
|---|---|---|---|---|---|
| 2005 | | | | | |
| Oct. 31 | Adj. Entry | J2 | | 25 | 25 |

### C. R. Byrd, Capital    No. 301

| Date | Explanation | Ref. | Debit | Credit | Balance |
|---|---|---|---|---|---|
| 2005 | | | | | |
| Oct. 1 | | J1 | | 10,000 | 10,000 |

### C. R. Byrd, Drawings    No. 306

| Date | Explanation | Ref. | Debit | Credit | Balance |
|---|---|---|---|---|---|
| 2005 | | | | | |
| Oct. 20 | | J1 | 500 | | 500 |

### Service Revenue    No. 400

| Date | Explanation | Ref. | Debit | Credit | Balance |
|---|---|---|---|---|---|
| 2005 | | | | | |
| Oct. 21 | | J1 | | 10,000 | 10,000 |
| 31 | Adj. Entry | J2 | | 400 | 10,400 |
| 31 | Adj. Entry | J2 | | 200 | 10,600 |

### Advertising Supplies Expense    No. 611

| Date | Explanation | Ref. | Debit | Credit | Balance |
|---|---|---|---|---|---|
| 2005 | | | | | |
| Oct. 31 | Adj. Entry | J2 | 1,500 | | 1,500 |

### Amortization Expense    No. 711

| Date | Explanation | Ref. | Debit | Credit | Balance |
|---|---|---|---|---|---|
| 2005 | | | | | |
| Oct. 31 | Adj. Entry | J2 | 83 | | 83 |

| Insurance Expense | | | | | No. 722 | | Rent Expense | | | | | No. 729 |
| Date | Explanation | Ref. | Debit | Credit | Balance | Date | Explanation | Ref. | Debit | Credit | Balance |
|---|---|---|---|---|---|---|---|---|---|---|---|
| 2005 | | | | | | 2005 | | | | | |
| Oct. 31 | Adj. Entry | J2 | 50 | | 50 | Oct. 4 | | J1 | 900 | | 900 |

| Salaries Expense | | | | | No. 726 | | Interest Expense | | | | | No. 905 |
| Date | Explanation | Ref. | Debit | Credit | Balance | Date | Explanation | Ref. | Debit | Credit | Balance |
|---|---|---|---|---|---|---|---|---|---|---|---|
| 2005 | | | | | | 2005 | | | | | |
| Oct. 28 | | J1 | 4,000 | | 4,000 | Oct. 31 | Adj. Entry | J2 | 25 | | 25 |
| 31 | | J2 | 400 | | 4,400 | | | | | | |

Computer systems handle the adjusting process like any other transaction. The accountant inputs the adjustment at the time required. The main difference between adjusting entries and regular transactions is that with adjusting entries, part of the computer system may perform the required calculation (for items such as amortization or interest) before sending these figures to the journalizing process.

Such systems are also able to display information before and after changes were made. Management may be interested in such information to highlight the impact that adjustments have on the various accounts and financial statements.

**ACCOUNTING IN ACTION ▶ Ethics Insight**

Executives from U.S. drugstore chain Rite Aid were charged with perpetrating a massive fraud that involved, among other deceptions, falsifying adjusting journal entries to inflate income. The former CFO is alleged to have told Rite Aid's accountants to make improper adjusting entries in the preparation of the interim financial statements from 1997 through 2000. Federal prosecutors called it "a wide-ranging accounting fraud scheme that resulted in the largest earnings restatement ever": US$1.6 billion.

*Source:* Stephen Taub, "Rite Aid's Former CFO, Three Other Executives, Charged with Perpetrating Massive Fraud," *CFO.com.*

## BEFORE YOU GO ON . . .

▶ Review It

1. What are the three types of adjusting entries?
2. What is the purpose of amortization?
3. Does net book value equal fair market value? Explain why or why not.
4. Using Forzani's statement of operations (income statement), find the amount of amortization expense recorded for 2003 and 2002. The answer to this question is provided at the end of the chapter.

*Related exercise material:* BE3–8, BE3–9, BE3–10, E3–8, E3–9, and E3–10.

# The Adjusted Trial Balance and Financial Statements

After all adjusting entries have been journalized and posted, another trial balance is prepared from the general ledger accounts. This is called an **adjusted trial balance**. The procedures for preparing an adjusted trial balance are the same as those described in Chapter 2 for preparing a trial balance.

**study objective 7**

Describe the nature and purpose of an adjusted trial balance and prepare one.

## Preparing the Adjusted Trial Balance

An adjusted trial balance proves the equality of the total debit balances and the total credit balances in the ledger after all adjustments have been made. The proof provided by an adjusted trial balance, like the proof contained in a trial balance, applies only to the mathematical accuracy of the ledger. The adjusted trial balance provides all data that are needed for the preparation of financial statements.

The adjusted trial balance for Pioneer Advertising Agency is presented in Illustration 3-6. It has been prepared from the ledger accounts shown in the previous section. The amounts affected by the adjusting entries are highlighted in colour in the adjusted trial balance columns. Compare these amounts to those in the unadjusted trial balance in Illustration 3-3.

**Illustration 3-6 ▶**

Adjusted trial balance

| PIONEER ADVERTISING AGENCY Adjusted Trial Balance October 31, 2005 | | |
|---|---|---|
| | Debit | Credit |
| Cash | $15,200 | |
| Accounts receivable | 200 | |
| Advertising supplies | 1,000 | |
| Prepaid insurance | 550 | |
| Office equipment | 5,000 | |
| Accumulated amortization—office equipment | | $    83 |
| Notes payable | | 5,000 |
| Accounts payable | | 2,500 |
| Unearned revenue | | 800 |
| Salaries payable | | 400 |
| Interest payable | | 25 |
| C. R. Byrd, capital | | 10,000 |
| C. R. Byrd, drawings | 500 | |
| Service revenue | | 10,600 |
| Advertising supplies expense | 1,500 | |
| Amortization expense | 83 | |
| Insurance expense | 50 | |
| Salaries expense | 4,400 | |
| Rent expense | 900 | |
| Interest expense | 25 | |
| | $29,408 | $29,408 |

## Preparing Financial Statements

Financial statements can be prepared directly from the adjusted trial balance. The preparation of financial statements from the adjusted trial balance of Pioneer Advertising Agency and the interrelationship of data are presented in Illustrations 3-7 and 3-8.

As shown in Illustration 3-7, the income statement is prepared from the revenue and expense accounts. The statement of owner's equity is derived from the owner's capital and drawings accounts, and from the net income (or net loss) shown in the income statement. As shown in Illustration 3-8, the balance sheet is then prepared from the asset and liability accounts and the ending owner's capital balance, as reported in the statement of owner's equity.

**Illustration 3-7 ▼**

Preparation of the income statement and statement of owner's equity from the adjusted trial balance

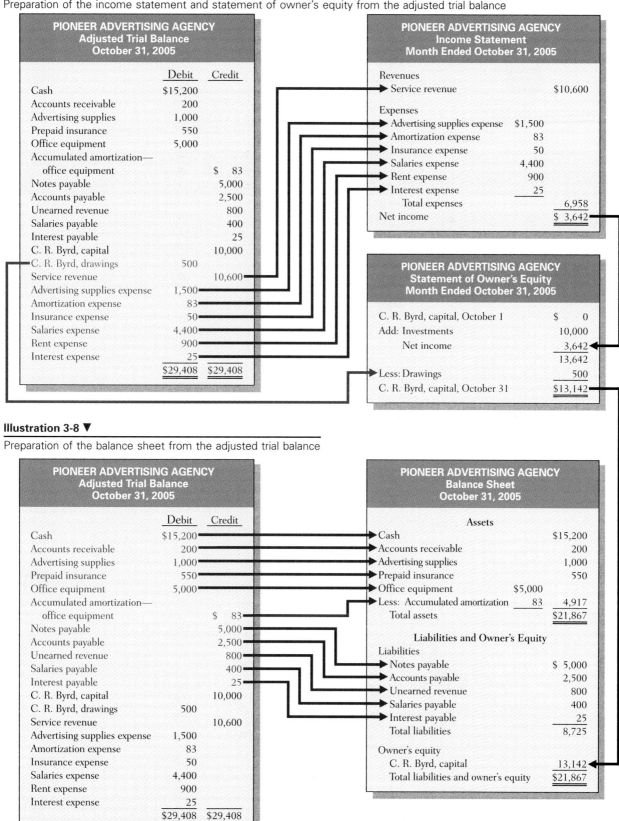

**Illustration 3-8 ▼**

Preparation of the balance sheet from the adjusted trial balance

## BEFORE YOU GO ON . . .

▶**Review It**

1. What is the purpose of an adjusted trial balance?
2. How is an adjusted trial balance prepared?

*Related exercise material: E3–11.*

---

### APPENDIX 3A ▶ ALTERNATIVE TREATMENT OF PREPAID EXPENSES AND UNEARNED REVENUES

**study objective 8**

Identify and prepare adjusting entries for the alternative treatment of prepayments.

In our discussion of adjusting entries for prepaid expenses and unearned revenues, we illustrated transactions which already had entries in balance sheet accounts. In the case of prepaid expenses, the prepayment was debited to an asset account. In the case of unearned revenue, the cash received was credited to a liability account. **Recording your first entry in a balance sheet account improves internal control over assets and imitates the real flow of costs (i.e., from asset to expense).**

Some businesses use an alternative treatment, which is also acceptable. At the time an expense is prepaid, an expense account is debited (increased) and cash is credited (decreased). At the time of a receipt for future services, cash is debited (increased) and a revenue account is credited (increased). The circumstances that justify such entries and the different adjusting entries that may be required are described in the following sections.

## Prepaid Expenses

Prepaid expenses become expired costs through either the passage of time, as in the case of insurance, or consumption, as in the case of advertising supplies. If at the time of purchase the company expects to consume the supplies before the next financial statement date, it may be more convenient to first debit (increase) an expense account rather than an asset account.

Assume that Pioneer Advertising expects that all of the supplies purchased on October 5 will be used before the end of the month. A debit of $2,500 to Advertising Supplies Expense, rather than to the asset account Advertising Supplies, on October 5, will eliminate the need for an adjusting entry on October 31, if all the supplies are used. At October 31, the Advertising Supplies Expense account will show a balance of $2,500, which is the cost of supplies used between October 5 and October 31.

But what if the company does not use all the supplies and an inventory of $1,000 of advertising supplies remains on October 31? Obviously, an adjusting entry is needed. The following adjusting entry is made:

| A = L + OE | | | | |
|---|---|---|---|---|
| +1,000    +1,000 | Oct. 31 | Advertising Supplies | 1,000 | |
| | |    Advertising Supplies Expense | | 1,000 |
| Cash flows: no effect | |    To record supply inventory. | | |

After posting of the adjusting entry, the accounts show the following:

| Advertising Supplies | | Advertising Supplies Expense | | |
| --- | --- | --- | --- | --- |
| Oct. 31 Adj.  1,000 | | Oct.  5         2,500 | Oct. 31 Adj.  1,000 | |
| | | Oct. 31 Bal.   1,500 | | |

After adjustment, the asset account Advertising Supplies shows a balance of $1,000, which is equal to the cost of supplies on hand at October 31. In addition, Advertising Supplies Expense shows a balance of $1,500, which is equal to the cost of supplies used between October 5 and October 31. If the adjusting entry is not made, expenses will be overstated and net income will be understated by $1,000 in the October income statement. Also, both assets and owner's equity will be understated by $1,000 on the October 31 balance sheet.

A comparison of the entries and accounts for advertising supplies is shown below:

| Prepayment Debited to Asset Account (as in chapter) | | | | Prepayment Debited to Expense Account (as in appendix) | | |
| --- | --- | --- | --- | --- | --- | --- |
| Oct.  5 | Advertising Supplies | 2,500 | | Oct.  5 | Advertising Supplies Expense | 2,500 |
| | Accounts Payable | | 2,500 | | Accounts Payable | 2,500 |
| 31 | Advertising Supplies Expense | 1,500 | | 31 | Advertising Supplies | 1,000 |
| | Advertising Supplies | | 1,500 | | Advertising Supplies Expense | 1,000 |

After posting of the entries, the accounts appear as follows:

**Prepayment Debited to Asset Account (as in chapter)**

| Advertising Supplies | | |
| --- | --- | --- |
| Oct.  5          2,500 | Oct. 31 Adj.  1,500 | |
| Oct. 31 Bal.   1,000 | | |

| Advertising Supplies Expense | |
| --- | --- |
| Oct. 31 Adj.  1,500 | |

**Prepayment Debited to Expense Account (as in appendix)**

| Advertising Supplies | |
| --- | --- |
| Oct. 31 Adj.  1,000 | |

| Advertising Supplies Expense | |
| --- | --- |
| Oct.  5          2,500 | Oct. 31 Adj.  1,000 |
| Oct. 31 Bal.   1,500 | |

Note that the **account balances under each alternative are the same** at October 31 (Advertising Supplies $1,000, and Advertising Supplies Expense $1,500).

# Unearned Revenues

Unearned revenues are earned either as time passes, as in the case of unearned rent, or by providing the service, as in the case of unearned fees. Rather than first debiting (increasing) cash and crediting (increasing) an unearned revenue (liability) account, a revenue account may be credited (increased) when cash is received for future services, and a different adjusting entry may be necessary.

To illustrate, assume that when Pioneer Advertising received $1,200 for future services on October 4, the services were expected to be performed before October 31. In such a case, Service Revenue would be credited. If revenue is in fact earned before October 31, no adjustment is needed. However, if at the statement date $800 of the services have not been provided, an adjusting entry is required. The following adjusting entry is made:

| A | = | L | + | OE |
|---|---|---|---|---|
|   |   | +800 |   | -800 |

Cash flows: no effect

| | | | | |
|---|---|---|---|---|
| Oct. 31 | Service Revenue | | 800 | |
| | Unearned Revenue | | | 800 |
| | To record unearned revenue. | | | |

After posting of the adjusting entry, the accounts show:

| Unearned Revenue | | | Service Revenue | | | | |
|---|---|---|---|---|---|---|---|
| | Oct. 31 Adj. | 800 | Oct. 31 Adj. | 800 | Oct. 4 | 1,200 | |
| | | | | | Oct. 31 Bal. | 400 | |

The liability account Unearned Revenue shows a balance of $800, which is equal to the services that will be provided in the future. In addition, the balance in Service Revenue equals the services provided in October. If the adjusting entry is not made, both revenues and net income will be overstated by $800 in the October income statement. On the October 31 balance sheet, liabilities will also be understated by $800, and owner's equity will be overstated by $800.

A comparison of the entries and accounts for service revenue and unearned revenue is presented below:

| Unearned Revenue Credited to Liability Account (as in chapter) | | | | Unearned Revenue Credited to Revenue Account (as in appendix) | | | |
|---|---|---|---|---|---|---|---|
| Oct. 4 | Cash | 1,200 | | Oct. 4 | Cash | 1,200 | |
| | Unearned Revenue | | 1,200 | | Service Revenue | | 1,200 |
| 31 | Unearned Revenue | 400 | | 31 | Service Revenue | 800 | |
| | Service Revenue | | 400 | | Unearned Revenue | | 800 |

After posting the entries, the accounts will show:

| Unearned Revenue Credited to Liability Account (as in chapter) | | | | Unearned Revenue Credited to Revenue Account (as in appendix) | | | |
|---|---|---|---|---|---|---|---|
| Unearned Revenue | | | | Unearned Revenue | | | |
| Oct. 31 Adj. | 400 | Oct. 4 | 1,200 | | | Oct. 31 Adj. | 800 |
| | | Oct. 31 Bal. | 800 | | | | |
| Service Revenue | | | | Service Revenue | | | |
| | | Oct. 31 Adj. | 400 | Oct. 31 Adj. | 800 | Oct. 4 | 1,200 |
| | | | | | | Oct. 31 Bal. | 400 |

Note that the balances in the accounts are the same under the two alternatives (Unearned Revenue $800, and Service Revenue $400).

Alternative adjusting entries do not apply to accruals or estimates because no entries occur before these types of adjusting entries are made.

# Demonstration Problem

Julie Szo opens the Green Thumb Lawn Care Company on April 1. At April 30, the trial balance shows the following balances for selected accounts:

| | |
|---|---|
| Prepaid Insurance | $ 3,600 |
| Equipment | 28,000 |
| Notes Payable | 20,000 |
| Unearned Revenue | 4,200 |
| Service Revenue | 1,800 |

Analysis reveals the following additional data about these accounts:

1. Prepaid insurance is the cost of a 12-month insurance policy, effective April 1.
2. The equipment is expected to have a useful life of four years.
3. The note payable is dated April 1. It is a six-month, 4% note.
4. Seven customers paid for the company's six-month lawn-service package of $600, beginning in April. These customers were serviced in April.
5. Lawn services performed for other customers but not recorded at April 30 totalled $1,500.

*Instructions*

Prepare the adjusting entries for the month of April. Show calculations.

## Solution to Demonstration Problem

Additional Demonstration Problems

| GENERAL JOURNAL | | | | J2 |
|---|---|---|---|---|
| Date | Account Titles and Explanation | Ref. | Debit | Credit |
| | *Adjusting Entries* | | | |
| Apr. 30 | Insurance Expense | | 300 | |
| |   Prepaid Insurance | | | 300 |
| |     To record insurance expired: $3,600 ÷ 12 = $300 per month. | | | |
| 30 | Amortization Expense | | 583 | |
| |   Accumulated Amortization—Equipment | | | 583 |
| |     To record monthly amortization: $28,000 ÷ 4 = $7,000 ÷ 12 = $583 per month. | | | |
| 30 | Interest Expense | | 67 | |
| |   Interest Payable | | | 67 |
| |     To accrue interest on notes payable: $20,000 × 4% × $\frac{1}{12}$ = $67. | | | |
| 30 | Unearned Revenue | | 700 | |
| |   Service Revenue | | | 700 |
| |     To record service revenue: $600 ÷ 6 months = $100; $100 per month × 7 customers = $700. | | | |
| 30 | Accounts Receivable | | 1,500 | |
| |   Service Revenue | | | 1,500 |
| |     To accrue revenue earned but not billed or collected. | | | |

**Action Plan**

- Note that adjustments are being made for one month.
- Look at how the amounts are currently recorded in the accounts before trying to determine what adjustments are necessary.
- Select account titles carefully. Use existing titles whenever possible.
- Determine what the balance in the ledger accounts will be after the adjusting entries are posted. Make sure the adjustment is made in the right direction to result in the desired balance.

# Summary of Study Objectives

1. *Explain the time period assumption, revenue recognition principle, and matching principle.* The time period assumption divides the economic life of a business into artificial time periods. The revenue recognition principle states that revenue should be recognized (recorded) in the accounting period in which it is earned. The matching principle states that expenses should be recognized (recorded) when they make their contribution to revenues.

2. *Explain the accrual basis of accounting.* The accrual basis of accounting means that events that change a company's financial statements are recorded in the periods in which the events occur, rather than in the periods in which the company receives or pays cash.

3. *Explain why adjusting entries are needed and identify the major types of adjusting entries.* Adjusting entries are made at the end of an accounting period. They ensure that revenues are recorded in the period in which they are earned. Expenses are recognized in the period in which services or goods are used or consumed, in order to match expenses with revenues. The major types of adjusting entries are prepayments (prepaid expenses and unearned revenues), accruals (accrued revenues and accrued expenses), and estimates (e.g., amortization).

4. *Identify and prepare adjusting entries for prepayments.* Prepayments are either prepaid expenses or unearned revenues. Adjusting entries for prepayments record the portion of the prepayment that applies to the expense or revenue of the current accounting period. The adjusting entry for prepaid expenses debits (increases) an expense account and credits (decreases) an asset account. The adjusting entry for unearned revenues debits (decreases) a liability account and credits (increases) a revenue account.

5. *Identify and prepare adjusting entries for accruals.* Accruals are either accrued revenues or accrued expenses.

Adjusting entries for accruals record revenues and expenses applicable to the current accounting period that have not yet been recognized through daily journal entries. The adjusting entry for an accrued revenue debits (increases) a receivable account and credits (increases) a revenue account. The adjusting entry for an accrued expense debits (increases) an expense account and credits (increases) a liability account.

6. *Identify and prepare the adjusting entry for amortization.* Amortization is the process of allocating the cost of a long-lived asset to expense over the periods when the asset provides benefits. The journal entry is a debit to amortization expense and a credit to accumulated amortization, a contra asset account.

7. *Describe the nature and purpose of an adjusted trial balance and prepare one.* An adjusted trial balance shows the balances of all accounts, including those that have been adjusted, at the end of an accounting period. Its purpose is to show the effects of all financial events that have occurred during the accounting period. An adjusted trial balance makes it easier to prepare the financial statements.

8. *Identify and prepare adjusting entries for the alternative treatment of prepayments (Appendix 3A).* Prepayments may initially be debited (increased) to an expense account. Unearned revenues may initially be credited (increased) to a revenue account. At the end of the period, these accounts may be overstated. The adjusting entries for prepaid expenses are a debit (increase) to an asset account and a credit (decrease) to an expense account. Adjusting entries for unearned revenues are a debit (decrease) to a revenue account and a credit (increase) to a liability account. It does not matter which alternative is used to record and adjust prepayments, as the ending account balances should be the same under each.

# Glossary

Key Term Matching Activity

**Accrual basis of accounting** Accounting basis in which transactions are recorded in the period in which the events occur. Revenues are recorded when earned. Expenses are recorded in the same period as the revenue to which they are related. (p. 102)

**Accrued expenses** Expenses incurred but not yet paid in cash or recorded. (p. 110)

**Accrued revenues** Revenues earned but not yet received in cash or recorded. (p. 109)

**Adjusted trial balance** A list of accounts and their balances after all adjustments have been made. (p. 117)

**Adjusting entries** Entries made at the end of an accounting period to ensure that the time period assump-

tion and the revenue recognition and matching principles are followed. (p. 103)

**Amortization** The allocation of the cost of a long-lived asset to expense over its useful life in a rational and systematic manner. (p. 113)

**Cash basis of accounting** Accounting basis in which transactions are recorded in the period in which cash is received or paid. Revenue is recorded when cash is received. An expense is recorded when cash is paid. (p. 102)

**Contra account** An account that is offset against another account on the income statement or balance sheet. (p. 114)

**Fiscal year** An accounting period that is one year in length. It does not need to coincide with the calendar year. (p. 101)

**Interim periods** Accounting time periods of less than one year in duration. (p. 101)

**Matching principle** The principle that efforts (expenses) should be matched with accomplishments (revenues). (p. 101)

**Net book value** The difference between the cost of an amortizable asset and its accumulated amortization; in other words, it is the unallocated or unexpired portion of the amortizable asset's cost. (p. 114)

**Prepaid expenses** Expenses paid in cash and recorded as assets before they are used or consumed. (p. 105)

**Revenue recognition principle** The principle that revenue should be recognized in the accounting period in which it is earned. (p. 101)

**Time period assumption** An assumption that the economic life of a business can be divided into artificial time periods: normally a month, quarter, or year. (p. 101)

**Unearned revenues** Revenues received in cash and recorded as liabilities before they are earned. (p. 107)

*Note*: All Questions, Exercises, and Problems below with an asterisk (*) relate to material in Appendix 3A.

# Self-Study Questions

Chapter 3 Self-Test

Answers are at the end of the chapter.

(SO 1) K  1. The time period assumption states that:
(a) revenue should be recognized in the accounting period in which it is earned.
(b) expenses should be matched with revenues.
(c) the economic life of a business can be divided into artificial time periods.
(d) the fiscal year should correspond with the calendar year.

(SO 1) K  2. The principle which states that efforts (expenses) should be recorded in the same period as the related accomplishments (revenues) is the:
(a) matching principle.
(b) cost principle.
(c) time period assumption.
(d) revenue recognition principle.

(SO 2) K  3. Which of the following statements about the accrual basis of accounting is false?
(a) Expenses are recorded when goods or services are used or consumed.
(b) Revenue is recognized in the period in which it is earned.
(c) The accrual basis is in accordance with generally accepted accounting principles.
(d) Revenue is recorded only when cash is received, and expenses are recorded only when cash is paid.

(SO 3) K  4. Adjusting entries are made to ensure that:
(a) expenses are matched to revenues in the period in which the revenue is generated.
(b) revenues are recorded in the period in which they are earned.
(c) balance sheet and income statement accounts have up-to-date balances at the end of an accounting period.
(d) All of the above.

(SO 4) AP  5. The trial balance shows Supplies $1,350 and Supplies Expense $0. If $600 of supplies are on hand at the end of the period, the adjusting entry is:

| | | |
|---|---|---|
| (a) Supplies | 600 | |
| Supplies Expense | | 600 |
| (b) Supplies | 750 | |
| Supplies Expense | | 750 |
| (c) Supplies Expense | 750 | |
| Supplies | | 750 |
| (d) Supplies Expense | 600 | |
| Supplies | | 600 |

(SO 4) K  6. Adjustments for unearned revenues:
(a) decrease liabilities and increase revenues.
(b) increase liabilities and increase revenues.
(c) increase assets and increase revenues.
(d) decrease revenues and decrease assets.

(SO 5) K  7. Adjustments for accrued revenues:
(a) increase assets and increase liabilities.
(b) increase assets and increase revenues.
(c) decrease assets and decrease revenues.
(d) decrease liabilities and increase revenues.

(SO 5) AP  8. Kathy Kiska earned a salary of $400 for the last week of September. She will be paid in October. The adjusting entry for Kathy's employer at September 30 is:

| | | |
|---|---|---|
| (a) Salaries Expense | 400 | |
| Salaries Payable | | 400 |
| (b) Salaries Expense | 400 | |
| Cash | | 400 |
| (c) Salaries Payable | 400 | |
| Cash | | 400 |
| (d) No entry is required. | | |

(SO 6) K    9. Accumulated Amortization is:
(a) an expense account.
(b) an owner's equity account.
(c) a liability account.
(d) a contra asset account.

(SO 7) K    10. Which of the following statements about the adjusted trial balance is *incorrect*?
(a) An adjusted trial balance proves the equality of the total debit balances and the total credit balances in the ledger after all adjustments are made.
(b) The adjusted trial balance provides the primary basis for the preparation of financial statements.
(c) The adjusted trial balance lists the account balances divided into assets and liabilities.
(d) The adjusted trial balance is prepared after the adjusting entries have been journalized and posted.

*11. The trial balance shows Supplies $0 and Supplies Expense $1,350. If $600 of supplies are on hand at the end of the period, the adjusting entry is:    (SO 8) AP

| (a) Supplies | 600 | |
| Supplies Expense | | 600 |
| (b) Supplies Expense | 750 | |
| Supplies | | 750 |
| (c) Supplies | 750 | |
| Supplies Expense | | 750 |
| (d) Supplies Expense | 600 | |
| Supplies | | 600 |

# Questions

(SO 1) C    1. (a) How does the time period assumption affect an accountant's analysis of business transactions?
(b) Explain the terms "fiscal year," "calendar year," and "interim period."

(SO 1) C    2. The Higher Education College collects tuition for the fall term from registered students on the first day of classes in September. The fall term runs from September to December. In what month(s) should the college recognize the revenue earned from tuition fees? Explain your reasoning.

(SO 1) C    3. Pierce Dussault, a lawyer, accepts a legal engagement in March, performs the work in April, and is paid in May. If Dussault's law firm prepares monthly financial statements, when should it recognize revenue from this engagement? Why?

(SO 1) C    4. In completing the engagement in question 3, Dussault incurred $500 of salary expenses specifically related to this engagement in March, $2,500 in April, and none in May. How much expense should be deducted from revenue in the month(s) the revenue is recognized? Why?

(SO 2) C    5. How does the cash basis of accounting differ from the accrual basis of accounting? Which method provides decision-makers with more useful information about the company? Why?

(SO 3) C    6. Why are adjusting entries needed? Include in your explanation a description of the assumption and two generally accepted accounting principles that relate to adjusting the accounts.

(SO 3) C    7. Financial statements are usually prepared as at the end of the month or fiscal year. Is it always possible to prepare and record adjusting entries on the last day of the month or year? If not, explain why and describe how accountants compensate for this problem.

8. Why might a trial balance not contain up-to-date and complete financial information?    (SO 3) C

9. Identify the five types of adjustments and explain, for each type, the reason an adjustment is required.    (SO 3) C

10. The name Prepaid Expense implies that this type of account is an expense and belongs on an income statement. Instead the account appears on the balance sheet as an asset. Using the definition of an asset, explain why this is appropriate. What does the balance in this account represent?    (SO 4) C

11. The name Unearned Revenue implies that this type of account is a revenue and belongs on the income statement. Instead the account appears on the balance sheet as a liability. Using the definition of a liability, explain why this is appropriate. What does the balance in this account represent?    (SO 4) C

12. A company has revenue earned but not yet received or recorded. Explain why it is necessary to make an adjusting entry. Which accounts are debited and which are credited in the adjusting entry?    (SO 3, 5) C

13. A company has a utility expense that has been incurred but not yet paid or recorded. Explain why it is necessary to make an adjusting entry. Which accounts are debited and which are credited in the adjusting entry?    (SO 3, 5) C

14. A company makes an accrued revenue adjusting entry for $900 and an accrued expense adjusting entry for $600. Which financial statement items were overstated or understated before these entries? Explain.    (SO 5) AP

15. "Amortization is a valuation process that results in the reporting of the market value of the asset." Do you agree? Explain.    (SO 6) C

16. Explain the difference between amortization expense and accumulated amortization.    (SO 6) C

(SO 6) C  17. What is a contra account? Why do we use a contra account to record accumulated amortization instead of directly reducing the long-lived asset?

(SO 6) AP  18. Cheung Company purchased equipment for $12,000. Annual amortization expense is $4,000. Show the presentation of the equipment and the accumulated amortization on the balance sheet at the end of the first and second fiscal years.

(SO 4, 5, 6) C  19. For each of the following items before adjustment, indicate the type of adjusting entry (prepaid expense, unearned revenue, accrued revenue, accrued expense, estimate) that is needed to correct the misstatement. If an item could result in more than one type of adjusting entry, indicate each of the types.
(a) Assets are understated.
(b) Liabilities are overstated.
(c) Liabilities are understated.
(d) Expenses are understated.
(e) Assets are overstated.
(f) Revenue is understated.

(SO 4, 5, 6) K  20. One half of the adjusting entry is given below. Indicate the account title for the other half of the entry.

(a) Salaries Expense is debited.
(b) Amortization Expense is debited.
(c) Interest Payable is credited.
(d) Supplies is credited.
(e) Accounts Receivable is debited.
(f) Unearned Revenue is debited.

(SO 4, 5, 6) C  21. "An adjusting entry may affect more than one balance sheet or income statement account." Do you agree? Why or why not?

(SO 7) C  22. What is the purpose of preparing an adjusted trial balance? What is it used for?

(SO 7) C  23. Net income is shown on the income statement and the statement of owner's equity. It is also indirectly included on the balance sheet. Do you agree or disagree? Why?

(SO 8) C  *24. Some companies debit an expense account at the time the expense is prepaid instead of debiting an asset account. Will this result in a different net income or different amount of total assets on the balance sheet than if they had instead debited an asset account at the time the amount was paid?

# Brief Exercises

**BE3–1**  Calculate the missing information in each of the following independent situations:

Calculate missing data for supplies.
(SO 4) AP

|  | A Co. | B Co. | C Co. | D Co. |
|---|---|---|---|---|
| Supplies on hand, May 31, 2004 | $ 475 | $ 875 | $ 640 | $   ? |
| Supplies purchased during the year | 1,695 | ? | 2,865 | 2,970 |
| Supplies on hand, May 31, 2005 | 250 | 1,295 | ? | 1,190 |
| Supplies used during the year | ? | 2,810 | 2,715 | 3,295 |

**BE3–2**  Spahn Cleaning Company had $745 of cleaning supplies on hand on January 1, 2005. During 2005 it purchased additional cleaning supplies for $3,680 on credit. On December 31, 2005, there were $830 of cleaning supplies on hand.

Prepare and post transaction and adjusting entries for supplies.
(SO 4) AP

(a) Prepare the journal entry to record the purchase of supplies during the year.
(b) Calculate the amount of cleaning supplies used during the year.
(c) Prepare the adjusting journal entry required at December 31, 2005.
(d) Using T accounts, enter the January 1, 2005, balance in Cleaning Supplies and Cleaning Supplies Expense, post the two journal entries, and indicate the adjusted balance in each account.

**BE3–3**  On June 1, 2004, Bere Co. paid $9,780 for a one-year insurance policy. Bere Co. has a December 31 fiscal year end.

Prepare and post transaction and adjusting entries for insurance.
(SO 4) AP

(a) Prepare the June 1, 2004, journal entry.
(b) Calculate the amount expiring per month and the number of months remaining in the policy at December 31, 2004.
(c) Calculate the amount of insurance that expired during 2004 and the unexpired cost as at December 31, 2004.
(d) Prepare the adjusting entry on December 31, 2004.
(e) Using T accounts, post the above two entries and indicate the adjusted balance in each account.

**Prepare and post transactions and adjusting entries for unearned revenue.**
(SO 4) AP

**BE3–4**  On August 1, 2004, the Hindi Insurance Co. received $1,560 cash from Savita Verma for a one-year insurance policy. Hindi Insurance Co. has a December 31 fiscal year end. Complete the following for Hindi Insurance Co.:

(a) Prepare the August 1, 2004, journal entry.
(b) Calculate the amount earned per month and the number of months remaining in the policy at December 31, 2004.
(c) Calculate the amount of revenue earned during 2004 and the amount unearned at December 31, 2004.
(d) Prepare the adjusting entry on December 31, 2004.
(e) Using T accounts, post the above two entries and indicate the adjusted balance in each account.

**Prepare and post transactions and adjusting entries for accrued revenue.**
(SO 5) AP

**BE3–5**  Zieborg Maintenance Co. has a $375 monthly contract with Crispy Treat Co. for general maintenance services. Zieborg invoices Crispy on the first of the month for the previous month's services provided. Crispy must then pay for the previous month's services by the 10th of the following month.

(a) Zieborg has a November 30 fiscal year end. Why will it need to prepare an adjusting entry on November 30?
(b) Prepare Zieborg's adjusting entry.
(c) Will Zieborg need to record a journal entry on December 1 when it invoices Crispy? Why or why not?
(d) Zieborg receives $375 from Crispy on December 9 for services provided in November. Prepare Zieborg's journal entry.

**Prepare transaction and adjusting entries for salaries.**
(SO 5) AP

**BE3–6**  The total payroll for Classic Autos Co. is $5,000 every Friday ($1,000 per day) for employee salaries earned during a five-day week (Monday through Friday, inclusive). Salaries were last paid on Friday, December 28. This year the company's fiscal year end, December 31, falls on a Monday. Salaries will be paid next on Friday, January 4, at which time employees will receive pay for the five-day work week (including the New Year's holiday). Prepare the journal entries required to record the following:

(a) The payment of salaries on December 28
(b) The adjusting journal entry to accrue salaries at year end
(c) The payment of salaries on January 4

**Prepare transaction and adjusting entries for interest.**
(SO 5) AP

**BE3–7**  On July 1, 2004, a company purchased a truck for use in its business for $40,000, paying $18,000 cash and signing a 6% note payable for the remainder. The interest and principal of the note are due on December 31, 2005. Prepare the journal entry to record the following:

(a) The purchase of the truck on July 1, 2004
(b) The accrual of the interest at the company's December 31, 2004, fiscal year end
(c) The repayment of the interest and note on December 31, 2005

**Prepare transaction and adjusting entries for amortization; show financial statement presentation.**
(SO 6) AP

**BE3–8**  On January 1, 2004, Creed Co. purchased a delivery truck for $45,000 cash. It estimates the truck will have a six-year useful life. Creed Co. has a December 31 fiscal year end.

(a) Prepare the January 1, 2004, journal entry.
(b) Prepare the December 31, 2004, adjusting entry.
(c) Prepare the December 31, 2005, adjusting entry.
(d) Indicate the balance sheet presentation of the delivery truck at December 31, 2004, and at December 31, 2005, and the amount of amortization expense in the 2004 and 2005 income statements.

**Identify the impact transactions have on cash and net income.**
(SO 2, 4, 5, 6) AP

**BE3–9**  Indicate the impact of each of the following transactions on cash and net income. The first transaction has been completed for you as an example.

| Transaction | Cash | Net Income |
| --- | --- | --- |
| 1. Purchased supplies for cash, $100. | –$100 | $0 |
| 2. Recorded the use of $60 of the supplies purchased in (1) in an adjusting journal entry. | | |
| 3. Performed services on account, $1,000. | | |
| 4. Received $800 from customers in payment of their account in (3). | | |
| 5. Purchased office equipment for cash, $500. | | |
| 6. Recorded amortization of office equipment for the period, $10. | | |

**BE3–10** The Riko Company has the following adjustment data at December 31. Indicate (a) the type of adjustment (prepaid expense, unearned revenue, accrued revenue, accrued expense, or amortization), and (b) the status of the accounts before adjustment (overstated or understated).

*Identify types of adjusting entries and account relationships.*
*(SO 4, 5, 6) C*

1. Supplies of $600 are on hand. The unadjusted balance in the Supplies account is $800.
2. Services provided but unbilled total $900.
3. Interest of $200 has accrued on a note payable.
4. Rent collected in advance totalling $800 has been earned.
5. Amortization of $100 is estimated on the office equipment.
6. Prepaid insurance that totals $350 has expired.
7. Salaries of $800 are unpaid and unrecorded.

*BE3–11** Refer to BE3–2. Assume that instead of debiting purchases of cleaning supplies to the Cleaning Supplies account, Spahn Cleaning debits purchases of supplies to the Cleaning Supplies Expense account. Spahn Cleaning Company's trial balance at December 31 shows Cleaning Supplies $745 and Cleaning Supplies Expense $3,680. On December 31, there are $830 of supplies on hand.

*Prepare and post adjusting entry for supplies.*
*(SO 8) AP*

(a) Prepare the adjusting entry at December 31. Using T accounts, enter the balances in the accounts, post the adjusting entry, and indicate the adjusted balance in each account.
(b) Compare the adjusted balances in BE3–2, where an asset account was originally debited, with the adjusted balances in this brief exercise, where an expense account was originally debited. Does it matter whether an original entry is recorded to an asset account or an expense account?

*BE3–12** Paboudjian Apartments receives $600 from a tenant as one month's rent in advance for the month of May.

*Prepare transaction and adjusting entries for unearned revenue.*
*(SO 4, 8) AP*

(a) Assuming the company records all prepayments in balance sheet accounts:
   1. Prepare the original journal entry Paboudjian should record when it receives the rent on May 1.
   2. Prepare the adjusting journal entry Paboudjian should record at the end of May, when the month's rent has been earned.
(b) Assuming the company records all prepayments in income statement accounts:
   1. Prepare the original journal entry Paboudjian should record when it receives the rent on May 1.
   2. Prepare the adjusting journal entry Paboudjian should record at the end of May, when the month's rent has been earned.
(c) Compare and comment upon the ending account balances for each alternative, (a) and (b).

# Exercises

**E3–1** The following independent situations require professional judgement to determine when to recognize revenue from the transactions:

*Identify point of revenue recognition.*
*(SO 1) AP*

(a) **Air Canada** sells you an advance purchase airline ticket in September for your flight home at Christmas.
(b) **Leon's Furniture** sells you a home theatre on a "no money down, no interest, and no payments for one year" promotional deal.
(c) The **Toronto Blue Jays** sell season tickets to games in the Skydome on-line. Fans can purchase the tickets at any time, although the season doesn't officially begin until April. It runs from April through October.
(d) The **RBC Financial Group** loans you money in August. The loan and the interest are repayable in full in November.
(e) In August, you order a sweater from **Sears** using its on-line catalogue. Sears ships the sweater to you in September and you charge it to your Sears credit card. You receive and pay the Sears bill in October.

*Instructions*
Identify when revenue should be recognized in each of the above situations.

Determine income using cash and accrual bases. Comment on usefulness. (SO 2) AP

**E3–2** In its first year of operations, Brisson Company earned $26,000 in service revenue. Of this revenue, $4,000 was on account and the remainder, $22,000, was received in cash from customers.

The company incurred operating expenses of $15,000. Of these expenses, $13,500 was paid in cash. At year end, $1,500 was still owing on account. In addition, Brisson prepaid $2,000 for insurance that covered the last half of the first year and the first half of the second year.

*Instructions*

(a) Calculate the first year's net income under the cash basis of accounting. Calculate the first year's net income under the accrual basis of accounting.
(b) Which basis of accounting (cash or accrual) provides the most useful information for decision-makers?

Prepare and post transaction and adjusting entries for prepayments. (SO 4) AP

Interactive Homework

**E3–3** Action Quest Games initially records all prepaid costs as assets and all revenue collected in advance as liabilities. The following information is available for the year ended December 31, 2005:

1. Purchased a one-year insurance policy on May 1, 2005, for $4,620 cash.
2. Paid $6,875 for five months' rent in advance on October 1, 2005.
3. Signed a contract for cleaning services starting December 1, 2005, for $1,050 per month. Paid for the first three months on December 1.
4. On September 15, 2005, received $3,600 cash from a corporation that sponsors a game each month for the most improved students attending a nearby school. The $3,600 was for nine sessions playing the game on the first Friday of each month starting in October. (Use the account Unearned Revenue.)
5. During the year, sold $1,500 of gift certificates. Determined that on December 31, 2005, $475 of these gift certificates had not yet been redeemed. (Use the account Unearned Gift Certificate Sales.)

*Instructions*

(a) For each of the above, prepare a journal entry to record the initial transaction.
(b) For each of the above, prepare the adjusting journal entry required on December 31, 2005.
(c) Post each of these entries to T accounts and calculate the final balance in each account. (*Note:* Posting to the Cash account is not necessary).

Prepare adjusting and subsequent journal entries for accruals. (SO 5) AP

Interactive Homework

**E3–4** Action Quest Games has the following information available regarding accruals that must be recorded for the year ended December 31, 2005:

1. The December utility bill for $420 was unrecorded on December 31. Action Quest paid the bill on January 17, 2005.
2. Action Quest is open seven days a week and employees are paid a total of $3,360 every Thursday. December 31, 2005, is a Saturday so employees will have worked two days since their last pay day. (The weekly amount can be divided by seven to calculate the daily rate.) Employees will be paid next on January 5, 2006.
3. Action Quest has a 6% note payable with its bank for $45,000. Interest is payable on a monthly basis on the first of the month.
4. Action Quest receives a 5% commission from Pizza Shop next door for all pizzas sold to customers using Action Quest's facility. The amount owing for December is $920, which Pizza Shop will pay on January 4, 2006.
5. Action Quest sold some equipment on November 1, 2005, in exchange for a $6,000, 8% note receivable. The principal and interest are due on February 1, 2006.

*Instructions*

(a) For each of the above, prepare the adjusting entry required at December 31, 2005.
(b) For each of the above, prepare the journal entry to record the subsequent cash transaction in 2006. Assume all payments and receipts are made as indicated.

Prepare transaction and adjusting entries. (SO 4, 5) AP

**E3–5** Selected accounts of the Nie Company are shown below:

| Supplies Expense | | | | Salaries Payable | | |
|---|---|---|---|---|---|---|
| July 31 | 500 | | | | July 31 | 1,200 |

| Supplies | | | | Unearned Revenue | | |
|---|---|---|---|---|---|---|
| July 1 Bal. | 1,100 | July 31 | 500 | July 31 | 900 | July 1 Bal. | 1,500 |
| 10 | 200 | | | | | 20 | 700 |

| Accounts Receivable | | | Service Revenue | | |
|---|---|---|---|---|---|
| July 31 | 500 | | | July 14 | 1,200 |
| | | | | 31 | 900 |
| Salaries Expense | | | | 31 | 500 |
| July 15 | 1,200 | | | | |
| 31 | 1,200 | | | | |

## Instructions

After analysing the accounts, journalize (a) the July transactions, and (b) the adjusting entries that were made on July 31. July transactions were all for cash.

**E3–6** A partial adjusted trial balance of the Thietke Company at January 31, 2005, shows the following:

*Analyse adjusted data.*
*(SO 4, 5) AP*

**THIETKE COMPANY**
**Adjusted Trial Balance**
**January 31, 2005**

| | Debit | Credit |
|---|---|---|
| Supplies | $ 700 | |
| Prepaid insurance | 2,400 | |
| Salaries payable | | $ 800 |
| Unearned revenue | | 750 |
| Supplies expense | 950 | |
| Insurance expense | 400 | |
| Salaries expense | 1,800 | |
| Service revenue | | 2,000 |

## Instructions

Answer the following questions, assuming the company's fiscal year begins January 1:

(a) If the amount in Supplies Expense is the January 31 adjusting entry, and $850 of supplies was purchased in January, what was the balance in Supplies on January 1?

(b) If the amount in Insurance Expense is the January 31 adjusting entry, and the original insurance premium was for one year, what was the total premium, and when was the policy purchased?

(c) If $2,500 of salaries was paid in January, what was the balance in Salaries Payable at December 31, 2004?

(d) If $1,600 was received in January for services performed in January, what was the balance in Unearned Revenue at December 31, 2004?

**E3–7** The following information is available regarding Hallal Company:

*Prepare transaction and adjusting entries, and determine amounts to be presented in the financial statements.*
*(SO 4, 5) AP*

1. On its December 31, 2003, balance sheet, the company had prepaid rent of $20,000 ($4,000 per month), which covered the period January 1–May 31, 2004.

2. On May 1, 2004, it negotiated a new lease agreement that covered a three-year period at a rent of $5,000 per month, effective June 1, and immediately paid a "security deposit" of $5,000. This amount will be refunded to the company after the termination of the lease (only, of course, if the premises are in reasonable condition when vacated).

3. On June 1, 2004, Hallal Company paid the rent for the first six months of the new lease ($30,000) in advance.

4. On December 1, the $30,000 rent payment for the next six months (i.e., for the period December 1, 2004–May 31, 2005) was due. However, because of an administrative error, this was not actually paid until January 2, 2005.

## Instructions

(a) Prepare general journal entries to record the 2004 transactions.

(b) Prepare any adjusting journal entries required to update the rent accounts at December 31, 2004.

(c) How much rent expense should be reported on the company's income statement for the year ending December 31, 2004?

(d) Indicate what (if anything) should be reported about rent on Hallal Company's balance sheet as at December 31, 2004. Be specific.

Prepare adjusting entries for amortization; calculate accumulated amortization and net book value.
(SO 6) AP

**E3–8** Action Quest Games owns the following long-lived assets:

| Asset | Date Purchased | Estimated Useful Life | Cost |
|---|---|---|---|
| Furniture | January 1, 2005 | 3 years | $ 9,600 |
| Lighting equipment | January 1, 2003 | 8 years | 18,000 |
| Computer equipment | December 31, 2003 | 4 years | 11,600 |

*Instructions*

(a) Prepare amortization adjusting entries for Action Quest Games for the year ended December 31, 2005.

(b) For each asset, calculate its accumulated amortization and net book value at December 31, 2005.

Prepare adjusting entries.
(SO 4, 5, 6) AP

**E3–9** The ledger of Bourque Rental Agency on March 31 of the current year includes the following selected accounts before adjusting entries have been prepared:

| | Debit | Credit |
|---|---|---|
| Prepaid insurance | $ 3,600 | |
| Supplies | 2,800 | |
| Equipment | 24,000 | |
| Accumulated amortization—equipment | | $ 6,400 |
| Notes payable | | 20,000 |
| Unearned rent revenue | | 9,300 |
| Rent revenue | | 60,000 |
| Wage expense | 14,000 | |

An analysis of the accounts shows the following:

1. The equipment is amortized at the rate of $400 per month.
2. One-third of the unearned rent was earned during the quarter.
3. Interest of $500 is accrued on the notes payable.
4. Supplies on hand total $850.
5. Insurance expires at the rate of $300 per month.

*Instructions*

Prepare the adjusting entries at March 31, assuming that adjusting entries are made quarterly.

Prepare adjusting entries from analysis of trial balances.
(SO 4, 5, 6) AP

**Interactive Homework**

**E3–10** The trial balances before and after adjustment for the Lim Company at the end of its fiscal year are as follows:

**LIM COMPANY**
**Trial Balance**
**August 31, 2005**

| | Before Adjustment | | After Adjustment | |
|---|---|---|---|---|
| | Dr. | Cr. | Dr. | Cr. |
| Cash | $10,400 | | $10,400 | |
| Accounts receivable | 8,800 | | 9,275 | |
| Office supplies | 2,450 | | 700 | |
| Prepaid insurance | 3,775 | | 2,355 | |
| Office equipment | 14,100 | | 14,100 | |
| Accumulated amortization— office equipment | | $ 3,525 | | $ 4,700 |
| Accounts payable | | 5,800 | | 5,800 |
| Salaries payable | | 0 | | 1,125 |
| Unearned rent revenue | | 1,600 | | 700 |
| E. Lim, capital | | 15,600 | | 15,600 |
| Service revenue | | 34,000 | | 34,475 |
| Rent revenue | | 11,000 | | 11,900 |
| Salaries expense | 17,000 | | 18,125 | |
| Office supplies expense | 0 | | 1,750 | |
| Rent expense | 15,000 | | 15,000 | |
| Insurance expense | 0 | | 1,420 | |
| Amortization expense | 0 | | 1,175 | |
| Totals | $71,525 | $71,525 | $74,300 | $74,300 |

*Instructions*

Prepare the adjusting entries that were made.

**E3–11** The adjusted trial balance for the Lim Company is given in E3–10.

*Instructions*

Prepare the income statement and statement of owner's equity for the year, and the balance sheet at August 31, 2005.

Prepare financial statements from adjusted trial balance. (SO 7) AP

*\*E3–12* At the Devereaux Company, prepaid costs are debited to expense when paid, and unearned revenues are credited to revenue when received. During January of the current year, the following transactions occurred:

Prepare and post transaction and adjusting entries for prepayments. (SO 8) AP

Jan.   2  Paid $2,400 for fire insurance protection for the year.
     10  Paid $1,700 for supplies.
     15  Received $5,100 for services to be performed in the future.

On January 31, it is determined that $1,500 of the service revenue has been earned and that there are $800 of supplies on hand.

*Instructions*

(a) Journalize and post the January transactions. Use T accounts.
(b) Journalize and post the adjusting entries at January 31.
(c) Determine the ending balance in each of the accounts.

*\*E3–13* Refer to the information provided in E3–3 for Action Quest Games.

Prepare and post transaction and adjusting entries for prepayments. (SO 8) AP

*Instructions*

(a) For each of the transactions listed in E3–3, prepare a journal entry assuming Action Quest records all prepaid costs as expenses and all revenue collected in advance as revenues.
(b) Prepare the adjusting journal entry on December 31, 2005.
(c) Post each of these entries to T accounts and calculate the final balance in each account. (*Note:* Posting to the Cash account is not necessary).
(d) Compare your balances in (c) above to those obtained in E3–3, part (c). Comment on your findings.

# Problems: Set A

**P3–1A** Ouellette & Associates began operations on January 1, 2005. Its fiscal year end is December 31. It only prepares financial statements and adjusts its accounts annually. Selected transactions during 2005 follow:

Prepare transaction and adjusting entries for prepayments. (SO 4) AP

1. On January 1, 2005, bought office supplies for $4,100 cash. A physical count at December 31, 2005, revealed $900 of supplies still on hand.
2. Bought a $3,780 one-year insurance policy for cash on August 1, 2005. The policy came into effect on this date.
3. On November 15, Ouellette received a $1,200 advance cash payment from a client for accounting services expected to be provided in the future. As at December 31, one-quarter of these services had not been performed.
4. On December 15, the company rented out excess office space for a six-month period starting on this date, and it received a $540 cheque for the first month's rent.

*Instructions*

For each of the above situations, prepare the journal entry for the original transaction and any adjusting journal entry required at December 31, 2005.

Convert income from cash to accrual basis.
(SO 2, 4, 5) AP

**P3–2A** Your examination of the records of a company that uses the cash basis of accounting tells you that the company's reported income in 2004 is $45,000. If this firm had followed accrual basis accounting practices, it would have reported the following year-end balances:

|  | 2004 | 2003 |
|---|---|---|
| Accounts receivable | $3,600 | $2,700 |
| Prepaid insurance | 1,500 | 1,300 |
| Accounts payable | 1,500 | 2,200 |
| Unearned revenues | 1,400 | 1,500 |

*Instructions*

Determine the company's net income on an accrual basis for 2004. Show all your calculations.

Prepare transaction and adjusting entries.
(SO 4, 5, 6) AP

**P3–3A** The following independent situations for the Theatre Brunswick for the year ended December 31, 2004, may require an original journal entry, an adjusting journal entry, or both:

1. Office supplies on hand at the Theatre Brunswick amounted to $1,460 at the beginning of the year. On July 1, additional office supplies were purchased for cash at a cost of $1,720. At the end of the year, a physical count showed that supplies on hand amounted to $990.
2. On January 1, 2004, the theatre purchased a used truck for use in its business for $23,500, paying cash in full. The truck was estimated to have a useful life of five years.
3. Theatre Brunswick has nine plays each season, which start in September 2004 and end in May 2005 (one play per month). Season tickets sell for $135 each and there were 200 sold in August for the upcoming 2004–05 season. Theatre Brunswick credited Unearned Season Ticket Revenue for the full amount received.
4. Theatre Brunswick rents the theatre to a local children's choir which uses the space for rehearsals twice a week at a rate of $500 per month. The choir was short of cash at the beginning of December and sent Theatre Brunswick a cheque for $350 and a promise to pay the balance in January. On January 4, 2005, Theatre Brunswick received a cheque for the balance owing from December plus all of January's rent.
5. At the beginning of March, the theatre borrowed $10,000 from the Bank of Montreal at an annual interest rate of 6.5%. The principal and interest are to be repaid in one years' time.
6. Every Wednesday, the total payroll for the theatre is $3,000 for employee wages earned during a six-day work week (each employee gets one day off per week). This year, December 31 falls on a Friday. Wages were last paid (and recorded) on Wednesday, December 29. No adjusting entry has yet been recorded for the period December 30-31.
7. Upon reviewing its books on December 31, 2004, the theatre noted that the telephone bill for the month of December had not yet been received. A call to Aliant helped determine that the telephone bill was $375. The bill was paid on January 12.

*Instructions*

Prepare the journal entry (or entries) required to record (a) the original transaction during the year for (1), (2), (3), (4), (5), and (6); (b) the year-end adjusting entry for all of the above; and (c) the cash transactions in 2005 for (4), (5), (6), and (7).

Prepare adjusting entries.
(SO 4, 5, 6) AP

**P3–4A** A review of the ledger of Greenberg Company at December 31, 2004, produces the following important data for the preparation of annual adjusting entries:

1. Prepaid Advertising has a balance of $14,160. This consists of payments on two advertising contracts. The contracts provide for monthly advertising in two trade magazines. The terms of the contracts are as follows:

| Contract | Date | Amount | Number of Magazine Issues |
|---|---|---|---|
| A650 | Apr. 1 | $ 6,240 | 12 |
| B974 | Aug. 1 | 7,920 | 24 |
|  |  | $14,160 |  |

The first advertisement runs in the month in which the contract is signed.

2. Unearned Rent Revenue has a balance of $396,000. The company began subleasing office space in its new building on November 1. Each tenant (nine in total) is required to make a $5,000 security deposit which is refundable after the lease has been satisfactorily ended. At December 31, the company had the following rental contracts that were paid in full for the entire term of the lease:

| Date | Term (in months) | Monthly Rent | Number of Leases | Total Rent Paid |
|---|---|---|---|---|
| Nov. 1 | 6 | $4,500 | 5 | $135,000 |
| Nov. 1 | 6 | 9,000 | 4 | 216,000 |
| | | | | $351,000 |

3. Notes Payable has a balance of $85,000. This consists of a note for one year at an annual interest rate of 8%, dated June 1.
4. Salaries Payable has a balance of $0. There are nine salaried employees. Salaries are paid every Saturday for a six-day work week (Monday–Saturday). Six employees receive a salary of $750 per week, and three employees earn $550 per week. December 31 is a Friday.
5. The company has two delivery trucks. The first, purchased on January 2, 2001, has an estimated five-year useful life and cost $32,000. The second, purchased June 1, 2002, has an estimated six-year useful life and cost $39,900.

*Instructions*

Prepare the adjusting entries at December 31, 2004. Show all your calculations.

**P3–5A** During the first week of January 2005, Chisata Moritaka began an interior design business, Exotic Designs. She kept no formal accounting records; however, she did keep a list of cash receipts and disbursements. The business was so successful that she required additional financing to keep up. She approached her bank for a loan and was asked to submit a balance sheet and income statement prepared on an accrual basis.

Prepare accrual-based income statement from cash-based information. (SO 2, 4, 5, 6) AP

Knowing very little about accounting, she hired you to prepare the statements the bank wants. She supplied you with the following information for the year ended December 31, 2005:

| | Receipts | Disbursements |
|---|---|---|
| Investment by owner | $28,500 | |
| Equipment | | $17,600 |
| Supplies | | 8,400 |
| Rent payments | | 9,900 |
| Insurance premium | | 1,920 |
| Advertising—all ads completed | | 3,400 |
| Wages of assistant | | 19,900 |
| Telephone | | 1,020 |
| Payments to owner | | 24,000 |
| Design revenue received | 60,270 | |
| | 88,770 | 86,140 |
| Cash balance | | 2,630 |
| | $88,770 | $88,770 |

Additional information:

1. The equipment has an estimated five-year life.
2. Supplies on hand on December 31 were worth $1,630.
3. Rent payments included $750 per month of rent and a $900 deposit refundable at the end of the two-year lease.
4. The insurance premium was for a one-year period expiring on March 31, 2006.
5. Wages earned the last week in December and to be paid in January 2006 amounted to $525.
6. Design revenue earned but not yet collected amounted to $3,950.
7. Chisata used her personal automobile for business purposes, travelling 12,000 km at 30 cents per km. She was not paid for use of her car, but would like to be paid for it.

*Instructions*

(a) Prepare an accrual-based income statement for the year ended December 31, 2005.
(b) Prepare the December 31, 2005, balance sheet.

**Prepare and post adjusting entries, and prepare adjusted trial balance.**
(SO 4, 5, 6, 7) AP

**P3–6A** Atlantic Tours has prepared the following trial balance prior to preparing the month-end adjustments:

**ATLANTIC TOURS**
**Trial Balance**
**June 30, 2005**

| | Debit | Credit |
|---|---|---|
| Cash | $  3,000 | |
| Prepaid insurance | 7,320 | |
| Supplies | 965 | |
| Office equipment | 13,440 | |
| Accumulated amortization—office equipment | | $   3,360 |
| Buses | 140,400 | |
| Accumulated amortization—buses | | 46,800 |
| Accounts payable | | 1,985 |
| Notes payable | | 54,000 |
| Unearned fees | | 14,000 |
| Eldon Kaplan, capital | | 45,000 |
| Eldon Kaplan, drawings | 3,400 | |
| Fees earned | | 17,110 |
| Salaries expense | 9,560 | |
| Advertising expense | 825 | |
| Rent expense | 2,175 | |
| Gas and oil expense | 1,170 | |
| | $182,255 | $182,255 |

Other data:

1. The insurance policy has a one-year term that began June 1, 2005.
2. The office equipment has an estimated useful life of eight years. The buses have an estimated useful life of six years.
3. A physical count shows $240 of supplies on hand at June 30.
4. The note payable has an annual interest rate of 7%. Interest is paid at the start of each month.
5. Deposits of $1,400 each were received for advance tour reservations from 10 school groups. At June 30, three of these deposits have been earned.
6. Bus drivers are paid a combined total of $425 per day. At June 30, three days' salaries are unpaid.
7. A senior citizens' organization that had not made an advance deposit took a Coastal Tour on June 30 for $1,150. This group was not billed for the tour until July 3.
8. Additional advertising costs of $620 have been incurred, but the bills have not been received by June 30. (Use the Accounts Payable account.)

*Instructions*

(a) Journalize the monthly adjusting entries at June 30, 2005.
(b) Prepare a ledger. Enter the trial balance amounts and post the adjusting entries.
(c) Prepare an adjusted trial balance at June 30, 2005.

**Prepare and post adjusting entries, and prepare adjusted trial balance and financial statements.**
(SO 4, 5, 6, 7) AP

**P3–7A** The Highland Cove Resort has a fiscal year end of August 31. The company's trial balance prior to adjustments is listed below:

### HIGHLAND COVE RESORT
### Trial Balance
### August 31, 2005

|  | Debit | Credit |
|---|---|---|
| Cash | $ 18,870 | |
| Prepaid insurance | 6,360 | |
| Supplies | 3,495 | |
| Land | 25,000 | |
| Cottages | 145,000 | |
| Accumulated amortization—cottages | | $ 34,800 |
| Furniture | 28,600 | |
| Accumulated amortization—furniture | | 10,725 |
| Accounts payable | | 6,500 |
| Unearned rent revenue | | 36,200 |
| Mortgage payable | | 60,000 |
| Keath Yhap, capital | | 85,000 |
| Keath Yhap, drawings | 44,000 | |
| Rent revenue | | 247,500 |
| Salaries expense | 153,000 | |
| Interest expense | 4,400 | |
| Utilities expense | 37,600 | |
| Repair expense | 14,400 | |
| | $480,725 | $480,725 |

Other data:

1. The insurance policy was purchased on May 31, 2005, and expires on May 31, 2006.
2. A count of supplies on August 31 shows $760 of supplies on hand.
3. The cottages have an estimated useful life of 25 years.
4. The furniture has an estimated useful life of eight years.
5. Customers must pay a $100 deposit if they wish to book a cottage during peak times. An analysis of these bookings indicates 362 deposits were received (all credited to Unearned Rent Revenue) and all but 45 of the deposits have been earned by August 31, 2005.
6. The mortgage interest rate is 8% per year. Interest has been paid to July 31, 2005.
7. Salaries accrued to the end of August were $1,100.
8. The August utility bill of $1,840 is unrecorded and unpaid.
9. On August 25, a local business contracted with Highland Cove to rent one of the cottages for six months starting October 1 at a rate of $1,500 per month. An advance payment equal to two months' rent is to be paid on September 5.
10. On August 31, Highland Cove has earned $1,360 of rent revenue from customers who are currently using the cottages but won't pay the amount owing until they check out in September. This amount is in addition to any deposits earned in item (5) above.

*Instructions*

(a) Journalize the adjusting entries on August 31.
(b) Prepare a ledger, enter the trial balance amounts, and post the adjusting entries.
(c) Prepare an adjusted trial balance at August 31.
(d) Prepare an income statement and a statement of owner's equity for the year ended August 31, and a balance sheet as at August 31, 2005.

Prepare adjusting entries
and financial statements.
(SO 4, 5, 6, 7) AP

**P3–8A** The adjusted and unadjusted trial balances of the Yount Advertising Agency as at December 31, 2005, are shown below:

**YOUNT ADVERTISING AGENCY**
**Trial Balance**
**December 31, 2005**

| | Unadjusted Dr. | Unadjusted Cr. | Adjusted Dr. | Adjusted Cr. |
|---|---|---|---|---|
| Cash | $ 11,000 | | $ 11,000 | |
| Accounts receivable | 18,650 | | 19,750 | |
| Art supplies | 7,200 | | 1,265 | |
| Prepaid insurance | 2,352 | | 980 | |
| Printing equipment | 66,000 | | 66,000 | |
| Accumulated amortization | | $ 28,500 | | $ 34,000 |
| Accounts payable | | 4,202 | | 4,852 |
| Interest payable | | 0 | | 300 |
| Note payable | | 10,000 | | 10,000 |
| Unearned advertising revenue | | 7,100 | | 6,200 |
| Salaries payable | | 0 | | 1,625 |
| T. Yount, capital | | 37,800 | | 37,800 |
| T. Yount, drawings | 22,000 | | 22,000 | |
| Advertising revenue | | 59,450 | | 61,450 |
| Salaries expense | 12,000 | | 13,625 | |
| Insurance expense | 0 | | 1,372 | |
| Interest expense | 700 | | 1,000 | |
| Amortization expense | 0 | | 5,500 | |
| Art supplies expense | 0 | | 5,935 | |
| Rent expense | 7,150 | | 7,800 | |
| | $147,052 | $147,052 | $156,227 | $156,227 |

*Instructions*

(a) Journalize the annual adjusting entries that were made.
(b) Prepare an income statement and a statement of owner's equity for the year ended December 31, 2005, and a balance sheet at December 31.
(c) Calculate the annual interest rate on the note. The note payable has been outstanding for 10 months.
(d) Determine the balance in Salaries Payable on December 31, 2004. The company paid $15,500 in salaries in 2005.

Prepare and post adjusting
entries; prepare adjusted
trial balance and financial
statements; and comment.
(SO 4, 5, 6, 7) AP

**P3–9A** On the next page is an alphabetical list of Scholz Consulting Co.'s accounts at its fiscal year end of March 31, 2005, prior to adjustments.

**SCHOLZ CONSULTING CO.**
**Trial Balance**
**March 31, 2005**

| | Debit | Credit |
|---|---|---|
| Accounts payable | | $ 3,495 |
| Accounts receivable | $ 7,270 | |
| Accumulated amortization—computer equipment | | 2,465 |
| Accumulated amortization—furniture | | 878 |
| Cash | 2,985 | |
| Computer equipment | 7,395 | |
| Consulting fees earned | | 106,750 |
| Furniture | 8,780 | |
| Greta Scholz, capital | | 12,672 |
| Greta Scholz, drawings | 59,500 | |
| Note payable | | 5,500 |
| Prepaid insurance | 1,980 | |
| Rent expense | 9,625 | |
| Salaries expense | 33,475 | |
| Supplies | 3,290 | |
| Telephone expense | 1,700 | |
| Unearned consulting fees | | 4,240 |
| | $136,000 | $136,000 |

Other data:

1. A one-year insurance policy was purchased on May 31, 2004.
2. On March 31, 2004, there were $845 of supplies on hand. During the year, $2,445 of additional supplies were purchased. A count of supplies on March 31, 2005 shows $710 of supplies on hand.
3. The computer equipment has an estimated useful life of three years.
4. The furniture has an estimated useful life of 10 years.
5. As at March 31, 2005, an analysis shows $1,825 of the unearned consulting fees were still unearned.
6. On December 1, 2004, the company obtained a nine-month, 7.5% note payable for $5,500. Interest and principal are due on the maturity date.
7. Salaries accrued to March 31 were $655.
8. On March 15 the company signed a contract to provide consulting services to Xendor Inc., starting April 1, 2005. The contract is for three months at a rate of $4,100 per month. Payment is due at the start of each month.
9. On March 31, 2005, the company had earned but not billed or received consulting revenue of $2,675.
10. Rent of $875 for March 2005 had not been recorded or paid.

*Instructions*

(a) Prepare adjusting journal entries for the year ended March 31, 2005, as required.
(b) Prepare an adjusted trial balance in financial statement account order.
(c) Prepare an income statement and statement of owner's equity for the year ended March 31, 2005, and a balance sheet at March 31, 2005.
(d) Comment on the company's results of operations and financial position. Include specific references to items in the financial statements in your analysis.

*P3–10A In P3–1A, when journal entries were originally recorded for Ouellette & Associates, prepaid costs were debited to an asset account and unearned revenues were credited to a liability account. This problem repeats P3–1A, assuming instead that prepaid costs are debited originally to an expense account and unearned revenues credited to a revenue account.

Prepare transaction and adjusting entries for prepayments.
(SO 8) AP

*Instructions*

Prepare the journal entry for the original transaction and any adjusting journal entry required at December 31, 2005, for each of the situations outlined in P3–1A, assuming this alternative treatment of prepaid expenses and unearned revenues.

Prepare adjusting entries,
adjusted trial balance, and
financial statements.
(SO 7, 8) AP

*P3–11A  The Global Graphics Company was organized on January 1, 2005, by Betty Batke. Global Graphics records all prepayments in income statement accounts. At the end of the first six months of operations, the trial balance contained the following accounts in alphabetical order:

**GLOBAL GRAPHICS COMPANY**
**Trial Balance**
**June 30, 2005**

|  | Debit | Credit |
|---|---|---|
| Accounts payable |  | $   7,400 |
| Accounts receivable | $  13,000 |  |
| Advertising expense | 1,900 |  |
| Betty Batke, capital |  | 35,000 |
| Betty Batke, drawings | 18,000 |  |
| Cash | 8,500 |  |
| Consulting revenue |  | 5,200 |
| Equipment | 42,500 |  |
| Graphic revenue |  | 54,900 |
| Insurance expense | 2,400 |  |
| Note payable |  | 22,000 |
| Rent expense | 3,500 |  |
| Salaries expense | 29,950 |  |
| Supplies expense | 2,950 |  |
| Utilities expense | 1,800 |  |
|  | $124,500 | $124,500 |

Analysis reveals the following additional data:

1. The $2,950 balance in Supplies Expense represents supplies purchased in January and in May. At June 30, there were $880 of supplies on hand.
2. The note payable was issued on March 1. It is an 8%, six-month note; interest and principal are payable on the maturity date.
3. The balance in Insurance Expense is the premium on a one-year policy that is dated February 1, 2005.
4. At June 30, consulting revenue of $1,250 was unearned.
5. Graphic revenue earned but unbilled at June 30 totals $2,475.
6. Amortization is $8,500 per year.
7. July rent of $500 was paid on June 30 and is included in Rent Expense.

*Instructions*

(a) Journalize the adjusting entries at June 30. (Adjustments are recorded every six months.)
(b) Prepare an adjusted trial balance.
(c) Prepare an income statement and statement of owner's equity for the six months ended June 30, and a balance sheet at June 30, 2005.

# Problems: Set B

Prepare transaction and
adjusting entries for
prepayments.
(SO 4) AP

P3–1B  Burke Bros. began operations on January 1, 2005. Its fiscal year end is December 31. It only prepares financial statements and adjusts its accounts annually. Selected transactions during 2005 follow:

1. On January 1, 2005, bought office supplies for $3,100 cash. A physical count at December 31, 2005, revealed $670 of supplies still on hand.
2. Bought a $5,040 one-year insurance policy for cash on June 1, 2005. The policy came into effect on this date.
3. On November 15, Burke received a $1,275 advance cash payment from three clients for services expected to be provided in the future. As at December 31, services had been performed for two of the clients ($425 each).
4. On December 15, the company paid $4,500 rent in advance for the month of January 2006.

*Instructions*

Prepare the journal entry for the original transaction and any adjusting journal entry required at December 31, 2005, for each of the above situations.

**P3–2B**  Your examination of the records of a company that follows the cash basis of accounting tells you that the company's reported cash basis income in 2004 is $44,800. If the company had followed accrual basis accounting practices, it would have reported the following year-end balances:

*Convert income from cash to accrual basis. (SO 2, 4, 5, 6) AP*

|  | 2004 | 2003 |
|---|---|---|
| Accounts payable | $ 1,810 | $ 1,640 |
| Accounts receivable | 2,900 | 3,200 |
| Accumulated amortization | 17,500 | 15,000 |
| Prepaid insurance | 1,620 | 1,330 |
| Unearned revenues | 1,400 | 1,560 |

*Instructions*

Determine the company's net income on an accrual basis for 2004. Show all your calculations.

**P3–3B**  The following independent situations for the Théâtre Dupuis for the year ended November 30, 2004, may require an original journal entry, an adjusting journal entry, or both:

*Prepare transaction and adjusting entries. (SO 4, 5, 6) AP*

1. Office supplies on hand at Théâtre Dupuis amounted to $500 at the beginning of the year. During the year, additional office supplies were purchased for cash at a cost of $1,550. At the end of the year, a physical count showed that supplies on hand amounted to $300.
2. On December 1, 2003, the theatre purchased a truck for use in its business for $39,000, paying cash in full. The estimated useful life of the truck is four years.
3. Théâtre Dupuis has eight plays each season, which start in October 2004 and end in May 2005 (one play per month). Season tickets sell for $160 each and 150 were sold in September for the upcoming 2004–05 season. Théâtre Dupuis credited Unearned Season Ticket Revenue for the full amount received.
4. At the beginning of June, the theatre borrowed $5,000 from La Caisse Populaire Desjardins at an annual interest rate of 8.5%. The principal and interest are to be repaid in a year's time.
5. Upon reviewing the books on November 30, 2004, it was noted that the utility bill for the month of November had not yet been received. A call to Hydro-Québec revealed that the utility bill was $1,350. The bill was paid on December 10.
6. Théâtre Dupuis rents the theatre to a local seniors' choir which uses the space for rehearsals twice a week at a rate of $400 per month. The new treasurer of the choir accidentally sent a cheque for $40 at the beginning of November. The treasurer promised to send a cheque in December for the balance when she returns from her vacation. On December 4, Théâtre Dupuis received a cheque for the balance owing from November plus all of December's rent.
7. The total payroll for the theatre is $6,000 every two weeks for employee wages earned during a five-day week (Monday through Friday, inclusive). This year, November 30 falls on a Tuesday. Wages were paid (and recorded) on Friday, November 26. No adjusting entry has yet been recorded for the period November 29–30.

*Instructions*

Prepare the journal entry (or entries) required to record (a) the original transaction during the year for (1), (2), (3), (4), (6), and (7); (b) the year-end adjusting entry, for all of the above; and (c) the subsequent cash transactions for (4), (5), (6), and (7).

**P3–4B**  A review of the ledger of the Hashmi Company at December 31, 2004, produces the following data pertaining to the preparation of annual adjusting entries:

*Prepare adjusting entries. (SO 4, 5, 6) AP*

1. Prepaid Insurance has an unadjusted balance of $16,200. The company has separate insurance policies on its buildings and its motor vehicles. Policy B4564 on the building was purchased on July 1, 2004, for $10,320. The policy has a term of two years. Policy A2958 on the vehicles was purchased on January 1, 2004, for $5,880. This policy also has a term of two years.
2. Unearned Subscription Revenue has a balance of $61,200. The company began selling magazine subscriptions in 2004. The selling price of a subscription is $60 for 12 monthly issues. A review of subscription contracts reveals the following:

| Subscription Date | Number of Subscriptions |
|---|---|
| October 1 | 220 |
| November 1 | 310 |
| December 1 | 490 |
| | 1,020 |

3. Salaries Payable has a balance of $0. There are nine salaried employees, each of whom is paid every Monday for the previous week. Six employees receive a salary of $625 each per week, and three employees earn $750 each per week. December 31 is a Friday. Employees do not work weekends. All employees worked the last five days of December.

4. The company has a note receivable issued on September 1, 2004, for $8,000. The annual interest rate is 7.75% and the note matures on June 1, 2005. Interest and principal are to be paid in full on the maturity date.

5. The company owns two buildings. The first, purchased on September 1, 1993, has an estimated 30-year useful life and cost $125,250. The second, purchased on May 1, 2001, has an estimated 40-year useful life and cost $165,000.

*Instructions*

(a) Prepare a calculation to show why the balance (before adjustments) in the Prepaid Insurance account is $16,200.

(b) Prepare the adjusting entries at December 31, 2004. Show all your calculations.

*Prepare accrual-based income statement from cash-based information.*
*(SO 2, 4, 5, 6) AP*

**P3–5B** During the first week of November 2004, Danielle Charron opened a ski tuning and repair shop, The Radical Edge, on a busy ski hill. She didn't do any bookkeeping, but she kept careful track of all her cash receipts and cash payments. She supplies you with the following information at the end of the ski season, April 30, 2005:

| | Cash Receipts | Cash Payments |
|---|---|---|
| Investment by Danielle Charron | $20,000 | |
| Payment for repair equipment | | $ 9,520 |
| Rent payments | | 1,575 |
| Newspaper advertising paid | | 460 |
| Utility bills paid | | 950 |
| Part-time helper's wages paid | | 3,600 |
| Cash receipts from ski and snowboard repair services | 33,250 | |
| Subtotals | 53,250 | 16,105 |
| Cash balance | | 37,145 |
| Totals | $53,250 | $53,250 |

You learn that the repair equipment has an estimated useful life of eight years. The company rents space at a cost of $225 per month on a one-year lease. The lease contract requires payment of the first and last months' rent in advance, which Danielle paid. The part-time helper is owed $120 at April 30, 2005, for unpaid wages. At April 30, 2005, customers owe The Radical Edge $720 for services they have received but have not yet paid for.

*Instructions*

(a) Prepare an accrual basis income statement for the six months ended April 30, 2005.

(b) Prepare the April 30, 2005, balance sheet.

**P3–6B** Orosco Security Service has prepared the following trial balance prior to the preparation of its year-end adjusting entries:

### OROSCO SECURITY SERVICE
### Trial Balance
### December 31, 2005

| | Debit | Credit |
|---|---|---|
| Cash | $ 12,400 | |
| Accounts receivable | 3,200 | |
| Prepaid insurance | 3,804 | |
| Prepaid rent | 1,225 | |
| Supplies | 2,571 | |
| Automobiles | 58,000 | |
| Accumulated amortization—automobiles | | $ 14,500 |
| Office furniture | 16,000 | |
| Accumulated amortization—office furniture | | 4,000 |
| Notes payable | | 46,000 |
| Unearned revenue | | 3,600 |
| C. Orosco, capital | | 56,000 |
| C. Orosco, drawings | 38,400 | |
| Service revenue | | 101,605 |
| Salaries expense | 57,000 | |
| Interest expense | 3,105 | |
| Rent expense | 14,700 | |
| Repair expense | 6,000 | |
| Gas and oil expense | 9,300 | |
| | $225,705 | $225,705 |

Other data:
1. Orosco had provided services totalling $2,750 that were unrecorded because the bills for these services had not yet been prepared.
2. The annual insurance policy of $3,804 was paid on April 1, 2005.
3. A physical count of supplies at December 31, 2005, shows $572 of supplies on hand.
4. The automobiles were purchased on January 2, 2004, and have an estimated useful life of four years.
5. The office furniture was purchased on July 2, 2002, and has an estimated useful life of ten years.
6. Interest on the 9% note payable is paid on the first day of each quarter (January, April, July, and October 1).
7. Drivers' salaries total $225 per day. At December 31, three days' salaries are unpaid.
8. One of Orosco's customers paid for a six-month contract at a rate of $600 per month in advance. The contract began on November 1, 2005, and Orosco credited Unearned Revenue at the time.
9. On December 28, 2005, Orosco paid $1,225 for January 2006 rent.

*Instructions*
(a) Journalize the annual adjusting entries at December 31, 2005.
(b) Prepare a ledger. Enter the trial balance amounts and post the adjusting entries.
(c) Prepare an adjusted trial balance at December 31, 2005.

Prepare and post adjusting
entries, and prepare
adjusted trial balance and
financial statements.
(SO 4, 5, 6, 7) AP

**P3–7B** The Super Motel has a fiscal year end of May 31. The company's trial balance prior to adjustments is listed below:

**SUPER MOTEL**
**Trial Balance**
**May 31, 2005**

|  | Debit | Credit |
|---|---|---|
| Cash | $ 2,200 | |
| Prepaid insurance | 5,460 | |
| Supplies | 2,440 | |
| Land | 30,000 | |
| Lodge | 84,000 | |
| Accumulated amortization—lodge | | $ 29,400 |
| Furniture | 17,200 | |
| Accumulated amortization—furniture | | 6,880 |
| Accounts payable | | 4,700 |
| Unearned rent revenue | | 8,750 |
| Mortgage payable | | 63,000 |
| Sara Sutton, capital | | 30,500 |
| Sara Sutton, drawings | 33,500 | |
| Rent revenue | | 101,160 |
| Salaries expense | 49,350 | |
| Interest expense | 4,620 | |
| Insurance expense | 1,820 | |
| Utilities expense | 13,300 | |
| Advertising expense | 500 | |
| | $244,390 | $244,390 |

Other data:

1. The company pays $5,460 for its annual insurance policy on September 30 each year.
2. A count of supplies on May 31 shows $670 of supplies on hand.
3. The lodge was purchased on May 31, 1997, and has an estimated useful life of 20 years.
4. The furniture was purchased on June 1, 2002, and has an estimated useful life of five years.
5. Customers must pay a $50 deposit if they wish to book a room in advance during peak times. An analysis of these bookings indicates that 175 deposits were received (all credited to Unearned Rent Revenue) and 65 of the deposits have been earned by May 31, 2005.
6. The mortgage interest rate is 8% per year. Interest has been paid to May 1, 2005; the next payment is due on June 1.
7. Salaries accrued to the end of May were $975.
8. The May utility bill of $1,210 is unrecorded and unpaid.
9. On May 28, a local business contracted with Super Motel to rent one of the rooms for four months starting June 1 at a rate of $1,400 per month. An advance payment equal to two months' rent is to be paid on June 1.
10. On May 31, Super Motel has earned $980 of rent revenue from customers who are currently using the rooms but won't pay the amount owing until they check out in June. This amount is in addition to any deposits earned in item (5) above.

*Instructions*

(a) Journalize the adjusting entries on May 31.
(b) Prepare a ledger. Enter the trial balance amounts and post the adjusting entries.
(c) Prepare an adjusted trial balance at May 31.
(d) Prepare an income statement and statement of owner's equity for the year ended May 31 and a balance sheet at May 31.

**P3–8B** The unadjusted and adjusted trial balances of Irabu Co. as at September 30, 2005, are shown below:

**IRABU CO.**
**Trial Balance**
**September 30, 2005**

| | Unadjusted | | Adjusted | |
|---|---|---|---|---|
| | Dr. | Cr. | Dr. | Cr. |
| Cash | $ 3,250 | | $ 3,250 | |
| Accounts receivable | 6,335 | | 7,435 | |
| Supplies | 1,750 | | 1,265 | |
| Prepaid rent | 1,500 | | 1,050 | |
| Equipment | 15,040 | | 15,040 | |
| Accumulated amortization | | $ 5,640 | | $ 6,110 |
| Notes payable | | 6,000 | | 6,000 |
| Accounts payable | | 4,250 | | 4,460 |
| Interest payable | | 0 | | 60 |
| Unearned rent revenue | | 775 | | 550 |
| Salaries payable | | 0 | | 840 |
| Yosuke Irabu, capital | | 14,000 | | 14,000 |
| Yosuke Irabu, drawings | 2,700 | | 2,700 | |
| Commission revenue | | 14,020 | | 15,120 |
| Rent revenue | | 400 | | 625 |
| Salaries expense | 13,000 | | 13,840 | |
| Interest expense | 0 | | 60 | |
| Amortization expense | 0 | | 470 | |
| Supplies expense | 0 | | 485 | |
| Utilities expense | 610 | | 820 | |
| Rent expense | 900 | | 1,350 | |
| | $45,085 | $45,085 | $47,765 | $47,765 |

*Instructions*

(a) Journalize the quarterly adjusting entries that were made.

(b) Prepare an income statement and a statement of owner's equity for the three months ending September 30 and a balance sheet at September 30.

(c) If the note bears interest at 12%, how many months has it been outstanding?

(d) A friend of yours is considering purchasing the company from Yosuke Irabu and asks you to comment on the company's results of operations and financial position. Is the company performing well or not? Does the financial position appear healthy or weak? Use specific information from the financial statements to support your answer.

Prepare and post adjusting entries; prepare adjusted trial balance and financial statements; and comment. (SO 4, 5, 6, 7) AP

**P3–9B** Below is an alphabetical list of Mahadeo Consulting Co.'s accounts at its fiscal year end of May 31, 2005, prior to adjustments:

**MAHADEO CONSULTING CO.**
**Trial Balance**
**May 31, 2005**

| | |
|---|---:|
| Accounts payable | $ 1,476 |
| Accounts receivable | 2,485 |
| Accumulated amortization—computer equipment | 2,545 |
| Accumulated amortization—furniture | 964 |
| Cash | 3,795 |
| Computer equipment | 7,635 |
| Consulting fees earned | 117,350 |
| Furniture | 9,640 |
| Mohammed Mahadeo, capital | 18,752 |
| Mohammed Mahadeo, drawings | 66,850 |
| Note receivable | 6,500 |
| Prepaid insurance | 1,872 |
| Rent expense | 10,120 |
| Salaries expense | 32,950 |
| Supplies | 2,960 |
| Telephone expense | 1,560 |
| Unearned consulting fees | 5,280 |

Other data:

1. A one-year insurance policy was purchased on December 1, 2004.
2. On May 31, 2004, there were $555 of supplies on hand. During the year, $2,405 of additional supplies were purchased. A count of supplies on May 31, 2005, shows $705 of supplies on hand.
3. The computer equipment has an estimated useful life of three years.
4. The furniture has an estimated useful life of 10 years.
5. As at May 31, 2005, an analysis shows that $1,550 of the unearned consulting fees were still unearned.
6. The note receivable, issued on April 1, 2005, bears an annual interest rate of 8.25%. Interest and principal are receivable in full on the December 1, 2005, maturity date.
7. Salaries accrued to May 31 were $980.
8. On May 21, the company signed a contract to provide consulting services to Mawani Inc., starting June 1, 2005. The contract is for three months at a rate of $3,600 per month. Payment is due at the start of each month.
9. On May 31, 2005, the company had earned but not billed or received consulting revenue of $3,225.
10. Rent of $920 for May 2005 had not been recorded or paid.

*Instructions*

(a) Prepare adjusting journal entries for the year ended May 31, 2005, as required.
(b) Prepare an adjusted trial balance in proper account order.
(c) Prepare an income statement and statement of owner's equity for the year ended May 31, 2005, and a balance sheet at May 31, 2005.
(d) Comment on the company's results of operations and financial position. Include specific references to items in the financial statements in your analysis.

Prepare transaction and adjusting entries for prepayments. (SO 8) AP

*__P3–10B__ In P3–1B, when journal entries were originally recorded for Burke Bros., prepaid costs were debited to an asset account and unearned revenues were credited to a liability account. This problem repeats P3–1B, assuming instead that prepaid costs are debited originally to an expense account and unearned revenues credited to a revenue account.

*Instructions*

Prepare the journal entry for the original transaction and any adjusting journal entry required at December 31, 2005, for each of the situations outlined in P3–1B, assuming this alternative treatment of prepaid expenses and unearned revenues.

Continuing Cookie Chronicle ◀ 147

**\*P3–11B** The Royal Graphics Company was organized on July 1, 2005, by Jan Bejar. Royal Graphics records all prepayments in income statement accounts. At the end of the first six months of operations, the trial balance contained the following accounts:

*Prepare adjusting entries, adjusted trial balance, and financial statements.*
*(SO 7, 8) AP*

**ROYAL GRAPHICS COMPANY**
**Trial Balance**
**December 31, 2005**

| | Debit | Credit |
|---|---|---|
| Accounts payable | | $ 11,000 |
| Accounts receivable | $ 7,450 | |
| Advertising expense | 1,825 | |
| Cash | 7,250 | |
| Consulting fees earned | | 7,100 |
| Equipment | 46,200 | |
| Graphic fees earned | | 55,500 |
| Insurance expense | 2,220 | |
| Jan Bejar, capital | | 34,625 |
| Jan Bejar, drawings | 17,400 | |
| Note payable | | 18,000 |
| Rent expense | 3,325 | |
| Salaries expense | 35,585 | |
| Supplies expense | 3,230 | |
| Utilities expense | 1,740 | |
| | $126,225 | $126,225 |

Analysis reveals the following additional data:

1. The $3,230 balance in Supplies Expense represents supplies purchased in July and in October. At December 31, $2,485 of supplies had been used.
2. The note payable was issued November 1. It is a 5%, three-month note, with interest and principal payable at maturity.
3. The balance in Insurance Expense is the premium on a one-year policy that is dated September 1, 2005.
4. Consulting fees are credited to revenue when received. At December 31, consulting fees of $1,400 are unearned.
5. Amortization is $2,100 per year.
6. Utilities of $205 are owed at December 31.
7. January 2006 rent of $475 was paid on December 31, 2005, and is included in Rent Expense.

*Instructions*

(a) Journalize the adjusting entries at December 31. (Adjustments are recorded every six months.)
(b) Prepare an adjusted trial balance.
(c) Prepare an income statement and statement of owner's equity for the six months ended December 31, and a balance sheet at December 31, 2005.

# Continuing Cookie Chronicle

(*Note*: This is a continuation of the Cookie Chronicle from Chapters 1 and 2. From the information gathered through Chapter 2, follow the instructions below using the general ledger accounts you have already prepared.)

It is the end of November and Natalie has been in touch with her grandmother. Her grandmother asked Natalie for financial statements because she believes it's important that Natalie, at some point in time, repay the loan she received from her grandmother. Natalie also feels that it's important to know the financial position of her business each month. The following additional information will help you prepare Cookie Creations' financial statements:

1. A count reveals that $75 of brochures and posters remain at the end of November.
2. A count reveals that $25 of baking supplies were used during November.

3. Natalie estimates that all of her baking equipment will have a useful life of five years or 60 months. (Assume Natalie decides to record a full month's worth of amortization regardless of when the equipment was obtained by the business.)
4. Natalie's grandmother has decided to charge interest of 6% on the note payable extended on November 16. The loan plus interest is to be repaid in 24 months. (Assume that half a month of interest accrued during November.)
5. On November 30, a friend of Natalie's asks her to teach a class at the neighbourhood school. Natalie agrees and teaches a group of 35 grade one students how to make Santa Claus cookies. The next day Natalie prepares an invoice for $250 and leaves it with the school principal. The principal says that he will pass the invoice along to head office and it will be paid sometime in December.
6. Natalie receives a cellphone bill for $50. She only uses her cellphone for business. The bill is for services provided during November and is due December 15.

*Instructions*

Using the information that you have gathered through Chapter 2, and based on the new information above, do the following:

(a) Prepare and post the adjusting journal entries.
(b) Prepare an adjusted trial balance.
(c) Prepare an income statement and statement of owner's equity for the month ended November 30, 2004, and a balance sheet as at November 30, 2004.

# Cumulative Coverage—Chapters 2 to 3

On August 31, 2004, the account balances of Pitre Equipment Repair were as follows:

**PITRE EQUIPMENT REPAIR**
**Trial Balance**
**August 31, 2004**

|  | Debit | Credit |
|---|---|---|
| Cash | $ 4,880 | |
| Accounts receivable | 3,720 | |
| Supplies | 800 | |
| Store equipment | 15,000 | |
| Accumulated amortization | | $ 1,500 |
| Accounts payable | | 3,100 |
| Unearned service revenue | | 400 |
| Salaries payable | | 700 |
| R. Pitre, capital | | 18,700 |
| | $24,400 | $24,400 |

During September, the following transactions were completed:

Sept.  8  Paid $1,100 for employees' salaries, of which $400 is for September and $700 for August.
10  Received $1,200 cash from customers on account.
12  Received $3,400 cash for services performed in September.
15  Purchased additional store equipment on account, $3,000.
17  Purchased additional supplies on account, $1,500.
20  Paid creditors $4,500 on account.
22  Paid September rent, $500.
25  Paid salaries, $1,200.
27  Performed services on account and billed customers for services provided, $900.
29  Received $650 from customers for future services.

Adjustment data consist of the following:

1. Supplies on hand cost $1,800.
2. Accrued salaries payable total $400.
3. Amortization is $250 per month.
4. Unearned service revenue of $350 is earned.

*Instructions*
(a) Enter the September 1 balances in general ledger accounts.
(b) Journalize the September transactions.
(c) Post to the ledger accounts.
(d) Prepare a trial balance at September 30.
(e) Journalize and post adjusting entries.
(f) Prepare an adjusted trial balance.
(g) Prepare an income statement and a statement of owner's equity for September, and a balance sheet at September 30, 2004.

## BROADENING YOUR PERSPECTIVE

# Financial Reporting and Analysis

 Practice Tools

## Financial Reporting Problem

**BYP3–1** The financial statements of **The Forzani Group** are presented in Appendix A at the end of this textbook.

*Instructions*
(a) What title does Forzani use for its income statement?
(b) What different types of revenues were reported by Forzani (see note 12)?
(c) Does Forzani report any prepayments on its balance sheet? If so, identify each item that is a prepaid expense or unearned (deferred) revenue. Indicate what other account title would likely be used in preparing adjusting entries for these accounts.
(d) Does Forzani report any accruals on its balance sheet? If so, identify each item that is an accrued revenue or accrued expense. Indicate what other account title would likely be used in preparing adjusting entries for these accounts.
(e) What are the cost, accumulated amortization, and net book value of Forzani's capital assets at February 2, 2003 (see note 3)?

## Interpreting Financial Statements

**BYP3–2** **Rogers Cable Inc.** is Canada's largest cable television service provider. Rogers is also a leading North American provider of high-speed Internet service. Rogers' balance sheet included a current liability of $35,256,000 at December 31, 2002, called Unearned Revenue. An excerpt from the notes to the financial statements follows:

ROGERS CABLE INC.
Notes to the Financial Statements
December 31, 2002

 ROGERS

Note 2 (k): Significant accounting policies—Revenue recognition

The Company earns revenue from several sources. The principal sources of revenue to the Company and recognition of these revenues for financial statement purposes are as follows:

(i) Installation revenues in connection with cable and Internet services are recorded as revenue to the extent of direct selling costs incurred.

(ii) Monthly fees in connection with cable and Internet services are recorded as revenue on a pro rata basis over the month.

(iii) Revenue from pay-per-view movies, video rentals and other transactional sales of products are recorded as revenue as the services or products are provided.

Unearned revenue included subscriber deposits and amounts received from subscribers related to services and subscriptions to be provided in future periods.

*Instructions*

(a) Adjusting entries can be classified as prepayments, accruals, or estimates. Is Unearned Revenue an example of a prepayment, accrual, or estimate?

(b) When an amount is received from a subscriber for services to be provided in the future, what account would be debited? What account would be credited?

(c) When should the revenue be recognized from the subscriber deposits recorded in the Unearned Revenue account? When revenue is recognized, what account would be debited? What account would be credited? If this journal entry was omitted, what would be the effect on the company's financial position (use the basic accounting equation and explain what elements would be overstated or understated)?

(d) Rogers is following an assumption and two generally accepted accounting principles with the policy explained in the notes. Name the assumption and the two principles and explain how they relate to each other.

## Accounting on the Web

**BYP3–3** A financial decision-maker should never rely only on the financial information reported in an annual report. It is important to know the latest financial news. This problem demonstrates how to search for financial news on the Web.

*Instructions*

Specific requirements of this Internet case are available on the Weygandt website.

# Critical Thinking

## Collaborative Learning Activity

**BYP3–4** Air Canada sells tickets for airline flights to passengers at a number of different points of sale. For example, you can purchase a ticket in advance (seat sale fare) that may be non-refundable or include restrictions about making changes; you can purchase a fully refundable full-fare ticket up to the time of flight departure; or you can fly standby at the last minute.

Air Canada's management team is brainstorming its options in terms of recognizing the revenue from its ticket sales. One person says the airline should record the revenue when it advertises the seat sale, because these are such great fares it's clear that every seat will be sold. Another states that revenue should be recognized when passengers pick up their tickets and pay for the flight. "What about when the boarding passes are collected at the gate?" a third asks. "Or when passengers arrive at their destinations?" a fourth adds.

*Instructions*

With the class divided into groups, do the following:

(a) Each group will be assigned, or should choose, one of the above revenue recognition options. Evaluate the effect of the option on recorded revenues, expenses, and net income for the period in question.

(b) Briefly review your option and compare it to the other options described in the above case. After doing the comparison, decide on the point at which you think Air Canada should recognize the revenue from flight ticket sales. Explain why you believe this point of revenue recognition is the best, referring to relevant generally accepted accounting principles in your answer.

# Communication Activity

**BYP3–5** There are many people today who believe that cash-based income is a better indicator of a company's future success than net income. This notion gained popularity after many reports of corporate financial scandals where management was easily able to manipulate estimates and accruals to influence net income.

*Instructions*

Write a memo discussing whether you believe cash-based income is a more reliable performance measure than accrual-based net income. Include in your memo the answers to the following questions:

(a) What is the difference between accrual-based and cash-based net income?

(b) Do you believe that it is possible for management to manipulate net income? If yes, identify one way that management might be able to increase net income by manipulating estimates or accruals.

(c) Do you believe that it is possible for management to manipulate cash-based income? If yes, identify one way that management might be able to increase cash flow.

# Ethics Case

**BYP3–6** Die Hard Company is a pesticide manufacturer. Its sales declined greatly this year due to the passage of legislation that outlawed the sale of several of Die Hard's chemical pesticides. In the coming year, Die Hard will have new, environmentally safe chemicals to replace these discontinued products. Sales in the next year are expected to greatly exceed those of any previous year. The drop in sales and profits appears to be a one-year aberration. But even so, the company president fears that a large drop in the current year's profits could cause a significant drop in the market price of Die Hard's shares, and could make the company a takeover target.

To avoid this possibility, the company president calls in Carole Chiasson, the company's controller, to discuss this period's year-end adjusting entries. He urges her to accrue every possible revenue and to defer as many expenses as possible when preparing this period's December 31 year-end adjusting entries. He says to Carole, "We need the revenues this year, and next year we can easily absorb expenses deferred from this year." Carole didn't record the adjusting entries until January 17, but she dated the entries December 31 as if they were recorded then. Carole also made every effort to comply with the president's request.

*Instructions*

(a) Who are the stakeholders in this situation?

(b) What are the ethical considerations of (1) the president's request, and (2) Carole's dating the adjusting entries December 31?

(c) Can Carole accrue revenues and defer expenses and still be ethical?

*Answers to Self-Study Questions*
1. c    2. a    3. d    4. d    5. c    6. a    7. b    8. a    9. d    10. c    *11. a

*Answer to Forzani Review It Question 4*
Forzani reported amortization expense of $29,624 thousand and $22,574 thousand in fiscal 2003 and 2002, respectively.

Remember to go back to the Navigator Box at the beginning of the chapter to check off your completed work.

## concepts for review >>

Before studying this chapter, you should understand or, if necessary, review:

  a. How to apply the revenue recognition and matching principles. (Ch. 3, p. 101)
  b. How to make adjusting entries. (Ch. 3, pp. 105–114)
  c. How to prepare an adjusted trial balance. (Ch. 3, p. 118)
  d. How the balance sheet, income statement, and statement of owner's equity are connected. (Ch. 3, pp. 118–119)

# Breezing through Month End with Style

WINNIPEG, Man.—Owned and operated by the Gorenstein family of Winnipeg, Moulé has four gallery-style retail stores in Vancouver and Winnipeg. Each one features gifts, jewellery, and other treasures from around the world. The items have been crafted by talented artists working in glass, ceramics, metal, and other media. Founded in 1987, Moulé also designs and manufactures a signature line of soft, feminine, and sophisticated women's apparel. The clothing is sold in Moulé stores and distributed across North America and as far away as Japan.

Month end finds Moulé's chief operations officer, Laurie Gorenstein, running off extra reports for things like sales, GST and PST, commissions, and inventory on the Smart Vendor computer software he uses for most of the company's accounting (Moulé uses a different program to track its payables). "Basically, I receive all the invoices from the stores at month end, do a second count, and check it against the figures in the computer. Then I run the general ledger and the trial balance."

"My accountant checks them, and we make any updates or corrections necessary—such as a cheque posted to the wrong account—with an adjusting or correcting entry," he continues. By checking things monthly, "it usually comes out pretty smoothly." Monthly financial statements then follow.

"So it really is pretty easy," confides Mr. Gorenstein. Once a year, the load gets a little heavier when the books are closed—as with many businesses, Moulé's fiscal year ends December 31—and the year's financial statements are prepared. At this point, he's very glad of the care taken to find discrepancies and to make adjustments at month end. If errors are left undetected, "then they come back to haunt you months later and you can spend forever trying to sort them out."

For example, when the company recently installed a new computer system, "it took a while to get things up to speed," says Mr. Gorenstein. "In the first few months after we made the switch, a lot of things somehow got posted to Travel instead of Purchases. We had to go through all the cheques and VISA card statements for a three-month period to find out where the mistakes occurred. Fortunately, this doesn't happen often!"

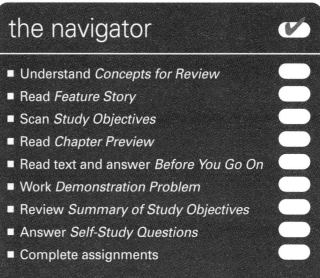

## the navigator

- Understand *Concepts for Review*
- Read *Feature Story*
- Scan *Study Objectives*
- Read *Chapter Preview*
- Read text and answer *Before You Go On*
- Work *Demonstration Problem*
- Review *Summary of Study Objectives*
- Answer *Self-Study Questions*
- Complete assignments

chapter 4

# Completion of the Accounting Cycle

## study objectives >>

the navigator

After studying this chapter, you should be able to:

1. Describe the purpose of a work sheet.
2. Demonstrate the process of closing the books.
3. Describe and produce a post-closing trial balance.
4. List the steps in the accounting cycle.
5. Explain and demonstrate the approaches to preparing correcting entries.
6. Identify and prepare the various sections of a classified balance sheet.
7. Illustrate measures used to evaluate liquidity.
8. Prepare a work sheet (Appendix 4A).
9. Prepare reversing entries (Appendix 4B).

In Chapter 3, we prepared financial statements directly from the adjusted trial balance. In this chapter we will explain the role of the remaining steps in the accounting cycle—especially the closing process. Once again, we will use the Pioneer Advertising Agency as an example.

Then we will look at correcting entries. It is easy to make errors because of the many details involved in the end-of-period accounting procedures. Locating and correcting errors can cost much time and effort, as Laurie Gorenstein of Moulé notes in the feature story. We end by discussing the classification and use of balance sheets.

This chapter is organized as follows:

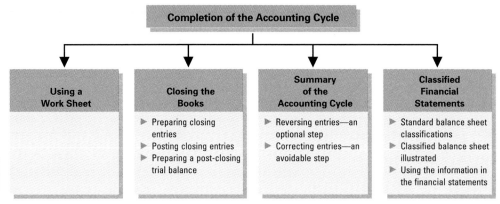

| Completion of the Accounting Cycle |
|---|

| Using a Work Sheet | Closing the Books | Summary of the Accounting Cycle | Classified Financial Statements |
|---|---|---|---|
| | ▶ Preparing closing entries<br>▶ Posting closing entries<br>▶ Preparing a post-closing trial balance | ▶ Reversing entries—an optional step<br>▶ Correcting entries—an avoidable step | ▶ Standard balance sheet classifications<br>▶ Classified balance sheet illustrated<br>▶ Using the information in the financial statements |

the navigator

# Using a Work Sheet

study objective 1

Describe the purpose of a work sheet.

In our discussion in Chapter 3, we used an adjusted trial balance to arrive at the accounts and amounts used to prepare financial statements. Accountants frequently use a device known as a work sheet to determine these. A work sheet is a multiple-column form that may be used in the adjustment process and in preparing financial statements. Work sheets can be prepared manually, but today most are done by accounting software or electronic spreadsheet programs.

As its name suggests, the work sheet is a working tool for the accountant. **A work sheet is not a permanent accounting record**; it is neither a journal nor a part of the general ledger. The work sheet is merely a device used to make it easier to prepare adjusting entries and financial statements. In small companies that have relatively few accounts and adjustments, a work sheet may not be needed. In companies with numerous accounts and many adjustments, it is almost indispensable.

The basic form of a work sheet and the procedure for preparing it (five steps) are shown in Illustration 4-1. The steps required to prepare the work sheet must be performed in the proper sequence. The steps to prepare a work sheet are explained in more detail in Appendix 4A to this chapter and on the Student Navigator CD that comes with this text.

Work Sheet Walkthrough

Although **the use of a work sheet is optional**, it is useful. Financial statements, for example, can be easily prepared from the work sheet, reducing errors. A work sheet also makes it easier to prepare interim (e.g., monthly or quarterly) financial information for internal use: because adjusting entries can be prepared and entered in the work sheet, interim financial statements can easily be developed.

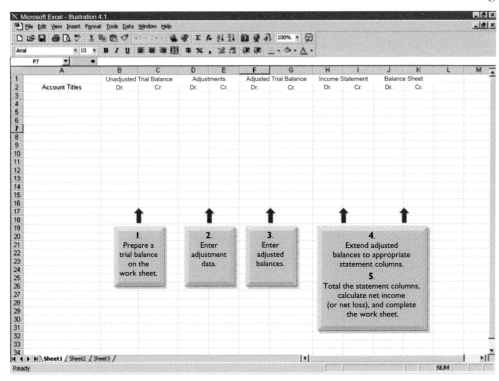

**Illustration 4-1 ◄**

Form and procedure for a work sheet

# Closing the Books

At the end of the accounting period, the accounts are made ready for the next period. This is called closing the books. When closing the books, it is necessary to distinguish between temporary and permanent accounts. Temporary accounts apply only to a single accounting period. They include all income statement (revenue and expense) accounts and the owner's drawings account. In previous chapters, you learned that revenue, expense, and drawings accounts are subdivisions of the owner's capital account, which is reported in the owner's equity section of the balance sheet. These accounts are called temporary accounts because they temporarily (for the period) provide detail about the changes in the owner's capital account. **All temporary accounts are closed.**

In contrast, permanent accounts apply to one or more future accounting periods. They comprise all balance sheet accounts, including the owner's capital account. **Permanent accounts are not closed.** Instead, their balances are carried forward into the next accounting period. Illustration 4-2 identifies the accounts in each category.

study objective 2

Demonstrate the process of closing the books.

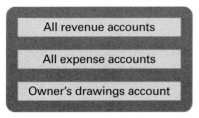

| TEMPORARY | PERMANENT |
|---|---|
| These accounts are closed. | These accounts are not closed. |
| All revenue accounts | All asset accounts |
| All expense accounts | All liability accounts |
| Owner's drawings account | Owner's capital account |

**Illustration 4-2 ◄**

Temporary versus permanent accounts

## Preparing Closing Entries

Accounting Cycle
Tutorial—Preparing
Financial Statements
and Closing Books

At the end of the accounting period, the temporary account balances are transferred to the equity account of the owner of the proprietorship, owner's capital, by preparing closing entries. Closing entries formally record in the ledger the transfer of net income (or net loss) and the owner's drawings to the owner's capital account. This updates the owner's capital balance, as shown in the statement of owner's equity. **These entries produce a zero balance in each temporary account.** These accounts are then ready to accumulate data in the next accounting period separately from the data of earlier periods.

Journalizing and posting closing entries is a required step in the accounting cycle. This step is performed after financial statements have been prepared. In contrast to the steps in the cycle that you have already studied, closing entries are generally journalized and posted only at the end of a company's annual accounting period. Moulé, introduced in the feature story, closes its books once a year. This practice simplifies the preparation of annual financial statements, because all temporary accounts contain data for the entire year.

In preparing closing entries, each income statement account could be closed directly to the owner's capital account. This is common in computerized accounting systems where the closing process occurs automatically when it is time to start a new accounting period. However, in manual accounting systems, this practice can result in excessive detail in the permanent owner's capital account. Instead, it is more efficient to first close the revenue and expense accounts to another temporary account, **income summary.** The total net income or net loss is then transferred from this account to owner's capital.

Closing entries may be prepared directly from (1) the adjusted balances in the general ledger or adjusted trial balance, (2) the income statement and statement of owner's equity, or (3) the work sheet, if available. If a work sheet is used, the data for the closing entries would appear in the income statement columns and in the drawings account in the balance sheet debit column.

Separate closing entries could be prepared for each temporary account. However, the compound entries shown in the first two of the following four entries are more efficient:

1. To close revenue accounts: Debit each individual revenue account for its balance, and credit income summary for total revenues.
2. To close expense accounts: Debit income summary for total expenses, and credit each individual expense account for its balance.
3. To close income summary: Debit income summary for the balance in the account, and credit owner's capital (if there is a net loss, credit income summary for the amount of the loss, and debit owner's capital).
4. To close drawings: Debit owner's capital and credit drawings for the latter's balance.

Closing entries are journalized in the general journal. A centre caption titled "Closing Entries" may be inserted in the journal between the last adjusting entry and the first closing entry to identify these entries. Then the closing entries are posted to the ledger accounts.

In Illustration 4-3, the four entries are shown with T accounts in a diagram of the closing process for a proprietorship.

### Closing Entries Illustrated

To illustrate the journalizing and posting of closing entries, we will continue using the example of Pioneer Advertising Agency introduced in Chapters 2 and 3. For illustrative purposes, we have also assumed that the company has chosen October 31 as its fiscal year end. Pioneer Advertising's adjusted trial balance on October 31, first shown in Chapter 3 (Illustration 3-6), is shown again in Illustration 4-4.

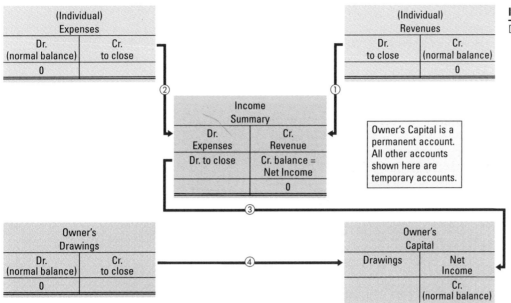

**Illustration 4-3 ◄**

Diagram of closing process

**Key:**
① Close revenues to Income Summary.   ③ Close Income Summary to Owner's Capital.
② Close expenses to Income Summary.   ④ Close Owner's Drawings to Owner's Capital.

**Illustration 4-4 ◄**

Adjusted trial balance

### PIONEER ADVERTISING AGENCY
### Adjusted Trial Balance
### October 31, 2005

|  | Debit | Credit |
|---|---|---|
| Cash | $15,200 | |
| Accounts receivable | 200 | |
| Advertising supplies | 1,000 | |
| Prepaid insurance | 550 | |
| Office equipment | 5,000 | |
| Accumulated amortization—office equipment | | $ 83 |
| Notes payable | | 5,000 |
| Accounts payable | | 2,500 |
| Unearned revenue | | 800 |
| Salaries payable | | 400 |
| Interest payable | | 25 |
| C. R. Byrd, capital | | 10,000 |
| C. R. Byrd, drawings | 500 | |
| Service revenue | | 10,600 |
| Advertising supplies expense | 1,500 | |
| Amortization expense | 83 | |
| Insurance expense | 50 | |
| Salaries expense | 4,400 | |
| Rent expense | 900 | |
| Interest expense | 25 | |
| | $29,408 | $29,408 |

We will use the adjusted account balances shown here to prepare the four required closing entries. The temporary accounts involved in the closing process have been highlighted in red. Although C. R. Byrd, Capital is not a temporary account, it has been highlighted because it is involved in the closing process. Remember that the capital account balance in the trial balance is the opening balance (plus any investments made by the owner during the period), not the ending balance that appears in the statement of owner's equity and balance sheet. This permanent account is not closed but the net income (loss) and drawings for the period must be recorded to update the account to its ending capital balance.

The closing entries at October 31 follow:

| GENERAL JOURNAL | | | | | J3 |
|---|---|---|---|---|---|
| Date | Account Titles and Explanation | Ref. | Debit | | Credit |
| | Closing Entries | | | | |
| 2005 | (1) | | | | |
| Oct. 31 | Service Revenue | 400 | 10,600 | | |
| | Income Summary | 350 | | | 10,600 |
| | To close revenue account. | | | | |
| | (2) | | | | |
| 31 | Income Summary | 350 | 6,958 | | |
| | Advertising Supplies Expense | 611 | | | 1,500 |
| | Amortization Expense | 711 | | | 83 |
| | Insurance Expense | 722 | | | 50 |
| | Salaries Expense | 726 | | | 4,400 |
| | Rent Expense | 729 | | | 900 |
| | Interest Expense | 905 | | | 25 |
| | To close expense accounts. | | | | |
| | (3) | | | | |
| 31 | Income Summary | 350 | 3,642 | | |
| | C. R. Byrd, Capital | 301 | | | 3,642 |
| | To close net income. | | | | |
| | (4) | | | | |
| 31 | C. R. Byrd, Capital | 301 | 500 | | |
| | C. R. Byrd, Drawings | 306 | | | 500 |
| | To close drawings account. | | | | |

Be careful when preparing closing entries: (1) Remember that the reason for making closing entries is to bring the temporary accounts to zero balances. Avoid unintentionally doubling the revenue, expense, drawings, and income summary account balances, rather than bringing them to zero. (2) Do not close owner's drawings with the expenses. An owner's drawings are not an expense and are not a factor in determining net income.

## Posting Closing Entries

The posting of the closing entries is shown below.

| GENERAL LEDGER | | | | | | | | | | | |
|---|---|---|---|---|---|---|---|---|---|---|---|
| | Cash | | | | No. 101 | | Accounts Receivable | | | | No. 112 |
| Date | Explanation | Ref. | Debit | Credit | Balance | Date | Explanation | Ref. | Debit | Credit | Balance |
| 2005 | | | | | | 2005 | | | | | |
| Oct. 1 | | J1 | 10,000 | | 10,000 | Oct. 21 | | J1 | 10,000 | | 10,000 |
| 4 | | J1 | 1,200 | | 11,200 | 31 | | J1 | | 10,000 | 0 |
| 4 | | J1 | | 900 | 10,300 | 31 | Adj. Entry | J2 | 200 | | 200 |
| 4 | | J1 | | 600 | 9,700 | | Advertising Supplies | | | | No. 129 |
| 20 | | J1 | | 500 | 9,200 | Date | Explanation | Ref. | Debit | Credit | Balance |
| 28 | | J1 | | 4,000 | 5,200 | 2005 | | | | | |
| 31 | | J1 | 10,000 | | 15,200 | Oct. 5 | | J1 | 2,500 | | 2,500 |
| | | | | | | 31 | Adj. Entry | J2 | | 1,500 | 1,000 |

## GENERAL LEDGER

| | Prepaid Insurance | | | No. 130 | |
|---|---|---|---|---|---|
| Date | Explanation | Ref. | Debit | Credit | Balance |
| 2005 | | | | | |
| Oct.  4 | | J1 | 600 | | 600 |
| 31 | Adj. Entry | J2 | | 50 | 550 |

| | Office Equipment | | | No. 151 | |
|---|---|---|---|---|---|
| Date | Explanation | Ref. | Debit | Credit | Balance |
| 2005 | | | | | |
| Oct.  3 | | J1 | 5,000 | | 5,000 |

| | Accumulated Amortization— Office Equipment | | | No. 152 | |
|---|---|---|---|---|---|
| Date | Explanation | Ref. | Debit | Credit | Balance |
| 2005 | | | | | |
| Oct. 31 | Adj. Entry | J2 | | 83 | 83 |

| | Notes Payable | | | No. 200 | |
|---|---|---|---|---|---|
| Date | Explanation | Ref. | Debit | Credit | Balance |
| 2005 | | | | | |
| Oct.  3 | | J1 | | 5,000 | 5,000 |

| | Accounts Payable | | | No. 201 | |
|---|---|---|---|---|---|
| Date | Explanation | Ref. | Debit | Credit | Balance |
| 2005 | | | | | |
| Oct.  5 | | J1 | | 2,500 | 2,500 |

| | Unearned Revenue | | | No. 209 | |
|---|---|---|---|---|---|
| Date | Explanation | Ref. | Debit | Credit | Balance |
| 2005 | | | | | |
| Oct.  4 | | J1 | | 1,200 | 1,200 |
| 31 | Adj. Entry | J2 | 400 | | 800 |

| | Salaries Payable | | | No. 212 | |
|---|---|---|---|---|---|
| Date | Explanation | Ref. | Debit | Credit | Balance |
| 2005 | | | | | |
| Oct. 31 | Adj. entry | J2 | | 400 | 400 |

| | Interest Payable | | | No. 230 | |
|---|---|---|---|---|---|
| Date | Explanation | Ref. | Debit | Credit | Balance |
| 2005 | | | | | |
| Oct. 31 | Adj. Entry | J2 | | 25 | 25 |

| | C. R. Byrd, Capital | | | No. 301 | |
|---|---|---|---|---|---|
| Date | Explanation | Ref. | Debit | Credit | Balance |
| 2005 | | | | | |
| Oct.  1 | | J1 | | 10,000 | 10,000 |
| 31 | Closing Entry | J3 | | 3,642 | 13,642 |
| 31 | Closing Entry | J3 | 500 | | 13,142 |

| | C. R. Byrd, Drawings | | | No. 306 | |
|---|---|---|---|---|---|
| Date | Explanation | Ref. | Debit | Credit | Balance |
| 2005 | | | | | |
| Oct. 20 | | J1 | 500 | | 500 |
| 31 | Closing Entry | J3 | | 500 | 0 |

| | Income Summary | | | No. 350 | |
|---|---|---|---|---|---|
| Date | Explanation | Ref. | Debit | Credit | Balance |
| 2005 | | | | | |
| Oct. 31 | Closing Entry | J3 | | 10,600 | 10,600 |
| 31 | Closing Entry | J3 | 6,958 | | 3,642 |
| 31 | Closing Entry | J3 | 3,642 | | 0 |

| | Service Revenue | | | No. 400 | |
|---|---|---|---|---|---|
| Date | Explanation | Ref. | Debit | Credit | Balance |
| 2005 | | | | | |
| Oct. 21 | | J1 | | 10,000 | 10,000 |
| 31 | Adj. Entry | J2 | | 400 | 10,400 |
| 31 | Adj. Entry | J2 | | 200 | 10,600 |
| 31 | Closing Entry | J3 | 10,600 | | 0 |

| | Advertising Supplies Expense | | | No. 611 | |
|---|---|---|---|---|---|
| Date | Explanation | Ref. | Debit | Credit | Balance |
| 2005 | | | | | |
| Oct. 31 | Adj. Entry | J2 | 1,500 | | 1,500 |
| 31 | Closing Entry | J3 | | 1,500 | 0 |

| | Amortization Expense | | | No. 711 | |
|---|---|---|---|---|---|
| Date | Explanation | Ref. | Debit | Credit | Balance |
| 2005 | | | | | |
| Oct. 31 | Adj. Entry | J2 | 83 | | 83 |
| 31 | Closing Entry | J3 | | 83 | 0 |

| | Insurance Expense | | | No. 722 | |
|---|---|---|---|---|---|
| Date | Explanation | Ref. | Debit | Credit | Balance |
| 2005 | | | | | |
| Oct. 31 | Adj. Entry | J2 | 50 | | 50 |
| 31 | Closing Entry | J3 | | 50 | 0 |

| | Salaries Expense | | | No. 726 | |
|---|---|---|---|---|---|
| Date | Explanation | Ref. | Debit | Credit | Balance |
| 2005 | | | | | |
| Oct. 28 | | J1 | 4,000 | | 4,000 |
| 31 | Adj. Entry | J2 | 400 | | 4,400 |
| 31 | Closing Entry | J3 | | 4,400 | 0 |

| | Rent Expense | | | No. 729 | |
|---|---|---|---|---|---|
| Date | Explanation | Ref. | Debit | Credit | Balance |
| 2005 | | | | | |
| Oct.  4 | | J1 | 900 | | 900 |
| 31 | Closing Entry | J3 | | 900 | 0 |

| | Interest Expense | | | No. 905 | |
|---|---|---|---|---|---|
| Date | Explanation | Ref. | Debit | Credit | Balance |
| 2005 | | | | | |
| Oct. 31 | Adj. Entry | J2 | 25 | | 25 |
| 31 | Closing Entry | J3 | | 25 | 0 |

Stop and check your work after the closing entries are posted: (1) The balance in the income summary account, immediately before the final closing entry to transfer the balance to the owner's capital account, should equal the net income (or net loss) reported in the income statement (see Illustration 3-7 in Chapter 3). (2) All temporary accounts (revenues, expenses, owner's drawings, and income summary) should have zero balances. (3) The balance in the capital account should equal the ending balance reported in the statement of owner's equity and balance sheet (see Illustration 3-7 and 3-8 in Chapter 3).

### ACCOUNTING IN ACTION ▶ @-Business

Garry Beattie, CMA and owner of HBM Integrated Technology Inc., believes that the closing process should be completed within five days of the end of the month. Accounting done in a timely, efficient manner through streamlined, computerized accounting systems can save a business time and money. "With good technology, you can provide better information faster," he says. In fact, Beattie says that studies show that posting journal entries daily can save four hours of work per week.

The five-day close is possible for anyone, since many multinational companies, such as Cisco Systems, do it in less than one day.

*Source:* Rosemary Godin, "Five-Day Close Saves Time on Balance Sheets, Says Halifax CMA," *Bottom Line*, January 2003.

## Preparing a Post-Closing Trial Balance

**study objective 3**

Describe and produce a post-closing trial balance.

After all closing entries have been journalized and posted, another trial balance is prepared from the ledger. It is called a post-closing trial balance. The post- (or after-) closing trial balance is a list of permanent accounts and their balances after closing entries have been journalized and posted. The purpose of this trial balance is to prove the equality of the permanent account balances that are carried forward into the next accounting period. Since all temporary accounts will have zero balances, the post-closing trial balance will contain only permanent (balance sheet) accounts.

To prepare a post-closing trial balance, we list the accounts and their balances. The post-closing trial balance for Pioneer Advertising Agency is shown below. Note that the balances listed below are the same as those reported in the company's balance sheet. Pioneer Advertising's balance sheet was last seen in Chapter 3 (Illustration 3-8) and is shown again later in this chapter, in Illustration 4-14.

**Illustration 4-5 ▶**

Post-closing trial balance

**Helpful hint** Total debits in a post-closing trial balance will not equal total assets on the balance sheet if contra accounts, such as accumulated amortization, are present. Accumulated amortization is deducted from assets on the balance sheet but added to the credit column in a trial balance.

| PIONEER ADVERTISING AGENCY<br>Post-Closing Trial Balance<br>October 31, 2005 | Debit | Credit |
|---|---|---|
| Cash | $15,200 | |
| Accounts receivable | 200 | |
| Advertising supplies | 1,000 | |
| Prepaid insurance | 550 | |
| Office equipment | 5,000 | |
| Accumulated amortization—office equipment | | $    83 |
| Notes payable | | 5,000 |
| Accounts payable | | 2,500 |
| Unearned revenue | | 800 |
| Salaries payable | | 400 |
| Interest payable | | 25 |
| C. R. Byrd, capital | | 13,142 |
| | $21,950 | $21,950 |

A post-closing trial balance provides evidence that the journalizing and posting of closing entries has been properly completed. It also shows that the accounting equation is in balance at the end of the accounting period or the beginning of the next accounting period. The post-closing trial balance can be dated at the end of the period (October 31 as in Pioneer Advertising's case) or the beginning of the next period (November 1) to serve as an opening trial balance. We have chosen to do the former here.

As in the case of the trial balance, the post-closing trial balance does not prove that all transactions have been recorded or that the ledger is correct. For example, the post-closing trial balance will still balance if a transaction is not journalized and posted, or if a transaction is journalized and posted twice. That is why it is so important, as Laurie Gorenstein of Moulé states in the feature story, to find and correct all errors before the books are closed.

## BEFORE YOU GO ON . . .

### ▶Review It

1. How do permanent accounts differ from temporary accounts?
2. What four different types of entries are required in closing the books?
3. What are the content and purpose of a post-closing trial balance?

### ▶Do It

The adjusted trial balance for the Nguyen Company shows the following: H. Nguyen, Drawings $5,000; H. Nguyen, Capital $42,000; Service Revenue $18,000; and Operating Expenses $10,000. Prepare the closing entries at December 31.

### Action Plan

- Debit each individual revenue account for its balance and credit the total to the income summary account.
- Credit each individual expense account for its balance and debit the total to the income summary account.
- Stop and check your work: Does the balance in the income summary account equal the reported net income (loss)?
- If there is net income, debit the balance in the income summary account and credit the amount to the owner's capital account (do the opposite if the result is a net loss).
- Credit the balance in the drawings account and debit the amount to the owner's capital account. Do not close drawings with the expenses.
- Stop and check your work: Do the temporary accounts have zero balances? Does the ending capital balance equal the balance reported on the statement of owner's equity and balance sheet?

### Solution

| Dec. 31 | Service Revenue | 18,000 | |
| | Income Summary | | 18,000 |
| | To close revenue account. | | |
| 31 | Income Summary | 10,000 | |
| | Operating Expenses | | 10,000 |
| | To close expense account. | | |
| 31 | Income Summary | 8,000 | |
| | H. Nguyen, Capital | | 8,000 |
| | To close income summary. | | |
| 31 | H. Nguyen, Capital | 5,000 | |
| | H. Nguyen, Drawings | | 5,000 |
| | To close drawings. | | |

*Related exercise material:* BE4–1, BE4–2, BE4–3, E4–1, E4–2, and E4–3.

# Summary of the Accounting Cycle

study objective 4

List the steps in the accounting cycle.

The steps in the accounting cycle are shown in Illustration 4-6. You can see that the cycle begins with the analysis of business transactions and ends with the preparation of a post-closing trial balance. The steps in the cycle are performed in sequence and are repeated in each accounting period.

**Illustration 4-6** ►

Steps in the accounting cycle

Accounting
Cycle Tutorial

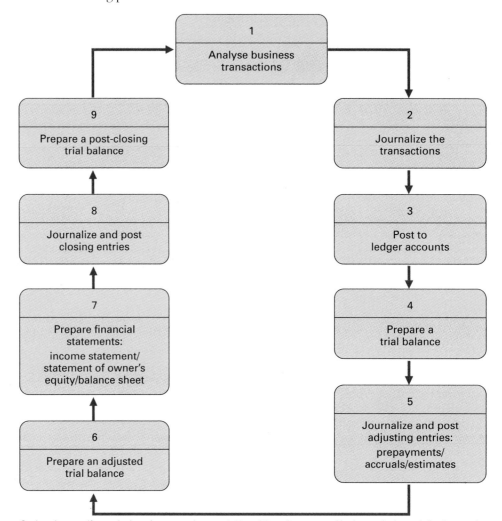

Optional steps: If a work sheet is prepared, steps 4, 5, and 6 are incorporated in the work sheet. Adjusting entries are journalized and posted after step 7. If reversing entries are prepared, they occur between steps 9 and 1.

Steps 1 and 2 may occur daily during the accounting period, as explained in Chapter 2. Steps 3 through 7 are performed on a periodic basis, such as monthly, quarterly, or annually. Steps 8 and 9, closing entries and a post-closing trial balance, are usually done only at the end of a company's annual accounting period.

There are also two optional steps in the accounting cycle. A work sheet may be used to prepare trial balances, adjusting entries, and financial statements. If a work sheet is used, adjusting entries are not formally recorded or posted until after the financial statements are prepared. In addition, reversing entries may be used, as the following section explains.

## Reversing Entries—An Optional Step

Some accountants prefer to reverse certain adjusting entries at the beginning of a new accounting period. A reversing entry is made at the beginning of the next accounting period. It is the exact opposite of the adjusting entry made in the previous period. The preparation of reversing entries is an optional bookkeeping procedure that is not a required step in the accounting cycle. Accordingly, we have chosen to cover this topic in Appendix 4B at the end of the chapter.

## Correcting Entries—An Avoidable Step

Unfortunately, errors may occur in the recording process. Errors should be corrected as soon as they are discovered by journalizing and posting correcting entries. If the accounting records have no errors, no correcting entries are necessary.

> **study objective 5**
>
> Explain and demonstrate the approaches to preparing correcting entries.

You should understand several differences between correcting entries and adjusting entries. First, adjusting entries are an integral part of the accounting cycle. Correcting entries, on the other hand, are unnecessary if the records have no errors. Second, **adjustments are journalized and posted only at the end of an accounting period. In contrast, correcting entries are made whenever an error is discovered.** Finally, adjusting entries always affect at least one balance sheet account (not Cash) and one income statement account. In contrast, correcting entries may involve any combination of accounts in need of correction. Both adjusting and correcting entries must be journalized and posted before closing entries.

To determine the correcting entry, it is useful to compare the incorrect entry with the entry that should have been made. Doing this helps identify the accounts and amounts that should—and should not—be corrected. After comparison, a correcting entry is made to correct the accounts. This approach is shown in the following two cases:

**Case 1.** On May 10, a $50 cash collection on account from a customer is journalized and posted as a debit to Cash $50 and as a credit to Service Revenue $50. The error is discovered on May 20 when the customer pays the remaining balance in full.

| Incorrect Entry (May 10) | | |
|---|---|---|
| Cash | 50 | |
|    Service Revenue | | 50 |

| Correct Entry (May 10) | | |
|---|---|---|
| Cash | 50 | |
|    Accounts Receivable | | 50 |

A comparison of the incorrect entry with the correct entry that should have been made (but was not) reveals that the debit to Cash of $50 is correct. However, the $50 credit to Service Revenue should have been credited to Accounts Receivable. As a result, both Service Revenue and Accounts Receivable are overstated in the ledger. The following correcting entry is required:

| | Correcting Entry | | |
|---|---|---|---|
| May 20 | Service Revenue | 50 | |
| |    Accounts Receivable | | 50 |
| |      To correct entry of May 10. | | |

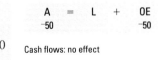

| A | = | L | + | OE |
|---|---|---|---|---|
| -50 | | | | -50 |

Cash flows: no effect

**Case 2.** On May 18, office equipment that costs $450 is purchased on account. The transaction is journalized and posted as a debit to Delivery Equipment $45 and as a credit to Accounts Payable $45. The error is discovered on June 3 when the monthly statement for May is received from the creditor.

| Incorrect Entry (May 18) | | | Correct Entry (May 18) | | |
|---|---|---|---|---|---|
| Delivery Equipment | 45 | | Office Equipment | 450 | |
| Accounts Payable | | 45 | Accounts Payable | | 450 |

A comparison of the two entries shows that three accounts are incorrect. Delivery Equipment is overstated by $45; Office Equipment is understated by $450; and Accounts Payable is understated by $405 ($450 − $45). The correcting entry is as follows:

A  =  L  +  OE
+450    +405
−45

Cash flows: no effect

<u>Correcting Entry</u>

| June 3 | Office Equipment | 450 | |
| | Delivery Equipment | | 45 |
| | Accounts Payable | | 405 |
| | To correct May 18 entry. | | |

Instead of preparing a correcting entry, many accountants simply reverse the incorrect entry and then record the correct entry. Even though this approach will result in more entries and postings, it is an easier and often more logical procedure.

### ACCOUNTING IN ACTION ▶ International Insight

Even banks can make errors, as the Bank of Ireland discovered recently. Due to a processing error, credit card transactions were posted twice to the credit card accounts of Bank of Ireland customers between December 27 and 30. "Bah! Humbug!" said the irritated bank customers. The bank apologized to the affected customers and posted correcting entries on January 2.

*Source:* "B of I Doubles Up on Credit Card Bills," *Irish Times,* January 10, 2003, 59.

## BEFORE YOU GO ON . . .

### ▶Review It

1. What are the required and optional steps in the accounting cycle?
2. Distinguish between an adjusting and a correcting journal entry.

### ▶Do It

The Chip 'N' Dough Company made the following adjusting journal entry to record $5,200 of amortization expense on a delivery truck at year end:

| Feb. 28 | Amortization Expense | 5,200 | |
| | Cash | | 5,200 |
| | To record amortization on delivery truck. | | |

Prepare the required correcting entry.

#### Action Plan

- Determine the correct entry that should have been made.
- Compare it to the incorrect entry made and make the required corrections.

#### Solution

| Feb. 28 | Cash | 5,200 | |
| | Accumulated Amortization—Truck | | 5,200 |
| | To correct amortization adjustment. | | |

*Related exercise material:* BE4–4, BE4–5, and E4–4.

# Classified Financial Statements

The financial statements illustrated up to this point were simplified. We classified items as assets, liabilities, and owner's equity in the balance sheet, and as revenues and expenses in the income statement. However, financial statements are more useful to management, creditors, and potential investors when the accounts are classified into significant subgroups. In the remainder of this chapter, we will introduce you to the primary balance sheet classifications. The classified income statement will be presented in Chapter 5.

## Standard Balance Sheet Classifications

A classified balance sheet for a proprietorship generally contains the following standard classifications:

| Assets | Liabilities and Owner's Equity |
|---|---|
| Current assets | Current liabilities |
| Long-term investments | Long-term liabilities |
| Property, plant, and equipment | Owner's equity |
| Intangible assets | |

These sections help the financial statement user determine such matters as (1) the availability of assets to meet debts as they come due, and (2) the claims of short- and long-term creditors on total assets. A classified balance sheet also makes it easier to compare companies in the same industry, such as Forzani and Foot Locker. Each of the sections of a classified balance sheet is explained below.

### Current Assets

Current assets are cash and other resources that will be realized within one year of the balance sheet date. They may be realized in cash or as items sold or consumed in the business. For example, accounts receivable are current assets because they will be realized in cash as the amounts are collected within the year. A prepayment such as supplies is a current asset because of the expected use or consumption of the supplies by the business within one year.

In a service company, it is customary to recognize four types of current assets: (1) cash and cash equivalents (e.g., noncash items such as treasury bills and money market funds), (2) temporary investments (e.g., debt and equity securities), (3) receivables (e.g., notes receivable, accounts receivable, and interest receivable), and (4) prepaid expenses (e.g., rent, insurance, and supplies). A fifth category of current assets, inventories (merchandise available for sale), will be introduced when merchandising companies are discussed in Chapter 5.

Current assets are listed in the order of liquidity—that is, in the order in which they are expected to be converted into cash. This arrangement is shown in the presentation used by Canada Post, in Illustration 4-7.

A company's current assets are important in assessing its short-term debt paying ability, as explained later in the chapter.

Illustration 4-7 ▶

Current assets section

**CANADA POST**
**Balance Sheet (partial)**
**December 31, 2002**
**(in millions)**

| | |
|---|---:|
| Current assets | |
| Cash and cash equivalents | $ 450 |
| Short-term investments | 29 |
| Accounts receivable and other receivables | 517 |
| Prepaid expenses | 71 |
| Current portion of note receivable | 18 |
| Current portion of future income taxes | 47 |
| | 1,132 |

## Long-Term Investments

Like current assets, long-term investments are resources that can be realized in cash. However, the conversion into cash is not expected within one year. This category, often just called *investments*, normally includes shares and bonds of other corporations that cannot be, or are not intended to be, converted into cash quickly. Note that these are investments (assets) acquired by the company. They are to be distinguished from investments (owner's equity) made by the owner in the company.

Imperial Tobacco's investments appear in the partial balance sheet in Illustration 4-8:

Illustration 4-8 ▶

Long-term investments section

**IMPERIAL TOBACCO CANADA LIMITED**
**Balance Sheet (partial)**
**December 31, 2002**
**(in millions)**

| | |
|---|---:|
| Investments | |
| Securities—fixed income | $ 65 |
| Securities—equity | 43 |
| Other | 210 |
| Investments in a company under common control | 484 |
| | 802 |

## Property, Plant, and Equipment

**Alternative terminology**
Property, plant, and equipment are also known as *capital assets* or *fixed assets*.

Property, plant, and equipment are long-lived, tangible resources that are used in the business and not intended for sale. This category includes land, buildings, equipment, and furniture.

Although the order of listing property, plant, and equipment can vary among companies, **these assets are normally listed in the balance sheet in order of permanency.** Land is usually listed first because it has an indefinite life, followed by the asset with the longest useful life (normally buildings), and so on.

Since property, plant, and equipment benefit future periods, their cost is matched to expense over their useful lives through amortization, as we learned in Chapter 3. Assets which are amortized should be reported at their net book value (cost minus accumulated amortization).

La Senza Corporation reports the net book value (or net carrying amount as La Senza calls it) of its property, plant, and equipment on its balance sheet and gives the cost and accumulated amortization in a note to the financial statements, as shown in the following illustration. Note that except for land (which has an unlimited useful life), all other property, plant, and equipment items are amortized. This includes leasehold improvements, which are long-lived additions or renovations made to leased property.

Illustration 4-9 ◄

Property, plant, and equipment section

### LA SENZA CORPORATION
### Notes to the Financial Statements (partial)
### February 1, 2003
### (in thousands)

**6. Fixed assets**

|  | Cost | Accumulated Amortization | Net Carrying Amount |
|---|---|---|---|
| Land | $ 1,307 | $ – | $ 1,307 |
| Building | 4,540 | 885 | 3,655 |
| Furniture and fixtures | 23,267 | 13,536 | 9,731 |
| Furniture and fixtures under capital lease | 7,468 | 1,649 | 5,819 |
| Leasehold improvements | 69,157 | 44,414 | 24,743 |
| Leasehold improvements under capital lease | 32,327 | 7,829 | 24,498 |
| Computer equipment | 15,308 | 7,648 | 7,660 |
| Computer equipment under capital lease | 935 | 60 | 875 |
|  | $154,309 | $76,021 | $78,288 |

## Intangible Assets

Intangible assets are noncurrent resources that do not have physical substance. They include goodwill, patents, copyrights, trademarks, trade names, and licences that give the company exclusive right of use. Similar to buildings and equipment, intangible assets with estimated useful lives are amortized. Similar to land, intangible assets with indefinite lives are not amortized.

Illustration 4-10 shows how Shaw Communications reported intangible assets in its balance sheet. All of Shaw Communications' intangible assets have indefinite lives so no amortization was deducted from these.

Illustration 4-10 ◄

Intangible assets section

### SHAW COMMUNICATIONS INC.
### Balance Sheet (partial)
### August 31, 2002
### (in thousands)

| Intangible assets | |
|---|---|
| Broadcast licences | $4,877,256 |
| Goodwill | 145,865 |
| | 5,023,121 |

## Current Liabilities

Current liabilities are listed first in the liabilities and owner's equity section of the balance sheet. Current liabilities are obligations that are expected to be paid within the coming year from current assets or through the creation of other current liabilities. Current liabilities include notes payable, accounts payable, salaries payable, interest payable, sales taxes payable, and current maturities of long-term liabilities (payments to be made within the next year on long-term debt).

Current liabilities are often listed in order of currency. That is, the liabilities that come due first are listed first. However, for many companies the arrangement of items within the current liabilities section is the result of custom rather than a prescribed rule. The current liabilities section from Sears Canada's balance sheet is shown in Illustration 4-11.

**Illustration 4-11 ▶**

Current liabilities section

| SEARS CANADA INC.<br>Balance Sheet (partial)<br>December 28, 2002<br>(in millions) | SEARS |
|---|---|
| **Current liabilities** | |
| Accounts payable | $  799.0 |
| Accrued liabilities | 517.3 |
| Income and other taxes payable | 99.1 |
| Principal payments on long-term obligations due within one year | 6.2 |
| Current portion of deferred credit | 30.0 |
| | 1,451.6 |

Users of financial statements look closely at the relationship between current assets and current liabilities. This relationship is important in evaluating a company's ability to pay its current liabilities. We will talk more about this later in the chapter when we learn how to use the information in the financial statements.

## Long-Term Liabilities

Obligations expected to be paid after one year are classified as **long-term liabilities**. Liabilities in this category can include (1) bonds payable, (2) mortgages payable, (3) notes payable, (4) lease liabilities, and (5) obligations under employee pension plans. Many companies report long-term debt that matures after one year as a single amount in the balance sheet. Then they show the details of the debt in the notes that accompany the financial statements. As Illustration 4-12 shows, Andrés Wines reported long-term debt of $21,913 thousand on a recent balance sheet, with selected information detailed in a note.

**Illustration 4-12 ▶**

Long-term liabilities section

| ANDRÉS WINES LTD.<br>Notes to the Financial Statements (partial)<br>March 31, 2002<br>(in thousands) | ANDRĒS |
|---|---|
| 5. Bank indebtedness and long-term debt | |
| Term bank loan A | $16,811 |
| Term bank loan B | 7,800 |
| Other debt | 646 |
| | 25,257 |
| Less:  Current portion | 3,344 |
| | 21,913 |

## Equity

As discussed briefly in Chapter 1, the content of the equity section varies with the form of business organization. In a proprietorship, there is one capital account under the heading **owner's equity**. In a partnership, there is a capital account for each partner under the heading **partners' equity**. For a corporation, **shareholders' equity** is divided into two sections:

share capital and retained earnings. Amounts invested in the business by the shareholders are recorded in one of the share capital accounts. Income kept for use in the business is recorded in the retained earnings account. The share capital and retained earnings accounts are combined and reported as shareholders' equity on the balance sheet. We'll learn more about these corporation equity accounts in later chapters.

As noted in Chapter 1, it is difficult to gain access to proprietorship and partnership financial statements. Public corporations, on the other hand, issue financial statements for use by present and potential investors, among others. In its balance sheet, WestJet Airlines Ltd., a corporation, reported its shareholders' equity section as in Illustration 4-13:

**Illustration 4-13 ◄**

Shareholders' equity section

| WESTJET AIRLINES LTD. Balance Sheet (partial) December 31, 2002 (in thousands) | |
|---|---|
| Shareholders' equity | |
| Share capital | $211,564 |
| Retained earnings | 144,192 |
| | 355,756 |

## Classified Balance Sheet Illustrated

Using the adjusted trial balance for Pioneer Advertising Agency presented in Illustration 4-4 or the post-closing trial balance presented in Illustration 4-5, we can prepare the classified balance sheet at October 31, 2005, shown in Illustration 4-14. Note that Pioneer Advertising has only one noncurrent asset, office equipment. Pioneer Advertising rents its premises so it does not report other property, plant, and equipment, such as land or building. As discussed earlier in this chapter, if it did, it would present the longest-lived asset (e.g., land) first. Also note that, for illustrative purposes, we have assumed that $1,000 of the notes payable is due currently and $4,000 is long-term.

The balance sheet is most often presented in report form, as in Illustration 4-14 on the following page, with the assets shown above the liabilities and owner's equity. The balance sheet may also be presented in account form, with the assets section placed on the left and the liabilities and owner's equity sections on the right. The majority of Canadian companies use the report form of presentation of the balance sheet.

Another, more complete example of a classified balance sheet for a different company is presented in Illustration 4-17 on page 173.

## Using the Information in the Financial Statements

Now that you are familiar with the components of the classified balance sheet, you should look more closely at The Forzani Group's balance sheet, reproduced in Appendix A at the end of this book. While you will note some variations of presentation, the format is very similar to the reporting practices of companies illustrated in this chapter.

Users of financial statements look closely at many relationships between the figures on the balance sheet. One important relationship is the one between current assets and current liabilities. The difference between current assets and current liabilities is called working capital. Working capital is important in order to evaluate a company's liquidity—it represents the company's ability to pay obligations that become due within the next year. When current assets exceed current liabilities at the balance sheet date, the likelihood of paying the liabilities is good. When the reverse is true, short-term creditors may not be paid.

study objective 7

Illustrate measures used to evaluate liquidity.

Illustration 4-14 ▶

Classified balance sheet

## PIONEER ADVERTISING AGENCY
### Balance Sheet
### October 31, 2005

### Assets

| | | |
|---|---:|---:|
| Current assets | | |
| Cash | | $15,200 |
| Accounts receivable | | 200 |
| Advertising supplies | | 1,000 |
| Prepaid insurance | | 550 |
| Total current assets | | 16,950 |
| Property, plant, and equipment | | |
| Office equipment | $5,000 | |
| Less:  Accumulated amortization | 83 | 4,917 |
| Total assets | | $21,867 |

### Liabilities and Owner's Equity

| | |
|---|---:|
| Current liabilities | |
| Notes payable | $ 1,000 |
| Accounts payable | 2,500 |
| Unearned revenue | 800 |
| Salaries payable | 400 |
| Interest payable | 25 |
| Total current liabilities | 4,725 |
| Long-term liabilities | |
| Notes payable | 4,000 |
| Total liabilities | 8,725 |
| Owner's equity | |
| C. R. Byrd, capital | 13,142 |
| Total liabilities and owner's equity | $21,867 |

Forzani's working capital is $100,725 thousand, as shown in Illustration 4-15, where amounts are in thousands.

**Illustration 4-15 ▶**

Working capital

| Current Assets | − | Current Liabilities | = | Working Capital |
|---|---|---|---|---|
| $318,440 | − | $217,715 | = | $100,725 |

The relationship can also be expressed as a ratio, called the current ratio. The current ratio is calculated by dividing current assets by current liabilities. The current ratio for Forzani at February 2, 2003, is as follows ($ in thousands):

**Illustration 4-16 ▶**

Current ratio

| Current Assets | ÷ | Current Liabilities | = | Current Ratio |
|---|---|---|---|---|
| $318,440 | ÷ | $217,715 | = | 1.5:1 |

It is important to be aware that norms vary between companies and between industries. Ratios should never be interpreted without considering certain factors. The current ratio and other ratios should be assessed (1) in reference to general economic and industry conditions, (2) in connection with other specific financial information about the company over time, and (3) in comparison with other firms in the same or related industries. We will discuss how to analyse ratios further in Chapter 18.

Illustration 4-17 ◀

Classified balance sheet

## FRANKLIN COMPANY
## Balance Sheet
## December 31, 2005

### Assets

| | | |
|---|---:|---:|
| **Current assets** | | |
| Cash and cash equivalents | $ 6,600 | |
| Temporary investments | 2,000 | |
| Accounts receivable | 7,000 | |
| Inventories | 4,000 | |
| Supplies | 2,100 | |
| Prepaid insurance | 400 | |
| Total current assets | | $ 22,100 |
| **Long-term investments** | | |
| Equity investment | $ 5,200 | |
| Debt investment | 2,000 | |
| Total long-term investments | | 7,200 |
| **Property, plant, and equipment** | | |
| Land | $40,000 | |
| Buildings | $75,000 | |
| Less: Accumulated amortization | 15,000 | 60,000 |
| Office equipment | $24,000 | |
| Less: Accumulated amortization | 5,000 | 19,000 |
| Total property, plant, and equipment | | 119,000 |
| **Intangible assets** | | |
| Patents (net of amortization) | | 3,100 |
| Total assets | | $151,400 |

### Liabilities and Owner's Equity

| | | |
|---|---:|---:|
| **Current liabilities** | | |
| Notes payable | $11,000 | |
| Accounts payable | 2,100 | |
| Salaries payable | 1,600 | |
| Unearned revenue | 900 | |
| Interest payable | 450 | |
| Current portion of mortgage payable | 1,000 | |
| Total current liabilities | | $ 17,050 |
| **Long-term liabilities** | | |
| Notes payable | $1,300 | |
| Mortgage payable | 9,000 | |
| Total long-term liabilities | | 10,300 |
| Total liabilities | | 27,350 |
| **Owner's equity** | | |
| B. Franklin, capital | | 124,050 |
| Total liabilities and owner's equity | | $151,400 |

# BEFORE YOU GO ON . . .

## ▶Review It

1. What are the major sections in a classified balance sheet?
2. What is working capital? How might it be expressed as a ratio?

3. Using Forzani's balance sheet, identify the components of its current assets and current liabilities at February 2, 2003. Can you tell if current assets and current liabilities are listed in order of liquidity, or in some other order? The answer to these questions is provided at the end of this chapter.

*Related exercise material:* BE4–6, BE4–7, BE4–8, E4–5, E4–6, E4–7, and E4–8.

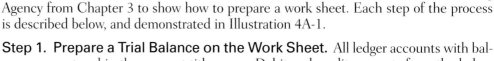

## APPENDIX 4A ▶ USING A WORK SHEET IN AN ELECTRONIC WORLD

As discussed in the chapter, a work sheet is a multiple-column form that may be used in the adjustment process and in preparing financial statements. The five steps for preparing a work sheet are described in the next section. The steps must be performed in the sequence shown.

## Steps in Preparing a Work Sheet

study objective 8

Prepare a work sheet.

We will use the October 31 trial balance and adjustment data for Pioneer Advertising Agency from Chapter 3 to show how to prepare a work sheet. Each step of the process is described below, and demonstrated in Illustration 4A-1.

**Step 1. Prepare a Trial Balance on the Work Sheet.** All ledger accounts with balances are entered in the account title space. Debit and credit amounts from the ledger are entered in the trial balance columns.

**Step 2. Enter the Adjustments in the Adjustment Columns.** When a work sheet is used, all adjustments are entered in the adjustment columns. In entering the adjustments, relevant trial balance accounts should be used. If additional accounts are needed, they should be inserted on the lines immediately below the trial balance totals.

In a manually prepared work sheet, each adjustment is cross-referenced (usually by letter) to make it easier to journalize the adjusting entry in the general journal. This has been done in Illustration 4A-1. It is important to realize that year-end adjustments must still be journalized, but not until after the work sheet is completed and the financial statements have been prepared. The books should not be filled with interim adjustments unless they need to show the adjusted information on a more permanent basis.

Work Sheet
Walkthrough

The adjustments on Pioneer Advertising Agency's work sheet are the same as the adjustments shown on pages 115 to 116 of Chapter 3. They are recorded in the adjustment columns of the work sheet as follows:

(a) An additional account, Advertising Supplies Expense, is debited $1,500 for the cost of supplies used, and Advertising Supplies is credited $1,500.
(b) An additional account, Insurance Expense, is debited $50 for the insurance that has expired, and Prepaid Insurance is credited $50.
(c) Unearned Revenue is debited $400 for fees, and Service Revenue is credited $400.
(d) Accounts Receivable is debited $200 for fees earned but not billed, and Service Revenue is credited $200.
(e) Two additional accounts relating to interest are needed. Interest Expense is debited $25 for accrued interest, and Interest Payable is credited $25.
(f) Salaries Expense is debited $400 for accrued salaries, and an additional account, Salaries Payable, is credited $400.

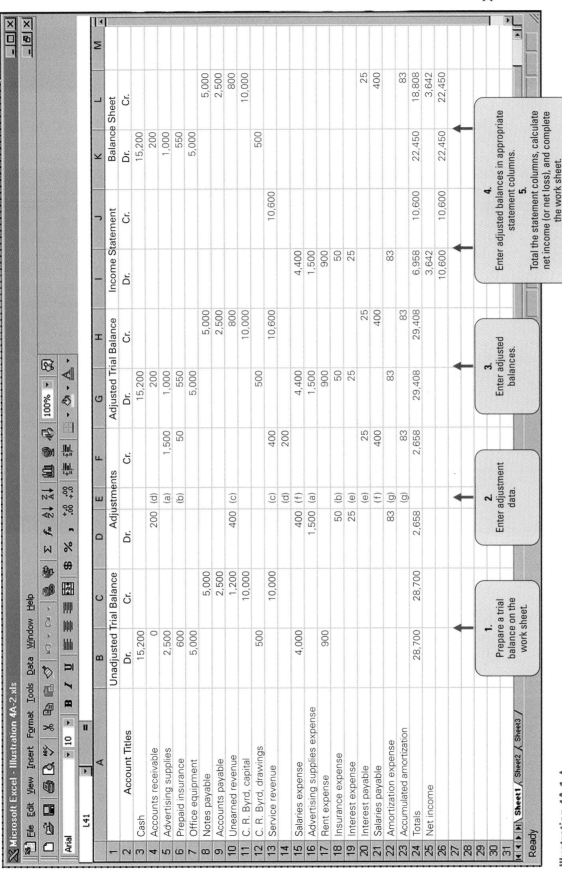

**Illustration 4A-1** ▲

Preparing a work sheet—
Steps 1–5

(g) Two additional accounts are needed. Amortization Expense is debited $83 for the month's amortization, and Accumulated Amortization—Office Equipment is credited $83.

Note in the illustration that after all the adjustments have been entered, the adjustment columns are totalled (automatically if the worksheet is computer generated) and the equality of the column totals is proven.

### Step 3.  Enter the Adjusted Balances in the Adjusted Trial Balance Columns.

The adjusted balance of an account is obtained by combining the amounts entered in the first four columns of the work sheet for each account. For example, the Prepaid Insurance account in the trial balance columns has a $600 debit balance and a $50 credit in the adjustment columns. These two amounts combine to result in a $550 debit balance in the adjusted trial balance columns. For each account on the work sheet, the amount in the adjusted trial balance columns is equal to the account balance that will appear in the ledger after the adjusting entries have been journalized and posted. The balances in these columns are the same as those in the adjusted trial balance in Illustration 4-4.

After all account balances have been entered in the adjusted trial balance columns, the columns are totalled and their equality is proven. The agreement of the column totals makes it easier to complete the work sheet. If these columns are not in agreement, the error(s) must be found before you proceed. If the errors are not found, the statement columns will not balance and the financial statements will be incorrect.

**Helpful hint** Every adjusted trial balance amount must appear in one of the four statement columns.

### Step 4.  Enter the Adjusted Trial Balance Amounts in the Appropriate Financial Statement Columns.

The fourth step is to enter adjusted trial balance amounts in the income statement or balance sheet columns of the work sheet. Balance sheet accounts are entered in the appropriate balance sheet debit and credit columns. For instance, Cash is entered in the balance sheet debit column and Notes Payable is entered in the credit column.

Because the work sheet does not have columns for the statement of owner's equity, the balance in owner's capital is entered in the balance sheet credit column. In addition, the balance in the owner's drawings account is entered in the balance sheet debit column because it is an owner's equity account with a debit balance.

The amounts in revenue and expense accounts such as Service Revenue and Salaries Expense are entered in the appropriate income statement columns.

### Step 5.  Total the Statement Columns, Calculate the Net Income (or Net Loss), and Complete the Work Sheet.

Each of the financial statement columns must be totalled. The net income or loss for the period is then found by calculating the difference between the totals of the two income statement columns. If total credits exceed total debits, net income has resulted. In such a case, as shown in Illustration 4A-1, the words "Net income" are inserted in the account title space. The amount is then entered in the income statement debit column and the balance sheet credit column. The debit amount balances the income statement columns, and the credit amount balances the balance sheet columns. In addition, the credit in the balance sheet column indicates the increase in owner's equity that results from net income. Conversely, if total debits in the income statement columns exceed total credits, a net loss has occurred. In such a case, the amount of the net loss is entered in the income statement credit column and the balance sheet debit column.

After the net income or net loss has been entered, new column totals are determined. The totals shown in the debit and credit income statement columns will now match. The totals shown in the debit and credit balance sheet columns will also match. If either the income statement columns or the balance sheet columns are not equal after the net income or net loss has been entered, there is an error in the work sheet.

# Preparing Financial Statements from a Work Sheet

After a work sheet has been completed, all the data required to prepare the financial statements are at hand. The income statement is prepared from the income statement columns. The balance sheet and statement of owner's equity are prepared from the balance sheet columns.

Note that the amount shown for owner's capital in the work sheet is the account balance before considering drawings and net income (or loss). When there have been no additional investments of capital by the owner during the period, this amount is the balance at the beginning of the period.

Using a work sheet, accountants can prepare financial statements before adjusting entries have been journalized and posted. However, the completed work sheet is not a substitute for formal financial statements. Data in the financial statement columns of the work sheet are not properly arranged for statement purposes. Also, as noted earlier, the financial statement presentation for some accounts differs from their statement columns on the work sheet. A work sheet is basically an accountant's working tool. It is not distributed to management or other parties.

## APPENDIX 4B ▶ REVERSING ENTRIES

After the financial statements are prepared and the books are closed, it is often helpful to reverse some of the adjusting entries before recording the regular transactions of the next period. Such entries are called reversing entries. **A reversing entry is made at the beginning of the next accounting period and is the exact opposite of the adjusting entry made in the previous period.** The recording of reversing entries is an **optional** step in the accounting cycle.

The purpose of reversing entries is to simplify the recording of future transactions related to an adjusting entry. As you may recall from Chapter 3, the payment of salaries on November 11 after an adjusting entry resulted in two debits: one to Salaries Payable and the other to Salaries Expense. With reversing entries, the entire later payment can be debited to Salaries Expense. You don't have to remember what has gone on before. The use of reversing entries does not change the amounts reported in the financial statements. What it does is simplify the recording of future transactions.

# Accounting with and without Reversing Entries

Reversing entries are most often used to reverse accruals: accrued revenues and accrued expenses. They are seldom needed for prepayments (prepaid expenses or unearned revenues) or for estimates. To illustrate the optional use of reversing entries for accrued expenses, we will use the salaries expense transactions for Pioneer Advertising Agency. The transaction and adjustment data were as follows:

study objective 9

Prepare reversing entries.

1. October 28 (initial salary entry): Salaries earned of $4,000 between October 17 and October 28 are paid.
2. October 31 (adjusting entry): Salaries earned on October 31 (Monday) are $400. These will be paid in the November 11 payroll.
3. November 11 (subsequent salary entry): Salaries paid are $4,000. Of this amount

$400 applies to accrued salaries payable and $3,600 was earned between November 1 and November 11.

The comparative entries with and without reversing entries are shown below.

| When Reversing Entries Are Not Used (as in the chapter) | | | | When Reversing Entries Are Used (as in the appendix) | | |
| --- | --- | --- | --- | --- | --- | --- |
| Initial Salary Entry | | | | Initial Salary Entry | | |
| Oct. 28 | Salaries Expense | 4,000 | | Oct. 28 | Salaries Expense | 4,000 | |
| | Cash | | 4,000 | | Cash | | 4,000 |
| Adjusting Entry | | | | Adjusting Entry | | |
| Oct. 31 | Salaries Expense | 400 | | Oct. 31 | Salaries Expense | 400 | |
| | Salaries Payable | | 400 | | Salaries Payable | | 400 |
| Closing Entry | | | | Closing Entry | | |
| Oct. 31 | Income Summary | 4,400 | | Oct. 31 | Income Summary | 4,400 | |
| | Salaries Expense | | 4,400 | | Salaries Expense | | 4,400 |
| Reversing Entry | | | | Reversing Entry | | |
| Nov. 1 | No reversing entry is made. | | | Nov. 1 | Salaries Payable | 400 | |
| | | | | | Salaries Expense | | 400 |
| Subsequent Salary Entry | | | | Subsequent Salary Entry | | |
| Nov. 11 | Salaries Payable | 400 | | Nov. 11 | Salaries Expense | 4,000 | |
| | Salaries Expense | 3,600 | | | Cash | | 4,000 |
| | Cash | | 4,000 | | | | |

The first three entries are the same whether or not reversing entries are used. The last two entries are different. The November 1 **reversing entry** eliminates the $400 balance in Salaries Payable that was created by the October 31 adjusting entry. The reversing entry also creates a $400 credit balance in the Salaries Expense account. As you know, it is unusual for an expense account to have a credit balance. The balance is correct in this instance, though, because it anticipates that the entire amount of the first salary payment in the new accounting period will be debited to Salaries Expense. This debit will eliminate the credit balance, and the resulting debit balance in the expense account will equal the actual salaries expense in the new accounting period ($3,600 in this example).

When reversing entries are made, all cash payments of expenses can be debited to the expense account. This means that on November 11 (and every payday) Salaries Expense can be debited for the amount paid without regard to any accrued salaries payable. Being able to make the same entry each time simplifies the recording process: future transactions can be recorded as if the related adjusting entry had never been made.

The posting of the entries with reversing entries is shown below, using T accounts.

| Salaries Expense | | | | | Salaries Payable | | | |
| --- | --- | --- | --- | --- | --- | --- | --- | --- |
| Oct.28 Paid | 4,000 | Oct.31 Clos. | 4,400 | | Nov. 1 Rev. | 400 | Oct.31 Adj. | 400 |
| 31 Adj. | 400 | | | | | | Nov. 1 Bal. | 0 |
| Oct.31 Bal. | 0 | | | | | | | |
| Nov.11 Paid | 4,000 | Nov. 1 Rev. | 400 | | | | | |
| Nov.11 Bal. | 3,600 | | | | | | | |

# Demonstration Problem

At the end of its first month of operations, the Paquet Answering Service has the following unadjusted trial balance, with the accounts presented in alphabetical order rather than in financial statement order:

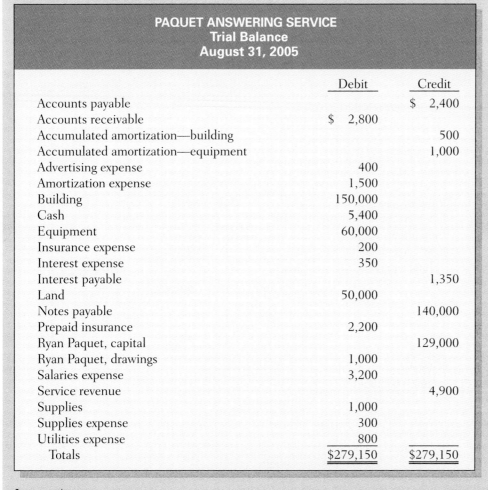

**PAQUET ANSWERING SERVICE**
**Trial Balance**
**August 31, 2005**

| | Debit | Credit |
|---|---|---|
| Accounts payable | | $ 2,400 |
| Accounts receivable | $ 2,800 | |
| Accumulated amortization—building | | 500 |
| Accumulated amortization—equipment | | 1,000 |
| Advertising expense | 400 | |
| Amortization expense | 1,500 | |
| Building | 150,000 | |
| Cash | 5,400 | |
| Equipment | 60,000 | |
| Insurance expense | 200 | |
| Interest expense | 350 | |
| Interest payable | | 1,350 |
| Land | 50,000 | |
| Notes payable | | 140,000 |
| Prepaid insurance | 2,200 | |
| Ryan Paquet, capital | | 129,000 |
| Ryan Paquet, drawings | 1,000 | |
| Salaries expense | 3,200 | |
| Service revenue | | 4,900 |
| Supplies | 1,000 | |
| Supplies expense | 300 | |
| Utilities expense | 800 | |
| Totals | $279,150 | $279,150 |

*Instructions*

(a) Prepare a classified balance sheet for Paquet Answering Service at August 31, 2005. Assume that $5,000 of the notes payable is currently due.

(b) Journalize the closing entries.

## Solution to Demonstration Problem

(a)

### PAQUET ANSWERING SERVICE
### Balance Sheet
### August 31, 2005

#### Assets

| | | | |
|---|---|---|---|
| Current assets | | | |
| Cash | | | $  5,400 |
| Accounts receivable | | | 2,800 |
| Prepaid insurance | | | 2,200 |
| Supplies | | | 1,000 |
| Total current assets | | | 11,400 |
| Property, plant, and equipment | | | |
| Land | | $ 50,000 | |
| Building | $150,000 | | |
| Less:  Accumulated amortization | 500 | 149,500 | |
| Equipment | $ 60,000 | | |
| Less:  Accumulated amortization | 1,000 | 59,000 | 258,500 |
| Total assets | | | $269,900 |

#### Liabilities and Owner's Equity

| | | |
|---|---|---|
| Current liabilities | | |
| Notes payable | | $  5,000 |
| Accounts payable | | 2,400 |
| Interest payable | | 1,350 |
| Total current liabilities | | 8,750 |
| Long-term liabilities | | |
| Notes payable | | 135,000 |
| Total liabilities | | 143,750 |
| Owner's equity | | |
| Ryan Paquet, capital | | 126,150 |
| Total liabilities and owner's equity | | $269,900 |

(b)

| | | | | |
|---|---|---|---|---|
| Aug. 31 | Service Revenue | | 4,900 | |
| | Income Summary | | | 4,900 |
| | To close revenue account. | | | |
| 31 | Income Summary | | 6,750 | |
| | Advertising Expense | | | 400 |
| | Amortization Expense | | | 1,500` |
| | Insurance Expense | | | 200 |
| | Interest Expense | | | 350 |
| | Salaries Expense | | | 3,200 |
| | Supplies Expense | | | 300 |
| | Utilities Expense | | | 800 |
| | To close expense accounts. | | | |
| 31 | Ryan Paquet, Capital | | 1,850 | |
| | Income Summary | | | 1,850 |
| | To close income summary. | | | |

| Aug. 31 | Ryan Paquet, Capital | | 1,000 | |
|---|---|---|---|---|
| | Ryan Paquet, Drawings | | | 1,000 |
| | To close drawings. | | | |

| Income Summary | | | Ryan Paquet, Capital | |
|---|---|---|---|---|
| 6,750 | 4,900 | | 1,850 | Bal. 129,000 |
| Bal. 1,850 | 1,850 | | 1,000 | |
| | Bal. 0 | | | Bal. 126,150 |

# Summary of Study Objectives

1. *Describe the purpose of a work sheet.* The work sheet is a device used to make it easier to prepare adjusting entries and financial statements.

2. *Demonstrate the process of closing the books.* Closing the books occurs at the end of an accounting period by journalizing and posting the closing entries. In closing the books, separate entries are made to close revenues and expenses to income summary, then income summary to owner's capital, and finally, owner's drawings to owner's capital. Only temporary accounts (revenue, expense, income summary, and owner's drawings) are closed, so these accounts begin the new period with a zero balance.

3. *Describe and produce a post-closing trial balance.* A post-closing trial balance contains the balances in permanent (balance sheet) accounts that are carried forward to the next accounting period. The purpose of this balance, as with other trial balances, is to prove the equality of these account balances.

4. *List the steps in the accounting cycle.* The steps in the accounting cycle are (1) analyse business transactions, (2) journalize the transactions, (3) post to ledger accounts, (4) prepare a trial balance, (5) journalize and post adjusting entries, (6) prepare an adjusted trial balance, (7) prepare financial statements, (8) journalize and post closing entries, and (9) prepare a post-closing trial balance.

5. *Explain and demonstrate the approaches to preparing correcting entries.* One approach for determining the correcting entry is to compare the incorrect entry with the correct entry. After comparison, a correcting entry is made to correct the accounts. An equally acceptable alternative is to reverse the incorrect entry and then record the correct entry.

6. *Identify and prepare the various sections of a classified balance sheet.* In a classified balance sheet, assets are classified as current assets; long-term investments; property, plant, and equipment; and intangible assets. Liabilities are classified as either current or long-term. There is also an owner's equity section, which varies with the form of business organization.

7. *Illustrate measures used to evaluate liquidity.* The excess of current assets over current liabilities is called working capital. This can also be expressed as the current ratio (current assets ÷ current liabilities), and used to assess short-term liquidity.

8. *Prepare a work sheet (Appendix 4A).* The steps in preparing a work sheet are (1) prepare a trial balance on the work sheet, (2) enter the adjustments in the adjustment columns, (3) enter adjusted balances in the adjusted trial balance columns, (4) enter adjusted trial balance amounts in appropriate financial statement columns, and (5) total the statement columns, calculate net income (or net loss), and complete the work sheet.

9. *Prepare reversing entries (Appendix 4B).* A reversing entry is the direct opposite of the adjusting entry made in the preceding period. It is made at the beginning of a new accounting period to simplify the recording of later transactions related to the adjusting entry. In most cases, only accrued adjusting entries are reversed.

## Glossary

Key Term Matching Activity

**Classified balance sheet**  A balance sheet that contains a number of classifications or sections. (p. 167)

**Closing entries**  Entries made at the end of an accounting period to transfer the balances of temporary accounts (revenues, expenses, and drawings) to the permanent owner's equity account, owner's capital. (p. 158)

**Closing the books**  The process of journalizing and posting closing entries to update the capital account and prepare the temporary accounts for the next period's postings. (p. 157)

**Correcting entries**  Entries to correct errors made in recording transactions. (p. 165)

**Current assets**  Cash and other resources that are expected to be realized in cash or sold or consumed in the business within one year. (p. 167)

**Current liabilities**  Obligations expected to be paid from current assets or through the creation of other current liabilities within the next year. (p. 169)

**Current ratio**  A measure of short-term debt-paying ability determined by dividing current assets by current liabilities. (p. 172)

**Income summary**  A temporary account used in closing revenue and expense accounts. (p. 158)

**Intangible assets**  Assets of a long-lived nature that do not have physical substance. They include goodwill, patents, copyrights, trademarks, trade names, and licences. (p. 169)

**Liquidity**  The ability of a company to pay obligations that are expected to become due within the next year. (p. 171)

**Long-term investments**  Investments in shares and bonds of other companies not expected to be realized in cash within the next year. (p. 168)

**Long-term liabilities**  Obligations expected to be paid after one year. (p. 170)

**Permanent accounts**  Balance sheet accounts whose balances are carried forward to the next accounting period. (p. 157)

**Post-closing trial balance**  A list of debit and credit balances of the permanent (balance sheet) accounts after closing entries have been journalized and posted. (p. 162)

**Property, plant, and equipment**  Tangible assets of a long-lived nature that are used in the operations of the business and are not intended for sale. They include land, buildings, equipment, and furniture. (p. 168)

**Reversing entry**  An entry made at the beginning of the next accounting period that is the exact opposite of the adjusting entry made in the previous period. (p. 165)

**Temporary accounts**  Revenue, expense, and drawings accounts whose balances are transferred to owner's capital at the end of an accounting period. (p. 157)

**Working capital**  The excess of current assets over current liabilities. (p. 171)

**Work sheet**  A multiple-column form that may be used in the adjustment process and in preparing financial statements. (p. 156)

*Note:*  All Questions, Exercises, and Problems below with an asterisk (∗) relate to material in Appendices 4A and 4B.

## Self-Study Questions

Chapter 4 Self-Test

Answers are at the end of the chapter.

(SO 1) K    1. Which of the following statements regarding the work sheet is *incorrect*?
(a) The work sheet is essentially a working tool of the accountant.
(b) The work sheet is distributed to investors and other interested parties.
(c) The work sheet cannot be used as a basis for posting to ledger accounts.
(d) Financial statements can be prepared directly from the work sheet before journalizing and posting the adjusting entries.

(SO 2) K    2. An account that will have a zero balance after closing entries have been journalized and posted is:

(a) Service Revenue.
(b) Advertising Supplies.
(c) Prepaid Insurance.
(d) Accumulated Amortization.

3. To close an expense account, the expense account is: (SO 2) K
(a) debited, and income summary credited.
(b) credited, and income summary debited.
(c) debited, and owner's capital credited.
(d) credited, and owner's drawings debited.

4. After the closing entries have been posted, the balance in the owner's capital account should equal: (SO 2) K
(a) the net income reported on the income statement.
(b) the opening capital balance reported on the statement of owner's equity.

(c) the ending capital balance reported on the statement of owner's equity and balance sheet.

(d) the opening capital balance plus any investments made by the owner during the period.

(SO 3) K   5. Which types of accounts will appear in the post-closing trial balance?

(a) Permanent (balance sheet) accounts

(b) Temporary (revenue, expense, and drawings) accounts

(c) Contra accounts

(d) All accounts

(SO 4) K   6. Which of the following is an optional step in the accounting cycle?

(a) Journalizing and posting closing entries

(b) Preparing an adjusted trial balance

(c) Preparing a post-closing trial balance

(d) Preparing a work sheet

(SO 5) AP   7. Cash of $100 is received at the time a service is provided. The transaction is journalized and posted as a debit to Cash of $100 and a credit to Accounts Receivable of $100. The correcting entry is:

(a) debit Service Revenue $100 and credit Accounts Receivable $100.

(b) debit Accounts Receivable $100 and credit Service Revenue $100.

(c) debit Cash $100 and credit Service Revenue $100.

(d) debit Accounts Receivable $100 and credit Cash $100.

8. Current assets are listed:   (SO 6) K

(a) by liquidity.   (c) by longevity.

(b) by importance.   (d) alphabetically.

9. A company reports current assets of $10,000 and current liabilities of $8,000. Its current ratio is:   (SO 7) AP

(a) $2,000.

(b) 80%.

(c) 1.25:1.

(d) More information is needed to calculate the ratio.

*10. In a work sheet, net income is entered in the following columns:   (SO 8) K

(a) income statement (Dr.) and balance sheet (Dr.).

(b) income statement (Cr.) and balance sheet (Dr.).

(c) income statement (Dr.) and balance sheet (Cr.).

(d) income statement (Cr.) and balance sheet (Cr.).

*11. On December 31, the Mott Company correctly made an adjusting entry to recognize $2,000 of accrued salaries payable. On January 8 of the next year, total salaries of $3,400 were paid. Assuming the correct reversing entry was made on January 1, the entry on January 8 will result in a credit to Cash of $3,400, and the following debit(s):   (SO 9) AP

(a) Salaries Payable $1,400, and Salaries Expense $2,000.

(b) Salaries Payable $2,000, and Salaries Expense $1,400.

(c) Salaries Expense $3,400.

(d) Salaries Payable $3,400.

the navigator

# Questions

(SO 1) C   1. A work sheet is a permanent accounting record and its use is required in the accounting cycle. Do you agree? Explain.

(SO 1) C   2. Why is it necessary to prepare formal financial statements if all of the data are in the statement columns of the work sheet?

(SO 2) C   3. How do closing entries differ from adjusting entries?

(SO 2) C   4. Identify the account(s) debited and credited in each of the four closing entries.

(SO 2) C   5. Describe the purpose of the Income Summary account and identify the types of summary data that are posted to this account.

(SO 2) C   6. Why is the owner's drawings account not closed with the expense accounts? Why is a separate entry required for this account?

(SO 3) C   7. What are the content and purpose of a post-closing trial balance?

(SO 3) K   8. Which of the following accounts would not appear in the post-closing trial balance: (a) Interest Payable, (b) Equipment, (c) Amortization Expense, (d) Ben Alschuler, Drawings, (e) Unearned Revenue, (f)

Accumulated Amortization—Equipment, and (g) Service Revenue?

9. Indicate, in the sequence in which they are made, the three required steps in the accounting cycle that involve journalizing.   (SO 4) K

10. How do correcting entries differ from adjusting entries?   (SO 5) C

11. What is the purpose of classifying assets and liabilities into categories on the balance sheet?   (SO 6) C

12. Define current assets. What basis is used for arranging individual items within the current assets section?   (SO 6) C

13. Distinguish between the three categories of non-current assets: long-term investments; property, plant, and equipment; and intangible assets.   (SO 6) C

14. How do current liabilities differ from long-term liabilities?   (SO 6) C

15. (a) What is the term used to describe the equity section of a corporation? (b) Identify the two equity accounts in a corporation and state the purpose of each.   (SO 6) K

16. What is liquidity? Identify one measure of liquidity.   (SO 7) C

(SO 8) C  *17. How is net income or loss calculated on a work sheet? How is this number entered on the work sheet if the company has net income? How is it entered if the company has a net loss?

(SO 8) C  *18. Why is it necessary to journalize and post adjusting entries if they have already been entered on the work sheet?

*19. Distinguish between a reversing entry and an adjusting entry. Are reversing entries required?  (SO 9) C

*20. Why is it helpful to use reversing entries to reverse accruals but not for prepayments or estimates?  (SO 9) C

# Brief Exercises

**List steps in preparing work sheet.**
**(SO 1) K**

**BE4–1**  The steps in using a work sheet are presented in random order below. List the steps in the proper order by writing the numbers 1 to 5 in the blank spaces.

(a) _____ Total the statement columns, calculate net income (loss), and enter it on the work sheet.
(b) _____ Enter adjustment data.
(c) _____ Prepare a trial balance on the work sheet.
(d) _____ Enter adjusted balances.
(e) _____ Enter adjusted balances in appropriate statement columns.

**Prepare and post closing entries.**
**(SO 2) AP**

**BE4–2**  The income statement for the Mosquera Golf Club for the month ending July 31 shows Green Fees Earned $16,000; Salaries Expense $8,400; and Maintenance Expense $2,500. The statement of owner's equity for the month ending July 31 shows N. Mosquera, Capital, July 1 $50,000; and N. Mosquera, Drawings $6,000. Prepare closing entries. Post the closing entries and calculate the balance in each account.

**Identify post-closing trial balance accounts.**
**(SO 3) C**

**BE4–3**  The following selected accounts and balances (in thousands) appear in the financial statements of **The Jean Coutu Group (PJC) Inc.**:

| | | | |
|---|---|---|---|
| Accounts payable | $296,044 | Long-term debt | $ 324,083 |
| Accounts receivable | 231,142 | Other revenues | 213,981 |
| Amortization expense | 43,541 | Prepaid expenses | 8,493 |
| Bank overdraft | 46,360 | Property, plant, and equipment | 415,495 |
| Interest on long-term debt expense | 12,613 | Sales | 3,372,205 |

Identify the accounts that would be included in a post-closing trial balance.

**List steps in accounting cycle.**
**(SO 4) K**

**BE4–4**  The required steps in the accounting cycle are listed below in random order. List the steps in the proper sequence by writing the numbers 1 to 9 in the blank spaces.

(a) _____ Prepare a post-closing trial balance.
(b) _____ Prepare an adjusted trial balance.
(c) _____ Analyse business transactions.
(d) _____ Prepare a trial balance.
(e) _____ Journalize the transactions.
(f) _____ Journalize and post the closing entries.
(g) _____ Prepare the financial statements.
(h) _____ Journalize and post the adjusting entries.
(i) _____ Post to the ledger accounts.

**Indicate impact of error on financial statements and prepare correcting entries.**
**(SO 5) AP**

**BE4–5**  At Hébert Company, the following errors were discovered after the transactions had been journalized and posted:

1. A collection on account from a customer for $780 was recorded as a debit to Cash of $780 and a credit to Service Revenue of $780.
2. The purchase of office supplies on account for $1,580 was recorded as a debit to Equipment of $1,850 and a credit to Accounts Payable of $1,850.

(a) Indicate the impact of each error on the balance sheet and income statement by stating whether assets, liabilities, owner's equity, revenues, expenses, and net income are understated (U), overstated (O), or not affected (NA).
(b) Prepare the correcting entries.

**BE4–6** The standard balance sheet classifications for assets and liabilities are as follows:

1. Current assets
2. Long-term investments
3. Property, plant, and equipment
4. Intangible assets
5. Current liabilities
6. Long-term liabilities

Classify balance sheet accounts.
(SO 6) K

Match the balance sheet classification above with the accounts listed below by inserting the appropriate number in the space provided:

(a) _____ Supplies
(b) _____ Accounts Payable
(c) _____ Equipment
(d) _____ Prepaid Insurance
(e) _____ Note Payable (due in 5 years)
(f) _____ Unearned Revenue
(g) _____ Accounts Receivable
(h) _____ Accumulated Amortization—Equipment
(i) _____ Patents
(j) _____ Debt Investment (due in 2 years)

**BE4–7** The adjusted trial balance of Reuben Company includes the following accounts: Accounts Receivable $12,500; Prepaid Insurance $3,900; Cash $18,400; Supplies $5,200; and Temporary Investments $8,200. Prepare the current assets section of the balance sheet as at December 31, 2005, listing the accounts in proper sequence.

Prepare current assets section of balance sheet.
(SO 6) AP

**BE4–8** Ontario-based CoolBrands International Inc. is the third largest frozen yogurt and ice cream company in the world. It reported current assets of $131,839 thousand and $93,937 thousand at August 31, 2002 and 2001, respectively. It reported current liabilities of $74,485 thousand and $50,529 thousand at August 31, 2002 and 2001, respectively. Calculate Cool-Brands working capital and current ratio for 2002 and 2001. Was CoolBrands' liquidity stronger or weaker in 2002 than it was in 2001?

Calculate working capital and current ratio; compare liquidity.
(SO 7) AP

*****BE4–9** The accountant for Coulombe Company is almost finished preparing the work sheet for the year ended July 31, 2005. The total of the accounts in the income statement and balance sheet columns are presented below. Calculate the net income or loss, write this number in the proper columns and calculate the final totals for these columns. Clearly indicate whether the company had net income or a net loss.

Complete work sheet.
(SO 8) AP

|  | Income Statement | | Balance Sheet | |
|---|---|---|---|---|
|  | Dr. | Cr. | Dr. | Cr. |
| Totals | 17,450 | 21,600 | 29,700 | 25,550 |
| Net income or loss |  |  |  |  |
| Totals |  |  |  |  |

*****BE4–10** The accountant for Orange Line Company is almost finished preparing the work sheet for the year ended August 31, 2005. The total of the accounts in the income statement and balance sheet columns are presented below. Calculate the net income or loss, write this in the proper columns and calculate the final totals for these columns. Clearly indicate whether the company had a net income or net loss.

Complete work sheet.
(SO 8) AP

|  | Income Statement | | Balance Sheet | |
|---|---|---|---|---|
|  | Dr. | Cr. | Dr. | Cr. |
| Totals | 35,800 | 29,750 | 56,150 | 62,200 |
| Net income or loss |  | 6 050 | 6050 |  |
| Totals | 35 800 | 35800 | 62 200 | 62 800 |

*****BE4–11** The following accounts appear in the adjusted trial balance columns of the work sheet for the Khanna Company: Accounts Payable; Accounts Receivable; Accumulated Amortization; Amortization Expense; H. Khanna, Capital; H. Khanna, Drawings; Prepaid Expenses; Rent Expense; Service Revenue; and Unearned Service Revenue. Indicate the financial statement column (income statement Dr., balance sheet Cr., etc.) each balance should be extended to (recorded in).

Identify work sheet columns for selected accounts.
(SO 8) C

*****BE4–12** At October 31, Orlaida Company made an accrued expense adjusting entry of $1,200 for salaries. Prepare the reversing entry on November 1 and indicate the balances in Salaries Payable and Salaries Expense after posting the reversing entry.

Prepare and post reversing entry.
(SO 9) AP

*****BE4–13** At December 31, interest receivable totalled $4,500. On January 10, interest of $5,000 was received. (a) Assuming that reversing entries are made at January 1, give the January 1 and January 10 entries. (b) Repeat part (a), assuming reversing entries are not made. (c) Compare the balances of the Interest Receivable and Interest Revenue accounts after all entries are made and posted in (a) and (b).

Prepare entries with and without reversing entries.
(SO 9) AP

# Exercises

**E4–1**  Selected T accounts for Roth Beauty Salon are presented below. All June 30 postings are from closing entries.

| Salaries Expense | | | |
|---|---|---|---|
| June 10 | 3,200 | June 30 | 8,800 |
| 28 | 5,600 | | |
| June 30 Bal. | 0 | | |

| J. Roth, Capital | | | |
|---|---|---|---|
| | | June 1 Bal. | 12,000 |
| June 30 | 2,500 | 30 | 3,000 |
| | | June 30 Bal. | 12,500 |

| Supplies Expense | | | |
|---|---|---|---|
| June 12 | 600 | June 30 | 1,300 |
| 24 | 700 | | |
| June 30 Bal. | 0 | | |

| J. Roth, Drawings | | | |
|---|---|---|---|
| June 13 | 1,000 | June 30 | 2,500 |
| 25 | 1,500 | | |
| June 30 Bal. | 0 | | |

| Service Revenue | | | |
|---|---|---|---|
| June 30 | 16,100 | June 15 | 7,700 |
| | | 24 | 8,400 |
| | | June 30 Bal. | 0 |

| Income Summary | | | |
|---|---|---|---|
| June 30 | 13,100 | June 30 | 16,100 |
| 30 | 3,000 | | |
| | | June 30 Bal. | 0 |

| Rent Expense | | | |
|---|---|---|---|
| June 1 | 3,000 | June 30 | 3,000 |
| June 30 Bal. | 0 | | |

*Instructions*

(a) Prepare the closing entries that were made.

(b) Which account(s) from which financial statement(s) should the ending balance of J. Roth, Capital account agree with?

**E4–2**  At the end of its fiscal year, the adjusted trial balance of Rafael Company is as follows:

**RAFAEL COMPANY**
**Adjusted Trial Balance**
**July 31, 2005**

| | Debit | Credit |
|---|---|---|
| Cash | $ 7,160 | |
| Accounts receivable | 14,840 | |
| Prepaid expenses | 1,620 | |
| Supplies | 470 | |
| Equipment | 15,900 | |
| Accumulated amortization—equipment | | $ 5,400 |
| Accounts payable | | 4,245 |
| Interest payable | | 525 |
| Unearned service revenue | | 2,750 |
| Notes payable (due on July 1, 2007) | | 15,000 |
| D. Rafael, capital | | 29,500 |
| D. Rafael, drawings | 14,000 | |
| Service revenue | | 73,800 |
| Amortization expense | 2,700 | |
| Salaries expense | 55,700 | |
| Interest expense | 1,350 | |
| Rent expense | 15,900 | |
| Supplies expense | 1,580 | |
| | $131,220 | $131,220 |

*Instructions*

(a) Prepare the closing entries, and post them to the appropriate accounts.

(b) Prepare a post-closing trial balance at July 31, 2005.

**E4–3** A list of adjusted accounts for Summit's Bowl-A-Drome Alley is presented in E4–7.

*Instructions*

(a) Journalize the closing entries at December 31.
(b) Post the closing entries.
(c) Prepare a post-closing trial balance at December 31, 2005.

*Prepare and post closing entries and prepare post-closing trial balance.*
*(SO 2, 3) AP*

**E4–4** The Choi Company has an inexperienced accountant. During the first two weeks on the job, the accountant made the following errors in journalizing transactions. All incorrect entries were posted.

*Prepare correcting entries.*
*(SO 5) AP*

1. A payment on account of $830 to a creditor was debited to Accounts Payable $380 and credited to Cash $380.
2. The purchase of supplies on account for $560 was debited to Equipment $56 and credited to Accounts Payable $56.
3. A $400 withdrawal of cash for L. Choi's personal use was debited to Salaries Expense $400 and credited to Cash $400.
4. The purchase of $1,200 of office equipment with a three-year useful life was debited to Office Supplies.

*Instructions*

Prepare the correcting entries.

**E4–5** The adjusted trial balance for Rafael Company is presented in E4–2.

*Instructions*

(a) Prepare an income statement and statement of owner's equity for the year. Mr. Rafael invested $5,000 cash in the business during the year.
(b) Prepare a classified balance sheet at July 31, 2005.

*Prepare financial statements.*
*(SO 6) AP*

**Interactive Homework**

**E4–6 Sobeys Inc.** has the following selected accounts listed in a recent balance sheet:

*Identify balance sheet classifications.*
*(SO 6) K*

| | |
|---|---|
| Accounts payable and accrued liabilities | Long-term debt due within one year |
| Cash and cash equivalents | Mortgages and loans receivable |
| Employee future benefit obligation | Prepaid expenses |
| Income taxes payable | Property and equipment |
| Income taxes recoverable | Receivables |
| Inventories | Temporary investments |
| Long-term debt | |

*Instructions*

Identify the classification of each balance sheet account listed above.

**E4–7** Summit's Bowl-A-Drome Alley has the following adjusted accounts and balances at December 31, 2005:

*Prepare financial statements and comment on liquidity.*
*(SO 6, 7) AN*

| Debits | | Credits | |
|---|---|---|---|
| Accounts receivable | $ 13,780 | Accounts payable | $ 12,300 |
| Amortization expense | 7,360 | Accumulated amortization— | |
| Building | 128,800 | building | 45,600 |
| Cash | 18,040 | Accumulated amortization— | |
| Equipment | 62,400 | equipment | 17,770 |
| Insurance expense | 780 | Bowling revenues | 14,180 |
| Interest expense | 2,600 | Interest payable | 2,600 |
| Land | 64,000 | Mortgage payable | 94,780 |
| Prepaid insurance | 4,680 | T. Bolgos, capital | 115,000 |
| Supplies | 740 | Unearned bowling revenue | 950 |
| | $303,180 | | $303,180 |

*Instructions*

(a) Prepare an income statement and statement of owner's equity for the year ended December 31, 2005, and a classified balance sheet at December 31, 2005. Assume that $13,600 of the mortgage payable will be paid in 2006.
(b) Calculate working capital and the current ratio and comment on the company's liquidity.

Calculate working capital
and current ratio; comment
on liquidity.
(SO 7) AN

**E4–8 Theratechnologies**, located in Quebec, is a leader in the Canadian biopharmaceutical industry. The following data (in thousands) were taken from Theratechnologies' financial statements:

|                     | Nov. 30, 2002 | Nov. 30, 2001 | Nov. 30, 2000 |
|---------------------|---------------|---------------|---------------|
| Current assets      | $44,573       | $55,586       | $32,214       |
| Current liabilities | 9,161         | 7,827         | 4,027         |

*Instructions*

(a) Calculate the working capital and current ratio for each year.

(b) Discuss Theratechnologies' liquidity in 2002 compared to the prior two years.

Prepare work sheet.
(SO 8) AP

Interactive Homework

*E4–9 The unadjusted trial balance for Kwok Yuen Ho Company at its month end, April 30, 2005, is as follows:

**KWOK YUEN HO COMPANY**
**Trial Balance**
**April 30, 2005**

|                                       | Debit    | Credit   |
|---------------------------------------|----------|----------|
| Cash                                  | $14,752  |          |
| Accounts receivable                   | 7,120    |          |
| Prepaid rent                          | 3,040    |          |
| Equipment                             | 23,050   |          |
| Accumulated amortization—equipment    |          | $ 4,250  |
| Accounts payable                      |          | 5,672    |
| Notes payable                         |          | 5,700    |
| K. Ho, capital                        |          | 33,960   |
| K. Ho, drawings                       | 3,650    |          |
| Service revenue                       |          | 11,870   |
| Salaries expense                      | 9,840    |          |
|                                       | $61,452  | $61,452  |

Other data:

1. Revenue of $720 was earned but unrecorded as at April 30, 2005.
2. Prepaid rent included $760 for April's rent.
3. Amortization on equipment for the month of April was $671.
4. Interest of $57 had accrued on the note payable by April 30.

*Instructions*

Prepare the work sheet for the month ended April 30, 2005.

Prepare adjusting entries
from work sheet data.
(SO 8) AP

*E4–10 Selected work sheet data for Blanchard Company are presented below:

|                          | Trial Balance | | Adjusted Trial Balance | |
|--------------------------|---------|--------|--------|--------|
|                          | Dr.     | Cr.    | Dr.    | Cr.    |
| Accounts receivable      | (1)     |        | 34,000 |        |
| Prepaid insurance        | 26,000  |        | 18,000 |        |
| Supplies                 | 7,000   |        | (3)    |        |
| Accumulated amortization |         | 12,000 |        | (5)    |
| Salaries payable         |         |        |        | 5,000  |
| Service revenue          |         | 88,000 |        | 94,000 |
| Insurance expense        |         |        | (4)    |        |
| Amortization expense     |         |        | 10,000 |        |
| Supplies expense         |         |        | 4,000  |        |
| Salaries expense         | (2)     |        | 49,000 |        |

*Instructions*

(a) Fill in the missing amounts.

(b) Prepare the adjusting entries that were made.

**\*E4–11** On December 31, the unadjusted trial balance of Masterson Employment Agency shows the following selected data:

Prepare and post adjusting, closing, reversing, and subsequent entries.
(SO 2, 9) AP

 Interactive Homework

| | | | |
|---|---|---|---|
| Accounts receivable | $24,000 | Commission revenue | $92,000 |
| Interest expense | 7,750 | Interest payable | 0 |
| Masterson, capital | 48,000 | | |

Analysis shows that adjusting entries were made to (1) accrue $4,200 of commission revenue, and (2) accrue $1,550 of interest expense.

*Instructions*

(a) Prepare and post (1) the adjusting entries, and (2) the closing entries for the temporary accounts at December 31.
(b) Prepare and post the reversing entries on January 1.
(c) Prepare and post the entries to record (1) the collection of $6,000 of commissions (including the accrued commission from December 31) on January 10, and (2) the payment of $2,235 interest on January 31 (consisting of the accrued interest from December 31 plus January's interest).

**\*E4–12** Rosborough Company provides property management services to a variety of companies. At its fiscal year end of April 30, 2005, adjustments were required for the following two items:

Prepare adjusting, reversing, and subsequent entries.
(SO 2, 9) AN

1. On April 1, Rosborough Company agreed to provide property management services to a client for four months at $600 per month. The client will pay the full amount at the end of the contract.
2. Rosborough Company is required to pay property taxes every year on May 31 for the calendar year. The property tax bill for 2005, which is payable on May 31, 2005, is $3,912.

*Instructions*

(a) Prepare adjusting entries for each of the above items.
(b) Prepare reversing entries on May 1, 2005.
(c) Prepare and post entries to record the later receipt of cash in (1) above and payment of cash in (2) above.
(d) Compare the amount of property management revenue and property tax expense recorded after the fiscal year end when reversing entries are used as opposed to when they are not used.

# Problems: Set A

**P4–1A** The following T accounts show the balances before the accounts were closed and the closing entries which were posted to them:

Analyse account data and prepare closing entries.
(SO 2) AN

| Repair Service Revenue | | Other Expenses | |
|---|---|---|---|
| 185,000 | 185,000 | 20,000 | 20,000 |

| J. Lecoure, Drawings | | Repair Service Expense | |
|---|---|---|---|
| 60,000 | 60,000 | 120,000 | 120,000 |

| J. Lecoure, Capital | | Other Revenue | |
|---|---|---|---|
| 60,000 | 70,000 | 20,000 | 20,000 |
| | 65,000 | | |

| Income Summary | |
|---|---|
| ? | ? |

*Instructions*

(a) Reconstruct, in general journal format, the closing entries that were journalized and posted to the above T accounts. (*Hint:* Notice that some of the amounts in the above T accounts are repeated several times. Think about which ones are related to each other in terms of the closing entries.)
(b) Post the closing entries to the Income Summary account.

Prepare adjusting entries,
adjusted trial balance,
financial statements, and
closing entries.
(SO 2, 6) AP

**P4–2A**  The following is Campus Cycle Shop's trial balance at January 31, 2005, the company's fiscal year end:

**CAMPUS CYCLE SHOP**
**Trial Balance**
**January 31, 2005**

|  | Debit | Credit |
|---|---|---|
| Cash | $   8,200 |  |
| Accounts receivable | 1,630 |  |
| Prepaid insurance | 4,020 |  |
| Supplies | 2,990 |  |
| Land | 50,000 |  |
| Building | 90,000 |  |
| Accumulated amortization—building |  | $  11,250 |
| Equipment | 24,000 |  |
| Accumulated amortization—equipment |  | 6,000 |
| Accounts payable |  | 4,000 |
| Unearned revenue |  | 1,950 |
| Mortgage payable |  | 95,000 |
| K. Dude, capital |  | 66,000 |
| K. Dude, drawings | 101,100 |  |
| Service revenue |  | 231,065 |
| Salaries expense | 115,200 |  |
| Utilities expense | 12,000 |  |
| Interest expense | 6,125 |  |
|  | $415,265 | $415,265 |

Other data:

1. Service revenue earned but not recorded at January 31, 2005, was $1,550.
2. The 12-month insurance policy was purchased on September 1, 2004.
3. A physical count of supplies shows $670 on hand on January 31, 2005.
4. Annual amortization is $3,750 on the building and $2,000 on the equipment.
5. Salaries of $1,325 are accrued and unpaid at January 31, 2005.
6. Interest of $792 is accrued and unpaid on the mortgage payable at January 31, 2005.
7. By January 31, 2005, $1,700 of the unearned revenue has been earned.
8. During the next fiscal year, $4,500 of the mortgage payable is to be paid.

*Instructions*

(a) Prepare the adjusting entries.
(b) Prepare an adjusted trial balance.
(c) Prepare an income statement, statement of owner's equity, and classified balance sheet. K. Dude invested $3,000 cash in the business on November 17, 2004.
(d) Prepare the closing entries.

**P4–3A** The adjusted trial balance for Raisin Oatmeal Company is shown below:

Prepare financial statements, closing entries, and post-closing trial balance.
(SO 2, 3, 6) AP

### RAISIN OATMEAL COMPANY
### Adjusted Trial Balance
### December 31, 2005

|  | Debit | Credit |
|---|---|---|
| Cash | $ 6,600 |  |
| Accounts receivable | 13,500 |  |
| Prepaid insurance | 3,500 |  |
| Supplies | 1,140 |  |
| Land | 46,800 |  |
| Building | 87,580 |  |
| Accumulated amortization—building |  | $ 17,520 |
| Equipment | 26,000 |  |
| Accumulated amortization—equipment |  | 5,600 |
| Accounts payable |  | 13,220 |
| Salaries payable |  | 3,000 |
| Interest payable |  | 350 |
| Unearned revenue |  | 2,190 |
| Notes payable—long-term |  | 63,900 |
| Ricardo Ospina, capital |  | 45,000 |
| Ricardo Ospina, drawings | 49,200 |  |
| Service revenue |  | 139,800 |
| Salaries expense | 32,100 |  |
| Amortization expense—building | 3,500 |  |
| Amortization expense—equipment | 2,800 |  |
| Utilities expense | 2,175 |  |
| Interest expense | 5,115 |  |
| Insurance expense | 8,400 |  |
| Supplies expense | 2,170 |  |
|  | $290,580 | $290,580 |

*Instructions*

(a) Prepare an income statement, statement of owner's equity, and classified balance sheet. Mr. Ospina made an additional investment of $1,500 during the year.
(b) Prepare the closing entries.
(c) Prepare general ledger accounts and post the closing entries.
(d) Prepare a post-closing trial balance.

Prepare financial statements, closing entries, and post-closing trial balance.
(SO 2, 3, 6) AP

**P4–4A** The adjusted trial balance for Cormier Company at its fiscal year end is as follows:

**CORMIER COMPANY**
**Adjusted Trial Balance**
**December 31, 2005**

|  | Debit | Credit |
|---|---|---|
| Cash | $ 3,600 |  |
| Temporary investments | 3,000 |  |
| Accounts receivable | 5,400 |  |
| Interest receivable | 600 |  |
| Prepaid insurance | 2,800 |  |
| Supplies | 2,000 |  |
| Note receivable | 7,500 |  |
| Office equipment | 34,000 |  |
| Accumulated amortization—office equipment |  | $ 8,000 |
| Patent | 22,000 |  |
| Note payable |  | 18,000 |
| Accounts payable |  | 6,000 |
| Salaries payable |  | 3,500 |
| Interest payable |  | 800 |
| Unearned revenue |  | 2,000 |
| P. Cormier, capital |  | 32,800 |
| P. Cormier, drawings | 10,000 |  |
| Service revenue |  | 88,000 |
| Interest revenue |  | 600 |
| Amortization expense | 8,000 |  |
| Salaries expense | 40,000 |  |
| Rent expense | 14,000 |  |
| Insurance expense | 5,000 |  |
| Interest expense | 1,800 |  |
|  | $159,700 | $159,700 |

Other data:

1. In 2006, $10,000 of the notes payable becomes due.
2. The note receivable becomes due in 2007.
3. On July 18, 2005, Pierre Cormier invested $2,800 cash in the business.

*Instructions*

(a) Prepare an income statement, statement of owner's equity, and classified balance sheet.
(b) Prepare the closing entries.
(c) Open general ledger accounts and post the closing entries.
(d) Prepare a post-closing trial balance.

**P4–5A** Bob Thebeau, CA, was hired by Campus DVD Repair to prepare financial statements for April 2005. Thebeau accumulated all the ledger balances from the owner's records, which are as follows:

Analyse errors and prepare corrections.
(SO 5) AN

### CAMPUS DVD REPAIR
### Trial Balance
### April 30, 2005

|  | Debit | Credit |
|---|---|---|
| Cash | $ 4,961 |  |
| Accounts receivable | 3,200 |  |
| Supplies | 3,800 |  |
| Equipment | 10,639 |  |
| Accumulated amortization |  | $ 1,350 |
| Accounts payable |  | 2,100 |
| Salaries payable |  | 700 |
| Unearned revenue |  | 590 |
| S. Morris, capital |  | 16,900 |
| Service revenue |  | 5,550 |
| Salaries expense | 3,300 |  |
| Advertising expense | 400 |  |
| Miscellaneous expense | 290 |  |
| Amortization expense | 500 |  |
| Repair expense | 100 |  |
| Totals | $27,190 | $27,190 |

Bob Thebeau reviewed the records and found the following errors:

1. Cash received from a customer on account was recorded as $590 instead of $650.
2. The purchase on account of a computer that cost $3,000 was recorded as a debit to supplies and a credit to accounts payable for $3,000.
3. The computer in error 2 was purchased February 1, 2005, and is expected to have a three-year useful life. Amortization, estimated to be $250, has not been recorded.
4. A payment of $45 for a miscellaneous expense was entered as a debit to Advertising Expense of $45 and a credit to Cash of $45.
5. The first salary payment made in April was for $1,900, which included $700 of salaries payable on March 31. The payment was recorded as a debit to Salaries Expense of $1,900 and a credit to Cash of $1,900. (No reversing entries were made on April 1.)
6. A cash payment for a repair expense on equipment of $93 was recorded as a debit to Equipment of $39 and a credit to Cash of $39.
7. Rent expense of $1,100 is owed but has not yet been recorded.

*Instructions*
(a) Prepare an analysis of each error that shows (1) the incorrect entry, (2) the correct entry, and (3) the correcting entry.
(b) Prepare a correct trial balance.

**P4–6A** The following accounting errors were made in the records of Mróz Company, and were not discovered. Assume the other side of each entry was correctly recorded and posted.

Determine impact of errors on financial statements.
(SO 5) AN

1. A $500 debit to Prepaid Rent was debited to Rent Payable.
2. A $300 debit to Supplies was debited to Rent Expense.
3. A $450 credit to Cash was posted to the Cash account twice.
4. A debit to Utilities Expense of $91 was posted as a debit of $19.
5. A $580 credit to Service Revenue was posted as a $500 credit.
6. A $600 credit to Interest Income was posted to Interest Receivable as a debit.
7. A $250 debit to Accounts Payable was not posted.
8. A $300 advance from a customer was credited to Service Revenue.

*Instructions*

(a) For each item, indicate the effect and amount of the error—understatement (U), overstatement (O), or no effect (NE)—on the income statement and balance sheet components. Use the following format in answering this question. The first one has been done for you as an example.

| | Income Statement | | | Balance Sheet | | |
|---|---|---|---|---|---|---|
| Item | Revenue | Expenses | Net Income | Assets | Liabilities | Owner's Equity |
| 1. | NE | NE | NE | U $500 | U $500 | NE |

(b) Determine the total amount of the understatement or overstatement resulting from the above errors.

**Calculate working capital and current ratio and comment on liquidity.**
**(SO 7) AN**

**P4–7A  Sleeman Breweries Ltd.** is the largest craft brewer in Canada and the country's leading maker of premium beers. The 2002 balance sheet of Sleeman Breweries showed current assets of $52,722 thousand and current liabilities of $47,628 thousand, including a bank overdraft (negative cash balance) of $10,461 thousand. The 2001 balance sheet reported current assets of $44,511 thousand and current liabilities of $46,315 thousand, including bank indebtedness of $16,063 thousand.

*Instructions*

(a) Calculate Sleeman's working capital and current ratio for each year.
(b) What do each of the measures calculated in (a) show? Comment on Sleeman's liquidity.

**Prepare work sheet.**
**(S0 8) AP**

\*P4–8A  The unadjusted trial balance and adjustment data for Campus Cycle Shop are presented in P4–2A.

*Instructions*

Prepare a work sheet for the year ended January 31, 2005.

**Prepare work sheet, financial statements, and adjusting and closing entries.**
**(SO 2, 6, 8) AP**

\*P4–9A  The unadjusted trial balance for Lavigne Roofing at the end of its fiscal year is as follows:

**LAVIGNE ROOFING**
**Trial Balance**
**March 31, 2005**

| | Debit | Credit |
|---|---|---|
| Cash | $  7,480 | |
| Accounts receivable | 8,290 | |
| Prepaid insurance | 6,200 | |
| Roofing supplies | 7,580 | |
| Roofing equipment | 45,000 | |
| Accumulated amortization—roofing equipment | | $  15,000 |
| Office equipment | 13,500 | |
| Accumulated amortization—office equipment | | 5,400 |
| Accounts payable | | 4,650 |
| Unearned service revenue | | 6,000 |
| Notes payable | | 30,000 |
| J. Lavigne, capital | | 36,800 |
| J. Lavigne, drawings | 44,000 | |
| Service revenue | | 157,300 |
| Salaries expense | 102,800 | |
| Interest expense | 2,200 | |
| Rent expense | 13,475 | |
| Telephone expense | 1,925 | |
| Business taxes expense | 2,700 | |
| | $255,150 | $255,150 |

Other data:

1. The insurance policy was purchased on July 31, 2004, and expires on July 31, 2005.
2. A physical count reveals $1,210 of roofing supplies on hand.
3. The roofing equipment has an estimated useful life of nine years.
4. The office equipment has an estimated useful life of five years.
5. Four customers paid $1,500 each in advance. As at March 31, 2005, the company has completed three of these contracts.

6. The note payable has an interest rate of 8% per year. Interest has been paid to the end of February 2005. The company is required to pay $6,000 of the note payable every September 30.
7. Accrued salaries at the end of March 31 were $2,050.
8. The March telephone bill of $180 is unrecorded and unpaid.
9. Revenue earned but not billed or recorded at March 31, 2005, was $1,450.

*Instructions*

(a) Enter the unadjusted trial balance on a work sheet and complete the work sheet.
(b) Prepare an income statement and statement of owner's equity for the year ended March 31, 2005, and a classified balance sheet at March 31, 2005. J. Lavigne invested $7,500 cash in the business on October 16, 2004.
(c) Journalize the adjusting entries from the adjustment columns of the work sheet.
(d) Journalize the closing entries from the financial statement columns of the work sheet.

*P4–10A* Water World Park has a fiscal year ending on September 30. Selected data from the September 30 work sheet are presented below:

Prepare work sheet, classified balance sheet, adjusting and closing entries, and post-closing trial balance.
(SO 2, 3, 6, 8) AP

**WATER WORLD PARK**
**Work Sheet**
**Year Ended September 30, 2005**

| | Trial Balance | | Adjusted Trial Balance | |
| --- | --- | --- | --- | --- |
| | Dr. | Cr. | Dr. | Cr. |
| Cash | $ 41,400 | | $ 41,400 | |
| Accounts receivable | 0 | | 1,520 | |
| Supplies | 18,600 | | 1,200 | |
| Prepaid insurance | 31,900 | | 3,900 | |
| Land | 80,000 | | 80,000 | |
| Building | 500,000 | | 500,000 | |
| Accumulated amortization—building | | $ 125,000 | | $ 150,000 |
| Equipment | 120,000 | | 120,000 | |
| Accumulated amortization—equipment | | 36,200 | | 42,200 |
| Accounts payable | | 14,600 | | 15,850 |
| Wages payable | | 0 | | 2,960 |
| Interest payable | | 0 | | 2,040 |
| Property taxes payable | | 0 | | 3,000 |
| Unearned admission revenue | | 3,700 | | 1,000 |
| Mortgage payable | | 350,000 | | 350,000 |
| M. Berge, capital | | 159,700 | | 159,700 |
| M. Berge, drawings | 14,000 | | 14,000 | |
| Admission revenue | | 302,500 | | 305,200 |
| Concession revenue | | 16,720 | | 18,240 |
| Wages expense | 105,000 | | 107,960 | |
| Repairs expense | 30,500 | | 31,750 | |
| Advertising expense | 9,660 | | 9,660 | |
| Utilities expense | 16,900 | | 16,900 | |
| Property tax expense | 18,000 | | 21,000 | |
| Insurance expense | 0 | | 28,000 | |
| Interest expense | 22,460 | | 24,500 | |
| Amortization expense | 0 | | 31,000 | |
| Supplies expense | 0 | | 17,400 | |
| | $1,008,420 | $1,008,420 | $1,050,190 | $1,050,190 |

*Instructions*

(a) Complete the work sheet, using the partial information provided above.
(b) Prepare a classified balance sheet. (*Note:* In the next fiscal year, $50,000 of the mortgage payable is due for payment.)
(c) Journalize the adjusting entries.
(d) Journalize the closing entries.
(e) Prepare a post-closing trial balance.

Use work sheet relationships to determine missing amounts.
(SO 8) AN

*P4–11A* A work sheet for Steam Carpet Cleaners in which certain amounts have been removed and replaced by letters is presented below.

**STEAM CARPET CLEANERS**
**Work Sheet**
**January 31, 2005**

|  | Trial Balance Dr. | Trial Balance Cr. | Adjustments Dr. | Adjustments Cr. | Adjusted Trial Balance Dr. | Adjusted Trial Balance Cr. | Income Statement Dr. | Income Statement Cr. | Balance Sheet Dr. | Balance Sheet Cr. |
|---|---|---|---|---|---|---|---|---|---|---|
| Cash | (a) |  |  |  | 1,200 |  |  |  | 1,200 |  |
| Accounts receivable | 4,400 |  | (e) |  | 5,000 |  |  |  | 5,000 |  |
| Cleaning supplies | 1,950 |  |  | (i) | (m) |  |  |  | 900 |  |
| Prepaid insurance | (b) |  |  | (j) | 1,650 |  |  |  | 1,650 |  |
| Equipment | 7,000 |  |  |  | 7,000 |  |  |  | 7,000 |  |
| Accumulated amortization |  | 1,000 |  | (k) |  | 1,250 |  |  |  | 1,250 |
| Accounts payable |  | 1,200 |  |  |  | 1,200 |  |  |  | (x) |
| Unearned service revenue |  | 750 | 450 |  |  | 300 |  |  |  | 300 |
| H. Kohl, capital |  | 10,000 |  |  |  | 10,000 |  |  |  | 10,000 |
| H. Kohl, drawings | (c) |  |  |  | 900 |  |  |  | 900 |  |
| Service revenue |  | 6,000 |  | (l) |  | (q) |  | (u) |  |  |
| Rent expense | 200 |  |  |  | 200 |  | 200 |  |  |  |
| Salaries expense | (d) |  | (f) |  | (n) |  | 2,000 |  |  |  |
| Totals | 18,950 | 18,950 |  |  |  |  |  |  |  |  |
| Amortization expense |  |  | (g) |  | (o) |  | (s) |  |  |  |
| Insurance expense |  |  | 150 |  | 150 |  | 150 |  |  |  |
| Cleaning supplies expense |  |  | (h) |  | (p) |  | (t) |  |  |  |
| Salaries payable |  |  |  | 500 |  | (r) |  |  |  | 500 |
| Totals |  |  | 3,000 | 3,000 | 20,300 | 20,300 | 3,650 | (v) | 16,650 | (y) |
| Net income |  |  |  |  |  |  | 3,400 |  |  | (z) |
| Totals |  |  |  |  |  |  | 7,050 | (w) | 16,650 | 16,650 |

*Instructions*

Determine the amounts that should appear in each of the spaces labeled (a) through (z) in the work sheet. (*Hint:* You will not be able to determine the missing items in alphabetical order.)

Prepare and post transaction entries, with and without reversing entries.
(SO 9) AN

*P4–12A* The Farid Company had the following balances on its December 31, 2004, balance sheet:

| Interest receivable | $2,000 | Wages payable | $38,000 |
|---|---|---|---|
| Prepaid insurance | 5,000 | Unearned sales revenue | 45,000 |

During early 2005, $3,500 cash was collected for interest and $85,000 was paid out for wages.

The company's insurance policy expired in 2005, and a premium of $8,000 was paid for a new one-year policy. Sales of $420,000 in 2005 included $375,000 of cash sales and $45,000 of goods delivered to customers who had made advance payments during 2004.

*Instructions*

(a) Assuming that the company does not use reversing entries:
   1. Prepare journal entries to record the 2005 transactions noted above.
   2. Post your entries to T accounts, and calculate the balance in each account.
(b) Assuming that Farid uses reversing entries:
   1. Prepare the appropriate reversing entries on January 1, 2005, for the accrued interest and accrued wages.
   2. Prepare journal entries to record the transactions for 2005 noted above.
   3. Post your entries to T accounts and calculate the balance in each account.

*P4–13A The unadjusted trial balance for Veda's Video Arcade at its fiscal year end of February 28, 2005, is as follows:

Prepare adjusting, reversing, and subsequent cash entries.
(SO 9) AP

**VEDA'S VIDEO ARCADE**
**Trial Balance**
**February 28, 2005**

|  | Debit | Credit |
|---|---|---|
| Cash | $ 3,495 | |
| Accounts receivable | 0 | |
| Supplies | 2,400 | |
| Equipment | 130,000 | |
| Accumulated amortization—equipment | | $ 39,000 |
| Wages payable | | 0 |
| Interest payable | | 0 |
| Note payable | | 60,000 |
| Unearned game fee revenue | | 1,500 |
| Veda Gupta, capital | | 35,000 |
| Veda Gupta, drawings | 22,500 | |
| Game fee revenue | | 83,545 |
| Rent expense | 13,800 | |
| Wages expense | 42,600 | |
| Supplies expense | 0 | |
| Amortization expense | 0 | |
| Interest expense | 4,250 | |
|  | $219,045 | $219,045 |

Other data:

1. In addition to the amount recorded as game fee revenue, the company has earned another $1,200 that will be collected on March 17. On that day, the company will also collect an additional $500 for new fees earned during March.
2. There was $950 of supplies on hand on February 28, 2005.
3. The equipment has an estimated useful life of 10 years.
4. Accrued salaries to February 28 were $480. The next payday is March 10. On that date, the employees will be paid a total of $1,680.
5. The note payable has an 8.5% annual interest rate. Interest is paid quarterly. The last day interest was paid was December 31, 2004. The next payment is due on March 31, 2005.
6. On February 28, $600 of the unearned game fee revenue was still unearned.

*Instructions*

(a) Prepare adjusting journal entries for the year ended February 28, 2005, as required.
(b) Prepare reversing entries where appropriate.
(c) Prepare journal entries to record the March 2005 cash transactions.
(d) Now assume reversing entries were not prepared as in (b) above. Prepare journal entries to record the March 2005 cash transactions.

# Problems: Set B

P4–1B The following T accounts show the balances before the accounts were closed, and the closing entries which were posted to them:

Analyse account data and prepare closing entries.
(SO 2) AN

| Other Revenue | |
|---|---|
| 30,000 | 30,000 |

| Repair Service Expense | |
|---|---|
| 115,000 | 115,000 |

| R. Laporte, Drawings | |
|---|---|
| 50,000 | 50,000 |

| R. Laporte, Capital | |
|---|---|
| 50,000 | 800,000 |
| | 70,000 |

| Repair Service Revenue | | Other Expenses | |
|---|---|---|---|
| | 180,000 | 180,000 | 25,000 | 25,000 |

| Income Summary | |
|---|---|
| ? | ? |

*Instructions*

(a) Identify the normal account balance (debit or credit) of each of the above accounts.

(b) Reconstruct, in general journal format, the closing entries that were journalized and posted to the above T accounts. (*Hint:* Notice that some of the amounts in the above T accounts are repeated several times. Think about which ones are related to each other in terms of the closing entries.)

(c) Post the closing entries to the Income Summary account.

Prepare adjusting entries, adjusted trial balance, financial statements, and closing entries.
(SO 2, 6) AP

**P4–2B** The following is Edge Sports Repair Shop's trial balance at September 30, 2005, the company's fiscal year end:

**EDGE SPORTS REPAIR SHOP**
**Trial Balance**
**September 30, 2005**

| | Debit | Credit |
|---|---|---|
| Cash | $ 8,500 | |
| Accounts receivable | 1,450 | |
| Prepaid insurance | 4,140 | |
| Supplies | 3,780 | |
| Land | 55,000 | |
| Building | 95,000 | |
| Accumulated amortization—building | | $ 11,875 |
| Equipment | 36,000 | |
| Accumulated amortization—equipment | | 9,000 |
| Accounts payable | | 4,300 |
| Unearned revenue | | 2,270 |
| Mortgage payable | | 105,000 |
| L. Bachchan, capital | | 60,000 |
| L. Bachchan, drawings | 93,525 | |
| Service revenue | | 198,450 |
| Salaries expense | 75,900 | |
| Utilities expense | 11,100 | |
| Interest expense | 6,500 | |
| | $390,895 | $390,895 |

Other data:

1. Service revenue earned but not recorded at September 30, 2005, was $1,150.
2. The 12-month insurance policy was purchased on November 1, 2004.
3. A physical count of supplies shows $960 on hand on September 30, 2005.
4. Annual amortization is $2,375 on the building and $4,500 on the equipment.
5. Salaries of $1,075 are accrued and unpaid at September 30, 2005.
6. Interest of $700 is accrued and unpaid on the mortgage payable at September 30, 2005.
7. By September 30, 2005, $1,420 of the unearned revenue has been earned.
8. During the next fiscal year, $5,400 of the mortgage payable is to be paid.

*Instructions*

(a) Prepare the adjusting entries.

(b) Prepare an adjusted trial balance.

(c) Prepare an income statement, statement of owner's equity, and classified balance sheet. L. Bachchan invested $4,000 cash in the business on November 21, 2004.

(d) Prepare the closing entries.

**P4–3B** The adjusted trial balance for Zazu Pits Raisin Company is shown below:

*Prepare financial statements, closing entries, and post-closing trial balance.*
*(SO 2, 3, 6) AP*

### ZAZU PITS RAISIN COMPANY
### Adjusted Trial Balance
### December 31, 2005

|  | Debit | Credit |
|---|---|---|
| Cash | $ 10,200 | |
| Accounts receivable | 7,500 | |
| Prepaid insurance | 1,800 | |
| Supplies | 570 | |
| Land | 100,000 | |
| Building | 150,000 | |
| Accumulated amortization—building | | $ 24,000 |
| Equipment | 28,000 | |
| Accumulated amortization—equipment | | 8,400 |
| Accounts payable | | 12,000 |
| Salaries payable | | 2,850 |
| Interest payable | | 1,400 |
| Unearned revenue | | 2,190 |
| Mortgage payable—long-term | | 198,000 |
| Andric Zazu, capital | | 58,500 |
| Andric Zazu, drawings | 7,200 | |
| Service revenue | | 77,500 |
| Salaries expense | 47,040 | |
| Amortization expense—building | 3,000 | |
| Amortization expense—equipment | 2,800 | |
| Utilities expense | 5,280 | |
| Interest expense | 16,830 | |
| Insurance expense | 1,200 | |
| Supplies expense | 3,420 | |
| | $384,840 | $384,840 |

*Instructions*

(a) Prepare an income statement, statement of owner's equity, and classified balance sheet. Andric Zazu made an additional investment in the business of $4,000 during 2005.
(b) Prepare the closing entries.
(c) Open general ledger accounts and post the closing entries.
(d) Prepare a post-closing trial balance.

Prepare financial statements, closing entries, and post-closing trial balance.
(SO 2, 3, 6) AP

**P4–4B** The adjusted trial balance for Matrix Consulting Services is as follows:

### MATRIX CONSULTING SERVICES
### Adjusted Trial Balance
### March 31, 2005

|  | Debit | Credit |
|---|---|---|
| Cash | $ 5,800 | |
| Temporary investments | 4,000 | |
| Accounts receivable | 6,200 | |
| Interest receivable | 800 | |
| Prepaid insurance | 4,400 | |
| Supplies | 2,300 | |
| Note receivable | 10,000 | |
| Computer equipment | 39,000 | |
| Accumulated amortization—computer equipment | | $ 18,000 |
| Patent | 16,000 | |
| Note payable | | 20,000 |
| Accounts payable | | 8,000 |
| Salaries payable | | 2,600 |
| Interest payable | | 1,000 |
| Unearned revenue | | 1,200 |
| Neo Anderson, capital | | 36,000 |
| Neo Anderson, drawings | 12,000 | |
| Service revenue | | 79,800 |
| Interest revenue | | 600 |
| Amortization expense | 6,000 | |
| Salaries expense | 39,000 | |
| Advertising expense | 12,000 | |
| Supplies expense | 3,700 | |
| Insurance expense | 4,000 | |
| Interest expense | 2,000 | |
| | $167,200 | $167,200 |

Other data:

1. Of the notes payable, $10,000 becomes due on July 1, 2005, the rest on July 1, 2006.
2. The note receivable becomes due on June 1, 2006.
3. On September 20, 2004, Neo Anderson invested $3,600 cash in the business.

*Instructions*

(a) Prepare an income statement and statement of owner's equity for the year ended March 31, 2005, and a classified balance sheet as at March 31, 2005.
(b) Prepare the closing entries.
(c) Open general ledger accounts and post the closing entries.
(d) Prepare a post-closing trial balance.

**P4–5B** Eric Mayers, CA, was hired by Interactive Computer Repair to prepare financial statements for March 2005. Mayers accumulated all the ledger balances from the owner's records, which are as follows:

Analyse errors and prepare corrections.
(SO 5) AN

### INTERACTIVE COMPUTER REPAIR
### Trial Balance
### March 31, 2005

| | Debit | Credit |
|---|---|---|
| Cash | $ 6,100 | |
| Accounts receivable | 3,800 | |
| Supplies | 900 | |
| Equipment | 11,490 | |
| Accumulated amortization | | $ 1,815 |
| Accounts payable | | 3,000 |
| Salaries payable | | 700 |
| Unearned revenue | | 935 |
| H. Maurice, capital | | 14,160 |
| Service revenue | | 6,450 |
| Salaries expense | 3,100 | |
| Advertising expense | 600 | |
| Miscellaneous expense | 220 | |
| Amortization expense | 700 | |
| Repair expense | 150 | |
| Totals | $27,060 | $27,060 |

Eric Mayers reviewed the records and found the following errors:

1. Cash received from a customer on account was recorded as $570 instead of $750.
2. The purchase on account of a printer that cost $395 was recorded as a debit to Supplies and a credit to Accounts Receivable for $395.
3. A payment of $30 for advertising expense was entered as a debit to Miscellaneous Expense of $50 and a credit to Cash of $50.
4. The first salary payment made in March was for $2,000, which included $700 of salaries payable on February 28. The payment was recorded as a debit to Salaries Expense of $2,000 and a credit to Cash of $2,000. (No reversing entries were made on March 1.)
5. A cash payment for a repair expense on equipment of $110 was recorded as a debit to Equipment of $90 and a credit to Cash of $90.
6. Rent of $1,050 is overdue. The company has neither paid nor recorded this amount.

*Instructions*

(a) Prepare an analysis of each error that shows (1) the incorrect entry, (2) the correct entry, and (3) the correcting entry.
(b) Prepare a correct trial balance.

**P4–6B** The following accounting errors were made in the records of Fu Company and were not discovered. Unless otherwise specified, assume the other side of each entry was correctly recorded and posted:

Determine impact of errors on financial statements.
(SO 5) AN

1. A $900 debit to Prepaid Insurance was debited to Insurance Expense.
2. A $600 debit to Accounts Receivable was debited to Cash.
3. A $350 cash sale was posted to the Cash and Service Revenue accounts twice.
4. The amortization adjusting entry was recorded and posted as $920, rather than $290.
5. A $680 posting to Accounts Receivable and Service Revenue was posted erroneously as $800.
6. A $750 credit to Interest Revenue was posted to Interest Expense as a credit.
7. A $500 collection in advance was not posted to the Cash and Unearned Service Revenue accounts.
8. A $300 rent prepayment was debited to Rent Expense.
9. A $1,500 cash withdrawal by the owner was debited to Salaries Expense.

*Instructions*

(a) For each item, indicate the effect and amount of the error—understatement (U), overstatement (O), or no effect (NE)—on the income statement and balance sheet components. Use the following format in answering this question. The first one has been done for you as an example.

|  | Income Statement | | | Balance Sheet | | |
|---|---|---|---|---|---|---|
| Item | Revenue | Expenses | Net Income | Assets | Liabilities | Owner's Equity |
| 1. | NE | O $900 | U $900 | U $900 | NE | U $900 |

(b) Determine the total amount of the understatement or overstatement resulting from the above errors.

Calculate working capital and current ratio and comment on liquidity.
(SO 7) AN

**P4–7B**  Big Rock Brewery creates and sells a premium natural unpasteurized beer. The 2002 balance sheet of Big Rock Breweries showed current assets of $6,492,345 and current liabilities of $5,257,882. The 2001 balance sheet reported current assets of $6,455,188 and current liabilities of $4,475,706. The 2000 balance sheet had current assets of $4,912,062 and current liabilities of $5,005,165.

*Instructions*

(a) Calculate Big Rock's working capital and current ratio for each year.
(b) What do each of the measures calculated in (a) show? Comment on Big Rock's liquidity.

Prepare work sheet
(S0 8) AP

*P4–8B*  The unadjusted trial balance and adjustment data for Edge Sports Repair Shop are presented in P4–2B.

*Instructions*

Prepare a work sheet for the year ended September 30, 2005.

Prepare work sheet, financial statements, and adjusting and closing entries.
(SO 2, 6, 8) AP

*P4–9B*  The unadjusted trial balance for Mason P.I. at the end of its fiscal year is as follows:

**MASON P.I.**
**Trial Balance**
**October 31, 2005**

|  | Trial Balance | |
|---|---|---|
|  | Debit | Credit |
| Cash | $ 9,618 | |
| Accounts receivable | 5,620 | |
| Prepaid insurance | 2,400 | |
| Office supplies | 1,050 | |
| Vehicle | 24,000 | |
| Accumulated amortization—vehicle | | $ 8,000 |
| Office equipment | 6,000 | |
| Accumulated amortization—office equipment | | 2,400 |
| Accounts payable | | 2,350 |
| Unearned service revenue | | 3,000 |
| Notes payable | | 10,000 |
| Allison Mason, capital | | 20,000 |
| Allison Mason, drawings | 29,000 | |
| Service revenue | | 54,480 |
| Salaries expense | 10,800 | |
| Interest expense | 917 | |
| Rent expense | 4,800 | |
| Telephone expense | 825 | |
| Gas and oil expense | 5,200 | |
| | $100,230 | $100,230 |

Other data:

1. The insurance policy was purchased on June 30, 2005, and expires on June 30, 2006.
2. A physical count reveals $410 of supplies on hand.
3. The vehicle has an estimated useful life of six years.
4. The office equipment has an estimated useful life of five years.

5. Six customers paid $500 each in advance. As at October 31, 2005 the company has completed four of these contracts.
6. The note payable has an interest rate of 10% per year. Interest has been paid to the end of September 2005. The company is required to pay $2,500 of the note payable every January 31.
7. Accrued salaries at October 31 were $850.
8. The October telephone bill of $95 is unrecorded and unpaid.
9. Revenue earned but not billed or recorded at October 31, 2005, was $945.

*Instructions*
(a) Enter the unadjusted trial balance on a work sheet and complete the work sheet.
(b) Prepare an income statement and statement of owner's equity for the year ended October 31, 2005, and a classified balance sheet at October 31, 2005. Allison Mason invested $3,500 in the business on July 18, 2005.
(c) Journalize the adjusting entries from the adjustment columns of the work sheet.
(d) Journalize the closing entries from the financial statement columns of the work sheet.

*P4–10B  Kumar Management Services manages condominiums for owners (service revenue) and rents space in its own office building (rent revenue). The trial balance and adjusted trial balance columns of the work sheet at the end of the fiscal year are as follows:

Prepare work sheet, classified balance sheet, adjusting and closing entries, and post-closing trial balance.
(SO 2, 3, 6, 8) AP

### KUMAR MANAGEMENT SERVICES
### Work Sheet
### Year Ended December 31, 2005

|  | Trial Balance | | Adjusted Trial Balance | |
|---|---|---|---|---|
|  | Dr. | Cr. | Dr. | Cr. |
| Cash | $ 14,310 |  | $ 14,310 |  |
| Accounts receivable | 23,600 |  | 25,100 |  |
| Supplies | 3,150 |  | 690 |  |
| Prepaid insurance | 3,100 |  | 1,400 |  |
| Land | 56,000 |  | 56,000 |  |
| Building | 106,000 |  | 106,000 |  |
| Accumulated amortization— building |  | $ 22,500 |  | $ 25,000 |
| Equipment | 49,000 |  | 49,000 |  |
| Accumulated amortization— equipment |  | 16,000 |  | 20,000 |
| Accounts payable |  | 10,400 |  | 11,100 |
| Salaries payable |  | 0 |  | 845 |
| Interest payable |  | 0 |  | 1,250 |
| Property taxes payable |  | 0 |  | 1,755 |
| Unearned rent revenue |  | 5,000 |  | 2,800 |
| Mortgage payable |  | 100,000 |  | 100,000 |
| N. Kumar, capital |  | 113,150 |  | 113,150 |
| N. Kumar, drawings | 28,500 |  | 28,500 |  |
| Service revenue |  | 75,600 |  | 77,100 |
| Rent revenue |  | 24,000 |  | 26,200 |
| Salaries expense | 30,000 |  | 30,845 |  |
| Repairs expense | 8,675 |  | 9,375 |  |
| Advertising expense | 17,000 |  | 17,000 |  |
| Utilities expense | 15,800 |  | 15,800 |  |
| Property tax expense | 5,265 |  | 7,020 |  |
| Insurance expense | 0 |  | 1,700 |  |
| Interest expense | 6,250 |  | 7,500 |  |
| Amortization expense— building | 0 |  | 2,500 |  |
| Amortization expense— equipment | 0 |  | 4,000 |  |
| Supplies expense | 0 |  | 2,460 |  |
|  | $366,650 | $366,650 | $379,200 | $379,200 |

### Instructions

(a) Complete the work sheet, using the partial information provided above.
(b) Prepare a classified balance sheet. (*Note:* In the next year, $10,000 of the mortgage payable is due for payment.)
(c) Journalize the adjusting entries.
(d) Journalize the closing entries.
(e) Prepare a post-closing trial balance.

**Use work sheet relationships to determine missing amounts.**
**(SO 8) AN**

*P4–11B* A work sheet for Nohe's Carpet Cleaners in which certain amounts have been removed and replaced by letters is presented below:

**NOHE'S CARPET CLEANERS**
**Work Sheet**
**April 30, 2005**

| | Trial Balance Dr. | Trial Balance Cr. | Adjustments Dr. | Adjustments Cr. | Adjusted Trial Balance Dr. | Adjusted Trial Balance Cr. | Income Statement Dr. | Income Statement Cr. | Balance Sheet Dr. | Balance Sheet Cr. |
|---|---|---|---|---|---|---|---|---|---|---|
| Cash | (a) | | | | 1,300 | | | | 1,300 | |
| Accounts receivable | 1,200 | | (e) | | 1,500 | | | | 1,500 | |
| Cleaning supplies | 1,400 | | | (i) | (m) | | | | 500 | |
| Prepaid insurance | (b) | | | (j) | 2,090 | | | | 2,090 | |
| Equipment | 7,160 | | | | 7,160 | | | | 7,160 | |
| Accumulated amortization | | 1,200 | | (k) | | 1,450 | | | | 1,450 |
| Accounts payable | | 2,115 | | | | 2,115 | | | | (z) |
| Unearned revenue | | 800 | 500 | | | 300 | | | | 300 |
| J. Nohe, capital | | 9,250 | | | | 9,250 | | | | 9,250 |
| J. Nohe, drawings | (c) | | | | 1,100 | | | | 1,100 | |
| Service revenue | | 4,000 | | (l) | | (q) | | (u) | | |
| Rent expense | 975 | | | | 975 | | 975 | | | |
| Salaries expense | (d) | | (f) | | (n) | | 2,550 | | | |
| Totals | 17,365 | 17,365 | | | | | | | | |
| Amortization expense | | | (g) | | (o) | | (s) | | | |
| Insurance expense | | | 190 | | 190 | | 190 | | | |
| Cleaning supplies expense | | | (h) | | (p) | | (t) | | | |
| Salaries payable | | | | 600 | | (r) | | | | 600 |
| Totals | | | 2,740 | 2,740 | 18,515 | 18,515 | 4,865 | (v) | (x) | 13,715 |
| Net income | | | | | | | 0 | 65 | (y) | |
| Totals | | | | | | | 4,865 | (w) | 13,715 | 13,715 |

### Instructions

Determine the amounts that should appear in each of the spaces labeled (a) through (z) in the work sheet. (*Hint:* You will not be able to determine the missing items in alphabetical order.)

**Prepare and post transaction entries, with and without reversing entries.**
**(SO 9) AN**

*P4–12B* The Friendly Food Company had the following balances on its December 31, 2004, balance sheet:

| | | | |
|---|---|---|---|
| Rent receivable | $3,000 | Property taxes payable | $ 3,250 |
| Prepaid insurance | 4,800 | Unearned service revenue | 35,000 |

During early 2005, $5,000 cash was collected for rent, and $8,500 was paid out for property taxes.

The company's insurance policy expired in 2005, and a premium of $9,000 was paid for a new one-year policy. Services provided of $455,000 in 2005 included $420,000 of services provided for cash and $35,000 of services to customers who had made advance payments during 2004.

*Instructions*

(a) Assuming that the company does not use reversing entries:
    1. Prepare journal entries to record the transactions noted above for 2005.
    2. Post your entries to T accounts and calculate the balance in each account.
(b) Assuming that the company uses reversing entries:
    1. Prepare the appropriate reversing entries for January 1, 2005, for the accrued rent and accrued property taxes.
    2. Prepare journal entries to record the transactions noted above for 2005.
    3. Post your entries to T accounts and calculate the balance in each account.

\*P4–13B The unadjusted trial balance for Larry's Laser Games at its fiscal year end of April 30, 2005, is as follows:

Prepare adjusting, reversing, and subsequent cash entries.
(SO 9) AP

**LARRY'S LASER GAMES**
**Trial Balance**
**April 30, 2005**

| | Debit | Credit |
|---|---|---|
| Cash | $ 3,495 | |
| Accounts receivable | 0 | |
| Supplies | 2,575 | |
| Equipment | 135,000 | |
| Accumulated amortization—equipment | | $ 40,500 |
| Wages payable | | 0 |
| Interest payable | | 0 |
| Note payable | | 80,000 |
| Unearned game fee revenue | | 1,875 |
| Larry Ng, capital | | 32,800 |
| Larry Ng, drawings | 24,500 | |
| Game fee revenue | | 83,545 |
| Rent expense | 14,400 | |
| Wages expense | 53,250 | |
| Supplies expense | 0 | |
| Amortization expense | 0 | |
| Interest expense | 5,500 | |
| | $238,720 | $238,720 |

Other data:

1. In addition to the amount recorded in Game Fee Revenue, the company has earned another $850 that will be collected on May 21. On that day, the company will also collect an additional $600 for new fees earned during May.
2. There was $770 of supplies on hand on April 30, 2005.
3. The equipment has an estimated useful life of 10 years.
4. Accrued salaries to April 30 were $550. The next pay day is May 10. On that date, the employees will be paid a total of $1,925.
5. The note payable has a 7.5% annual interest rate. Interest is paid quarterly. The last day interest was paid was March 31, 2005. The next payment is due on June 30, 2005.
6. On April 30, $475 of the unearned game fee revenue was still unearned.

*Instructions*

(a) Prepare adjusting journal entries for the year ended April 30, 2005, as required.
(b) Prepare reversing entries where appropriate.
(c) Prepare journal entries to record the May and June 2005 cash transactions.
(d) Now assume reversing entries were not prepared as in (b) above. Prepare journal entries to record the May and June 2005 cash transactions.

# Continuing Cookie Chronicle

(Note: The Continuing Cookie Chronicle was started in Chapter 1 and continued in Chapters 2 and 3. From the information gathered through Chapter 3, follow the instructions below using the general ledger accounts you have already prepared.)

Natalie is gearing up for the Christmas season. During the month of December, the following transactions happen:

Dec.  1  Natalie hires an assistant to help with cookie making and to do some administrative duties. Natalie and her assistant agree on an hourly rate of $8.

4  Natalie teaches the class that was booked on November 25 and receives the balance outstanding.

8  She collects the amount due from the neighbourhood school that was accrued at the end of November, 2004.

10  She receives $625 in advance from the local school board for five classes that are to be given during December and January.

15  She pays for the cellphone bill accrued in the adjusting journal entries in November 2004.

16  Natalie issues a cheque to her brother for payment of the website he set up in November 2004.

18  She receives a deposit of $50 on a cookie class that is scheduled for early January.

24  Natalie adds up all of the additional revenue for the classes taught during the month. She has not had time to account for each class individually. She determines that during the period December 1 to 24 she taught $3,500 worth of cookie-making classes. For these classes, she has collected $3,000 in cash and sent out invoices for $500. (This is in addition to the December 4 and the December 10 transactions.)

24  Natalie adds up all of the sugar, flour, and chocolate chips she purchased during the month. In total she paid $1,250 for these baking supplies.

24  Natalie issues a cheque to her assistant for $800. Her assistant worked approximately 100 hours from the time she started working for Natalie until December 24.

24  Because Natalie has had such a busy December doing school work and giving lessons, she decides to take the rest of the month off. She also withdraws $500 in cash to make a personal car loan payment.

As at December 31, the following adjusting entry data is available:

1. A count reveals that $50 of brochures and posters remain at the end of December.
2. Another month's worth of amortization needs to be recorded on the baking equipment purchased in November. (Recall that the baking equipment has a useful life of five years or 60 months.)
3. One month's worth of amortization needs to be recorded for the website. (Recall that the website has a useful life of two years or 24 months.)
4. An additional month's worth of interest on her grandmother's loan needs to be accrued. (Recall that the interest rate is 6%.)
5. One month's worth of insurance has expired.
6. Natalie is unexpectedly telephoned on December 28 to give a cookie class at the neighbourhood community centre. In January, she invoices the centre for $375 and the manager of the centre tells Natalie that the invoice will be paid sometime in early January.
7. A count on December 31 reveals that $1,000 of baking supplies were used during December.
8. Natalie receives her cellphone bill, $75. The bill is for services provided during the month of December and is due January 15. (Recall that the cellphone is only used for business.)
9. Because the cookie-making class occurred unexpectedly on December 28 and is for such a large group of children, Natalie's assistant helps out. Her assistant works seven hours at a rate of $8 per hour.
10. An analysis of the unearned revenue account reveals that two of the five classes paid for by the local school board on December 10 have still not been taught by the end of December. The $50 deposit received on December 18 for another class also remains unearned.

*Instructions*

Using the information that you have gathered through Chapter 3, and the new information above, do the following:

(a) Prepare and post the December 2004 transactions. (Use the general ledger accounts that you prepared in Chapter 3.)
(b) Prepare a trial balance as at December 31, 2004.
(c) Prepare and post adjusting journal entries for the month of December.
(d) Prepare an adjusted trial balance as at December 31, 2004.
(e) Prepare an income statement and a statement of owner's equity for the two months ended December 31, 2004, and a classified balance sheet as at December 31, 2004.
(f) Natalie has decided that her year end will be December 31, 2004. Prepare and post closing entries as at December 31, 2004.
(g) Prepare a post-closing trial balance.

# Cumulative Coverage—Chapters 2 to 4

Lee Chan opened Lee's Window Washing on July 1, 2005. During July, the following transactions were completed:

July   1  Invested $14,000 cash in the business.
       1  Purchased a used truck for $26,000, paying $4,000 cash and the balance on account.
       1  Paid $500 rent for the month.
      3  Purchased cleaning supplies for $800 on account.
      5  Paid $1,800 on a one-year insurance policy, effective July 1.
    12  Billed customers $3,800 for cleaning services.
    18  Paid $3,000 of amount owed on truck, and $400 of amount owed on cleaning supplies.
    20  Paid $1,600 for employee salaries.
    21  Collected $1,400 from customers billed on July 12.
    25  Billed customers $3,000 for cleaning services.
    31  Paid gas and oil for the month on the truck, $250.
    31  Withdrew $1,600 cash for personal use.

*Instructions*

(a) Journalize and post the July transactions.
(b) Prepare a trial balance at July 31.
(c) Journalize and post the following adjustments:
    1. Earned but unbilled fees at July 31 were $1,500.
    2. Amortization on truck for the month was $700.
    3. One-twelfth of the insurance expired.
    4. An inventory count shows $400 of cleaning supplies on hand at July 31.
    5. Accrued but unpaid employee salaries were $400.
(d) Prepare an adjusted trial balance.
(e) Prepare the income statement and statement of owner's equity for July, and a classified balance sheet at July 31, 2005.
(f) Journalize and post the closing entries, and complete the closing process.
(g) Prepare a post-closing trial balance at July 31.

**BROADENING YOUR PERSPECTIVE**

# Financial Reporting and Analysis

Practice
Tools

## Financial Reporting Problem

**BYP4–1**  The financial statements and accompanying notes of **The Forzani Group** are presented in Appendix A at the end of this book.

*Instructions*
(a) How is Forzani's balance sheet classified? What classifications does it use?
(b) How are Forzani's assets and liabilities ordered (e.g., in order of liquidity, permanency)?
(c) Forzani's working capital and current ratio for the fiscal year 2003 are calculated in the chapter. Calculate its working capital and current ratio for the fiscal year 2002. Compare them to the 2003 results.

## Interpreting Financial Statements

**BYP4–2**  The following information was reported by **The Gap, Inc.** in its 2002 annual report:

|  | 2002 | 2001 | 2000 | 1999 | 1998 |
|---|---|---|---|---|---|
| Total assets (in US millions) | $9,902 | $7,591 | $7,013 | $5,189 | $3,964 |
| Working capital (in US millions) | $3,013 | $1,023 | $(151) | $445 | $319 |
| Current ratio | 2.11:1 | 1.48:1 | 0.95:1 | 1.25:1 | 1.21:1 |

*Instructions*
(a) Determine the percentage of the overall increase in The Gap's total assets from 1998 to 2002. What was the average increase per year?
(b) Comment on the change in The Gap's liquidity. Does working capital or the current ratio appear to provide a better indication of The Gap's liquidity? What might explain the change in The Gap's liquidity during the period?
(c) Do you believe that The Gap's creditors should be concerned about its liquidity?
(d) If you were a creditor of The Gap and noted that it did not have enough current assets to cover its current liabilities in 2000, what additional information might you request to help you assess its liquidity?

## Accounting on the Web

**BYP4–3**  This case explores the advantages of e-commerce and the use of Internet technology in financial processes.

*Instructions*
Specific requirements of this Internet case are available on the Weygandt website.

# Critical Thinking

## Collaborative Learning Activity

**BYP4–4** Everclean Janitorial Service was started two years ago by Jean-Guy Richard. Because business has been exceptionally good, Jean-Guy decided on July 1, 2005, to expand operations by acquiring an additional truck and hiring two more assistants.

To finance the expansion, Jean-Guy obtained a bank loan on July 1, 2005, for $25,000, with an interest rate of 6%. Of the loan amount, $10,000 is due on July 1, 2006. The balance is due on July 1, 2007. The terms of the loan require that the borrower have working capital of at least $10,000 at December 31, 2005. If these terms are not met, the entire amount of the bank loan will be refinanced at 10% interest.

At December 31, 2005, the accountant for Everclean Janitorial Service prepared the following balance sheet:

**EVERCLEAN JANITORIAL SERVICE**
**Balance Sheet**
**December 31, 2005**

**Assets**

| | | |
|---|---:|---:|
| Current assets | | |
| Cash | | $ 6,500 |
| Accounts receivable | | 9,000 |
| Janitorial supplies | | 5,200 |
| Prepaid insurance | | 4,800 |
| Total current assets | | 25,500 |
| Property, plant, and equipment | | |
| Cleaning equipment (net) | $22,000 | |
| Delivery trucks (net) | 34,000 | 56,000 |
| Total assets | | $81,500 |

**Liabilities and Owner's Equity**

| | | |
|---|---:|---:|
| Current liabilities | | |
| Notes payable | | $10,000 |
| Accounts payable | | 2,500 |
| Total current liabilities | | 12,500 |
| Long-term liability | | |
| Notes payable | | 15,000 |
| Total liabilities | | 27,500 |
| Owner's equity | | |
| Jean-Guy Richard, capital | | 54,000 |
| Total liabilities and owner's equity | | $81,500 |

Jean-Guy presented the balance sheet to the bank's loan officer on January 2, 2006, confident that the company had met the terms of the loan. However, the loan officer was not impressed. She said, "We need financial statements which have been audited."

An auditor was hired and immediately realized that the balance sheet had been prepared from a trial balance and not from an adjusted trial balance. The adjustment data at the balance sheet date consisted of the following:

1. Earned but unbilled janitorial services were $5,700.
2. Janitorial supplies on hand were $2,300.
3. Prepaid insurance was a one-year policy dated January 1, 2005.

4. December expenses incurred but unpaid at December 31 were $700.
5. Interest on the bank loan was not recorded.
6. The amounts for property, plant, and equipment were reported net of accumulated amortization of $4,000 for cleaning equipment and of $5,000 for delivery trucks, as at January 1, 2005. Amortization for 2005 was $2,000 for cleaning equipment and $5,000 for delivery trucks.

*Instructions*

With the class divided into groups, do the following:

(a) Prepare a correct balance sheet.
(b) Were the terms of the bank loan met? Explain.

## Communication Activity

**BYP4–5** The accounting cycle is important for understanding the accounting process.

*Instructions*

Write a memo to your instructor that lists and briefly explains each of the steps in the accounting cycle in the order in which they should be completed. Your memo should also discuss the optional steps in the accounting cycle.

## Ethics Case

**BYP4–6** As the controller of Breathless Perfume Company, you discover a significant misstatement that overstated net income in the prior year's financial statements. The misleading financial statements are contained in the company's annual report, which was issued to banks and other creditors less than a month ago.

After much thought about the consequences of telling the president, Eddy Lieman, about this misstatement, you gather your courage to inform him. Eddy says, "Hey! What they don't know won't hurt them. But, just so we set the record straight, we'll adjust this year's financial statements for last year's misstatement. We can absorb that misstatement better this year than last year anyway! Just don't make that kind of mistake again."

*Instructions*

(a) Who are the stakeholders in this situation?
(b) What are the ethical issues in this situation?
(c) As a controller, what would you do in this situation?

*Answers to Self-Study Questions*

1. b   2. a   3. b   4. c   5. a   6. d   7. b   8. a   9. c   *10. c   *11. c

*Answer to Forzani Review It Question 3*

Forzani's current assets include Cash, $523; Accounts Receivable, $38,275; Inventory, $268,519; and Prepaid and Other Expenses, $11,123. Its current liabilities include Indebtedness Under Revolving Credit Facility (bank debt), $4,204; Accounts Payable and Accrued Liabilities, $209,873; and the Current Portion of Long-Term Debt, $3,638. All amounts are listed in thousands. Forzani's current assets and current liabilities appear to be listed in order of liquidity, with the most current or liquid account listed first.

Remember to go back to the Navigator Box at the beginning of the chapter to check off your completed work.

## concepts for review >>

Before studying this chapter, you should understand or, if necessary, review:

a. How to close revenue, expense, and drawings accounts. (Ch. 4, p. 158)

b. The steps in the accounting cycle. (Ch. 4, p. 164)

# Taking Stock—from Backpacks to Kayaks

VANCOUVER, B.C.—Backpacks and jackets sporting the jagged peaks of the Mountain Equipment Co-op logo are a familiar sight on Canadian campuses. Founded in 1971, MEC has eight retail stores across Canada and a huge market around the world with its catalogue and website sales. It ships everything from climbing ropes to kayaks to bike helmets, to destinations as far away as Japan and South America.

*Mountain Equipment Co-op: www.mec.ca*

With tens of thousands of items in inventory and new ones being added all the time, it's no surprise that MEC relies on a sophisticated perpetual inventory system to keep track of the flow of goods. "Because of the sheer size of our inventory, there really is no other way to do it," says Tim Crossin, who handles inventory costing at MEC.

Managing inventory is, in fact, a challenge for any retailer. The system in place at MEC, which runs on JDA software, provides continuous and up-to-date information. It identifies merchandise that has been sold and merchandise still on hand available to be sold, as well as in-house inventory—fabric and supplies MEC uses to make its own products. MEC uses this information to ensure a smooth flow of gear into its stores from its suppliers and to minimize stock outages.

"Once in-store quantities of any given item fall below a pre-determined level, the system sends a message to our distribution centre, automatically triggering a new shipment for that item," explains Mr. Crossin. "To reconcile our system data with vendor data we match our vendor invoices with quantities actually ordered and received."

The system also provides MEC with snapshot financial reports at regular intervals on such things as sales, expenses, and total value of inventory, and keeps track of GST and PST collected.

Unlike most retail operations, MEC is not out to make a profit. As a co-op, it exists to serve its members, who pay a lifetime membership fee of $5 and vote for the organization's directors. "Still, when you're as close to the line as we are—we plan for a surplus of only 3 or 4 percent—you can't afford to make mistakes," points out Mr. Crossin. Accounting for inventory—from backpacks to kayaks—is a vital part of MEC's fiscal fitness routine.

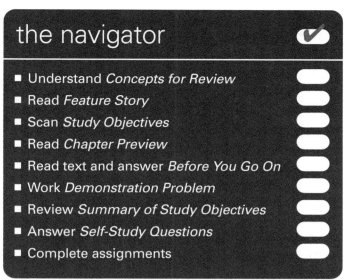

## the navigator

- Understand *Concepts for Review*
- Read *Feature Story*
- Scan *Study Objectives*
- Read *Chapter Preview*
- Read text and answer *Before You Go On*
- Work *Demonstration Problem*
- Review *Summary of Study Objectives*
- Answer *Self-Study Questions*
- Complete assignments

# c h a p t e r  5
# Accounting for Merchandising Operations

## study objectives >>

After studying this chapter, you should be able to:

1. Describe the differences between a service company and a merchandising company.
2. Explain and complete the entries for purchases under a perpetual inventory system.
3. Explain and complete the entries for sales revenue under a perpetual inventory system.
4. Explain and perform the steps in the accounting cycle for a merchandising company.
5. Distinguish between, and be able to prepare, a multiple-step and a single-step income statement.
6. Calculate the gross profit margin and profit margin.
7. Prepare the entries for purchases and sales of inventory under a periodic inventory system and calculate cost of goods sold (Appendix 5A).
8. Explain the accounting for purchase and sales discounts (Appendix 5B).

The first four chapters of this text focused mostly on service companies like the fictional Pioneer Advertising. Other examples of service companies include Air Canada, Canada Post, College Pro Painters, and the Bank of Montreal. Mountain Equipment Co-op (MEC), as indicated in the feature story, buys (or makes) and sells goods instead of performing services to earn a profit. Merchandising companies that purchase and sell directly to consumers—such as MEC, Forzani, Hudson's Bay, Indigo Books & Music, and Toys "R" Us—are called retailers.

The steps in the accounting cycle for a merchandising company are the same as the steps for a service enterprise. However, merchandising companies need additional accounts and entries in order to record merchandising transactions.

This chapter is organized as follows:

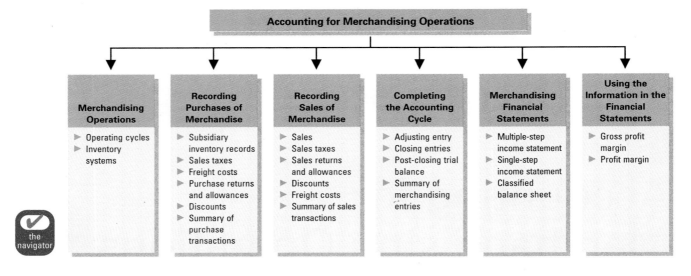

## Merchandising Operations

Measuring net income for a merchandising company is basically the same as for a service company. That is, net income (or loss) results when expenses are matched with revenues. In a merchandising company, the primary source of revenues is the sale of merchandise. These revenues called **sales revenue**, or simply sales. Unlike expenses for a service company, expenses for a merchandising company are divided into two categories: (1) cost of goods sold, and (2) operating expenses.

The cost of goods sold is the total cost of merchandise sold during the period. This expense is directly related to the revenue earned from the sale of the goods. Sales revenue less cost of goods sold is called **gross profit**. For example, when a pocket calculator that costs $15 is sold for $25, the gross profit is $10. Merchandisers report gross profit on sales in the income statement.

After gross profit is calculated, operating expenses are deducted to determine net income (or net loss). **Operating expenses** are expenses that are incurred in the process of earning sales revenue. Examples of operating expenses are salaries, advertising, insurance, and amortization. The operating expenses of a merchandising company include many of the same expenses found in a service company.

The way to measure income for a merchandising company is diagrammed in Illustration 5-1. The items in the two blue boxes are used only by a merchandising company. They are not used by a service company.

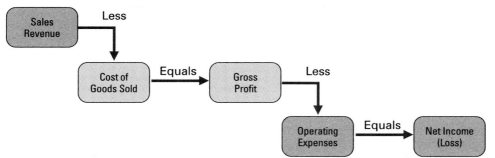

**Illustration 5-1 ◄**

Income measurement process for a merchandising company

## Operating Cycles

While measuring income for a merchandising company is basically the same as for a service company, the operating cycles differ. An operating cycle is the average time it takes to go from cash to cash in producing revenues. The normal operating cycle of a merchandising company is longer than that of a service company. The purchase of merchandise inventory and its eventual sale lengthens the cycle. The operating cycles of service and merchandising companies can be contrasted as shown in Illustration 5-2. Note that the added asset account for a merchandising company is an inventory account. It is usually titled Merchandise Inventory. Merchandise inventory is reported as a current asset on the balance sheet.

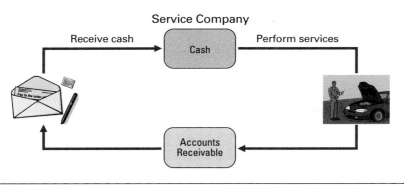

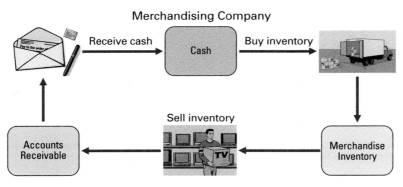

## Inventory Systems

A merchandising company keeps track of its inventory to determine what is available for sale (inventory) and what has been sold (cost of goods sold). One of two systems is used to account for inventory and cost of goods sold: a **perpetual inventory system** or a **periodic inventory system**.

### Perpetual Inventory System

In a **perpetual inventory system**, detailed records of each inventory purchase and sale are maintained. This system continuously—perpetually—shows the quantity and cost of the inventory purchased, sold, and on hand. For example, a Ford dealership has separate inventory records for each automobile, truck, and van on its lot. With the use of bar codes and optical scanners, a grocery store can keep a daily running record of every box of cereal, or other product, that it buys and sells. That's also why Mountain Equipment Co-op in our feature story uses a perpetual inventory system.

9 780471 642527 0

---

**ACCOUNTING IN ACTION ▶ @–Business Insight**

Bar codes were invented in 1973 by George Laurer, primarily to speed up check-outs and reduce cashier errors in the grocery story industry. Although there are many bar code formats, the most common bar code in North America is the UPC (Universal Product Code). The UPC contains machine-readable symbols: the first digit is a system identifier, the next five or six digits are assigned manufacturer numbers, the following five or six digits are product numbers, and the last digit is a check digit. When a code is read by a bar code reader and transmitted to a computer, the computer finds the disk file item record associated with that item number. In the disk file are the price, vendor name, quantity on hand, description, and so on. The computer does a "price look-up" by reading the bar code, and then it creates a register of the items and adds the price to the subtotal of groceries purchased. It also subtracts the quantity from the "on hand" total.

---

When inventory items are sold under a perpetual inventory system, the cost of the goods sold (the original purchase cost of the merchandise) is obtained from the inventory records. This cost is transferred from the Merchandise Inventory account (an asset) to the Cost of Goods Sold account (an expense). Under a perpetual inventory system, the cost of goods sold and reduction in inventory are recorded each time a sale occurs.

Inventory is usually the largest current asset for a merchandiser. Effective inventory control over goods on hand is critical for success. A perpetual inventory system provides strong internal control over inventories. Since the inventory records show the quantities that should be on hand, the goods can be counted at any time to see whether the amount of goods actually on hand agrees with the inventory records. Any shortages uncovered can be investigated. For control purposes, a physical inventory count is always taken at least once a year under the perpetual inventory system.

A perpetual inventory system does result in more clerical work and additional costs, even with an automated system, to maintain the detailed inventory records. However, for many businesses, the advantages of this detailed information outweigh the disadvantages. With access to this information, management can answer the inquiries of salespersons and customers about merchandise availability. Management can also maintain optimum inventory levels and avoid running out of stock. Mountain Equipment Co-op's sophisticated perpetual inventory system automatically reorders inventory for the company when in-store quantities fall below a pre-set level.

### Periodic Inventory System

In a periodic inventory system, detailed inventory records of the goods on hand are not kept throughout the period. The cost of goods sold is **determined only at the end of the accounting period**—that is, periodically. A physical inventory count is taken to determine the quantity and cost of the goods on hand at the end of the accounting period. We will learn more about how to determine the quantity and cost of inventory later in this chapter and in the next chapter.

Once the cost of the goods on hand at the end of the period is determined, we can calculate the cost of the goods sold. To determine the cost of goods sold in a periodic inventory system, the following steps are necessary: (1) Determine the cost of goods on hand at the beginning of the accounting period (beginning inventory). (2) Add to it the cost of goods purchased. (3) Subtract the cost of goods on hand at the end of the accounting period (ending inventory).

Illustration 5-3 presents the formula to calculate cost of goods sold.

**Illustration 5-3 ◄**

Formula for cost of goods sold

This calculation is, in effect, also used in a perpetual inventory system. However, the determination of cost of goods sold occurs at each sale date in a perpetual inventory system, rather than only at the end of the accounting period as in a periodic inventory system.

Illustration 5-4 compares the sequence of activities and the timing of the cost of goods sold calculation under the two inventory systems.

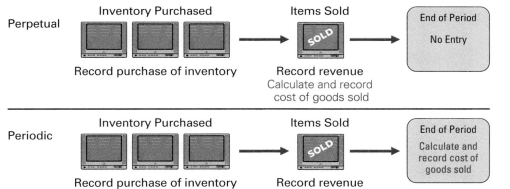

**Illustration 5-4 ◄**

Comparing perpetual and periodic inventory systems

Perpetual inventory systems have traditionally been used by companies that sell merchandise with high unit values. Examples are automobiles, furniture, and major home appliances. However, the widespread use of electronic scanners with computers has expanded this list to include nearly any product.

Periodic inventory systems are widely used by companies that sell thousands of low-unit-value items (e.g., nails) that turn over rapidly. Periodic systems are also used by companies with homogeneous goods, such as sawmill companies, where it is not possible to separately identify each piece of lumber among others of the same size and grade.

Many small businesses also use a periodic inventory system, because the cost of the detailed record keeping required for a perpetual inventory systems outweighs the benefits. They can adequately control merchandise and manage day-to-day operations without perpetual inventory records. Periodically, they count their merchandise to determine quantities on hand and establish costs for accounting purposes.

Because the perpetual inventory system is widely used, we illustrate it in this chapter. The periodic system, still used by some small businesses, is described in Appendix 5A to this chapter.

# Recording Purchases of Merchandise

**study objective 2**

Explain and complete the entries for purchases under a perpetual inventory system.

Purchases of inventory may be made for cash or on account (credit). The purchase is normally recorded by the buyer when the goods are received from the seller. Every purchase should be supported by business documents that provide written evidence of the transaction. In larger companies, each order's origin is documented with a **purchase order**. A purchase order is a document used to place an order for goods (or services) with a supplier.

Cash purchases should be supported by a cash register receipt indicating the items purchased. Both cash purchases and credit purchases are also supported by a **purchase invoice**. This document indicates the total purchase price and other relevant information. However, the buyer does not prepare a separate purchase invoice. Instead, the copy of the sales invoice sent by the seller becomes the purchase invoice for the buyer. In Illustration 5-5, the computer-generated sales invoice prepared by Highpoint Electronic serves as both a sales invoice for the seller (Highpoint Electronic) and a purchase invoice for the buyer (Chelsea Video).

**Illustration 5-5** ▼

Sales/purchase invoice

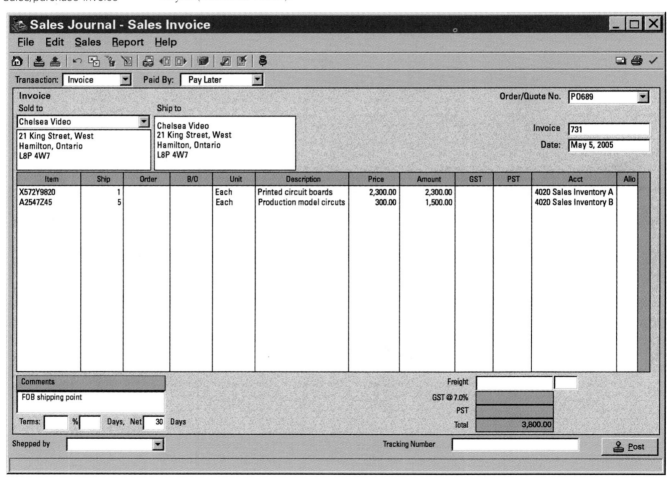

The buyer, Chelsea Video, would make the following entry to record the purchase of merchandise from Highpoint Electronic:

| May 4 | Merchandise Inventory | 3,800 | |
| | Accounts Payable | | 3,800 |
| | To record goods purchased on account per invoice #731, terms n/30. | | |

A = L + OE
+3,800  +3,800

Cash flows: no effect

Under a perpetual inventory system, when merchandise is purchased for resale to customers, the current asset account Merchandise Inventory is debited for the cost of the goods. Mountain Equipment Co-op debits Merchandise Inventory for the 9,000 different products it purchases or makes for resale.

Not all purchases are automatically debited to Merchandise Inventory. Purchases of assets acquired for use and not for resale—such as supplies, equipment, and similar items—should be debited to specific asset accounts rather than to Merchandise Inventory. For example, MEC would debit the Supplies account for the supplies it purchases and uses to make shelf signs and labels. The fabric and supplies it purchases to make clothing for resale, however, are recorded differently. These are part of the cost of a product for resale and are debited to Merchandise Inventory.

## Subsidiary Inventory Records

Imagine a business like MEC recording purchases and sales of its 9,000 products in only one general ledger account—Merchandise Inventory. It would be virtually impossible to determine the balance remaining of any particular inventory item at any specific time.

Instead, companies like MEC use a subsidiary ledger to organize and track individual items. A subsidiary ledger is a group of accounts that share a common characteristic (for example, all inventory accounts). The subsidiary ledger frees the general ledger from the details of individual balances. It is common to have subsidiary ledgers for accounts receivable (to track individual customer balances), inventory, accounts payable (to track individual creditor balances), and payroll (to track individual employee pay records).

A subsidiary ledger is an addition to, and an expansion of, the general ledger, as shown below:

**Illustration 5-6 ◄**

Relationship of general ledger and subsidiary ledgers

In this illustration, both Merchandise Inventory and Accounts Payable are control accounts with subsidiary ledgers. Cash is not a control account because there is no subsidiary ledger related to this account.

Purchases and sales of merchandise are recorded and posted to each individual inventory subsidiary ledger account. At any point in time, the inventory subsidiary ledger shows detailed information about the quantity and cost of each inventory item.

The detailed individual data from the inventory subsidiary ledger are summarized in the Merchandise Inventory account in the general ledger. The general ledger account that summarizes the subsidiary ledger data is called a control account. At all times, the control account balance must equal the total of all the individual inventory account balances.

Additional information about how to record and balance subsidiary and control account transactions can be found in Appendix C at the end of this textbook.

## Sales Taxes

Sales taxes include the federal Goods and Services Tax and the Provincial Sales Tax. GST is paid by merchandising companies on the goods they purchase for resale. However, this cost does not form part of the cost of the merchandise, because companies can recover any GST they paid on purchases by offsetting it against the GST they collected from customers.

PST is not paid by a merchandiser—it is paid only by the final consumer. Therefore, retail businesses do not have to pay PST on any merchandise purchased for resale.

As stated in Chapter 2, accounting transactions described in this textbook are presented without the added complexity of sales taxes. That is why Invoice No. 731, shown in Illustration 5-5, omitted GST, which would normally be added to the invoice price. Sales taxes are discussed in more detail in Appendix B at the end of this textbook.

## Freight Costs

**Alternative terminology**
Other common shipping terms include FCA (free carrier), CIF (cost, insurance, freight), and CPT (carriage paid to).

The purchase agreement should indicate whether the seller or the buyer must pay the cost of transporting the goods to the buyer's place of business. When a carrier such as a railroad, trucking company, or airline is used, the transportation company prepares a freight bill (often called a bill of lading) in accordance with the purchase agreement. Freight terms may vary but generally say who pays the freight and who assumes the risk during transit. For example, the terms may be expressed as either **FOB shipping point** or **FOB destination**. The letters FOB mean "free on board." FOB shipping point means that the goods are placed free on board the carrier by the seller, and the buyer pays the freight costs. Conversely, FOB destination means that the goods are placed free on board to the buyer's place of business, and the seller pays the freight. For example, the purchase invoice in Illustration 5-5 shown earlier in this chapter indicates that freight is FOB shipping point. Thus, the buyer (Chelsea Video) pays the freight charges. Illustration 5-7 illustrates these shipping terms.

**Illustration 5-7 ▼**

Terms of shipping

When the buyer pays for the freight costs, Merchandise Inventory is debited for the cost of the transportation. **Any freight paid by the buyer is part of the cost of the merchandise purchased.** This is because the inventory cost should include any freight charges necessary to deliver the goods to the buyer. Freight costs paid by MEC on its kayaks and canoes, for example, form part of the cost of these products.

To illustrate the buyer's journal entry to record the cost of shipping, assume that, upon delivery of the goods on May 4, Chelsea Video pays the Public Carrier Co. $150 for freight charges. The entry on Chelsea Video's books is:

| A | = | L | + | OE |
|---|---|---|---|---|
| +150 | | | | |
| −150 | | | | |

▼ Cash flows: −150

| | | | | |
|---|---|---|---|---|
| May 4 | Merchandise Inventory | | 150 | |
| | Cash | | | 150 |
| | To record payment of freight on goods purchased. | | | |

## Purchase Returns and Allowances

A buyer may be dissatisfied with the merchandise received. The goods may be damaged or defective, of inferior quality, or perhaps they do not meet the buyer's specifications. In such cases, the buyer may return the goods to the seller. The buyer will receive a cash refund if the purchase was made for cash. Credit is granted if the purchase was made on credit. Each type of return is known as a **purchase return**. Alternatively, the buyer may choose to keep the merchandise if the seller is willing to grant an allowance (deduction) from the purchase price. This transaction is known as a **purchase allowance**.

Assume that Chelsea Video returned goods costing $300 to Highpoint Electronic on May 9. The entry by Chelsea Video for the returned merchandise is as follows:

| May 9 | Accounts Payable | 300 | |
| | Merchandise Inventory | | 300 |
| | To record return of goods to Highpoint Electronic. | | |

A = L + OE
-300  -300

Cash flows: no effect

Chelsea Video increased Merchandise Inventory when the goods were originally purchased. So Chelsea Video decreases Merchandise Inventory when it returns the goods, or when it is granted an allowance.

## Discounts

The terms of a credit purchase may include an offer of a **quantity discount** for a bulk purchase. A quantity discount provides a reduction in price according to the volume of the purchase. Quantity discounts are not recorded or accounted for separately. For example, Highpoint may offer a 10% price discount on orders of 25 or more items. Then, if 25 printed circuit boards were ordered, the price per board would be $2,070 ($2,300 × 90%) rather than $2,300. Only the $2,070 amount would be recorded by Chelsea Video.

Quantity discounts are not the same as **purchase discounts**, which are offered to customers for early payment of the balance due. Purchase discounts are noted on the invoice by the use of credit terms specifying the amount and time period for the purchase discount. They also indicate the length of time the buyer has to pay the full invoice price. For example, credit terms might be stated as 1/10, n/30 (read "one ten, net thirty"). This means that a 1% cash discount may be taken on the invoice price (less any returns or allowances) if payment is made within 10 days of the invoice date (the discount period). Otherwise, the invoice price is due 30 days from the invoice date.

When the seller chooses not to offer a discount for prompt payment, credit terms will specify only the maximum time period for paying the balance due. For example, the time period may be stated as n/30, n/60, or EOM (end of month). In the invoice in Illustration 5-5, credit terms are n/30. This means that payment is due within 30 days of the invoice date. There is no discount offered for early payment.

In contrast to quantity discounts, purchase discounts are recorded separately. Not every company uses purchase discounts, although they are common to certain industries. Consequently, the accounting entries for purchase discounts are presented in Appendix 5B to this chapter for those who wish to study this topic further.

## Summary of Purchase Transactions

A summary of the effects of the previous transactions on Merchandise Inventory is provided in the following T account (with transaction descriptions in parentheses). Chelsea Video originally purchased $3,800 worth of inventory for resale. It paid $150 in freight charges. It then returned $300 worth of goods. This results in a balance in Merchandise Inventory of $3,650.

|  | Merchandise Inventory | | | |
|---|---|---|---|---|
| (Purchase) May 4 | 3,800 | May 9 | 300 | (Purchase return) |
| (Freight)    4 | 150 | | | |
| Bal. | 3,650 | | | |

---

## BEFORE YOU GO ON . . .

▶**Review It**

1. How does the measurement of net income in a merchandising company differ from measuring income in a service company?
2. In what ways is a perpetual inventory system different from a periodic inventory system?
3. Under the perpetual inventory system, what entries are made to record purchases, freight costs, purchase returns and allowances, and quantity discounts?

*Related exercise material:* BE5–1, BE5–2, BE5–3, and E5–1.

---

# Recording Sales of Merchandise

**study objective 3**

Explain and complete the entries for sales revenue under a perpetual inventory system.

Sales revenue, like service revenue, is recorded when it is earned. This is in accordance with the revenue recognition principle. Typically, sales revenue is earned when the goods are transferred from the seller to the buyer. At this point, the sales transaction is completed and the sales price has been established.

Sales may be made on credit or for cash. Every sales transaction should be supported by a business document that provides written evidence of the sale. **Cash register tapes** provide evidence of cash sales. A **sales invoice**, like the one shown in Illustration 5-5, can provide support for a credit or cash sale. The original copy of the invoice goes to the customer. A copy is kept by the seller for use in recording the sale. The invoice shows the date of sale, customer name, sales price, total amount due, and other relevant information.

## Sales

**Two entries are made for each sale in a perpetual inventory system.** The first entry records the sales revenue: Cash (or Accounts Receivable, if a credit sale) is increased by a debit, and Sales is increased by a credit for the selling (invoice) price of the goods. The second entry records the cost of the merchandise sold: Cost of Goods Sold is increased by a debit, and Merchandise Inventory is decreased by a credit for the cost of the goods. As a result, the Merchandise Inventory account will always show the amount of inventory that should be on hand.

To illustrate a credit sales transaction using the sales invoice shown earlier in Illustration 5-5, Highpoint Electronic's $3,800 sale to Chelsea Video on May 4 is recorded as follows. Assume the merchandise cost Highpoint Electronic $2,400 when it was originally purchased.

| A | = | L | + | OE |
|---|---|---|---|---|
| +3,800 | | | | +3,800 |

Cash flows: no effect

| May 4 | Accounts Receivable | 3,800 | |
|---|---|---|---|
| | Sales | | 3,800 |
| | To record credit sale to Chelsea Video per invoice #731. | | |

| May | 4 | Cost of Goods Sold | 2,400 | |
|-----|---|---------------------|-------|---|
| | | Merchandise Inventory | | 2,400 |
| | | To record cost of merchandise sold to Chelsea Video per invoice #731. | | |

| A | = | L | + | OE |
|---|---|---|---|----|
| -2,400 | | | | -2,400 |

Cash flows: no effect

For internal purposes, merchandisers may use more than one sales account, just as they use more than one inventory account. For example, Highpoint Electronic may keep separate sales accounts for its TV sets, VCRs, DVD players, CD players, and microwave ovens. By using separate sales accounts for major product lines, company management can monitor sales trends more closely and respond more strategically to changes in sales patterns. For example, if DVD player sales are increasing while CD player sales are decreasing, the company can re-evaluate its advertising and pricing policies on each of these items.

However, on its income statement presented to outside investors, a merchandiser would normally provide only a single sales figure—the sum of all of its individual sales accounts. This is done for two reasons. First, providing detail on individual sales accounts would add too much length to the income statement. Second, companies do not want their competitors to know the details of their operating results.

## Sales Taxes

Sales taxes are collected by merchandising companies on the goods that they sell. When a company collects sales taxes from selling a good or service, **these sales taxes are not recorded as revenue**. For example, if a company sells merchandise for $100 plus $15 HST, only $100 is recorded as Sales. The $15 HST collected is recorded in Sales Tax Payable, a liability account. The sales tax amount ($15 in this case) is collected on behalf of the federal and provincial governments, and must be periodically remitted to these collecting authorities. Until the sales tax is paid to the government, it is a liability to the company.

Companies can offset the GST (or HST in this case) paid against the GST collected. The difference (the net amount) results in either GST Recoverable from, or GST Payable to, the federal government. As stated earlier, accounting for sales taxes is complicated and is explained in Appendix B at the end of this textbook.

## Sales Returns and Allowances

We now look at the "flip side" of purchase returns and allowances, that is, sales returns and allowances recorded on the books of the seller.

Highpoint Electronic records a $300 credit for Chelsea Video's returned goods in two entries: (1) The first is an increase in Sales Returns and Allowances and a decrease in Accounts Receivable for the $300 selling price. (2) The second is an increase in Merchandise Inventory (assume a $140 original cost) and a decrease in Cost of Goods Sold. The entries are as follows:

| May | 9 | Sales Returns and Allowances | 300 | |
|-----|---|------------------------------|-----|---|
| | | Accounts Receivable | | 300 |
| | | To record credit granted to Chelsea Video for returned goods. | | |

| A | = | L | + | OE |
|---|---|---|---|----|
| -300 | | | | -300 |

Cash flows: no effect

| | 9 | Merchandise Inventory | 140 | |
|-----|---|------------------------|-----|---|
| | | Cost of Goods Sold | | 140 |
| | | To record cost of returned goods. | | |

| A | = | L | + | OE |
|---|---|---|---|----|
| +140 | | | | +140 |

Cash flows: no effect

Note that if in the first journal entry, the sales return or allowance had been on a cash sale, a cash refund would normally be made and Cash would be credited instead of Accounts Receivable.

The second entry assumes that the merchandise is not damaged and can be sold again. If the goods are returned because they are damaged or defective, the second entry still credits Cost of Goods Sold (since the goods have not been sold), but the debit is to a loss (expense) account, Loss from Damaged Goods, rather than to the asset account Merchandise Inventory if the inventory is no longer saleable. If the inventory can be repaired and resold, it is debited to Merchandise Inventory. Some companies maintain a separate Merchandise Inventory account to record used or damaged goods for resale.

**Helpful hint** Remember that the increases, decreases, and normal balances of contra accounts are the opposite of the accounts they correspond to.

Sales Returns and Allowances is a contra revenue account to Sales. The normal balance of Sales Returns and Allowances is a debit. A contra account is used instead of debiting sales in order to show the amount of sales returns and allowances in the accounts. This information is important to management. Excessive returns and allowances suggest inferior merchandise, inefficiencies in filling orders, errors in billing customers, and mistakes in the delivery or shipment of goods. Also, a decrease (debit) recorded directly to Sales could distort comparisons between total sales in different accounting periods.

**ACCOUNTING IN ACTION ▶ Business Insight**

Returned goods can represent as much as 15% of total sales volume. Most companies do a poor job of dealing with returned goods, often destroying perfectly good merchandise. A new piece of software changed this for the cosmetic company Estée Lauder. When boxes of Estée Lauder lipstick and other products are returned by a retailer, each bar code is scanned, and each item's expiration date and condition are determined. The item is then either scrapped or sorted for resale to employees, to "seconds" stores, or to poor countries. The system paid for its $1.5-million development cost in nine months because it enabled the company to resell two-and-one-half times as many items at less than half the cost of the old system.

*Source:* "Cash from Trash," *The Economist,* February 6, 1999, 66.

## Discounts

Quantity discounts and sales discounts given on sales prices affect the seller, as well as the buyer. No separate entry is made to record a **quantity discount**. Merchandise is recorded at cost—the price actually paid—whether it is the full retail price, a sale price, or a volume discount price.

Like a purchase discount, the seller may offer the customer a cash discount for the prompt payment of the balance due. From the seller's point of view, this is called a sales discount. Further discussion of sales discounts can be found in Appendix 5B at the end of the chapter.

## Freight Costs

Freight terms—FOB destination and FOB shipping point—on the sales invoice indicate who assumes responsibility for shipping costs. If the term is FOB destination, the seller assumes the responsibility of getting the goods to their intended destination. Freight costs incurred by the seller on outgoing merchandise are an operating expense to the seller. These costs are debited to a Freight Out or Delivery Expense account. When the freight charges are paid by the seller, the seller will usually set a higher invoice price for the goods to cover the expense of shipping.

In the sale of electronic equipment to Chelsea Video, the freight terms (FOB shipping point) indicate that Chelsea Video must pay the cost of shipping the goods from Highpoint Electronic's location in Toronto to Chelsea Video's location in Hamilton. The seller (Highpoint Electronic) makes no journal entry to record the cost of shipping, since this cost was incurred by Chelsea and not by Highpoint.

# Summary of Sales Transactions

A summary of the effects of the previous transactions on Sales, and its contra account, is provided in the following T accounts. Highpoint Electronic sold merchandise for $3,800, with $300 of it later returned. In contrast to the purchase transactions illustrated on page 222, which affected only one account, Merchandise Inventory, sales transactions are recorded in two different accounts. In addition, cost of goods sold is also calculated and recorded at the time of each sale transaction in a perpetual inventory system.

|  | Sales |  |  | Sales Returns and Allowances |  |
|---|---|---|---|---|---|
|  | May 4 | 3,800 | May 9 | 300 |  |

|  | Cost of Goods Sold |  |  |  |
|---|---|---|---|---|
| May 4 | 2,400 | May 9 | 140 |  |
| Bal. | 2,260 |  |  |  |

---

## BEFORE YOU GO ON . . .

### ▶Review It

1. Under a perpetual inventory system, what are the two entries that must be recorded at the time of each sale?
2. Why is it important to use the Sales Returns and Allowances account, rather than simply reduce the Sales account, when goods are returned?
3. What journal entries (if any) are recorded by the seller and the buyer when the shipping terms are FOB destination? FOB shipping point?

### ▶Do It

On September 4, New Idea Company buys merchandise on account from Junot Company. The selling price of the goods is $1,500, and the cost to Junot Company was $800. On September 8, goods with a selling price of $200 and a cost of $80 are returned and restored to inventory. Record the transaction on the books of both companies.

#### Action Plan

- Buyer: Record purchases of inventory at cost. Reduce the Merchandise Inventory account for returned goods.
- Seller: Record both the sale and the cost of goods sold at the time of the sale. Record returns in the contra account Sales Returns and Allowances and reduce Cost of Goods Sold when merchandise is returned to inventory.

#### Solution

New Idea Company (Buyer)

| Sept. 4 | Merchandise Inventory | 1,500 | |
|---|---|---|---|
| | Accounts Payable | | 1,500 |
| | To record goods purchased on account. | | |
| 8 | Accounts Payable | 200 | |
| | Merchandise Inventory | | 200 |
| | To record return of goods. | | |

Junot Company (Seller)

| Sept. 4 | Accounts Receivable | 1,500 | |
|---|---|---|---|
| | Sales | | 1,500 |
| | To record credit sale. | | |

| | | | |
|---|---|---|---|
| 4 | Cost of Goods Sold | 800 | |
| |     Merchandise Inventory | | 800 |
| |         To record cost of goods sold. | | |
| 8 | Sales Returns and Allowances | 200 | |
| |     Accounts Receivable | | 200 |
| |         To record credit granted for receipt of returned goods. | | |
| 8 | Merchandise Inventory | 80 | |
| |     Cost of Goods Sold | | 80 |
| |         To record cost of goods returned. | | |

*Related exercise material:* BE5–4, BE5–5, E5–2, E5–3, and E5–4.

# Completing the Accounting Cycle

study objective 4

Explain and perform the steps in the accounting cycle for a merchandising company.

Up to this point, we have illustrated the basic entries for recording transactions for purchases and sales in a perpetual inventory system. Now, it is time to consider the remaining steps in the accounting cycle for a merchandising company. Each of the required steps described in Chapter 4 for a service company also applies to a merchandising company.

## Adjusting Entry

A merchandising company generally has the same types of adjusting entries as a service company. But, for control purposes, a merchandiser using a perpetual inventory system may require one additional adjustment to make the recorded inventory agree with the actual inventory on hand.

In a perpetual inventory system, the Merchandise Inventory account balance should equal the cost of the merchandise on hand (ending inventory) at all times. As mentioned earlier in the chapter, a **physical inventory count** adds an important control feature to the perpetual inventory system. Even though the Merchandise Inventory account provides a record of the inventory on hand, it only indicates what *should* be there, not what actually is there. If inventory errors have occurred, or if inventory has been stolen or damaged, it is important that management be aware of this at an early stage so that preventive controls can be put in place.

Taking a physical inventory involves the following:

1. Counting the units on hand for each item of inventory.
2. Applying unit costs to the total units on hand for each item of inventory.
3. Totalling the costs for each item of inventory to determine the total cost of goods on hand.

If Highpoint Electronic's accounting records show an ending inventory balance of $40,500 at the end of May and a physical inventory count indicates only $40,000 on hand, the following journal entry should be prepared. The inventory shortage increases the Cost of Goods Sold account. Although this inventory hasn't been *sold*, inventory losses are part of the cost of the goods.

A = L + OE
-500          -500

Cash flows: no effect

| | | | |
|---|---|---|---|
| May 31 | Cost of Goods Sold | 500 | |
| |     Merchandise Inventory | | 500 |
| |         To record difference between inventory records and | | |
| |         physical units on hand. | | |

The non-existent inventory is removed from the Merchandise Inventory account so that accuracy is maintained and performance measures using inventory are not distorted.

## Closing Entries

An adjusted trial balance, using assumed data, is shown below for Highpoint Electronic at May 31, the company's year end. The accounts used only by a merchandising company are highlighted in red.

**Illustration 5-8 ◄**

Adjusted trial balance

| HIGHPOINT ELECTRONIC<br>Adjusted Trial Balance<br>May 31, 2005 | Debit | Credit |
|---|---|---|
| Cash | $ 9,500 | |
| Accounts receivable | 16,100 | |
| Merchandise inventory | 40,000 | |
| Prepaid insurance | 1,800 | |
| Store equipment | 80,000 | |
| Accumulated amortization | | $ 24,000 |
| Accounts payable | | 20,400 |
| Salaries payable | | 5,000 |
| R. A. Lamb, capital | | 83,000 |
| R. A. Lamb, drawings | 15,000 | |
| Sales | | 480,000 |
| Sales returns and allowances | 20,000 | |
| Cost of goods sold | 316,000 | |
| Salaries expense | 45,000 | |
| Rent expense | 19,000 | |
| Utilities expense | 17,000 | |
| Advertising expense | 16,000 | |
| Amortization expense | 8,000 | |
| Freight out | 7,000 | |
| Insurance expense | 2,000 | |
| Totals | $612,400 | $612,400 |

For a merchandising company, like a service company, all temporary accounts (revenues, expenses, and drawings) are closed. In journalizing, the steps are as follows: (1) All temporary accounts with credit balances are debited for their individual balances. The total is credited to Income Summary. Note that Sales is a new account that must be closed to the income summary account. (2) All temporary accounts with debit balances are credited for their individual balances. The total is debited to Income Summary. Three new accounts are included in this entry: Sales Returns and Allowances, a contra revenue account with a debit balance;

Cost of Goods Sold; and Freight Out. (3) The Income Summary account is closed to the owner's capital account. If there is net income, Income Summary would be debited and owner's capital credited. If there is a net loss, the reverse would happen. (4) Drawings, a temporary account with a debit balance, is credited separately to the owner's capital account, as indicated in the following closing entries:

| | | | |
|---|---|---|---|
| May 31 | Sales | 480,000 | |
| |    Income Summary | | 480,000 |
| |       To close income statement accounts with | | |
| |       credit balances. | | |
| 31 | Income Summary | 450,000 | |
| |    Sales Returns and Allowances | | 20,000 |
| |    Cost of Goods Sold | | 316,000 |
| |    Salaries Expense | | 45,000 |
| |    Rent Expense | | 19,000 |
| |    Utilities Expense | | 17,000 |
| |    Advertising Expense | | 16,000 |
| |    Amortization Expense | | 8,000 |
| |    Freight Out | | 7,000 |
| |    Insurance Expense | | 2,000 |
| |       To close income statement accounts with | | |
| |       debit balances. | | |
| 31 | Income Summary | 30,000 | |
| |    R. A. Lamb, Capital | | 30,000 |
| |       To close income summary to capital. | | |
| 31 | R. A. Lamb, Capital | 15,000 | |
| |    R. A. Lamb, Drawings | | 15,000 |
| |       To close drawings to capital. | | |

**Margin notes:**

A = L + OE
−480,000
+480,000
Cash flows: no effect

A = L + OE
−450,000
+20,000
+316,000
+45,000
+19,000
+17,000
+16,000
+8,000
+7,000
+2,000
Cash flows: no effect

A = L + OE
−30,000
+30,000
Cash flows: no effect

A = L + OE
−15,000
+15,000
Cash flows: no effect

After the closing entries are posted, all temporary accounts have zero balances. In addition, the R. A. Lamb, Capital account should have an ending balance of $98,000 (beginning balance of $83,000 + net income of $30,000 − drawings of $15,000), equal to that reported on the statement of owner's equity and balance sheet.

## Post-Closing Trial Balance

After the closing entries are posted, a post-closing trial balance should be prepared. You will recall that the purpose of this trial balance is to ensure that debits equal credits in the permanent (balance sheet) accounts after all temporary accounts have been closed. The only new account in the post-closing trial balance is the current asset account Merchandise Inventory.

    Preparation of a post-closing trial balance does not differ from the process described in Chapter 4 and is not illustrated again here.

## Summary of Merchandising Entries

A summary of the entries for the merchandising accounts using a perpetual inventory system follows:

| | Transactions | Recurring Journal Entries | Debit | Credit |
|---|---|---|---|---|
| **Sales** { | Selling merchandise to customers. | Cash or Accounts Receivable<br>    Sales | XX | <br>XX |
| | | Cost of Goods Sold<br>    Merchandise Inventory | XX | <br>XX |
| | Granting sales returns or allowances to customers. | Sales Returns and Allowances<br>    Cash or Accounts Receivable | XX | <br>XX |
| | | Merchandise Inventory<br>    Cost of Goods Sold | XX | <br>XX |
| | Paying freight costs on sales, FOB destination. | Freight Out<br>    Cash | XX | <br>XX |
| | Receiving payment from customers on account. | Cash<br>    Accounts Receivable | XX | <br>XX |
| **Purchases** { | Purchasing merchandise for resale. | Merchandise Inventory<br>    Cash or Accounts Payable | XX | <br>XX |
| | Paying freight costs on merchandise purchased, FOB shipping point. | Merchandise Inventory<br>    Cash | XX | <br>XX |
| | Receiving purchase returns or allowances from suppliers. | Cash or Accounts Payable<br>    Merchandise Inventory | XX | <br>XX |
| | Paying creditors on account. | Accounts Payable<br>    Cash | XX | <br>XX |

| | Transactions | End of Period Journal Entries | Debit | Credit |
|---|---|---|---|---|
| **Adjusting Entry** { | Physical count determined that inventory in general ledger is higher than inventory actually on hand. | Cost of Goods Sold<br>    Merchandise Inventory | XX | <br>XX |
| **Closing Entries** { | Close temporary accounts with credit balances. | Sales<br>    Income Summary | XX | <br>XX |
| | Close temporary accounts with debit balances (drawings closed separately). | Income Summary<br>    Sales Returns and Allowances<br>    Cost of Goods Sold<br>    Freight Out<br>    Other expenses | XX | <br>XX<br>XX<br>XX<br>XX |
| | Close Income Summary account (assuming net income). | Income Summary<br>    Capital | XX | <br>XX |
| | Close drawings account. | Capital<br>    Drawings | XX | <br>XX |

## BEFORE YOU GO ON . . .

### ►Review It

1. Why is an adjustment to the Merchandise Inventory account sometimes necessary?
2. How do closing entries for a merchandising company differ from closing entries for a service company?
3. What merchandising account(s) will appear in the post-closing trial balance?

### ►Do It

The trial balance of the Yee Clothing Company at December 31 shows Merchandise Inventory $25,000; Yee, Capital $12,000; Sales $162,400; Sales Returns and Allowances $4,800; Cost of Goods Sold $110,000; Rental Revenue $6,000; Freight Out $1,800; Rent Expense $8,800; Salaries Expense $22,000; and Yee, Drawings $3,600. Prepare the closing entries for the above accounts.

#### Action Plan

- Debit each temporary account with a credit balance and credit the total to the Income Summary account.

- Credit each temporary account with a debit balance and debit the total to the Income Summary account.
- Stop and check your work: Does the balance in the Income Summary account equal the reported net income (loss)?
- Assuming net income, debit the balance in the Income Summary account and credit the amount to the owner's capital account. (Do the opposite if the result is a net loss.)
- Credit the balance in the drawings account and debit the amount to the owner's capital account. Do not close drawings with the expenses.
- Stop and check your work: Does the balance in the owner's capital account equal the ending balance reported in the statement of owner's equity and balance sheet?

### Solution

| | | | |
|---|---|---:|---:|
| Dec. 31 | Sales | 162,400 | |
| | Rental Revenue | 6,000 | |
| |     Income Summary | | 168,400 |
| |         To close income statement accounts with | | |
| |         credit balances. | | |
| 31 | Income Summary | 147,400 | |
| |     Sales Returns and Allowances | | 4,800 |
| |     Cost of Goods Sold | | 110,000 |
| |     Freight Out | | 1,800 |
| |     Rent Expense | | 8,800 |
| |     Salaries Expense | | 22,000 |
| |         To close income statement accounts with | | |
| |         debit balances. | | |
| 31 | Income Summary | 21,000 | |
| |     Yee, Capital | | 21,000 |
| |         To close Income Summary account. | | |
| 31 | Yee, Capital | 3,600 | |
| |     Yee, Drawings | | 3,600 |
| |         To close drawings account. | | |

*Related exercise material*: BE5–6, BE5–7, and E5–5.

# Merchandising Financial Statements

study objective 5

Distinguish between, and be able to prepare, a multi-ple-step and a single-step income statement.

Merchandisers use the classified balance sheet introduced in Chapter 4. In addition, two forms of income statement are widely used by merchandising companies. How merchandisers use them is explained below.

## Multiple-Step Income Statement

The multiple-step income statement has its name because it shows the steps in determining net income (or net loss). It shows three main steps: (1) Cost of goods sold is subtracted from net sales to determine gross profit. (2) Operating expenses are deducted from gross profit to determine income from operations. These first two steps involve the company's principal operating activities. A multiple-step income statement also distinguishes between **operating** and **non-operating** activities in the third step. (3) The results of activities not related to operations are added (other revenue) or deducted (other expenses) to determine net income.

## Net Sales

The multiple-step income statement begins by presenting sales revenues. As a contra revenue account, Sales Returns and Allowances is deducted from Sales in the income statement to arrive at **net sales**. The sales revenue section for Highpoint Electronic (using data presented in the adjusted trial balance in Illustration 5-8) is as follows:

| | |
|---|---|
| Sales revenue | |
| Sales | $480,000 |
| Less: Sales returns and allowances | 20,000 |
| Net sales | 460,000 |

This presentation discloses the key aspects of the company's principal revenue-producing activities. Many companies condense this information and report only the net sales figure in their income statement.

## Gross Profit

From Illustration 5-1, you learned that cost of goods sold is deducted from sales revenue to determine **gross profit**. On the basis of the sales data presented above and a cost of goods sold of $316,000, the gross profit for Highpoint Electronic is $144,000, calculated as follows:

| | |
|---|---|
| Net sales | $460,000 |
| Cost of goods sold | 316,000 |
| Gross profit | 144,000 |

## Income from Operations

Operating expenses are the next component in measuring net income for a merchandiser. As indicated earlier, these expenses are similar in merchandising and service companies. At Highpoint Electronic, operating expenses total $114,000 (from Illustration 5-8, $45,000 + $19,000 + $17,000 + $16,000 + $8,000 + $7,000 + $2,000). Income from operations, or the results of the company's normal operating activities, is determined by subtracting operating expenses from gross profit:

| | |
|---|---|
| Gross profit | $144,000 |
| Operating expenses | 114,000 |
| Income from operations | $ 30,000 |

Sometimes operating expenses are subdivided into selling expenses and administrative expenses. **Selling expenses** are those associated with making sales. They include expenses for sales promotion, as well as the expenses of completing the sale (e.g., freight costs). **Administrative expenses** relate to general operating activities such as management, accounting, and legal costs.

## Non-Operating Activities

Highpoint Electronic had no activities other than those from primary operations. If there are no non-operating activities, the company's income from operations becomes its net income—or "bottom line." However, most companies also have non-operating activities. **Non-operating activities** consist of (1) revenues and expenses from auxiliary operations and (2) gains and losses that are unrelated to the company's operations. The results of non-operating activities are shown in two sections: **other revenues** and **other expenses**. For a merchandising company, these sections will typically include the following items:

**Illustration 5-9 ▶**

Items reported in non-operating sections

Non-Operating Activities

| Other Revenues | Other Expenses |
|---|---|
| Interest from notes receivable and short-term investments | Interest expense on notes and loans payable |
| Dividend revenue from equity investments | Casualty losses from vandalism and accidents |
| Rent revenue from subleasing a portion of the store | Losses from the sale of property, plant, and equipment |
| Gain from the sale of property, plant, and equipment | Losses from strikes by employees and suppliers |

When the two non-operating sections are included, the heading "Income from Operations" precedes them. It clearly identifies the results of the company's normal operations.

In the non-operating activities sections, items are generally reported at their net amount. Thus, if a company received a $2,500 insurance settlement on vandalism losses of $2,700, the loss is reported at $200. Note, too, that the results of the two non-operating sections are netted. The difference is added to, or subtracted from, income from operations to determine net income. It is not uncommon for companies to combine these two non-operating sections into a single "Other Revenues and Expenses" section.

These sections are shown in Illustration 5-10, using assumed non-operating data, for Highpoint Electronic.

**Illustration 5-10 ▶**

Multiple-step income statement

**HIGHPOINT ELECTRONIC**
**Income Statement**
**Year Ended May 31, 2005**

| | | | |
|---|---|---|---|
| **Calculation of gross profit** | Sales revenue | | |
| |   Sales | | $480,000 |
| |   Less: Sales returns and allowances | | 20,000 |
| |   Net sales | | 460,000 |
| | Cost of goods sold | | 316,000 |
| | Gross profit | | 144,000 |
| **Calculation of income from operations** | Operating expenses | | |
| |   Salaries expense | $45,000 | |
| |   Rent expense | 19,000 | |
| |   Utilities expense | 17,000 | |
| |   Advertising expense | 16,000 | |
| |   Amortization expense | 8,000 | |
| |   Freight out | 7,000 | |
| |   Insurance expense | 2,000 | |
| |     Total operating expenses | | 114,000 |
| | Income from operations | | 30,000 |
| **Calculation of non-operating activities** | Other revenues | | |
| |   Interest revenue | $ 3,000 | |
| |   Gain on sale of equipment | 600 | |
| |     Total non-operating revenues | 3,600 | |
| | Other expenses | | |
| |   Interest expense | $ 1,800 | |
| |   Casualty loss from vandalism | 200 | |
| |     Total non-operating expenses | 2,000 | |
| |     Net non-operating revenue | | 1,600 |
| | Net income | | $ 31,600 |

## Net Income

Net income is the final outcome of all the company's operating and non-operating activities. Highpoint's net income, as shown in Illustration 5-10, is $31,600.

## Single-Step Income Statement

Another income statement format is the single-step income statement. The statement has this name because only one step, subtracting total expenses from total revenues, is required in determining net income (or net loss).

In a single-step statement, all data are classified under two categories: (1) revenues, and (2) expenses. The **revenues** category includes both operating revenues and other revenues. The **expenses** category includes cost of goods sold, operating expenses, and other expenses.

A condensed single-step statement for Highpoint Electronic is shown in Illustration 5-11.

**Illustration 5-11** ◀

Single-step income statement

**HIGHPOINT ELECTRONIC**
**Income Statement**
**Year Ended May 31, 2005**

| | | |
|---|---:|---:|
| Revenues | | |
| Net sales | | $460,000 |
| Interest revenue | | 3,000 |
| Gain on sale of equipment | | 600 |
| Total revenues | | 463,600 |
| Expenses | | |
| Cost of goods sold | $316,000 | |
| Operating expenses | 114,000 | |
| Interest expense | 1,800 | |
| Casualty loss from vandalism | 200 | |
| Total expenses | | 432,000 |
| Net income | | $ 31,600 |

There are two primary reasons for using the single-step format: (1) A company does not realize any type of profit or income until total revenues exceed total expenses, so it makes sense to divide the statement into these two categories. (2) The format is simpler and easier to read than the multiple-step format.

## Classified Balance Sheet

In the balance sheet, merchandise inventory is reported as a current asset immediately following accounts receivable. Recall from Chapter 4 that items are listed under current assets in their order of liquidity. Merchandise inventory is less liquid than accounts receivable because the goods must first be sold before revenue can be collected from the customer. Illustration 5-12 presents the assets section of a classified balance sheet for Highpoint Electronic.

**Illustration 5-12 ▶**

Assets section of a
classified balance sheet

**HIGHPOINT ELECTRONIC**
**Balance Sheet (partial)**
**May 31, 2005**

### Assets

| | | |
|---|---:|---:|
| Current assets | | |
| Cash | | $ 9,500 |
| Accounts receivable | | 16,100 |
| Merchandise inventory | | 40,000 |
| Prepaid insurance | | 1,800 |
| Total current assets | | 67,400 |
| Property, plant, and equipment | | |
| Store equipment | $80,000 | |
| Less: Accumulated amortization | 24,000 | 56,000 |
| Total assets | | $123,400 |

**Helpful hint**   The $40,000 is
the cost of the inventory on
hand, not its expected selling
price.

The remaining two financial statements, the statement of owner's equity and cash flow statement (to be discussed in Chapter 17) are the same as those of a service company. They are not shown in this chapter.

## BEFORE YOU GO ON . . .

▶ **Review It**

1. What are non-operating activities and how are they reported in the income statement?
2. How does a single-step income statement differ from a multiple-step income statement?

*Related exercise material:* BE5–8, E5–6, E5–7, and E5–8.

# Using the Information in the Financial Statements

**study objective 6**

**Calculate the gross profit margin and profit margin.**

Inventory has a significant effect on a company's profitability because cost of goods sold is usually the largest expense on the income statement. We will examine two ratios to help evaluate a company's profitability: the gross profit margin and the profit margin.

## Gross Profit Margin

A company's gross profit may be expressed as a percentage, called the gross profit margin. This is done by dividing the amount of gross profit by net sales. For Highpoint Electronic, the gross profit margin is 31.3%, as calculated in Illustration 5-13:

**Illustration 5-13 ▶**

Gross profit margin

| Gross Profit | ÷ | Net Sales | = | Gross Profit Margin |
|:---:|:---:|:---:|:---:|:---:|
| $144,000 | ÷ | $460,000 | = | 31.3% |

The gross profit margin is generally considered to be more useful than the gross profit amount. The margin expresses a more meaningful (relative) relationship between net sales and gross profit. For example, a gross profit amount of $1,000,000 may sound impressive. But, if it is the result of a gross profit margin of only 7%, it is not so impressive.

Gross profit represents the merchandising profit of a company. It is not a measure of the overall profitability, because operating expenses have not been deducted. The amount and trend of gross profit are closely watched by management and other interested parties. They compare current gross profit to amounts reported in past periods. They also compare the company's gross profit margin to the margin of competitors and to industry averages. Such comparisons provide information about the effectiveness of a company's purchasing and the soundness of its pricing policies.

## Profit Margin

Net income is often expressed as a percentage of sales, similar to the gross profit margin. The **profit margin** measures the percentage of each dollar of sales that results in net income. It is calculated by dividing net income by net sales. Highpoint Electronic's profit margin of 6.9% is calculated in Illustration 5-14:

| Net Income | ÷ | Net Sales | = | Profit Margin |
| :---: | :---: | :---: | :---: | :---: |
| $31,600 | ÷ | $460,000 | = | 6.9% |

**Illustration 5-14 ◄**
Profit margin

How do the gross profit margin and profit margin differ? The gross profit margin measures the amount by which the selling price exceeds the cost of goods sold. The profit margin measures the extent by which the selling price covers *all* expenses (including the cost of goods sold). A company can improve its profit margin by increasing its gross profit margin, or by controlling its operating expenses (and non-operating activities), or by doing both.

---

**ACCOUNTING IN ACTION ► Business Insight**

In its death spiral toward bankruptcy, Kmart appeared to make two very costly strategic errors. First, in an effort to attract customers, it decided to reduce selling prices on over 30,000 items. The problem was that this reduced its gross profit margin—and didn't even have the intended effect of increasing sales because Wal-Mart quickly matched these price cuts. Since Wal-Mart operates much more efficiently than Kmart, Wal-Mart could afford to absorb these price cuts and still operate at a profit. Kmart couldn't. Its second error was to try to increase its profit margin by reducing operating costs. Kmart decided to cut its advertising expenditures. This resulted in a reduction in customers—and sales revenue.

---

## BEFORE YOU GO ON . . .

**►Review It**

1. Distinguish between the gross profit margin and profit margin.
2. Calculate The Forzani Group Ltd.'s gross profit margin and profit margin for fiscal 2002 and 2003. Indicate whether these ratios improved or deteriorated in 2003. The answers to these questions are provided at the end of this chapter.

*Related exercise material:* BE5–9, BE5–10, and E5–9.

the navigator

**study objective 7**

Prepare the entries for purchases and sales of inventory under a periodic inventory system and calculate cost of goods sold.

As described in this chapter, there are two basic systems of accounting for inventories: (1) the perpetual inventory system, and (2) the periodic inventory system. In the chapter, we focused on the characteristics of the perpetual inventory system. In this appendix, we discuss and illustrate the periodic inventory system.

**One key difference between the two inventory systems is when the cost of goods sold is calculated.** In a periodic inventory system, revenues from the sale of merchandise are recorded when sales are made, in the same way as in a perpetual inventory system, but no attempt is made on the date of sale to record the cost of the merchandise sold. Instead, a physical inventory count is taken at or near the end of the period. This count determines the cost of the merchandise on hand. We will use this and other information to determine the cost of the goods sold during the period.

There are other differences between the perpetual and periodic inventory systems. Under a periodic inventory system, purchases of merchandise are recorded in the Purchases expense account, rather than the Merchandise Inventory asset account. Also, under a periodic system, it is customary to record purchase returns and allowances and freight in separate accounts. That way, accumulated amounts are known for each.

To illustrate the recording of merchandise transactions under a periodic inventory system, we will use the purchase and sale transactions between Highpoint Electronic (the seller) and Chelsea Video (the buyer) from earlier in this chapter.

## Recording Sales of Merchandise

The sale of $3,800 of merchandise to Chelsea Video on May 4 shown in the sales invoice in Illustration 5-5 is recorded by the seller, Highpoint Electronic, as follows:

A   =   L   +   OE
+3,800              +3,800

Cash flows: no effect

| May  4 | Accounts Receivable | 3,800 | |
| | Sales | | 3,800 |
| | To record credit sale to Chelsea Video per invoice #731. | | |

### Sales Returns and Allowances

The $300 return of goods on May 9 is recorded by Highpoint Electronic as follows:

A   =   L   +   OE
−300              −300

Cash flows: No effect

| May  9 | Sales Returns and Allowances | 300 | |
| | Accounts Receivable | | 300 |
| | To record credit granted to Chelsea Video for returned goods. | | |

These two sales entries are exactly the same as those illustrated earlier in the chapter, with one exception. In a perpetual inventory system, two journal entries are made for each transaction. The first entry records the accounts receivable and sales revenue (or return), as illustrated above. The second journal entry records the cost of the sale by transferring the inventory to the cost of goods sold account (or the opposite in the case of a return).

In a periodic inventory system, there is only one journal entry made at the time of the sale—the entry to record the sales revenue—and at the time of the return—the entry to record the sales return. The cost of the sale is not recorded. Instead, the cost of goods sold is determined by calculation at the end of the period.

# Recording Purchases of Merchandise

Based on the sales invoice (Illustration 5-5) and receipt of the merchandise ordered from Highpoint Electronic, Chelsea Video records the $3,800 purchase as follows:

| May 4 | Purchases | 3,800 | |
| |     Accounts Payable | | 3,800 |
| |       To record goods purchased on account per | | |
| |       invoice #731, terms n/30. | | |

```
A   =   L    +   OE
       +3,800     -3,800
Cash flows: no effect
```

Purchases is a temporary expense account reported on the income statement. Its normal balance is a debit.

## Freight Costs

When the buyer pays for the freight costs, the account Freight In is debited. For example, upon delivery of the goods, Chelsea pays the Public Carrier Co. $150 for freight charges on its purchase from Highpoint Electronic. The entry on Chelsea's books is as follows:

| May 4 | Freight In | 150 | |
| |     Cash | | 150 |
| |       To record payment of freight on goods purchased. | | |

```
A    =   L   +   OE
-150              -150
Cash flows: -150
```

Like Purchases, Freight In is a temporary expense account whose normal balance is a debit. Just as freight was a part of the cost of the merchandise inventory in a perpetual inventory system, **freight in is part of the cost of goods purchased** in a periodic inventory system. Freight in is added to net purchases to determine the cost of goods purchased. In accordance with the cost principle, the cost of goods purchased should include any freight charges for bringing the goods to the buyer.

## Purchase Returns and Allowances

Chelsea Video returns $300 worth of goods. The following entry recognizes the purchase return:

| May 9 | Accounts Payable | 300 | |
| |     Purchase Returns and Allowances | | 300 |
| |       To record return of goods to Highpoint Electronic. | | |

```
A   =   L    +   OE
       -300      +300
Cash flows: no effect
```

Purchase Returns and Allowances is a temporary account whose normal balance is a credit. It is a contra account, whose balance is deducted from the balance in Purchases. Purchases less purchase returns and allowances results in net purchases.

    In each of the above cases, recording purchases of merchandise used a temporary expense account rather than the Merchandise Inventory account used in a perpetual inventory system. The Purchases and Freight In accounts were debited rather than Merchandise Inventory in the first two entries, and Purchases Returns and Allowances was credited in the last entry rather than the Merchandise Inventory account. As we will see later in this appendix, these temporary accounts are needed to calculate the cost of goods sold.

# Comparison of Entries—Perpetual vs. Periodic

The periodic inventory system entries for sales and purchases are shown in Illustration 5A-1 next to the perpetual inventory system entries that were shown earlier in the chapter. Having these entries side by side should help you compare the differences. The entries that are different in the two inventory systems are highlighted.

| ENTRIES ON CHELSEA VIDEO'S BOOKS (BUYER) | | |
| --- | --- | --- |
| Transaction | Perpetual Inventory System | Periodic Inventory System |
| May  4  Purchase of merchandise on credit. | Merchandise Inventory  3,800<br>    Accounts Payable              3,800 | Purchases                    3,800<br>    Accounts Payable              3,800 |
| May  4  Freight cost on purchases. | Merchandise Inventory   150<br>    Cash                           150 | Freight In                    150<br>    Cash                           150 |
| May  9  Purchase returns and allowances. | Accounts Payable          300<br>    Merchandise Inventory          300 | Accounts Payable          300<br>    Purchase Returns<br>    and Allowances                300 |

| ENTRIES ON HIGHPOINT ELECTRONIC'S BOOKS (SELLER) | | |
| --- | --- | --- |
| Transaction | Perpetual Inventory System | Periodic Inventory System |
| May  4  Sale of merchandise on credit. | Accounts Receivable      3,800<br>    Sales                         3,800 | Accounts Receivable      3,800<br>    Sales                         3,800 |
| | Cost of Goods Sold       2,400<br>    Merchandise Inventory         2,400 | No entry |
| May  9  Return of merchandise sold. | Sales Returns<br>and Allowances            300<br>    Accounts Receivable           300 | Sales Returns<br>and Allowances            300<br>    Accounts Receivable           300 |
| | Merchandise Inventory    140<br>    Cost of Goods Sold            140 | No entry |

**Illustration 5A-1** ▲

Comparison of journal entries under perpetual and periodic inventory systems

# Cost of Goods Sold

In a periodic inventory system, as we've seen in the entries above, temporary accounts are used to accumulate the increases and decreases in purchases and sales throughout the period. A continuous account of the changes in inventory is not recorded when purchase or sales transactions occur. The dollar amount of merchandise on hand is not known, and neither is the cost of goods sold.

To determine the cost of goods sold in a periodic inventory system, three steps are required: (1) Determine the cost of goods purchased. (2) Determine the cost of goods on hand at the beginning and end of the accounting period. (3) Calculate the cost of goods sold. We will discuss each of these steps in the following sections.

## Determining Cost of Goods Purchased

Earlier in this chapter, we used three accounts—Purchases, Purchase Returns and Allowances, and Freight In—to record the purchase of inventory under a periodic inventory system. The procedure for determining the cost of goods purchased is as follows:

1. The balance in Purchase Returns and Allowances is subtracted from the balance in Purchases. The result is **net purchases**.
2. The balance in Freight In is added to net purchases. The result is **cost of goods purchased**.

To illustrate, assume that Highpoint Electronic shows the following balances for the accounts above: Purchases, $325,000; Purchase Returns and Allowances, $17,200; and Freight In, $12,200. Net purchases is $307,800, and cost of goods purchased is $320,000, calculated as follows:

| | | |
|---|---|---|
| Purchases | | $325,000 |
| (1) Less: Purchase returns and allowances | | 17,200 |
| Net purchases | | 307,800 |
| (2) Add: Freight in | | 12,200 |
| Cost of goods purchased | | 320,000 |

## Determining Cost of Goods on Hand

To determine the cost of the inventory on hand, Highpoint Electronic must take a physical inventory. As described earlier in this chapter, we use these steps to take a physical inventory:

1. Count the units on hand for each item of inventory.
2. Apply unit costs to the total units on hand for each item of inventory.
3. Total the costs for each item of inventory to determine the total cost of goods on hand.

The total cost of goods on hand is known as the ending inventory. Highpoint's physical inventory count on May 31, 2005, determines that the cost of its goods on hand, or ending inventory, is $40,000. This ending inventory amount will be used to calculate the cost of goods sold (as shown in the next section) and will be recorded as part of the closing process in the Merchandise Inventory account, as you will learn later in this appendix.

## Calculating Cost of Goods Sold

There are two steps involved in calculating the cost of goods sold:

1. Add the cost of goods purchased to the cost of goods on hand at the beginning of the period (beginning inventory). The result is the cost of goods available for sale.
2. Subtract the cost of goods on hand at the end of the period (ending inventory) from the cost of goods available for sale. The result is the cost of goods sold.

For Highpoint Electronic, the cost of goods available for sale is $356,000 and the cost of goods sold is $316,000 as shown below:

| | | |
|---|---|---|
| Inventory, June 1 | | $ 36,000 |
| Purchases | $325,000 | |
| Less: Purchase returns and allowances | 17,200 | |
| Net purchases | 307,800 | |
| Add: Freight in | 12,200 | |
| Cost of goods purchased | | 320,000 |
| Cost of goods available for sale | | 356,000 |
| Inventory, May 31 | | 40,000 |
| Cost of goods sold | | $316,000 |

**Illustration 5A-2 ◄**
Calculation of cost of goods sold

Once cost of goods sold is calculated, gross profit, operating expenses, and net income are reported in a multiple-step or single-step income statement in a periodic inventory system in the same manner as under a perpetual inventory system. The only reporting difference in a multiple-step income statement is that the cost of goods sold section contains more detail in a periodic inventory system—the same detail shown in Illustration 5A-2—than in a perpetual inventory system where only one line is reported for the cost of goods sold.

Use of the periodic inventory system does not affect the content of the balance sheet. As under the perpetual system, merchandise inventory is reported in the current assets section, and at the same amount.

## Completing the Accounting Cycle

After preparing the financial statements, closing entries and a post-closing trial balance complete the accounting cycle. It is now time to consider these two remaining steps.

For a merchandising company, as for a service enterprise, all accounts that affect the determination of net income are closed to the owner's capital account, whether a perpetual or periodic inventory system is used.

In a periodic inventory system, the closing entries are the same as those we previously learned about, with one exception: the treatment of Merchandise Inventory. In the adjusted trial balance, the balance reported for inventory is its beginning balance, not the ending balance reported in a perpetual inventory system. During the year (or period in question), **no entries are made to the Merchandise Inventory account** since the temporary Purchases and related accounts are used. The beginning inventory remains unchanged in the account all year. At year end, entries must be made to eliminate the beginning inventory ($36,000 at June 1, 2004, for Highpoint) and to record this year's new ending inventory ($40,000 at May 31, 2005, for Highpoint).

Two journal entries close the Merchandise Inventory account in a periodic inventory system:

1. The beginning inventory balance is debited to the Income Summary account and credited to Merchandise Inventory to bring the account balance to zero.
2. The ending inventory balance is debited to Merchandise Inventory and credited to the Income Summary account to record the current end-of-period balance in the account.

The two entries for Highpoint Electronic are as follows:

| A | = | L | + | OE |
|---|---|---|---|---|
| -36,000 | | | | -36,000 |

Cash flows: no effect

| A | = | L | + | OE |
|---|---|---|---|---|
| +40,000 | | | | +40,000 |

Cash flows: no effect

| | | | | |
|---|---|---|---|---|
| May 31 | Income Summary | | 36,000 | |
| |    Merchandise Inventory | | | 36,000 |
| |     To close beginning inventory. | | | |
| 31 | Merchandise Inventory | | 40,000 | |
| |    Income Summary | | | 40,000 |
| |     To close ending inventory. | | | |

After the closing entries are posted, the Merchandise Inventory account will show the following:

| Merchandise Inventory | |
|---|---|
| June 1 Bal.   36,000 | May 31 Close   36,000 |
| **May 31 Close   40,000** | |
| May 31 Bal.   40,000 | |

As a permanent balance sheet account, Merchandise Inventory is not actually closed through this process, as temporary accounts are. Instead, the closing process updates the inventory account for the change in inventory during the period. This is similar to the effect the closing process has on the owner's capital account. The ending inventory and capital balances must be updated to agree with the balance sheet at the end of the period. It is these ending balances that are reported on the balance sheet, not the opening balances found in the adjusted trial balance.

The remaining closing entries are as we saw in prior chapters and are not illustrated here. To summarize:

1. The Merchandise Inventory account is credited for its beginning inventory balance, and debited to the Income Summary account.
2. The Merchandise Inventory account is debited for its ending inventory balance, and credited to the Income Summary account.

3. Temporary accounts with credit balances (including the Sales account and the Purchase Returns and Allowances account) are debited for their individual account balances and the total credited to the Income Summary account.

4. Temporary accounts with debit balances (including the Sales Returns and Allowances, Purchases, Purchase Returns and Allowances, and Freight In accounts) are credited for their individual account balances and the total is debited to the Income Summary account.

5. The Income Summary account is debited for its balance (if net income exists) and credited to the owner's capital account. The reverse happens if there is a net loss.

6. The drawings account is credited and its balance is debited to owner's capital.

Closing entries for accounts with credit balances (items 2 and 3), and accounts with debit balances (items 1 and 4) are often combined for convenience. After the closing entries are posted, a post-closing trial balance is prepared. Note that in the post-closing trial balance, the balance after closing in the current asset account Merchandise Inventory equals ending inventory. **This amount now becomes the beginning inventory of the new period.**

Preparation of a post-closing trial balance is the same as described in earlier chapters and is not explained again here.

---

## APPENDIX 5B ► DISCOUNTS

# Discounts for Early Payment

In addition to the quantity discounts discussed earlier in the chapter, there are two other types of discounts from the price of goods: **purchase discounts** and **sales discounts**. Both purchase and sales discounts offer a cash discount for early payment—a purchase discount for the buyer and a sales discount for the seller. The incentive offers advantages to both the buyer and the seller: the buyer saves money, and the seller is able to shorten the operating cycle by converting accounts receivable to cash earlier.

The credit terms on the invoice specify the amount of the cash discount and the time period during which it is available. They also indicate the date by which the buyer is expected to pay the full invoice price. For example, credit terms may specify a payment period of 2/10, n/30, which is read "two-ten, net thirty." This means that a 2% cash discount may be taken on the invoice price, net of any returns or allowances, if payment is made within 10 days of the invoice date. This is called the **discount period**, or period within which the reduced payment can be made. If the invoice is not paid within the discount period, the full invoice price, less any returns or allowances, is due 30 days from the invoice date. Other credit terms are also possible, such as 1/20, n/30 (1% discount if paid within 20 days).

When the seller chooses not to offer a cash discount for early payment, credit terms will specify only the maximum time period for paying the balance due. For example, the invoice in Illustration 5-5 shown in the chapter includes credit terms of n/30. This means that the invoice price, less any returns or allowances, must be paid within 30 days.

> **study objective 8**
>
> Explain the accounting for purchase and sales discounts.

## Purchase Discounts

A purchase discount lets the buyer claim a cash discount for early payment. To illustrate the accounting for a purchase discount, we will continue to use the purchase invoice shown in Illustration 5-5 in the chapter, where Chelsea Video purchased $3,800 of merchandise from Highpoint Electronic. However, we will assume that instead of the credit terms of n/30 displayed on the purchase invoice, the credit terms are 2/10, n/30.

The journal entry to record the purchase of merchandise by Chelsea Video on May 4 is the same as that illustrated in the chapter using a perpetual inventory system:

A = L + OE
+3,800   +3,800

Cash flows: no effect

| May 4 | Merchandise Inventory | 3,800 | |
| | Accounts Payable | | 3,800 |
| | To record goods purchased on account per invoice #731, terms 2/10, n/30. | | |

The merchandise purchased and amount owed are recorded at the full invoice price on this date because, at this point in time, it is not known with certainty that the invoice will be paid within the 10-day discount period. This is called the **gross method** of recording discounts.

Recall that Chelsea Video returned goods to Highpoint Electronic on May 9. The following entry is the same as the one earlier in the chapter for purchase returns and allowances:

A = L + OE
-300   -300

Cash flows: no effect

| May 9 | Accounts Payable | 300 | |
| | Merchandise Inventory | | 300 |
| | To record return of goods to Highpoint Electronic. | | |

After this transaction, Chelsea Video owes Highpoint Electronic $3,500 (gross invoice price of $3,800 less purchase returns and allowances of $300). The company has two options: pay the invoice by May 14 within the 10-day discount period, or pay the invoice by June 3 within the total 30-day payment period.

Let's assume first that Chelsea Video pays the amount owing on May 14, the last day of the discount period. When an invoice is paid within the discount period, the buyer automatically deducts the discount amount from its payment. The cash discount is $70 ($3,500 × 2%), and the amount of cash paid by Chelsea Video to Highpoint Electronic is $3,430 ($3,500 − $70). The amount of the discount decreases Merchandise Inventory because inventory is recorded at cost. By paying within the discount period, the merchandiser has reduced its cost.

Chelsea Video's entry to record its May 14 payment to Highpoint Electronic is:

A = L + OE
-3,430   -3,500
-70

Cash flows: -3,430

| May 14 | Accounts Payable | 3,500 | |
| | Cash | | 3,430 |
| | Merchandise Inventory | | 70 |
| | To record payment of invoice #731 within discount period. | | |

It makes sense to take advantage of any available purchase discount. Passing up a discount is viewed as paying interest for the use of the money. For example, if Chelsea Video passed up the discount, it would have paid 2% for the use of $3,500 for 20 days. This is the equivalent of an annual interest rate of 36.5% (2% × 365/20). Obviously, it would be better for Chelsea Video to borrow at bank interest rates than to lose the purchase discount.

So as not to miss purchase discounts, unpaid invoices should be filed by due dates. This procedure helps the purchaser remember the discount date, prevents early payment of bills, and maximizes the time that cash can be used for other purposes.

Let's now assume that, contrary to best practices, Chelsea Video did not take advantage of the purchase discount and instead makes full payment of $3,500 on June 3. The journal entry to record this payment would be:

A = L + OE
-3,500   -3,500

Cash flows: -3,500

| June 3 | Accounts Payable | 3,500 | |
| | Cash | | 3,500 |
| | To record payment of invoice #731 with no discount taken. | | |

Some companies use a different method than the gross method to record purchase discounts. It is called the **net method**. The net method records the purchase at the invoice price, net of the discount. For example, on May 4, the inventory and account payable would be recorded net of the discount amount, at $3,430. If the account is paid within the discount period, Accounts Payable and Cash are debited and credited for the net amount, $3,430. If the discount is not taken, the discount lost, $70, is recorded in a Purchase Discounts Lost account.

The net method is theoretically preferable to the gross method because it (1) better measures the true inventory cost and related liability, and (2) highlights the discounts lost. Despite this, most companies believe that the net method is complicated and is not worth the benefits. The simpler gross method is far more commonly used. Consequently, we focus on the gross method in this text.

## Purchase Discounts in a Periodic Inventory System

The above transactions assumed the use of a perpetual inventory system, similar to that discussed in the chapter material. If Chelsea Video used a periodic inventory system, as described in Appendix 5A, accounting for the purchase discount would be relatively unchanged. The only difference is that a separate temporary account is used to record the discount. You will recall that the Merchandise Inventory account is not used in a periodic inventory system. Rather, inventory transactions are recorded in one of three temporary accounts: Purchases, Purchase Returns and Allowances, or Freight In.

Recording a purchase discount in a periodic inventory system results in a credit (increase) to a fourth temporary account called Purchase Discounts. This account is a contra expense account to Purchases, with a normal credit balance. Purchase discounts are subtracted from purchases, along with purchase returns and allowances, to determine net purchases.

# Sales Discounts

A sales discount is a cash discount offered by the seller to the buyer for early payment of an amount due. Like a purchase discount, a sales discount is based on the invoice price less returns and allowances, if any. Although no new account is added to record purchase discounts in a perpetual inventory system—the discount is recorded as a reduction in the Merchandise Inventory account—a new account, called Sales Discounts, is added to record sales discounts.

Sales Discounts is a contra revenue account, with a normal debit balance. This account is used, instead of debiting Sales, to disclose the amount of cash discounts taken by customers. It is subtracted from the balances in Sales and Sales Returns and Allowances, to determine net sales.

To illustrate the accounting for a sales discount, we will continue with the Highpoint Electronic/Chelsea Video illustration. Highpoint Electronic's journal entry to record the sale of merchandise to Chelsea Video on May 4 is the same as in the chapter, using a perpetual inventory system:

A = L + OE
+3,800      +3,800

Cash flows: no effect

A = L + OE
-2,400      -2,400

Cash flows: no effect

| May 4 | Accounts Receivable | 3,800 | |
| | Sales | | 3,800 |
| | To record credit sale to Chelsea Video per | | |
| | invoice #731, terms 2/10, n/30. | | |
| 4 | Cost of Goods Sold | 2,400 | |
| | Merchandise Inventory | | 2,400 |
| | To record cost of merchandise sold | | |
| | to Chelsea Video per invoice #731. | | |

On May 9, Chelsea Video returned $300 of goods to Highpoint Electronic. These goods cost Highpoint Electronic $140. The following two entries are unchanged from those shown earlier in the chapter for sales returns and allowances:

A = L + OE
-300      -300

Cash flows: no effect

A = L + OE
+140      +140

Cash flows: no effect

| May 9 | Sales Returns and Allowances | 300 | |
| | Accounts Receivable | | 300 |
| | To record credit granted to Chelsea Video for | | |
| | returned goods. | | |
| 9 | Merchandise Inventory | 140 | |
| | Cost of Goods Sold | | 140 |
| | To record cost of returned goods. | | |

In a perpetual inventory system, two journal entries are made to record sales transactions. If a periodic inventory system was used instead, the second journal entry recording the effect on the cost of goods sold would not be made on May 4 and May 9. The first journal entry would remain unchanged.

The entry by Highpoint Electronic to record the cash receipt from Chelsea Video on May 14 within the discount period, adds the new Sales Discount account to the entry as follows:

A = L + OE
+3,430      -70
-3,500

⬆ Cash flows: +3,430

| May 14 | Cash | 3,430 | |
| | Sales Discounts | 70 | |
| | Accounts Receivable | | 3,500 |
| | To record collection of invoice #731 within | | |
| | discount period. | | |

If the discount is not taken, Highpoint Electronic increases Cash and decreases Accounts Receivable by $3,500 at the date of collection. Entries to record sales discounts are the same whether a perpetual or periodic inventory system is in use.

## Summary of Discount Transactions

**Illustration 5B-1 ▼**

Comparison of journal entries for purchase and sales discounts

The following illustration summarizes the entries for purchase and sales discounts using the gross method in a perpetual and periodic inventory system. Note that the entries the perpetual and periodic inventory systems only differ for the account used to record the purchase discount on the buyer's books. There is no difference between any of the other entries.

| PURCHASE DISCOUNTS: ENTRIES ON CHELSEA VIDEO'S BOOKS (BUYER) | | | | | |
| --- | --- | --- | --- | --- | --- |
| | Perpetual Inventory System | | | Periodic Inventory System | |
| Payment within discount period. | Accounts Payable | 3,500 | | Accounts Payable | 3,500 | |
| | Cash | | 3,430 | Cash | | 3,430 |
| | Merchandise Inventory | | 70 | Purchase Discounts | | 70 |
| Payment after discount period. | Accounts Payable | 3,500 | | Accounts Payable | 3,500 | |
| | Cash | | 3,500 | Cash | | 3,500 |

| ENTRIES ON HIGHPOINT ELECTRONIC'S BOOKS (SELLER) | | | | | |
|---|---|---|---|---|---|
| | Perpetual Inventory System | | | Periodic Inventory System | |
| Collection within discount period. | Cash | 3,430 | | Cash | 3,430 | |
| | Sales Discounts | 70 | | Sales Discounts | 70 | |
| | Accounts Receivable | | 3,500 | Accounts Receivable | | 3,500 |
| Collection after discount period. | Cash | 3,500 | | Cash | 3,500 | |
| | Accounts Receivable | | 3,500 | Accounts Receivable | | 3,500 |

# Demonstration Problem

The adjusted trial balance data for the year ended December 31, 2005, for Dykstra Company are as follows:

Additional
Demonstration
Problems

| DYKSTRA COMPANY Adjusted Trial Balance December 31, 2005 | | |
|---|---|---|
| | Debit | Credit |
| Cash | $ 14,500 | |
| Accounts receivable | 15,100 | |
| Merchandise inventory | 29,000 | |
| Prepaid insurance | 2,500 | |
| Land | 150,000 | |
| Building | 500,000 | |
| Accumulated amortization—building | | $ 40,000 |
| Equipment | 95,000 | |
| Accumulated amortization—equipment | | 18,000 |
| Accounts payable | | 10,600 |
| Property taxes payable | | 4,000 |
| Mortgage payable—currently due | | 25,000 |
| Mortgage payable—long-term | | 530,000 |
| Gene Dykstra, capital | | 81,000 |
| Gene Dykstra, drawings | 12,000 | |
| Sales | | 627,200 |
| Sales returns and allowances | 6,700 | |
| Cost of goods sold | 353,800 | |
| Salaries expense | 61,000 | |
| Property tax expense | 24,000 | |
| Utilities expense | 18,000 | |
| Advertising expense | 12,000 | |
| Amortization expense | 29,000 | |
| Freight out | 7,600 | |
| Insurance expense | 4,500 | |
| Interest revenue | | 2,500 |
| Interest expense | 3,600 | |
| Totals | $1,338,300 | $1,338,300 |

*Instructions*

(a) Prepare an income statement for the year ended December 31, 2005.
(b) Prepare a statement of owner's equity for Dykstra Company for the year ended December 31, 2005. No additional investments were made by Mr. Dykstra during the year.
(c) Prepare a classified balance sheet as at December 31, 2005.

**Action Plan**

- Remember that the major subtotal headings in the income statement are net sales, cost of goods sold, gross profit, income from operations, and net income (loss).
- Prepare the income statement in steps:
  1. Net sales less cost of goods sold equals gross profit.
  2. Gross profit less operating expenses equals income from operations.
  3. Income from operations plus or minus non-operating revenue or expense items equals net income.

## Solution to Demonstration Problem

(a)

### DYKSTRA COMPANY
### Income Statement
### Year Ended December 31, 2005

| | | | |
|---|---|---:|---:|
| Sales revenues | | | |
| Sales | | | $627,200 |
| Less: Sales returns and allowances | | | 6,700 |
| Net sales | | | 620,500 |
| Cost of goods sold | | | 353,800 |
| Gross profit | | | 266,700 |
| Operating expenses | | | |
| Salaries expense | $61,000 | | |
| Property tax expense | 24,000 | | |
| Utilities expense | 18,000 | | |
| Advertising expense | 12,000 | | |
| Amortization expense | 29,000 | | |
| Freight out | 7,600 | | |
| Insurance expense | 4,500 | | |
| Total operating expenses | | | 156,100 |
| Income from operations | | | 110,600 |
| Other revenues | | | |
| Interest revenue | $2,500 | | |
| Other expenses | | | |
| Interest expense | 3,600 | | (1,100) |
| Net income | | | $109,500 |

(b)

### DYKSTRA COMPANY
### Statement of Owner's Equity
### Year Ended December 31, 2005

| | |
|---|---:|
| Gene Dykstra, capital, January 1, 2005 | $ 81,000 |
| Add:    Net income | 109,500 |
| | 190,500 |
| Deduct:  Drawings | 12,000 |
| Gene Dykstra, capital, December 31, 2005 | $178,500 |

(c)

**DYKSTRA COMPANY**
**Balance Sheet**
**December 31, 2005**

### Assets

| | | |
|---|---|---|
| Current assets | | |
| Cash | | $ 14,500 |
| Accounts receivable | | 15,100 |
| Merchandise inventory | | 29,000 |
| Prepaid insurance | | 2,500 |
| | | 61,100 |
| Property, plant, and equipment | | |
| Land | | 150,000 |
| Building | $500,000 | |
| Less: Accumulated amortization | 40,000 | 460,000 |
| Equipment | $95,000 | |
| Less: Accumulated amortization | 18,000 | 77,000 |
| | | 687,000 |
| Total assets | | $748,100 |

### Liabilities

| | | |
|---|---|---|
| Current liabilities | | |
| Accounts payable | | $ 10,600 |
| Property taxes payable | | 4,000 |
| Mortgage payable | | 25,000 |
| | | 39,600 |
| Long-term liabilities | | |
| Mortgage payable | | 530,000 |
| Total liabilities | | 569,600 |

### Owner's Equity

| | | |
|---|---|---|
| Gene Dykstra, capital | | 178,500 |
| Total liabilities and owner's equity | | $748,100 |

the navigator

# Summary of Study Objectives

1. *Describe the differences between a service company and a merchandising company.* A service company performs services. It has service or fee revenue and operating expenses. A merchandising company sells goods. It has sales revenue, cost of goods sold, gross profit, and operating expenses.

2. *Explain and complete the entries for purchases under a perpetual inventory system.* The Merchandise Inventory account is debited for all purchases of merchandise and freight, if freight is paid by the buyer. It is credited for purchase returns and allowances.

3. *Explain and complete the entries for sales revenue under a perpetual inventory system.* When inventory is sold, two entries are required: (1) Accounts Receivable (or Cash) is debited and Sales is credited for the selling price of the merchandise. (2) Cost of Goods Sold is debited and Merchandise Inventory is credited for the cost of the inventory items sold.

4. *Explain and perform the steps in the accounting cycle for a merchandising company.* Each of the required steps in the accounting cycle for a service company applies to a merchandising company. An additional adjusting journal entry may be required under a perpetual inventory system. The Merchandise Inventory account must be adjusted to agree with the physical inventory count if any difference exists.

5. *Distinguish between, and be able to prepare, a multiple-step and a single-step income statement.* A multiple-step income statement shows numerous steps in determining net income. Step 1 deducts cost of goods sold from net sales to determine gross profit. Step 2 deducts operating expenses from gross profit to determine income from operations. Step 3 adds or deducts any non-operating activities to determine net income. In a single-step income statement, all data are classified under two categories (revenues or expenses), and net income is determined by one step.

6. *Calculate the gross profit margin and profit margin.* The gross profit margin, calculated by dividing gross profit by net sales, measures the gross profit earned for each dollar of sales. The profit margin, calculated by dividing net income by net sales, measures the net income (total profit) earned for each dollar of sales. Both are measures of profitability that are closely watched by management and other interested parties.

7. *Prepare the entries for purchases and sales of inventory under a periodic inventory system and calculate cost of goods sold (Appendix 5A).* In a perpetual inventory system, only one account—Merchandise Inventory—is used to record inventory transactions. In a periodic inventory system, separate temporary accounts are used to record (a) cash and credit purchases (Purchases); (b) purchase returns and allowances (Purchase Returns and Allowances); and (c) freight costs paid by the buyer

(Freight In). Purchases − purchase returns and allowances = net purchases. Net purchases + freight in = cost of goods purchased.

In a perpetual inventory system, two journal entries are required to record the sale and the cost of the goods sold. In a periodic inventory system, only one journal entry is made to record the sale. Cost of goods sold is not recorded at the time of the sale. Instead it is calculated as follows at the end of the period: beginning inventory + cost of goods purchased = cost of goods available for sale. Cost of goods available for sale − ending inventory = cost of goods sold.

8. *Explain the accounting for purchase and sales discounts (Appendix 5B).* Purchase discounts (for the buyer) and sales discounts (for the seller) are cash reductions to the net invoice price for early payment. In a perpetual inventory system, the purchase discount is recorded as a reduction of the cost in the Merchandise Inventory account. In a periodic inventory system, the purchase discount is recorded in a separate account called Purchase Discounts. The Purchase Discounts account is deducted from purchases, along with purchase returns and allowances, in order to determine net purchases.

Sales discounts are recorded in a separate account called Sales Discounts in both a perpetual and a periodic inventory system. The Sales Discounts account balance is deducted from sales, along with sales returns and allowances, in order to determine net sales.

# Glossary

### Key Term Matching Activity

**Contra revenue account** An account that is offset against (deducted from) a revenue account on the income statement. (p. 224)

**Control account** An account in the general ledger that summarizes the detail for a subsidiary ledger and controls it. (p. 219)

**Cost of goods available for sale** Term used in a periodic inventory system. It is calculated by adding the cost of goods purchased to beginning inventory. (p. 239)

**Cost of goods purchased** Term used in a periodic inventory system. It is calculated by adding freight in to net purchases. (p. 238)

**Cost of goods sold** The total cost of merchandise sold during the period. In a perpetual inventory system, it is recorded. In a periodic inventory system, it is calculated by deducting ending inventory from the cost of goods available for sale. (p. 214)

**FOB destination** Freight terms indicating that the seller will pay for the shipping costs of the goods. (p. 220)

**FOB shipping point** Freight terms indicating that the seller will be responsible for the shipping costs of the goods only until they reach their shipping point. Since this is normally the seller's place of business (shipping point),

there is no cost to the seller. The buyer pays freight costs from the shipping point to the destination. (p. 220)

**Gross profit** Sales revenue less cost of goods sold. (p. 214)

**Gross profit margin** Gross profit expressed as a percentage of net sales. It is calculated by dividing gross profit by net sales. (p. 234)

**Income from operations** Income from a company's principal operating activity, determined by subtracting operating expenses from gross profit. (p. 231)

**Multiple-step income statement** An income statement that shows numerous steps to determine net income or net loss. (p. 230)

**Net purchases** Term used in a periodic inventory system. It is calculated by deducting purchase returns and allowances from purchases. (p. 238)

**Net sales** Sales less sales returns and allowances. (p. 231)

**Operating cycle** The time required to go from cash to cash in producing revenues. (p. 215)

**Operating expenses** Expenses incurred in the process of earning sales revenues. They are deducted from gross profit in the income statement. (p. 214)

**Other expenses** A non-operating activities section of the income statement that shows expenses from auxiliary operations and losses unrelated to the company's operations. (p. 231)

**Other revenues** A non-operating activities section of the income statement that shows revenues from auxiliary operations and gains unrelated to the company's operations. (p. 231)

**Periodic inventory system** An inventory system in which detailed records are not maintained. The cost of goods sold is determined only at the end of the accounting period. (p. 216)

**Perpetual inventory system** A detailed inventory system in which the quantity and cost of each inventory item are maintained. The records continuously show the inventory that should be on hand. (p. 216)

**Profit margin** Net income expressed as a percentage of net sales. It is calculated by dividing net income by net sales. (p. 235)

**Purchase discount** A discount, based on the invoice price less any returns and allowances, given to a buyer for early payment of a balance due. (p. 221)

**Purchase returns (allowances)** The return (or reduction in price) of unsatisfactory purchased merchandise. It results in a debit to cash or accounts payable. (p. 221)

**Quantity discount** A cash discount, reducing the invoice price, given to the buyer for volume purchases. (p. 221)

**Sales discount** A reduction, based on the invoice price less any returns and allowances, given by a seller for prompt payment of a credit sale. (p. 224)

**Sales returns and allowances** The return, or reduction in price, of unsatisfactory sold merchandise. It results in a credit to cash or accounts receivable. (p. 223)

**Sales revenue** The primary source of revenue in a merchandising company. (p. 214)

**Single-step income statement** An income statement that shows only one step (revenues less expenses) in determining net income (or net loss). (p. 233)

**Subsidiary ledger** A group of accounts that provide details of a control account in the general ledger. (p. 219)

---

*Note:* All Questions, Exercises, and Problems below with an asterisk (∗) relate to material in the appendices to the chapter.

# Self-Study Questions

Chapter 5 Self-Test

Answers are at the end of the chapter.

**(SO 1) K**  1. Gross profit will result if:
  (a) operating expenses are less than net income.
  (b) sales revenue is greater than operating expenses.
  (c) sales revenue is greater than cost of goods sold.
  (d) operating expenses are greater than cost of goods sold.

**(SO 2) K**  2. When goods are purchased for resale by a company using the perpetual inventory system:
  (a) purchases are debited to Merchandise Inventory.
  (b) purchases are debited to Purchases.
  (c) purchase returns are debited to Merchandise Inventory.
  (d) freight costs are debited to Freight Out.

**(SO 3) K**  3. To record the sale of goods for cash in a perpetual inventory system:
  (a) only one journal entry is necessary to record the cost of goods sold and reduction of inventory.
  (b) only one journal entry is necessary to record the receipt of cash and the sales revenue.
  (c) two journal entries are necessary: one to record the receipt of cash and sales revenue, and one to record the cost of the goods sold and reduction of inventory.
  (d) two journal entries are necessary: one to record the receipt of cash and reduction of inventory, and one to record the cost of the goods sold and sales revenue.

**(SO 3) K**  4. A contra sales account that normally has a debit balance is:
  (a) Sales Returns and Allowances.
  (b) Sales.
  (c) Freight Out.
  (d) Cost of Goods Sold.

**(SO 4) K**  5. The steps in the accounting cycle for a merchandising company are the same as those for a service company *except*:
  (a) an additional adjusting journal entry for inventory may be needed in a merchandising company.
  (b) closing journal entries are not required for a merchandising company.
  (c) a post-closing trial balance is not required for a merchandising company.
  (d) a multiple-step income statement is required for a merchandising company.

**(SO 5) K**  6. Which of the following appears on both a single-step and a multiple-step income statement?
  (a) Merchandise inventory
  (b) Gross profit
  (c) Income from operations
  (d) Cost of goods sold

(SO 6) AP  7. Net sales are $400,000, cost of goods sold is $310,000, operating expenses are $60,000, and other revenues are $5,000. What are the gross profit margin and profit margin?
(a) 7.5% and 8.8%          (c) 22.5% and 8.8%
(b) 22.5% and 7.4%         (d) 77.5% and 8.8%

(SO 7) K  *8. When goods are purchased for resale by a company using a periodic inventory system:
(a) purchases are debited to Merchandise Inventory.
(b) purchases are debited to Purchases.
(c) purchase returns are debited to Purchase Returns and Allowances.
(d) freight costs are debited to Purchases.

*9. If beginning inventory is $60,000, purchases are $400,000, purchase returns and allowances are $25,000, freight in is $5,000, and ending inventory is $50,000, what is the cost of goods sold?      (SO 7) C
(a) $385,000           (c) $410,000
(b) $390,000           (d) $430,000

*10. A credit sale of $750 is made on June 13, terms 2/10, n/30, on which a return of $50 is granted on June 16. What amount is received as payment in full on June 22?      (SO 8) K
(a) $686               (c) $735
(b) $700               (d) $750

# Questions

(SO 1) C  1. How do the components of revenues and expenses differ between a merchandising company and a service company?

(SO 1) C  2. Explain the income measurement process in a merchandising company.

(SO 1) C  3. What is meant by the term "operating cycle"? Why is the normal operating cycle for a merchandising company likely to be longer than that for a service company?

(SO 1) C  4. Distinguish between a perpetual and a periodic inventory system.

(SO 1) C  5. What types of businesses are most likely to use a perpetual inventory system?

(SO 2) C  6. What is the purpose of an inventory subsidiary ledger? What are the advantages of using one?

(SO 2) C  7. What is the relationship between the inventory subsidiary ledger and the Merchandise Inventory account in the general ledger?

(SO 2, 3) C  8. Distinguish between FOB shipping point and FOB destination. What freight term will result in a debit to Merchandise Inventory by the purchaser? A debit to Freight Out by the seller?

(SO 2, 3) C  9. Inventory was purchased on credit in April and paid for in May. It was sold in June. In which month should the company record this cost as an expense? Why?

(SO 3) C  10. Explain why sales returns are not debited directly to the Sales account.

(SO 4) C  11. "The steps in the accounting cycle for a merchandising company are different from those in the accounting cycle for a service enterprise." Do you agree or disagree?

(SO 4) C  12. Song Yee wonders why a physical inventory count is necessary in a perpetual inventory system. After all, the accounting records show how much inventory is on hand. Explain why a physical inventory count is required in a perpetual inventory system.

13. What additional accounts must be closed for a merchandising company using a perpetual inventory system as compared with a service company?      (SO 4) K

14. Ford Company reports net sales of $800,000, gross profit of $580,000, other expenses of $5,000, and net income of $300,000. What is the company's income from operations? What are its operating expenses?      (SO 5) AP

15. Identify the sections of a multiple-step income statement that relate to (a) operating activities, and (b) non-operating activities.      (SO 5) K

16. Why is interest expense a non-operating expense and not an operating expense?      (SO 5) C

17. How does the single-step form of income statement differ from the multiple-step form?      (SO 5) C

18. What factors affect a company's gross profit margin: that is, what can cause the gross profit margin to increase and what can cause it to decrease?      (SO 6) C

19. How do the gross profit margin and profit margin differ?      (SO 6) C

*20. How is cost of goods sold calculated and recorded in a periodic inventory system?      (SO 7) K

*21. In a periodic system, purchases of inventory are recorded in the Purchases account. Why are purchases of supplies or equipment not also recorded in the Purchases account?      (SO 7) C

*22. In a periodic inventory system, closing entries are posted to the Merchandise Inventory account. What is the purpose of these entries?      (SO 7) C

*23. Why do companies offer a cash discount?      (SO 8) C

*24. The Fukushima Company received an invoice for $16,000, terms 1/10, n/30. It will have to borrow from its bank in order to pay the invoice in 10 days. The interest rate Fukushima pays on its bank loans is 7.25%. Should it take advantage of the cash discount offered or not? Support your answer with calculations.      (SO 8) C

# Brief Exercises

**BE5–1** The components in the income statements of companies A, B, and C are presented below. Determine the missing amounts.

Calculate missing amounts in determining net income. (SO 1) AP

| | Sales | Cost of Goods Sold | Gross Profit | Operating Expenses | Net Income |
|---|---|---|---|---|---|
| Company A | $ 75,000 | $ ? | $ 31,500 | $ ? | $10,800 |
| Company B | 108,000 | 70,000 | ? | ? | 29,500 |
| Company C | ? | 71,900 | 109,600 | 39,500 | ? |

**BE5–2** The Big C Company sells three types of cookies. The company uses a perpetual inventory system and a subsidiary ledger to keep track of the inventory. Determine the balance in the inventory control account in the general ledger if the company had the following items on hand on March 31:

Calculate balance in inventory control account. (SO 2) AP

| Inventory Item | Packages on Hand | Cost per Package |
|---|---|---|
| Oatmeal | 200 | $1.75 |
| Chocolate Chip | 600 | 2.10 |
| Ginger Snaps | 500 | 1.50 |

**BE5–3** Prepare the journal entries to record the following purchase transactions in Xiaoyan Company's books. Xiaoyan uses a perpetual inventory system.

Journalize purchase transactions—perpetual system. (SO 2) AP

(a) On January 3, Xiaoyan purchased $9,000 of merchandise from Feng Company, terms n/30.
(b) On January 6, Xiaoyan returned $1,000 of the merchandise purchased on January 3 because it did not need it.
(c) On January 12, Xiaoyan paid the balance owing to Feng.

**BE5–4** Prepare journal entries to record the following sales transactions in Feng Company's books. Feng uses a perpetual inventory system.

Journalize sales transactions—perpetual system. (SO 3) AP

(a) On January 3, Feng sold $9,000 of merchandise to Xiaoyan Company, terms n/30. The cost of the merchandise sold was $6,000.
(b) On January 6, Xiaoyan returned $1,000 of the merchandise purchased on January 3 because it did not need it. The cost of the merchandise returned was $800, and it was restored to inventory.
(c) On January 12, Feng received the balance due from Xiaoyan.

**BE5–5** The Big C Company (see BE5–2) has decided to expand its sales to include Double Chocolate Chip cookies. It purchases 1,000 packages from its supplier at a cost of $2.50 per package, terms n/30, FOB shipping point. The freight charges are $120 cash. Big C immediately sells 50 packages to a regular customer for $4.90 cash per package. Prepare journal entries to record these transactions. What are the quantity, cost per package, and total cost of this inventory item on hand after these transactions?

Journalize purchase and sales transactions. Calculate balances. (SO 2, 3) AP

**BE5–6** At its August 31 year end, the inventory records of Dren Company showed merchandise inventory of $98,000. Through a physical count, the company determined that its actual inventory on hand was $97,100. Record the necessary adjusting entry.

Prepare adjusting entry. (SO 4) AP

**BE5–7** Prasad Company has the following merchandise account balances at its July 31 year end: Sales, $180,000; Sales Returns and Allowances, $2,000; Cost of Goods Sold, $100,000; Merchandise Inventory, $40,000; Freight Out, $2,500; and Prasad, Capital, $150,000. Prepare the closing entries.

Prepare closing entries. (SO 4) AP

**BE5–8** Explain where each of the following items would appear on (1) a multiple-step income statement, and (2) a single-step income statement: (a) gain on sale of equipment, (b) interest expense, (c) cost of goods sold, (d) rent revenue, and (e) amortization expense.

Indicate income statement presentation. (SO 5) C

**BE5–9** Assume Crisp Company has the following account balances: Sales, $500,000; Sales Returns and Allowances, $15,000; Cost of Goods Sold, $350,000; Operating Expenses, $110,000; Other Revenues, $8,000; and Other Expenses, $12,000. Calculate the following: (a) net sales, (b) gross profit, (c) income from operations, and (d) net income.

Calculate net sales, gross profit, income from operations, and net income. (SO 5, 6) AP

Calculate profitability ratios.
(SO 6) AP

**BE5–10**  Ry Company reported net sales, $550,000; cost of goods sold, $300,000; and operating expenses, $200,000. Calculate the following ratios: (a) gross profit margin, and (b) profit margin.

Journalize purchase transactions—periodic system.
(SO 7) AP

*BE5–11  From the information in BE5–3, prepare the journal entries to record the purchase transactions on Xiaoyan Company's books, assuming a periodic inventory system is used instead of a perpetual inventory system.

Journalize sales trans-
actions—periodic system.
(SO 7) AP

*BE5–12  From the information in BE5–4, prepare the journal entries to record the purchase transactions on Feng Company's books, assuming a periodic inventory system is used instead of a perpetual inventory system.

Calculate net purchases and
cost of goods purchased.
(SO 7) AP

*BE5–13  Bassing Company uses a periodic inventory system and has these account balances: Purchases, $400,000; Purchase Returns and Allowances, $11,000; and Freight In, $16,000. Determine net purchases and cost of goods purchased.

Calculate cost of goods
sold and gross profit.
(SO 7) AP

*BE5–14  In addition to the information given in BE5–13, Bassing Company has beginning inventory of $60,000, ending inventory of $90,000, and net sales of $630,000. Determine the cost of goods sold and gross profit.

Journalize purchase transactions with purchase
discount.
(SO 8) AP

*BE5–15  From the information in BE5–3, prepare the journal entry to record the January 12 payment on Xiaoyan Company's books, assuming the terms of the sale were 2/10, n/30. First assume Xiaoyan uses a perpetual inventory system, and then assume Xiaoyan uses a periodic inventory system.

Journalize sales trans-
actions with sales discount.
(SO 8) AP

*BE5–16  From the information in BE5–4, prepare the journal entry to record the January 12 cash receipt on Feng Company's books, assuming the terms of sale were 2/10, n/30. Does it make a difference if Feng uses the periodic or perpetual inventory system?

# Exercises

Journalize inventory transactions—perpetual system.
(SO 2) AP

**E5–1**  Information related to Olaf Co. is shown below:

1. On April 5, purchased merchandise from DeVito Company for $18,000, terms n/30, FOB shipping point.
2. On April 6, paid freight costs of $900 on merchandise purchased from DeVito.
3. On April 7, purchased supplies for $2,600 cash.
4. On April 8, returned damaged merchandise to DeVito Company and was granted a $3,000 purchase allowance.
5. On May 2, paid the amount due to DeVito Company in full.

*Instructions*

Prepare the journal entries to record these transactions on the books of Olaf Co., assuming a perpetual inventory system is used.

Journalize inventory
transactions on buyer's and
seller's books—perpetual
system.
(SO 3) AP

**E5–2**  The following merchandise transactions occurred in December. Both companies use a perpetual inventory system.

1. On December 3, Pippen Company sold and shipped merchandise to Thomas Co. for $480,000, terms n/30, FOB shipping point. This merchandise cost Pippen Company $320,000.
2. On December 8, Thomas Co. was granted a sales allowance of $24,000 for defective merchandise purchased on December 3. No merchandise was returned.
3. On December 31, Pippen Company received the balance due from Thomas Co.

*Instructions*

(a) Prepare the journal entries to record these transactions on the books of Pippen Company.
(b) Prepare the journal entries to record these transactions on the books of Thomas Co.

Journalize and post inventory transactions—perpetual
system.
(SO 2, 3) AP

**E5–3**  Collegiate Office Supply sells various office furniture items and uses a perpetual inventory system. At the beginning of October, it had no office chairs in stock. The following events occurred during October and November:

Oct. 6 Purchased 100 office chairs from Katts Ltd. for $78 each, terms n/30, FOB shipping point.
  7 Paid $200 cash to Freight Company for the delivery of the chairs.
  9 Sold 30 chairs to Butler Inc. for $135 each on credit, terms n/30, FOB destination. (*Hint:* Note that the freight charges from the October 7 transaction will increase the cost per chair.)
  10 Paid $30 cash to Freight Company for the delivery of the chairs to Butler Inc.
  11 Granted Butler Inc. credit for five returned chairs. The chairs were returned to inventory.
  31 Counted the inventory and determined there were actually 74 chairs on hand.
Nov. 5 Paid Katts Ltd. for the chairs purchased on October 6.
  8 Received payment from Butler Inc. for the amount owing.

*Instructions*

(a) Journalize the above transactions and events.
(b) Post the appropriate entries to the Merchandise Inventory and Cost of Goods Sold accounts and determine their ending balances.

**E5–4** An inexperienced accountant for Churchill Company made the following errors in recording merchandising transactions:

Prepare correcting entries. (SO 2, 3) AN

Interactive Homework

1. A $150 cash refund to a customer for faulty merchandise was debited to Sales $150 and credited to Cash $150.
2. A $250 credit purchase of supplies was debited to Merchandise Inventory $250 and credited to Cash $250.
3. A $50 purchase return on account was recorded as a debit to Accounts Payable $50 and a credit to Sales $50.
4. A cash payment of $300 for freight on merchandise purchases was debited to Freight Expense $300 and credited to Cash $300.
5. A $200 credit sale of merchandise with a cost of $125 was debited to Accounts Receivable for $200, credited to Merchandise Inventory for $125, and credited to Sales for $75.

*Instructions*

Prepare correcting entries for each error. Churchill Company uses a perpetual inventory system.

**E5–5** On June 10, Pele Company purchased $5,000 of merchandise from Duvall Company FOB shipping point, terms n/30. Pele paid $300 of freight costs to Hoyt Movers on June 11. Damaged goods totalling $500 were returned to Duvall for credit on June 12. On July 7, Pele paid Duvall Company in full. On July 15, Pele sold all of the remaining merchandise purchased from Duvall for $8,500 cash. On that same date, Pele paid $250 of freight costs to AAA Transit to deliver the goods to the customer. On July 17, Pele gave its customer a $300 cash sales allowance for damaged goods. Pele uses a perpetual inventory system.

Record inventory transactions and closing entries—perpetual system. (SO 2, 4) AP

*Instructions*

(a) Journalize each of the above transactions on the books of Pele Company.
(b) Prepare closing entries on July 31 for the temporary accounts.

**E5–6** Financial information is presented below for three different companies:

Calculate missing amounts. (SO 5) AN

| | Natural Cosmetics | Mattar Grocery | Allied Wholesalers |
|---|---|---|---|
| Sales | $90,000 | $    (e) | $144,000 |
| Sales returns and allowances | (a) | 5,000 | 12,000 |
| Net sales | 81,000 | 95,000 | (i) |
| Cost of goods sold | 56,000 | (f) | (j) |
| Gross profit | (b) | 38,000 | 24,000 |
| Operating expenses | 15,000 | (g) | 18,000 |
| Income from operations | (c) | (h) | (k) |
| Other expenses | 4,000 | 7,000 | (l) |
| Net income | (d) | 11,000 | 5,000 |

*Instructions*

Determine the missing amounts.

Prepare multiple-step and single-step income statements—perpetual system.
(SO 5) AP

**Interactive Homework**

**E5–7** In its income statement for the year ended December 31, 2005, Chevalier Company reported the following condensed data:

| | | | |
|---|---|---|---|
| Operating expenses | $1,125,000 | Loss on sale of equipment | $ 10,000 |
| Cost of goods sold | 985,000 | Sales | 2,400,000 |
| Interest expense | 70,000 | Sales returns and allowances | 41,000 |
| Interest revenue | 45,000 | | |

**Instructions**

(a) Prepare a multiple-step income statement.
(b) Prepare a single-step income statement.

Classify accounts of merchandising company.
(SO 5) K

**E5–8** You are provided with the following list of accounts from the adjusted trial balance for Swirsky Company:

Accounts payable
Accounts receivable
Accumulated amortization—office building
Accumulated amortization—store equipment
Advertising expense
Amortization expense
B. Swirsky, capital
B. Swirsky, drawings
Cash
Freight out
Insurance expense
Interest expense
Interest payable

Land
Merchandise inventory
Mortgage payable
Office building
Prepaid insurance
Property tax payable
Salaries expense
Salaries payable
Sales returns and allowances
Store equipment
Unearned sales revenue
Utilities expense

**Instructions**

For each account, identify whether it should be reported on the balance sheet, statement of owner's equity, or multiple-step income statement. Please specify where the account should be classified. For example, Accounts Payable would be classified under current liabilities on the balance sheet.

Calculate profitability ratios.
(SO 6) AN

**E5–9** Best Buy Co., Inc. is North America's number one specialty retailer of consumer electronics, personal computers, entertainment software, and appliances. The company reported the following information for the three most recent fiscal years (in U.S. millions):

| | 2003 | 2002 | 2001 |
|---|---|---|---|
| Sales | $20,946 | $17,711 | $15,189 |
| Cost of goods sold | 15,710 | 13,941 | 12,177 |
| Operating income | 1,010 | 908 | 611 |
| Net income | 99 | 570 | 396 |

**Instructions**

Calculate the gross profit margin and profit margin for Best Buy for each of the three years. Also calculate profit margin using operating income as opposed to net income. Comment on whether the ratios have improved or deteriorated over the last three years.

Journalize inventory transactions and calculate cost of goods sold— periodic system.
(SO 7) AP

**Interactive Homework**

**\*E5–10** Data for Collegiate Office Supply are presented in E5–3.

**Instructions**

(a) Repeat the instructions for E5–3, assuming a periodic inventory system is used instead of a perpetual inventory system.
(b) Calculate the cost of goods sold for October.
(c) Compare the balance in the Cost of Goods Sold account determined in E5–3 to the amount calculated in (b) above.

*E5–11 Below are a series of cost of goods sold sections for four companies:

Determine missing amounts for cost of goods sold section.
(SO 7) AN

|  | Co. 1 | Co. 2 | Co. 3 | Co. 4 |
|---|---|---|---|---|
| Beginning inventory | $ 250 | $ 120 | $1,000 | $ (j) |
| Purchases | 1,500 | 1,080 | (g) | 43,590 |
| Purchase returns and allowances | 65 | (d) | 440 | (k) |
| Net purchases | (a) | 1,030 | 7,210 | 42,090 |
| Freight in | 110 | (e) | (h) | 2,240 |
| Cost of goods purchased | (b) | 1,230 | 7,940 | (l) |
| Cost of goods available for sale | 1,795 | 1,350 | (i) | 49,530 |
| Ending inventory | 310 | (f) | 1,450 | 6,230 |
| Cost of goods sold | (c) | 1,230 | 7,490 | 43,300 |

Instructions

Fill in the missing amounts to complete the cost of goods sold sections.

*E5–12 The following selected information is presented for Okanagan Company for the year ended January 31, 2005:

Prepare multiple-step income statement and closing entries.
(SO 7) AP

| | | | |
|---|---|---|---|
| Accounts receivable | $ 25,000 | O. G. Pogo, drawings | $ 42,000 |
| Freight in | 10,000 | Purchases | 200,000 |
| Freight out | 7,000 | Purchase returns and allowances | 6,000 |
| Insurance expense | 12,000 | Rent expense | 20,000 |
| Interest expense | 6,000 | Salaries expense | 61,000 |
| Merchandise inventory, beginning | 42,000 | Salaries payable | 2,500 |
| Merchandise inventory, ending | 61,000 | Sales | 315,000 |
| O. G. Pogo, capital | 105,000 | Sales returns and allowances | 13,000 |

Instructions

(a) Prepare a multiple-step income statement.
(b) Prepare closing entries.

*E5–13 On September 20, Glatiotis Company purchased $10,000 of merchandise from Kreuz Company, terms 2/10, n/30. Glatiotis Company pays freight costs of $350 on September 21. Damaged goods totalling $500 are returned to Kreuz Company for credit on September 22. On September 30, Glatiotis Company pays Kreuz Company in full.

Journalize purchase and sales transactions with discounts.
(SO 8) AP

Interactive Homework

Instructions

(a) Prepare journal entries for each transaction in the books of Glatiotis Company, assuming (1) a perpetual inventory system is used, and (2) a periodic inventory system is used.
(b) Prepare journal entries for each transaction for Kreuz Company assuming (1) a perpetual inventory system is used, and (2) a periodic inventory system is used. The merchandise purchased by Glatiotis on September 20 cost Kreuz $6,000. The merchandise returned by Glatiotis on September 20 cost Kreuz $350. The merchandise was repaired and returned to inventory.

*E5–14 The Furano Company had the following merchandise transactions in May:

Journalize purchase and sales transactions with discounts.
(SO 8) AP

May 2 Purchased $1,200 of merchandise from Digital Suppliers, terms 2/10, n/30.
3 Returned $200 of the merchandise to Digital as it did not meet specifications.
9 Paid Digital the balance owing.
12 Sold three-quarters of the remaining merchandise to SunDial Company for $1,500, terms, 2/10, n/30.
14 SunDial complained that some of the merchandise was slightly damaged. Furano issued SunDial a credit memo for $100 as a sales allowance.
22 Received the correct balance owing from SunDial.

Instructions

(a) Prepare journal entries for Furano Company assuming it uses a perpetual inventory system.
(b) Prepare journal entries for Furano Company assuming it uses a periodic inventory system.

# Problems: Set A

Journalize inventory
transactions—perpetual
system.
(SO 2, 3) AP

**P5–1A** Travel Warehouse distributes suitcases to retail stores and extends credit terms of n/30 to all of its customers. At the end of June, Travel Warehouse's inventory consisted of 40 suitcases purchased at $30 each. During the month of July, the following merchandising transactions occurred:

July   1  Purchased 50 suitcases on account for $30 each from Trunk Manufacturers, FOB destination, terms n/30. The appropriate party also made a cash payment of $100 for freight on this date.

      3  Sold 40 suitcases on account to Satchel World for $55 each.

      4  Issued a $55 credit memorandum to Satchel World for the return of a damaged suitcase. The suitcase was determined to be no longer saleable and was destroyed.

      9  Paid Trunk Manufacturers in full.

    12  Received balance owing from Satchel World.

    17  Sold 30 suitcases on account to The Going Concern for $55 each.

    18  Purchased 60 suitcases on account for $1,700 from Holiday Manufacturers, FOB shipping point, terms n/30. The appropriate party also made a cash payment of $100 for freight on this date.

    20  Received $300 credit for 10 suitcases returned to Holiday Manufacturers.

    21  Received payment in full from The Going Concern.

    21  Sold 40 suitcases on account to Fly-By-Night for $55 each.

    23  Granted Fly-By-Night $275 credit for five suitcases returned costing $150. The suitcases were in good condition and were restored to inventory.

    30  Paid Holiday Manufacturers in full.

    31  Received the balance owing from Fly-By-Night.

*Instructions*

Journalize the transactions for the month of July for Travel Warehouse using the perpetual inventory system.

Journalize and post
inventory transactions—
perpetual system. Prepare
partial income statement
and balance sheet.
(SO 2, 3, 5) AP

**P5–2A** The Nisson Distributing Company completed the following merchandising transactions in the month of April 2005. At the beginning of April, Nisson's ledger showed Cash $9,000; and M. Nisson, Capital $9,000.

Apr.   2  Purchased 100 tables for resale from Kananaskis Supply Co. for $8,900, terms n/30, FOB shipping point.

     3  Paid $100 cash for freight charges on the merchandise purchased from Kananaskis Supply Co.

     4  Sold 80 of these tables on account for $10,800, FOB destination, terms n/30.

     5  Paid $200 freight on the April 4 sale.

     6  Issued a credit memorandum for the return of four tables sold on April 4. Tables were returned to inventory.

    14  Purchased merchandise for cash, $3,800.

    16  Received a $500 refund from a supplier for returned goods on the cash purchase of April 14.

    18  Purchased merchandise from Testa Distributors for $4,200, FOB destination, terms n/30.

    20  Received credit from Testa for merchandise returned, $300.

    23  Sold merchandise for cash, $6,400. The cost of this merchandise was $5,200.

    26  Purchased merchandise for $2,300 cash.

    27  Paid Kananaskis Supply Co. the amount due.

    28  Received collections for balance owing from customer billed on April 4.

    29  Made refunds to cash customers for merchandise, $90. The returned merchandise had a cost of $60. The merchandise was returned to inventory for future resale.

    30  Sold merchandise on account for $3,700, FOB shipping point, terms n/30. Nisson's cost for this merchandise was $2,800.

*Instructions*

(a) Journalize the transactions assuming Nisson uses a perpetual inventory system.

(b) Set up general ledger accounts, enter the beginning cash and capital balances, and post the transactions.

(c) Prepare a partial multiple-step income statement, up to gross profit, for the month of April 2005.
(d) Prepare the current assets section of the balance sheet at the end of April.

**P5–3A** The unadjusted trial balance of World Enterprises for the year ending December 31, 2005, is shown below:

*Prepare adjusting and closing entries—perpetual system. Prepare financial statements.*
*(SO 4, 5) AP*

**WORLD ENTERPRISES**
**Trial Balance**
**December 31, 2005**

|  | Debit | Credit |
|---|---|---|
| Cash | $ 14,000 | |
| Accounts receivable | 30,600 | |
| Merchandise inventory | 27,500 | |
| Supplies | 1,650 | |
| Prepaid insurance | 1,800 | |
| Office furniture | 26,800 | |
| Accumulated amortization—office furniture | | $ 8,900 |
| Store equipment | 42,000 | |
| Accumulated amortization—store equipment | | 9,000 |
| Accounts payable | | 34,400 |
| Unearned sales revenue | | 3,000 |
| Note payable | | 36,000 |
| Seok Kim, capital | | 59,700 |
| Seok Kim, drawings | 45,850 | |
| Sales | | 238,500 |
| Sales returns and allowances | 4,600 | |
| Cost of goods sold | 157,000 | |
| Salaries expense | 31,600 | |
| Rent expense | 6,100 | |
| | $389,500 | $389,500 |

Other data:
1. The 12-month insurance policy was purchased on August 1, 2005.
2. There are $750 of supplies on hand on December 31, 2005.
3. Amortization expense for the year is $3,000 for store equipment and $1,500 for office furniture.
4. Salaries of $1,210 are accrued and unpaid at December 31, 2005.
5. Accrued interest expense at December 31, 2005, is $2,800.
6. Of the unearned sales revenue, $1,950 has been earned by December 31, 2005. The cost of goods sold incurred in earning this revenue is $1,275.
7. A physical count of merchandise inventory indicates $25,600 on hand on December 31, 2005.
8. Of the note payable, $6,000 is to be paid during 2006.
9. Seok Kim invested $5,000 cash in the business on July 18, 2005.

*Instructions*
(a) Prepare the adjusting journal entries.
(b) Prepare a multiple-step income statement, statement of owner's equity, and classified balance sheet.
(c) Prepare the closing entries.

Prepare financial
statements and adjusting
and closing entries—
perpetual system.
(SO 4, 5) AP

**P5–4A** Moulton Department Store is located in midtown Metropolis. Over the past several years, net income has been declining because of suburban shopping centers. At the end of the company's fiscal year on November 30, 2005, the following accounts appeared in alphabetical order in its unadjusted and adjusted trial balances:

| | Trial Balances | |
| --- | --- | --- |
| | Unadjusted | Adjusted |
| Accounts payable | $ 47,310 | $ 47,310 |
| Accounts receivable | 11,770 | 11,770 |
| Accumulated amortization—delivery equipment | 15,680 | 18,816 |
| Accumulated amortization—building | 32,300 | 41,800 |
| Amortization expense—delivery equipment | 0 | 3,136 |
| Amortization expense—building | 0 | 9,500 |
| Building | 125,000 | 125,000 |
| C. Moulton, capital | 84,200 | 84,200 |
| C. Moulton, drawings | 12,000 | 12,000 |
| Cash | 8,000 | 8,000 |
| Cost of goods sold | 633,220 | 633,520 |
| Delivery equipment | 57,000 | 57,000 |
| Delivery expense | 8,200 | 8,200 |
| Insurance expense | 0 | 10,500 |
| Interest expense | 8,000 | 8,000 |
| Interest revenue | 5,000 | 5,000 |
| Land | 50,000 | 50,000 |
| Merchandise inventory | 36,200 | 35,900 |
| Mortgage payable | 96,000 | 96,000 |
| Prepaid insurance | 13,500 | 3,000 |
| Property tax expense | 0 | 3,500 |
| Property taxes payable | 0 | 3,500 |
| Salaries expense | 139,000 | 139,000 |
| Sales | 845,000 | 849,000 |
| Sales commissions expense | 8,000 | 10,500 |
| Sales commissions payable | 0 | 2,500 |
| Sales returns and allowances | 10,000 | 10,000 |
| Unearned sales revenue | 5,000 | 1,000 |
| Utilities expense | 10,600 | 10,600 |

Analysis reveals a mortgage payment of $6,000 is currently due.

*Instructions*

(a) Journalize the adjusting entries that were made.
(b) Prepare a multiple-step income statement, statement of owner's equity, and classified balance sheet.
(c) Journalize the closing entries that are necessary.

**P5–5A** The trial balance of Club Canada Wholesale Company contained the following accounts at December 31, the company's fiscal year end:

*Prepare adjusting and closing entries. Prepare adjusted trial balance and financial statements—perpetual system. (SO 4, 5) AP*

**CLUB CANADA WHOLESALE COMPANY**
**Trial Balance**
**December 31, 2005**

|  | Debit | Credit |
|---|---|---|
| Cash | $ 23,400 | |
| Accounts receivable | 7,600 | |
| Merchandise inventory | 72,400 | |
| Prepaid insurance | 3,630 | |
| Supplies | 3,780 | |
| Notes receivable | 30,000 | |
| Land | 72,000 | |
| Building | 197,000 | |
| Accumulated amortization—building | | $ 54,000 |
| Equipment | 83,500 | |
| Accumulated amortization—equipment | | 42,400 |
| Accounts payable | | 37,500 |
| Unearned revenue | | 7,550 |
| Mortgage payable | | 186,000 |
| E. Martel, capital | | 137,465 |
| E. Martel, drawings | 72,500 | |
| Sales | | 923,470 |
| Interest revenue | | 1,200 |
| Sales returns and allowances | 18,050 | |
| Cost of goods sold | 712,100 | |
| Interest expense | 8,525 | |
| Repairs expense | 5,900 | |
| Salaries expense | 69,800 | |
| Utilities expense | 9,400 | |
| | $1,389,585 | $1,389,585 |

Other data:

1. Interest revenue earned but not recorded on December 31 was $300.
2. Of the insurance, $3,400 has expired by December 31.
3. A physical count of supplies shows $1,170 on hand on December 31, 2005.
4. Annual amortization is $5,250 on the building and $9,200 on the equipment.
5. The note receivable matures on March 10, 2007.
6. Interest of $1,325 is accrued and unpaid on the mortgage payable at December 31, 2005.
7. Unearned revenue of $5,800 has been earned by December 31, 2005. The cost of goods sold incurred in earning this revenue was $4,500.
8. Merchandise inventory actually on hand at December 31, 2005, is $70,200.
9. Of the mortgage payable, $5,900 is to be paid during the next fiscal year.

*Instructions*

(a) Prepare the adjusting entries.
(b) Prepare an adjusted trial balance.
(c) Prepare an income statement, statement of owner's equity and classified balance sheet.
(d) Prepare the closing entries.

Prepare financial state-
ments, closing entries, and
calculate ratios—perpetual
system.
(SO 4, 5, 6) AP

**P5–6A** The adjusted trial balance at fiscal year end for Rikard's, an upscale men's clothing store, is as follows:

### RIKARD'S
### Adjusted Trial Balance
### August 31, 2005

| | Debit | Credit |
|---|---|---|
| Cash | $ 5,890 | |
| Accounts receivable | 2,570 | |
| Merchandise inventory | 87,400 | |
| Prepaid insurance | 2,205 | |
| Supplies | 1,680 | |
| Store equipment | 32,600 | |
| Accumulated amortization—store equipment | | $ 13,040 |
| Office furniture | 18,500 | |
| Accumulated amortization—office furniture | | 7,400 |
| Note payable | | 22,900 |
| Accounts payable | | 29,100 |
| Salaries payable | | 3,500 |
| Interest payable | | 450 |
| Unearned sales revenue | | 1,460 |
| Rikard Martinson, capital | | 47,950 |
| Rikard Martinson, drawings | 76,000 | |
| Sales | | 455,600 |
| Sales returns and allowances | 4,555 | |
| Cost of goods sold | 273,360 | |
| Amortization expense | 5,110 | |
| Salaries expense | 48,000 | |
| Rent expense | 14,000 | |
| Supplies expense | 5,040 | |
| Insurance expense | 1,575 | |
| Loss on sale of equipment | 625 | |
| Interest expense | 2,290 | |
| | $581,400 | $581,400 |

Other data:

1. Of the notes payable, $5,000 becomes due on February 28, 2006; the balance is due in 2007.
2. On July 6, 2005, Rikard invested $1,500 cash in the business.

*Instructions*

(a) Prepare a multiple-step income statement, statement of owner's equity, and classified balance sheet.
(b) Prepare closing entries.
(c) Calculate the gross profit margin and profit margin.

**P5–7A IPSCO Inc.,** headquartered in Regina, Saskatchewan, produces steel mill and fabricated products for the oil and natural gas, manufacturing, agricultural, and transportation industries in Canada and the US.

Selected financial information related to IPSCO's inventories from its December 31 consolidated financial statements (in U.S. thousands) follows:

| | 2002 | 2001 |
|---|---|---|
| Sales | $1,081,709 | $949,263 |
| Cost of sales | 976,392 | 807,895 |
| Net income | 20,279 | 38,868 |
| Current assets | 476,270 | 440,115 |
| Current liabilities | 171,458 | 208,916 |

*Instructions*

(a) Calculate the gross profit margin, profit margin, and current ratio.
(b) Evaluate IPSCO's performance in 2002 compared to 2001.

**\*P5–8A** Data for Travel Warehouse are presented in P5–1A.

Journalize inventory transactions—periodic system.
(SO 7) AP

*Instructions*

Journalize the July transactions for Travel Warehouse, assuming a periodic inventory system is used instead of a perpetual inventory system.

**\*P5–9A** Joanie Kane, a former professional golfer, operates Kane's Pro Shop at Crowtree Golf Course. At the beginning of the current season on April 1, the ledger of Kane's Pro Shop showed Cash $2,500; Merchandise Inventory $3,500; and Joanie Kane, Capital $6,000. The following transactions occurred during April 2005:

Journalize and post inventory transactions, and prepare trial balance and partial income statement—periodic system.
(SO 7) AP

Apr. 5 Purchased golf bags, clubs, and balls on account from Balata Co. for $1,700, FOB shipping point, terms n/60.
 7 Paid freight on Balata Co. purchases, $90.
 9 Received credit from Balata Co. for merchandise returned, $150.
 10 Sold merchandise on account to members for $950, terms n/30.
 12 Purchased golf shoes, sweaters, and other accessories on account from Arrow Sportswear for $770, terms n/30.
 14 Paid Balata Co. in full.
 17 Received $75 credit from Arrow Sportswear for returned merchandise.
 20 Made sales on account to members for $790, terms n/30.
 21 Paid Arrow Sportswear in full.
 24 Purchased supplies on account for $590, terms n/30.
 27 Granted credit to members for clothing that did not fit, $50.
 30 Made cash sales, $670.
 30 Received payments on accounts from members, $1,250.

*Instructions*

(a) Journalize the April transactions for Kane's Pro Shop using a periodic inventory system.
(b) Enter the beginning balances in the ledger accounts and post the April transactions.
(c) Prepare a trial balance as at April 30, 2005.
(d) Prepare a multiple-step income statement up to gross profit, assuming merchandise inventory on hand at April 30 is $4,350.

**\*P5–10A** At the end of Bud's Bakery's fiscal year on November 30, 2005, the following accounts appeared in alphabetical order in its adjusted trial balance:

Prepare multiple-step income statement and closing entries—periodic system.
(SO 7) AP

| | | | |
|---|---|---|---|
| Accounts payable | $ 32,310 | Interest expense | $ 11,315 |
| Accounts receivable | 13,770 | Land | 45,000 |
| Accumulated amortization— | | Merchandise inventory | 34,360 |
| building | 61,200 | Mortgage payable | 146,000 |
| Accumulated amortization— | | Prepaid insurance | 4,500 |
| delivery equipment | 19,880 | Property tax expense | 3,500 |
| Accumulated amortization— | | Property tax payable | 3,500 |
| store equipment | 44,000 | Purchases | 630,700 |
| Amortization expense | 14,000 | Purchase returns and allowances | 3,315 |
| Building | 175,000 | Salaries expense | 141,000 |
| Bud Hachey, capital | 156,800 | Salaries payable | 8,000 |
| Bud Hachey, drawings | 12,000 | Sales | 849,000 |
| Cash | 8,000 | Sales returns and allowances | 10,000 |
| Delivery equipment | 57,000 | Store equipment | 125,000 |
| Delivery expense | 8,200 | Unearned sales revenue | 3,000 |
| Freight in | 5,060 | Utilities expense | 19,600 |
| Insurance expense | 9,000 | | |

Additional facts:

1. Bud's Bakery uses a periodic system.
2. Merchandise inventory at November 30, 2005, is $37,350.
3. Bud invested $1,050 cash in the business during the year.

*Instructions*

(a) Prepare a multiple-step income statement and a statement of owner's equity for the year ended November 30, 2005.
(b) Prepare the closing journal entries.
(c) Post closing entries to the capital account. Compare the final balance to the closing owner's equity on the statement of owner's equity.

**Journalize and post inventory transactions with discounts and prepare partial income statement—perpetual system.**
(SO 8) AP

*P5–11A  Presented below are selected transactions for the Norlan Company during September and October of the current year. On September 1 Norlan's ledger showed Cash, $70,000; and C. Norlan, Capital, $70,000.

Sept.  2  Purchased merchandise on account from Hillary Company at a cost of $60,000, FOB shipping point, terms 2/10, n/30.
       4  Paid $2,000 of freight charges to Trucking Company on the merchandise purchased from Hillary Company on September 2.
       5  Returned damaged goods having a gross invoice cost of $7,000 to Hillary Company. Received a credit for this.
      11  Paid Hillary Company the balance owing for the September 2 purchase.
      15  Sold all of the remaining merchandise purchased from Hillary Company to Irvine Company for $90,000, FOB shipping point, terms 2/10, n/30.
      17  Issued Irvine Company a credit of $4,000 for returned goods. These goods had cost Norlan Company $2,400 and were returned to inventory.
      25  Received the balance owing from Irvine Company for the September 15 sale.
Oct.   1  Purchased merchandise on account from Kimmel Company at a cost of $50,000, FOB destination, terms 1/15, n/30.
       3  Obtained a purchase allowance of $2,000 from Kimmel Company to compensate for some minor damage to goods purchased on October 1.
       4  Sold all of the merchandise purchased from Kimmel Company to Kieso Company for $80,000, FOB destination, terms 2/10, n/30.
       7  Issued Kieso Company a sales allowance of $1,500 because some of the goods did not meet Kieso's exact specifications.
      29  Received a cheque from Kieso Company for the balance owing on the October 4 sale.
      31  Paid Kimmel Company the amount owing on the October 1 purchase.
      31  A physical count of inventory on October 31 determines that $2,400 is on hand.

*Instructions*

(a) Prepare journal entries to record the above transactions for Norlan Company, assuming it uses a perpetual inventory system.
(b) Open ledger accounts, post the transactions, and calculate the balance in each account.
(c) Prepare a partial multiple-step income statement, up to gross profit, for the two months ended October 31.

**Journalize and post inventory transactions with discounts and prepare partial income statement—periodic system.**
(SO 8) AP

*P5–12A  Data for Norlan Company are presented in P5–11A.

*Instructions*

Repeat the instructions for P5–11A assuming a periodic inventory system is used instead of a perpetual inventory system. Compare the partial income statement to the one prepared in P5–11A and note any similarities and differences.

# Problems: Set B

**Journalize inventory transactions—perpetual system.**
(SO 2, 3) AP

P5–1B  Phantom Book Warehouse distributes hardcover books to retail stores and extends credit terms of n/30 to all of its customers. At the end of May, Phantom's inventory consists of 240 books purchased at $6 each. During the month of June, the following merchandise transactions occurred:

June  1  Purchased 160 books on account for $5 each from Reader's World Publishers, FOB shipping point, terms n/30. The appropriate party also made a cash payment of $50 for the freight on this date.

June 3 Sold 120 books on account to the Book Nook for $10 each. The cost of each book was $6.
6 Received $50 credit for 10 books returned to Reader's World Publishers.
9 Paid Reader's World Publishers in full.
15 Received payment in full from the Book Nook.
17 Sold 120 books on account to Read-A-Lot Bookstore for $10 each. The cost of the books sold was $682.
18 Issued a $50 credit memorandum to Read-A-Lot Bookstore for the return of five damaged books. The books were determined to be no longer saleable and were destroyed.
20 Purchased 110 books on account for $5 each from Read More Publishers, FOB destination, terms n/30. The appropriate party also made a cash payment of $50 for the freight on this date.
24 Received payment in full from Read-A-Lot Bookstore.
26 Paid Read More Publishers in full.
27 Sold 110 books on account to Readers Bookstore for $10 each. The total cost of the books sold was $616.
28 Granted Readers Bookstore $150 credit for 15 books returned. These books were restored to inventory.
30 Received the balance owing from Readers Bookstore.

### Instructions

Journalize the transactions for the month of June for Phantom Book Warehouse, assuming it uses a perpetual inventory system.

**P5–2B** Copple Hardware Store completed the following merchandising transactions in the month of May. At the beginning of May, Copple's ledger showed Cash, $5,000; and Brad Copple, Capital, $5,000.

*Journalize and post inventory transactions—perpetual system. Prepare partial income statement and balance sheet.*
*(SO 2, 3, 5) AP*

May 1 Purchased 120 tool sets for resale from Lathrop Wholesale Supply Co. for $5,800, terms n/30, FOB shipping point.
3 Paid $200 cash for freight charges on the merchandise purchased from Lathrop Wholesale Supply Co.
4 Sold 30 of these tool sets on account for $2,250, FOB destination, terms n/30.
5 Paid $100 freight on the May 4 sale.
6 Issued a credit memorandum for the return of three tool sets sold on May 4. The tool sets were returned to inventory.
11 Purchased supplies for cash, $900.
12 Purchased merchandise for cash, $2,400.
15 Received refund for poor-quality merchandise from supplier on cash purchase, $230.
17 Purchased merchandise from Harlow Distributors for $1,900, FOB shipping point, terms n/30.
19 Paid freight on May 17 purchase, $250.
20 Received credit from Harlow Distributors for merchandise returned, $250.
24 Sold merchandise for cash, $6,200. The merchandise sold had a cost of $4,600.
25 Purchased merchandise from Horicon Inc. for $1,000, FOB destination, terms n/30.
27 Received collections in full from customers billed on May 4.
29 Made cash refunds to customers for returned merchandise, $100. The returned merchandise had a cost of $70 and was restored to inventory.
30 Paid Lathrop Wholesale Supply for balance owing.
31 Sold merchandise on account for $1,600, FOB shipping point, terms n/30. The cost of the merchandise sold was $1,000.
31 Paid Harlow Distributors for the balance owing.

### Instructions

(a) Journalize the transactions assuming Copple uses a perpetual inventory system.
(b) Set up general ledger accounts, enter the beginning cash and capital balances, and post the transactions.
(c) Prepare a partial multiple-step income statement, up to gross profit, for the month of May 2005.
(d) Prepare the current assets section of the balance sheet at May 31, 2005.

Prepare adjusting and
closing entries—perpetual
system. Prepare financial
statements.
(SO 4, 5) AP

**P5–3B** The unadjusted trial balance of Global Enterprises for the year ending December 31, 2005, is shown below:

### GLOBAL ENTERPRISES
### Trial Balance
### December 31, 2005

|  | Debit | Credit |
|---|---|---|
| Cash | $ 13,000 | |
| Accounts receivable | 31,700 | |
| Merchandise inventory | 28,750 | |
| Supplies | 2,940 | |
| Prepaid insurance | 1,980 | |
| Land | 30,000 | |
| Building | 150,000 | |
| Accumulated amortization—building | | $ 18,750 |
| Office equipment | 45,000 | |
| Accumulated amortization—office equipment | | 9,100 |
| Accounts payable | | 35,600 |
| Unearned sales revenue | | 4,000 |
| Mortgage payable | | 161,250 |
| Ingrid Rochefort, capital | | 79,275 |
| Ingrid Rochefort, drawings | 45,850 | |
| Sales | | 263,770 |
| Sales returns and allowances | 5,275 | |
| Cost of goods sold | 171,225 | |
| Salaries expense | 30,950 | |
| Utilities expense | 5,100 | |
| Interest expense | 9,975 | |
| | $571,745 | $571,745 |

Other data:

1. The 12-month insurance policy was purchased on February 1, 2005.
2. There were $650 of supplies on hand on December 31, 2005.
3. Amortization expense for the year is $2,850 for office equipment and $4,000 for the building.
4. Salaries of $940 are accrued and unpaid at December 31, 2005.
5. Accrued interest expense at December 31, 2005, is $925.
6. Unearned sales revenue of $975 is still unearned at December 31, 2005. On the sales that were earned, the cost of goods sold incurred was $2,000.
7. A physical count of merchandise inventory indicates $26,200 on hand on December 31, 2005.
8. Of the mortgage payable, $9,000 is to be paid during 2006.
9. Ingrid Rochefort invested $7,500 cash in the business on May 21, 2005.

*Instructions*

(a) Prepare the adjusting entries.
(b) Prepare a multiple-step income statement, statement of owner's equity, and classified balance sheet.
(c) Prepare the closing entries.

**P5–4B** At the end of the Starz Department Store's fiscal year on December 31, 2005, the following accounts appeared in two of its trial balances:

Prepare financial statements and adjusting and closing entries—perpetual system. (SO 4, 5) AP

| | Trial Balances | |
|---|---|---|
| | Unadjusted | Adjusted |
| Accounts payable | $ 78,700 | $ 79,700 |
| Accounts receivable | 50,300 | 50,300 |
| Accumulated amortization—building | 42,100 | 52,500 |
| Accumulated amortization—equipment | 30,200 | 42,900 |
| Amortization expense—building | | 10,400 |
| Amortization expense—equipment | | 12,700 |
| Building | 190,000 | 190,000 |
| Cash | 20,800 | 20,800 |
| Cost of goods sold | 412,700 | 415,200 |
| D. Veitch, capital | 226,600 | 226,600 |
| D. Veitch, drawings | 28,000 | 28,000 |
| Equipment | 110,000 | 110,000 |
| Insurance expense | | 7,200 |
| Interest expense | 6,000 | 11,000 |
| Interest payable | | 5,000 |
| Interest revenue | 4,000 | 4,000 |
| Land | 50,000 | 50,000 |
| Merchandise inventory | 75,000 | 72,500 |
| Mortgage payable | 80,000 | 80,000 |
| Prepaid insurance | 9,600 | 2,400 |
| Property taxes expense | | 4,800 |
| Property taxes payable | | 4,800 |
| Salaries expense | 108,000 | 108,000 |
| Sales | 621,000 | 626,500 |
| Sales commissions expense | 10,200 | 15,500 |
| Sales commissions payable | | 5,300 |
| Sales returns and allowances | 8,000 | 8,000 |
| Unearned sales revenue | 7,000 | 1,500 |
| Utilities expense | 11,000 | 12,000 |

Analysis reveals that $20,000 of the mortgage payable is due for payment next year.

*Instructions*

(a) Journalize the adjusting entries that were made.

(b) Prepare a multiple-step income statement, statement of owner's equity, and classified balance sheet.

(c) Journalize the closing entries that are necessary.

Prepare adjusting and
closing entries. Prepare
adjusted trial balance and
financial statements—
perpetual system.
(SO 4, 5) AP

**P5–5B**  The trial balance of Poorten Wholesale Centre contained the following accounts at
November 30, the company's fiscal year end:

**POORTEN WHOLESALE CENTRE**
**Trial Balance**
**November 30, 2005**

|  | Debit | Credit |
|---|---|---|
| Cash | $    16,700 | |
| Accounts receivable | 15,700 | |
| Merchandise inventory | 48,000 | |
| Supplies | 5,500 | |
| Notes receivable | 25,000 | |
| Land | 60,000 | |
| Building | 85,000 | |
| Accumulated amortization—building | | $    17,000 |
| Delivery equipment | 48,000 | |
| Accumulated amortization—delivery equipment | | 16,000 |
| Accounts payable | | 48,500 |
| Unearned revenue | | 7,000 |
| Mortgage payable | | 51,000 |
| K. Poorten, capital | | 161,000 |
| K. Poorten, drawings | 12,000 | |
| Sales | | 750,300 |
| Interest revenue | | 1,325 |
| Sales returns and allowances | 4,200 | |
| Cost of goods sold | 497,500 | |
| Advertising expense | 26,400 | |
| Delivery expense | 16,700 | |
| Interest expense | 3,700 | |
| Repairs expense | 12,100 | |
| Salaries expense | 161,625 | |
| Utilities expense | 14,000 | |
|  | $1,052,125 | $1,052,125 |

Other data:

1. Interest revenue earned but not recorded on November 30 is $350.
2. A physical count of supplies shows $3,250 on hand on November 30, 2005.
3. Annual amortization is $4,250 on the building and $8,000 on the equipment.
4. The note receivable matures on December 31, 2006.
5. Interest of $1,075 is accrued and unpaid on the mortgage payable at November 30, 2005.
6. Unearned revenue of $4,200 has been earned by November 30, 2005. The cost of goods
   sold incurred in earning this revenue was $2,800.
7. Merchandise inventory actually on hand at November 30, 2005, is $42,400.
8. Of the mortgage payable, $4,500 is to be paid during the next fiscal year.

*Instructions*

(a) Prepare the adjusting entries.
(b) Prepare an adjusted trial balance.
(c) Prepare an income statement, statement of owner's equity, and classified balance sheet.
(d) Prepare the closing entries.

Prepare financial
statements, closing
entries, and calculate
ratios—perpetual system.
(SO 4, 5, 6) AP

**P5–6B**  The adjusted trial balance at fiscal year end for Betty's Boutique, an upscale women's
clothing store, is as follows:

**BETTY'S BOUTIQUE**
**Adjusted Trial Balance**
**March 31, 2005**

| | Debit | Credit |
|---|---|---|
| Cash | $ 10,240 | |
| Accounts receivable | 4,870 | |
| Merchandise inventory | 78,200 | |
| Prepaid insurance | 1,280 | |
| Supplies | 840 | |
| Store equipment | 30,800 | |
| Accumulated amortization—store equipment | | $ 12,320 |
| Office furniture | 16,700 | |
| Accumulated amortization—office furniture | | 6,680 |
| Note payable | | 21,500 |
| Accounts payable | | 24,200 |
| Salaries payable | | 2,100 |
| Interest payable | | 360 |
| Unearned sales revenue | | 1,640 |
| Betty Tainch, capital | | 47,950 |
| Betty Tainch, drawings | 90,800 | |
| Sales | | 545,500 |
| Sales returns and allowances | 5,445 | |
| Cost of goods sold | 327,300 | |
| Amortization expense | 4,750 | |
| Salaries expense | 56,000 | |
| Rent expense | 26,000 | |
| Supplies expense | 5,040 | |
| Insurance expense | 1,280 | |
| Loss on sale of equipment | 555 | |
| Interest expense | 2,150 | |
| | $662,250 | $662,250 |

Other data:

1. Of the notes payable, $5,000 becomes due on January 31, 2006; the balance is due in 2007.
2. On August 7, 2004, Betty invested $1,000 cash in the business.

*Instructions*

(a) Prepare a multiple-step income statement, statement of owner's equity, and classified balance sheet.
(b) Prepare closing entries.
(c) Calculate the gross profit margin and profit margin.

**P5–7B Danier Leather Inc.** is the second largest publicly traded specialty leather apparel retailer in the world. The company is headquartered in Toronto and has been profitable every year since it entered the retail business in 1974. The following information (in thousands) is available its 2002 and 2001 fiscal year ends:

Calculate ratios and comment.
(SO 6) AN

| | 2002 | 2001 |
|---|---|---|
| Current assets | $ 44,154 | $ 42,945 |
| Current liabilities | 10,552 | 15,252 |
| Sales revenue | 179,977 | 165,418 |
| Cost of sales | 92,098 | 82,818 |
| Net earnings | 10,725 | 12,078 |

*Instructions:*

(a) Calculate the gross profit margin, the profit margin, and the current ratio for Danier Leather for 2002 and 2001. Comment on whether the ratios have improved or deteriorated over the two years.
(b) Compare the 2002 ratios to the following industry averages: gross profit margin, 38.2%; profit margin, 4.1%; and current ratio, 2.5:1. State whether Danier Leather's ratios are better or worse than those of its industry.

Journalize inventory transactions—periodic system.
(SO 7) AP

*P5–8B  Data for Phantom Book Warehouse are presented in P5–1B.

*Instructions*

Journalize the July transactions for Phantom Book Warehouse assuming a periodic inventory system is used instead of a perpetual inventory system.

Journalize and post
inventory transactions, and
prepare trial balance and
partial income statement—
periodic system.
(SO 7) AP

*P5–9B  At the beginning of the current season, the ledger of Kicked-Back Tennis Shop included Cash, $2,500; Merchandise Inventory, $1,700; and J. Noya, Capital, $4,200. The following transactions were completed during April 2005:

Apr.  4  Purchased racquets and balls from Robert Co., $1,460, FOB shipping point, terms n/30.
      6  Paid freight on Robert Co. purchase, $65.
      8  Sold merchandise to members for $950, terms n/30.
     10  Received credit of $35 from Robert Co. for a damaged racquet that was returned.
     11  Purchased tennis shoes from Niki Sports for cash, $460.
     12  Purchased store supplies for $650 cash from Discount Supplies.
     13  Paid Robert Co. in full.
     14  Purchased tennis shirts and shorts from Martina's Sportswear for $725, FOB shipping point, terms n/60.
     15  Received cash refund of $55 from Niki Sports for damaged merchandise that was returned.
     16  Returned $60 of the supplies purchased on April 12 and received a cash refund.
     17  Paid freight on Martina's Sportswear purchase, $30.
     18  Sold merchandise to members for $850, terms n/30.
     19  Purchased store equipment for use in the business from DomCo. for $1,800, terms n/30.
     20  Received $500 in cash from members in settlement of their accounts.
     21  Paid Martina's Sportswear in full.
     27  Granted credit of $40 to members for tennis clothing that did not fit.
     30  Sold merchandise to members for $1,025, terms n/30.
     30  Received cash payments on account from members, $600.

*Instructions*

(a) Journalize the April transactions for the Kicked-Back Tennis Shop using a periodic inventory system.
(b) Enter the beginning balances in the general ledger accounts and post the April transactions.
(c) Prepare a trial balance as at April 30, 2005.
(d) Prepare a multiple-step income statement up to gross profit, assuming merchandise inventory on hand at April 30 is $2,450.

Prepare multiple-step
income statement and
closing entries—periodic
system.
(SO 7) AP

*P5–10B  At the end of the company's fiscal year on December 31, 2005, the following accounts appeared in alphabetical order in Tse's Tater Tot's adjusted trial balance:

| | | | |
|---|---:|---|---:|
| Accounts payable | $ 86,300 | Interest expense | $ 5,400 |
| Accounts receivable | 49,200 | Merchandise inventory | 40,500 |
| Accumulated amortization— | | Mortgage payable | 80,000 |
| building | 51,800 | Prepaid insurance | 2,400 |
| Accumulated amortization— | | Property tax expense | 4,800 |
| equipment | 42,900 | Property tax payable | 4,800 |
| Amortization expense | 23,400 | Purchases | 441,600 |
| Building | 190,000 | Purchase returns and allowances | 6,400 |
| Cash | 23,000 | Salaries expense | 122,500 |
| Equipment | 110,000 | Salaries payable | 3,500 |
| Freight in | 5,600 | Sales | 623,000 |
| H. Tse, capital | 178,600 | Sales returns and allowances | 8,000 |
| H. Tse, drawings | 28,000 | Unearned sales revenue | 2,300 |
| Insurance expense | 7,200 | Utilities expense | 18,000 |

Additional facts:

1. Tse's Tater Tots uses a periodic system.
2. Merchandise inventory on December 31, 2005, is $72,600.
3. H. Tse invested $2,200 in the business during 2005.

*Instructions*

(a) Prepare a multiple-step income statement and statement of owner's equity for the year ended December 31, 2005.
(b) Prepare the closing journal entries.
(c) Post the closing entries to the inventory and capital accounts. What is the ending balance reported in Merchandise Inventory and H. Tse, Capital?

**\*P5–11B** Presented below are selected transactions for the Leeland Company during October and November of the current year. On October 1, Leeland's ledger showed Cash, $90,000; and D. Leeland, Capital, $90,000.

Journalize and post inventory transactions with discounts and prepare partial income statement—perpetual system. (SO 8) AP

Oct. 2 Purchased merchandise on account from Gregory Company at a cost of $75,000, FOB shipping point, terms 2/10, n/30.
4 Paid freight charges to Rail Company of $1,800 on the merchandise purchased from Gregory Company on October 2.
5 Returned damaged goods having a gross invoice cost of $6,000 to Gregory Company. Received a credit for this.
11 Paid Gregory Company the balance owing for the October 2 purchase.
17 Sold all of the remaining merchandise purchased from Gregory Company to Kurji Company for $92,500, FOB shipping point, terms 2/10, n/30.
19 Issued Kurji Company a sales allowance of $2,500 because some of the goods did not meet Kurji's exact specifications.
27 Received the balance owing from Kurji Company for the October 17 sale.
Nov. 1 Purchased merchandise on account from Romeo Company at a cost of $85,000, FOB destination, terms 1/15, n/30.
2 The appropriate company paid freight charges of $2,200.
3 Obtained a purchase allowance of $3,000 from Romeo Company to compensate for some minor damage to the goods purchased on November 1.
5 Sold all of the merchandise purchased from Romeo Company to Barlow Company for $109,300, FOB destination, terms 2/10, n/30.
6 The appropriate company paid freight charges of $2,600.
7 Issued Barlow a credit of $7,000 for goods returned. These goods had cost Leeland $5,250 and were returned to inventory.
29 Received a cheque from Barlow Company for the balance owing on the November 5 sale.
30 Paid Romeo Company the amount owing on the November 1 purchase.
30 A physical count of inventory on November 30 determines that $5,250 is on hand.

*Instructions*

(a) Prepare journal entries to record the above transactions for Leeland Company assuming it uses a perpetual inventory system.
(b) Open ledger accounts, post the transactions, and calculate the balance in each account.
(c) Prepare a partial multiple-step income statement, up to gross profit, for the two months ended November 30.

**\*P5–12B** Data for Leeland Company are presented in P5–11B.

Journalize and post inventory transactions with discounts and prepare partial income statement—periodic system. (SO 8) AP

*Instructions*

Repeat the requirements for P5–11B assuming a periodic inventory system is used instead of a perpetual system. Compare the partial income statement to the one prepared in P5–11B and note any similarities and differences.

# Continuing Cookie Chronicle

(Note: The Continuing Cookie Chronicle was started in Chapter 1 and continued in Chapters 2 through 4. From the information gathered through Chapter 4, follow the instructions below using the general ledger accounts you have already prepared.)

Because Natalie has had such a successful first few months, she is considering other opportunities to develop her business. One opportunity is the sale of fine European mixers. The owner of Mixer Deluxe has approached Natalie to become the exclusive Canadian distributor of these fine mixers. The current cost of a mixer is approximately $525 Canadian, and Natalie would sell each one for $1,050. Natalie comes to you for advice on how to account for these mixers. Each appliance has a serial number and can be easily identified.

Natalie asks you the following questions:

1. "Would you consider these mixers to be inventory? Or, should they be classified as supplies or equipment?"
2. "I've learned a little about keeping track of inventory using both the perpetual and the periodic systems of accounting for inventory. Which system do you think is better? Which one would you recommend for the type of inventory that I want to sell?"
3. "How often do I need to count inventory if I maintain it using the perpetual system? Do I need to count inventory at all?"

In the end, Natalie decides to use the perpetual method of accounting for inventory, and the following transactions happen during the month of January:

Jan.  4 She buys five deluxe mixers on account from Kzinski Supply Co. for $2,625, FOB shipping point, terms n/30.
  6 She pays $100 freight on the January 4 purchase.
  7 Natalie returns one of the mixers to Kzinski because it was damaged during shipping. Kzinski issues Cookie Creations a credit note for the cost of the mixer plus $20 for the cost of freight that was paid on January 6 for one mixer.
  8 She collects the amount due from the neighbourhood community centre that was accrued at the end of December, 2004.
  12 She sells three deluxe mixers on account for $3,150, FOB destination, terms n/30.
  13 Natalie pays her cellphone bill previously accrued in the December adjusting journal entries.
  14 She pays $75 of delivery charges for the three mixers that were sold on January 12.
  14 She buys four deluxe mixers on account from Kzinski Supply Co. for $2,100, FOB shipping point, terms n/30.
  17 Natalie is concerned that there is not enough cash available to pay for all of the mixers purchased.  She invests an additional $1,000 cash in Cookie Creations.
  18 She pays $80 freight on the January 14 purchase.
  20 She sells two deluxe mixers for $2,100 cash.
  28 Natalie issues a cheque to her assistant for all the help the assistant has given her during the month. Her assistant worked 20 hours in January and is also paid for amounts owing at December 31, 2004. (Recall that Natalie's assistant earns $8 an hour.)
  28 Natalie collects amounts due from customers in the January 12 transaction.
  31 She pays Kzinski all amounts due.
  31 She withdraws $750 cash for personal use.

As at January 31, the following adjusting entry data is available:

1. A count of brochures and posters reveals that none were used in January.
2. A count of baking supplies reveals that none were used in January.
3. Another month's worth of amortization needs to be recorded on the baking equipment bought in November. (Recall that the baking equipment has a useful life of five years or 60 months.)
4. One month's worth of amortization needs to be recorded on the website. (Recall that the website has a useful life of two years or 24 months.)
5. An additional month's worth of interest on her grandmother's loan needs to be accrued. (The interest rate is 6%.)
6. One month's worth of insurance has expired.
7. Natalie receives her cellphone bill, $75. The bill is for services provided in January and is due February 15. (Recall that the cellphone is only used for business purposes.)
8. An analysis of the unearned revenue account reveals that Natalie has not had time to teach any of these lessons this month because she has been so busy selling mixers. As a result there is no change to the unearned revenue account. Natalie hopes to book the outstanding lessons in February.
9. An inventory count of mixers at the end of January reveals that Natalie has three mixers remaining.

*Instructions*

Using the information that you have gathered through Chapter 4, and the new information above, do the following:

(a) Answer Natalie's questions.
(b) Prepare and post the January 2005 transactions.
(c) Prepare a trial balance.
(d) Prepare and post the adjusting journal entries required.
(e) Prepare an adjusted trial balance.
(f) Prepare a multiple-step income statement and statement of owner's equity for the month ended January 31, 2005.
(g) Prepare a classified balance sheet as at January 31, 2005.

# Cumulative Coverage—Chapters 2 to 5

The Board Shop, owned by Andrew John, sells skateboards in the spring/summer season and snowboards in the fall/winter season. The shop has an August 31 fiscal year end and uses a perpetual inventory system. On August 1, 2005, the company had the following balances in its general ledger:

| | | | |
|---|---:|---|---:|
| Cash | $ 15,740 | Notes payable | $ 36,000 |
| Accounts receivable | 2,975 | Andrew John, capital | 47,250 |
| Inventory | 112,700 | Andrew John, drawings | 42,000 |
| Store supplies | 2,660 | Sales | 761,300 |
| Prepaid insurance | 4,140 | Sales returns and allowances | 11,420 |
| Store equipment | 53,800 | Cost of goods sold | 517,680 |
| Accumulated amortization— | | Salaries expense | 92,900 |
| store equipment | 13,450 | Advertising expense | 9,625 |
| Accounts payable | 22,120 | Rent expense | 17,050 |
| Unearned sales revenue | 4,820 | Interest expense | 2,250 |

During August, the last month of the fiscal year, the company had the following transactions:

Aug.  1 Paid $1,550 for August's rent.
    4 Sold merchandise costing $8,500 for $12,250 cash.
    5 Purchased merchandise on account from Orange Line Co., FOB shipping point, for $24,500.
    5 Paid freight charges of $500 on merchandise purchased from Orange Line Co.
    8 Purchased store supplies on account for $345.
    9 Refunded a customer $425 cash for returned merchandise. The merchandise had cost $290 and was returned to inventory.
   10 Sold merchandise on account for $16,750, FOB shipping point, to Spider Company. The merchandise had a cost of $11,340.
   11 Paid Orange Line Co. for half of the merchandise purchased on August 5.
   12 Spider Company returned $750 of the merchandise it had purchased. Board Shop issued Spider a credit memo. The merchandise had a cost of $510 and was returned to inventory.
   15 Paid salaries, $4,200.
   17 Andrew John withdrew $3,800 cash.
   19 Spider Company paid the amount owing.
   22 Purchased $9,900 of merchandise from Rainbow Option Co. on account.
   23 Returned $800 of the merchandise to Rainbow Option Co. and received a credit memo.
   24 Received $525 cash in advance from customers for merchandise to be delivered in September.
   25 Paid Rainbow Option Co. the amount owing.
   26 Purchased merchandise for $4,500 cash.
   29 Paid for $1,200 of advertising.
   30 Collected $775 of the August 1 accounts receivable.
   31 Paid $2,500 on account.

*Instructions*

(a) Create a general ledger account for each of the above accounts and enter the August 1 balances.
(b) Journalize and post the August transactions.
(c) Prepare a trial balance at August 31.
(d) Journalize and post the following adjustments:
    1. Five months of the 12-month insurance policy has expired.
    2. A count shows $570 of store supplies on hand at August 31.
    3. The store equipment has an estimated eight-year useful life.
    4. The note payable has an annual interest rate of 7.5%. Two months of interest has accrued on August 31.
    5. Of the note payable, $5,000 must be paid on December 1 each year.
    6. An analysis of the Unearned Sales Revenue account showed that $3,570 has been earned by August 31. A corresponding $2,430 for Cost of Goods Sold will also need to be recorded for these sales.
    7. Salaries earned but not paid at August 31 total $3,500.
    8. A count of the merchandise inventory on August 31 shows $128,260 on hand.
(e) Prepare an adjusted trial balance at August 31.
(f) Prepare a multiple-step income statement, statement of owners equity, and classified balance sheet.
(g) Journalize and post closing entries.
(h) Prepare a post-closing trial balance at August 31.

## BROADENING YOUR PERSPECTIVE

# Financial Reporting and Analysis

Practice
Tools

## Financial Reporting Problem

**BYP5–1**  The financial statements for **The Forzani Group Ltd.** are reproduced in Appendix A at the end of this text.

*Instructions*

(a) Is The Forzani Group a service company or a merchandising company?
(b) Significant accounting policies are identified in Note 2 to the consolidated financial statements. In reference to Note 2 (b), does The Forzani Group recognize any volume rebates and/or supplier discounts? If so, how are they recognized?
(c) Are any non-operating revenues and non-operating expenses included in The Forzani Group's income statement (called "statement of operations" by Forzani)?
(d) Determine the following values:
    1. Percentage change in revenue from 2002 to 2003
    2. Percentage change in "operating earnings before undernoted items" from 2002 to 2003
    3. Gross profit margin for each of the 2002 and 2003 fiscal years
    4. Profit margin for each of the 2002 and 2003 fiscal years
(e) What conclusions concerning the relative profitability can be drawn from the data from part (d) above?

## Interpreting Financial Statements

**BYP5–2** **Sleeman Breweries Ltd.** is the third largest brewer of premium and value quality beers in Canada. Selected information from Sleeman Breweries' income statement (statement of operations) for the past three years follows (in thousands):

|  | 2002 | 2001 | 2000 |
|---|---|---|---|
| Net revenue | $157,053 | $141,615 | $134,439 |
| Cost of goods sold | 79,059 | 69,472 | 70,082 |
| Operating expense | 59,483 | 57,323 | 51,038 |
| Income tax expense | 6,190 | 5,055 | 4,350 |

*Instructions*

(a) Calculate gross profit and net income for each of the three years.
(b) Calculate the percentage change in net revenue and net income from 2000 to 2002.
(c) Calculate the gross profit margin for each of the three years. Comment on any trend in this percentage.
(d) Calculate the profit margin for each of the three years. Comment on any trend in this percentage.
(e) How well has Sleeman Breweries managed operating expenses over the three-year period?

## Accounting on the Web

**BYP5–3** A lot of information about specific companies is available on the Internet. This case searches for financial information about the **Hudson's Bay Company** and its competitors.

*Instructions*
Specific requirements of this Internet case are available on the Weygandt website.

# Critical Thinking

## Collaborative Learning Activity

**BYP5–4** Three years ago, Kathy Morin and her brother-in-law, Carl Gibbons, opened Lemire Department Store. For the first two years, business was good, but the following condensed income results for 2005 were disappointing:

**LEMIRE DEPARTMENT STORE**
**Income Statement**
**Year Ended December 31, 2005**

| | |
|---|---|
| Net sales | $700,000 |
| Cost of goods sold | 560,000 |
| Gross profit | 140,000 |
| Operating expenses | 120,000 |
| Net income | $ 20,000 |

Kathy believes the problem lies in the relatively low gross profit margin of 20%. Carl believes the problem is that operating expenses are too high. Kathy thinks the gross profit margin can be improved by making the following changes:

1. Increase average selling prices by 17%. This increase is expected to lower the sales volume so that total sales will increase only 8%.
2. Buy merchandise in larger quantities to get trade discounts and take advantage of all purchase discounts. These changes are expected to increase the gross profit margin by 3%.

Kathy does not anticipate that these changes will have any effect on operating expenses. Carl thinks expenses can be cut by making the following changes:

1. Cut sales salaries of $60,000 in half and give sales personnel a commission of 2% of net sales.
2. Reduce store deliveries to one day per week rather than twice a week. This change will reduce delivery expenses of $40,000 by 40%.

Carl feels that these changes will not have any effect on net sales. Kathy and Carl come to you for help in deciding on the best way to improve net income.

*Instructions*

With the class divided into groups, do the following:

(a) Prepare (1) a condensed income statement for 2006 assuming only Kathy's changes are implemented, and (2) another one for 2006 assuming only Carl's ideas are adopted.
(b) What is your recommendation to Kathy and Carl, based upon the results in part (a)?
(c) Prepare a condensed income statement for 2006 assuming both sets of proposed changes are made.

## Communication Activity

**BYP5–5** Consider the following events, listed in chronological order:

1. Dexter Maersk decides to buy a custom-made snowboard and calls The Great Canadian Snowboard Company to inquire about its products.
2. Dexter asks The Great Canadian Snowboard Company to manufacture a custom board for him.
3. The company sends Dexter a purchase order to fill out, which he immediately completes, signs, and sends back with a required 25% down payment.
4. The Great Canadian Snowboard Company receives Dexter's purchase order and down payment, and begins working on the board.
5. The Great Canadian Snowboard Company has its fiscal year end. At this time, Dexter's board is 75% completed.
6. The company completes the snowboard for Dexter and notifies him that he can take delivery.
7. Dexter picks up his snowboard from the company and takes it home.
8. Dexter tries the snowboard out and likes it so much that he carves his initials in it.
9. The Great Canadian Snowboard Company bills Dexter for the cost of the snowboard, less the 25% down payment.
10. The company receives partial payment from Dexter.
11. The company receives payment of the balance due from Dexter.

*Instructions*

In a memo to the president of The Great Canadian Snowboard Company, answer these questions:

(a) When should The Great Canadian Snowboard Company record the revenue and cost related to the snowboard? Refer to the revenue recognition and matching principles in your answer.
(b) Suppose that, with his purchase order, Dexter was not required to make a down payment. Would that change your answer to part (a)?

## Ethics Case

**BYP5–6** Rita Pelzer was just hired as the Assistant Controller of Liu Stores. The company is a specialty chain store with nine retail stores concentrated in one metropolitan area. Among other things, the payment of all invoices is centralized in one of the departments Rita will manage. Her primary responsibilities are to maintain the company's high credit rating by paying all bills when due and to take advantage of all cash discounts.

Jamie Caterino, the former Assistant Controller, who has been promoted to Controller, is training Rita in her new duties. He instructs Rita to continue the practice of preparing all cheques "net of discount" and dating the cheques the last day of the discount period. "But," Jamie continues, "we always hold the cheques at least four days beyond the discount period before mailing them. That way we get another four days of interest on our money. Most of our creditors need our business and don't complain. And, if they scream about our missing the discount period, we blame it on the mail room or the post office. Believe me, everybody does it. By the way, welcome to our team!"

*Instructions*

(a) What are the ethical considerations in this case?
(b) Who are the stakeholders that are harmed or benefited in this situation?
(c) Should Rita continue the practice started by Jamie? Does she have any choice?

---

*Answers to Self-Study Questions*

1. c    2. a    3. c    4. a    5. a    6. d    7. c    *8. b    *9. b    *10. a

*Answer to Forzani Review It Question 2*

Forzani's gross profit margin for 2002 is 26.1% ($198,033 ÷ $758,257). The company's gross profit margin improved significantly in 2003, to 34.7% ($320,469 ÷ $923,795). Forzani's profit margin for 2002 is 2.7% ($20,629 ÷ $758,257). The profit margin also improved in 2003, to 3.3% ($30,531 ÷ $923,795). All dollar amounts are given in thousands.

Remember to go back to the Navigator Box at the beginning of the chapter to check off your completed work.

## concepts for review >>

Before studying this chapter, you should understand or, if necessary, review:

a. The cost principle (Ch. 1, pp. 7–8) and matching principle of accounting. (Ch. 3, p. 101)
b. The difference between calculating cost of goods sold in a perpetual inventory system and in a periodic inventory system. (Ch. 5, pp. 216–217)
c. How to journalize inventory transactions in a perpetual inventory system. (Ch. 5, pp. 228–229)
d. How to prepare financial statements for a merchandising company. (Ch. 5, pp. 230–234)

# Minding the Books on Campus

*North Atlantic's Prince Philip Drive Campus Bookstore: www.northatlantic.nf.ca*

ST. JOHN'S, Nfld.—Like campus bookstores across Canada, the bookstore at the College of the North Atlantic's Prince Philip Drive Campus does most of its business in the fall term. In fact, 45% of its $1.3 million in annual sales are recorded in the first three weeks of September. But with four terms each year, the bookstore—the largest of the college's 16 campus bookstores—buys books year-round for the 3,000 students it serves.

As general manager Ed Pinto explains, the number of copies to be ordered for each title depends on the age of the book and the likelihood of used sales. "A few months before the start of a semester, we send a request to the Department Heads' Office for itemized enrolment," he says. "If a textbook is new, 100% of an order is processed. For books that are one to two years old or more, we cut the order based on past performance."

To keep track of the 1,200 items in its inventory—which also includes stationery and novelty items bearing the school's logo—the Prince Philip Drive Campus Bookstore uses a computerized perpetual inventory system running on Vigilant point-of-sale software. As books and other items are scanned at the cash register, information stored in the system is automatically updated.

Every month, Mr. Pinto prints out a valuation report giving itemized figures for quantities in stock, latest cost, average cost, total inventory value, list price, and gross margin percentage. The bookstore finds it easier to use the average cost flow assumption to track inventory because of price fluctuations with its purchases. "If we have to reorder a title in the same semester we do not change the price to students even if our cost has gone up," says Mr. Pinto.

To confirm that the report matches actual quantities on hand, Mr. Pinto and his staff do a physical count of the entire inventory twice a year—once on March 31, the college's year end, and again in October.

Sometimes there is more merchandise on hand than required. "We normally return any surplus books to the publisher for credit," says Mr. Pinto. "When that's not possible, we reduce the price to clear the inventory and document the markdown in our records."

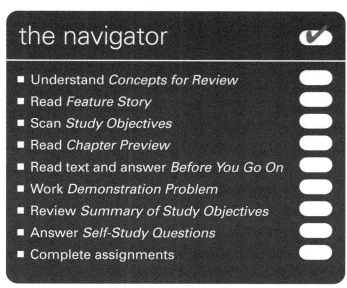

## the navigator ✔

- Understand *Concepts for Review*
- Read *Feature Story*
- Scan *Study Objectives*
- Read *Chapter Preview*
- Read text and answer *Before You Go On*
- Work *Demonstration Problem*
- Review *Summary of Study Objectives*
- Answer *Self-Study Questions*
- Complete assignments

c h a p t e r   6

# Inventory Costing

## study objectives >>

After studying this chapter, you should be able to:

1. Describe the steps in determining inventory quantities.
2. Explain the basis of accounting for inventories and use the inventory cost flow assumptions.
3. Demonstrate the effects on the financial statements of each of the inventory cost flow assumptions.
4. Determine the effects of inventory errors on the financial statements.
5. Demonstrate the presentation and analysis of inventory.
6. Apply the inventory cost flow assumptions to perpetual inventory records (Appendix 6A).
7. Use the two methods of estimating inventories (Appendix 6B).

For companies such as the Prince Philip Drive Campus Bookstore, accounting for 1,200 inventory items can be time-consuming and complex. In this chapter, we explain the procedures for determining inventory quantities. We discuss the cost flow assumptions for determining the cost of goods sold and the cost of inventory on hand. We also discuss the effects of inventory errors on a company's financial statements and conclude by illustrating methods to report and analyse inventory. The chapter is organized as follows:

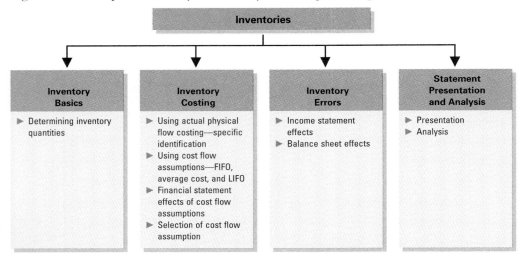

# Inventory Basics

Inventories are goods purchased for resale. Inventory affects both the balance sheet (through the current asset account Merchandise Inventory) and the income statement (through the expense account Cost of Goods Sold).

In the **balance sheet** of merchandising companies, inventory is frequently the most significant current asset. Of course, its amount and relative importance can vary, even for companies in the same industry. For example, Sears recently reported total inventory of $754 million, representing 29% of total current assets. For the same period, Hudson's Bay reported $1.5 billion of inventory, representing 58% of total current assets.

In the **income statement**, cost of goods sold is vital in determining the results of operations for a particular period. You will recall from Chapter 5 that the income statement for a merchandiser contains three features not found in the income statement of a service company: (1) sales revenue, (2) cost of goods sold, and (3) gross profit. Gross profit (net sales − cost of goods sold) is closely watched by management, owners, and other interested parties.

## Determining Inventory Quantities

**study objective 1**

Describe the steps in determining inventory quantities.

To prepare financial statements, we must know the number of units of inventory owned by the company at the statement date before we can assign a cost to them. Determining inventory quantities requires two steps: (1) taking a physical inventory of goods on hand, and (2) determining the ownership of goods.

## Taking a Physical Inventory

You will recall from Chapter 5 that merchandisers account for their inventory transactions by using either a perpetual or a periodic inventory system. In a **perpetual inventory system**, the accounting records continuously—perpetually—show the quantity of inventory that should be on hand. A physical count is done at some point in the year to verify the accuracy of the accounting records. The College of the North Atlantic's Prince Philip Drive Campus Bookstore, described in the feature story, takes a physical inventory twice a year to be sure that the actual quantities on hand agree with the accounting records.

In a **periodic inventory system**, inventory quantities are not maintained on a continuous basis. Instead they are determined at the end of each reporting period by a physical count. Whether inventory quantities are maintained by the perpetual or the periodic inventory system, a physical inventory count is necessary to determine the goods on hand or to confirm their accuracy.

Taking a physical inventory involves actually counting, weighing, or measuring each kind of inventory on hand. Taking an inventory can be a formidable task for many companies, especially if they have thousands of inventory items, like the Prince Philip Drive Campus Bookstore. An inventory count is generally more accurate when goods are not being sold or received during the counting. This is why companies often count their inventory when the business is closed or when business is slow.

To minimize errors in taking the inventory, a company should ensure that it has a good system of internal control in place. **Internal control** consists of policies and procedures to optimize resources, prevent and detect errors, safeguard assets, and enhance the accuracy and reliability of accounting records. Some internal control procedures for counting inventory include the following:

1. The counting should be done by employees who do not have custodial or record-keeping responsibility for the inventory.
2. Each counter should establish the authenticity of each inventory item. For example, does each box contain a television set? Does each storage tank contain gasoline?
3. There should be a second count by another employee or auditor. Counting should take place in teams of two.
4. Prenumbered inventory tags should be used. All inventory tags should be accounted for.
5. At the end of the count, a designated supervisor should check that all inventory items are tagged and that no items have more than one tag.

We will learn more about internal controls in Chapter 7.

After the physical inventory is taken, the quantity of each kind of inventory is listed on inventory summary sheets. To ensure accuracy, the listing should be verified by a second employee, or auditor.

Unit costs are then applied to the quantities in order to determine the total cost of the inventory—this will be explained later in the chapter. To estimate the cost of inventory when a physical count cannot be taken (if the inventory is destroyed, for example) or when it is inconvenient (during interim periods), estimating methods are applied. These methods (the gross profit and retail inventory methods) are discussed in Appendix 6B.

### ACCOUNTING IN ACTION ► Ethics Insight

Over the years, inventory has played a role in many fraud cases. A classic one involved salad oil. Management filled storage tanks mostly with water, and since oil rises to the top, the auditors thought the tanks were full of oil. In this instance, management also said the company had more tanks than it really did—numbers were repainted on the tanks to confuse the auditors.

In recent years, the management of women's apparel maker The Leslie Fay Company was convicted of falsifying inventory records to boost net earnings and management bonuses. In another case, Frost Fence was forced into bankruptcy after it was discovered that $17 million in inventory was on the company's books but not in its storage yard.

## Determining Ownership of Goods

Before we can begin to calculate the cost of inventory, we need to consider the ownership of goods. Specifically, we need to be sure that we have not included in the inventory quantities any goods that do not belong to the company, or forgotten any that do.

**Goods in Transit.**  Goods are considered **in transit** when they are in the hands of a public carrier such as a railway, airline, trucking, or shipping company at the statement date. Goods in transit should be included in the inventory of the party that has legal title to the goods. Legal title is determined by the terms of sale described below, as we learned in Chapter 5.

1. **FOB (free on board) shipping point.** Ownership of the goods passes to the buyer when the public carrier accepts the goods from the seller.
2. **FOB destination.** Ownership of the goods remains with the seller until the goods reach the buyer.

Inventory quantities may be seriously miscounted if goods in transit at the statement date are ignored. The company may have purchased goods that have not yet been received, or it may have sold goods that have not yet been delivered. Assume that Hill Company has 20,000 units of inventory on hand on December 31. It has the following goods in transit: (1) sales of 1,500 units shipped December 31, FOB destination, and (2) purchases of 2,500 units shipped FOB shipping point by the seller on December 31. Hill has legal title to both the units sold and the units purchased. If units in transit are ignored, inventory quantities would be understated by 4,000 units (1,500 + 2,500). As we will see later in this chapter, inaccurate inventory quantities affect not only the inventory amount on the balance sheet, but also the cost of goods sold reported in the income statement.

**Consigned Goods.**  In some lines of business, it is customary to hold goods belonging to other parties and sell them, for a fee, without ever taking ownership of the goods. These are called consigned goods. Under a consignment arrangement, the holder of the goods (called the *consignee*) does not own the goods. Ownership remains with the shipper of the goods (called the *consignor*) until the goods are actually sold to a customer. Because consigned goods are not owned by the consignee, they should not be included in the consignee's physical inventory count. Conversely, the consignor should include merchandise held by the consignee as part of the consignor's inventory.

For example, artists often display their paintings and other works of art at galleries on consignment. In such cases, the art gallery does not take ownership of the art—it still belongs to the artist. Therefore, if an inventory count is taken, any art on consignment should not be included in the art gallery's inventory. When the art sells, the gallery then takes a commission and pays the artist the remainder. Many craft stores, second-hand clothing stores, sporting goods stores, and antique dealers sell goods on consignment to keep their inventory costs down and to avoid the risk of purchasing an item they won't be able to sell.

**Other Situations.**  Sometimes goods are not physically on the premises, because they have been taken home *on approval* by a customer. Goods on approval should be added to the physical inventory count because they still belong to the seller. The customer will either return the item or decide to buy it.

In other cases, goods are sold but the seller is holding them for alteration, or until they are picked up or delivered to the customer. These goods should not be included in the physical count, because legal title to ownership has passed to the customer. Damaged or unsaleable goods should be separated from the physical count and any loss should be recorded. We will discuss losses in the valuation of inventories later in the chapter.

## BEFORE YOU GO ON . . .

### ▶Review It

1. What steps are involved in determining inventory quantities?
2. How is ownership determined for goods in transit at the balance sheet date?
3. Who has title to consigned goods?

### ▶Do It

The Too Good To Be Threw Company completed its inventory count. It arrived at a total inventory value of $200,000, counting everything currently on hand in its warehouse. You have been given the information listed below. Discuss how this information affects the reported cost of inventory.

1. Goods costing $15,000 held on consignment were included in the inventory.
2. Purchased goods of $10,000 that were in transit (terms FOB shipping point) and were not included in the count.
3. Sold inventory with a cost of $12,000 that was in transit (terms FOB shipping point) and was not included in the count.

#### Action Plan

- Apply the rules of ownership to goods held on consignment.
- Apply the rules of ownership to goods in transit:
  ° FOB shipping point: Goods sold or purchased and shipped FOB shipping point belong to the buyer.
  ° FOB destination: Goods sold or purchased and shipped FOB destination belong to the seller until they reach their destination.

#### Solution

The $15,000 of goods held on consignment should be deducted from Too Good To Be Threw's inventory count. The goods worth $10,000 that were purchased FOB shipping point should be added to the company's inventory count. The goods sold for $12,000 that were in transit FOB shipping point were correctly excluded from Too Good To Be Threw's ending inventory, since title passed when the goods were handed over to the railway company. Inventory therefore totals $195,000 ($200,000 − $15,000 + $10,000).

*Related exercise material:* BE6–1, BE6–2, E6–1, and E6–2.

# Inventory Costing

**study objective 2**

Explain the basis of accounting for inventories, and use the inventory cost flow assumptions.

After the quantity of units of inventory has been determined, unit costs are applied to those quantities to determine the total cost of the goods sold and the cost of the ending inventory. When all inventory items have been purchased at the same unit cost, this determination is simple. However, when items have been purchased at different costs during the period, it is difficult to decide which particular item at which unit cost remains in inventory and which particular item at which unit cost has been sold.

For example, assume that throughout the calendar year Fraser Valley Electronics buys at different prices 1,000 Astro Condenser units for resale. Some Astro Condensers cost $10 when originally purchased last year. Units purchased in April cost $11, those purchased in August cost $12, and those acquired in November cost $13. Now suppose Fraser Valley Electronics has 450 Astro Condensers remaining in inventory at the end of December. Should these inventory items be assigned a cost of $10, $11, $12, $13, or some combination of all four? To determine the cost of goods sold as well as the cost of ending inventory, we must have some means of allocating the purchase cost to each item in inventory and each item that has been sold.

The cost of goods available for sale (beginning inventory plus cost of goods purchased) gives us our starting point. It is these costs that must be allocated between cost of goods sold and ending inventory, as shown in Illustration 6-1.

**Illustration 6-1 ▶**

Allocation of cost of goods available for sale

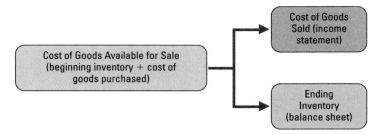

The cost of inventory items must be allocated in a consistent and rational way. The cost and matching principles of accounting help by guiding the determination, and allocation, of the cost of the goods available for sale.

1. Following the **cost principle**, cost is the primary basis of accounting for inventories. This includes all costs incurred to acquire goods and make them ready for sale. These are called inventoriable costs.
2. Following the **matching principle**, the major objective in accounting for inventories is the matching of appropriate costs with sales revenue.

Under a perpetual inventory system, this allocation is made as each item is sold. Under a periodic inventory system, the allocation is made at the end of the period. There are four allocation methods used to allocate cost of goods available for sale between cost of goods sold and ending inventory: specific identification; first-in, first-out (FIFO); average; and last-in, first-out (LIFO). These are discussed in the following sections.

## Using Actual Physical Flow Costing—Specific Identification

The specific identification method tracks the **actual physical flow** of the goods. Each item of inventory is marked, tagged, or coded with its specific unit cost. Items still in inventory at the end of the year are specifically costed to determine the total cost of the ending inventory. Assume, for example, that Fraser Valley Electronics buys three portable DVD players at costs of $700, $750, and $800. During the year, two are sold at a selling price of $1,200 each. At December 31, the company determines that the $750 DVD player is still on hand. The ending inventory is $750 and the cost of goods sold is $1,500 ($700 + $800).

**Illustration 6-2 ▶**

Specific identification

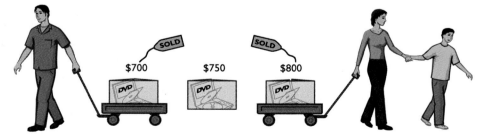

Specific identification is possible when a company sells a limited number of high-unit-cost items that can be clearly identified from purchase through to sale. Examples are cars, electronics, jewellery, and furniture.

When possible, specific identification is the ideal method for allocating cost of goods available for sale. This method reports ending inventory at actual cost and matches the actual cost of goods sold against sales revenue. However, there are also drawbacks to this method. For example, specific identification may allow management to manipulate net income. To see how, assume that Fraser Valley Electronics wants to maximize its net income just before year end. When selling one of the three DVD players referred to earlier, management could choose the player with the lowest cost ($700) to match against revenues ($1,200). Or, it could minimize net income by selecting the highest-cost ($800) player.

Ordinarily, however, the identity of goods purchased at a specific cost is lost between the date of purchase and the date of sale. For example, book, grocery, and hardware stores sell thousands of relatively low-unit-cost items of inventory. These are often indistinguishable from one another. It may be impossible or impractical to track each item's cost. In that case, as the next section will show, we must make assumptions about which units were sold.

## Using Cost Flow Assumptions—FIFO, Average Cost, and LIFO

Because specific identification is often impractical, cost flow assumptions are allowed. These differ from specific identification as they assume flows of costs that may be unrelated to the physical flow of goods. For this reason, we call them **cost flow assumptions**. They are as follows:

1. First-in, first-out (FIFO)
2. Average cost
3. Last-in, first-out (LIFO)

Any of the three cost flow assumptions can be applied in a perpetual inventory system or a periodic inventory system. We will discuss the periodic inventory system here. Appendix 6A explains the use of these cost flow assumptions under a perpetual inventory system.

We have chosen to use the periodic inventory system to illustrate cost flow assumptions in this chapter for several reasons. First, many companies that use a perpetual inventory system use it only to keep track of *quantities* on hand. They then determine cost of goods sold at the end of the period using one of the three cost flow assumptions under a periodic inventory system. Second, the FIFO cost flow assumption gives the same results under the periodic and perpetual inventory systems. Third, most companies that use the average cost flow assumption use it under a periodic inventory system. The Prince Philip Drive Campus Bookstore in the feature story is able to use the average cost flow assumption under a perpetual inventory system because it has sophisticated computer software to facilitate this system—unlike many other companies. Finally, it is simpler to demonstrate the cost flow assumptions under the periodic inventory system, which makes them easier to understand.

To illustrate these three inventory cost flow assumptions in a periodic inventory system, we will assume that Fraser Valley Electronics has the information below for one of its products, a Z202 Astro Condenser:

### FRASER VALLEY ELECTRONICS
### Z202 Astro Condensers

| Date | Explanation | Units | Unit Cost | Total Cost |
|---|---|---|---|---|
| Jan. 1 | Beginning inventory | 100 | $10 | $ 1,000 |
| Apr. 15 | Purchase | 200 | 11 | 2,200 |
| Aug. 24 | Purchase | 300 | 12 | 3,600 |
| Nov. 27 | Purchase | 400 | 13 | 5,200 |
| | Total | 1,000 | | $12,000 |

The company had a total of 1,000 units available for sale during the year. A physical inventory count at the end of the year determined that 450 units remain on hand at the end of the year. Consequently, it can be calculated that 550 (1,000 − 450) units were sold during the year. The questions are (1) which unit costs of the 1,000 units available for sale should be allocated to the 550 units sold, to determine the cost of the goods sold, and (2) which unit costs should be allocated to the 450 units remaining, to determine the cost of the ending inventory.

The total cost of the 1,000 units available for sale was $12,000. We will demonstrate the allocation of this pool of costs, using FIFO, average cost, and LIFO in the next sections. Note that throughout these sections, the total cost of goods available for sale will remain unchanged regardless of which inventory cost flow assumption is used. The pool of costs doesn't change with the choice of cost flow assumption—just the allocation of these costs between the cost of goods sold and ending inventory.

## First-In, First-Out (FIFO)

Under the **first-in, first-out (FIFO)** cost flow assumption, the cost of the **earliest goods** purchased is the first to be recognized as the cost of goods sold. This does not necessarily mean that the oldest units are sold first, only that the cost of the oldest units is recognized first. Note that there is no accounting requirement that the cost flow assumption match the actual movement of the goods. Nonetheless, FIFO often matches the actual physical flow of merchandise, because it generally is good business practice to sell the oldest units first.

In the periodic inventory system, we ignore the dates of each of the sales. Instead, we make the allocation **at the end of a period** and assume that the entire pool of costs is available for allocation at that time. The allocation of the cost of goods available for sale at Fraser Valley Electronics under periodic FIFO is shown in Illustration 6-3.

**Illustration 6-3 ▶**

Periodic system—FIFO

| Pool of Costs — Cost of Goods Available for Sale | | | | |
|---|---|---|---|---|
| Date | Explanation | Units | Unit Cost | Total Cost |
| Jan. 1 | Beginning inventory | 100 | $10 | $ 1,000 |
| Apr. 15 | Purchase | 200 | 11 | 2,200 |
| Aug. 24 | Purchase | 300 | 12 | 3,600 |
| Nov. 27 | Purchase | 400 | 13 | 5,200 |
| | Total | 1,000 | | $12,000 |

| Cost of Goods Sold | | | | Ending Inventory | | | |
|---|---|---|---|---|---|---|---|
| Date | Units | Unit Cost | Total Cost | Date | Units | Unit Cost | Total Cost |
| Jan. 1 | 100 | $10 | $1,000 | Nov. 27 | 400 | $13 | $5,200 |
| Apr. 15 | 200 | 11 | 2,200 | Aug. 24 | 50 | 12 | 600 |
| Aug. 24 | 250 | 12 | 3,000 | Total | 450 | | $5,800 |
| Total | 550 | | $6,200 | | | | |

Proof:
$6,200 + $5,800 = $12,000

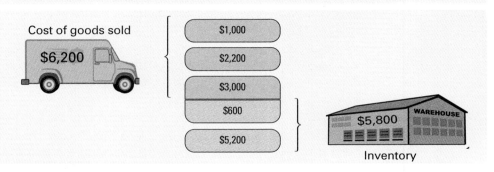

The cost flow assumption—FIFO, in this case—always indicates the order of selling. That is, with FIFO the order in which the goods are assumed to be sold is first-in, first-out. To determine the cost of goods sold, simply start at the first (beginning inventory) and count forward until the total number of units sold (550) is reached. The result is that of the 300 units purchased on August 24, only 250 units are assumed sold.

After calculating the cost of goods sold, we must next allocate a cost to the remaining inventory. Under FIFO, the cost of the ending inventory is obtained by taking the unit cost of the most recent purchase and working backward until all units of inventory have been costed. In this example, the last purchase was 400 units at $13 on November 27. These are assumed to remain in ending inventory, in addition to 50 units at $12 from the second most recent purchase on August 24. Recall that there are 450 units of ending inventory in total.

Another way to determine the cost of goods sold is to calculate ending inventory and subtract it from the cost of goods available for sale, as shown in Illustration 6-4.

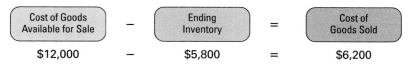

| Cost of Goods Available for Sale | − | Ending Inventory | = | Cost of Goods Sold |
|---|---|---|---|---|
| $12,000 | − | $5,800 | = | $6,200 |

**Illustration 6-4 ◄**

Calculation of cost of goods sold

This approach is consistent with how you learned to calculate cost of goods sold in the multiple-step statement of earnings described in Appendix 5A. Most companies calculate cost of goods sold in this manner—they count and cost ending inventory and then use this value to determine cost of goods sold.

Because of the potential for calculation errors, we recommend that both the cost of goods sold and the ending inventory amounts be calculated separately. The cost of goods sold and ending inventory total can then be compared to the cost of goods available for sale amount to check the accuracy of your calculations (e.g., $6,200 + $5,800 = $12,000).

## Average Cost

The average cost flow assumption assumes that the goods available for sale are identical or nondistinguishable. Under this assumption, the allocation of the cost of goods available for sale is on the basis of the **weighted average unit cost**. This average cost is not calculated by taking a simple average ([$10 + $11 + $12 + $13] ÷ 4 = $11.50 per unit), but rather by weighting the quantities purchased at each unit cost. The formula and calculation of weighted average unit cost are presented in Illustration 6-5:

| Cost of Goods Available for Sale | ÷ | Total Units Available for Sale | = | Weighted Average Unit Cost |
|---|---|---|---|---|
| $12,000 | ÷ | 1,000 | = | $12 |

**Illustration 6-5 ◄**

Calculation of weighted average unit cost

The weighted average unit cost is then applied (1) to the units sold to determine the cost of goods sold and (2) to the units on hand to determine the cost of the ending inventory. The allocation of the cost of goods available for sale at Fraser Valley Electronics using weighted average cost is shown in Illustration 6-6.

**Illustration 6-6 ◄**

Periodic system—weighted average cost

| Pool of Costs Cost of Goods Available for Sale | | | | |
|---|---|---|---|---|
| Date | Explanation | Units | Unit Cost | Total Cost |
| Jan.  1 | Beginning inventory | 100 | $10 | $ 1,000 |
| Apr. 15 | Purchase | 200 | 11 | 2,200 |
| Aug. 24 | Purchase | 300 | 12 | 3,600 |
| Nov. 27 | Purchase | 400 | 13 | 5,200 |
|  | Total | 1,000 | | $12,000 |

| | Cost of Goods Sold | | | Ending Inventory | | |
|---|---|---|---|---|---|---|
| Units | Weighted Average Unit Cost | Total Cost | | Units | Weighted Average Unit Cost | Total Cost |
| 550 × | $12 | = $6,600 | | 450 × | $12 | = $5,400 |

**Proof:**
$6,600 + $5,400 = $12,000

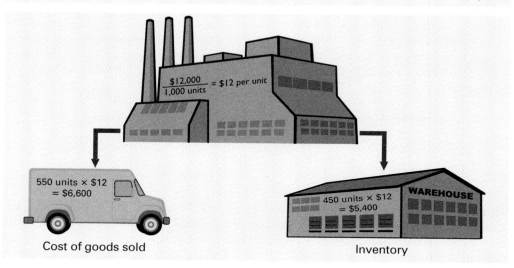

$$\frac{\$12,000}{1,000 \text{ units}} = \$12 \text{ per unit}$$

550 units × $12 = $6,600

Cost of goods sold

450 units × $12 = $5,400    **WAREHOUSE**

Inventory

## Last-In, First-Out (LIFO)

The **last-in, first-out (LIFO)** cost flow assumption assumes that the **latest goods** purchased are the first to be sold. For most companies, LIFO seldom matches the actual physical flow of inventory. Only for goods in piles, such as sand, hay, or gravel, would LIFO match the physical flow of inventory. But, as explained earlier, this does not mean that the LIFO cost flow assumption cannot be used in other cases. It is the flow of costs that is important, not the physical flow of goods. The allocation of the cost of goods available for sale at Fraser Valley Electronics under LIFO is shown in Illustration 6-7.

**Illustration 6-7 ▶**

Periodic system—LIFO

| | Pool of Costs Cost of Goods Available for Sale | | | | |
|---|---|---|---|---|---|
| Date | Explanation | Units | Unit Cost | Total Cost | |
| Jan.  1 | Beginning inventory | 100 | $10 | $ 1,000 | |
| Apr. 15 | Purchase | 200 | 11 | 2,200 | |
| Aug. 24 | Purchase | 300 | 12 | 3,600 | |
| Nov. 27 | Purchase | 400 | 13 | 5,200 | |
| | Total | 1,000 | | $12,000 | |

| Cost of Goods Sold | | | | Ending Inventory | | | |
|---|---|---|---|---|---|---|---|
| Date | Units | Unit Cost | Total Cost | Date | Units | Unit Cost | Total Cost |
| Nov. 27 | 400 | $13 | $5,200 | Jan.  1 | 100 | $10 | $1,000 |
| Aug. 24 | 150 | 12 | 1,800 | Apr. 15 | 200 | 11 | 2,200 |
| Total | 550 | | $7,000 | Aug. 24 | 150 | 12 | 1,800 |
| | | | | Total | 450 | | $5,000 |

**Proof:**
$7,000 + $5,000 = $12,000

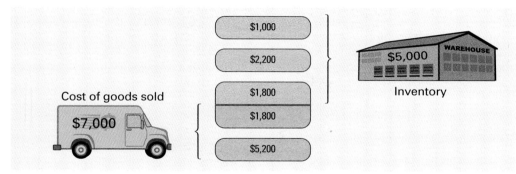

Remember that, under a periodic inventory system, all goods bought during the period are assumed to be available for the first sale, regardless of the purchase dates. Under LIFO, the cost of the last goods in is the first to be assigned to cost of goods sold. Using our example, start at the end of the period and count backwards until you reach the total number of units sold (550). The result is that 400 units from the November 27, or last, purchase are assumed to be sold first. Only 150 units from the next (August 24) purchase are needed to reach the total 550 units sold.

Note that because goods purchased late in a period are assumed to be available for the first sale in a periodic inventory system, income could be manipulated by a last-minute end-of-period purchase of inventory.

Since it is assumed that the first goods sold were those that were most recently purchased, ending inventory under LIFO is based on the costs of the oldest units purchased. That is, the cost of the ending inventory is obtained by taking the unit cost of the earliest goods available for sale and working forward until all units of inventory have been costed. In our example, therefore, the 450 units of ending inventory must be costed using the earliest purchase prices. The first purchase was 100 units at $10 in the January 1 beginning inventory. Then 200 units were purchased at $11. The remaining 150 units are costed at $12 per unit, the August 24 purchase price.

## Financial Statement Effects of Cost Flow Assumptions

Companies can choose specific identification, or any of the three cost flow assumptions—all are acceptable for use. For example, Ault Foods, Canadian Tire, and Sobeys use FIFO. The Prince Philip Drive Campus Bookstore, Andrés Wines, and Mountain Equipment Co-op use average cost. Alberta Natural Gas, Cominco, and Suncor use LIFO. A company may also use more than one cost flow assumption at the same time. Finning International, for example, uses specific identification to account for its equipment inventory, FIFO to account for about two-thirds of its inventory of parts and supplies, and average cost to account for the remainder.

About an equal number of companies in Canada use FIFO and the average cost flow assumptions. Only a very few companies, about 2%, use LIFO. The Canadian companies that do use LIFO tend to use it to harmonize their reporting practices to the U.S., where use of the LIFO cost flow assumption is greater.

Although the FIFO and average cost flow assumptions are more commonly used in Canada, to understand global financial reporting, students need to have some understanding of the impact of the LIFO cost flow assumption. The reasons companies have for adopting different inventory cost flow assumptions are varied, but they usually involve one of the following factors:

1. Income statement effects
2. Balance sheet effects

> **study objective 3**
>
> Demonstrate the effects on the financial statements of each of the inventory cost flow assumptions.

## Income Statement Effects

To understand why companies might choose a particular cost flow assumption, let's compare the effects of each assumption on the financial statements of Fraser Valley Electronics. The condensed income statements in Illustration 6-8 assume that Fraser Valley sold its 550 units for $11,500 and that its operating expenses were $2,000.

**Illustration 6-8 ▶**

Comparative effects of cost flow assumptions

| FRASER VALLEY ELECTRONICS Condensed Income Statement | | | | | |
|---|---|---|---|---|---|
| | FIFO | | Average Cost | | LIFO |
| Sales | | $11,500 | | $11,500 | | $11,500 |
| Beginning inventory | $ 1,000 | | $ 1,000 | | $ 1,000 | |
| Purchases | 11,000 | | 11,000 | | 11,000 | |
| Cost of goods available for sale | 12,000 | | 12,000 | | 12,000 | |
| Ending inventory | 5,800 | | 5,400 | | 5,000 | |
| Cost of goods sold | | 6,200 | | 6,600 | | 7,000 |
| Gross profit | | 5,300 | | 4,900 | | 4,500 |
| Operating expenses | | 2,000 | | 2,000 | | 2,000 |
| Net income | | $ 3,300 | | $ 2,900 | | $ 2,500 |

The cost of goods available for sale ($12,000) is the same under each of the three inventory cost flow assumptions. But both the ending inventories and the cost of goods sold are different. This difference is because of the unit costs that are allocated to each. Each dollar of difference in ending inventory results in a corresponding dollar difference in cost of goods sold and net income. For Fraser Valley, there is an $800 difference between FIFO and LIFO.

In periods of changing prices, the choice of cost flow assumption can have a significant impact on net income. In a period of rising prices, as is the case here, FIFO produces a higher income. This happens because the expenses matched against revenues are the lower unit costs of the first units purchased. As indicated in Illustration 6-8, FIFO reports the highest income ($3,300) and LIFO the lowest ($2,500). Average cost falls somewhere in the middle ($2,900). To management, higher net income is an advantage. It causes external users to view the company more favourably. Also, if management bonuses are based on net income, FIFO will provide the higher income for higher bonuses.

If prices are falling, the results from the use of FIFO and LIFO are reversed. FIFO will report the lowest income and LIFO the highest. If prices are stable, all three cost flow assumptions will report the same results.

**LIFO provides the best income statement valuation.** It matches current costs with current revenues. This is because, under LIFO, the cost of goods sold is assumed to be the cost of the goods most recently acquired. Even though LIFO does result in the best match of revenues and expense, it can also result in some income statement distortions if beginning inventory is ever liquidated. This cost flow assumption is seldom used in Canada. The use of LIFO is not permitted for income tax purposes in this country, and most firms do not wish to maintain two sets of inventory records—one for accounting purposes and another for tax purposes.

## Balance Sheet Effects

**FIFO produces the best balance sheet valuation.** A major advantage of FIFO is that in a period of rising prices, the costs allocated to ending inventory will approximate the inventory's current, or replacement, cost. For example, for Fraser Valley, 400 of the 450 units in the ending inventory are costed at the November 27 unit cost of $13. Since management needs to replace inventory once sold, a valuation that approximates replacement cost is helpful for decision-making.

A major shortcoming of LIFO is evident during periods of rising prices, because the costs allocated to ending inventory may be understated in terms of current costs. The understatement becomes even larger if the inventory includes goods purchased in one or more prior accounting periods. This is true for Fraser Valley Electronics. The cost of the ending inventory includes the $10 unit cost of the beginning inventory.

## Summary of Effects

The following illustration summarizes the key differences that result from the different cost flow assumptions during a period of rising prices. The effects will be the opposite of those in the illustration if prices are falling. There is no distinction between assumptions if prices are constant.

| | FIFO | Average | LIFO |
|---|---|---|---|
| Cost of goods sold | Lowest | Results will fall in between FIFO and LIFO | Highest |
| Gross profit/Net income | Highest | Results will fall in between FIFO and LIFO | Lowest |
| Cash flow (pretax) | Same | Same | Same |
| Ending inventory | Highest | Results will fall in between FIFO and LIFO | Lowest |

**Illustration 6-9 ◄**

Financial statement effects of cost flow assumptions during a period of rising prices

We have seen that both inventory on the balance sheet and net income on the income statement are higher when FIFO is used in a period of rising prices. Do not confuse this with cash flow. All three cost flow assumptions produce exactly the same cash flow. Revenues and purchases are not affected by the choice of cost flow assumption. The only thing affected is the allocation between ending inventory and cost of goods sold, which does not involve cash.

It is also worth remembering that all three cost flow assumptions will give exactly the same results over the life cycle of the business or its product. That is, the allocation between cost of goods sold and ending inventory may vary within a period, but over time will give the same cumulative results. Although much has been written about the impact of the choice of inventory cost flow assumption on a variety of performance measures, in reality there is little real economic distinction among them *over time*.

## Selection of Cost Flow Assumption

Accounting should provide information that is useful to decision-makers. We have learned that the choice of cost flow assumption can lead to substantially different financial statement effects, depending on the direction of prices. Is the financial reporting objective of providing useful information for decision-making achieved if managers can choose a cost flow assumption based on its desired influence on their financial results? The answer to this is "No."

While the accounting profession does permit a choice among acceptable methods, the reason is to **accommodate differences in the circumstances of the company and the industry**. It is not to permit managers to manipulate the company's financial position at will. The CICA recommends that in those cases "where the choice of method of inventory valuation is an important factor in determining income, the most suitable method for determining cost is that which results in charging against operations costs which most fairly match the sales revenue for the period."

Whichever cost flow assumption is chosen by a company, it should be used from one period to the next. Consistency makes financial statements comparable over successive time periods. Using FIFO in one year and average cost in the next year would make it difficult to compare the net incomes for the two years.

Although consistency is preferred, a company may change its cost flow assumption. Such a change and its effects on net income should be disclosed in the financial statements. This conforms with the **full disclosure principle**, which requires all relevant information to be disclosed. The full disclosure principle is discussed further in Chapter 11.

## BEFORE YOU GO ON . . .

### ▶Review It

1. How do the cost, matching, and full disclosure principles apply to inventory costs?
2. How are the three cost flow assumptions applied in allocating cost of goods available for sale?
3. Which inventory cost flow assumption produces the highest net income in a period of rising prices? The highest balance sheet valuation? The highest cash flow?
4. What factors should be considered by management when choosing an inventory cost flow assumption?
5. Which inventory cost flow assumption does The Forzani Group Ltd. use? The answer to this question is provided at the end of this chapter.

### ▶Do It

The accounting records of the Cookie Cutters Company show the following data:

|  |  |
|---|---|
| Beginning inventory | 4,000 units at $3 |
| Purchases | 6,000 units at $4 |
| Sales | 8,000 units at $8 |

Determine the cost of goods sold and ending inventory under a periodic inventory system using (a) FIFO, (b) average cost, and (c) LIFO.

#### Action Plan

- Ignore selling price in allocating cost.
- Allocate costs between goods sold and goods on hand for each cost flow assumption.
- For FIFO, allocate the earliest costs to the goods sold and the latest costs to the goods on hand.
- For average cost, determine the weighted average unit cost (cost of goods available for sale ÷ number of units available for sale). Multiply this cost by the number of units sold and the number of units on hand.
- For LIFO, allocate the latest costs to the goods sold and the earliest costs to the goods on hand.
- Prove your work: cost of goods sold + ending inventory = cost of goods available for sale.

#### Solution

(a) Ending inventory = 4,000 + 6,000 − 8,000 = 2,000 units
   FIFO cost of goods sold: (4,000 × $3) + (4,000 × $4) = $28,000
   FIFO ending inventory: 2,000 × $4 = $8,000
   Proof: $28,000 + $8,000 = $36,000
(b) Weighted average unit cost: [(4,000 × $3) + (6,000 × $4)] ÷ 10,000 = $3.60
   Average cost of goods sold: 8,000 × $3.60 = $28,800
   Average ending inventory: 2,000 × $3.60 = $7,200
   Proof: $28,800 + $7,200 = $36,000
(c) LIFO cost of goods sold: (6,000 × $4) + (2,000 × $3) = $30,000
   LIFO ending inventory: 2,000 × $3 = $6,000
   Proof: $30,000 + $6,000 = $36,000

the navigator

*Related exercise material:* BE6–3, BE6–4, BE6–5, BE6–6, E6–3, E6–4, E6–5, and E6–6.

# Inventory Errors

Unfortunately, errors sometimes occur in taking or costing inventory. Some errors are caused by counting or pricing the inventory incorrectly. Other errors occur because of improper recognition of the transfer of legal title for goods in transit. When errors happen, they affect both the income statement and the balance sheet.

> **study objective 4**
>
> Determine the effects of inventory errors on the financial statements.

## Income Statement Effects

The cost of goods available for sale (beginning inventory plus cost of goods purchased) is allocated between cost of goods sold and ending inventory. Therefore, an error in any one of these components will affect both the income statement (through cost of goods sold and net income) and the balance sheet (ending inventory and owner's capital).

The dollar effects on cost of goods sold and net income can be determined by entering the incorrect data in the income statement formula, and then substituting the correct data.

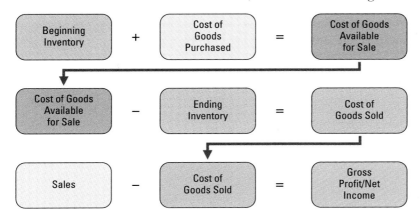

**Illustration 6-10 ▼**

Income formula

The overall effects of inventory errors on the current year's income statement are summarized below. U stands for understatement, O for overstatement, and NE for no effect.

| Nature of Error | Beginning Inventory | + | Cost of Goods Purchased | = | Cost of Goods Available for Sale | − | Ending Inventory | = | Cost of Goods Sold | Sales | − | Cost of Goods Sold | = | Gross Profit/Net Income |
|---|---|---|---|---|---|---|---|---|---|---|---|---|---|---|
| Understate beginning inventory | U | + | NE | = | U | − | NE | = | U | NE | − | U | = | O |
| Overstate beginning inventory | O | + | NE | = | O | − | NE | = | O | NE | − | O | = | U |
| Understate cost of goods purchased | NE | + | U | = | U | − | NE | = | U | NE | − | U | = | O |
| Overstate cost of goods purchased | NE | + | O | = | O | − | NE | = | O | NE | − | O | = | U |
| Understate ending inventory | NE | + | NE | = | NE | − | U | = | O | NE | − | O | = | U |
| Overstate ending inventory | NE | + | NE | = | NE | − | O | = | U | NE | − | U | = | O |

If **beginning inventory** is understated, cost of goods sold will be understated (assuming no other offsetting errors have occurred). On the other hand, an understatement of **ending inventory** will overstate cost of goods sold, because ending inventory must be deducted to determine cost of goods sold.

Cost of goods sold is deducted from sales to determine gross profit, and ultimately net income. An understatement in cost of goods sold will produce an overstatement in net income. An overstatement in cost of goods sold will produce an understatement in net income.

Since the ending inventory of one period becomes the beginning inventory of the next period, **an error in ending inventory of the current period will have a reverse effect on net income of the next period.** This is shown in Illustration 6-11. Note that the $3,000 understatement of ending inventory in 2005 will result in an overstatement of cost of goods sold and an understatement of net income. It also results in an understatement of beginning inventory in 2006, an understatement of cost of goods sold, and an overstatement of net income of the same amount.

**Illustration 6-11 ▼**

Effects of inventory errors on income statements of two successive years

| CONDENSED INCOME STATEMENTS | | | | | | | |
|---|---|---|---|---|---|---|---|
| | 2005 | | | | 2006 | | |
| | Incorrect | | Correct | | Incorrect | | Correct |
| Sales | | $80,000 | | $80,000 | | $90,000 | | $90,000 |
| Beginning inventory | $20,000 | | $20,000 | | $12,000 | | $15,000 | |
| Cost of goods purchased | 40,000 | | 40,000 | | 68,000 | | 68,000 | |
| Cost of goods available for sale | 60,000 | | 60,000 | | 80,000 | | 83,000 | |
| Ending inventory | 12,000 | | 15,000 | | 23,000 | | 23,000 | |
| Cost of goods sold | | 48,000 | | 45,000 | | 57,000 | | 60,000 |
| Gross profit | | 32,000 | | 35,000 | | 33,000 | | 30,000 |
| Operating expenses | | 10,000 | | 10,000 | | 20,000 | | 20,000 |
| Net income | | $22,000 | | $25,000 | | $13,000 | | $10,000 |

($3,000)
Net income
understated

$3,000
Net income
overstated

The combined net income for two years is correct because the errors cancel each other out.

Over the two years, total net income is correct. The errors offset one another. Notice that total income using incorrect data is $35,000 ($22,000 + $13,000). This is the same as the total income of $35,000 ($25,000 + $10,000) using correct data. Nevertheless, the distortion of the year-by-year results can have a serious impact on financial analysis and management decisions.

Note that an error in the beginning inventory does not result in a corresponding error in the ending inventory. The accuracy of the ending inventory depends entirely on correctly taking and costing the inventory at the balance sheet date.

## Balance Sheet Effects

The effects of errors on the balance sheet can be determined by using the basic accounting equation: assets = liabilities + owner's equity. In the following table, U is for understatement, O is for overstatement, and NE is for no effect.

| Nature of Error | Assets | = | Liabilities | + | Owner's Equity |
|---|---|---|---|---|---|
| Understate ending inventory | U | = | NE | + | U |
| Overstate ending inventory | O | = | NE | + | O |

Errors in beginning inventory have no impact on the balance sheet, if ending inventory is correctly calculated in the current period. Understating ending inventory (assuming no other offsetting errors) will understate net income. If net income is understated, then owner's equity will be understated (because net income is part of owner's equity).

The effect of an error in ending inventory on the next period was shown in Illustration 6-11. If the error is not corrected, total net income for the two periods would be correct. Thus, total assets and owner's equity reported on the balance sheet at the end of 2006 will also be correct.

Regardless of the nature of the error (and there are many possible combinations of errors), using the income statement and balance sheet equation will help ensure that you don't miss the total effect of inventory errors.

## BEFORE YOU GO ON . . .

### ►Review It

1. How do inventory errors affect financial statements?

### ►Do It

On December 31, Silas Company counted and recorded $600,000 of inventory. This count did not include $90,000 of goods in transit, shipped to Silas FOB shipping point. Determine the correct December 31 inventory. If Silas reports ending inventory of $600,000 on its balance sheet, which financial statement accounts may be in error, and what would the amount and direction of the error be?

#### Action Plan

- Use income statement relationships to determine the impact of an error on the income statement.
- Use the accounting equation to determine the impact of an error on the balance sheet.

#### Solution

The correct inventory count should have been $690,000 ($600,000 + $90,000).

*Income statement accounts:* Purchases are understated (U) by $90,000. However, since ending inventory is also understated, cost of goods sold and net income will be correct. [Beginning inventory + cost of goods purchased (U $90,000) − ending inventory (U $90,000) = cost of goods sold.]

*Balance sheet accounts:* Merchandise Inventory (ending) is understated by $90,000, as is Accounts Payable. [Assets (U $90,000) = liabilities (U $90,000) + owner's equity.]

*Related exercise material:* BE6–7, BE6–8, E6–7, and E6–8.

# Statement Presentation and Analysis

Presenting inventory on the financial statements is important because inventory is usually the largest current asset (ending inventory) on the balance sheet and the largest expense (cost of goods sold) on the income statement. In addition, these reported numbers are critical for analysing a company's effectiveness in managing its inventory. In the next sections, we will discuss the presentation and analysis of inventory.

> **study objective 5**
>
> Demonstrate the presentation and analysis of inventory.

## Presentation

Before reporting inventory on the financial statements, we must first ensure that it is properly valuated.

## Valuating Inventory at the Lower of Cost and Market (LCM)

Inventory values sometimes fall due to changes in technology or style. For example, suppose you manage a retail store that sells computers. At the end of the year, the value of the computers has dropped almost 25%. Do you think your inventory should be stated at cost, in accordance with the cost principle, or at its lower market value?

As you probably reasoned, this situation requires a departure from the cost basis of accounting. When the value of inventory is lower than its cost, the inventory is written down to its market value. This is done by valuating the inventory at the **lower of cost and market** (**LCM**) in the period in which the decline occurs. LCM is an example of the accounting concept of conservatism. **Conservatism** means that when choosing among alternatives, the best choice is the one that is least likely to overstate assets and net income.

The term *market* in the "lower of cost and market" phrase is not specifically defined in Canada. It may include **replacement cost** or **net realizable value**, among other definitions. The majority of Canadian companies use net realizable value to define market for LCM. For a merchandising company, **net realizable value is the selling price less any costs required to make the goods ready for sale**.

LCM is applied to the items in inventory after specific identification or one of the cost flow assumptions (FIFO, average, or LIFO) has been applied to determine the inventory cost.

Assume that Wacky World has the following lines of merchandise with costs and market values as indicated. LCM produces the following results:

|  | Cost | Market | Lower of Cost and Market |
|---|---|---|---|
| **Television sets** | | | |
| Consoles | $ 60,000 | $ 55,000 | |
| Portables | 45,000 | 52,000 | |
| | 105,000 | 107,000 | |
| **Video equipment** | | | |
| VCRs | 48,000 | 45,000 | |
| CD Players | 15,000 | 14,000 | |
| | 63,000 | 59,000 | |
| Total inventory | $168,000 | $166,000 | $166,000 |

LCM can be applied separately to each individual item, to categories of items (e.g., television sets and video equipment), or to total inventory. However, it is common practice to use total inventory rather than individual items or major categories in determining the LCM valuation. Although it is the least conservative, this approach still yields conservative results and allows increases in value (e.g., television sets) to offset decreases (e.g., video equipment), in part or in full. It is also the method that must be used for income tax purposes.

Using total inventory, the journal entry to record the loss for Wacky World would be the following:

A  =  L  +  OE
−2,000         −2,000

Cash flows: no effect

| | | |
|---|---|---|
| Loss Due to Decline in Net Realizable Value of Inventory | 2,000 | |
| Merchandise Inventory | | 2,000 |
| To record decline in inventory value from original cost of $168,000 to market value of $166,000. | | |

The loss would be reported as Other Expenses on the income statement. LCM should be applied consistently from period to period.

**ACCOUNTING IN ACTION ► Business Insight**

FALCONBRIDGE

In its 2002 third quarter financial statements, Falconbridge Limited wrote down the value of its metal inventory by $11 million, after taxes. Falconbridge's president and chief executive officer, Aaron Regent, commented that global economic conditions were uncertain and business confidence low. He said that this had a negative impact on demand for metals, particularly copper and zinc. On receiving the news, analysts immediately cut share price targets for Falconbridge by 12%.

## Classifying Inventory

How a company classifies its inventory depends on whether the firm is a merchandiser or a manufacturer. A merchandiser *buys* its inventory. A manufacturer *produces* its inventory. In a **merchandising company**, inventory consists of many different items. Textbooks, paper, and pens, for example, are just a few of the inventory items on hand in a bookstore. These items have two common characteristics: (1) they are owned by the company, and (2) they are in a form ready for sale to customers. Only one inventory classification, **merchandise inventory**, is needed to describe the many different items that make up the total inventory.

In a **manufacturing company**, some goods may not yet be ready for sale. As a result, inventory is usually classified into three categories: raw materials, work in process, and finished goods. For example, Bombardier classifies the steel, fibreglass, upholstery material, and other components that are on hand waiting to be used in production as **raw materials**. Motorized consumer products such as Ski-Doos and Sea-Doos that are on the assembly line in various stages of production are classified as **work in process**. Ski-Doos and Sea-Doos that are completed and ready for sale are identified as **finished goods**.

The accounting principles and concepts discussed in this chapter apply to the inventory classifications of both merchandising and manufacturing companies.

## Presentation

In the balance sheet, inventory is classified as a current asset. It usually follows receivables. In the income statement, inventory affects the cost of goods sold, which is subtracted from sales. There should be disclosure of (1) the major inventory classifications, (2) the basis of valuation (cost or lower of cost and market), and (3) the cost flow assumption (specific identification, FIFO, average, or LIFO).

Forzani reported inventory of $268,519 thousand under current assets in its 2003 balance sheet. It reported cost of sales (another term for cost of goods sold) of $603,326 thousand in its income statement. Note 2 (b) to Forzani's financial statements, reproduced in Appendix A at the end of this textbook, discloses that inventory is valuated at the lower of cost and net realizable value. Cost is determined using the weighted average cost flow assumption. Net realizable value is defined as the expected selling price.

## Analysis

In our economy, inventories are an important barometer of business activity. The amount of inventory and the time required to sell the goods are two closely watched indicators. During downturns in the economy, there can be an initial build-up of inventories, as it takes longer to sell existing quantities. Inventories generally decrease with an upturn in business activity.

A delicate balance must be maintained between too little inventory and too much inventory. On one hand, management wants to have a variety and quantity of merchandise on hand so that customers have a wide selection of items in stock. But having too much inventory on hand can cost the company money in storage costs, interest costs (on funds tied up in inventory), and costs due to the obsolescence of technology-driven goods or shifts in fashion. On the other hand, low inventory levels can result in stockouts, lost sales, and disgruntled customers.

Inventory is a significant component of the current ratio, a liquidity ratio which was introduced in Chapter 4. In Chapter 5, we introduced the gross profit margin, which helps determine the profitability of the cost of goods sold. In this section, we add another liquidity ratio that is commonly used to evaluate inventory levels, the inventory turnover ratio. We also present a related measure, the average days to sell the inventory.

## Inventory Turnover

The inventory turnover ratio measures the number of times, on average, inventory is sold during the period. It is calculated by dividing cost of goods sold by average inventory.

Whenever a ratio compares a balance sheet figure (e.g., inventory) to an income statement figure (e.g., cost of goods sold), the balance sheet figure must be averaged. Average balance sheet figures are determined by adding beginning and ending balances together and dividing by two. Averages are used to ensure that the balance sheet figures (which represent end-of-period amounts) cover the same period of time as the income statement figures (which represent amounts for the entire period). Illustration 6-12 shows the formula for calculating the inventory turnover ratio for The Forzani Group for fiscal 2003 (dollar amounts in thousands).

**Illustration 6-12 ▶**

Inventory turnover

| Cost of goods sold | ÷ | Average inventory | = | Inventory turnover |
|---|---|---|---|---|
| $603,326 | ÷ | $\dfrac{\$268{,}519 + \$229{,}270}{2}$ | = | 2.4 times |

Generally, the greater the number of times per year the inventory turns over, the more efficiently sales are being made.

## Days Sales in Inventory

It is informative to convert the inventory turnover ratio into a period of time, describing the age of the inventory. This ratio, called days sales in inventory, is calculated by dividing 365 days by the inventory turnover, as in Illustration 6-13.

**Illustration 6-13 ▶**

Days sales in inventory

| Days in year | ÷ | Inventory turnover | = | Days sales in inventory |
|---|---|---|---|---|
| 365 days | ÷ | 2.4 | = | 152 days |

This means that Forzani's inventory, on average, is in stock for 152 days. One has to be careful in interpreting this ratio: it should be compared to the company's ratio in prior years, and to the industry average. However, you must recognize that this average will differ for each type of inventory item (e.g., sneakers vs. bicycles). What we see here is a total average only.

---

## BEFORE YOU GO ON . . .

### ▶Review It

1. When is it appropriate to report inventory at the lower of cost and market?
2. What inventory information should be disclosed in the financial statements?
3. How can you tell if a company has too much or too little inventory on hand?

*Related exercise material:* BE6–9, BE6–10, BE6–11, E6–9, and E6–10.

Each of the inventory cost flow assumptions described in the chapter for a periodic inventory system can be used in a perpetual inventory system. To illustrate the application of the three cost flow assumptions (FIFO, average cost, and LIFO), we will use the data below and shown earlier in this chapter for Fraser Valley Electronics' Astro Condensers.

> study objective 6
>
> Apply the inventory cost flow assumptions to perpetual inventory records.

### FRAZER VALLEY ELECTRONICS
### Z202 Astro Condensers

| Date | Explanation | Units | Cost | Unit Cost | Total in Units |
|---|---|---|---|---|---|
| Jan. 1 | Beginning inventory | 100 | $10 | $ 1,000 | 100 |
| Apr. 15 | Purchases | 200 | 11 | 2,200 | 300 |
| May 1 | Sales | 150 | | | 150 |
| Aug. 24 | Purchases | 300 | 12 | 3,600 | 450 |
| Sept. 1 | Sales | 400 | | | 50 |
| Nov. 27 | Purchases | 400 | 13 | 5,200 | 450 |
| | | | | $12,000 | |

# First-In, First-Out (FIFO)

Under perpetual FIFO, the cost of the oldest goods on hand prior to each sale is allocated to the cost of goods sold. Therefore, the cost of goods sold on May 1 is assumed to consist of all the January 1 beginning inventory and 50 units of the items purchased on April 15. Similarly, the cost of goods sold on September 1 is assumed to consist of the remaining 150 units purchased on April 15, plus 250 of the items purchased on August 24, as shown in Illustration 6A-1.

| Date | Purchases Units | Purchases Cost | Purchases Total | Cost of Goods Sold Units | Cost of Goods Sold Cost | Cost of Goods Sold Total | Balance Units | Balance Cost | Balance Total |
|---|---|---|---|---|---|---|---|---|---|
| Jan. 1 | | | | | | | 100 | $10 | $1,000 |
| Apr. 15 | 200 | $11 | $ 2,200 | | | | 100<br>200 | 10<br>11 | } 3,200 |
| May 1 | | | | 100<br>50 | $10<br>11 | } $1,550 | 150 | 11 | 1,650 |
| Aug. 24 | 300 | 12 | 3,600 | | | | 150<br>300 | 11<br>12 | } 5,250 |
| Sept. 1 | | | | 150<br>250 | 11<br>12 | } 4,650 | 50 | 12 | 600 |
| Nov. 27 | 400 | 13 | 5,200 | | | | 50<br>400 | 12<br>13 | } 5,800 |
| | 900 | | $11,000 | 550 | | $6,200 | | | |

**Illustration 6A-1 ◀**

Perpetual system—FIFO

Proof:
$6,200 + $5,800 = $12,000

Note that the total cost of goods available for sale allocated between ending inventory and cost of goods sold is $12,000 (beginning inventory of $1,000 + purchases of $11,000), as shown in the margin proof. The results under FIFO in a perpetual system are the **same as in a periodic system** (see Illustration 6-3 where, similarly, the ending inventory is $5,800 and the cost of goods sold is $6,200). Regardless of the system, the first costs in are the ones assigned to cost of goods sold.

# Average Cost

The average cost flow assumption in a perpetual inventory system is called **moving average cost**. The average cost is calculated in the same manner as we calculated the weighted average unit cost: by dividing the cost of goods available for sale by the units available for sale. The difference is that under the perpetual cost flow assumption a new average is calculated **after each purchase**. The average cost is then applied to (1) the units sold, to determine the cost of goods sold, and (2) the remaining units on hand, to determine the ending inventory amount. The application of the moving average cost flow assumption by Fraser Valley Electronics is shown in Illustration 6A-2.

**Illustration 6A-2 ▶**

Perpetual system—moving average cost

| Date | Units | Cost | Total | Units | Cost | Total | Units | Cost | Total |
|------|-------|------|-------|-------|------|-------|-------|------|-------|
|      | | **Purchases** | | | **Cost of Goods Sold** | | | **Balance** | |
| Jan.  1 |     |         |             |     |         |             | 100 | $10.00 | $1,000.00 |
| Apr. 15 | 200 | $11.00  | $ 2,200.00  |     |         |             | 300 | 10.67  | 3,200.00  |
| May   1 |     |         |             | 150 | $10.67  | $1,600.00   | 150 | 10.67  | 1,600.00  |
| Aug. 24 | 300 | 12.00   | 3,600.00    |     |         |             | 450 | 11.56  | 5,200.00  |
| Sept.  1 |    |         |             | 400 | 11.56   | 4,622.22    | 50  | 11.56  | 577.78    |
| Nov. 27 | 400 | 13.00   | 5,200.00    |     |         |             | 450 | 12.84  | 5,777.78  |
|         | 900 |         | $11,000.00  | 550 |         | $6,222.22   |     |        |           |

**Proof:**
$6,222.22 + $5,777.78 = $12,000

As indicated above, a new average is calculated each time a purchase is made. On April 15, after 200 units are purchased for $2,200, a total of 300 units that cost $3,200 ($1,000 + $2,200) is on hand. The average unit cost is $3,200 divided by 300 units, or $10.67. Accordingly, the unit cost of the 150 units sold on May 1 is shown at $10.67, and the total cost of goods sold is $1,600. This unit cost is used in costing units sold until another purchase is made, when a new unit cost is calculated.

On August 24, following the purchase of 300 units for $3,600, there are 450 units on hand that cost $5,200 ($1,600 + $3,600). The new average cost is $11.56 ($5,200 ÷ 450), used to cost the September 1 sale. After the November 27 purchase of 400 units for $5,200, there are 450 units on hand that cost $5,777.78 ($577.78 + $5,200). The new average cost is $12.84 ($5,777.78 ÷ 450).

In practice, these average unit costs may be rounded to the nearest cent, or even to the nearest dollar. This illustration used the exact unit cost amounts, as would a computerized schedule, even though the unit costs have been rounded to the nearest digit for presentation in Illustration 6A-2. However, it is important to remember that this is an *assumed* cost flow, and using four digits, or even cents, suggests a false level of accuracy.

Compare the moving average cost under the perpetual inventory system to Illustration 6-6 (shown earlier in the chapter) which shows the weighted average cost under a periodic inventory system.

# Last-In, First-Out (LIFO)

Under the LIFO cost flow assumption using a perpetual system, the cost of the most recent purchase prior to sale is allocated to the units sold. Therefore, the cost of the goods sold on May 1 is assumed to consist of the units from the latest purchase, on April 15, at the cost of $11 per unit. The cost of the goods sold on September 1 counts backwards, first allocating the 300 units purchased on August 24, then the 50 remaining units from the April 15 purchase, and finally the 50 units necessary to equal the 400 units sold from the beginning inventory. The LIFO perpetual cost flow assumption is detailed in Illustration 6A-3.

| | Purchases | | | Cost of Goods Sold | | | Balance | | |
|---|---|---|---|---|---|---|---|---|---|
| Date | Units | Cost | Total | Units | Cost | Total | Units | Cost | Total |
| Jan. 1 | | | | | | | 100 | $10 | $1,000 |
| Apr. 15 | 200 | $11 | $ 2,200 | | | | 100 | 10 | } 3,200 |
| | | | | | | | 200 | 11 | |
| May 1 | | | | 150 | $11 | $1,650 | 100 | 10 | } 1,550 |
| | | | | | | | 50 | 11 | |
| Aug. 24 | 300 | 12 | 3,600 | | | | 100 | 10 | } |
| | | | | | | | 50 | 11 | } 5,150 |
| | | | | | | | 300 | 12 | } |
| Sept. 1 | | | | 300 | 12 | } | 50 | 10 | 500 |
| | | | | 50 | 11 | } 4,650 | | | |
| | | | | 50 | 10 | } | | | |
| Nov. 27 | 400 | 13 | 5,200 | | | | 50 | 10 | } 5,700 |
| | | | | | | | 400 | 13 | } |
| | 900 | | $11,000 | 550 | | $6,300 | | | |

**Illustration 6A-3 ◄**

Perpetual system—LIFO

Proof:
$6,300 + $5,700 = $12,000

The ending inventory in this LIFO perpetual illustration is $5,700 and cost of goods sold is $6,300, as compared to the LIFO periodic example in Illustration 6-7, where the ending inventory is $5,000 and cost of goods sold is $7,000.

The use of LIFO in a perpetual system will usually produce cost allocations that differ from using LIFO in a periodic system. In a perpetual system, the latest units purchased *before each sale* are allocated to cost of goods sold. In a periodic system, the latest units bought *during the period* are allocated to cost of goods sold. When a purchase is made after the last sale, the LIFO periodic system will apply this purchase to the previous sale. See Illustration 6-7, where the 400 units at $13 purchased on November 27 are applied to the sale of 550 units. As shown under the LIFO perpetual system, the 400 units at $13 purchased on November 27 are all applied to the ending inventory.

If we compare the cost of goods sold and ending inventory figures for all three perpetual cost flow assumptions, we find the same proportionate outcomes that we saw with periodic cost flow assumptions. That is, in a period of rising prices (prices rose in this problem), FIFO will always give the highest ending inventory valuation and LIFO the lowest. LIFO will always give the highest cost of goods sold figure (and lowest net income) and FIFO the lowest cost of goods sold (and highest net income). Of course, if prices are falling, the reverse situation will result. Finally, remember that the sum of cost of goods sold and ending inventory always equals the cost of goods available for sale, which is the same with each cost flow assumption.

| | FIFO | Average | LIFO |
|---|---|---|---|
| Cost of goods sold | $ 6,200 | $ 6,222 | $ 6,300 |
| Ending inventory | 5,800 | 5,778 | 5,700 |
| Cost of goods available for sale | $12,000 | $12,000 | $12,000 |

**Illustration 6A-4 ◄**

Comparison of cost flow assumptions

<table>
<tr><td>

**study objective 7**

Use the two methods of estimating inventories.

</td></tr>
</table>

We assumed in the chapter that a company would be able to physically count its inventory. But what if it cannot? What if the inventory were destroyed by fire? In that case, we would use an estimate.

Two circumstances explain why inventories are sometimes estimated. First, management that uses a periodic inventory system may want monthly or quarterly financial statements, without the time and expense of monthly or quarterly physical inventory counts. Second, a casualty such as fire or flood may make it impossible to take a physical inventory. The need to estimate inventories is associated primarily with a periodic inventory system because of the absence of detailed inventory records.

There are two widely used methods of estimating inventories: (1) the gross profit method, and (2) the retail inventory method.

# Gross Profit Method

The gross profit method estimates the cost of ending inventory by applying the gross profit margin to net sales. It is commonly used to prepare interim (e.g., monthly) financial statements in a periodic inventory system. This method is relatively simple but effective.

To use this method, a company needs to know its net sales, cost of goods available for sale (beginning inventory + cost of goods purchased), and gross profit margin. With the gross profit margin, the company estimates its gross profit for the period by multiplying net sales by the gross profit margin.

The formulas for using the gross profit method are given in Illustration 6B-1.

**Illustration 6B-1 ▶**

Gross profit method formulas

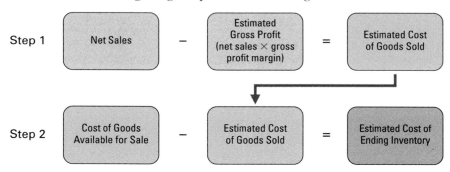

To illustrate, assume that Lalonde Company wants to prepare an income statement for the month of January. Its records show net sales of $200,000, beginning inventory of $40,000, and cost of goods purchased of $120,000. In the preceding year, the company had a 30% gross profit margin. It expects to earn the same margin this year. Given these facts and assumptions, the estimated cost of the ending inventory at January 31 under the gross profit method is $20,000, calculated as follows:

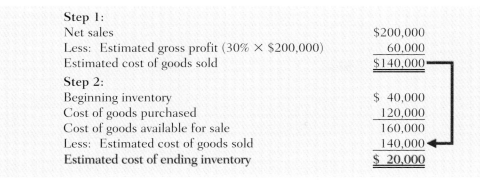

**Step 1:**

| | |
|---|---|
| Net sales | $200,000 |
| Less: Estimated gross profit (30% × $200,000) | 60,000 |
| Estimated cost of goods sold | $140,000 |

**Step 2:**

| | |
|---|---|
| Beginning inventory | $ 40,000 |
| Cost of goods purchased | 120,000 |
| Cost of goods available for sale | 160,000 |
| Less: Estimated cost of goods sold | 140,000 |
| **Estimated cost of ending inventory** | $ 20,000 |

The gross profit method is based on the assumption that the gross profit margin will remain constant from one year to the next. It may not remain constant, though, because of a change in merchandising policies or in market conditions. In such cases, the margin should be adjusted to reflect current operating conditions. In some cases, a better estimate can be obtained by applying this method on a department or product-line basis.

The gross profit method should not be used in preparing a company's financial statements at the end of the year. These statements should be based on a physical inventory count. Accountants and managers frequently use the gross profit method to test the reasonableness of the ending inventory amount, however.

# Retail Inventory Method

A retail store such as Canadian Tire has thousands of types of merchandise at low unit costs. In such cases, the application of unit costs to inventory quantities is difficult and time-consuming. An alternative is to use the **retail inventory method** to estimate the cost of inventory. In most retail concerns, a relationship between cost and sales price can be established. The cost-to-retail percentage is then applied to the ending inventory at retail prices to determine the cost of the inventory.

To use the retail inventory method, a company's records must show both the cost and the retail value of the goods available for sale. The formulas for using the retail inventory method are presented in Illustration 6B-2.

**Helpful hint** In determining inventory at retail, selling prices on the unit are used. Tracing actual unit costs to invoices is unnecessary.

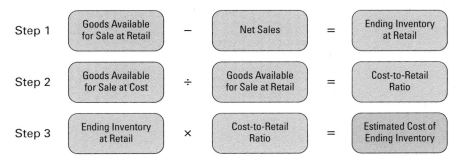

**Illustration 6B-2** ◀

Retail inventory method formulas

The logic of the retail method can be demonstrated by using unit cost data. Assume that 10 units purchased at $7 each ($70 in total) are priced to sell for $10 per unit ($100 in total). The cost-to-retail ratio is 70% ($70 ÷ $100). If four units remain unsold, their retail value is $40 and their cost is $28 ($40 × 70%). This amount agrees with the total cost of goods on hand on a per-unit basis (4 × $7).

The application of the retail method for Zboyovsky Co., using assumed data, is shown below.

|  | At Cost | At Retail |
|---|---|---|
| Beginning inventory | $14,000 | $ 21,500 |
| Goods purchased | 61,000 | 78,500 |
| Goods available for sale | 75,000 | 100,000 |
| Net sales |  | 70,000 |
| (1)  Ending inventory at retail |  | $ 30,000 |
| (2)  Cost-to-retail ratio = $75,000 ÷ $100,000 = 75% |  |  |
| (3)  Estimated cost of ending inventory ($30,000 × 75%) | $22,500 |  |

The retail inventory method also simplifies taking a physical inventory at the end of the year. The goods on hand can be valued at the prices marked on the merchandise. The cost-to-retail ratio is then applied to the goods on hand at retail to determine the ending inventory at cost. This value can be used for reporting purposes in the year-end financial statements.

The major disadvantage of the retail method is that it is an averaging technique. It may produce an incorrect inventory valuation if the mix of the ending inventory is not representative of the mix in the goods available for sale. Assume, for example, that the cost-to-retail ratio of 75% in the Zboyovsky Co. illustration consists of equal proportions of inventory items that have cost to retail ratios of 70%, 75%, and 80%, respectively. If the ending inventory contains only items with a 70% ratio, an incorrect inventory cost will result. This problem can be minimized by applying the retail method on a department or product-line basis.

# Demonstration Problem

Additional
Demonstration
Problems

Englehart Company has the following inventory, purchases, and sales data for the month of March:

| | | |
|---|---|---|
| Inventory, March 1 | 200 units @ $4.00 | $  800 |
| Purchases | | |
| March 10 | 500 units @ $4.50 | 2,250 |
| March 20 | 400 units @ $4.75 | 1,900 |
| March 30 | 300 units @ $5.00 | 1,500 |

Englehart Company uses a periodic inventory system. The physical inventory count on March 31 shows 500 units on hand.

## Instructions

Determine the cost of goods sold for March and the cost of ending inventory at March 31, under (a) FIFO, (b) average cost, and (c) LIFO.

## Solution to Demonstration Problem

The cost of goods available for sale is $6,450, calculated as follows:

| | | | |
|---|---|---|---|
| Inventory, March 1 | | 200 units @ $4.00 | $  800 |
| Purchases | | | |
| March 10 | | 500 units @ $4.50 | 2,250 |
| March 20 | | 400 units @ $4.75 | 1,900 |
| March 30 | | 300 units @ $5.00 | 1,500 |
| Total cost of goods available for sale | | 1,400 | $6,450 |

The number of units sold is 900 (1,400 units available for sale − 500 units on hand).

(a)

## FIFO

Cost of goods sold:

| Date | Units | Unit Cost | Total Cost |
|---|---|---|---|
| Inventory, Mar. 1 | 200 | $4.00 | $ 800 |
| Mar. 10 | 500 | 4.50 | 2,250 |
| Mar. 20 | 200 | 4.75 | 950 |
| | 900 | | $4,000 |

Ending inventory:

| Date | Units | Unit Cost | Total Cost |
|---|---|---|---|
| Mar. 30 | 300 | $5.00 | $1,500 |
| Mar. 20 | 200 | 4.75 | 950 |
| | 500 | | $2,450 |

Proof: $4,000 + $2,450 = $6,450

(b)

## Average Cost

Weighted average unit cost: $6,450 ÷ 1,400 units = $4.607 per unit
Cost of goods sold: 900 units × $4.607 = $4,146
Ending inventory: 500 units × $4.607 = 2,304

Proof: $4,146 + $2,304 = $6,450

(c)

## LIFO

Cost of goods sold:

| Date | Units | Unit Cost | Total Cost |
|---|---|---|---|
| Mar. 30 | 300 | $5.00 | $1,500 |
| Mar. 20 | 400 | 4.75 | 1,900 |
| Mar. 10 | 200 | 4.50 | 900 |
| | 900 | | $4,300 |

Ending inventory:

| Date | Units | Unit Cost | Total Cost |
|---|---|---|---|
| Mar. 1 | 200 | $4.00 | $ 800 |
| Mar. 10 | 300 | 4.50 | 1,350 |
| | 500 | | $2,150 |

Proof: $4,300 + $2,150 = $6,450

the
navigator

**Action Plan**
- Ignore the dates of sale in a periodic inventory system. Assume everything happens at the end of the period.
- Allocate costs between goods sold and goods on hand for each cost flow assumption.
- For FIFO, allocate the earliest costs to the goods sold and the latest costs to the goods on hand.
- For average, calculate the weighted average unit cost. Multiply this cost by the number of units sold and the number of units on hand.
- For LIFO, allocate the latest costs to the goods sold and the earliest costs to the goods on hand.
- Prove your work: cost of goods sold + ending inventory = cost of goods available for sale.

# Summary of Study Objectives

1. *Describe the steps in determining inventory quantities.* The steps in determining inventory quantities are (1) taking a physical inventory of goods on hand and (2) determining the ownership of goods in transit, on consignment, and in similar situations.

2. *Explain the basis of accounting for inventories and use the inventory cost flow assumptions.* The primary basis of accounting for inventories is cost. Cost includes all costs incurred to acquire goods and put them in a condition ready for sale. The cost of goods available for sale (beginning inventory + cost of goods purchased) may be allocated to cost of goods sold and ending inventory by specific identification or by one of the three cost flow assumptions—FIFO (first-in, first-out), average, or LIFO (last-in, first-out).

Specific identification allocates the exact cost of each merchandise item to cost of goods sold and ending inventory. FIFO assumes a first-in, first-out cost flow for sales. The FIFO cost flow assumption allocates the cost of the earliest goods purchased to cost of goods sold, and the cost of the most recent goods purchased to ending inventory. Average cost assumes an average cost flow for both cost of goods sold and ending inventory. Goods available for sale in dollars and units are used to determine the weighted average cost. This unit cost is then applied to the number of units sold and the number of units remaining in ending inventory. LIFO assumes a last-in, first-out cost flow for sales. The LIFO cost flow assumption allocates the cost of the most recent goods purchased to cost of goods sold, and the cost of the earliest goods purchased to ending inventory.

3. *Demonstrate the effects on the financial statements of each of the inventory cost flow assumptions.* When prices are rising, FIFO results in a lower cost of goods sold and higher net income than average and LIFO. The reverse is true when prices are falling. LIFO produces the best income statement valuation. It results in a cost of goods sold that best matches current costs with current revenues. FIFO produces the best balance sheet valuation. It results in an ending inventory that is closest to current value or replacement cost. FIFO and average are the most commonly used. LIFO can produce undesirable income effects in certain circumstances and is not permitted for income tax purposes.

4. *Determine the effects of inventory errors on the financial statements.* In the income statement of the current year, an error in beginning inventory will have a reverse effect on net income (e.g., an overstatement of beginning inventory results in an overstatement of cost of goods sold and an understatement of net income). An error in the cost of goods purchased will have a reverse effect on net income (e.g., an overstatement of purchases results in an overstatement of cost of goods sold and an understatement of net income). An error in ending inventory will

have a similar effect on net income (e.g., an overstatement of ending inventory results in an understatement of cost of goods sold and an overstatement of net income). If ending inventory errors are not corrected in the following period, their effect on net income for the second period is reversed. Total net income for the two years will be correct. In the balance sheet, ending inventory errors will have the same effects on total assets and total owner's equity, and no effect on liabilities.

5. *Demonstrate the presentation and analysis of inventory.* Ending inventory is reported as a current asset on the balance sheet. Cost of goods sold is reported on the income statement. Additional disclosure includes information about the major inventory classifications, the basis of valuation, and the cost flow assumption. The lower of cost and market basis (LCM) may be used when the net realizable value (market) is less than cost. Under LCM, the loss is recognized in the period in which the price decline occurs. The inventory turnover ratio is calculated as cost of goods sold divided by average inventory. It can be converted to days in inventory by dividing 365 days by the inventory turnover.

6. *Apply the inventory cost flow assumptions to perpetual inventory records (Appendix 6A).* Under FIFO, the cost of the earliest goods on hand is allocated to cost of goods sold. The cost of the most recent goods purchased is allocated to ending inventory. Under average, a new average (moving average) cost is calculated after each purchase and applied to the number of units sold and the number of units remaining in ending inventory. Under LIFO, the cost of the most recent purchase is allocated to cost of goods sold. The cost of the earliest goods purchased is allocated to ending inventory.

Each of these assumptions is applied in the same cost flow order as in a periodic inventory system. The main difference is that in a perpetual inventory system, the cost flow assumption is applied at the date of each sale to determine the cost of goods sold. In a periodic inventory system, the cost flow assumption is applied at the end of the period.

7. *Use the two methods of estimating inventories (Appendix 6B).* The two methods of estimating inventories are the gross profit method and the retail inventory method. Under the gross profit method, the gross profit margin is applied to net sales to determine the estimated cost of goods sold. The estimated cost of goods sold is subtracted from the cost of goods available for sale to determine the estimated cost of the ending inventory. Under the retail inventory method, a cost-to-retail ratio is calculated by dividing the cost of goods available for sale by the retail value of the goods available for sale. This ratio is then applied to the ending inventory at retail to determine the estimated cost of the ending inventory.

the
navigator

# Glossary

 **Key Term Matching Activity**

**Average cost** Inventory cost flow assumption which assumes that the goods available for sale are identical or nondistinguishable. They have the same average cost per unit, calculated by dividing the cost of the goods available for sale by the units available for sale. (p. 285)

**Consigned goods** Goods shipped by a consignor, who retains ownership, to a party called the consignee. (p. 280)

**Days sales in inventory** A measure of the average number of days inventory is held. It is calculated as 365 days divided by the inventory turnover ratio. (p. 296)

**First-in, first-out (FIFO)** Inventory cost flow assumption which assumes that the costs of the earliest goods acquired are the first to be recognized as cost of goods sold. The costs of the latest goods acquired are assumed to remain in ending inventory. (p. 284)

**Full disclosure principle** The requirement that all information relevant for decision-making be disclosed. (p. 290)

**Gross profit method** A method for estimating the cost of the ending inventory by applying the gross profit margin to net sales. (p. 300)

**Inventoriable costs** All costs incurred to acquire goods and make them ready for sale. (p. 282)

**Inventory turnover** A liquidity measure of the number of times, on average, inventory is sold during the period. It is calculated by dividing cost of goods sold by average inventory. (p. 296)

**Last-in, first-out (LIFO)** Inventory cost flow assumption which assumes that the costs of the latest units purchased are the first to be allocated to cost of goods sold. The costs of the earliest units purchased are allocated to ending inventory. (p. 286)

**Lower of cost and market (LCM)** A basis for stating inventory at the lower of the original cost and the current market value (usually defined as net realizable value). (p. 294)

**Net realizable value** The estimated amount for which an asset can be sold, less any costs necessary to make it saleable. (p. 294).

**Replacement cost** The cost of replacing an asset. (p. 294)

**Retail inventory method** A method used to estimate the cost of the ending inventory by applying a cost-to-retail ratio to the ending inventory at retail prices. (p. 301)

**Specific identification** An actual physical flow inventory costing method in which items are specifically costed to arrive at the cost of goods sold and the cost of the ending inventory. (p. 282).

*Note:* All Questions, Exercises, and Problems below with an asterisk (*) relate to material in the appendices to the chapter.

# Self-Study Questions

 **Chapter 6 Self-Test**

Answers are at the end of the chapter.

(SO 1) K  1. A physical inventory count is normally taken:
   (a) in a periodic inventory system.
   (b) in a perpetual inventory system.
   (c) at the end of the company's fiscal year.
   (d) All of the above

(SO 1) K  2. Which of the following should not be included in the physical inventory of a company?
   (a) Goods held on consignment from another company
   (b) Goods shipped on consignment to another company
   (c) Goods in transit purchased from a manufacturer and shipped FOB shipping point
   (d) Goods in transit sold to a customer and shipped FOB shipping point

(SO 2) AP  3. Kam Company uses a periodic inventory system and has the following:

| | Units | Unit Cost | Total Cost |
|---|---|---|---|
| Inventory, Jan. 1 | 8,000 | $11 | $ 88,000 |
| Purchase, June 19 | 13,000 | 12 | 156,000 |
| Purchase, Nov. 8 | 5,000 | 13 | 65,000 |
| | 26,000 | | $309,000 |

If 9,000 units are on hand at December 31, the cost of the ending inventory under FIFO is:
   (a) $100,000.          (c) $196,000.
   (b) $113,000.          (d) $209,000.

(SO 2) AP  4. Using the data in (3) above, the cost of goods sold (rounded) under average cost is:
   (a) $106,962.          (c) $180,000.
   (b) $108,000.          (d) $202,038.

(SO 3) C  5. In periods of rising prices, the average cost flow assumption will produce:
   (a) higher net income than FIFO.
   (b) the same net income as FIFO.
   (c) lower net income than FIFO.
   (d) lower net income than LIFO.

(SO 4) C  6. In Fran Company, ending inventory is understated by $4,000. The effects of this error on the current year's cost of goods sold and net income, respectively, are:
(a) understated, overstated.
(b) overstated, understated.
(c) overstated, overstated.
(d) understated, understated.

(SO 5) K  7. The lower of cost and market rule for inventory is an example of the application of:
(a) the conservatism concept.
(b) the historical cost principle.
(c) the materiality constraint.
(d) the economic entity assumption.

(SO 5) AP  8. If a company's cost of goods sold is $120,000, its beginning inventory is $15,000, and its ending inventory is $25,000, what are its inventory turnover and days sales in inventory?
(a) 0.2 times and 1,825 days.
(b) 4.8 times and 76 days.
(c) 6 times and 61 days.
(d) 8 times and 46 days.

*9. In a perpetual inventory system:  (SO 6) C
(a) LIFO cost of goods sold will be the same as in a periodic inventory system.
(b) average cost of goods sold will be the same as in a periodic inventory system.
(c) FIFO cost of goods sold will be the same as in a periodic inventory system.
(d) All of the above

*10. Somers Company has sales of $150,000 and a cost of goods available for sale of $135,000. If the gross profit margin is 30%, the estimated cost of the ending inventory under the gross profit method is:  (SO 7) AP
(a) $15,000.          (c) $40,500.
(b) $20,000.          (d) $105,000.

*11. Retail Home Company reports the following selected information: cost of goods available for sale, at cost, $60,000, at retail, $100,000; and net sales at retail, $80,000. What is the estimated cost of Retail Home Company's ending inventory under the retail method?  (SO 7) AP
(a) $12,000          (c) $40,000
(b) $20,000          (d) $60,000

# Questions

(SO 1) C  1. Your friend Tom Wetzel has been hired to help take the physical inventory in Kikujiro's Hardware Store. Explain to Tom what this job will involve.

(SO 1) C  2. Janine Company ships merchandise to Carbonear Corporation on December 30. The merchandise reaches the buyer on January 5. Indicate the terms of sale that will result in the goods being included in (a) Janine's December 31 inventory, and (b) Carbonear's December 31 inventory.

(SO 1) C  3. What are consigned goods? Which company, the consignee or the consignor, should include consigned goods in its inventory balance? Explain why.

(SO 2) C  4. Dave Wier believes that the allocation of goods available for sale should be based on the actual physical flow of the goods. Explain to Dave why this may be both impractical and inappropriate.

(SO 2) K  5. Which inventory cost flow assumption:
(a) usually matches the actual physical flow of merchandise?
(b) assumes that the first units purchased are the first to be sold?
(c) assumes that the goods available for sale are identical?

(SO 2) C  6. Compare the financial statement effects on (a) cash, (b) ending inventory, (c) cost of goods sold, and (d) net income of using the FIFO and average cost flow assumptions during a period of declining prices.

(SO 2) C  7. Explain how the cost of goods sold can be manipulated when the specific identification method is used.

8. In a period of rising prices, the inventory reported in Plato Company's balance sheet is close to the replacement cost of the inventory. York Company's inventory is considerably below its current cost. Identify the inventory cost flow assumption being used by each company. Which company has probably been reporting the higher gross profit?  (SO 3) C

9. "The selection of an inventory cost flow assumption depends on whether prices are rising or falling." Do you agree? Explain. Once an assumption has been chosen, what accounting characteristic applies?  (SO 3) C

10. Swift Company has been using the FIFO cost flow assumption during a long period of inflation. During the same period, the owner of Swift has been withdrawing a substantial amount of its net income. What adverse effects may result from this policy?  (SO 3) C

11. Mila Company discovers in 2004 that its ending inventory at December 31, 2004, was understated by $5,000. What effect will this error have on (a) 2004 net income, (b) 2005 net income, and (c) the combined net income for the two years?  (SO 4) C

12. If an error in ending inventory in one year will have the reverse effect in the following year, does this error need to be corrected when it is discovered?  (SO 4) C

13. Lucy Ritter is studying for the next accounting midterm examination. What should Lucy know about (a) departing from the cost basis of accounting for inventories, and (b) the meaning of "market" in the lower of cost and market method?  (SO 5) C

(SO 5) C 14. "The key to successful business operations is effective inventory management." Do you agree? Explain.

(SO 5) AN 15. Under what circumstances might the inventory turnover ratio be too high—that is, what possible negative consequences might occur?

(SO 5) C 16. Would an increase in the days sales in inventory ratio from one year to the next be viewed as an improvement or a deterioration in the company's efficiency in managing its inventory?

(SO 5) K 17. The Wabanaki Company's balance sheet shows inventories of $162,800. What additional disclosures should be made?

*18. "When perpetual inventory records are kept, the results under the FIFO and average cost flow assumptions are the same as they would be in a periodic inventory system." Do you agree? (SO 6) C

*19. How does the average cost flow assumption of inventory costing differ when it's used in a perpetual inventory system and in a periodic inventory system? (SO 6) K

*20. When is it necessary to estimate inventories? (SO 7) K

*21. Both the gross profit method and the retail inventory method are based on averages. For each method, indicate the average used, how it is determined, and how it is applied. (SO 7) C

# Brief Exercises

**BE6–1** Helgeson Company has identified the following items for possible inclusion when taking a physical inventory. Indicate whether each item should be included in or excluded from the inventory.

1. Goods shipped on consignment by Helgeson to another company
2. Goods in transit to Helgeson from a supplier, shipped FOB destination
3. Goods sold to a customer but being held for delivery
4. Goods from another company held on consignment by Helgeson
5. Goods in transit to a customer, shipped FOB destination

*Identify items to be included in taking a physical inventory.*
*(SO 1) K*

**BE6–2** Mary Ann's Hat Shop recently purchased a shipment of hats from a wholesaler. The cost of the hats was $3,000. Mary Ann's was also required to pay freight charges of $70. In addition, Mary Ann's paid $100 to cover the travel expenses of an employee who negotiated the purchase of the hats. Calculate the cost of this inventory. Briefly explain your reasoning.

*Calculate inventory cost.*
*(SO 1) AP*

**BE6–3** On January 3, Piano Company purchased three model EBS electronic pianos for $1,000 each. On January 20, it purchased two additional model EBS electronic pianos for $1,200 each. An inventory count on January 31 revealed that three of the pianos were still on hand. Piano Company uses a periodic inventory system. Calculate the cost of goods sold and ending inventory on January 31 under (a) FIFO, (b) average, (c) LIFO, and (d) specific identification. Assume for (d) that one of the pianos sold during January was purchased on January 3 and the other was purchased on January 20.

*Apply specific identification and periodic cost flow assumptions.*
*(SO 2) AP*

**BE6–4** In its first month of operations, Quilt Company made three purchases of merchandise in the following sequence: 250 units at $6, 400 units at $7, and 350 units at $8. There are 400 units on hand at the end of the period. Quilt uses a periodic inventory system. Calculate the cost to be allocated to cost of goods sold and ending inventory under (a) FIFO, (b) average, and (c) LIFO.

*Apply periodic cost flow assumptions.*
*(SO 2) AP*

**BE6–5** For each statement which follows, identify the inventory cost flow assumption which best fits the description, assuming a period of rising prices:

1. It results in a balance sheet inventory closest to replacement cost.
2. It matches recent costs against revenue.
3. It is the best choice because each product has unique features that affect cost.
4. It understates the current value of the inventory on the balance sheet.

*Identify inventory cost flow assumptions.*
*(SO 3) AN*

**BE6–6** Interactive.com just started business and is trying to decide which inventory cost flow assumption to use. Assuming prices are falling, as they often do in the information technology business, answer the following questions for Interactive.com:

(a) Which cost flow assumption gives the highest ending inventory? Why?
(b) Which cost flow assumption gives the highest cost of goods sold? Why?
(c) Which cost flow assumption will result in the highest cash flow? Explain.
(d) What factors are important to Interactive.com in its selection of the most appropriate cost flow assumption?

*Compare financial effects of inventory cost flow assumptions.*
*(SO 3) AN*

**Determine effects of inventory error.**
(SO 4) AP

**BE6–7**  Creole Company reports net income of $90,000 in 2004. Ending inventory was understated by $7,000. What is the correct net income for 2004? What effect, if any, will this error have on total assets and owner's equity reported in the balance sheet at December 31, 2004?

**Determine effect of ending inventory error on balance sheet for two years.**
(SO 4) AP

**BE6–8**  Johal Company counted and recorded its ending inventory as at December 31, 2004, incorrectly overstating its correct value by $25,000. Assuming that this misstatement was not discovered and corrected, what is the impact of this error on assets, liabilities, and owner's equity at the end of 2004? At the end of 2005?

**Determine LCM valuation.**
(SO 5) AP

**BE6–9**  Svenska Electronic Centre accumulates the following cost and market data at December 31:

| Inventory Categories | Cost | Market |
|---|---|---|
| Cameras | $12,000 | $10,200 |
| DVD players | 9,000 | 9,500 |
| VCRs | 14,000 | 12,800 |

Calculate the lower of cost and market valuation, applying LCM to total inventory.

**Calculate inventory turnover and days sales in inventory.**
(SO 5) AP

**BE6–10**  Ry Company reported net sales of $550,000; cost of goods sold of $300,000; beginning inventory of $22,250; and ending inventory of $27,750. Calculate the inventory turnover and days sales in inventory ratios for Ry Company.

**Determine impact of transactions on inventory turnover.**
(SO 5) AN

**BE6–11**  Indicate whether the following transactions would increase (+), decrease (−), or have no effect (NE) on the inventory turnover ratio:

(a) _____  Beginning inventory was understated.
(b) _____  Cost of goods purchased was reduced by moving to a new, cheaper supplier.
(c) _____  Operating expenses increased.

**Apply perpetual inventory cost flow assumptions.**
(SO 6) AP

*__BE6–12__  Poirier Department Store uses a perpetual inventory system. Data for a product include the following purchases:

| Date | Units | Unit Cost |
|---|---|---|
| May 7 | 50 | $10 |
| July 28 | 30 | 15 |

On June 1, Poirier sold 32 units for $20 each, and on August 27, Poirier sold 33 more units for $22 each. What are the cost of goods sold and ending inventory under (a) FIFO, (b) average, and (c) LIFO?

**Apply perpetual FIFO and average cost flow assumptions.**
(SO 6) AP

*__BE6–13__  Yip Company uses a perpetual inventory system. The sequence of sales and purchases is as follows in its first month of operations: (1) 250 units purchased at $6; (2) 400 units purchased at $7; (3) 275 units sold at $10; (4) 350 units purchased at $8; and (5) 325 units sold at $12. Calculate the cost of goods sold and ending inventory under (a) FIFO and (b) average.

**Journalize transactions in periodic and perpetual inventory systems.**
(SO 6) AP

*__BE6–14__  At the beginning of the year, Seller Company had 700 units with a cost of $3 per unit in its beginning inventory. The following inventory transactions occurred during the month of January:

Jan.  3 Sold 500 units on account for $5 each.
      9 Purchased 1,000 units on account for $4 per unit.
     15 Sold 800 units for $8 each, cash.

Prepare journal entries assuming that Seller Company uses (a) FIFO under the periodic inventory assumption and (b) FIFO under the perpetual inventory system.

**Apply gross profit method.**
(SO 7) AP

*__BE6–15__  The Jansen Company had beginning inventory of $60,000, net sales of $350,000, and cost of goods purchased of $250,000. In the preceding year, the company had a gross profit margin of 40%. Calculate the estimated cost of the ending inventory using the gross profit method.

**Apply retail inventory method.**
(SO 7) AP

*__BE6–16__  On June 30, Fabricville has the following data related to the retail inventory method: Goods available for sale at cost $35,000 and at retail $50,000, and net sales $40,000. Calculate the estimated cost of the ending inventory, using the retail inventory method.

# Exercises

**E6–1** The Shippers Company had the following inventory situations to consider at January 31, its year end:

Identify items in inventory. (SO 1) K

1. Goods held on consignment for MailBoxes Etc. since December 12
2. Goods shipped on consignment to Rinehart Holdings on January 5
3. Goods that are still in transit purchased FOB destination from a supplier on January 25
4. Goods that are still in transit purchased FOB shipping point from a supplier on January 25
5. Goods that are still in transit shipped to a customer, FOB destination, on January 29
6. Goods that are still in transit shipped to a customer, FOB shipping point, on January 29
7. Office supplies on hand at January 31

*Instructions*

Identify which of the above items should be included in inventory. If the item should not be included in inventory, state where it should be recorded.

**E6–2** First Bank is considering giving Moghul Company a loan. Before doing so, it decides that further discussions with Moghul's accountant may be desirable. One area of particular concern is the inventory account. A physical inventory count revealed a year-end balance of $283,000. Discussions with the accountant reveal the following:

Determine correct inventory amount. (SO 1) AN

Interactive Homework

1. Moghul sold goods that cost $35,000 to Novotna Company, FOB shipping point, on December 28. The goods are not expected to arrive at their destination, in India, until January 12. The goods were not included in the physical inventory because they were not in the warehouse.
2. The physical count of the inventory did not include goods that cost $95,000 that were shipped to Moghul, FOB destination, on December 27 and were still in transit at year end.
3. Moghul received goods that cost $28,000 on January 2. The goods were shipped on December 26 by Cellar Co., FOB shipping point. The goods were not included in the physical count.
4. Moghul sold goods that cost $49,000 to Sterling of Canada, FOB destination, on December 30. The goods were received by Sterling on January 8. They were not included in Moghul's physical inventory.
5. Moghul received goods that cost $44,000 on January 2 that were shipped, FOB destination, on December 29. The shipment was a rush order that was supposed to arrive December 31. This purchase was not included in the ending inventory of $283,000.
6. Included in Moghul's ending inventory balance of $283,000 are $31,000 of goods held on consignment for Board Company.

*Instructions*

Determine the correct inventory amount at December 31.

**E6–3** On December 1, Discount Electronics has three DVD players left in stock. All are identical and priced to sell at $750. Of the three DVD players in stock, one with serial #1012 was purchased on June 1 at a cost of $500, another with serial #1045 was purchased on November 1 for $450. The last player, serial #1056, was purchased on November 30 for $400.

Calculate cost of goods sold using specific identification and periodic FIFO. (SO 2) AN

*Instructions*

(a) Calculate the cost of goods sold using the FIFO periodic inventory cost flow assumption, assuming that two of the three players were sold by the end of December, Discount Electronics' year end.
(b) If Discount Electronics used the specific identification method instead of FIFO, how might it alter its income by "selectively choosing" which particular players to sell to the two customers? What would Discount's cost of goods sold be if the company wanted to maximize income? What would Discount's cost of goods sold be if the company wanted to minimize income?
(c) Which inventory cost flow assumption do you recommend that Discount use? Explain why.

Calculate inventory and cost of goods sold using periodic FIFO and average cost.
(SO 2) AP

Interactive Homework

**E6–4** Zambia Company uses a periodic inventory system. Its records show the following for the month of May, with 20 units on hand at May 31:

|       |      |           | Units | Unit Cost | Total Cost |
|-------|------|-----------|-------|-----------|------------|
| May   | 1    | Inventory | 30    | $ 8       | $240       |
|       | 15   | Purchases | 45    | 11        | 495        |
|       | 24   | Purchases | 15    | 12        | 180        |
|       |      | Total     | 90    |           | $915       |

*Instructions*

Calculate the cost of goods sold and ending inventory at May 31 using the FIFO and average cost flow assumptions.

Calculate inventory and cost of goods sold using periodic FIFO and average cost. Answer questions about results.
(SO 2, 3) AP

**E6–5** Dene Company reports the following for the month of June:

|        |     |           | Units | Unit Cost | Total Cost |
|--------|-----|-----------|-------|-----------|------------|
| June   | 1   | Inventory | 150   | $5        | $ 750      |
|        | 12  | Purchases | 200   | 6         | 1,200      |
|        | 16  | Purchases | 480   | 8         | 3,840      |
|        | 23  | Purchases | 170   | 9         | 1,530      |
|        | 30  | Inventory | 180   |           |            |

*Instructions*

(a) Calculate the cost of the ending inventory and the cost of goods sold using a periodic inventory system under (1) FIFO and (2) average.
(b) Which cost flow assumption gives the higher ending inventory? Why?
(c) Which cost flow assumption results in the higher cost of goods sold? Why?
(d) Why is the average unit cost not $7?

Calculate inventory and cost of goods sold using periodic LIFO. Answer questions about results.
(SO 2, 3) AP

**E6–6** Inventory data for Dene Company are presented in E6–5.

*Instructions*

(a) Calculate the cost of the ending inventory and the cost of goods sold using the LIFO cost flow assumption in a periodic inventory system.
(b) Will the results in (a) be higher or lower than the results under (1) FIFO and (2) average cost? Explain why.

Determine effects of inventory errors.
(SO 4) AP

Interactive Homework

**E6–7** Seles Hardware reported cost of goods sold as follows:

|                                | 2004      | 2005      |
|--------------------------------|-----------|-----------|
| Beginning inventory            | $ 20,000  | $ 30,000  |
| Cost of goods purchased        | 160,000   | 175,000   |
| Cost of goods available for sale | 180,000 | 205,000   |
| Ending inventory               | 30,000    | 35,000    |
| Cost of goods sold             | $150,000  | $170,000  |

Seles made two errors: (1) 2004 ending inventory was overstated by $4,000, and (2) 2005 ending inventory was understated by $3,000.

*Instructions*

(a) Calculate the correct cost of goods sold for each year.
(b) Describe the impact of the error on cost of goods sold for each year, and in total for the two years.

Prepare correct income statements and comment.
(SO 4) AN

**E6–8** Aruba Company reported the following income statement data for the years ended December 31:

|  | 2004 | 2005 |
|---|---|---|
| Sales | $210,000 | $250,000 |
| Cost of goods sold |  |  |
|   Beginning inventory | 32,000 | 44,000 |
|   Cost of goods purchased | 173,000 | 202,000 |
|   Cost of goods available for sale | 205,000 | 246,000 |
|   Ending inventory | 44,000 | 52,000 |
|   Cost of goods sold | 161,000 | 194,000 |
| Gross profit | $ 49,000 | $ 56,000 |

Aruba uses a periodic inventory system. The inventories at January 1, 2004, and December 31, 2005, are correct. However, the ending inventory at December 31, 2004, was overstated by $5,000.

*Instructions*

(a) Prepare the correct income statement data for the two years.
(b) What is the combined effect of the inventory error on total gross profit for the two years?
(c) Calculate the gross profit margin for each of the two years, before and after the correction.
(d) In a letter to the president of Aruba Company, explain what has happened: the nature of the error and its effect on the financial statements.

**E6–9** This information is available for Danier Leather Inc. for three recent years (in thousands): Calculate inventory turnover and days sales in inventory. (SO 5) AP

|  | 2003 | 2002 | 2001 |
|---|---|---|---|
| Inventory | $ 37,029 | $ 38,662 | $ 39,227 |
| Sales | 175,487 | 179,977 | 165,418 |
| Cost of sales | 88,788 | 92,098 | 82,818 |

*Instructions*

Calculate the inventory turnover, days sales in inventory, and gross profit margin for Danier Leather Inc. for 2003 and 2002. Comment on any trends.

**E6–10** Cody Camera Shop uses the lower of cost and market basis for its inventory. The following data are available at December 31: Determine LCM valuation. (SO 5) AP

| | Units | Unit Cost | Market |
|---|---|---|---|
| Cameras: |  |  |  |
|   Minolta | 5 | $175 | $160 |
|   Canon | 7 | 140 | 142 |
| Light Meters: |  |  |  |
|   Vivitar | 12 | 135 | 129 |
|   Kodak | 10 | 115 | 120 |

Interactive Homework

*Instructions*

(a) Determine the total cost of the ending inventory.
(b) Determine the total market value of the ending inventory.
(c) What amount should be reported on Cody Camera Shop's financial statements, assuming the lower of cost and market rule is applied to total inventory?

**\*E6–11** Inventory data for Dene Company are presented in E6–5. Apply perpetual cost flow assumptions. (SO 6) AP

*Instructions*

(a) Calculate the cost of goods sold and the cost of the ending inventory under (1) FIFO, (2) average, and (3) LIFO, using a perpetual inventory system. Assume there were sales of 250 units on June 14 for $10 each and 570 units on June 26 for $12 each.
(b) How do the results in (a) differ from the results in E6–5 and E6–6?
(c) Why is the average unit cost not $7 (simple average) or $7.32 (weighted average) with a perpetual system?

Apply periodic and
perpetual cost flow
assumptions.
(SO 2, 6) AP

*E6–12    Powder! sells an Xpert snowboard that is popular with snowboard enthusiasts. Below is information relating to Powder!'s purchases and sales of Xpert snowboards during September:

| Date | Transaction | Units | Unit Price | Total Sales Price | Total Purchase Cost |
|------|-------------|-------|-----------|-------------------|---------------------|
| Sept. 1 | Beginning inventory | 26 | $297 | | $ 7,722 |
| 5 | Purchase | 28 | 302 | | 8,456 |
| 12 | Sale | (32) | 449 | $14,368 | |
| 19 | Purchase | 30 | 304 | | 9,120 |
| 22 | Sale | (50) | 449 | 22,450 | |
| 25 | Purchase | 15 | 310 | | 4,650 |
| | Totals | 17 | | $36,818 | $29,948 |

**Instructions**

(a) Calculate the cost of goods sold and the ending inventory using FIFO and average, assuming Powder! uses a perpetual inventory system.
(b) What would the cost of goods sold and ending inventory be if Powder! used each of these cost flow assumptions in a periodic inventory system?

Journalize transactions in
perpetual and periodic
inventory systems.
(SO 2, 6) AP

*E6–13    Refer to the data provided for Powder! in E6–12. Powder! makes all sales for cash and purchases on account.

**Instructions**

(a) Prepare journal entries to record the purchases and sales for Powder! in a perpetual inventory system under each of the following cost flow assumptions: (1) FIFO and (2) average.
(b) Prepare journal entries to record the purchases and sales for Powder! in a periodic inventory system under each of the following cost flow assumptions: (1) FIFO and (2) average.

Determine inventory loss
using gross profit method.
(SO 7) AP

*E6–14    The inventory of Farhad Company was destroyed by fire on March 1. From an examination of the accounting records, the following data for the first two months of the year are obtained: Sales $51,000, Sales Returns and Allowances $1,000, Purchases $31,200, Freight In $1,200, and Purchase Returns and Allowances $1,400.

**Instructions**

Determine the inventory lost by fire, assuming a beginning inventory of $25,000 and a gross profit margin of 30%.

Determine ending
inventory at cost using
retail method.
(SO 7) AP

*E6–15    Agnew Shoe Store uses the retail inventory method for its two departments: Women's Shoes and Men's Shoes. The following information is obtained for each department:

| Item | Women's Shoes | Men's Shoes |
|------|---------------|-------------|
| Beginning inventory at cost | $ 31,550 | $ 45,000 |
| Goods purchased at cost | 152,150 | 132,750 |
| Net sales | 177,000 | 185,000 |
| Beginning inventory at retail | 45,000 | 60,000 |
| Goods purchased at retail | 179,000 | 177,000 |

**Instructions**

Calculate the estimated cost of the ending inventory for each shoe department under the retail inventory method.

Determine ending
inventory using the gross
profit method and the
retail method. Compare
results.
(SO 7) AN

*E6–16    Nancy's Running Store has two departments: running shoes and running clothes. The selling price of running clothes is double their cost; the selling price of running shoes is 1.6 times the cost. During the previous year, the company had an overall gross profit margin of 43.75%. The information for the first six months of the current year is as follows:

| | Running Shoes | Running Clothes |
|------|---------------|-----------------|
| Beginning inventory at cost | $ 48,000 | $ 35,000 |
| Sales for the six months | 249,600 | 207,000 |
| Purchases at cost | 144,000 | 92,500 |

*Instructions*

(a) Estimate the cost of the ending inventory using the gross profit method.
(b) Estimate the cost of the ending inventory using the retail method.
(c) Do the two methods result in the same estimate? Why or why not? Which method would you recommend in this situation?

# Problems: Set A

**P6–1A** Kananaskis Country Company is trying to determine the value of its ending inventory as at February 28, 2005, the company's year end. The following transactions occurred, and the accountant asked for your help in determining whether these transactions should be recorded or not:

Determine items and amounts to be recorded in inventory.
(SO 1) AN

1. On February 26, Kananaskis shipped goods costing $950 to a customer and charged the customer $1,300. The goods were shipped with terms FOB destination and the receiving report indicates that the customer received the goods on March 3.
2. On February 26, Seller Company shipped goods to Kananaskis with terms FOB shipping point. The invoice price was $375 plus $30 for freight. The receiving report indicates that the goods were received by Kananaskis on March 2.
3. Kananaskis had $630 of inventory isolated in the warehouse. The inventory is designated for a customer who has requested that the goods be shipped on March 10.
4. Also in Kananaskis' warehouse is $400 of inventory that Craft Producers shipped to Kananaskis on consignment.
5. On February 26, Kananaskis issued a purchase order to acquire goods costing $750. The goods were shipped FOB destination. The receiving report indicates that Kananaskis received the goods on March 2.
6. On February 26, Kananaskis shipped goods to a customer with terms FOB shipping point. The invoice price was $350 plus $25 for freight. The cost of the items was $280. The receiving report indicates that the goods were received by the customer on March 2.
7. On February 28, Kananaskis was holding merchandise that had been sold to a customer on February 25 but needed some minor alterations before the customer would take possession. The customer has paid for the goods and will pick them up on March 3 after the alterations are complete. This inventory cost $490 and was sold for $880.
8. Kananaskis shipped $875 of inventory on consignment to Banff Company on February 20. By February 28, Banff Company had sold $365 of this inventory for Kananaskis.

*Instructions*

For each of the above transactions, specify whether the item in question should be included in ending inventory, and if so, at what amount. Explain your reasoning.

**P6–2A** Ng Company had a beginning inventory on January 1 of 200 units of Product SXL at a cost of $8 per unit. During the year, the following purchases were made:

Apply periodic cost flow assumptions. Prepare income statements and answer questions.
(SO 2, 3) AN

| | Units | Unit Cost |
|---|---|---|
| Mar. 15 | 700 | $ 9 |
| July 20 | 500 | 10 |
| Sept. 4 | 500 | 11 |
| Dec. 2 | 100 | 12 |

At the end of the year there were 300 units on hand. Ng Company uses a periodic inventory system.

*Instructions*

(a) Determine the cost of goods available for sale.
(b) Determine (1) the cost of the ending inventory and (2) the cost of goods sold under each of the three cost flow assumptions: (1) FIFO, (2) average, and (3) LIFO.
(c) Ng Company sold product SXL for $19 per unit and operating costs were $4 per unit sold. Prepare an income statement for each of the three cost flow assumptions.
(d) What cost flow assumption do you recommend Ng Company use if its primary objective is to minimize the income taxes that the owner will have to pay? Explain.
(e) Which assumption would have the most favourable impact on the company's cash flow?

Calculate ending inventory
using periodic FIFO and
average cost, prepare
income statements, and
answer questions.
(SO 2, 3) AN

**P6–3A** The management of Réal Novelty is re-evaluating the appropriateness of its present inventory cost flow assumption, average cost. It requests your help in determining the results of operations for the year ended December 31, 2005, if the FIFO cost flow assumption had been used. For 2005, the accounting records show the following data:

| Inventories | | Purchases and Sales | |
|---|---|---|---|
| Beginning (15,000 units) | $33,750 | Total net sales | $900,000 |
| Ending (20,000 units) | ? | Total cost of goods purchased | 585,500 |

Purchases were made quarterly, as follows:

| Quarter | Units | Unit Cost | Total Cost |
|---|---|---|---|
| 1 | 60,000 | $2.30 | $138,000 |
| 2 | 50,000 | 2.50 | 125,000 |
| 3 | 50,000 | 2.60 | 130,000 |
| 4 | 70,000 | 2.75 | 192,500 |
| | 230,000 | | $585,500 |

Operating expenses were $147,000. The periodic inventory system is used.

*Instructions*

(a) Prepare condensed income statements for 2005 under periodic FIFO and average cost.
(b) Write a business letter which answers the following questions for management:
  1. Which cost flow assumption produces the more meaningful inventory amount for the balance sheet? Why?
  2. Which cost flow assumption produces the more meaningful net income? Why?
  3. Which assumption produces the more realistic gross profit figure? Why?
  4. How much additional cash will be available for management under average cost than under FIFO? Why?
  5. What factors should management consider in choosing its inventory cost flow assumption?

Journalize transactions for
purchaser and seller using
periodic average cost.
Apply lower of cost and
market.
(SO 2, 3, 5) AP

**P6–4A** You are provided with the following information for Amelia Company. Amelia purchases all its high-tech items from Karina Company and makes sales to a variety of customers. All transactions are settled in cash. Returns are usually not damaged and are restored immediately to inventory for resale. Both Amelia and Karina use a periodic inventory system and the average cost flow assumption. Increased competition has reduced the price of the product.

**AMELIA COMPANY**

| Date | Transaction | Units | Unit Price |
|---|---|---|---|
| July 1 | Beginning inventory | 25 | $10.00 |
| 5 | Purchase | 60 | 9.00 |
| 8 | Sale | 65 | 11.00 |
| 10 | Sale return | 10 | 11.00 |
| 15 | Purchase | 45 | 8.00 |
| 16 | Purchase return | 5 | 8.00 |
| 20 | Sale | 60 | 9.00 |
| 25 | Purchase | 10 | 6.50 |

*Instructions*

(a) Prepare the required journal entries for the month of July for Amelia Company.
(b) Prepare the required journal entries for the month of July for Karina Company.
(c) Determine the ending inventory amount for Amelia using the average cost flow assumption.
(d) By July 31, Amelia Company learns that the product has a net realizable value of $7 per unit. What amount should ending inventory be valued at on the July 31 balance sheet? Discuss the accounting concept that is relevant in making this decision.
(e) What impact will the application of this concept have on Amelia's net income?

Indicate effect of errors
and identify cost flow
assumptions.
(SO 3, 4) AN

**P6–5A** JL Company maintains its inventory records on a periodic basis. At the end of 2003, the inventory was properly stated. But, in taking a physical inventory at the end of 2004, a batch of inventory was not included in the count. The inventory was properly stated at the end of 2005.

*Instructions*

(a) Indicate the effect of the error (overstatement, understatement, or no effect) on the following:
    1. Cost of goods sold for each of 2004 and 2005
    2. Net income for each of 2004 and 2005
    3. Owner's equity at the end of 2004 and 2005
    4. Ending inventory for each of 2004 and 2005
    5. Inventory turnover for each of 2004 and 2005

(b) Identify the inventory cost flow assumption most closely related to each of the following statements, assuming a period of falling prices:
    1. It overstates current value on a balance sheet.
    2. It matches recent costs against revenue.
    3. It results in a balance sheet inventory value closest to replacement cost.
    4. It smooths out the effect of price fluctuations.

**P6–6A** The records of Alyssa Company show the following data:

*Illustrate impact of inventory errors. Calculate inventory turnover. (SO 4, 5) AN*

| Account | 2003 | 2004 | 2005 |
|---|---|---|---|
| Sales | $300,000 | $320,000 | $330,000 |
| Beginning inventory | 35,000 | 24,000 | 31,000 |
| Cost of goods purchased | 200,000 | 240,000 | 230,000 |
| Ending inventory | 24,000 | 31,000 | 40,000 |
| Operating expenses | 60,000 | 64,000 | 66,000 |

Subsequent to its July 31, 2005, year end, Alyssa discovered two errors:

1. Ending inventory for the year ended July 31, 2003, was actually $30,000 not $24,000.
2. The cost of goods purchased for the year ended July 31, 2004, included $20,000 of merchandise that should have been recorded as a purchase in the year ended July 31, 2005.

*Instructions*

(a) Prepare both incorrect and corrected income statements for Alyssa for the years ended July 31, 2003, 2004, and 2005.
(b) What is the impact of these errors on the owner's equity at July 31, 2005?
(c) Calculate both the correct and incorrect inventory turnover ratios for 2003, 2004, and 2005.

**P6–7A** Financial information (in U.S. millions) is available for two major corporations for the three years ended December 31:

*Calculate ratios and comment. (SO 5) AN*

| PepsiCo Inc. | 2002 | 2001 | 2000 |
|---|---|---|---|
| Net sales | $25,112 | $23,512 | $22,337 |
| Cost of sales | 11,497 | 10,750 | 10,226 |
| Net income | 3,313 | 2,662 | 2,543 |
| Inventory | 1,342 | 1,310 | 1,192 |
| Current assets | 6,413 | 5,853 | 5,617 |
| Current liabilities | 6,052 | 4,998 | 4,795 |

| Coca-Cola Company | 2002 | 2001 | 2000 |
|---|---|---|---|
| Net sales | $19,564 | $17,545 | $17,354 |
| Cost of sales | 7,105 | 6,044 | 6,204 |
| Net income | 3,050 | 3,969 | 2,177 |
| Inventory | 1,294 | 1,055 | 1,066 |
| Current assets | 7,352 | 7,171 | 6,620 |
| Current liabilities | 7,341 | 8,429 | 9,321 |

*Instructions*

(a) Calculate the inventory turnover, days sales in inventory, current ratio, gross profit margin, and profit margin for each company for 2002 and 2001.
(b) Comment on each company's profitability and liquidity.

Apply perpetual cost flow
assumptions. Calculate
gross profit.
(SO 6) AP

*P6–8A  You are provided with the following information for Lahti Company for the month ended October 31, 2004:

| Date | | Description | Units | Unit Price |
|---|---|---|---|---|
| Oct. | 1 | Beginning inventory | 60 | $25 |
| | 9 | Purchase | 120 | 26 |
| | 10 | Purchase return | 5 | 26 |
| | 15 | Sale | 150 | 35 |
| | 22 | Purchase | 70 | 27 |
| | 29 | Sale | 75 | 40 |

Lahti Company uses a perpetual inventory system.

*Instructions*

(a) Calculate the ending inventory and cost of goods sold using FIFO, average, and LIFO cost flow assumptions.
(b) Calculate and compare the gross profit earned by Lahti using each of the three cost flow assumptions.
(c) How would the results of the three alternatives change if Lahti had experienced declining prices when purchasing additional inventory?

Calculate and journalize
perpetual FIFO and
average cost. Answer
questions about financial
statement effects.
(SO 3, 6) AN

*P6–9A  The Reliable Electronic Mart began operations on May 1, 2005, and uses a perpetual inventory system. During May, the company had the following cash purchases and sales for its Model 25 digital camera:

| | Purchases | | | Sales | |
|---|---|---|---|---|---|
| Date | Units | Unit Cost | | Units | Unit Price |
| May 1 | 5 | $ 90 | | | |
| 4 | | | | 2 | $195 |
| 8 | 4 | 99 | | | |
| 12 | | | | 4 | 225 |
| 15 | 3 | 103 | | | |
| 20 | | | | 2 | 245 |
| 25 | | | | 2 | 245 |

*Instructions*

(a) Determine the cost of goods sold and ending inventory under a perpetual inventory system using (1) FIFO and (2) average cost.
(b) Prepare all required journal entries using (1) FIFO and (2) average cost.
(c) Calculate gross profit using (1) FIFO and (2) average cost.
(d) Which cost flow assumption produces (1) the higher ending inventory valuation, (2) the higher gross profit, and (3) the higher cash flow?
(e) What factors should the owner of Reliable Electronic Mart consider when choosing a cost flow assumption?

Apply perpetual and
periodic average cost flow
assumption. Prepare
partial income statement.
(SO 2, 3, 6) AP

*P6–10A  Yuan Company uses the perpetual inventory system. Assume that all transactions are settled in cash. You are provided with the following information for Yuan Company for the month of January 2005:

| Date | | Description | Units | Unit Price |
|---|---|---|---|---|
| Jan. | 1 | Beginning inventory | 125 | $17 |
| | 2 | Purchase | 100 | 21 |
| | 6 | Sale | 175 | 40 |
| | 9 | Purchase | 50 | 24 |
| | 15 | Sale | 75 | 45 |
| | 23 | Purchase | 110 | 28 |

*Instructions*

(a) Calculate the ending inventory and cost of goods sold using the average cost flow assumption.
(b) Prepare all required journal entries using average cost.
(c) Prepare a partial income statement to gross profit using average cost.
(d) Yuan Company is considering changing to a periodic inventory system. Repeat (a), (b), and (c) above using the average cost flow assumption in a periodic inventory system.

(e) Compare the ending inventory and cost of goods sold using the average cost flow assumption in a perpetual system and in a periodic system. Are the numbers the same or different? Explain why.

*P6–11A* Chung Company lost all of its inventory in a fire on December 28, 2005. The accounting records showed the following gross profit data for November and December:

Determine inventory loss using gross profit method. (SO 7) AP

|  | November | December (to 12/28) |
|---|---|---|
| Net sales | $500,000 | $600,000 |
| Beginning inventory | 22,700 | 26,270 |
| Purchases | 325,745 | 390,235 |
| Purchase returns and allowances | 11,700 | 12,900 |
| Freight in | 4,573 | 4,100 |
| Ending inventory | 26,270 | ? |

Chung is fully insured for fire losses but must prepare a report for the insurance company.

**Instructions**

Determine the amount of inventory lost by Chung as a result of the fire.

*P6–12A* Varocher's Book Store uses the retail inventory method to estimate its monthly ending inventories. The following information is available at October 31, 2005:

Determine ending inventory using retail method. (SO 7) AP

|  | Cost | Retail |
|---|---|---|
| Beginning inventory | $ 275,000 | $ 423,000 |
| Purchases | 1,180,000 | 1,800,000 |
| Purchase returns and allowances | 23,600 | 36,000 |
| Freight in | 5,000 |  |
| Sales |  | 1,845,000 |
| Sales returns and allowances | 27,000 |  |

**Instructions**

(a) Determine the estimated cost of the ending inventory at October 31, 2005, using the retail inventory method.

(b) Assume Varocher took a physical inventory count on October 31 at selling prices that totalled $363,500. Calculate the store's loss from theft and other causes, at retail and at cost.

*P6–13A* Country Lace Clothing Company has a periodic inventory system and uses the gross profit method to estimate inventories for monthly financial statements. The business has had an average gross profit margin of 30% for the last five years. It performs a physical count of inventory every March 31, the company's fiscal year end. Data for the year ended March 31, 2005, are presented below:

Determine ending inventory using gross profit method and comment. Prepare partial income statement. (SO 7) AP

| Inventory, March 31, 2004 | $ 63,000 | Sales | $312,000 |
|---|---|---|---|
| Purchases | 200,000 | Sales returns and allowances | 13,000 |
| Purchase returns and allowances | 6,000 | Inventory, March 31, 2005 | 56,000 |
| Freight in | 10,000 |  |  |

**Instructions**

(a) Prepare a partial income statement to gross profit and calculate the actual gross profit margin for the year ended March 31, 2005.

(b) Use the gross profit method to estimate the March 31, 2005, inventory. Compare this amount to the actual inventory and comment on your findings.

(c) The owner of Country Lace is considering investing in a perpetual inventory system. Would you recommend this or not? Why?

# Problems: Set B

Determine items and
amounts to be recorded in
inventory.
(SO 1) AN

**P6–1B** Banff Company is trying to determine the value of its ending inventory as at February 28, 2005, the company's year end. The accountant counted everything that was in the warehouse as at February 28, which resulted in an ending inventory valuation of $48,000. However, she didn't know how to treat the following transactions, so she didn't record them:

1. On February 26, Banff shipped goods costing $800 to a customer. The goods were shipped FOB shipping point. The receiving report indicates that the customer received the goods on March 2.
2. On February 27, Wah Company shipped goods to Banff, FOB destination. The invoice price was $350 plus $25 for freight. The receiving report indicates that the goods were received by Banff on March 2.
3. Banff had $620 of inventory at a customer's warehouse "on approval." The customer was going to let Banff know whether it wanted the merchandise by the end of the week, March 7.
4. Banff also had $570 of inventory on consignment at a Jasper craft shop.
5. On February 25, Banff ordered goods costing $750. The goods were shipped FOB shipping point on February 27. The receiving report indicates that Banff received the goods on March 1.
6. On February 28, Banff packaged goods and moved them to the shipping department for shipping to a customer, FOB destination. The invoice price was $425 plus $20 for freight. The cost of the items was $360. The receiving report indicates that the goods were received by the customer on March 2.
7. Banff had damaged goods set aside in the warehouse because they were not saleable. These goods originally cost $400. Banff initially expected to sell these items for $600.
8. On February 20, Banff Company had received $875 of inventory on consignment from Kananaskis Company. By February 28, Banff Company had sold $365 of this inventory for Kananaskis.
9. On February 28, Banff was holding merchandise that had been sold to a customer on February 25 but needed some engraving completed before the customer would take possession. The customer has paid for the goods and will pick them up on March 3 after the engraving is finished. This inventory cost $940 and was sold for $1,340.

*Instructions*

(a) For each of the above transactions, specify whether the item in question should be included in ending inventory, and if so, at what amount. Explain your reasoning.
(b) How much is the revised ending inventory valuation?

Apply periodic cost flow
assumptions. Prepare
income statement and
answer questions.
(SO 2, 3) AN

**P6–2B** Savita Company had a beginning inventory on January 1, 2005, of 100 units of product E2-D2 at a cost of $16 per unit. During the year, purchases were as follows:

|          | Units | Unit Cost |
|----------|-------|-----------|
| Feb. 20  | 350   | $18       |
| May  5   | 600   | 20        |
| Aug. 12  | 300   | 21        |
| Dec.  8  | 150   | 22        |

Savita uses a periodic inventory system. At the end of the year there were 225 units on hand.

*Instructions*

(a) Determine the cost of goods available for sale.
(b) Determine the (1) cost of goods sold and (2) ending inventory under each of the three cost flow assumptions: (1) FIFO, (2) average, and (3) LIFO.
(c) Savita Company sold product E2-D2 for $37 per unit and operating costs were $9 per unit sold. Prepare an income statement for each of the three cost flow assumptions.
(d) What cost flow assumption do you recommend that Savita use if it needs to give its financial statements to the bank as part of a loan application? Explain.
(e) Will one cost flow assumption consistently provide a higher net income than the other two assumptions? Explain. If not, can Savita Company choose a different cost flow assumption each year in order to always have the highest possible net income? Explain.

**P6–3B** The management of Tumatoe Company asks for your help in determining the comparative effects of the FIFO and average periodic inventory cost flow assumptions. For 2005, the accounting records show the following data:

Calculate ending inventory using periodic FIFO and average cost. Prepare income statements, and answer questions.
(SO 2, 3) AN

| | |
|---|---|
| Inventory, January 1 (10,000 units) | $ 35,000 |
| Cost of 110,000 units purchased | 462,500 |
| Selling price of 95,000 units sold | 665,000 |
| Operating expenses | 120,000 |

Units purchased consisted of 40,000 units at $4.00 on May 10; 50,000 units at $4.25 on August 15; and 20,000 units at $4.50 on November 20.

*Instructions*

(a) Prepare condensed income statements for 2005 under FIFO and average cost.

(b) Write a business letter which answers the following questions for management:
   1. Which inventory cost flow assumption produces the more meaningful inventory amount for the balance sheet? Why?
   2. Which inventory cost flow assumption produces the more meaningful net income? Why?
   3. Which inventory cost flow assumption is more likely to approximate the actual physical flow of the goods? Why?
   4. How much more cash would be available to management under average cost than under FIFO? Why?
   5. What factors should influence management's choice of cost flow assumption?

**P6–4B** You are provided with the following information concerning the transactions for Schwinghamer Co. Schwinghamer purchases all items from Pataki Co. and makes sales to a variety of customers. All transactions are settled in cash. Returns are normally not damaged and are restored immediately to inventory for resale. Both companies use a periodic inventory system and the FIFO cost flow assumption.

Journalize transactions for purchaser and seller using periodic FIFO. Apply lower of cost and market.
(SO 2, 3, 5) AP

### SCHWINGHAMER CO.

| Date | Transaction | Units | Unit Price |
|---|---|---|---|
| Oct. 1 | Beginning inventory | 60 | $15 |
| 5 | Purchase | 120 | 14 |
| 8 | Sale | 150 | 24 |
| 10 | Sale return | 25 | 24 |
| 15 | Purchase | 40 | 13 |
| 16 | Purchase return | 5 | 13 |
| 20 | Sale | 75 | 18 |
| 25 | Purchase | 10 | 11 |

*Instructions*

(a) Prepare the required journal entries for the month of October for Schwinghamer Co., the purchaser.

(b) Prepare the required journal entries for the month of October for Pataki Co., the seller, to record the purchases made by Schwinghamer.

(c) Determine the ending inventory amount for Schwinghamer, using the FIFO cost flow assumption.

(d) By October 31, Schwinghamer Co. learns that the product has a net realizable value of $10 per unit. What amount should ending inventory be valued at on the October 31 balance sheet? Discuss the accounting concept that is relevant in making this decision.

(e) What impact will the application of this concept have on Shwinghamer's net income?

**P6–5B** Chandra Company maintains its inventory records on a periodic basis. At the end of 2004, the ending inventory was overstated by $25,000 by including inventory that had been sold but not yet shipped. The inventory was properly stated at the end of 2005.

Indicate effect of errors and identify cost flow assumptions.
(SO 3, 4) AN

*Instructions*

(a) Indicate the effect of the error (overstatement, understatement, or no effect) on the following:
   1. Cost of goods sold for each of 2004 and 2005
   2. Net income for each of 2004 and 2005
   3. 2004 and 2005 combined income

4. Assets for each of 2004 and 2005
5. Owner's equity for each of 2004 and 2005
6. Inventory turnover for each of 2004 and 2005

(b) Identify the inventory cost flow assumption most closely related to each of the following statements, assuming a period of rising prices:
1. It understates current value on a balance sheet.
2. It matches recent costs against revenue.
3. It results in a balance sheet inventory value closest to replacement cost.
4. It smooths out the effect of price fluctuations.

**Illustrate impact of inventory errors. Calculate inventory turnover.**
**(SO 4, 5) AN**

**P6–6B** The records of Pelletier Company show the following data:

| Account | 2003 | 2004 | 2005 |
|---|---|---|---|
| Sales | $300,000 | $330,000 | $350,000 |
| Beginning inventory | 25,000 | 27,000 | 46,000 |
| Cost of goods purchased | 250,000 | 260,000 | 320,000 |
| Ending inventory | 27,000 | 46,000 | 50,000 |
| Operating expenses | 55,000 | 60,000 | 63,000 |

Subsequent to its July 31, 2005, year end, Pelletier discovered two errors:
1. Ending inventory in 2003 was understated by $3,000.
2. The cost of goods purchased for the year ended July 31, 2005, included $25,000 of merchandise that should have been recorded as a purchase in the year ended July 31, 2004.

*Instructions*

(a) Prepare both incorrect and corrected income statements for the years ended July 31, 2003, 2004, and 2005.
(b) What is the combined effect of the errors at July 31, 2005, before correction?
(c) Calculate both the correct and the incorrect inventory turnover ratios for 2003, 2004, and 2005.

**Calculate ratios and comment.**
**(SO 5) AN**

**P6–7B** The following information (in thousands) is available for Markham-based **CoolBrands International Inc.** for the years ended August 31:

| | 2002 | 2001 | 2000 |
|---|---|---|---|
| Cost of goods sold | $129,246 | $98,190 | $47,569 |
| Inventory | 25,361 | 16,539 | 7,047 |
| Current assets | 131,839 | 93,937 | 57,104 |
| Current liabilities | 74,485 | 50,529 | 27,051 |

The industry averages for the inventory turnover, days sales in inventory, and current ratios are as follows:

| | 2002 | 2001 |
|---|---|---|
| Inventory turnover | 8 times | 12 times |
| Days sales in inventory | 45.6 days | 30.4 days |
| Current ratio | 1.42:1 | 1.35:1 |

*Instructions*

(a) Calculate the inventory turnover, days sales in inventory, and current ratios for 2002 and 2001. Comment on CoolBrands' liquidity.
(b) CoolBrands uses FIFO to determine the cost of its inventory. If prices are rising, how would you expect the inventory turnover, days sales in inventory, and current ratios to change (e.g., increase or decrease) if CoolBrands used LIFO instead of FIFO?

**\*P6–8B** You are provided with the following information for Danielle Company for the month ended June 30, 2004:

Apply perpetual cost flow assumptions. Calculate gross profit.
(SO 6) AP

| Date | Description | Units | Unit Price |
|---|---|---|---|
| June 1 | Beginning inventory | 25 | $60 |
| 4 | Purchase | 85 | 64 |
| 10 | Sale | 90 | 90 |
| 18 | Purchase | 35 | 68 |
| 25 | Sale | 50 | 95 |
| 26 | Sale return | 5 | 95 |
| 28 | Purchase | 20 | 72 |

Danielle Company uses a perpetual inventory system.

*Instructions*

(a) Calculate the ending inventory and cost of goods sold using FIFO, average, and LIFO cost flow assumptions.
(b) Calculate and compare the gross profit earned by Danielle using each of the three cost flow assumptions.
(c) How would the results of the three alternatives change if Danielle had experienced declining prices when purchasing additional inventory?

**\*P6–9B** The Grinder Company sells a variety of skateboards and accessories. Below is information for Grinder's purchases and sales of GrindKing, one of its top brands of skateboards, during April 2005:

Calculate and journalize perpetual FIFO and average cost. Answer questions about financial statement effects.
(SO 3, 6) AN

| Date | Purchases Units | Purchases Unit Cost | Sales Units | Sales Unit Price |
|---|---|---|---|---|
| Apr. 1 | 26 | $198 | | |
| 5 | | | 12 | $299 |
| 12 | 56 | 202 | | |
| 16 | | | 50 | 299 |
| 19 | 47 | 204 | | |
| 22 | | | 62 | 309 |
| 26 | 32 | 205 | | |

Grinder uses a perpetual inventory system. All purchases and sales are on account.

*Instructions*

(a) Determine the cost of goods sold and ending inventory under a perpetual inventory system using (1) FIFO and (2) average cost.
(b) Prepare all required journal entries using (1) FIFO and (2) average cost.
(c) Calculate gross profit using (1) FIFO and (2) average cost.
(d) Which cost flow assumption produces (1) the higher ending inventory valuation, (2) the higher gross profit, and (3) the higher cash flow?
(e) What factors should the owner of Grinder consider when choosing a cost flow assumption?

**\*P6–10B** Matthew Company uses the perpetual inventory system. Assume that all transactions are settled in cash. You are provided with the following information for Matthew Company for the month of January 2005:

Apply perpetual and periodic FIFO cost flow assumption. Prepare partial income statement.
(SO 2, 3, 6) AP

| Date | Description | Units | Unit Price |
|---|---|---|---|
| Jan. 1 | Beginning inventory | 25 | $12 |
| 5 | Purchase | 125 | 14 |
| 7 | Sale | 110 | 25 |
| 14 | Purchase | 30 | 16 |
| 20 | Sale | 60 | 25 |
| 25 | Purchase | 20 | 18 |

*Instructions*

(a) Calculate the ending inventory and cost of goods sold using the FIFO cost flow assumption.
(b) Prepare all required journal entries using FIFO.
(c) Prepare a partial income statement to gross profit using FIFO.
(d) Matthew Company is considering changing to a periodic inventory system. Repeat (a), (b), and (c) above using the FIFO cost flow assumption in a periodic inventory system.
(e) Compare the ending inventory and cost of goods sold using FIFO in a perpetual system to FIFO in a periodic system. Are the numbers the same or different? Explain why.

Determine inventory loss using gross profit method. (SO 7) AP

*P6–11B** Thierry Company lost 80% of its inventory in a fire on March 23, 2005. The accounting records showed the following gross profit data for February and March:

| | February | March (to 3/23) |
|---|---|---|
| Sales | $325,000 | $292,500 |
| Sales returns and allowances | 6,500 | 5,850 |
| Purchases | 218,000 | 196,000 |
| Purchase returns and allowances | 4,360 | 3,920 |
| Freight in | 3,270 | 2,940 |
| Beginning inventory | 17,500 | 25,200 |
| Ending inventory | 25,200 | ? |

Thierry is fully insured for fire losses but must prepare a report for the insurance company.

*Instructions*

Determine both the estimated total inventory and the inventory lost in the March fire.

Determine ending inventory using retail method. (SO 7) AP

*P6–12B** Lincoln Department Store uses the retail inventory method to estimate its monthly ending inventories. The following information is available for two of its departments at August 31, 2005:

| | Clothing | | Jewellery and Cosmetics | |
|---|---|---|---|---|
| | Cost | Retail | Cost | Retail |
| Sales | | $1,375,000 | | $895,000 |
| Sales returns and allowances | | 27,000 | | 5,400 |
| Purchases | $770,000 | 1,440,000 | $560,000 | 918,000 |
| Purchase returns and allowances | 36,000 | 65,500 | 12,200 | 19,700 |
| Freight in | 7,900 | | 5,700 | |
| Beginning inventory | 50,600 | 92,000 | 29,000 | 48,000 |

At December 31, Lincoln Department Store takes a physical inventory count at retail. The actual retail values of the inventories in each department on August 31, 2005, are as follows: Clothing $116,250 and Jewellery and Cosmetics $54,300.

*Instructions*

(a) Determine the estimated cost of the ending inventory for each department on August 31, 2005, using the retail inventory method.
(b) Calculate the store's loss on August 31, 2005, from theft and other causes, at retail and at cost.

Determine ending inventory using retail method and comment. Prepare partial income statement. (SO 7) AP

*P6–13B** Outback Clothing Company has a periodic inventory system and uses the retail method to estimate inventories at cost for financial statements. It performs a physical count of inventory every January 31, the company's fiscal year end. Data for the year ended January 31, 2005, are presented below:

| | Cost | Retail |
|---|---|---|
| Sales | | $710,000 |
| Sales returns and allowances | | 14,200 |
| Purchases | $443,300 | 715,000 |
| Purchase returns and allowances | 7,200 | 11,600 |
| Freight in | 12,800 | |
| Inventory, January 31, 2004 | 39,875 | 72,500 |

*Instructions*

(a) Use the retail method to estimate the January 31, 2005, inventory at cost and at retail.
(b) The physical inventory count at January 31, 2005, at retail prices was $70,400. Compare this to the estimated inventory and comment on your findings.
(c) Prepare a partial income statement to gross profit and calculate the gross profit margin for the year ended January 31, 2005.
(d) The owner of Outback Clothing is considering investing in a perpetual inventory system. Would you recommend this or not? Why?

# Continuing Cookie Chronicle

(*Note*: This is a continuation of the Cookie Chronicle from Chapters 1 through 5.)

Natalie is busy establishing both divisions of her business (cookie classes and mixer sales) and completing her business diploma. She has decided to concentrate her efforts on mixers for the next while, and try to sell at least one mixer a month.

The cost of the fine European mixers is expected to increase. Natalie has just negotiated new terms with Kzinski that include shipping costs in the negotiated purchase price (mixers will be shipped FOB destination). The invoice price will also be in Canadian dollars, which means Kzinski cannot guarantee the invoice price. It will depend on the foreign exchange rate when Kzinski prepares its invoices for Cookie Creations (Kzinski sets its mixer price in Euros). Natalie must choose a cost flow assumption for her mixer inventory.

The following transactions occur in February to May, 2005:

Feb. 2 Natalie buys two deluxe mixers on account from Kzinski Supply Co. for $1,100 ($550 each), FOB destination, terms n/30.
16 She sells one deluxe mixer for $1,050 cash.
25 She pays the amount owing to Kzinski.
Mar. 2 She buys one deluxe mixer on account from Kzinski Supply Co. for $567, FOB destination, terms n/30.
30 Natalie sells two deluxe mixers for a total of $2,100 cash.
31 She pays the amount owing to Kzinski.
Apr. 1 She buys two deluxe mixers on account from Kzinski Supply Co. for $1,122 ($561 each), FOB destination, terms n/30.
13 She sells three deluxe mixers for a total of $3,150 cash.
30 Natalie pays the amounts owing to Kzinski.
May 4 She buys three deluxe mixers on account from Kzinski Supply Co. for $1,720 ($573.33 each), FOB destination, terms n/30.
27 She sells one deluxe mixer for $1,050 cash.

*Instructions*

(a) Using the FIFO cost flow assumption in a perpetual inventory system, prepare a schedule to track the purchases and sales, and the balance of the mixers inventory account. Use the format from Illustration 6A-1. Recall from Chapter 5 that at the end of January, Cookie Creations had three mixers on hand at a cost of $545 each.
(b) From the information gathered in (a), prepare journal entries for each of the transactions.
(c) Using the average cost flow assumption in a perpetual inventory system, prepare a schedule to track the purchases and sales, and the balance of the mixers inventory account. Use the format from Illustration 6A-2. Recall from Chapter 5 that at the end of January, Cookie Creations had three mixers on hand at a cost of $545 each.
(d) From the information gathered in (c), prepare journal entries for each of the transactions.
(e) Natalie is thinking of getting a bank loan. If this is the only factor Natalie has to consider in choosing an inventory cost flow assumption, which cost flow assumption would you recommend Natalie use? Why?

# Financial Reporting and Analysis

Practice
Tools

## Financial Reporting Problem

**BYP6–1**   Refer to the financial statements and Notes to Consolidated Financial Statements of **The Forzani Group Ltd.** in Appendix A.

*Instructions*

(a) How does Forzani value its inventory?
(b) Which inventory cost flow assumption does Forzani use? Is this cost flow assumption applied in a perpetual or periodic inventory system?
(c) Do you think that using a different cost flow assumption than the one identified in (b) above would materially affect Forzani's results? Explain.
(d) Calculate inventory as a percentage of current assets and cost of sales as a percentage of total revenue for 2003 and 2002. Comment on the results.
(e) Forzani's inventory turnover and days sales in inventory were calculated for fiscal 2003 in Illustrations 6-12 and 6-13. Calculate these same two ratios for fiscal 2002. Forzani's inventory at the end of fiscal 2001 was $157,923 thousand. Comment on whether Forzani's inventory management improved or deteriorated in 2003.

## Interpreting Financial Statements

**BYP6–2**   The following information was taken from the financial statements of **Indigo Books & Music Inc.** (in thousands):

|  | 2003 | 2002 | 2001 |
|---|---|---|---|
| Cost of product, purchasing, selling and administration | $737,228 | $698,660 | $729,800 |
| Inventories | 202,455 | 223,467 | 193,977 |

Additional information:

1. Inventories are valuated, using the retail inventory method, at the lower of cost and net realizable value less a normal profit margin.
2. The cost of product, purchasing, selling, and administration includes the following amounts for 2002 and 2001 (in thousands). This information was not separately disclosed in 2003:

|  | 2002 | 2001 |
|---|---|---|
| Provision for future markdowns | $ 2,876 | $24,722 |
| Inventory shrinkage | 23,988 | 28,600 |
|  | $26,864 | $53,322 |

The provision for future markdowns is for the required clearance of slow-moving, non-returnable inventory and a provision for damaged stock. Inventory shrinkage gives the actual experience during the period.

*Instructions*

(a) Calculate the percentage that the provision for future markdowns and inventory shrinkage is of the cost of product, purchasing, selling, and administration for the years 2002 and 2001. Comment on any trend.
(b) Calculate the company's inventory turnover and days sales in inventory ratios for 2003 and 2002. Use the cost of product, purchasing, selling, and administration as the cost of goods

sold. Comment on whether Indigo's inventory management improved or deteriorated in 2003.

(c) Indigo uses the retail inventory method to value its inventories. Indigo's main competitor, Amazon.Com, Inc., uses the FIFO cost flow assumption to value its inventories. Is one of these two methods more accurate than the other? Explain.

(d) Which company would have the better balance sheet valuation? Explain.

(e) Why would a company use the retail inventory method to value its inventory?

## Accounting on the Web

**BYP6–3** This problem uses an annual report to identify the inventory cost flow assumption and to calculate inventory ratios.

*Instructions*

Specific requirements of this Internet case are available on the Weygandt website.

# Critical Thinking

## Collaborative Learning Activity

**BYP6–4** Just-in-Time (JIT) Auto Parts manufactures auto parts. The company's inventories reported on its balance sheet at July 31, 2005, total $1,094.7 million. Assume that the following transactions occurred during July and August:

1. Office supplies were shipped to JIT Auto Parts by Office Maxx, FOB destination. The goods were shipped July 31 and received August 3.
2. JIT Auto Parts purchased specialty plastic from DuPont Canada for use in the manufacture of door mouldings. The goods were shipped FOB shipping point July 31 and received August 3.
3. Ford Motor Company of Canada, Limited, purchased 3,000 rear liftgate assemblies from JIT to be used in the manufacture of the Ford Windstar. They were shipped FOB shipping point July 29, and were received by Ford August 1.
4. Nadeau Furniture shipped office furniture to JIT Auto Parts, FOB destination, on July 27. The furniture was received August 3.
5. Inland Specialty Chemical shipped JIT Auto Parts chemicals that JIT uses in the manufacture of door mouldings and other items. The goods were sent FOB shipping point July 30 and received August 3.
6. JIT Auto Parts purchased new Cadillac Sevilles for its executives to drive. The cars were shipped FOB destination July 30 and received August 5.
7. JIT Auto Parts purchased steel, to be used in expanding its manufacturing plant, from IPSCO, FOB Regina (shipping point). The steel was shipped July 30, arrived in Ontario August 2, and at JIT Auto Parts' plant in Aurora on August 3.
8. JIT Auto Parts shipped instrument panels to Jaguar, FOB destination. The panels were shipped July 15 and arrived at Jaguar's headquarters in England August 7.

*Instructions*

With the class divided into groups, answer the following:

(a) Determine which of the above transactions affect JIT Auto Parts' inventory account. For each item that has an effect, would the transaction result in an increase or a decrease in the inventory account at July 31, 2005?

(b) For each transaction that does not affect JIT Auto Parts' inventory account, indicate who owns the relevant items and how they should be reported.

## Communication Activity

**BYP6–5** You are the controller of Small Toys. Mutahir Kazmi, the president, recently mentioned to you that he found an error in the 2004 financial statements that he believes has now corrected itself.

In discussions with the Purchasing Department, Mutahir determined that the 2004 ending inventory was understated by $1 million. However, the 2005 ending inventory is correct. Mutahir assumes that 2005 income is correct and comments to you, "What happened has happened—there's no point in worrying about it now."

*Instructions*

You conclude that Mutahir is wrong. Write a brief, tactful memo to him, clarifying the situation.

## Ethics Case

**BYP6–6** Discount Diamonds carries only one brand and size of diamond—all are identical. Each batch of diamonds purchased is carefully coded and marked with its purchase cost. The following data are available:

Mar.  1  Beginning inventory was 140 diamonds at a cost of $300 per diamond.
      3  Purchased 200 diamonds at a cost of $340 each.
      5  Sold 170 diamonds for $600 each.
    10  Purchased 340 diamonds at a cost of $370 each.
    25  Sold 500 diamonds for $650 each.

*Instructions*

(a) Assume that Discount Diamonds uses the specific identification method.
    1. Demonstrate how Discount Diamonds could maximize its gross profit for the month by selecting which diamonds to sell on March 5 and March 25.
    2. Demonstrate how Discount Diamonds could minimize its gross profit for the month by selecting which diamonds to sell on March 5 and March 25.
(b) Assume that Discount Diamonds uses the average cost flow assumption and a periodic inventory system. How much gross profit would Discount Diamonds report under this cost flow assumption?
(c) Who are the stakeholders in this situation? Is there anything unethical in choosing which diamonds to sell in a month?
(d) Which cost flow assumption should Discount Diamonds choose? Explain.

---

*Answers to Self-Study Questions*
1. d    2. a    3. b    4. d    5. c    6. b    7. a    8. c    *9. c    *10. b    *11. a

*Answer to Forzani Review It Question 5*
In Note 2 (b) to its financial statements, Forzani discloses that it uses the weighted average cost flow assumption.

Remember to go back to the Navigator Box at the beginning of the chapter to check off your completed work.

## concepts for review >>

Before studying this chapter, you should understand or, if necessary, review:

a. The role ethics play in financial reporting. (Ch. 1, p. 6)
b. How cash transactions are recorded. (Ch. 2, pp. 61–66)
c. How cash is classified on a balance sheet. (Ch. 4, pp. 167–168)

# Keeping Track of the Cash

CHARLOTTETOWN, P.E.I.—Located right in the heart of downtown Charlottetown, Beanz Espresso Bar is bustling with activity weekdays. On average, 1,200 customers stop by each day for its selection of specialty coffees, homemade soups, sandwiches, and baked goods. "Our back door leads into a federal government building, so we get a lot of office workers coming through," says owner Lori Kays, who launched the business with her husband and business partner Doug Hurry back in 1995. "But we really cater to every age group since we're open seven days a week."

Lunch is the busiest time for Beanz, which seats 65 on the main floor plus an additional 45 on its deck. The two cash registers are shared by the six staff members working behind the counter on any given shift. "In an ideal situation, one or two people would be designated to ring in orders, but when we get swamped, we all have to work together to keep things running smoothly," says Ms. Kays.

The prices of most items are pre-programmed in the machines, which reduces the chances of entry errors. Each register generates a sales report at the end of the day. Ms. Kays checks the day's cash receipts against the report to make sure they match. She also verifies the closing balances for the two floats—$250 for each till. "I tend to allow a few dollars' leeway since we round down amounts here and there when customers are short a few cents."

Any discrepancies beyond that and she goes through the register's internal tape to trace the source. "I will backtrack and try to make sure there weren't any payouts for which a receipt should have been turned in—we often make a run to the grocery store for something we need using cash from the till," she explains. "A lot of times it's just an item that's been rung in improperly."

Ms. Kays does all of her bookkeeping herself using Simply Accounting software. "I post my sales totals each day and reconcile everything with my bank statements once a month," she says. "At the end of every year, I do everything except the last few adjusting entries before sending things off to the accountants." Careful cash control throughout the year helps ensure everything adds up every time!

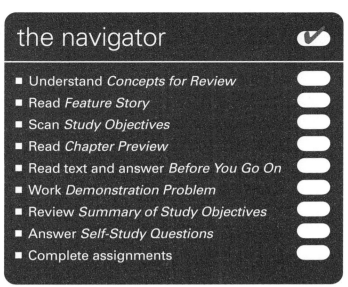

the navigator

- Understand *Concepts for Review*
- Read *Feature Story*
- Scan *Study Objectives*
- Read *Chapter Preview*
- Read text and answer *Before You Go On*
- Work *Demonstration Problem*
- Review *Summary of Study Objectives*
- Answer *Self-Study Questions*
- Complete assignments

chapter 7

# Internal Control and Cash

## study objectives >>

After studying this chapter, you should be able to:

1. Describe internal control.
2. Explain the principles of internal control and be able to identify weaknesses in their application and suggest improvements.
3. Explain and critique the application of internal control principles to cash receipts.
4. Explain and critique the application of internal control principles to cash disbursements.
5. Demonstrate the operation of a petty cash fund.
6. Describe the control features of a bank account.
7. Prepare a bank reconciliation.
8. Explain the reporting of cash.

As the feature story about Beanz Espresso Bar indicates, control of cash is important. Similarly, controls are needed to safeguard other types of assets. For example, Beanz Espresso Bar undoubtedly has controls to prevent the theft of food, computer equipment, and supplies.

In this chapter, we explain the essential features of an internal control system and describe how these controls apply to cash. The applications include some controls you may already be familiar with. Then we describe the use of a bank and explain how cash is reported on the balance sheet. The chapter is organized as follows:

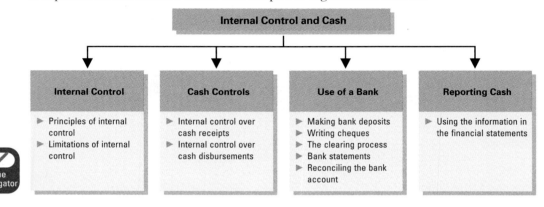

# Internal Control

**study objective 1**

Describe internal control.

Could there be dishonest employees where you work? Unfortunately, the answer sometimes is "Yes." The following real occurrences show this point well:

- The general accountant of a Canadian charity embezzled $2 million over a four-year period by diverting contributions into her personal bank account.
- The comptroller of a Canadian manufacturing company paid himself $2 million above his normal pay level by writing unauthorized cheques on the company's payroll account. He got rid of the cancelled cheques when they were returned from the bank and altered the books.
- An accounting clerk defrauded the Quebec Securities Commission of $600,000 over a four-year period. She intercepted cheques and deposited them in her own bank account.
- An assistant bank manager stole more than $10 million from a Toronto bank by making loans to fictitious companies.

These situations emphasize the need for a good system of internal control.

Internal control consists of the policies and procedures in an organization that help achieve the following objectives:

1. **Optimize the use of resources** to reduce inefficiencies and waste.
2. **Prevent and detect errors and irregularities** in the accounting process.
3. **Safeguard assets** from theft, robbery, and unauthorized use.
4. **Maintain reliable control systems** to enhance the accuracy and reliability of accounting records.

The importance of internal control to the efficient and effective operation of a business organization must not be underestimated. All federally incorporated companies are required, under the *Canada Business Corporations Act*, to maintain an adequate system of internal control. The CICA's Criteria of Control Board stresses that this internal control should address not only external financial reporting, but also the reliability of internal reporting.

**Helpful hint** Errors are unintentional mistakes. Irregularities are intentional mistakes and misrepresentations.

# Principles of Internal Control

To optimize resources, prevent and detect errors and irregularities, safeguard assets, and maintain reliable control systems, a company follows internal control principles. Of course, the specific control measures that are used depend on the size and nature of the business, and on management's control philosophy. However, the principles listed in Illustration 7-1 apply to most companies.

study objective 2

Explain the principles of internal control and be able to identify weaknesses in their application and suggest improvements.

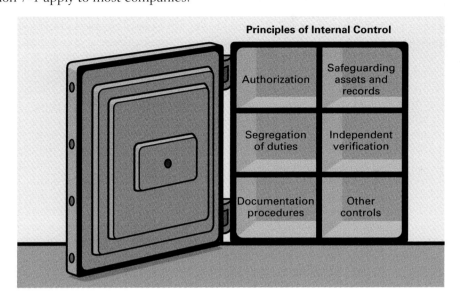

**Principles of Internal Control**

- Authorization
- Safeguarding assets and records
- Segregation of duties
- Independent verification
- Documentation procedures
- Other controls

**Illustration 7-1** ◀

Principles of internal control

These principles are explained in the following sections.

## Authorization of Transactions and Activities

Transactions and activities must be done, and approved, by the right individuals or departments. For example, the vice-president of finance should establish policies for making credit sales, not the vice-president of sales.

An essential characteristic of this internal control principle is the assignment of responsibility to specific employees. **Control is most effective when only one person is responsible for a task.** To illustrate, assume that the cash on hand at the end of the day at Beanz Espresso Bar in the feature story is $50 less than the cash recorded on the cash register. If only one person at the restaurant has operated the register, that person is likely responsible for the shortage. If two or more individuals have worked the register, as is the case when the restaurant is busy, it may be impossible to determine who is responsible for the error. Internal control would have been strengthened in this situation if each staff member had their own cash drawer. To identify any shortages quickly at the Beanz Espresso Bar, the owner, Lori Kays, checks the cash receipts against the cash register sales report at the end of each day.

## Segregation of Duties

Segregation of duties is essential in a system of internal control. There are two common applications of this principle:

1. Related activities should be assigned to different individuals.
2. Establishing the accountability (keeping the records) for an asset should be separate from the physical custody of that asset.

The rationale for segregation of duties is this: The work of one employee should, without a duplication of effort, provide a reliable basis for monitoring the work of another employee.

**Related Activities.**  Related activities that should be assigned to different individuals happen in both buying and selling. **When one individual is responsible for all of the related activities, the potential for errors and irregularities is increased.** Related purchasing activities include ordering merchandise, receiving the goods, and paying (or authorizing payment) for the merchandise. In purchasing, for example, orders could be placed with friends or with suppliers who give kickbacks. Or, only a cursory count and inspection could be made upon receiving the goods, which could lead to errors and/or acceptance of poor-quality merchandise. Payment might also be authorized without a careful review of the invoice. Even worse, fictitious invoices might be approved for payment. When the responsibility for ordering, receiving, and paying is assigned to different individuals, there is less risk of such abuses.

Similarly, related sales activities should be assigned to different individuals. Related selling activities include making a sale, shipping (or delivering) the goods to the customer, and billing the customer. When one person handles related sales transactions, a salesperson could make sales at unauthorized prices to increase sales commissions, a shipping clerk could ship goods to himself or herself, or a billing clerk could understate the amount billed for sales made to friends and relatives. These abuses are reduced by dividing the sales tasks: salespersons make the sale, shipping department employees ship the goods on the basis of the sales order, and billing department employees prepare the sales invoice after comparing the sales order with the report of goods shipped.

**Custody of Assets.**  To provide a valid basis of accountability for an asset, the accountant should not have physical custody of the asset or access to it. Similarly, the custodian of the asset should not maintain or have access to the accounting records. **When one employee (the accountant) keeps the records of an asset, and a different employee (the custodian) keeps the asset itself, the employee who keeps the asset is unlikely to use it dishonestly.** The separation of accounting responsibility from the custody of assets is especially important for cash and inventories, because these assets are vulnerable to unauthorized use or theft.

## Documentation Procedures

Documents provide evidence that transactions and events have happened. In the Beanz Espresso Bar, the cash register sales report and internal tape is the restaurant's documentation for a sale and the amount of cash received. Similarly, a shipping document indicates that goods have been shipped. A sales invoice indicates that the customer has been billed for the goods. Adding signatures (or initials) to the document(s) means that the individual(s) responsible for the transaction or event can be identified. Transactions should be documented when they happen. Documentation of events, such as those leading to adjusting or correcting entries, generally occurs when these entries are made.

Several procedures should be established for documents. First, whenever possible, **documents should be prenumbered and all documents should be accounted for.** Prenumbering helps to prevent a transaction from being recorded more than once. It also helps to prevent the transaction from not being recorded. Second, documents that are **source documents (the original receipts, etc.) for accounting entries should be promptly sent to the accounting department.** Thus, it helps to ensure timely recording of the transaction. This control measure contributes directly to the accuracy and reliability of the accounting records.

In an electronic accounting system, recording usually takes place automatically when an event happens. In these systems, special program controls are necessary to ensure the accuracy and reliability of data.

## Safeguarding Assets and Records

Physical controls are needed to adequately control access to, and use of, assets and records. Physical controls include mechanical and electronic controls to safeguard (protect) assets and enhance the accuracy and reliability of the accounting records. Examples of these controls are shown in Illustration 7-2.

**Physical Controls**

Illustration 7-2 ◄
Physical controls

Safes, vaults, and safety deposit boxes for cash and business papers

Locked warehouses and storage cabinets for inventories and records

Computer facilities with password or biometric access

Alarms to prevent break-ins

Television monitors and garment sensors to deter theft

Time clocks to record time worked

Program controls are built into computer systems to prevent intentional and unintentional errors and unauthorized access. To prevent unauthorized access, the computer system may require passwords to be entered and random personal questions to be correctly answered, or biometric controls such as fingerprint or retinal scans to be used, before system access is allowed. Once access has been allowed, other program controls validate calculations (math checks), detect an improper processing order (sequence checks), and identify data with, for example, a higher or lower value than a predetermined amount (limit checks).

### ACCOUNTING IN ACTION ► Ethics Insight

According to the 2001 *Canadian Retail Security Report*, retailers report that customer theft amounts to $3 million in losses a day. Theft by dishonest employees increases this figure by another $3 million a day and paperwork errors add nearly $2 million more.

Most retailers use physical controls to stem their losses. More than 90% now have loss prevention departments. Other measures include attaching security labels tor CDs and DVDs, preventing unauthorized access to computer equipment and data, using alarms and drop safes, employing mystery shoppers, and having more employee awareness programs.

*Source:* Retail Council of Canada, *2001 Canadian Retail Security Report.*

## Independent Verification

Most internal control systems include independent internal and/or external verification of performance and records. This means having someone else review, compare, and reconcile data. To obtain maximum benefit from independent verification:

1. The verification should be done periodically or on a surprise basis.
2. The verification should be done by someone who is independent of the employee responsible for the information.
3. Discrepancies and exceptions should be reported to a management level that can take corrective action.

**Internal Verification.**  Independent internal verification is especially useful when comparing the accounting records with existing assets. In the feature story, the reconciliation of the cash register sales report with the cash in the register by owner Lori Kays is an example of this internal control principle. Another common example is the reconciliation by an independent person of the cash balance according to the books with the cash balance according to the bank. We will learn about bank reconciliations later in this chapter.

In large companies, independent internal verification is often monitored by internal auditors. **Internal auditors** are company employees who continuously evaluate the effectiveness of the company's system of internal control. They periodically review the activities of departments and individuals to determine whether prescribed internal controls are being followed. They also recommend improvements. The importance of this function is illustrated by the fact that most fraud is discovered by a company through internal mechanisms, such as existing internal controls and internal audits. The alleged fraud at WorldCom, involving billions of dollars, for example, was uncovered by an internal auditor.

In smaller companies that lack an internal audit division, segregated functions are more important to ensure that the company's internal control objectives are still achieved. If the company is very small, such segregation may not be possible at all, or only possible to a limited extent. In such cases, the owner usually assumes responsibility for, or oversees, incompatible functions such as authorization and access to assets.

**External Verification.**  It is useful to contrast independent *internal* verification with independent external verification. **External auditors**, in contrast to internal auditors, are **independent** of the company. They are professional accountants and are hired by a company to report on whether or not the company's financial statements fairly present its financial position and results of operations. As part of the evaluation, they also examine internal control.

## Other Controls

Other control measures include the following:
1. **Bonding of employees who handle cash.** Bonding means obtaining insurance protection against misappropriation of assets by dishonest employees. This measure contributes to the safeguarding of cash in two ways: First, the insurance company carefully screens all individuals before adding them to the policy and may reject risky applicants. Second, bonded employees know that the insurance company will vigorously prosecute all offenders.
2. **Rotating employees' duties and requiring employees to take vacations.** These measures are designed to discourage employees from attempting any thefts since they will not be able to permanently conceal their improper actions. Many bank embezzlements, for example, have been discovered when the perpetrator was on vacation or assigned to a new position.

## Limitations of Internal Control

A company's system of internal control is generally designed to provide reasonable assurance that resources are optimized, errors and irregularities are detected, assets are properly safeguarded, and accounting records are reliable. **The concept of reasonable assurance is based on the belief that the costs of establishing control procedures should not exceed their expected benefit.**

To illustrate, consider shoplifting losses in retail stores. Such losses could be eliminated by having a security guard stop and search customers as they leave the store. Store managers have concluded, however, that the negative effects of adopting such a procedure cannot be justified. Instead, stores have attempted to control shoplifting losses by less extreme procedures such as (1) posting signs that state "We reserve the right to inspect all packages" and "All shoplifters will be prosecuted," (2) using hidden TV cameras and store detectives to monitor customer activity, and (3) using sensor equipment at exits.

The **human element** is an important factor in every system of internal control. A good system can become ineffective as a result of employee fatigue, carelessness, or indifference. For example, a receiving clerk may not bother to count goods received, or may just "fudge" the counts.

Occasionally, two or more individuals may work together to get around controls. Such **collusion** reduces the effectiveness of a system because it eliminates the protection offered by segregation of duties. If a supervisor and a cashier collaborate to understate cash receipts, the system of internal control may be beaten (at least in the short run).

The size of the business may also impose limitations on internal control. As mentioned earlier, in small companies it may be difficult to segregate duties or to provide independent internal verification. In these cases, independent external verification is even more important to provide the necessary assurance.

Computer systems provide unique internal control problems. In many instances, computerization has shifted the responsibility for internal control to programmers and end-users. For example, in point-of-sale systems, accountants are not required to record daily transactions. The computer automatically records the transaction when the cashier or clerk makes the sale. It is especially important to maintain effective control over authorization, documentation, and access in computerized systems.

### ACCOUNTING IN ACTION ► @–Business

Unfortunately, computer-related frauds are a major concern. The average computer crime loss is nearly $1 million, compared with an average loss of only $30,000 resulting from other types of white-collar crime.

Computer fraud can be perpetrated almost invisibly and done with electronic speed. Psychologically, stealing using an impersonal computer seems far less criminal than other crimes to some people. Therefore, the moral threshold to commit computer fraud is lower than for fraud involving a person-to-person interaction. Nonetheless, computer crime is still illegal and the *Criminal Code of Canada* and the *Copyright Act* contain provisions to deal with computer crimes.

## BEFORE YOU GO ON . . .

### ►Review It

1. What are the four objectives of internal control?
2. Identify and describe the principles of internal control.
3. What are the limitations of internal control?

### ►Do It

Li Song owns a small retail store. Li wants to establish good internal control procedures but is confused about the difference between segregation of duties and independent internal verification. Explain the differences to Li.

#### Action Plan

• Understand and explain the differences between (1) segregation of duties and (2) independent internal verification.

#### Solution

Segregation of duties involves assigning responsibility so that the work of one employee checks the work of another employee. Segregation of duties happens daily in executing and recording transactions. In contrast, independent internal verification in a small retail store would likely require

Li Song to take an active role in reviewing, comparing, and reconciling data prepared by one or several employees. Independent internal verification occurs after the fact, as in the case of reconciling cash register totals at the end of the day with cash on hand.

*Related exercise material:* BE7–1.

# Cash Controls

Just as cash is the beginning of a company's operating cycle, it is also usually the starting point for a company's system of internal control. Cash is easily concealed and transported, lacks owner identification, and is highly desirable. Because of these characteristics, cash is prone to theft or misuse. In fact, the Association of Certified Fraud Examiners reports that cash is the asset targeted for theft 90% of the time. In addition, because of the large volume of cash transactions, many errors can happen when handling and recording cash. To safeguard cash and ensure the accuracy of the accounting records, effective internal control over cash is essential.

**Cash** consists of coins, currency (paper money), cheques, money orders, travellers' cheques, and money on deposit in a bank or similar depository. The general rule is that if the bank will accept it for deposit, it is cash. Debit card transactions and bank credit card slips, such as Visa and MasterCard, are cash but nonbank (e.g., Diner's Club) credit card slips are not. (We will learn more about accounting for debit and credit card transactions in Chapter 8). Cheques that are postdated (payable in the future), staledated (more than six months old), or NSF (not sufficient funds) are not cash. Postage stamps and IOUs from employees are not cash either, because these items are not acceptable at face value on deposit.

In the following sections, we explain the application of internal control principles to cash receipts and disbursements.

## Internal Control over Cash Receipts

**study objective 3**

Explain and critique the application of internal control principles to cash receipts.

Cash receipts come from a variety of sources: cash sales; collections on account from customers; the receipt of interest, dividends, and rents; investments by owners; bank loans; and proceeds from the sale of property, plant, and equipment. Illustration 7-3 shows how the internal control principles explained earlier apply to cash receipt transactions.

As might be expected, companies vary considerably in how they apply these principles. To illustrate internal control over cash receipts, we will examine manual control measures for a retail store with over-the-counter, mail-in, and electronic receipts. These same control measures can be adapted for smaller retail stores. However, as noted previously, the owner or manager must take a more active role because there are fewer people among whom the responsibilities can be divided.

### Over-the-Counter Receipts

Control of over-the-counter receipts in retail businesses is centred on cash registers that are visible to customers. A cash sale should be "rung up" on a cash register **with the amount clearly visible to the customer.** This measure prevents the cashier from entering a lower amount. The customer receives an itemized cash register receipt and, if paying with cash, is expected to count the change received.

## Internal Control over Cash Receipts

**Illustration 7-3 ◀**

Application of internal control principles to cash receipts

### Authorization

Only designated personnel (cashiers) are authorized to handle cash receipts.

### Safeguarding Assets and Records

Store cash in safes and bank vaults; limit access to storage areas; use cash registers.

### Segregation of Duties

Different individuals receive cash, record cash receipts, and hold the cash.

### Independent Verification

Supervisors count cash receipts daily; comptroller's office compares total receipts to bank deposits daily.

### Documentation Procedures

Use remittance advices (mail receipts), cash register tapes, and deposit slips.

### Other Controls

Bond personnel who handle cash; require employees to take vacations; deposit all cash in a bank daily.

Actual cash payments are rare today. Most customers pay by debit or credit card. What's the difference between a debit card and a credit card? A debit card gives customers access to the money in their own bank accounts. A credit card gives customers access to money made available by a bank or other financial institution (essentially a short-term loan which has to be repaid). As soon as a debit card or a bank credit card is swiped, the bank immediately deposits the authorized amount into the retailer's bank account. At the same time, a two-part receipt is issued, with one copy for the customer and the other for the company.

Most companies track the different types of receipts automatically through their point-of-sale cash register system. That is, daily sales are listed by cash, debit card, credit card, cheque, or other payment type on the cash register tape.

A cash register tape is locked into the register until removed by a supervisor or manager. This tape accumulates the daily transactions and totals. At the end of the day (or shift, in some cases), the tape total is compared to the amount of cash and other payment evidence (e.g., debit and credit card slips) in the register. The findings are reported on a cash count sheet that is signed by both the cashier and the supervisor or manager. The count sheet should then be sent to the accounting department for matching with documentation prepared by the head cashier.

The register tapes, cash, and other documentation are then given to the head cashier, who prepares a daily cash summary that shows the total cash and other types of payment received, and the amount from each source. The head cashier sends one copy of the summary to the accounting department for entry into the journal.

The other copy of the daily cash summary goes to the comptroller's office, where it will later be compared with the daily bank deposit.

Next, the head cashier prepares a deposit slip for the cash received and makes the bank deposit. The total amount deposited should be equal to the total cash receipts reported on the daily cash summary. This will ensure that all cash receipts have been placed in the custody of the bank. A fundamental control over cash receipts occurs when **all cash receipts are deposited daily, intact, into the bank account.**

The Beanz Espresso Bar in the feature story violates this fundamental control when it uses cash directly from the cash register to pay for grocery store purchases. This makes it much more difficult to ensure that all revenues and expenses are recorded. In a later section in this chapter, we'll learn how a petty cash system improves internal control over small cash expenditures and ensures that cash receipts remain intact for depositing and recording.

Although some bank deposits are made to ABMs or through electronic funds transfers, a significant number are still deposited personally by an authorized employee. When the bank accepts a face-to-face bank deposit, it stamps (authenticates) the duplicate deposit slip. This deposit slip is returned to the company comptroller or an appointed designate, who then makes the comparison with the daily cash summary.

Often companies with recurring cash transactions use a special journal, called a **cash receipts journal**, to record all receipts of cash. A **special journal** is used to record similar types of transactions. The type of special journals used depends largely on the types of transactions that happen frequently. Special journals are illustrated in Appendix C at the end of this textbook.

## Mail-In Receipts

**Helpful hint**   When billing customers, many companies state "Pay by cheque; do not send cash through the mail." This is designed to reduce the risk that cash receipts will be misappropriated when received.

As an individual customer, you may be more familiar with over-the-counter receipts than with mail-in receipts. However, many companies receive payment from billings and credit sales through the mail. Think, for example, of the number of cheques received through the mail daily by a national retailer such as Sears.

All mail-in receipts should be opened in the presence of two mail clerks. These receipts are generally in the form of cheques. They are frequently accompanied by a remittance advice that states the purpose of the cheque (sometimes attached to the cheque, but often a part of the bill that the customer tears off and returns). Each cheque should be promptly stamped "For Deposit Only." This restrictive endorsement reduces the chances of the cheque being put to personal use. With this type of endorsement, banks will not give cash to an individual.

A list of the cheques received each day should be prepared in duplicate. This list shows the name of the issuer of the cheque, the purpose of the payment, and the amount of the cheque. Each mail clerk should sign the list to establish responsibility for the data. The original copy of the list, along with the cheques and remittance advices, is then sent to the cashier's department. There, the cheques are added to over-the-counter receipts (if any) when the daily cash summary and the daily bank deposit are prepared. In addition, a copy of the list is sent to the accounting department for comparison with the total mail receipts shown on the daily cash summary. This copy ensures that all mail receipts have been included. The accounting department will record a journal entry to debit Cash and credit Accounts Receivable or Sales, as required.

## Electronic Receipts

According to the Canadian Payments Association, the increase in payment options—on-line banking, telephone banking, ATMs, and automatic pre-authorized monthly bill payments—has resulted in a significant decline in customer payments by cheque. In 2001, only 2% of customers paid their accounts by cheque.

**Electronic funds transfer (EFT)** systems transfer funds between parties without the use of paper (e.g., deposits, cheques, etc.). In the case of electronic receipts, amounts are transferred from a customer's bank account to the retailer's bank account.

Debit and credit cards, discussed earlier in this chapter, are examples of electronic funds transfers. Debit cards result in funds being transferred from a customer's bank account to the retailer's bank account. Bank credit cards result in funds being transferred from the issuing bank (e.g., Bank of Montreal for MasterCard) to the retailer's bank account. In addition, some customers pay their accounts using EFT and on-line banking.

When a customer pays his or her account, the cash is instantly transferred from the customer's bank account to the company's bank account. Companies also transfer cash between bank accounts using EFT. In fact, 85% of banking transactions are done electronically in Canada.

Electronic funds transfers normally result in better internal control, since no cash or cheques are handled by company employees. The only evidence of these electronic cash receipts will be a line on the bank statement showing the amount, a reference number, and usually the name of the person paying.

Since the only documentation for these transactions is from the bank account, these transactions are journalized directly from the company's on-line bank statement.

## Internal Control over Cash Disbursements

Cash may be disbursed for a variety of reasons, such as to pay expenses and liabilities, or to purchase assets. **Generally, internal control over cash disbursements is more effective when payments are made by cheque, rather than by cash.** Payment by cheque should occur only after specified control procedures have been followed. The paid cheque provides proof of payment. Illustration 7-4 shows how the principles of internal control apply to cash disbursements.

### Internal Control over Cash Disbursements

**Authorization**

Only designated personnel are authorized to sign cheques.

**Safeguarding Assets and Records**

Store blank cheques in safes with limited access; print cheque amounts by machine in indelible ink.

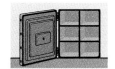

**Segregation of Duties**

Different individuals approve and make payments; cheque signers do not record disbursements.

**Independent Verification**

Compare cheques to invoices; reconcile bank statement monthly.

**Documentation Procedures**

Use prenumbered cheques and account for them in sequence; each cheque must have an approved invoice.

**Other Controls**

Stamp invoices PAID.

**Illustration 7-4 ◄**

Application of internal control principles to cash disbursements

## Cheques

As outlined in Illustration 7-4, the internal controls over cheques include the signing of cheques by an authorized person or persons—cheques often require two signatures. The cheque signer(s) should carefully review the supporting documentation for the payment before signing the cheque. There should be a clear segregation of duties between the cheque signing function and the accounts payable function. Cheques should be prenumbered, and all cheque numbers must be accounted for in the payment and recording process. Cheques should never be pre-signed, and blank cheques should be guarded.

Many large companies use purchase orders to improve their internal control over cash disbursements. A purchase order is an authorization form prepared for each expenditure, or for expenditures greater than a specified amount. The purchase order is usually prepared by the purchasing department.

When the good or service is received, the receiving report is matched with the purchase order. When the seller's invoice is subsequently received, it is matched to the purchase order and receiving report. An authorized person in the accounts payable department then approves the invoice for payment. A cheque is sent on the due date, and the invoice is stamped "Paid."

The accounting department records the payment of the invoice. Often companies with a significant number of cash disbursements use a special journal, called a **cash payments journal**, to record all disbursements of cash. Appendix C at the end of this textbook illustrates the use of special journals.

## Electronic Payments

Many companies make payments to suppliers and employees using electronic funds transfer systems. For example, when a company pays its employees' salaries using a direct deposit option, the cash is instantly transferred from the company's bank account to each employee's bank account. No cheques are issued.

In addition, pre-authorized payments, for things like loans and interest paid on a recurring basis, are often made electronically. As with electronic cash receipts, the only evidence of this payment will be a line on the bank statement showing the amount, reference, and usually the name of the company that was paid.

Internal controls over electronic payments must ensure that all such payments are properly authorized. A person independent of the accounts payable department should check that the payments agree with a list of authorized electronic payments. These payments are then journalized from the supporting accounts payable documentation.

## BEFORE YOU GO ON . . .

►**Review It**

1. How do the principles of internal control apply to cash receipts?
2. How do the principles of internal control apply to cash disbursements?

*Related exercise material:* BE7–2, BE7–3, BE7–4, E7–1, E7–2, and E7–3.

## Petty Cash Fund

study objective 5

Demonstrate the operation of a petty cash fund.

As you just learned, better internal control over cash disbursements is possible when payments are made by cheque or pre-authorized electronic payments. However, using cheques or EFT to pay for small amounts is both impractical and a nuisance. For example, a company would not want to write cheques to pay for postage, couriers, or taxis. A common way to handle such payments is to use a petty cash fund. A **petty cash fund** is used to pay relatively small amounts, while still maintaining satisfactory control. The petty cash fund is usually operated on an imprest system. The word "imprest" means an advance of a specified sum of money for a designated purpose. To account for an imprest petty cash fund, you must understand three steps: (1) how the fund is established, (2) how payments are made from the fund, and (3) how the fund is replenished.

**Establishing the Fund.**  Two essential steps are required to establish a petty cash fund: (1) appoint a petty cash custodian to be responsible for the fund, and (2) determine the size of the fund. Ordinarily, the amount is expected to be enough for likely payments during a three- to four-week period. To establish the fund, a cheque payable to the petty cash custodian is issued for the determined amount. If the Lee Company decides to establish a $100 petty cash fund on March 1, the entry recorded in the general journal is as follows:

| Mar. 1 | Petty Cash | 100 | |
| | Cash | | 100 |
| | To establish a petty cash fund. | | |

A = L + OE
+100
−100

Cash flows: −100

The custodian cashes the cheque and places the proceeds in a locked petty cash box or drawer. No additional entries are made to the Petty Cash account unless management changes the stipulated amount of the fund. For example, if Lee Company decides on March 15 to increase the size of the fund to $125, it will debit Petty Cash $25 and credit Cash $25.

**Making Payments from the Fund.** The custodian of the petty cash fund has the authority to make payments from the fund in accordance with management policies. Usually, management limits the size of expenditures that may be made. Likewise, it may not permit use of the fund for certain types of transactions (such as making short-term loans to employees). Each payment from the fund must be documented on a prenumbered petty cash receipt, signed by both the custodian and the person who receives payment. If other supporting documents such as a freight bill or invoice are available, they should be attached to the petty cash receipt.

> **Helpful hint** From the standpoint of internal control, the receipt satisfies two principles: (1) authorization (signature of custodian), and (2) documentation.

The receipts are kept in the petty cash box until the fund runs low and needs to be replenished. The sum of the petty cash receipts and money in the fund should equal the established total at all times. Surprise counts can be made by an independent person, such as a supervisor or internal auditor, to determine whether the fund is being used properly.

No accounting entry is made to record a payment at the time it is made from petty cash. It is considered both inefficient and unnecessary to do so. Instead, the accounting effects of each payment are recognized when the fund is replenished.

**Replenishing the Fund.** When the money in the petty cash fund reaches a minimum level, the fund is replenished. The request for reimbursement is made by the petty cash custodian. This individual prepares a schedule (or summary) of the payments that have been made and sends the schedule, supported by petty cash receipts and other documentation, to the comptroller's office. The receipts and supporting documents are examined in the comptroller's office to verify that they were proper payments from the fund. The request is approved and a cheque is prepared to restore the fund to its established amount. At the same time, all supporting documentation is stamped "Paid" so that it cannot be submitted again for payment.

> **Helpful hint** Replenishing involves three internal control procedures: segregation of duties, documentation, and independent verification.

To illustrate, assume that on March 15 the petty cash custodian requests a cheque for $87. The fund contains $13 cash and petty cash receipts for postage $44, freight $38 (assume a perpetual inventory system is used), and miscellaneous expenses $5. The entry to record the cheque is as follows:

| Mar. 15 | Postage Expense | 44 | |
| | Merchandise Inventory | 38 | |
| | Miscellaneous Expense | 5 | |
| | Cash | | 87 |
| | To replenish petty cash. | | |

A = L + OE
+38        −44
−87        −5

Cash flows: −87

Note that the Petty Cash account is not affected by the reimbursement entry. Replenishment changes what's in the fund by replacing the petty cash receipts with cash. It does not change the balance in the fund.

It may be necessary, in replenishing a petty cash fund, to recognize a cash shortage or overage. This results when the cash plus receipts plus cash in the petty cash box do not equal the established amount of the petty cash fund. To illustrate, assume in the example above that the custodian had only $12 in cash in the fund, plus the receipts as listed. The request for reimbursement would, therefore, have been for $88. The following entry would be made:

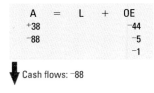

| Mar. 15 | Postage Expense | 44 | |
| | Merchandise Inventory | 38 | |
| | Miscellaneous Expense | 5 | |
| | Cash Over and Short | 1 | |
| |    Cash | | 88 |
| |      To replenish petty cash. | | |

Conversely, if the custodian had $14 in cash, the reimbursement request would have been for $86 and Cash Over and Short would have been credited for $1. A debit balance in Cash Over and Short is reported in the income statement as miscellaneous expense. A credit balance in the account is reported as miscellaneous revenue.

If the petty cash fund is not big enough, it is often increased (or decreased) when the fund is replenished. Assume that Lee Company decides to increase the size of its petty cash fund from $100 to $125 on March 15 when it replenishes the fund. The entry to record the reimbursement and change in fund size is as follows:

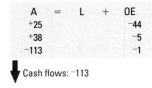

| Mar. 15 | Petty Cash | 25 | |
| | Postage Expense | 44 | |
| | Merchandise Inventory | 38 | |
| | Miscellaneous Expense | 5 | |
| | Cash Over and Short | 1 | |
| |    Cash | | 113 |
| |      To replenish petty cash and increase the fund | | |
| |      size by $25. | | |

In this entry, the Petty Cash account is affected, not because of the reimbursement, but because of the change in size of the fund. After this entry, the general ledger account shows a balance of $125 and the custodian must ensure that cash and paid-out receipts now total $125.

A petty cash fund should be replenished at the end of the accounting period regardless of the cash in the fund. Replenishment at this time is necessary in order to recognize the effects of the petty cash payments on the financial statements.

Internal control over a petty cash fund is strengthened by (1) having a supervisor make surprise counts of the fund to check whether the paid receipts and fund cash equal the imprest amount, and (2) cancelling the paid receipts so they cannot be resubmitted for reimbursement.

If the Beanz Espresso Bar, in the feature story, used a petty cash fund instead of making small payments directly from cash receipts, its internal control would be strengthened.

## BEFORE YOU GO ON . . .

### ▶Review It

   1. How does the use of a petty cash system strengthen internal control?
   2. When are entries required in a petty cash system?

### ▶Do It

The Bateer Company established a $50 petty cash fund on July 1. On July 30, the fund had $12 cash remaining and petty cash receipts for postage, $14; office supplies, $10; and delivery expense, $15. Prepare the journal entries to establish the fund on July 1 and replenish the fund on July 30.

## Action Plan

- To establish the fund, set up a separate general ledger account.
- Total the petty cash receipts to calculate the cash required to replenish the petty cash.
- Determine any cash over or short—the difference between the cash required and the total of the petty cash receipts.
- To replenish the fund, record the expenses incurred according to the petty cash receipts.

## Solution

| | | | | |
|---|---|---|---:|---:|
| July | 1 | Petty Cash | 50 | |
| | |     Cash | | 50 |
| | |         To establish a petty cash fund. | | |
| | 30 | Postage Expense | 14 | |
| | | Office Supplies | 10 | |
| | | Delivery Expense | 15 | |
| | |     Cash Over and Short | | 1 |
| | |     Cash | | 38 |
| | |         To replenish petty cash. | | |

*Related exercise material:* BE7–5, BE7–6, E7–4, and E7–5.

# Use of a Bank

**The use of a bank contributes significantly to good internal control over cash.** A company can safeguard its cash by using a bank as a depository and as a clearing house for cheques received and cheques written. Use of a bank reduces the amount of currency that must be kept on hand. In addition, the use of a bank facilitates the control of cash, because it creates a double record of all bank transactions—one by the business and the other by the bank. The asset account Cash, maintained by the depositor, is the opposite of the bank's liability account for each depositor. It should be possible to **reconcile (balance) these accounts** at any time.

Opening a bank chequing account is a relatively simple procedure. Typically, the bank runs a credit check on the new customer and the depositor is required to sign a **signature card**. The card contains the signature of each person authorized to sign cheques on the account. The signature card is used by bank employees to validate the signature on the cheques. As mentioned earlier in the chapter, many companies require two authorized signatures on each cheque to act as a check and balance on each other.

The bank provides the depositor with a book of serially numbered cheques and deposit slips imprinted with the depositor's name and address. Each cheque and deposit slip is imprinted with both a bank and a depositor identification number. This number, printed in magnetic ink, permits computer processing of the transaction.

Many companies have more than one bank account. For efficiency of operations and better control, national retailers like Sears may have local bank accounts. Similarly, a company may have a payroll bank account, as well as one or more general bank accounts. A company may also have accounts with different banks in order to have more than one source for short-term loans when needed.

## Making Bank Deposits

Bank deposits should be made by an authorized employee, such as the head cashier. Each deposit must be documented by a deposit slip, as shown in Illustration 7-5 on the following page.

Deposit slip (reproduced with permission of the Bank of Montreal)

Deposit slips are normally prepared in duplicate. The original is kept by the bank. The duplicate is stamped by the bank to establish its authenticity, then kept by the depositor. Deposits are also made by direct deposit, through ABMs, or through electronic funds transfers. In these cases, notification is found on the bank statement.

## Writing Cheques

A **cheque** is a written order signed by the depositor that instructs the bank to pay a specific sum of money to a designated recipient. There are three parties to a cheque: (1) the **maker** (or drawer) who issues the cheque, (2) the **bank** (or payer) on which the cheque is drawn, and (3) the **payee** to whom the cheque is payable. A cheque is a negotiable instrument that can be transferred to another party by endorsement.

Each cheque should clearly explain its purpose. For many businesses, the purpose of a cheque is detailed on the cheque stub, as shown in Illustration 7-6. The purpose of the cheque should also be apparent to the payee, either by referencing the invoice directly on the cheque—see the reference to invoice #27622 on the For line of the cheque in the illustration—or by attaching a copy of the invoice to the cheque.

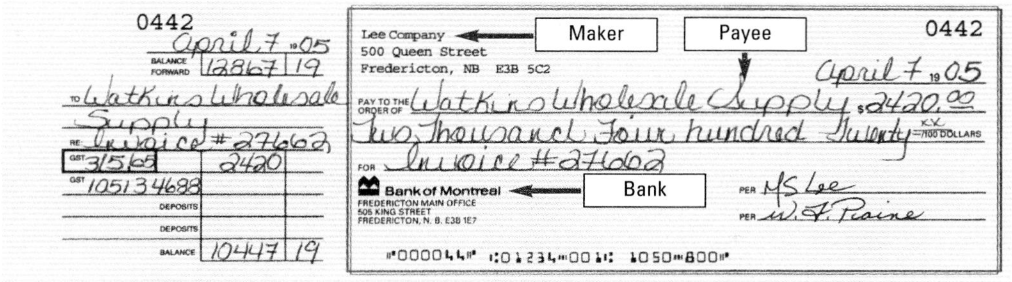

Illustration 7-6 ◄

Cheque (reproduced with permission of the Bank of Montreal)

Most business bank accounts do not allow ABM withdrawals because internal control is strengthened by making all payments by cheque. Other disbursements may include pre-arranged payments using EFT.

For both individuals and businesses, it is important to know the balance in the chequing account at all times. This is easily done in a computerized accounting system, where deposits and cheques are recorded as soon as they are received or issued. In smaller businesses, to keep the balance current, each deposit and cheque must be entered in the cheque book, as shown on the left side of Illustration 7-6.

## The Clearing Process

How does cash actually flow through the banking system? When cheques, debit cards, and pre-authorized or other payments occur, they may result in one financial institution owing money to another. For example, if a company (the maker) writes a cheque to a supplier (the payee), the payee deposits the cheque in its own bank account.

When the cheque is deposited, it is sent to a regional data centre for processing, usually the same day. When the cheque arrives at the regional data centre, it is "presented" to the payee's financial institution, where it is determined whether the cheque will be honoured or returned (for example, for insufficient funds or a stop payment order). This process is automated and happens very quickly. In most cases, the cheque will clear the maker's bank account before the end of the day. **Clearing** is the term used when a cheque or deposit is accepted by the maker's bank.

In some cases, a cheque cannot be cleared on the day it is deposited. For example, cheques that cannot be processed by automated equipment must be processed manually the next day. As well, cheques deposited at a branch on Saturday will not be cleared until the following Monday, because clearing takes place only on regular business days.

The clearing process for electronic payments is more direct than for cheques and other paper-based payment items, as there is no requirement to deliver a physical payment item in these cases.

The clearing process nets cash flows in one direction against cash flows in the opposite direction for each bank or financial institution. Then, the financial institutions involved settle the net amounts through central accounts each institution maintains at the Bank of Canada. More than 17 million payments totalling more than $133 billion are cleared on an average business day.

## Bank Statements

Each month, the depositor receives a bank statement from the bank. A **bank statement** shows the depositor's bank transactions and balance. A typical statement is presented in Illustration 7-7. It shows (1) cheques paid and other debits that reduce the balance in the

**Illustration 7-7** ▶

Bank statement (reproduced with permission of the Bank of Montreal)

depositor's account, (2) deposits and other credits that increase the balance in the depositor's account, and (3) the account balance after each day's transactions.

**Helpful hint**  Every deposit received by the bank is credited to the customer's account. The reverse happens when the bank "pays" a cheque issued by a company on the company's chequing account balance. Because payment reduces the bank's liability, the amount is debited to the customer's account with the bank.

## Bank of Montreal / Banque de Montréal

505 King Street
Fredericton, NB
E3B 1E7

| Transit No de dom | Date D/J M/M Y/A | Account Title Désignation de compte | Account Type Type de compte | Account No. No de compte | Page |
|---|---|---|---|---|---|
| 0123 | 30 04 05 | Operating Account | FBOA | 1050-800 | 58 |

Lee Company
500 Queen Street
Fredericton, NB    E3B 5C2

BALANCE FORWARD SOLDE REPORTÉ    Date 03 31    13,256.90

**TRANSACTION CODES* / CODES DE TRANSACTIONS***

|  |  |
|---|---|
| AD | Adjustments / Rectification |
| CB | Cheque Posted By Branch / Chèque inscrit par la succ. |
| CC | Certified Cheque / Chèque certifié |
| CD | Customer Deposit / Dépôt |
| CK | Cheque / Chèque |
| CM | Credit Memo / Avis de Crédit |
| CW | Telephone Banking / Services bancaires par téléphone |
| DC | Other Charges / Autres frais |
| DD | Direct Deposit/Pre-authorized Debit / Dépôt ou débit direct |
| DM | Debit Memo / Avis de débit |
| DN | Not Service Chargeable / Sans frais de gestion |
| DR | Overdraft / Découvert |
| DS | Service Chargeable / Avec frais de gestion |
| EC | Error Correction / Correction d'erreur |
| FX | Foreign Exchange / Change |
| GS | Tax / Taxe |
| IB | Instabank / Instabanque |
| IN | Interest / Intérêt |
| LI | Loan Interest / Intérêt sur prêt |
| LN | Loan Payment / Versement sur prêt |
| LP | Loan Advance / Avance sur prêt |
| LT | Large Volume Account List Total / Liste de chèque - compte superactif |
| MB | Multi-Branch Banking / Inter-Service |
| NR | Non-Resident Tax / Impôt de non-résident |
| NS | Cheque returned NSF / Chèque retourné - provision insuffisante |
| NT | Nesbitt Burns Entry / Transaction de Nesbitt Burns |
| OM | Other Machine / Autre machine |
| PR | Purchase at Merchant / Achat chez le commerçant |
| RC | NSF Charge / Frais pour provision insuffisante |
| RN | Merchandise Return / Retour de marchandise |
| RT | Returned Item / Article retourné |
| RV | Merchant Reversal / Correction - Commerçant |
| SC | Service Charge / Frais de gestion |
| SO | Standing Order / Ordre de virement |
| ST | Merchant Deposit / Dépôt du commerçant |
| TF | Transfer of Funds / Virement |
| TX | Tax / Taxe |
| WD | Withdrawal / Retrait |

Please see the reverse side for the Account Types
Les types de compte figurent au verso.

| CODE | Description/Message justificatif | Debits/Débits | Credits/Crédits | Mo. | Day Jour | Balance/Solde |
|---|---|---|---|---|---|---|
| CK | NO. 435 | 644.95 | | 04 | 01 | 12,611.95 |
| CD | | | 4,276.85 | 04 | 01 | 16,888.80 |
| DD | | | 2,137.50 | 04 | 04 | 19,026.30 |
| CK | NO. 438 | 776.65 | | 04 | 04 | 18,249.65 |
| CK | NO. 437 | 1,185.79 | | 04 | 05 | 17,063.86 |
| CK | NO. 436 | 3,260.00 | | 04 | 05 | 13,803.86 |
| CD | | | 1,350.47 | 04 | 06 | 15,154.33 |
| CD | | | 982.46 | 04 | 07 | 16,136.79 |
| CK | NO. 440 | 1,487.90 | | 04 | 07 | 14,648.89 |
| CK | NO. 439 | 1,781.70 | | 04 | 08 | 12,867.19 |
| CK | NO. 442 | 2,420.00 | | 04 | 08 | 10,447.19 |
| CD | | | 2,355.28 | 04 | 11 | 12,802.47 |
| CK | NO. 441 | 1,585.60 | | 04 | 11 | 11,216.87 |
| CD | | | 2,720.00 | 04 | 12 | 13,936.87 |
| CK | NO. 443 | 1,226.00 | | 04 | 12 | 12,710.87 |
| CD | | | 757.41 | 04 | 14 | 13,468.28 |
| CD | | | 1,218.56 | 04 | 15 | 14,686.84 |
| CD | | | 715.42 | 04 | 15 | 15,402.26 |
| RC | | 425.60 | | 04 | 18 | 14,976.66 |
| CK | NO. 444 | 3,477.11 | | 04 | 22 | 11,499.55 |
| CD | | | 1,578.90 | 04 | 25 | 13,078.45 |
| CK | | | 1,350.55 | 04 | 27 | 14,429.00 |
| DM | | 30.00 | | 04 | 28 | 14,399.00 |
| CD | | | 2,128.60 | 04 | 29 | 16,527.60 |
| CK | NO. 447 | 659.91 | | 04 | 29 | 15,867.69 |
| IN | | | 39.76 | 04 | 29 | 15,907.45 |

Prompt notification of any change of address would be appreciated. / Prière de signaler à la Banque tout changement d'adresse.

Please check this statement and report any errors or omissions within 30 days of its delivery
Prière de vérifier ce relevé de compte et de signaler toute erreur ou omission dans les 30 jours suivant sa réception.

Although not all the supporting documentation has been shown for this bank statement, you can trace the cheque for $2,420 shown in Illustration 7-6 to the bank statement's April 8 transaction. Note that although the cheque was written on April 7, it did not clear the bank until April 8. You can also trace the deposit slip for $1,218.56 shown in Illustration 7-5 to the bank statement's April 15 transaction. Other deposits and cheques could be traced similarly, by examining the supporting documentation kept on file by the company.

All paid cheques are listed in chronological order on the bank statement, with the date the cheque was paid and its amount indicated. A paid cheque is sometimes referred to as a **cleared** or **cancelled** cheque. Most banks offer depositors the option of receiving paid cheques with their bank statements. For those who decline, the bank keeps an electronic record of each cheque. The bank statement also includes bank memoranda that explain other debits and credits made by the bank to the depositor's account.

At first glance, it may appear that the debits and credits reported on the bank statement are backward. How can a cheque be a debit? And how can a deposit be a credit? Debits and credits are not really backward. To the company, cash is an asset account. Assets are increased by debits (e.g., for cash receipts) and decreased by credits (e.g., for cash payments). To the bank, on the other hand, the cash in your bank account is a liability account—an amount it must repay to you upon request. Liabilities are increased by credits and decreased by debits. When you deposit money in your bank account, the bank's liability to you increases. That is why the bank shows deposits as credits. When you write a cheque on your account, the bank pays out this amount and decreases (debits) its liability to you.

## Debit Memorandum

Banks charge a monthly fee for the use of their services, called a **bank service charge**. A debit memorandum that explains the charge is usually included with the bank statement and noted on the statement. The symbol DM (debit memo) is often used for such charges. Separate debit memoranda may also be issued for other bank services such as the cost of printing cheques, issuing traveller's cheques, certifying cheques, and transferring funds to other locations.

A debit memorandum is also used by the bank when a deposited cheque from a customer bounces because of insufficient funds. In such a case, the cheque is marked NSF (not sufficient funds) or RC (returned cheque) by the customer's bank, and is returned to the depositor's bank. The bank then debits the depositor's account, as shown by the symbol RC on the bank statement in Illustration 7-7. Note that this cheque for $425.60 was originally included in the deposit made on April 15, detailed in Illustration 7-5. Because the deposit was credited (added) to the bank account on April 15 and the cheque wasn't honoured, it must be debited (deducted) by the bank on April 18.

The bank sends the NSF cheque and debit memorandum to the depositor as notification of the charge. The company (depositor) then advises the customer who wrote the NSF cheque that the payment was ineffective and that a payment is still owed on the account. The company also usually passes the bank charges on to the customer by adding them to the customer's account balance. In summary, the overall effect of an NSF cheque to the depositor is to create an account receivable, and to reduce cash in the bank account.

Recording an account receivable assumes that the customer will honour the account due by replacing the bounced cheque with a valid cheque, or with cash. This happens in most cases. In the next chapter, we will discuss how to account for uncollectible accounts receivable when customers are unable to pay their accounts.

## Credit Memorandum

Credit memoranda (CM) identify interest earned on the bank account, electronic funds transfers into the depositor's account, and other amounts added to the depositor's account. For example, as explained earlier in the chapter, some retailers accept electronic payments for merchandise sold on account. Funds are electronically transferred from the customer's account to the retailer's account in payment of the bill.

Note that in Illustration 7-7, interest of $39.76, as indicated by the symbol IN, has been added to Lee Company's bank balance. A bank does not pay interest by sending a cheque to a company. Rather it deposits the interest earned directly into the company's bank account and notifies the company by a credit memo which is attached to the monthly bank statement.

# Reconciling the Bank Account

The bank and the depositor keep independent records of the depositor's chequing account. If you've never had a chequing account, you might assume that the balances you and the bank have will always agree. In fact, the two balances are seldom the same at any given time. It is necessary to make the balance per books (the balance recorded in a company's general ledger cash account) agree with the balance per bank (the balance recorded on the bank statement)—a process called **reconciling the bank account**.

The lack of agreement between the two balances is due to the following:

1. Time lags that prevent one of the parties from recording a transaction in the same period as the other
2. Errors by either party in recording transactions

Except in electronic banking applications, time lags happen often. For example, several days pass between the time a cheque is mailed to a payee and the date the cheque is presented to, and cleared (paid) by, the bank. Similarly, when the depositor uses the bank's night depository to make deposits, there will be a difference between the time the receipts are recorded by the depositor and the time they are recorded by the bank. There is also a time lag whenever the bank mails a debit or credit memorandum to the depositor.

Errors also occur. How often errors happen depends on the effectiveness of the internal controls of the depositor and the bank. Bank errors are rare. However, either party could inadvertently record a $450 cheque as $45 or $540. In addition, the bank might mistakenly charge a cheque to the wrong account if the code is missing or if the cheque cannot be scanned.

### ACCOUNTING IN ACTION ▶ Business Insight

Bank errors may be infrequent, but they can involve a story more suitable for *Ripley's Believe It or Not* than an accounting textbook. The Bank of Nova Scotia's discount brokerage arm accidentally put $17.1 million of somebody else's money into a Toronto doctor's Scotiabank account. It took four months to find and correct the error. Stories about banks misplacing customers' funds are a dime a dozen. But they usually involve misplaced debits, and rarely amounts as high as this.

*Source:* John Partridge, "Bank Error in Your Favour: Collect $17 Million." *The Globe and Mail,* April 11, 2000, A1.

## Reconciliation Procedure

**To obtain maximum benefit from a bank reconciliation, the reconciliation should be prepared by an employee who has no other responsibilities that relate to cash.** In the feature story about the Beanz Espresso Bar, the owner prepares the bank reconciliation. If the internal control principles of segregation of duties and internal verification are not followed when the reconciliation is prepared, cash embezzlements may go unnoticed. For example, a cashier who prepares the reconciliation can steal cash and conceal the theft by misstating the reconciliation. Thus, the bank accounts would reconcile and the theft would not be detected.

In reconciling the bank account, it is customary to reconcile the balance per books (found in the cash account in the general ledger) and balance per bank (found on the bank statement provided by the bank) to their adjusted (correct) cash balances. The reconciliation schedule is usually divided into two sections—one for the bank and one for the books (company). The starting point when preparing the reconciliation is to enter the balance per bank statement and balance per books on the schedule. Adjustments are then made to each section, as shown in Illustration 7-8.

**Illustration 7-8** ◄

Bank reconciliation procedures

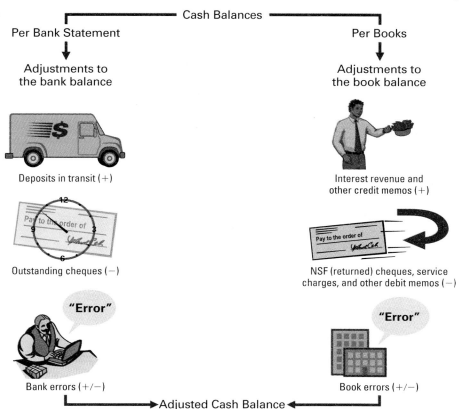

The following steps should reveal all the reconciling items that cause the difference between the two balances:

1. **Deposits in transit.** Compare the individual deposits on the bank statement with (1) the deposits in transit from the preceding bank reconciliation, and (2) the deposits according to company records or duplicate deposit slips. Deposits recorded by the depositor that have not been recorded by the bank are **deposits in transit**. They are added to the balance per bank.

    Before determining deposits in transit for the current period, you must check whether all deposits in transit outstanding from a prior period have cleared. For example, Lee Company used a night deposit slot to deposit $2,201.40 on April 30. Because April 30 fell on a Saturday in 2005, the bank did not receive or record this deposit until Monday, May 2. This amount would be treated as a deposit in transit at the end of April. However, this outstanding deposit cleared the bank in May and would no longer be a deposit in transit for the month of May. As at the end of May, this amount has been recorded by both the company and the bank.

2. **Outstanding cheques.** Compare the paid cheques shown on the bank statement or returned with the bank statement to (1) cheques outstanding from the preceding bank reconciliation, and (2) cheques issued by the company. Issued cheques recorded by the company that have not yet been paid by the bank are **outstanding cheques**. They are deducted from the balance per bank.

    Note that an outstanding cheque from a prior period means that the cheque was deducted from the books in the prior period, but not paid by the bank. If the cheque was paid by the bank in the current month, both sides (book and bank) are now reconciled, the cheque is no longer outstanding, and no further reconciling item is required. If the cheque has still not been presented to the bank for payment, it will continue to be outstanding.

3. **Errors.** Note any errors discovered in the previous steps. List them in the appropriate section of the reconciliation schedule. For example, if a paid cheque correctly written by the company for $1,226 was mistakenly recorded by the company for $1,262, the error of $36 is added to the balance per books. All errors made by the depositor are reconciling items in determining the adjusted cash balance per books. In contrast, all errors made by the bank are reconciling items in determining the adjusted cash balance per bank.

4. **Bank memoranda.** Trace bank memoranda to the depositor's records. Any unrecorded memoranda should be listed in the appropriate section of the reconciliation schedule. For example, a debit memorandum for bank service charges is deducted from the balance per books. A credit memorandum for interest earned is added to the balance per books.

## Bank Reconciliation Illustrated

The bank statement for Lee Company was shown in Illustration 7-7. It shows a balance per bank of $15,907.45 on April 30, 2005. On this date, the balance of cash per books is $12,584.69. Using the foregoing steps, the following reconciling items are determined:

1. **Deposits in transit:** April 30 deposit (recorded by bank on May 2):  $2,201.40
2. **Outstanding cheques:** No. 445, $3,000.00; No. 446, $1,401.30; No. 448, $1,502.70:  5,904.00
3. **Errors:** Cheque No. 443 was correctly written by Lee for $1,226.00 and was correctly paid by the bank. However, it was recorded as $1,262.00 by Lee:  36.00
4. **Bank memoranda:**
   (a) Debit—NSF cheque from J. R. Baron for $425.60:  425.60
   (b) Debit—Bank service charge, $30.00, re NSF cheque:  30.00
   (c) Credit—Interest earned:  39.76

The bank reconciliation is as follows:

**LEE COMPANY**
**Bank Reconciliation**
**April 30, 2005**

| | | |
|---|---:|---:|
| Cash balance per bank statement | | $15,907.45 |
| Add:  Deposit in transit | | 2,201.40 |
| | | 18,108.85 |
| Less:  Outstanding cheques | | |
| No. 445 | $3,000.00 | |
| No. 446 | 1,401.30 | |
| No. 448 | 1,502.70 | 5,904.00 |
| **Adjusted cash balance per bank** | | **$12,204.85** |
| Cash balance per books | | $12,584.69 |
| Add:  Error in recording cheque No. 443 | $ 36.00 | |
| Interest earned | 39.76 | 75.76 |
| | | 12,660.45 |
| Less:  NSF cheque | $425.60 | |
| Bank service charge | 30.00 | 455.60 |
| **Adjusted cash balance per books** | | **$12,204.85** |

## Entries from Bank Reconciliation

When determining the **adjusted cash balance per books**, each reconciling item should be recorded by the depositor. If these items are not journalized and posted, the Cash account will not show the correct balance. The entries for Lee Company on April 30 are as follows:

**Interest.** The entry to record the credit memorandum for the interest (IN) earned on the bank account for the month of April is:

| Apr. 30 | Cash | 39.76 | |
| |    Interest Revenue | | 39.76 |
| |      To record interest earned. | | |

**Book Error.** Cheque No. 443 was a payment on account to Asia Company, a supplier. The correcting entry is:

| Apr. 30 | Cash | 36.00 | |
| |    Accounts Payable | | 36.00 |
| |      To correct error in recording cheque No. 443. | | |

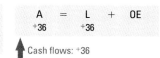

**NSF Cheque.** As indicated earlier, an NSF (RC) cheque becomes an account receivable to the depositor. The entry is:

| Apr. 30 | Accounts Receivable | 425.60 | |
| |    Cash | | 425.60 |
| |      To record NSF cheque from J. R. Baron. | | |

**Bank Service Charges.** Bank service charges are normally debited to Bank Charges Expense. Some companies use the account Interest Expense; others use Miscellaneous Expense because the charges are often nominal in amount. In this instance, however, because the bank service charge relates to processing J. R. Baron's NSF cheque, this charge will be passed on to J. R. Baron and added to his account. The entry is:

| Apr. 30 | Accounts Receivable | 30.00 | |
| |    Cash | | 30.00 |
| |      To record bank service charge for processing NSF cheque to J. R. Baron's account. | | |

The four entries above could also be combined into one compound entry. Our presentation assumes that all adjustments are made at the end of the month. In practice, many companies make journal entries throughout the month as they receive information from the bank about their account, or as they check their on-line bank account balances.

    Note that in prior chapters Cash was treated as an account that did not require adjustment. This was done to make learning easier, because the bank reconciliation process had not been explained.

    After the entries above are posted, the Cash account will show the following:

| | Cash | | | |
| --- | --- | --- | --- | --- |
| Apr. 30 | Bal. 12,584.69 | Apr. 30 | 425.60 |
| 30 | 39.76 | 30 | 30.00 |
| 30 | 36.00 | | |
| Apr. 30 | Bal. 12,204.85 | | |

The adjusted cash balance in the general ledger should agree with the adjusted cash balance per books in the bank reconciliation shown on page 351.

What entries does the bank make? **The bank cannot correct your errors on its books, and you cannot correct the bank's errors on your books.** If any bank errors are discovered in preparing the reconciliation, the bank should be notified. It can then make the necessary corrections on its records. The bank does not make any entries for deposits in transit or outstanding cheques. The bank will record these items when they clear.

## BEFORE YOU GO ON . . .

### ▶Review It

1. Why is it necessary to reconcile a bank account?
2. What steps are involved in the reconciliation procedure?
3. How are deposits in transit and outstanding cheques treated in the reconciling process?

### ▶Do It

The Cash account of Zhizhi Company showed a balance of $16,333 on December 31, 2005. The bank statement as of that date showed a balance of $18,084. After comparing the bank statement with the cash records, the following information was determined:

1. The bank returned an NSF cheque in the amount of $239 that Zhizhi had deposited on December 20. The cheque was a payment on a customer's account.
2. Electronic receipts received from customers on the last day of the month to pay their accounts totalled $2,300. These receipts have not yet been recorded by the company.
3. The bank issued a credit memo for interest of $9 earned on Zhizhi's account.
4. The bank issued a debit memo for bank service charges of $37. This amount included $25 for processing the NSF cheque (see #1 above) and $12 for the rental of a safety deposit box.
5. The company made an error in recording a customer's deposit. The company recorded the payment on account as $209, when it should have been $290. The bank correctly recorded the deposit at $290.
6. Deposits in transit as at December 31 amounted to $3,643.
7. Outstanding cheques for the month of December amounted to $3,000. Cheques still outstanding from the month of November totalled $280.

Prepare a bank reconciliation and any required journal entries for Zhizhi Company at December 31, 2005.

### Action Plan

- Prepare the bank reconciliation in two sections: one for the company and one for the bank.
- Determine which reconciling items each side knows about and adjust the other side accordingly.
- Be careful when you determine the direction of an error correction.
- Prepare journal entries only for the books side; not the bank side.
- The adjusted cash balances must agree with each other when complete, and with the general ledger account after the journal entries are posted.

Solution

**ZHIZHI COMPANY**
**Bank Reconciliation**
**December 31, 2005**

| | | |
|---|---:|---:|
| Cash balance per bank statement | | $18,084 |
| Add: Deposits in transit | | 3,643 |
| | | 21,727 |
| Less: Outstanding cheques ($3,000 + $280) | | 3,280 |
| Adjusted cash balance per bank | | $18,447 |
| | | |
| Cash balance per books | | $16,333 |
| Add: Electronic receipts from customers on account | $2,300 | |
| Interest earned | 9 | |
| Deposit error correction ($290 − $209) | 81 | 2,390 |
| | | 18,723 |
| Less: NSF cheque | $239 | |
| Bank service charges | 37 | 276 |
| Adjusted cash balance per books | | $18,447 |

| | | | |
|---|---|---:|---:|
| Dec. 31 | Cash | 2,300 | |
| |    Accounts Receivable | | 2,300 |
| |      To record electronic receipts on account. | | |
| 31 | Cash | 9 | |
| |    Interest Revenue | | 9 |
| |      To record interest earned on bank account. | | |
| 31 | Cash | 81 | |
| |    Accounts Receivable ($290 − $209) | | 81 |
| |      To correct deposit error. | | |
| 31 | Accounts Receivable ($239 + $25) | 264 | |
| |    Cash | | 264 |
| |      To re-establish accounts receivable for NSF cheque and related service charge. | | |
| 31 | Bank Charges Expense | 12 | |
| |    Cash | | 12 |
| |      To record bank service charges. | | |

| | | Cash | | | |
|---|---|---:|---|---|---:|
| Dec. 31 | Bal. | 16,333 | Dec. 31 | | 264 |
| | | 2,300 | | | 12 |
| | | 9 | | | |
| | | 81 | | | |
| Dec. 31 | Bal. | 18,447 | | | |

*Related exercise material*: BE7–7, BE7–8, BE7–9, BE7–10, BE7–11, E7–6, E7–7, E7–8, E7–9, E7–10, and E7–11.

# Reporting Cash

Cash on hand, cash in banks, and petty cash are normally combined and reported simply as Cash in the balance sheet. Because it is the most liquid asset owned by a company, cash is listed first in the current assets section of the balance sheet. **Many companies combine cash with cash equivalents.** Cash equivalents are short-term, highly liquid (easily sold) investments. They typically have maturities of three months or less when purchased. These investments include short-term deposits, short-term investments such as treasury bills and money-market funds, and short-term notes.

**study objective 8**

Explain the reporting of cash.

More than 70% of Canadian public companies present cash in this manner. The illustration below shows how Canadian Tire combines cash and cash equivalents on its balance sheet:

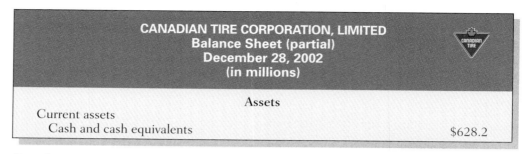

| CANADIAN TIRE CORPORATION, LIMITED |
| Balance Sheet (partial) |
| December 28, 2002 |
| (in millions) |

| Assets | |
| --- | --- |
| Current assets | |
| Cash and cash equivalents | $628.2 |

Canadian Tire reports that its cash and cash equivalents include cash on hand, balances with banks, and investments in money-market instruments.

Some companies may be in a cash deficit or negative position at year end. This can happen when the company is in an overdraft position at the bank. A **bank overdraft** occurs when withdrawals or payments exceed the amount in the bank account. This becomes a short-term loan from the bank, assuming that the bank does not reject the withdrawal or payment. Most companies have overdraft protection up to a certain amount with their banks. In an overdraft situation, the cash account shows a credit balance in the general ledger and is reported as a current liability called bank indebtedness.

A company may have cash that is **restricted** for a special purpose. An example is funds held on deposit until completion of an offer to buy real estate. Another example would be a plant expansion fund for financing the construction of an addition to the plant site. If the restricted cash is expected to be used within the next year, the amount should be reported as a current asset. When restricted funds will not be used in that time, they should be reported as a noncurrent asset.

In making loans to depositors, banks commonly require borrowers to keep minimum cash balances. These minimum balances, called **compensating balances**, provide the bank with support for the loans. They are a form of restriction on the use of cash. Compensating balances should be reported as a noncurrent asset and be disclosed in the financial statements.

## Using the Information in the Financial Statements

Management must perform a difficult balancing act to properly manage cash. On one hand, it is critical to ensure that enough cash is available to pay bills as they come due, to buy goods, and to take advantage of opportunities as they present themselves. On the other hand, cash itself is an unproductive asset unless invested in other assets (e.g., investments, inventory, and property, plant, and equipment). Too much cash on hand may indicate that management is not maximizing its return on assets.

The cash flow statement and the management report are two useful pieces of information to help readers assess management's effectiveness in managing and controlling cash. The cash flow statement, which will be discussed in Chapter 17, provides information about where cash came from and what it was used for.

A management report is included in all publicly distributed financial statements. The purpose of this report is to acknowledge management's responsibility for—among other items—the development of internal controls over the financial reporting process. In Appendix A at the end of this textbook, The Forzani Group Ltd. attaches a statement of Management's Responsibilities for Financial Reporting. This report includes the following statements to assure the reader that management takes its responsibility to produce reliable information seriously: "Management is responsible for the development and maintenance of systems of internal accounting and administrative controls. Such systems are designed to provide reasonable assurance that the financial information is accurate, relevant and reliable, and that the Company's assets are appropriately accounted for and adequately safeguarded."

## BEFORE YOU GO ON . . .

▶Review It

1. What is included as cash on a company's balance sheet?
2. What is meant by cash equivalents and compensating balances?
3. Does Forzani report cash or cash and cash equivalents in its 2003 balance sheet? At what amount? The answer to this question is provided at the end of the chapter.
4. How should a company report its responsibilities for internal control?

*Related exercise material:* BE7–12 and E7–12.

# Demonstration Problem

Trillo Company reports the following condensed information from its general ledger cash account and bank statement at June 30, 2005:

| Cash | | | |
|---|---|---|---|
| June 1 Bal. | 18,290 | | |
| June deposits | 17,000 | Cheques written | 20,510 |
| June 30 Bal. | 14,780 | | |

Additional
Demonstration
Problems

**TRILLO COMPANY**
**Bank Statement**
**June 30, 2005**

| | Cheques and Other Debits | Deposits and Other Credits | Balance |
|---|---|---|---|
| Balance, June 1 | | | 17,690 |
| Deposits | | 15,248 | 32,938 |
| Cheques cleared | 18,100 | | 14,838 |
| EFT insurance payment | 500 | | 14,338 |
| NSF cheque ($150 + $25) | 175 | | 14,163 |
| Service charge | 12 | | 14,151 |
| Interest earned | | 35 | 14,186 |

Additional information:

1. There was a deposit in transit of $600 at May 30, the preceding month, that cleared the bank in June. There were no outstanding cheques at the end of May.
2. The EFT payment for insurance is a pre-authorized monthly payment.
3. The NSF cheque was for $150, from Massif Co., a customer, in payment of its account. The bank added a $25 processing fee.

*Instructions*

(a) Prepare a bank reconciliation at June 30.
(b) Journalize the entries required by the reconciliation.

## Action Plan

- Compare the deposits on the bank statement with the deposits recorded in the books to determine the deposits in transit.
- Compare the cheques that cleared the bank statement with the cheques recorded in the books to determine the outstanding cheques.
- Note that any outstanding deposits or cheques from a prior period affect the amount reported by the bank which is used to determine outstanding items for the current period.
- Identify any items recorded on one side that are unrecorded on the other and adjust accordingly.
- All the journal entries should be based on the reconciling items per books.
- Make sure the Cash ledger account balance, after posting the reconciling items, agrees with the adjusted cash balance per books.

## Solution to Demonstration Problem

(a)

### TRILLO COMPANY
### Bank Reconciliation
### June 30, 2005

| | | |
|---|---|---:|
| Cash balance per bank statement | | $14,186 |
| Add:  Deposits in transit [$17,000 − ($15,248 − $600)] | | 2,352 |
| | | 16,538 |
| Less:  Outstanding cheques ($20,510 − $18,100) | | 2,410 |
| Adjusted cash balance per bank | | $14,128 |
| Cash balance per books | | $14,780 |
| Add:  Interest earned | | 35 |
| | | 14,815 |
| Less:  EFT insurance payment | $500 | |
| NSF cheque ($150 + $25) | 175 | |
| Bank service charge | 12 | 687 |
| Adjusted cash balance per books | | $14,128 |

(b)

|  | | | | |
|---|---|---|---:|---:|
| June 30 | Cash | | 35 | |
| | Interest Revenue | | | 35 |
| | To record bank interest earned. | | | |
| 30 | Insurance Expense | | 500 | |
| | Cash | | | 500 |
| | To record monthly insurance payment. | | | |
| 30 | Accounts Receivable | | 175 | |
| | Cash | | | 175 |
| | To re-establish accounts receivable for Massif Co. for NSF cheque and related service charge. | | | |
| 30 | Bank Charges Expense | | 12 | |
| | Cash | | | 12 |
| | To record bank service charges. | | | |

Check:

| Cash | | | |
|---|---:|---|---:|
| June 30  Bal. | 14,780 | June 30 | 500 |
| | 35 | | 175 |
| | | | 12 |
| June 30  Bal. | 14,128 | | |

the navigator

# Summary of Study Objectives

1. *Describe internal control.* Internal control consists of the policies and procedures within an organization to optimize its resources, prevent and detect errors and irregularities, safeguard its assets, and maintain reliable control systems.

2. *Explain the principles of internal control and be able to identify weaknesses in their application and suggest improvements.* The principles of internal control are authorization, segregation of duties, documentation, safeguarding of assets and records, independent verification, and other controls.

3. *Explain and critique the application of internal control principles to cash receipts.* Internal controls over cash receipts include (a) designating only personnel such as cashiers to handle cash, (b) assigning the duties of receiving cash, recording cash, and maintaining custody of cash to different individuals, (c) obtaining remittance advices for mail receipts, cash register tapes for over-the-counter receipts, and deposit slips for bank deposits, (d) using company safes and bank vaults to store cash with access limited to authorized personnel, and using cash registers to issue over-the-counter receipts, (e) depositing all cash intact daily, (f) making independent daily counts of register receipts and daily comparisons of total receipts with total deposits, and (g) bonding personnel that handle cash.

4. *Explain and critique the application of internal control principles to cash disbursements.* Internal controls over cash disbursements include (a) authorizing only specified individuals such as the comptroller to sign cheques, (b) assigning the duties of approving items for payment, paying for the items, and recording the payment to different individuals, (c) using prenumbered cheques and accounting for all cheques, with each cheque supported by an approved invoice, (d) storing blank cheques in a safe or vault, with access restricted to authorized personnel, and

using a cheque writer to imprint amounts on cheques, (e) comparing each cheque to the approved invoice before issuing the cheque, and making monthly reconciliations of bank and book balances, and (f) after payment, stamping each approved invoice "Paid."

5. *Demonstrate the operation of a petty cash fund.* To operate a petty cash fund, it is necessary to establish the fund, make payments from the fund, and replenish the fund. Journal entries are only made when the fund is established and replenished.

6. *Describe the control features of a bank account.* A bank account contributes to good internal control by providing physical controls for the storage of cash, reducing the amount of currency that must be kept on hand, and creating a double record of a depositor's bank transactions.

7. *Prepare a bank reconciliation.* In reconciling the bank account, the balance per books and balance per bank are reconciled to their adjusted balances. The steps in determining the reconciling items are to identify each of the following: deposits in transit, outstanding cheques, errors by the depositor or the bank, and unrecorded bank memoranda. Correcting entries must be made for any errors made by the depositor (the company). Entries are also required to update unrecorded bank memoranda (e.g., interest).

8. *Explain the reporting of cash.* Cash is listed first in the current assets section of the balance sheet. In many cases, cash is reported together with highly liquid, short-term investments (cash equivalents). Cash restricted for a special purpose is reported separately as a current asset or a noncurrent asset, depending on when the cash is expected to be used. The cash flow statement and the management report on the financial statements are useful tools to assess management's effectiveness in managing and controlling cash.

the navigator

# Glossary

Key Term Matching Activity

**Bank overdraft** Excess of withdrawals over the amount available in the bank account. (p. 354)

**Bank service charge** A fee charged by a bank for the use of its services. (p. 347)

**Bank statement** A statement received monthly from the bank that shows the depositor's bank transactions and balances. (p. 345)

**Cash** Resources such as coins, currency, cheques, and money orders that are acceptable at face value on deposit in a bank or similar depository. (p. 336)

**Cash equivalents** Highly liquid, short-term investments, with maturities of three months or less when purchased. (p. 353)

**Cash payments journal** A special journal used to record all cash paid. (p. 340)

**Cash receipts journal** A special journal used to record all cash received. (p. 338)

**Clearing** The process of exchanging and settling payment items that results in a transfer of funds from one financial institution to another. (p. 345)

**Compensating balances** Minimum cash balances required by a bank in support of bank loans. (p. 354)

**Deposits in transit** Deposits recorded by the depositor that have not been recorded by the bank. (p. 349)

**Electronic funds transfer (EFT)** A disbursement system that uses telephone, computer, or wireless means to transfer cash from one location to another. (p. 338)

**External auditors** Auditors who are independent of the organization. They examine internal control and attest to the reasonableness of financial statements or other financial information. (p. 334)

**Internal auditors** Company employees who evaluate the effectiveness of the company's system of internal control. (p. 334)

**Internal control** The policies and procedures adopted within a business to optimize resources, prevent and detect errors and irregularities, safeguard assets, and maintain reliable control systems. (p. 330)

**Outstanding cheques** Cheques issued and recorded by a company that have not been paid by the bank. (p. 349)

**Petty cash fund** A cash fund used to pay relatively small amounts. (p. 340)

**Special journal** A journal that is used to record similar types of transactions, such as all cash receipts or all cash payments. (p. 338)

# Self-Study Questions

 Chapter 7 Self-Test

Answers are at the end of the chapter.

(SO 1) K  1. Which of the following is not an objective of internal control?
  (a) Optimize resources.
  (b) Eliminate errors.
  (c) Safeguard assets.
  (d) Maintain reliable control systems.

(SO 2) K  2. The principles of internal control do not include:
  (a) authorization.
  (b) documentation procedures.
  (c) cost-benefit constraints.
  (d) independent verification.

(SO 2) K  3. Physical controls do not include:
  (a) safes and vaults to store cash.
  (b) bank reconciliations.
  (c) locked warehouses for inventories.
  (d) bank safety deposit boxes for important papers.

(SO 3) C  4. Which of the following items in a cash drawer at November 30 is not cash?
  (a) Debit card slips from sales to customers
  (b) Bank credit card slips from sales to customers
  (c) A customer cheque dated December 1
  (d) A customer cheque dated November 28

(SO 3) C  5. Permitting only designated personnel to handle cash receipts is an application of the principle of:
  (a) segregation of duties.
  (b) authorization.
  (c) independent verification.
  (d) other controls.

(SO 4) C  6. The use of prenumbered cheques in disbursing cash is an application of the principle of:
  (a) authorization.
  (b) segregation of duties.
  (c) physical controls.
  (d) documentation procedures.

(SO 5) AP  7. A cheque is written to replenish a $100 petty cash fund when the fund contains receipts of $94 and $3 in cash. In recording the cheque:
  (a) Cash Over and Short should be debited for $3.
  (b) Cash Over and Short should be credited for $3.
  (c) Petty Cash should be debited for $94.
  (d) Cash should be credited for $94.

(SO 6) C  8. The control features of a bank account do not include:
  (a) having bank auditors verify the correctness of the balance per books.
  (b) minimizing the amount of cash that must be kept on hand.
  (c) providing a double record of all bank transactions.
  (d) safeguarding cash by using a bank as a depository.

(SO 7) AP  9. Suzanne Terriault reports an ending cash balance of $410 in her cheque book at the end of the month and $500 in her bank statement. Reconciling items include deposits in transit of $250, outstanding cheques of $350, and service charges of $10. What is Suzanne's adjusted cash balance?
  (a) $390          (c) $410
  (b) $400          (d) $500

(SO 7) AP  10. A company mistakenly recorded a $459 cheque written in payment of an account as $495. The journal entry required to correct this would be:
  (a) debit Accounts Payable $36; credit Cash $36.
  (b) debit Cash $36; credit Accounts Payable $36.
  (c) debit Cash $36; credit Accounts Receivable $36.
  (d) No journal entry is required.

(SO 8) K  11. The statement that correctly describes the reporting of cash is:
  (a) Cash cannot be combined with cash equivalents.
  (b) Cash and cash equivalents are listed first in the current assets section.
  (c) Restricted cash funds are always reported as a current asset.
  (d) Compensating balances are reported as a current asset.

# Questions

(SO 2) C    1. "Internal control is concerned only with enhancing the accuracy of the accounting records." Do you agree? Explain.

(SO 2) K    2. What are the principles of internal control that most companies follow?

(SO 2) C    3. What are two common applications of the principle of segregation of duties?

(SO 2) C    4. How do documentation procedures contribute to good internal control?

(SO 2, 4) K    5. What internal control objectives are met by physical controls? Provide an example of how they apply to cash disbursements.

(SO 2) C    6. Explain the control principle of independent verification. What practices are important in applying this principle?

(SO 2) C    7. The management of Ly Company asks you, as the company accountant, to explain (a) the concept of reasonable assurance in internal control, and (b) the importance of the human factor in internal control. Explain them.

(SO 3) AN    8. At the corner grocery store, all sales clerks make change out of one cash register drawer using the same password. Is this a violation of internal control? Explain.

(SO 3) C    9. Creaghan's Department Stores has just installed electronic cash registers in its stores. How do cash registers improve internal control over cash receipts?

(SO 3) C    10. Explain the procedures that should be followed at the end of the day (or shift) to ensure proper internal control of over-the-counter cash receipts.

(SO 3) C    11. At Vink Wholesale Company, two mail clerks open all mail receipts. How does this strengthen internal control?

(SO 3) C    12. From a company's point of view, what are the similarities and differences between a customer using a debit card to pay for a purchase and a customer electronically transferring funds to pay an account on-line? What are the advantages to a company of allowing customers to use debit cards and electronic transfers?

(SO 4) C    13. "To have maximum effective internal control over cash disbursements, all payments should be made by cheque or by an electronic funds transfer." Is this true? Explain.

(SO 4) C    14. Ouellette Company's internal controls over cash disbursements require the comptroller to sign cheques imprinted by a computer after she compares the cheque to the approved invoice. Identify the internal control principles that are present in these procedures.

(SO 4) AN    15. Walter's Watches is a small retail store. Walter, the owner of the company, has recently hired a new employee, Wanda, who will be responsible for ordering merchandise, receiving the goods, and authorizing the merchandise invoices for payment. Describe the various ways Wanda could potentially commit a fraud with this arrangement.

(SO 5) C    16. (a) Identify the three activities that pertain to a petty cash fund, and indicate an internal control principle that is applicable to each activity. (b) When are journal entries required in the operation of a petty cash fund?

(SO 6) K    17. Explain the control features of a bank account, including the control benefits of (a) signature cards, (b) cheques, and (c) bank statements.

(SO 7) C    18. What is the purpose of a bank reconciliation? Who should be responsible for preparing it?

(SO 7) C    19. Paul Reimer is confused about the lack of agreement between the cash balance per books and the balance per bank. Explain the causes for the lack of agreement to Paul, and give an example of each cause.

(SO 7) C    20. The Diablo Company wrote cheque #2375 for $1,325 on March 16. As at March 31 the cheque had not cleared the company's bank account and was correctly listed as an outstanding cheque on the March 31 bank reconciliation. If the cheque has still not cleared the bank account on April 30, should it be included in the April bank reconciliation or not? Explain.

(SO 7) C    21. Omar Basabe asks for your help with an NSF cheque. Explain to Omar (a) what an NSF cheque is, (b) how it is treated in a bank reconciliation, and (c) whether it will require an adjusting entry.

(SO 8) C    22. (a) "Cash equivalents are the same as cash." Do you agree? Explain. (b) How should restricted cash funds be reported on the balance sheet?

# Brief Exercises

**Identify internal control objectives.**
**(SO 1, 2) C**

**BE7–1**  Natalie McPhail is the new owner of Liberty Parking—a parking garage. She has heard about internal control but is not clear about its importance for her business. Explain to Natalie the objectives of internal control, and give her one application of each objective for Liberty Parking.

**Calculate cash balance.**
**(SO 3) AP**

**BE7–2**  Sirois Company owns the following assets at the balance sheet date:

| | |
|---|---|
| Cash in bank—savings account | $ 6,000 |
| Cash on hand | 850 |
| Cash refund due from the Canada Customs and Revenue Agency | 1,000 |
| Cash in bank—chequing account | 12,000 |
| Postdated cheques | 500 |

What amount should be reported as cash in the balance sheet?

**Identify internal control principles applicable to cash receipts.**
**(SO 3) K**

**BE7–3**  The Miramichi Company has the following internal control procedures over cash receipts. Identify the internal control principle that is applicable to each procedure.

1. All over-the-counter receipts are recorded on cash registers.
2. All cashiers are bonded.
3. Daily cash counts are made by cashier department supervisors.
4. The duties of receiving cash, recording cash, and maintaining custody of cash are assigned to different individuals.
5. Only cashiers may operate cash registers.
6. All cash is deposited intact in the bank account daily.

**Identify internal control principles applicable to cash disbursements.**
**(SO 4) K**

**BE7–4**  Bujold Company has the following internal control procedures over cash disbursements. Identify the internal control principle that is applicable to each procedure.

1. Company cheques are prenumbered.
2. The bank statement is reconciled monthly by an internal auditor.
3. Blank cheques are stored in a safe in the comptroller's office.
4. Only the comptroller or assistant comptroller may sign cheques.
5. Cheque signers are not allowed to record cash disbursement transactions.
6. All payments, except for petty cash transactions, are made by cheque.

**Record petty cash transactions.**
**(SO 5) AP**

**BE7–5**  On March 20, Pugh's petty cash fund of $100 is replenished when the fund contains $10 in cash and receipts for postage $52, freight out $26, and supplies $10. Prepare the journal entry to record the replenishment of the petty cash fund.

**Record petty cash transactions.**
**(SO 5) AP**

**BE7–6**  On November 6, Clara's Snack Shop established a petty cash fund of $150. At the end of the month, the fund contained $23 in cash and receipts for printing $32, supplies $57, postage $19, and delivery expense $21. Prepare journal entries to establish the fund on November 6 and to replenish it on November 30.

**Indicate location of items in bank reconciliation.**
**(SO 7) AP**

**BE7–7**  For each of the items in the following list, identify where it is included on a bank reconciliation. Next to each item record the appropriate letter from this list: (a) increase to bank balance, (b) decrease to bank balance, (c) increase to company cash balance, (d) decrease to company cash balance, or (e) not included in the bank reconciliation.

_____ Bank debit memorandum for service charges
_____ EFT payment
_____ Outstanding cheques from the current month
_____ Outstanding cheques from the prior month that are still outstanding
_____ Outstanding cheques from the prior month that are no longer outstanding
_____ Bank error in recording a company cheque made out for $200 as $290
_____ Bank credit memorandum for interest revenue
_____ Company error in recording a deposit of $1,280 as $1,680
_____ Bank debit memorandum for an NSF cheque
_____ Deposit in transit from the current month
_____ Company error in recording a cheque made out for $360 as $630
_____ Bank error in recording a $2,575 deposit as $2,755

**BE7–8**  Referring to BE7–7, indicate (a) the items that will result in an adjustment to the company's records, and (b) why the other items do not require adjustment.

Identify reconciling items that require journal entries. (SO 7) C

**BE7–9**  In the month of November, Johal Company wrote and recorded cheques in the amount of $9,520. In December, it wrote and recorded cheques in the amount of $12,617. Of these cheques, $8,687 were presented to the bank for payment in November, and $10,989 in December. What is the amount for outstanding cheques at the end of November? At the end of December?

Analyse outstanding cheques. (SO 7) AP

**BE7–10**  On July 31, Manuliak Company had an unadjusted cash balance of $9,100. An examination of the July bank statement shows a balance of $7,920 on July 31; bank service charges $35; deposits in transit $2,152; interest earned $25; outstanding cheques $1,144; and an NSF cheque of $162. Prepare a bank reconciliation at July 31.

Prepare bank reconciliation. (SO 7) AP

**BE7–11**  Refer to the bank reconciliation prepared in BE7–10. Prepare the adjusting journal entries for Manuliak Company on July 31.

Prepare entries from bank reconciliation. (SO 7) AP

**BE7–12**  Dupré Company has the following cash balances: Cash in Bank $17,540; Payroll Bank Account $6,000; and Plant Expansion Fund Cash $25,000. Dupré maintains a $5,000 compensating bank balance in a separate account. Explain how each balance should be reported on the balance sheet.

Explain statement presentation of cash balances. (SO 8) C

# Exercises

**E7–1**  Per Paasche is the owner of Luna's Pizza. Luna's is operated strictly on a carry-out basis. Customers pick up their orders at a counter where a clerk exchanges the pizzas for cash. While at the counter, the customer can see other employees making the pizzas and the large ovens in which the pizzas are baked.

Identify principles of internal control. (SO 2, 3) C

*Instructions*

Identify the principles of internal control and give an example of each principle that you might observe when picking up your pizza. (*Note:* It may not be possible to observe all of the principles in action.)

**E7–2**  The following control procedures are used in the Sheridan Company for over-the-counter cash receipts:

Identify weaknesses in internal control over cash receipts, and suggest improvements. (SO 2, 3) AN

1. Cashiers are experienced, so they are not bonded.
2. All over-the-counter receipts are received by one of three clerks who share a cash register with a single cash drawer.
3. To minimize the risk of robbery, cash in excess of $100 is stored in an unlocked desk drawer in a back room until it is deposited in the bank.
4. At the end of each day, the total receipts are counted by the cashier on duty and reconciled to the cash register total.
5. The company accountant makes the bank deposit and then records the day's receipts.
6. If a customer has exact change and does not want a receipt, the sale is not rung through the cash register.

*Instructions*

(a) For each procedure, explain the weakness in internal control and identify the control principle that is violated.
(b) For each weakness, suggest a change in procedure that will result in better internal control.

**E7–3**  In the Abekah Company, cheques are not prenumbered. Both the purchasing agent and the comptroller are authorized to issue cheques. Each signer has access to unissued cheques kept in an unlocked file cabinet. The purchasing agent pays all bills for goods purchased for resale. Before making a payment, the purchasing agent determines that the goods have been received and verifies the mathematical accuracy of the vendor's invoice. After payment, the invoice is filed by the vendor, and the purchasing agent records the payment in the cash payments journal. The comptroller pays all other bills after receiving approval from authorized employees. After payment, the comptroller stamps all bills PAID, files them by payment date, and records the cheques in the cash payments journal. Abekah Company maintains one chequing account that is reconciled by the comptroller.

Identify weaknesses in internal control over cash disbursements, and suggest improvements. (SO 2, 4) S

*Instructions*

(a) List the weaknesses in internal control over cash disbursements.

(b) Write a memo to the company comptroller in which you recommend improvements.

**Record petty cash transactions.**
**(SO 5) AP**

**E7–4** Lang Company uses an imprest petty cash system. The fund was established on March 10 with a balance of $100. At the end of March, the following petty cash receipts were in the petty cash box:

| Date | Receipt No. | For | Amount |
|------|-------------|-----|--------|
| Mar. 15 | 1 | Postage stamps | $24 |
| 17 | 2 | Freight in (assume perpetual inventory system) | 19 |
| 19 | 3 | Miscellaneous expense | 12 |
| 21 | 4 | Delivery charges on outgoing freight | 38 |
| 24 | 5 | Miscellaneous expense | 5 |

There was $4 in the cash box when the fund was replenished and the amount in the fund was increased to $150 on March 25.

*Instructions*

Journalize the entries in March for the operation of the petty cash fund.

**Record petty cash transactions.**
**(SO 5) AP**

**Interactive Homework**

**E7–5** DesChene Company established a $300 petty cash fund on May 1. On May 31 the fund contained $123 cash and receipts for the following: office supplies, $37; printing, $42; parking, $36; drawings by the owner, $50; and postage, $10. Prepare journal entries to establish the fund on May 1, and to reimburse the fund and reduce it to $200 on May 31.

**Determine deposits in transit and other reconciling items.**
**(SO 7) AP**

**Interactive Homework**

**E7–6** On April 30, the bank reconciliation of the Hidden Valley Company shows a deposit in transit of $1,437. The May bank statement and the general ledger Cash account during May show the following:

| Bank Statement Deposits/Credits | | | Hidden Valley Company Deposits Made | |
|------|------|------|------|------|
| Date | Description | Amount | Date | Amount |
| May 2 | Deposit | $1,437 | May 6 | $2,255 |
| 10 | Deposit | 2,255 | 13 | 3,218 |
| 16 | Deposit | 3,218 | 20 | 954 |
| 20 | Deposit | 945 | 23 | 1,298 |
| 24 | Deposit | 1,298 | 31 | 1,531 |
| 31 | Interest Earned | 32 | | |

*Note:* The bank did not make any errors during May.

*Instructions*

(a) List the deposits in transit at May 31.

(b) List any other items that must be included in the bank reconciliation. Describe the impact of each item on the bank reconciliation.

**Determine outstanding cheques and other reconciling items.**
**(SO 7) AP**

**Interactive Homework**

**E7–7** On April 30, the bank reconciliation of Hidden Valley Company shows three outstanding cheques: No. 254 for $560: No. 255 for $280; and No. 257 for $410. The May bank statement and the general ledger Cash account during May show the following:

| Bank Statement Cheques Paid/Debits | | | Hidden Valley Company Cheques Written | | |
|------|------|------|------|------|------|
| Date | Cheque No. | Amount | Date | Cheque No. | Amount |
| May 2 | 254 | $560 | May 2 | 258 | $159 |
| 4 | 257 | 410 | 5 | 259 | 275 |
| 12 | 258 | 159 | 10 | 260 | 500 |
| 17 | 259 | 275 | 15 | 261 | 867 |
| 20 | 260 | 500 | 22 | 262 | 750 |
| 29 | 263 | 840 | 24 | 263 | 440 |
| 30 | 262 | 750 | 29 | 264 | 650 |
| 31 | SC | 54 | | | |

*Note:* The bank did not make any errors during May.

**Instructions**

(a) List the outstanding cheques at May 31.
(b) List any other items that must be included in the bank reconciliation. Describe the impact of each item on the bank reconciliation.

**E7–8** Refer to the data presented in E7–6 and E7–7. On May 31 Hidden Valley Company had an adjusted Cash balance of $6,543 in the general ledger. The bank statement showed a balance of $6,378 on May 31.

*Prepare bank reconciliation and related entries.*
*(SO 7) AP*

**Instructions**

(a) Prepare a bank reconciliation for Hidden Valley Company on May 31.
(b) Prepare the necessary journal entries to bring the Cash account to its adjusted balance on May 31. Assume all deposits made were to record the collection of accounts receivable, and any cheques written were for the payment of accounts payable.

**E7–9** Verwey Company reconciles its bank account on a monthly basis. The following information was available to reconcile the Cash account to the bank statement balance as at November 30, 2005:

*Prepare bank reconciliation and related entries.*
*(SO 7) AP*

*Interactive Homework*

1. Cash balance per the bank statement, November 30: $9,013
2. November bank service charge not recorded by the company: $24
3. Cash balance per the accounting records, November 30: $7,190
4. Deposits in transit on November 30: $1,575
5. Cheque number 373 was correctly written and posted by the bank as $672. Verwey Company had recorded the cheque as $762 in error. The cheque was written for the purchase of office supplies.
6. EFT deposits from customers in payment of their accounts on the bank statement during the month of November totalled $883. (*Note:* Verwey had not recorded these prior to receiving the bank statement.)
7. Outstanding cheques, November 30: $2,449

**Instructions**

(a) Prepare a bank reconciliation at November 30, 2005.
(b) Journalize the adjusting entries at November 30, 2005, on Verwey Company's books.

**E7–10** The information below relates to the Cash account in the ledger of Sharaf Company:

*Prepare bank reconciliation and related entries.*
*(SO 7) AP*

Adjusted balance August 31, 2005: $17,350
Cash deposited during September 2005: $64,329
Cheques written during September 2005: $63,746

The September bank statement shows a balance of $17,292 on September 30 and the following memoranda:

| Credits | | Debits | |
|---|---|---|---|
| EFT collections | $1,825 | NSF cheque: J. Hower | $410 |
| Interest earned on chequing account | 45 | Safety deposit box rent | 30 |

At September 30, deposits in transit were $4,910 and outstanding cheques totalled $3,839. The bank had incorrectly posted a cheque correctly written for $972 as $1,972. The cheque was payable to one of Sharaf's employees for his or her salary.

**Instructions**

(a) Calculate the unadjusted balance in the Cash account on September 30.
(b) Prepare the bank reconciliation at September 30.
(c) Prepare the required entries at September 30, assuming (1) the NSF cheque was from a customer on account, and (2) EFT collections were from customers paying their accounts.

**E7–11** The cash records of Shigahiro Company show the following:

*Calculate deposits in transit and outstanding cheques for two months.*
*(SO 7) AP*

1. The June 30 bank reconciliation indicated that deposits in transit totalled $1,050. During July, the general ledger account Cash showed deposits of $15,750, but the bank statement indicated that $15,820 of deposits were received during the month.

2. The June 30 bank reconciliation also reported outstanding cheques of $970. During the month of July, Shigahiro Company's books showed that cheques worth $17,200 were issued, yet the bank statement showed that only $16,660 of cheques cleared the bank in July.

3. In September, deposits per bank statement totalled $23,500, deposits per books totalled $22,900, and deposits in transit at September 30 totalled $3,800.

4. In September, cash disbursements per books were $19,700, cheques clearing the bank were $22,250, and outstanding cheques at September 30 were $2,275.

There were no bank debit or credit memoranda. No errors were made by either the bank or Shigahiro Company.

*Instructions*

Answer the following questions:

(a) In number 1, what were the deposits in transit at July 31?
(b) In number 2, what were the outstanding cheques at July 31?
(c) In number 3, what were the deposits in transit at August 31?
(d) In number 4, what were the outstanding cheques at August 31?

**Calculate cash and cash equivalents and report other items.**
**(SO 8) AP**

**E7–12** A new accountant at La Maison is trying to identify which of the following amounts should be reported as the current asset "Cash and Cash Equivalents" in the year-end balance sheet, as at April 30, 2005:

1. Currency and coin totalling $57 in a locked box used for petty cash transactions
2. A $10,000 guaranteed investment certificate, due May 31, 2005
3. April-dated cheques worth $300 that La Maison has received from customers but not yet deposited
4. An $85 cheque received from a customer in payment of her April account, but postdated May 1
5. A balance of $2,575 in the Royal Bank chequing account
6. A balance of $4,000 in the Royal Bank savings account
7. Prepaid postage of $75 in the postage meter
8. A $100 IOU from the company receptionist

*Instructions*

(a) What amount should La Maison report as its "Cash and Cash Equivalents" balance at April 30, 2005?
(b) In which financial statement and in which account should the items not included as "Cash and Cash Equivalents" be reported?

# Problems: Set A

**Identify internal control weaknesses over cash receipts.**
**(SO 2, 3) AN**

**P7–1A** Red River Theatre is located in the Red River Mall. A cashier's booth is located near the entrance to the theatre. Two cashiers are employed. One works from 1:00 to 5:00 p.m., the other from 5:00 to 9:00 p.m. Each cashier is bonded. The cashiers receive cash from customers and operate a machine that ejects serially numbered tickets. The rolls of tickets are inserted and locked into the machine by the theatre manager at the beginning of each cashier's shift.

After purchasing a ticket, which may be at different prices depending on the day or age group, the customer takes the ticket to an usher stationed at the entrance of the theatre lobby, about 10 metres from the cashier's booth. The usher tears the ticket in half, admits the customer, and returns the ticket stub to the customer. The other half of the ticket is dropped into a locked box by the usher.

At the end of each cashier's shift, the theatre manager removes the ticket rolls from the machine and makes a cash count. The cash count sheet is initialled by the cashier. At the end of the day, the manager deposits the receipts in total in a bank night deposit vault located in the mall. The manager also sends copies of the deposit slip and the initialled cash count sheets to the theatre company comptroller for verification, and to the company's accounting department. Receipts from the first shift are stored in a safe located in the manager's office.

*Instructions*

(a) Identify the internal control principles and their application to the cash receipts transactions of the Red River Theatre.

(b) If the usher and the cashier decide to collaborate to misappropriate cash, what actions might they take?

**P7–2A** Cedar Grove Middle School wants to raise money for a new sound system for its auditorium. The main fundraising event is a dance at which the famous disc jockey Obnoxious Al will play classic and not-so-classic dance tunes. Roger DeMaster, the music teacher, has been given the responsibility for coordinating the fundraising efforts. This is Roger's first experience with fundraising. He asks the Student Representative Council (SRC) to help him with the event.

*Identify internal control weaknesses over cash receipts and cash disbursements.*
*(SO 2, 3, 4) AN*

Roger had 500 unnumbered tickets printed for the dance. He left the tickets in a box on his desk and told the SRC students to take as many tickets as they thought they could sell for $5 each. In order to ensure that no extra tickets would be floating around, he told them to dispose of any unsold tickets. When the students received payment for the tickets, they were to bring the cash back to Roger. He then put it in a locked box in his desk drawer.

Some of the students were responsible for decorating the gymnasium for the dance. Roger gave each of them a key to the cash box. He told them that if they took money out to buy materials, they should put a note in the box saying how much they took and what it was used for. After two weeks, the cash box appeared to be getting full, so Roger asked Freda Stevens to count the money, prepare a deposit slip, and deposit the money in a bank account Roger had opened.

The day of the dance, Roger wrote a cheque from the account to pay Obnoxious Al. Al said that he accepted only cash and did not give receipts. So Roger took $200 out of the cash box and gave it to Al. At the dance, Roger had Sara Billings working at the entrance to the gymnasium. She collected tickets from students and sold tickets to those who had not prepurchased them. Roger estimated 400 students attended the dance.

The following day Roger closed out the bank account, which had $250 in it. He gave that amount plus the $180 in the cash box to Principal Skinner. Principal Skinner seemed surprised that, after generating roughly $2,000 in sales, the dance netted only $430 in cash. Roger did not know how to respond.

*Instructions*

Identify as many internal control weaknesses as you can in this scenario. Suggest how each could be addressed.

**P7–3A** MTR Company maintains a petty cash fund for small expenditures. The following transactions happened over a two-month period:

*Record and post petty cash transactions and identify internal control features.*
*(SO 2, 5) AP*

July    1   Established a petty cash fund by writing a cheque on its bank account for $250.
       15   Replenished the petty cash fund. On this date the fund had $12.60 in cash and the following petty cash receipts: freight out $94, postage expense $42.40, entertainment expense $46.60, and miscellaneous expense $51.20.

July   31   Replenished the petty cash fund. On this date, the fund had $9.90 in cash and the following petty cash receipts: freight out $82.10, charitable contributions expense $50, postage expense $67.80, and miscellaneous expense $42.10.

Aug.   15   Replenished the petty cash fund. On this date, the fund had $12 in cash and the following petty cash receipts: freight out $85.80, entertainment expense $73, postage expense $33, and supplies expense $47.60.
       16   Increased the amount of the petty cash fund to $350.
       31   Replenished the petty cash fund. On this date, the fund had $17 in cash and the following petty cash receipts: postage expense $165, entertainment expense $90.60, and freight out $73.20.

*Instructions*

(a) Journalize the petty cash transactions.
(b) Post to the Petty Cash account.
(c) What internal control features exist in a petty cash fund?

Prepare bank reconciliation
and related entries.
(SO 7) AP

**P7–4A** On May 31, 2005, Lisik Company had a cash balance per books of $6,760. The bank statement on that date showed a balance of $7,675. A comparison of the statement with the Cash account revealed the following facts:

1. The statement included a debit memo of $40 for the printing of additional company cheques.
2. Cash sales of $836 on May 12 were deposited in the bank. The cash receipts journal entry and the deposit slip were incorrectly made out and recorded by Lisik as $856. The bank detected the error on the deposit slip and credited Lisik Company for the correct amount.
3. The May 31 deposit of $963 was not included in the deposits on the May bank statement. The deposit had been placed in the bank's night deposit vault on May 31.
4. Outstanding cheques on April 30 totalled $1,450. Of these $1,120 cleared the bank in May. There were $946 of cheques written in May that were outstanding on May 31.
5. On May 18, the company issued cheque #1181 for $685 to M. Helms, on account. The cheque, which cleared the bank in May, was incorrectly journalized and posted by Lisik Company for $568.
6. A review of the bank statement revealed that Lisik Company received electronic payments from customers on account of $2,055 during May. The bank had also credited the account with $39 of interest revenue on May 31. Lisik had no prior notice of these amounts.
7. Included with the cancelled cheques was a cheque issued by Lasik Company for $600 that was incorrectly charged to Lisik Company by the bank.
8. On May 31, the bank statement showed an NSF charge of $715 for a cheque issued by W. Hoad, a customer, to Lisik Company on account. This amount included a $15 service charge by the bank.

*Instructions*

(a) Prepare the bank reconciliation at May 31, 2005.
(b) Prepare the necessary adjusting entries for Lisik Company at May 31, 2005.

Prepare bank reconciliation
and related entries.
(SO 7) AP

**P7–5A** The March bank statement showed the following for Yap Co.:

**YAP CO.**
**Bank Statement**
**March 31, 2005**

| Date | Deposits Amount | Cheques and Other Debits Number | Amount | Balance |
|---|---|---|---|---|
| Feb. 28 | | | | $14,368 |
| Mar.  1 | $2,530 | 3451 | $2,260 | 14,638 |
| 2 | | 3471 | 845 | 13,793 |
| 5 | 1,212 | | | 15,005 |
| 7 | | 3472 | 1,427 | 13,578 |
| 10 | | NSF—Jordan | 550 | 13,028 |
| 15 | | 3473 | 1,641 | 11,387 |
| 22 | | 3474 | 1,320 | 10,067 |
| 27 | 2,567 | | | 12,634 |
| 31 | IN 23 | SC | 49 | 12,608 |

Additional information:

1. The bank statement contained two debit memoranda:
   (a) An NSF cheque for of $550 that had been previously deposited by Yap was returned due to insufficient funds in the maker's bank account. This cheque was originally given to Yap by Mr. Jordan, a customer, in payment of his account. Yap believes it will be able to collect this amount from Mr. Jordan.
   (b) A service charge (SC) of $49 for bank services provided throughout the month
2. The bank statement contained one credit memorandum for interest (IN) earned on the account for the month in the amount of $23.
3. The bank made an error processing cheque #3474. No other errors were made by the bank.

Yap's list of cash receipts and cash payments showed the following for March:

| Cash Receipts | | | Cash Payments | | |
|---|---|---|---|---|---|
| Date | Amount | | Date | Cheque No. | Amount |
| Mar.  4 | $1,221 | | Mar.  7 | 3472 | $1,427 |
| 26 | 2,567 | | 15 | 3473 | 1,461 |
| 30 | 1,025 | | 22 | 3474 | 2,130 |
| Total | $4,813 | | 29 | 3475 | 487 |
| | | | | | $5,505 |

The bank portion of last month's bank reconciliation for Yap Co., at February 28, 2005, was as follows:

**YAP CO.**
**Bank Reconciliation**
**February 28, 2005**

| | | | |
|---|---|---|---|
| Cash balance per bank | | | $14,368 |
| Add:  Deposits in transit | | | 2,530 |
| | | | 16,898 |
| Less:  Outstanding cheques | | | |
| #3451 | | $2,260 | |
| #3470 | | 1,535 | |
| #3471 | | 845 | 4,640 |
| Adjusted cash balance per bank | | | $12,258 |

*Instructions*
(a) Determine Yap Co.'s unadjusted cash balance in its general ledger on March 31.
(b) What is the amount of the deposits in transit, if any, at March 31?
(c) What is the amount of the outstanding cheques, if any, at March 31?
(d) Prepare a bank reconciliation for Yap Co. for the month of March 2005.
(e) Prepare the required journal entries for Yap Co. on March 31, 2005.

**P7–6A** The bank portion of the bank reconciliation for Maloney Company at October 31, 2005, was as follows:

Prepare bank reconciliation and related entries.
(SO 7) AP

**MALONEY COMPANY**
**Bank Reconciliation**
**October 31, 2005**

| | | | |
|---|---|---|---|
| Cash balance per bank | | | $12,444.70 |
| Add:  Deposits in transit | | | 1,530.20 |
| | | | 13,974.90 |
| Less:  Outstanding cheques | | | |
| #2451 | | $1,260.40 | |
| #2470 | | 720.10 | |
| #2471 | | 844.50 | |
| #2472 | | 503.60 | |
| #2474 | | 1,050.00 | 4,378.60 |
| Adjusted cash balance per bank | | | $ 9,596.30 |

The adjusted cash balance per bank agreed with the cash balance per books at October 31.
The November bank statement showed the following:

**MALONEY COMPANY**
**Bank Statement**
**November 30, 2005**

| Date | Deposits Amount | Cheques and Other Debits Number | Amount | Balance |
|---|---|---|---|---|
| Oct. 31 | | | | $12,444.70 |
| Nov. 1 | $1,530.20 | 2470 | $ 720.10 | 13,254.80 |
| 2 | | 2471 | 844.50 | 12,410.30 |
| 4 | 1,211.60 | 2475 | 1,640.70 | 11,981.20 |
| 5 | | 2474 | 1,050.00 | 10,931.20 |
| 8 | 990.10 | 2476 | 2,830.00 | 9,091.30 |
| 10 | | 2477 | 600.00 | 8,491.30 |
| 13 | 2,575.00 | | | 11,066.30 |
| 15 | | 2479 | 1,750.00 | 9,316.30 |
| 18 | 1,472.70 | 2480 | 1,330.00 | 9,459.00 |
| 21 | 2,945.00 | | | 12,404.00 |
| 25 | 2,567.30 | NSF | 260.00 | 14,711.30 |
| 27 | | 2481 | 695.40 | 14,015.90 |
| 28 | 1,650.00 | | | 15,665.90 |
| 29 | EFT 2,479.00 | 2486 | 900.00 | 17,244.90 |
| 30 | 1,186.00 | 2483 | 575.50 | 17,855.40 |

Additional information from the bank statement:

1. The EFT of $2,479 is an electronic transfer from a customer in payment of its account. The amount includes $49 of interest which Maloney Company had not previously accrued.
2. The NSF for $260 is a $250 cheque from a customer, Pendray Holdings, in payment of its account, and a $10 processing fee.
3. The bank did not make any errors.

The cash records per books for November follow. Two errors were made by Maloney Company.

| Cash Payments | | | | | | | Cash Receipts | |
|---|---|---|---|---|---|---|---|---|
| Date | Number | Amount | Date | Number | Amount | | Date | Amount |
| Nov. 1 | 2475 | $1,640.70 | Nov. 20 | 2483 | 575.50 | | Nov. 3 | $ 1,211.60 |
| 2 | 2476 | 2,380.00 | 22 | 2484 | 829.50 | | 7 | 990.10 |
| 2 | 2477 | 600.00 | 23 | 2485 | 974.80 | | 12 | 2,575.00 |
| 4 | 2478 | 538.20 | 24 | 2486 | 900.00 | | 17 | 1,472.70 |
| 8 | 2479 | 1,750.00 | 29 | 2487 | 398.00 | | 20 | 2,954.00 |
| 10 | 2480 | 1,330.00 | 30 | 2488 | 1,200.00 | | 24 | 2,567.30 |
| 15 | 2481 | 695.40 | Total | | $14,424.10 | | 27 | 1,650.00 |
| 18 | 2482 | 612.00 | | | | | 29 | 1,186.00 |
| | | | | | | | 30 | 1,338.00 |
| | | | | | | | Total | $15,944.70 |

*Instructions*

(a) Determine the unadjusted cash balance per books as at November 30, 2005, before reconciliation.
(b) Prepare a bank reconciliation at November 30.
(c) Prepare the required entries based on the reconciliation. (*Note:* The correction of any errors in the recording of cheques should be made to Accounts Payable. The correction of any errors in the recording of cash receipts should be made to Accounts Receivable.)

Prepare bank reconciliation and related entries.
(SO 7) AP

**P7–7A** When the accountant of Kurji's Appliances prepared the bank reconciliation on April 30, 2005, there were three outstanding cheques: #286 for $217, #289 for $326, and #290 for $105. There were no deposits in transit as at April 30, 2005. The bank balance at April 30 was $4,261. Shown below is selected information from the May bank statement:

| Cheques Cleared | | |
|---|---|---|
| Date | Cheque No. | Amount |
| May  1 | 286 | $  217 |
| 8 | 305 | 402 |
| 20 | 306 | 105 |
| 22 | 308 | 1,648 |
| 22 | 289 | 326 |
| 23 | 304 | 2,735 |
| 31 | 309 | 175 |

| Other Bank Account Transactions | | |
|---|---|---|
| Date | Amount | Transaction |
| May  8 | $2,620 + | Deposit |
| 12 | 4,718 + | Deposit |
| 24 | 3,190 + | Deposit |
| 25 | 280 − | NSF cheque |
| 31 | 28 − | Service charge |
| 31 | 12 + | Interest |

The NSF cheque was originally received from a customer, M. Rafique, in payment of his account of $265. The bank included a $15 service charge for a total of $280.

Information from the company's accounting records appears below:

| Cash Receipts | |
|---|---|
| Date | Amount |
| May  5 | $2,260 |
| 12 | 4,718 |
| 23 | 3,190 |
| 31 | 1,004 |

| Cash Payments | | |
|---|---|---|
| Date | Cheque No. | Amount |
| May  5 | 304 | $2,735 |
| 5 | 305 | 402 |
| 19 | 306 | 150 |
| 19 | 307 | 3,266 |
| 19 | 308 | 1,648 |
| 31 | 309 | 175 |
| 31 | 310 | 1,800 |

Investigation reveals that cheque #306 was issued to pay the telephone bill. All deposits are for collections of accounts receivable. The bank made no errors.

*Instructions*

(a) Calculate the balance per bank statement at May 31 and the unadjusted Cash balance per company records at May 31.
(b) Prepare a bank reconciliation for Kurji's Appliances at May 31.
(c) Prepare the general journal entries necessary to adjust the book balance of Cash to the adjusted balance.
(d) What balance would Kurji's Appliances report as cash in the current assets section of its balance sheet on May 31, 2005?

**P7–8A**  Aura Whole Foods is a very profitable small business. It has not, however, thought much about internal control. For example, in an attempt to keep clerical and office expenses to a minimum, the company has combined the jobs of cashier and bookkeeper. As a result, K. Kilgora handles all cash receipts, keeps the accounting records, and prepares the monthly bank reconciliations.

The balance per bank statement on October 31, 2005, was $19,460. Outstanding cheques were #762 for $113.90, #783 for $160, #784 for $266.90, #862 for $170.73, #863 for $325.40, and #864 for $173.10. Included with the statement was an EFT receipt for $750 that indicated the collection of an account receivable on October 25. This EFT has not been recorded by the company.

The company's ledger showed one cash account, with a balance of $19,640.77. The balance included undeposited cash on hand. Because of the lack of internal controls, Kilgora took for personal use all of the undeposited receipts. He then prepared the following bank reconciliation in an effort to hide his theft of cash:

*Prepare bank reconciliation and identify internal control weaknesses.*
*(SO 2, 3, 4, 7) AN*

| Cash balance per books, October 31 | | $19,640.77 |
|---|---|---|
| Add: Outstanding cheques | | |
| #862 | $170.73 | |
| #863 | 325.40 | |
| #864 | 173.10 | 669.23 |
| | | 20,210.00 |
| Less: Bank credit memorandum | | 750.00 |
| Cash balance per bank statement, October 31 | | $19,460.00 |

*Instructions*

(a) Prepare a correct bank reconciliation. (*Hint:* The theft is the difference between the adjusted balance per books and bank.)
(b) Indicate the three ways that Kilgora attempted to hide the theft and the dollar amount for each method.
(c) What principles of internal control were violated in this case?

Calculate cash balance.
(SO 8) AP

**P7–9A** A first year co-op student is trying to determine the amount of cash that should be reported on a company's balance sheet. The following information was provided to the student at year end:

1. Cash on hand in the cash registers totals $5,000.
2. The petty cash fund is $500.
3. The balance in the commercial bank savings account is $100,000 and in the commercial bank chequing account, $25,000. The company also has a U.S. bank account, which contained the equivalent of $48,000 Canadian at year end.
4. A special bank account holds $150,000 that is restricted for capital asset replacement.
5. A line of credit of $50,000 is available at the bank on demand.
6. The amount due from employees (travel advances) totals $14,000.
7. Temporary investments held by the company include $32,000 in a money-market fund, $75,000 in treasury bills, and $40,000 in shares of The Forzani Group Ltd.
8. The company has a supply of unused postage stamps totalling $150.
9. The company has NSF cheques totalling $1,750 that were returned by the bank.
10. In a special account, the company has $9,250 of cash deposits (advances) paid by customers.

*Instructions*

(a) Calculate the Cash balance that should be reported on the year end balance sheet as a current asset.
(b) Would your answer for (a) change if the company combines its cash and cash equivalents?
(c) Identify where any items that were not reported in the Cash balance in (a) should be reported.

# Problems: Set B

Identify internal control weaknesses over cash receipts.
(SO 2, 3) AN

**P7–1B** The board of trustees of a local church is concerned about the internal accounting controls of its offering collections made at weekly services. Its members ask you to serve on a three-person audit team made up of yourself, the internal auditor of the university, and a CA who has just joined the church. At a meeting of the audit team and the board of trustees, you learn the following:

1. The church's board of trustees has delegated responsibility for the financial management and audit of the financial records to the finance committee. This group prepares the annual budget and approves major disbursements but is not involved in collections or record keeping. No audit has been done in recent years, because the same trusted employee has kept church records and served as financial secretary for 15 years. The church does not carry any fidelity insurance.
2. The collection at the weekly service is taken by a team of ushers who volunteer to serve for one month. The ushers take the collection plates to a basement office at the rear of the church. They hand their plates to the head usher and return to the church service. After all plates have been turned in, the head usher counts the cash received. The head usher

then places the cash in the church safe along with a notation of the amount counted. The head usher volunteers to serve for three months.

3. The next morning, the financial secretary opens the safe and recounts the collection. The secretary withholds from $150 to $200 in cash, depending on the cash expenditures expected for the week, and deposits the remainder of the collections in the bank. To make the deposit easier, church members who contribute by cheque are asked to make their cheques payable to Cash.

4. Each month the financial secretary reconciles the bank statement and submits a copy of the reconciliation to the board of trustees. The reconciliations have rarely contained any bank errors and have never shown any errors per books.

### Instructions

(a) Indicate the weaknesses in internal control in the handling of collections.

(b) List the improvements in internal control procedures that you plan to recommend at the next meeting of the audit team for (1) the ushers, (2) the head usher, (3) the financial secretary, and (4) the finance committee.

(c) What church policies should be changed to improve internal control?

**P7–2B** Segal Office Supply Company recently changed its system of internal control over cash disbursements. The system includes the following features:

*Identify internal controls over cash disbursements. (SO 2, 4) AN*

1. Instead of being unnumbered and manually prepared, all cheques are now prenumbered and written with an electronic cheque writer bought by the company. Before a cheque can be issued, each invoice must have the approval of Cindy Moonti, the purchasing agent, and Ian Methven, the receiving department supervisor. Cheques must be signed by either Frank Kepros, the comptroller, or Mary Arno, the assistant comptroller. Before signing a cheque, the signer is expected to compare the amount of the cheque with the amount on the invoice.

2. After signing a cheque, the signer stamps the invoice PAID and writes, in the stamp, the date, cheque number, and amount of the cheque. The paid invoice is then sent to the accounting department for recording.

3. Blank cheques are stored in a safe in the comptroller's office. The combination to the safe is known only by the comptroller and the assistant comptroller. Each month, the bank statement is reconciled by the assistant chief accountant.

### Instructions

Identify the internal control principles and their application to the cash disbursements of Segal Office Supply Company.

**P7–3B** Vickers Company maintains a petty cash fund for small expenditures. The following transactions happened over a two-month period:

*Record and post petty cash transactions and identify internal control features. (SO 2, 5) AP*

Jan.  1 Established the petty cash fund by writing a cheque on First Bank for $200.

15 Replenished the petty cash fund. On this date, the fund consisted of $3 in cash and the following petty cash receipts: freight out $94, postage expense $42.40, office supplies expense $47.10, and miscellaneous expense $11.90.

31 Replenished the petty cash fund. On this date, the fund consisted of $8 in cash and the following petty cash receipts: freight out $82.10, charitable contributions expense $40, postage expense $27.80, and miscellaneous expense $43.70.

Feb. 15 Replenished the petty cash fund. On this date, the fund consisted of $11 in cash and the following petty cash receipts: freight out $16, entertainment expense $43, postage expense $33, freight in $60 (assume perpetual inventory system), and miscellaneous expense $33.80.

16 Increased the amount of the petty cash fund to $300.

28 Replenished the petty cash fund. On this date, the fund consisted of $13 in cash and the following petty cash receipts: postage expense $140, travel expense $45.60, freight out $46.40, and office supplies expense, $57.20.

### Instructions

(a) Journalize the petty cash transactions.

(b) Post to the Petty Cash account.

(c) It was stated in the chapter that "better internal control over cash disbursements is possible when payments are made by cheque." Why, then, are some payments made from petty cash rather than by cheque? Does this mean that there is no internal control over payments from petty cash? Explain.

**Prepare bank reconciliation and related entries.**
**(SO 7) AP**

**P7–4B** The Agricultural Genetics Company's Cash account in its general ledger report a balance of $7,393 on May 31, 2005. The company's bank statement from the Western Bank reported a balance of $9,134 on the same date.

A comparison of the details in the bank statement to the details in the Cash account revealed the following facts:

1. The bank statement included a debit memo of $50 for bank service charges.
2. Cash sales of $638 on May 12 were deposited in the bank. The journal entry to record the cash sales and the deposit slip to deposit the cash were correctly made out for $638. The bank credited Agricultural Genetics Company for $386.
3. The May 31 deposit of $1,141 was not included in the deposits on the May bank statement. The deposit had been placed in the bank's night deposit vault on May 31.
4. Outstanding cheques on April 30 totalled $922. Of these, $689 cleared the bank in May. There were $1,446 of cheques written in May that were outstanding on May 31.
5. On May 18, the company issued cheque #1181 for $585 to L. Kingston, on account. The cheque, which cleared the bank in May, was incorrectly journalized and posted by Agricultural Genetics Company for $855.
6. A review of the bank statement revealed that the Agricultural Genetics Company received $2,031 of electronic payments from customers on account during May. The bank had also credited the company's account with $24 of interest revenue on May 31. Agricultural Genetics Company had no prior notice of these amounts.
7. On May 31, the bank statement showed an NSF charge of $820 for a cheque issued by Pete Dell, a customer, to Agricultural Genetics Company on account. This amount includes a $20 service charge by the bank.

*Instructions*

(a) Prepare the bank reconciliation at May 31, 2005.
(b) Prepare the necessary entries for Agricultural Genetics Company at May 31, 2005.

**Prepare bank reconciliation and related entries.**
**(SO 7) AP**

**P7–5B** The bank portion of the bank reconciliation for Huang Company at November 30, 2005, was as follows:

**HUANG COMPANY**
**Bank Reconciliation**
**November 30, 2005**

| | | | |
|---|---|---|---|
| Cash balance per bank | | | $14,367.90 |
| Add:  Deposits in transit | | | 2,530.20 |
| | | | 16,898.10 |
| Less:  Outstanding cheques | | | |
| | #3451 | $2,260.40 | |
| | #3470 | 1,100.00 | |
| | #3471 | 844.50 | |
| | #3472 | 1,426.80 | |
| | #3474 | 1,050.00 | 6,681.70 |
| Adjusted cash balance per bank | | | $10,216.40 |

The adjusted cash balance per bank agreed with the cash balance per books at November 30. The December bank statement showed the following:

**HUANG COMPANY**
**Bank Statement**
**December 31, 2005**

| Date | Deposits Amount | Cheques and Other Debits Number | Cheques and Other Debits Amount | Balance |
|---|---|---|---|---|
| Nov. 30 | | | | $14,367.90 |
| Dec.  1 | $2,530.20 | 3451 | $2,260.40 | 14,637.70 |
| 2 | | 3471 | 844.50 | 13,793.20 |
| 4 | 1,211.60 | 3475 | 1,640.70 | 13,364.10 |
| 7 | | 3472 | 1,426.80 | 11,937.30 |
| 8 | 2,365.10 | 3476 | 1,300.00 | 13,002.40 |
| 10 | | 3477 | 2,130.00 | 10,872.40 |
| 15 | 3,145.00 | 3479 | 3,080.00 | 10,937.40 |
| 16 | 2,672.70 | | | 13,610.10 |
| 21 | 2,945.00 | | | 16,555.10 |
| 26 | 2,567.30 | NSF | 1,027.10 | 18,095.30 |
| 27 | | 3480 | 600.00 | 17,495.30 |
| 29 | 2,836.00 | 3483 | 1,140.00 | 19,191.30 |
| 30 | 1,025.00 | 3482 | 475.50 | 19,740.80 |
| 31 | | 3485 | 540.80 | 19,200.00 |
| 31 | | SC | 45.00 | 19,155.00 |

Additional information:

1. The deposit of $3,145 on December 15 is an electronic transfer from a customer in payment of its account. The amount includes $65 of interest, which Huang Company had not previously accrued.
2. The NSF for $1,027.10 is a $1,007.10 cheque from a customer, Hilo Holdings, in payment of its account, and a $20 processing fee.
3. SC represents bank service charges for the month.

The bank did not make any errors, but errors were made by Huang Company. The cash records per the company's books for December showed the following:

| | | Cash Payments | | | | | Cash Receipts | |
|---|---|---|---|---|---|---|---|---|
| Date | Number | Amount | Date | Number | Amount | | Date | Amount |
| Dec.  1 | 3475 | $1,640.70 | 20 | 3482 | 475.50 | | Dec.  3 | $ 1,211.60 |
| 2 | 3476 | 1,300.00 | 22 | 3483 | 1,140.00 | | 7 | 2,365.10 |
| 2 | 3477 | 2,130.00 | 23 | 3484 | 1,274.00 | | 15 | 2,672.70 |
| 4 | 3478 | 538.20 | 24 | 3485 | 440.80 | | 20 | 2,954.00 |
| 8 | 3479 | 3,080.00 | 30 | 3486 | 1,389.50 | | 25 | 2,567.30 |
| 10 | 3480 | 600.00 | Total | | $14,816.10 | | 28 | 2,836.00 |
| 17 | 3481 | 807.40 | | | | | 30 | 1,025.00 |
| | | | | | | | 31 | 1,197.90 |
| | | | | | | | Total | $16,829.60 |

*Instructions*

(a) Determine the unadjusted cash balance per books as at December 31 before reconciliation.
(b) Prepare a bank reconciliation at December 31.
(c) Prepare the correcting entries based on the reconciliation. (*Note:* The correction of any errors in the recording of cheques should be made to Accounts Payable. The correction of any errors in the recording of cash receipts should be made to Accounts Receivable.)

Prepare bank reconciliation
and related entries.
(SO 7) AP

**P7–6B** You are provided with the following information for River Adventures Company:

### RIVER ADVENTURES COMPANY
### Bank Reconciliation
### April 30, 2005

| | | | |
|---|---|---|---|
| Cash balance per bank | | | $9,008.53 |
| Add: Deposits in transit | | 846.33 | |
| | | | 9,854.86 |
| Less: Outstanding cheques | | | |
| | #526 | $1,357.99 | |
| | #533 | 278.90 | |
| | #541 | 363.44 | |
| | #555 | 78.82 | 2,079.15 |
| Adjusted cash balance per bank | | | $7,775.71 |

The adjusted cash balance per bank agreed with the cash balance per books at April 30, 2005. The May bank statement showed the following:

### RIVER ADVENTURES COMPANY
### Bank Statement
### May 31, 2005

| | Deposits | Cheques and Other Debits | | |
|---|---|---|---|---|
| Date | Amount | Number | Amount | Balance |
| Apr. 30 | | | | $9,008.53 |
| May  3 | $   846.33 | 526 | $1,357.99 | 8,496.87 |
| 4 | | 541 | 363.44 | 8,133.43 |
| 6 | | 556 | 223.46 | 7,909.97 |
| 6 | 1,250.00 | 557 | 1,800.00 | 7,359.97 |
| 10 | 980.00 | | | 8,339.97 |
| 10 | | 559 | 1,650.00 | 6,689.97 |
| 13 | 426.00 | | | 7,115.97 |
| 13 | 1,650.00 | | | 8,765.97 |
| 14 | | 561 | 799.00 | 7,966.97 |
| 18 | | 562 | 2,045.00 | 5,921.97 |
| 18 | 222.00 | | | 6,143.97 |
| 19 | | 563 | 2,487.00 | 3,656.97 |
| 21 | | 564 | 603.00 | 3,053.97 |
| 25 | | 565 | 1,033.00 | 2,020.97 |
| 26 | 980.00 | | | 3,000.97 |
| 28 | 1,771.00 | NSF | 440.00 | 4,331.97 |
| 31 | | SC | 25.00 | 4,306.97 |

Additional information from the bank statement:

1. The deposit of $1,650 on May 13 is an electronic transfer from a customer in payment of its account. The amount includes $35 of interest, which River Adventures Company had not previously accrued.
2. The NSF for $440 is a $425 cheque from a customer, Ralph King, in payment of his account, and a $15 processing fee.
3. SC represents bank service charges for the month.
4. The bank made an error when processing cheque 564. The company also made one error during the month.

The company's cash payments and cash receipts for the month were as follows:

| Cash Receipts | | | Cash Payments | | |
|---|---|---|---|---|---|
| Date | Amount | | Date | Cheque No. | Amount |
| May  5 | $1,250.00 | | May  4 | 556 | $    223.46 |
| 8 | 980.00 | | 5 | 557 | 1,800.00 |
| 12 | 426.00 | | 7 | 558 | 943.00 |
| 18 | 222.00 | | 7 | 559 | 1,650.00 |
| 25 | 890.00 | | 8 | 560 | 890.00 |
| 28 | 1,771.00 | | 10 | 561 | 799.00 |
| 31 | 1,286.00 | | 15 | 562 | 2,045.00 |
| Total | $6,825.00 | | 18 | 563 | 2,487.00 |
| | | | 20 | 564 | 306.00 |
| | | | 25 | 565 | 1,033.00 |
| | | | 31 | 566 | 950.00 |
| | | | | | $13,126.46 |

*Instructions*

(a) Calculate the unadjusted Cash balance at May 31, 2005, according to River Adventures' general ledger.

(b) Prepare a bank reconciliation and the necessary journal entries for River Adventures as at May 31, 2005.

**P7–7B**  When the accountant of Haworth's Marine Centre prepared the bank reconciliation on September 30, 2005, there were three outstanding cheques: #387 for $628, #390 for $553, and #391 for $159. There was a $1,084 deposit in transit as at September 30, 2005. The bank balance at September 30 was $6,469. Shown below is selected information from the October bank statement:

Prepare bank reconciliation and related entries. (SO 7) AP

| Cheques Cleared | | | Other Bank Account Transactions | | |
|---|---|---|---|---|---|
| Date | Cheque No. | Amount | Date | Amount | Transaction |
| Oct.  1 | 387 | $    628 | Oct.  1 | $1,084 + | Deposit |
| 8 | 406 | 642 | 8 | 2,267 + | Deposit |
| 20 | 407 | 150 | 12 | 3,818 + | Deposit |
| 22 | 409 | 1,848 | 24 | 4,410 + | Deposit |
| 22 | 390 | 553 | 25 | 790 − | NSF cheque |
| 23 | 405 | 3,115 | 31 | 43 − | Service charge |
| 31 | 410 | 317 | 31 | 27 + | Interest |

The NSF cheque was originally received from a customer, Y. Fujii, in payment of her account of $760. The bank included a $30 service charge for $790 total.

Information from the company's accounting records appears below:

| Cash Receipts | | | Cash Payments | | |
|---|---|---|---|---|---|
| Date | Amount | | Date | Cheque No. | Amount |
| Oct.  5 | $2,267 | | Oct.  5 | 405 | $3,115 |
| 12 | 3,118 | | 5 | 406 | 642 |
| 23 | 4,410 | | 19 | 407 | 150 |
| 31 | 1,941 | | 19 | 408 | 3,266 |
| | | | 19 | 409 | 1,448 |
| | | | 31 | 410 | 317 |
| | | | 31 | 411 | 984 |

Investigation reveals that cheque #409 was issued to buy office equipment. All deposits are for collections of accounts receivable. The bank made no errors.

*Instructions*

(a) Calculate the balance per bank statement at October 31 and the unadjusted cash balance per company records at October 31.
(b) Prepare a bank reconciliation for Haworth's Marine Center at October 31.
(c) Prepare the general journal entries necessary to adjust the book balance of cash to the adjusted balance.
(d) What balance would Haworth's Marine Center report as cash in the current assets section of its balance sheet on October 31, 2005?

Prepare bank reconciliation and identify internal control features.
(SO 2, 3, 4, 7) AN

**P7–8B** Your newly hired assistant prepared the following bank reconciliation:

### CAREFREE COMPANY
### Bank Reconciliation
### March 31, 2005

| | | | | | |
|---|---|---|---|---|---|
| Book Balance | | $2,305 | Bank Balance | | $6,530 |
| Add: Deposit in transit | $ 750 | | Add: Error re: cheque #173 | | 45 [3] |
| EFT receipt from customer | 2,635 | | | | 6,575 |
| Interest earned | 15 | 3,400 | Deduct: Pre-authorized payments [4] | | |
| | | 5,705 | Hydro | $ 120 | |
| Deduct: Error re: Careless Company's | | | Telephone | 85 | |
| deposit to our account | $1,100 [1] | | NSF cheque | 220 | |
| Bank service charge | 45 [2] | 1,145 | Outstanding cheques | 1,650 | 2,075 |
| Adjusted book balance | | $4,560 | Adjusted bank balance | | $4,500 |

Notes:

1. The bank credited Carefree's account for a deposit made by Careless Company. Carefree and Careless are unrelated parties.
2. Of the bank service charge, $20 was due to the NSF cheque.
3. Carefree's cheque no. 173 was made for the proper amount of $249 in payment of an account payable; however, it was entered in the cash payments journal as $294.
4. Carefree authorized the bank to automatically pay its hydro and telephone bills, as directly submitted to the bank by the hydro and telephone companies. These amounts have not yet been recorded by Carefree.
5. A difference of $60 is undetermined.

*Instructions*

(a) Prepare a correct bank reconciliation.
(b) Prepare the required journal entries resulting from the corrected bank reconciliation.
(c) Identify the internal control features added by the bank reconciliation process.

Calculate cash balance.
(SO 8) AP

**P7–9B** A new CGA student has been asked to determine the balance that should be reported as cash and cash equivalents as at December 31, 2005, for one of the firm's clients. The following information is available:

1. Cash on hand in the cash registers on December 31 totals $1,600. Of this amount, $500 is kept on hand as a cash float.
2. The petty cash fund has an imprest amount of $200. Actual petty cash on hand at December 31 is $43. Paid-out receipts total $155. Of these receipts, $100 is in IOUs from company employees.
3. The balance in the bank chequing account at December 31 is $7,460.
4. Temporary investments include $5,000 in a BMO money-market fund and an investment of $2,500 in a six-month term deposit.
5. The company sold $250 of merchandise to a customer late in the day on December 31. The customer had forgotten her wallet and promised to pay the amount on January 1.
6. The company had a U.S. dollar bank account. At December 31 its U.S. funds were worth the equivalent of $2,241 Canadian.
7. At December 31, the company has Diner's Club credit card slips totalling $500 that have not yet been submitted to Diner's Club for payment.

8. The company received $500 of cash on December 31 as an advance deposit in trust on a property sale.
9. In order to hook up utilities, the company is required to deposit $1,000 in trust with Ontario Hydro. This amount must remain on deposit until a satisfactory credit history has been established. The company expects to have this deposit back within the year.

*Instructions*

(a) Calculate the Cash and Cash Equivalents balance that should be reported on the year end balance sheet as a current asset.
(b) Identify where any items that were not reported in the Cash and Cash Equivalents balance in (a) should be reported.

# Continuing Cookie Chronicle

(Note: This is a continuation of the Cookie Chronicle from Chapters 1 through 6.)

## Part 1

Natalie is struggling to keep up with the recording of her accounting transactions. She is spending a lot of time marketing and selling mixers and giving her cookie classes. Her friend John is an accounting student who runs his own accounting service. He has asked Natalie if she would like to have him do her accounting.

John and Natalie meet and discuss her business. John suggests that he do the following for Natalie:

1. Hold onto cash until there is enough to be deposited. (He would keep the cash locked up in his vehicle). He would also take all of the deposits to the bank at least twice a month.
2. Write and sign all of the cheques.
3. Record all of the deposits in the accounting records.
4. Record all of the cheques in the accounting records.
5. Prepare the monthly bank reconciliation.
6. Transfer all of Natalie's manual accounting records to his computer accounting program. John maintains all of the accounting information that he keeps for his clients on his laptop computer.
7. Prepare monthly financial statements for Natalie to review.
8. Write himself a cheque every month for the work he has done for Natalie.

*Instructions*

Identify the weaknesses in internal control that you see in the system which John is recommending (consider the principles of internal control identified in the chapter). Can you suggest any improvements if John is hired to do Natalie's accounting?

## Part 2

Natalie decides that she cannot afford to hire John to do her accounting. One way that she can ensure that her cash account does not have any errors and is accurate and up to date is to prepare a bank reconciliation at the end of each month.

Natalie would like you to help her. She asks you to prepare a bank reconciliation for June 2005 using the following information:

## GENERAL LEDGER—COOKIE CREATIONS

### Cash

| Date | Explanation | Ref. | Debit | Credit | Balance |
|------|-------------|------|-------|--------|---------|
| 2005 | | | | | |
| June 1 | Balance | | | | 2,657 |
| 1 | | | 750 | | 3,407 |
| 3 | Cheque #600 | | | 625 | 2,782 |
| 3 | Cheque #601 | | | 95 | 2,687 |
| 8 | Cheque #602 | | | 56 | 2,631 |
| 9 | | | 1,050 | | 3,681 |
| 13 | Cheque #603 | | | 425 | 3,256 |
| 20 | | | 155 | | 3,411 |
| 28 | Cheque #604 | | | 247 | 3,164 |
| 28 | | | 110 | | 3,274 |

### THE CANADA BANK
### Statement of Account—Cookie Creations
### June 30, 2005

| Date | Explanation | Cheques and Other Debits | Deposits | Balance |
|------|-------------|--------------------------|----------|---------|
| May 31 | Balance | | | 3,256 |
| June 1 | Deposit | | 750 | 4,006 |
| 6 | Cheque #600 | 625 | | 3,381 |
| 6 | Cheque #601 | 95 | | 3,286 |
| 8 | Cheque #602 | 56 | | 3,230 |
| 9 | Deposit | | 1,050 | 4,280 |
| 10 | NSF cheque | 100 | | |
| 10 | NSF – fee | 35 | | 4,145 |
| 14 | Cheque #603 | 452 | | 3,693 |
| 20 | Deposit | | 125 | 3,818 |
| 23 | EFT – Telus | 85 | | 3,733 |
| 28 | Cheque #599 | 361 | | 3,372 |
| 30 | Bank charges | 13 | | 3,359 |

Additional information:

1. On May 31, there were two outstanding cheques: # 595 for $238 and #599 for $361.
2. The Canada Bank made a posting error to the bank statement: cheque # 603 was issued for $425, not $452.
3. The deposit made on June 20 was for $125 that Natalie received for teaching a class. Natalie made an error in recording this transaction.
4. The electronic funds transfer (EFT) was for Natalie's cellphone use. Remember that she only uses this phone for business.
5. The NSF cheque was from Ron Black. Natalie received this cheque for teaching a class to Ron's children. Natalie contacted Ron and he assured her that she will receive a cheque in the mail for the outstanding amount of the invoice and the NSF bank charge.

*Instructions*

(a) Prepare Cookie Creations' bank reconciliation for June 2005.
(b) Prepare any necessary general journal entries.
(c) If a balance sheet is prepared for Cookie Creations at June 30, 2005, what balance will be reported as cash in the current assets section?

# Financial Reporting and Analysis

Practice
Tools

## Financial Reporting Problem

**BYP7–1**  The Forzani Group Ltd.'s financial statements, including the auditor's report, are presented in Appendix A at the end of this book.

*Instructions*

(a) What is the name of Forzani's external auditing firm?
(b) Who is primarily responsible for the financial statements? Explain.
(c) How much did cash increase during the current fiscal year?
(d) How much cash was provided by operating activities for the current year?
(e) Does Forzani have any compensating balances?
(f) How large was the balance of cash at the end of the current fiscal year? Express it (1) in dollars, (2) as a percentage of total assets, (3) as a percentage of current assets, and (4) as a percentage of current liabilities.

## Interpreting Financial Statements

**BYP7–2**  Shown below is selected information from Imperial Tobacco Canada Limited's balance sheet.

| IMPERIAL TOBACCO CANADA LIMITED<br>Balance Sheet (partial)<br>December 31, 2002<br>(in millions) | | |
| --- | --- | --- |
| | 2002 | 2001 |
| Current assets | | |
| Cash and cash equivalents | $  402 | $  581 |
| Trade and other accounts receivable | 223 | 148 |
| Future income taxes | 59 | 71 |
| Inventories | 443 | 490 |
| Total current assets | $1,127 | $1,290 |
| Total current liabilities | $  932 | $1,186 |

*Instructions*

(a) What is a cash equivalent? How do cash equivalents differ from other types of temporary investments?
(b) Calculate the (1) working capital and (2) current ratio for each year. The industry averages for the current ratio were 1.61:1 in 2002 and 1.06:1 in 2001. Comment on your results.
(c) Is it possible to have too much cash? Explain why or why not?

## Accounting on the Web

**BYP7–3** Internal control and governance are tightly linked. The management of a company, including the board of directors, must ensure that effective control exists in the organization. This problem reviews the annual report of a well-known Canadian retailer that demonstrates good corporate governance and control practices.

*Instructions*

Specific requirements of this Internet case are available on the Weygandt website.

# Critical Thinking

## Collaborative Learning Activity

**BYP7–4** From your employment or personal experiences, identify situations in which cash was received and disbursed.

*Instructions*

In groups of five or six students, do the following:
 (a) Identify the internal control principles used for cash receipts in the situations you have selected.
 (b) Identify the internal control principles used for cash disbursements in the situations you have selected.
 (c) Identify any weaknesses in internal control related to these cash receipts and disbursements.

## Communication Activity

**BYP7–5** As a new auditor for the public accounting firm of Rawls, Keoto, and Landry, you have been assigned to review the internal controls over the cash receipts by mail of Avalon Company. Your review reveals the following: cheques are promptly endorsed "For Deposit Only" but no list of the cheques is prepared by the person opening the mail. The mail is opened either by the cashier or by the employee who maintains the accounts receivable records, depending on who is less busy. Mail receipts are deposited in the bank weekly by the cashier.

*Instructions*

Write a letter to L. S. Osman, owner of the Avalon Company, explaining the weaknesses in internal control and your recommendations for improving the system.

## Ethics Case

**BYP7–6** Banks charge fees of up to $25 for "bounced" cheques—that is, cheques that exceed the balance in the account. It has been estimated that processing bounced cheques costs a bank roughly $1.50 per cheque. Thus, the profit margin on a bounced cheque is very high. Recognizing this, some banks process cheques from largest to smallest. By doing this, they maximize the number of cheques that bounce if a customer overdraws an account. One bank projected a $14-million increase in fee revenue as a result of processing the largest cheques first. In response to criticism, banks have responded that their customers prefer to have large cheques processed first because those tend to be the most important. At the other extreme, some banks will cover their customers' bounced cheques, effectively extending them overdraft protection.

*Instructions*

Answer each of the following situation:
(a) Who are the stakeholders in this situation?
(b) Antonio Freeman had a balance of $1,500 in his chequing account on a day when the bank received the following five cheques for processing against his account:

| Cheque Number | Amount | Cheque Number | Amount |
|---|---|---|---|
| 3150 | $   35 | 3165 | $890 |
| 3158 | 1,510 | 3169 | 180 |
| 3162 | 400 | | |

Assuming a $25 fee per cheque is assessed by the bank, how much fee revenue would the bank generate if it processed cheques (1) from largest to smallest, (2) from smallest to largest, and (3) in the order of the cheque numbers?
(c) Do you think that processing cheques from largest to smallest is an ethical business practice?
(d) Besides ethical issues, what other considerations must a bank make in deciding whether to process cheques from largest to smallest?
(e) If you were managing a bank, what policy would you adopt on bounced cheques?

---

## Answers to Self-Study Questions

1. b    2. c    3. b    4. c    5. b    6. d    7. a    8. a    9. b    10. b    11. b

## Answer to Forzani Review It Question 3

Forzani reports only cash in its 2003 balance sheet. It does not have any short-term investments. The reported cash amount at the end of February 2, 2003, is $523,000.

Remember to go back to the Navigator Box at the beginning of the chapter to check off your completed work.

**AUDITORS' REPORT**

**TO THE SHAREHOLDERS OF THE FORZANI GROUP LTD.**

We have audited the consolidated balance sheets of **The Forzani Group Ltd.** as at February 2, 2003 and January 27, 2002 and the consolidated statements of operations and retained earnings and cash flows for the years then ended. These consolidated financial statements are the responsibility of the Company's management. Our responsibility is to express an opinion on these consolidated financial statements based on our audits.

We conducted our audits in accordance with Canadian generally accepted auditing standards. Those standards require that we plan and perform an audit to obtain reasonable assurance whether the financial statements are free of material misstatement. An audit includes examining, on a test basis, evidence supporting the amounts and disclosures in the financial statements. An audit also includes assessing the accounting principles used and significant estimates made by management, as well as evaluating the overall financial statement presentation.

In our opinion, these consolidated financial statements present fairly, in all material respects, the financial position of the Company as at February 2, 2003 and January 27, 2002 and the results of its operations and its cash flows for the years then ended in accordance with Canadian generally accepted accounting principles.

Calgary, Alberta
March 7, 2003

*Deloitte & Touche LLP*

Chartered Accountants

A FOCUSED DIRECTION

## CONSOLIDATED BALANCE SHEETS

(in thousands)
(audited)

| As at | February 2, 2003 | January 27, 2002 |
|---|---|---|
| **ASSETS** | | |
| Current | | |
| Cash | $ 523 | $ 494 |
| Accounts receivable | 38,275 | 35,988 |
| Inventory | 268,519 | 229,270 |
| Prepaid and other expenses | 11,123 | 4,481 |
| | 318,440 | 270,233 |
| Capital assets (Note 3) | 142,236 | 120,525 |
| Goodwill and other intangibles (Note 4) | 38,684 | 37,394 |
| Other assets (Note 5) | 7,452 | 8,112 |
| | $506,812 | $ 436,264 |
| **LIABILITIES** | | |
| Current | | |
| Indebtedness under revolving credit facility (Note 6) | $ 4,204 | $ 17,094 |
| Accounts payable and accrued liabilities | 209,873 | 188,995 |
| Current portion of long-term debt | 3,638 | 14,032 |
| | 217,715 | 220,121 |
| Long-term debt (Note 7) | 32,062 | 35,454 |
| Deferred lease inducements | 52,251 | 46,623 |
| Future income tax liability (Note 10) | 1,061 | 2,021 |
| | 303,089 | 304,219 |
| **SHAREHOLDERS' EQUITY** | | |
| Share capital (Note 9) | 124,866 | 83,719 |
| Retained earnings | 78,857 | 48,326 |
| | 203,723 | 132,045 |
| | $506,812 | $ 436,264 |

On behalf of the Board:

Roman Doroniuk, C.A.

John M. Forzani

## CONSOLIDATED STATEMENTS OF OPERATIONS AND RETAINED EARNINGS

(in thousands, except share data)

(audited, except where otherwise noted)

| | For the 53 weeks ended February 2, 2003 | For the 52 weeks ended January 27, 2002 |
|---|---|---|
| Corporate and Franchise Retail Sales (unaudited – Note 12) | $ 1,053,449 | $ 876,434 |
| | | |
| **Revenue** | | |
| Corporate | $ 715,003 | $ 579,196 |
| Franchise | 208,792 | 179,061 |
| | 923,795 | 758,257 |
| Cost of sales | 603,326 | 497,758 |
| | | |
| **Gross margin** | 320,469 | 260,499 |
| | | |
| **Operating and administrative expenses** | | |
| Store operating | 177,252 | 142,788 |
| General and administrative | 60,230 | 55,215 |
| | 237,482 | 198,003 |
| | | |
| **Operating earnings before undernoted items** | 82,987 | 62,496 |
| | | |
| Amortization | 29,624 | 22,574 |
| Interest | 4,354 | 4,901 |
| Gain on sale of investments (Note 13) | (1,454) | - |
| | 32,524 | 27,475 |
| | | |
| **Earnings before income taxes** | 50,463 | 35,021 |
| | | |
| **Provision for (recovery of) income taxes (Note 10)** | | |
| Current | 22,133 | 6,434 |
| Future | (2,201) | 7,958 |
| | 19,932 | 14,392 |
| | | |
| **Net earnings** | 30,531 | 20,629 |
| | | |
| Retained earnings, opening | 48,326 | 27,697 |
| **Retained earnings, closing** | $ 78,857 | $ 48,326 |
| **Earnings per share** | $ 1.01 | $ 0.76 |
| **Diluted earnings per share** | $ 0.96 | $ 0.74 |
| **Total number of common shares outstanding** | 30,787,179 | 27,622,447 |
| **Weighted average number of common shares outstanding** | 30,082,408 | 27,085,234 |

39

A FOCUSED DIRECTION

## CONSOLIDATED STATEMENTS OF CASH FLOWS

(in thousands)

(audited)

| | For the 53 weeks ended February 2, 2003 | For the 52 weeks ended January 27, 2002 |
|---|---|---|
| **Cash provided by (used in) operating activities** | | |
| Net earnings | $30,531 | $ 20,629 |
| Items not involving cash | | |
| Amortization | 29,624 | 22,574 |
| Amortization of finance charges | 571 | 181 |
| Amortization of deferred lease inducements | (8,767) | (6,394) |
| Gain on sale of investment | (1,445) | - |
| Future income tax expense | (2,201) | 7,958 |
| **Cash flow from operations (Note 9 (c))** | 48,313 | 44,948 |
| **Changes in non-cash elements of working capital (Note 8)** | (27,300) | (24,161) |
| | 21,013 | 20,787 |
| **Cash provided by (used in) financing activities** | | |
| Proceeds from issuance of share capital | 40,416 | 1,311 |
| Principal repayment of long-term debt | (13,786) | (2,683) |
| (Decrease) increase in revolving credit facility | (12,890) | 17,094 |
| Proceeds from deferred lease inducements | 14,395 | 11,559 |
| | 28,135 | 27,281 |
| **Cash provided by (used in) investing activities** | | |
| Addition of capital assets | (50,085) | (40,791) |
| Addition of other assets | (1,186) | (1,710) |
| Acquisition of wholly owned subsidiary, net of cash acquired (Note 14) | - | (18,518) |
| Sale of investments | 1,690 | - |
| Disposal of capital assets | 276 | 347 |
| Disposal of other assets | 186 | 68 |
| | (49,119) | (60,604) |
| Increase (decrease) in cash | 29 | (12,536) |
| Net cash position, opening | 494 | 13,030 |
| **Net cash position, closing** | $    523 | $     494 |

Supplementary cash flow information (Note 8)

**NOTES TO CONSOLIDATED FINANCIAL STATEMENTS** (Tabular amounts in thousands, except share data)

## 1. Nature of Operations

The Forzani Group Ltd. "FGL" or "the Company" is Canada's largest sporting goods retailer. FGL currently operates 215 corporate stores under the banners: Sport Chek, Sport Mart, Coast Mountain Sports, and Forzani's. The Company is also the franchisor of 161 stores under the banners: Sports Experts, Intersport, R'n'R, Econosports and Atmosphere. FGL operates two websites, dedicated to the Canadian online sporting goods market, at www.sportchek.ca and www.sportmart.ca.

## 2. Significant Accounting Policies

The consolidated financial statements have been prepared by management in accordance with Canadian generally accepted accounting principles. The financial statements have, in management's opinion, been prepared within reasonable limits of materiality and within the framework of the accounting policies summarized below:

**(a)     Organization**

The consolidated financial statements include the accounts of The Forzani Group Ltd. and its subsidiaries, all of which are wholly owned.

**(b)     Inventory**

Inventory is valued at the lower of laid-down cost and net realizable value. Laid-down cost is determined using the weighted average cost method and includes invoice cost, duties, freight, and distribution costs. Net realizable value is defined as the expected selling price.

Volume rebates and other supplier discounts are included in income when earned.

**(c)     Capital assets**

Capital assets are recorded at cost and are amortized using the following methods and rates:

- Building - 4% declining-balance basis
- Building on leased land - 20 years straight-line basis
- Furniture, fixtures, equipment and automotive - straight-line basis over 3-5 years
- Leasehold improvements - straight-line basis over the lesser of the length of the lease and estimated useful life of the improvements, not exceeding 10 years

**(d)     Goodwill and other intangibles**

Goodwill represents the excess of the purchase price over the fair market value of the identifiable net assets acquired. Goodwill and other intangible assets, with indefinite lives, are not amortized, but tested for impairment at least annually, at year end, and, if required, asset values reduced accordingly.

The method used to assess impairment is a review of the profitability of the assets acquired.

Non-competition agreement costs are being amortized, on a straight-line basis, over the five-year life of the agreements.

**(e)     Other assets (see Note 5)**

Other assets include financing costs, system and interactive development costs, long-term receivables, and an investment in a wholesale distribution company.

Interactive development costs relate to the development of the sportchek.ca interactive web site, designed as a part of the Company's multi-channel retailing and branding strategy. These costs are being amortized over five years following the commencement of the web site's operations in June, 2001.

Financing costs represent fees incurred in establishing the Company's revolving credit facility. These costs are being amortized over the term of the facility.

System development costs relate to the implementation of software. Upon activation, costs are amortized over the estimated useful lives of the systems.

Long-term receivables are carried at cost less a valuation allowance.

A FOCUSED DIRECTION

The investment in shares of a wholesale distribution company is carried at cost and periodically reviewed for impairment. The method used to assess impairment is a review of the operation's profitability.

**(f)    Deferred lease inducements**

Deferred lease inducements represent cash and non-cash benefits that the Company has received from landlords pursuant to store lease agreements. These lease inducements are amortized against rent expense over the term of the lease, not exceeding 10 years.

**(g)    Revenue recognition**

Revenue includes sales to customers through corporate stores operated by the Company and sales to, and service fees from, franchise stores. Sales to customers through corporate stores operated by the Company are recognized at the point of sale, net of an estimated allowance for sales returns. Sales of merchandise to franchise stores are recognized at the time of shipment. Royalties and administration fees are recognized when earned, in accordance with the terms of the franchise agreements.

**(h)    Store opening expenses**

Operating costs incurred prior to the opening of new stores are expensed as incurred.

**(i)    Fiscal year**

The Company's fiscal year follows the retail calendar. The fiscal years for the consolidated financial statements presented are the 53-week period ended February 2, 2003 and the 52-week period ended January 27, 2002.

**(j)    Foreign currency translation**

Foreign currency accounts are translated to Canadian dollars as follows:

At the transaction date, each asset, liability, revenue or expense is translated into Canadian dollars by the use of the exchange rate in effect at that date. At the year-end date, monetary assets and liabilities are translated into Canadian dollars by using the exchange rate in effect at that date and the resulting foreign exchange gains and losses are included in income in the current period. The amendments to Foreign Currency Translation, of the Canadian Institute of Chartered Accountants, "CICA", Handbook Section 1650, applicable January 1, 2002, did not have an impact on the Company's operations.

**(k)    Financial instruments (see Notes 7 and 16)**

Accounts receivable, accounts payable and accrued liabilities, long-term debt and derivative transactions, constitute financial instruments. The Company also, in the normal course of business, enters into leases in respect of real estate and certain point-of-sale equipment.

The Company enters into forward contracts and options, with financial institutions, as hedges of other financial transactions and not for speculative purposes. The Company's policies do not allow leveraged transactions and are designed to minimize foreign currency risk. The Company's policies require all hedges to be linked with specific liabilities on the balance sheet and to be assessed, both at inception, and on an ongoing basis, as to their effectiveness in offsetting changes in the fair values or cash flows of the hedged liabilities.

**(l)    Measurement uncertainty**

The amounts recorded for amortization of capital assets, the provision for shrinkage and obsolescence of inventory are based on estimates. By their nature, these estimates are subject to measurement uncertainty and the impact on the consolidated financial statements of future periods could be material.

**(m)    Stock Option Plan**

The Company has a stock option plan as described in Note 9 (d). No compensation expense is recognized when stock options are issued to employees. Any consideration paid by employees on the exercise of stock options is credited to share capital.

**(n)    Income taxes (see Note 10)**

The Company follows the liability method under which future income taxes and obligations are determined based on differences between the financial reporting and tax basis of assets and liabilities, measured using tax rates substantively enacted at the balance sheet date.

FORZANI ANNUAL REPORT F2003

**(o)   Employee Profit Sharing Plan (see Note 9(e))**

The Company has an Employee Profit Sharing Plan that causes an amount no less than 1%, and no greater than 5%, of consolidated earnings before income taxes, to be paid to a Trustee for the purchase of shares of the Company. These shares are distributed to participating employees on a predetermined basis, upon retirement from the Company. Compensation expense is recognized when such contributions are made.

**(p)   Comparative Figures**

Certain 2002 comparative figures have been reclassified to conform with the current year's presentation.

### 3.   Capital Assets

| | 2003 | | | 2002 | | |
|---|---|---|---|---|---|---|
| | Cost | Accumulated Amortization | Net Book Value | Cost | Accumulated Amortization | Net Book Value |
| Land | $    638 | $      - | $    638 | $    638 | $      - | $    638 |
| Buildings | 6,280 | 1,637 | 4,643 | 6,036 | 1,406 | 4,630 |
| Building on leased land | 3,159 | 1,186 | 1,973 | 3,159 | 1,029 | 2,130 |
| Furniture, fixtures, equipment and automotive | 97,117 | 52,438 | 44,679 | 74,330 | 39,778 | 34,552 |
| Leasehold improvements | 145,150 | 54,847 | 90,303 | 119,079 | 40,504 | 78,575 |
| | $ 252,344 | $ 110,108 | $ 142,236 | $ 203,242 | $ 82,717 | $ 120,525 |

### 4.   Goodwill and Other Intangible Assets

| | 2003 | 2002 |
|---|---|---|
| Goodwill | $21,319 | $19,438 |
| Trademarks/Tradenames | 16,702 | 16,702 |
| Non-competition agreements | 3,000 | 3,000 |
| | 41,021 | 39,140 |
| Less accumulated amortization | 2,337 | 1,746 |
| | $38,684 | $37,394 |

During the prior fiscal year, the Company adopted new CICA standards on "Goodwill and Other Intangible Assets". Under the new accounting standards, goodwill and other intangible assets with indefinite lives are no longer amortized, but are tested for impairment at least annually. At year end, there was no impairment of goodwill and other intangible assets. Prior to the January 29, 2002 adoption of CICA Handbook requirements for goodwill and other intangible assets, the Company amortized pre-existing trademarks over ten years and pre-existing goodwill over five years, each on a straight-line basis.

In accordance with the transitional provisions of the new standards, CICA 3062, the following is a summary of the fiscal 2002 comparable 52-week period, net earnings and earnings per share, had the new standards been applied retroactively to January 29, 2001.

| | For the 52-week Period ended 27-Jan-02 (previously reported) | For the 52-week Period ended 27-Jan-02 (restated) |
|---|---|---|
| Earnings before income taxes | $35,021 | $35,021 |
| Amortization of goodwill | - | 552 |
| Earnings before income taxes | $35,021 | $35,573 |
| Provision for income taxes | 14,392 | 14,619 |
| Net earnings | $20,629 | $20,954 |
| Earnings per share | $0.76 | |
| Earnings per share adjusted | | $0.77 |

A FOCUSED DIRECTION

### 5.    Other Assets

|  | 2003 | 2002 |
|---|---|---|
| Interactive development | $2,649 | $2,649 |
| Deferred financing charges | 2,124 | 1,397 |
| System development | 1,471 | 1,121 |
|  | 6,244 | 5,167 |
| Less accumulated amortization | 2,246 | 960 |
|  | 3,998 | 4,207 |
| Long-term receivables | 950 | 1,005 |
| Investment in shares of a wholesale distribution company | 2,504 | 2,900 |
|  | $7,452 | $8,112 |

### 6.    Indebtedness

The Company has a $140 million credit facility with General Electric Capital Canada Inc. (G.E.) and National Bank of Canada, comprised of a $115 million revolving loan and a $25 million term loan repayable at maturity on December 20, 2003. Under the terms of the credit agreement, the interest rate payable on both the revolving and term loans is based on the Company's financial performance as determined by its interest coverage ratio. As at February 2, 2003, the interest rate paid was 4.5%. The facility is secured by general security agreements against all existing and future acquired assets of the Company. As at February 2, 2003, the Company is in compliance with all covenants.

Subsequent to the fiscal year end, on February 3, 2003, the Company extended its existing credit agreement to February 3, 2006. This agreement with G.E. was amended to: assign a 21.43% pro rata share of the revolving credit facility and term loan to each of National Bank of Canada and The Royal Bank of Canada and; grant an increase of the maximum revolving credit commitment to $150 million via the exercising of a single, irreversible option.

### 7.    Long-term Debt

|  | 2003 | 2002 |
|---|---|---|
| G.E. term loan (see Note 6) | $25,000 | $25,000 |
| Vendor take-back re: Sport Mart acquisition, with interest rates from prime plus 1% to prime plus 2% (see Note 14) | 7,039 | 15,000 |
| Various long-term debts, with interest rates from prime plus 1.5% to prime plus 2% | - | 5,490 |
| Mortgages, with monthly blended payments of $52,611, including interest at rates from approximately 7% to 10%, compounded semi-annually, supported by land and buildings, renewable July 1, 2004 and August 1, 2005. | 3,631 | 3,966 |
| Security Deposits | 30 | 30 |
|  | 35,700 | 49,486 |
| Less current portion | 3,638 | 14,032 |
|  | $32,062 | $35,454 |

Principal payments on the above mortgages due in the next five years, assuming the mortgages continue to be renewed on similar terms, are as follows:

| | |
|---|---|
| 2004 | $370 |
| 2005 | $404 |
| 2006 | $296 |
| 2007 | $169 |
| 2008 | $182 |

Based on estimated interest rates currently available to the Company for mortgages with similar terms and maturities, the fair value of the mortgages at February 2, 2003 amounted to approximately $3,600,000 (2002 - $3,966,000). Interest costs incurred for the 53-week period ended February 2, 2003 on long-term debt amounted to $2,330,983 (2002 - $2,312,906). The fair value of the other long-term debt components above, approximates book value.

## 8. Supplementary Cash Flow Information

| | 2003 | 2002 |
|---|---|---|
| Changes in non-cash elements of working capital | | |
| Accounts receivable | $ (2,287) | $ (3,044) |
| Inventory | (39,249) | (50,130) |
| Prepaid and other expenses | (6,642) | 942 |
| Accounts payable | 20,878 | 28,071 |
| | $(27,300) | $(24,161) |
| | | |
| Cash interest paid | $ 5,195 | $ 5,190 |
| Cash taxes paid | $ 14,897 | $ 790 |

## 9. Share Capital

**(a) Authorized**

An unlimited number of Class A shares

An unlimited number of Preferred shares, issuable in series

**(b) Issued**

Class A shares

| | Number | Consideration |
|---|---|---|
| Balance, January 28, 2001 | 26,918,448 | $ 82,408 |
| Shares issued upon employees exercising stock options | 703,999 | 1,311 |
| **Balance, January 27, 2002** | **27,622,447** | **83,719** |
| **Shares issued upon employees exercising stock options** | **664,732** | **2,817** |
| **Shares issued March 26, 2002 upon public stock offer** | | |
| **(net of issuance costs and related future income tax)** | **2,500,000** | **38,330** |
| | **30,787,179** | **$124,866** |

**(c) Earnings and Cash Flow Per Share** [1]

| | 2003 | 2002 |
|---|---|---|
| Earnings Per Share | | |
| Basic | $1.01 | $0.76 |
| Diluted | $0.96 | $0.74 |
| Cash Flow Per Share | | |
| Basic | $1.61 | $1.66 |
| Diluted | $1.53 | $1.61 |
| Weighted average number of common shares outstanding | | |
| Basic | 30,082,408 | 27,085,234 |
| Diluted | 31,678,044 | 27,944,114 |
| Common shares outstanding | | |
| Basic | 30,787,179 | 27,622,447 |
| Diluted | 32,382,815 | 28,481,327 |

Diluted calculations assume that options under the stock option plan have been exercised at the later of the beginning of the year or date of issuance, and that the funds derived therefrom would have been used to repurchase shares at the average market value of the Company's stock, 2003 - $19.55 (2002 - $8.33).

(1) Cash flow per share is a not a recognized measure under Canadian generally accepted accounting principles. Cash flow per share is defined to be cash flow from operations before non-cash changes in working capital divided by the weighted average shares outstanding. Management believes that cash flow per share is a key measure, as it demonstrates the Company's ability to generate cash flow necessary to fund future growth.

**(d) Stock Option Plan**

The Company has granted stock options to directors, officers and employees to purchase 2,437,968 Class A shares at prices between $3.00 and $22.06 per share. These options expire on dates between March 31, 2003 and June 5, 2007.

A summary of the status of the Company's stock option plan as of February 2, 2003 and January 27, 2002, and any changes during the year ending on those dates is presented in the following table:

A FOCUSED DIRECTION

| Stock Options | 2003 | | 2002 | |
|---|---|---|---|---|
| | Shares | Weighted Average Exercise Price | Shares | Weighted Average Exercise Price |
| Outstanding, beginning of year | 1,997,700 | $4.84 | 2,109,233 | $3.13 |
| Granted | 1,105,000 | $8.88 | 595,800 | $7.37 |
| Exercised | 664,732 | $4.24 | 703,999 | $1.86 |
| Forfeited | - | - | 3,334 | $3.81 |
| Outstanding, end of year | 2,437,968 | $6.81 | 1,997,700 | $4.84 |
| Options exercisable at year end | 1,103,482 | | 935,247 | |

The following table summarizes information about stock options outstanding at February 2, 2003:

| | Options Outstanding | | | Options Exercisable | |
|---|---|---|---|---|---|
| Range of Exercise Prices | Number Outstanding | Weighted Average Remaining Contractual Life | Weighted Average Exercise Price | Number of Shares Exercisable | Weighted Average Exercise Price |
| $3.00 - $3.90 | 1,162,000 | 0.9 years | $3.25 | 682,000 | $3.40 |
| $4.16 - $4.26 | 393,501 | 1.3 years | $4.23 | 193,500 | $4.20 |
| $6.18 - $14.65 | 697,467 | 3.8 years | $11.21 | 227,982 | $11.36 |
| $16.49 - $22.06 | 185,000 | 4.2 years | $18.00 | - | - |
| | 2,437,968 | | | 1,103,482 | |

The Company does not recognize an expense in the financial statements, for share options granted to employees and directors, when issued at market value.

Effective January 1, 2002 , Canadian generally accepted accounting principles require disclosure of the impact on net earnings, using the fair-value method, for stock options issued on or after January 1, 2002.  If the fair-value method had been used, the effect on the Company's net earnings and earnings per share, for the 53-week period ended February 2, 2003, would have been as follows, if the expense had been realized based on the number of stock options granted in the period (the pro forma amounts):

| | For the 53-week period ended February 2, 2003 |
|---|---|
| Net earnings  - as reported | $30,531 |
| - pro forma | $30,201 |
| | |
| Earnings per share  - as reported | $1.01 |
| - pro forma | $1.00 |
| | |
| Diluted earnings per share   - as reported | $0.96 |
| - pro forma | $0.95 |

(e)    **Employee Profit Sharing Plan**

Under the terms of the Employee Profit Sharing Plan the Company has accrued $1,000,000 for the purchase of shares, in trust, for distribution to participating employees.

### 10. Income Taxes

The components of the future income tax asset (liability) amount as at February 2, 2003 and January 27, 2002, are as follows:

|  | 2003 | 2002 |
|---|---|---|
| Current assets | $ (4,610) | $ (3,567) |
| Capital and other assets | (14,776) | (14,733) |
| Tax benefit of share issuance costs | 556 | - |
| Deferred lease inducements | 17,769 | 16,279 |
| Future income tax liability | $ (1,061) | $ (2,021) |

A reconciliation of income taxes at the combined statutory federal and provincial tax rate to the actual income tax rate is as follows:

|  | 2003 | | 2002 | |
|---|---|---|---|---|
| Federal and provincial income taxes | $19,222 | 38.10% | $ 13,856 | 39.60% |
| Increase (decrease) resulting from: | | | | |
| Effect of substantively enacted tax rate changes | 451 | 0.90% | 48 | 0.10% |
| Permanent differences | (60) | (0.10)% | 317 | 0.90% |
| Other, net | 319 | 0.60% | 171 | 0.50% |
| Provision for income taxes | $19,932 | 39.50% | $ 14,392 | 41.10% |

Federal Part I.3 tax and provincial capital tax expense in the amount of $960,000 (2002 - $790,000) is included in operating expenses.

### 11. Commitments

(a)     The Company is committed, at February 2, 2003, to minimum payments under long-term real property leases for the next five years as follows:

|  |  | Gross |
|---|---|---|
|  | 2004 | $55,251 |
|  | 2005 | $51,638 |
|  | 2006 | $50,165 |
|  | 2007 | $47,827 |
|  | 2008 | $47,005 |

In addition, the Company may be obligated to pay percentage rent under certain of the leases.

(b)     As at February 2, 2003, the Company has open letters of credit for purchases of inventory of approximately $3,031,000 (2002 - $3,735,000).

The Company has entered into long-term lease agreements for the rental of data processing hardware and software equipment. The leases, expiring at various dates until 2007, call for minimum lease payments of, $3,799,413 in 2004, $2,456,400 in 2005, $1,793,500 in 2006, and $218,700 in 2007.

### 12. Corporate and Franchise Retail Sales

Total corporate and franchise retail sales have been shown on the Consolidated Statements of Operations and Retained Earnings to indicate the size of the Company's total retail sales level (on an unaudited basis). Only revenue from corporately owned stores, wholesale sales to, and fees from, franchisees are included in the Consolidated Statements of Operations and Retained Earnings.

### 13. Sale of Investment

During the year, the Company sold its investment in a wholesale distribution operation. The Company held 668,668 common and 334,334 series C preferred shares, which were valued at $2,899,800. The Company received consideration of $1,690,100 and 234,771 shares in a publicly traded wholesale distribution company, resulting in a pre-tax gain of $1,445,000. Subsequent to the initial transaction, 13,400 shares of the 234,771 received were sold, for a gain of $9,000, resulting in an overall pre-tax gain on sale of investments, of $1,454,000.

A FOCUSED DIRECTION

### 14.     Acquisition

Effective August 1, 2001, the Company acquired all of the outstanding shares of Sport Mart Inc. This acquisition has been accounted for using the purchase method and accordingly the consolidated financial statements include the results of operations since the date of acquisition.

The purchase of all of the outstanding common; class B and preference shares, 9,891,267; 368 and 17,761,718 shares respectively, was made for a consideration of $35 million, consisting of $20 million cash and a vendor take-back loan of $15 million payable as to $8.5 million on August 1, 2002, $3.0 million on August 1, 2003 and $3.5 million on August 1, 2006. The loan is secured by a general security agreement and bears interest at rates of prime plus 2% on the first and second installments and prime plus 1% on the final installment. The assigned fair values of the underlying assets and liabilities acquired by the Company, as at August 1, 2001, are summarized as follows:

| | |
|---|---:|
| Current assets | $ 24,939 |
| Capital assets | 8,704 |
| Trademarks/trade names | 16,443 |
| Goodwill | 17,938 |
| Non-competition agreements | 3,000 |
| Total assets acquired | $ 71,024 |

| | |
|---|---:|
| Current liabilities | $(24,060) |
| Long-term liabilities | (8,710) |
| Future income tax liability | (3,254) |
| Total liabilities assumed | (36,024) |
| Total consideration | $ 35,000 |

### 15.     Contingencies

(a)     As part of its operations, the Company has entered into agreements with certain franchisees to buy back inventory in the event that the franchisees' bank realizes on related security. The maximum exposure to the Company is limited to the lesser of 75% of the book value of inventory or the franchisees' bank indebtedness. As at February 2, 2003, the maximum exposure was $25,874,232  (2002 - $20,320,000).

(b)     Claims and suits have been brought against the Company in the ordinary course of business. In the opinion of management, all such claims and suits are adequately covered by insurance, or if not so covered, the results are not expected to materially affect the Company's financial position. Any costs to the Company arising from these claims and suits will be charged to earnings in the year in which they occur.

### 16.     Financial Instruments

The carrying value of the Company's accounts receivable and accounts payable and accrued liabilities approximates, based on available information, fair value as at February 2, 2003.

The Company is exposed to credit risk on its accounts receivable from franchisees. The accounts receivable are net of applicable allowance for doubtful accounts, which are established based on the specific credit risks associated with individual franchisees and other relevant information. Concentration of credit risk with respect to receivables is limited, due to the large number of franchisees.

The Company purchases a portion of its inventory from foreign vendors with payment terms in non-Canadian dollars. To manage the foreign exchange risk associated with these purchases, the Company hedges its exposure to foreign currency by purchasing foreign exchange options and forward contracts to fix exchange rates and protect planned margins. The Company has the following derivative instruments outstanding at February 2, 2003 and January 27, 2002:

FORZANI ANNUAL REPORT F2003

|  | Notional amounts maturing in | | | |
|---|---|---|---|---|
|  | Less than 1 year | Over 1 year | **2003 total** | 2002 total |
| **Foreign exchange contracts ($CAD)** | | | | |
| United States dollar contracts | 12,712 | - | **12,712** | 10,958 |
| EURO contracts | 367 | - | **367** | 1,812 |
| Swiss Franc contracts | - | - | **-** | 8 |
| Total | 13,079 | - | **13,079** | 12,778 |

As at February 2, 2003, these instruments had unrealized losses of $0.2 million (2002 - $0.1 million gain).

The Company is exposed to interest risk on its credit facility and the term loan. Interest rate risk reflects the sensitivity of the Company's financial condition to movements in interest rates. For fiscal year 2003, a +/-1% change in interest rates would change interest expense by +/- $292 (2002 +/- $421).

### 17.   Segmented Financial Information

The Company operates principally in two business segments: corporately-owned and operated retail stores and as franchisor of retail stores. Identifiable assets, depreciation and amortization, interest expense and capital expenditures are not disclosed by segment as they are substantially corporate in nature.

|  | 2003 | 2002 |
|---|---|---|
| Revenues: | | |
| Corporate | $ 715,003 | $ 579,196 |
| Franchise | 208,792 | 179,061 |
|  | 923,795 | 758,257 |
| Operating Profit: | | |
| Corporate | 87,201 | 65,426 |
| Franchise | 16,163 | 12,396 |
|  | 103,364 | 77,822 |
|  | | |
| Non-segment specific administrative expenses | 20,377 | 15,326 |
| Amortization | 29,624 | 22,574 |
| Interest expense | 4,354 | 4,901 |
| Gain on sale of investments | (1,454) | - |
|  | 52,901 | 42,801 |
|  | | |
| Earnings before income taxes | 50,463 | 35,021 |
| Income tax expense | 19,932 | 14,392 |
| Net Earnings | $  30,531 | $   20,629 |

### 18.   Related Party Transaction

The Company has advanced $320,567 (2002-$398,750) to an officer for housing purchase assistance. The advance is being repaid over a four-year term commencing on January 28, 2002 and bears interest at bank prime rate.

# appendix B
# Sales Taxes

All businesses operating in Canada need to understand how sales taxes apply to their particular business in their particular province or territory. Sales taxes may take the form of the **Goods and Services Tax (GST)**, **Provincial Sales Tax (PST)**, or **Harmonized Sales Tax (HST)**. GST is levied by the federal government. PST is levied by the provinces and territories, with the exception of Alberta, the Northwest Territories, Nunavut, and Yukon, where no provincial sales tax is charged. Nova Scotia, New Brunswick, and Newfoundland and Labrador have combined the GST and PST into one harmonized sales tax, known as the HST.

As an agent of the federal and provincial governments, a business is required to collect sales taxes on the sale of certain goods and services. In addition, businesses pay sales taxes on most disbursements. We will discuss the collection, payment, recording, and remittance of each of these types of sales taxes in the following sections.

## Types of Sales Taxes

### Goods and Services Tax

The GST is a federal sales tax on most goods and services provided in Canada. A business must register for the GST if it provides taxable goods or services in Canada and if it has revenues of more than $30,000 in any year. Businesses that have to, or decide to, voluntarily register for the GST are called registrants. Registrants can claim a credit—called an **input tax credit (ITC)**—to offset the GST they pay or owe on purchases of goods or services against the GST they collect or are owed. GST returns are submitted quarterly for most registrants (monthly for large registrants) to the Canada Customs and Revenue Agency (CCRA). The taxes are payable to the Receiver General, who is the collection agent for the federal government.

The GST applies at a rate of 7% on most transactions. Transactions subject to GST are called **taxable supplies**. There are two other categories of goods and services with respect to the GST:

- zero-rated supplies, such as basic groceries and prescription drugs
- exempt supplies, such as educational services, health-care services, and financial services

No GST applies to zero-rated or exempt supplies. However, zero-rated suppliers can claim input tax credits.

Illustration B-1 provides the GST status of some typical goods and services.

| Taxable Supplies | Zero-Rated Supplies | Exempt Supplies |
|---|---|---|
| Building materials | Prescription drugs | Used house |
| Ready-to-eat pizza | Uncooked pizza | Dental services |
| Two doughnuts | Six or more doughnuts | Insurance policy |

The reason ready-to-eat pizza and two doughnuts have GST added to the purchase price is because they are considered convenience items and not basic groceries.

## Provincial Sales Tax

Provincial sales taxes are charged on retail sales of certain goods and services. In the provinces charging sales tax, except Quebec and Prince Edward Island, this tax is applied to the selling price of the item before GST is applied. Similarly, GST is charged on the selling price of the item before PST is applied, thus avoiding GST being charged on PST. In Quebec and Prince Edward Island, however, the provincial sales tax is cascaded—that is, applied to the total of the selling price plus GST. Quebec's sales tax is also known as the QST (Quebec Sales Tax).

The following example shows the calculation of cascaded sales tax, using a taxable item sold in Quebec for $100:

| | |
|---|---:|
| Selling price | $100.00 |
| GST ($100 × 7%) | 7.00 |
| QST [($100 + $7) × 7.5%] | 8.03 |
| Total | $115.03 |

Provincial sales taxes are remitted periodically to the Minister of Finance or Provincial Treasurer in each province.

PST rates vary by province and can change with each provincial budget. It is important to understand that the PST may not be applied at the same rate to all taxable goods and services. For example, in Ontario, the rates vary for insurance premiums and alcoholic beverages. Certain goods are exempt, such as children's clothing, textbooks, and residential rent, and may be purchased with no PST. Examples of exempt services that are not taxable include personal services such as dental and medical services. Because rates and exemptions vary by province, it is important, when starting a business, to check with provincial officials for details on how to calculate the provincial tax that must be applied to sales.

## Harmonized Sales Tax

The provinces of Newfoundland and Labrador, Nova Scotia, and New Brunswick charge Harmonized Sales Tax, or HST. Instead of charging GST and PST separately, only the HST is charged at a combined rate of 15%.

Similar to GST, HST returns are submitted quarterly for most registrants (monthly for large registrants) to the CCRA. The federal government then gives the provincial portion of the tax to the province.

To summarize, four provinces—British Columbia, Manitoba, Ontario, and Saskatchewan—apply PST and GST to the selling price of a taxable good or service. Two provinces—Prince Edward Island and Quebec—apply PST to the total of the purchase price and the GST. Three provinces—New Brunswick, Newfoundland and Labrador, and Nova Scotia—charge a combined GST and PST (harmonized) rate of 15% on the selling price. Four provinces and territories do not charge PST—Alberta, the Northwest Territories, Nunavut, and Yukon. In addition to the different ways of applying sales taxes, the rates of sales tax differ in each province and territory, as shown below:

| Province/Territory | GST (HST) Rate | PST Rate | Combined Rate |
|---|---|---|---|
| Alberta | 7.0% | 0.0% | 7.0% |
| British Columbia | 7.0% | 7.5% | 14.5% |
| Manitoba | 7.0% | 7.0% | 14.0% |
| New Brunswick | 15.0% | N/A | 15.0% |
| Newfoundland and Labrador | 15.0% | N/A | 15.0% |
| Northwest Territories | 7.0% | 0.0% | 7.0% |
| Nova Scotia | 15.0% | N/A | 15.0% |
| Nunavut | 7.0% | 0.0% | 7.0% |
| Ontario | 7.0% | 8.0% | 15.0% |
| Prince Edward Island | 7.0% | 10.0% | 17.7%[1] |
| Quebec | 7.0% | 7.5% | 15.025%[1] |
| Saskatchewan | 7.0% | 6.0% | 13.0% |
| Yukon | 7.0% | 0.0% | 7.0% |

[1] In Prince Edward Island and Quebec only, the GST is included in the provincial sales tax base.

**Illustration B-2 ◄**

Sales tax rates

# Sales Taxes Collected on Receipts

Sales taxes are collected by businesses from consumers on taxable goods and services. It is important to understand that sales taxes are not a source of revenue for a company. Sales taxes are collected by a company on behalf of the federal and provincial governments. Consequently, collected sales tax is a current liability to the company until remitted to the respective government at regular intervals.

## Services

Now let's look at how service companies record sales taxes on the services they provide. Assume that a law firm bills a client for legal services. Some service providers, such as law firms, do not have to charge PST in some provinces. In these provinces, the law firm would only charge 7% GST on the legal services provided.

The following entry would be made to record the billing of a client for $500 of services provided by a law firm in Ontario on May 28. In Ontario, legal services are exempt from PST, so only 7% GST would be charged on these services.

| | | | |
|---|---|---|---|
| May 28 | Accounts Receivable | 535 | |
| | Legal Fees Earned | | 500 |
| | GST Payable ($500 × 7%) | | 35 |
| | To record revenue earned from legal fees. | | |

| A | = | L | + | OE |
|---|---|---|---|---|
| +535 | | +35 | | +500 |

Cash flows: no effect

Note that the revenue recorded is $500, and not $535. The legal fees earned are exclusive of the GST amount collected, which is recorded as a current liability.

Assume instead that $250 of cleaning services were provided by a company in Saskatchewan for cash on July 24. These services are subject to both PST (6%) and GST (7%), and would be recorded as follows:

| A | = | L | + | OE |
|---|---|---|---|---|
| +282.50 | | +15.00 | | +250.00 |
| | | +17.50 | | |

Cash flows: +282.50

| July 24 | Cash | 282.50 | |
|---|---|---|---|
| | Cleaning Service Revenue | | 250.00 |
| | PST Payable ($250 × 6%) | | 15.00 |
| | GST Payable ($250 × 7%) | | 17.50 |
| | To record cleaning service revenue. | | |

If these same services were provided by a company in New Brunswick, where HST is 15%, the entry would be as follows:

| A | = | L | + | OE |
|---|---|---|---|---|
| +287.50 | | +37.50 | | +250.00 |

Cash flows: +287.50

| July 24 | Cash | 287.50 | |
|---|---|---|---|
| | Cleaning Service Revenue | | 250.00 |
| | HST Payable ($250 × 15%) | | 37.50 |
| | To record cleaning service revenue. | | |

## Goods

Entries are needed to record the sales taxes owed when goods are sold, or to reduce sales taxes payable when goods are returned.

### Sales

Assume that Staples sells $1,000 of office furniture, on credit, in the province of Ontario, where PST is 8%. GST is 7%. Staples uses a perpetual inventory system and the cost of the furniture to Staples was $800. The following two entries are required to record the sale and the cost of the sale on May 20:

| A | = | L | + | OE |
|---|---|---|---|---|
| +1,150 | | +70 | | +1,000 |
| | | +80 | | |

Cash flows: no effect

| May 20 | Accounts Receivable | 1,150 | |
|---|---|---|---|
| | Sales | | 1,000 |
| | GST Payable ($1,000 × 7%) | | 70 |
| | PST Payable ($1,000 × 8%) | | 80 |
| | To record sale of office furniture on account. | | |

| A | = | L | + | OE |
|---|---|---|---|---|
| -800 | | | | -800 |

Cash flows: no effect

| 20 | Cost of Goods Sold | 800 | |
|---|---|---|---|
| | Merchandise Inventory | | 800 |
| | To record cost of merchandise sold. | | |

Under the periodic inventory system, the second entry would not be recorded.

### Sales Returns and Allowances

If a $300 sales return and allowance were granted by Staples on May 25 for returned merchandise from the above sale, the entry to record the credit memorandum would appear as follows:

| A | = | L | + | OE |
|---|---|---|---|---|
| -345 | | -21 | | -300 |
| | | -24 | | |

Cash flows: no effect

| May 25 | Sales Returns and Allowances | 300 | |
|---|---|---|---|
| | GST Payable ($300 × 7%) | 21 | |
| | PST Payable ($300 × 8%) | 24 | |
| | Accounts Receivable | | 345 |
| | To record returned goods. | | |

| A | = | L | + | OE |
|---|---|---|---|---|
| +240 | | | | +240 |

Cash flows: no effect

| 25 | Merchandise Inventory ($300 ÷ $1,000 × $800) | 240 | |
|---|---|---|---|
| | Cost of Goods Sold | | 240 |
| | To record cost of merchandise returned. | | |

Note that the GST and PST payable accounts are debited, rather than debiting a receivable account, to indicate that this is a return of previously collected sales tax. This entry assumes that the merchandise was in good condition and returned to inventory. Note also that the GST and PST did not form part of the original cost of the merchandise, and therefore are not considered in restoring the cost of the merchandise to the inventory account.

Under the periodic inventory system, the second entry would not be recorded.

# Sales Taxes Paid on Disbursements

As a consumer of goods and services, a business must pay the applicable PST and GST charged by its suppliers on taxable goods and services.

## Purchase of Merchandise for Resale

When purchasing merchandise for resale, the treatment of the PST is different than that of the GST. PST is a single-stage tax collected from the final consumers of taxable goods and services. Consequently, wholesalers do not charge the tax to the retailer who will in turn resell the merchandise, at a higher price, to the final consumer. By presenting a vendor registration number, retailers are able to buy merchandise for resale, exempt of the PST.

Businesses must pay GST on the purchase of merchandise but can then offset the GST paid against any GST collected. Consequently, **when merchandise is purchased, the GST paid by a business is *not* part of the inventory cost.** The GST paid on purchases is debited to an account called GST Recoverable and is called an input tax credit.

In Quebec, the QST works somewhat like the GST. Businesses can offset QST paid against any QST collected. The QST paid on purchases is debited to an account called QST Recoverable and is called an input tax refund. Other differences also exist in the treatment of QST. This appendix will focus on PST and does not discuss the QST in any detail.

### Purchases

The following is an entry to record the purchase of goods for resale on May 4 at a price of $4,000, on account, using a perpetual inventory system:

| | | | |
|---|---|---|---|
| May 4 | Merchandise Inventory | 4,000 | |
| | GST Recoverable ($4,000 × 7%) | 280 | |
| | Accounts Payable | | 4,280 |
| | To record goods purchased on account. | | |

A = L + OE
+4,000  +4,280
+280

Cash flows: no effect

The cost of the merchandise, $4,000, is not affected by the GST, which is recorded as a receivable.

Under a periodic inventory system, the $4,000 debit would have been recorded to the Purchases account.

### Purchase Returns and Allowances

The entry to record a $300 return of merchandise on May 8 is as follows:

| | | | |
|---|---|---|---|
| May 8 | Accounts Payable | 321 | |
| | GST Recoverable ($300 × 7%) | | 21 |
| | Merchandise Inventory | | 300 |
| | To record the return of goods. | | |

A = L + OE
−21  −321
−300

Cash flows: no effect

Note that the GST Recoverable account is credited instead of the GST Payable account because this is a return of previously recorded GST.

Under the periodic inventory system, the credit of $300 would have been recorded to the Purchase Returns and Allowances account.

To summarize, PST is not paid on purchases of merchandise for resale. GST paid on purchases is normally recoverable and recorded as a current asset in the GST Recoverable account. Purchase returns and allowances require an adjustment of GST only, since PST was not paid on the original purchase.

## Operating Expenses

Although PST is not charged on goods purchased for resale, it is charged to businesses that use taxable goods and services in their operations. For example, a business must pay GST and PST when it buys office supplies. As with all purchases made by a registered business, the GST is recoverable (can be offset as an input tax credit against GST collected). Because the PST is not recoverable, the PST forms part of the asset or expense that is being acquired.

The following is the entry for a cash purchase of office supplies on May 18 in the amount of $200 in the province of Ontario where PST is 8% and GST is 7%:

| A | = | L | + | OE |
|---|---|---|---|---|
| +216 | | | | |
| +14 | | | | |
| −230 | | | | |

Cash flows: −230

| | May 18 | Office Supplies ($200 + $16[1] PST) | 216 | |
|---|---|---|---|---|
| | | GST Recoverable ($200 × 7%) | 14 | |
| | | Cash | | 230 |
| | | To record purchase of office supplies. | | |

[1] $200 × 8% = $16

In this situation, the cost of the supplies includes both the supplies and the PST. Because GST is recoverable, it does not form part of the asset cost.

This same purchase would be recorded as follows if it occurred in the province of Prince Edward Island, where GST is 7% and PST is charged on GST at 10%:

| A | = | L | + | OE |
|---|---|---|---|---|
| +221.40 | | | | |
| +14.00 | | | | |
| −235.40 | | | | |

Cash flows: −235.40

| | May 18 | Office Supplies ($200 + $21.40[2] PST) | 221.40 | |
|---|---|---|---|---|
| | | GST Recoverable ($200 × 7%) | 14.00 | |
| | | Cash | | 235.40 |
| | | To record purchase of office supplies. | | |

[2] $200 + $14 = $214 × 10% = $21.40

Remember that in Prince Edward Island the provincial sales tax base includes both the cost of the item and the GST. That is, the PST is determined by multiplying 10% by $214 ($200 + $14).

When HST is applied, it is treated in the same manner as GST. HST is recoverable and does not form part of the cost of the item purchased. The purchase of office supplies would be recorded as follows if it had occurred in the province of Newfoundland and Labrador where HST is 15%:

| A | = | L | + | OE |
|---|---|---|---|---|
| +200 | | | | |
| +30 | | | | |
| −230 | | | | |

Cash flows: −230

| | May 18 | Office Supplies | 200 | |
|---|---|---|---|---|
| | | HST Recoverable ($200 × 15%) | 30 | |
| | | Cash | | 230 |
| | | To record purchase of office supplies. | | |

Note that the same amount is paid for the supplies in Ontario and Newfoundland and Labrador, $230, but the amount recorded as the cost of the office supplies differs ($216 and $200).

## Property, Plant, and Equipment

Businesses incur costs other than those for merchandise and operating expenses, such as for the purchase of property, plant, and equipment. The PST and GST apply to these purchases in the same manner as described in the operating expenses section above. All

GST (or HST) paid is recoverable and is not part of the cost of the asset. The PST, however, is part of the cost of the asset being purchased as it is not recoverable.

The following is the entry for the purchase of office furniture on May 20 from Staples, on account, for $1,000 plus applicable sales taxes in Ontario. PST is 8% and GST is 7%.

| May 20 | Office Furniture ($1,000 + $80[1] PST) | 1,080 | |
| | GST Recoverable ($1,000 × 7%) | 70 | |
| | Accounts Payable | | 1,150 |
| | To record purchase of office furniture. | | |

[1] $1,000 x 8% = $80

| A | = | L | + | OE |
|---|---|---|---|---|
| +1,080 | | +1,150 | | |
| +70 | | | | |

Cash flows: no effect

Because the PST is not recoverable, the cost of the furniture is $1,080, inclusive of the PST.

Compare this entry made by the buyer to record the purchase, to the entry made by the seller to record the sale on page B4. Both companies record accounts payable and accounts receivable in the same amount, $1,150. However, the seller records both GST and PST payable while the buyer records only GST recoverable. The PST paid by the buyer is not recoverable, so it becomes part of the cost of the office furniture, $1,080.

In Prince Edward Island, where GST is 7% and PST is charged on GST at 10%, the same entry would be recorded as follows:

| May 20 | Office Furniture ($1,000 + $107[2] PST) | 1,107 | |
| | GST Recoverable ($1,000 x 7%) | 70 | |
| | Accounts Payable | | 1,177 |
| | To record purchase of office furniture. | | |

[2] $1,000 + $70 = $1,070 × 10% = $107

| A | = | L | + | OE |
|---|---|---|---|---|
| +1,107 | | +1,177 | | |
| +70 | | | | |

Cash flows: no effect

In P.E.I., PST is calculated on a cost base which includes the GST. Therefore, PST is calculated on $1,070 ($1,000 + $70).

In Nova Scotia, where HST is 15%, the entry would be recorded as follows:

| May 20 | Office Furniture | 1,000 | |
| | HST Recoverable ($1,000 × 15%) | 150 | |
| | Accounts Payable | | 1,150 |
| | To record purchase of office furniture. | | |

| A | = | L | + | OE |
|---|---|---|---|---|
| +1,000 | | +1,150 | | |
| +150 | | | | |

Cash flows: no effect

As we have noted before, the amount paid for the PST changes the amount recorded as the cost of the office furniture in each province: $1,080 in Ontario, $1,107 in Prince Edward Island, and $1,000 in Nova Scotia.

# Remittance of Sales Taxes

As mentioned in the introduction, businesses act as agents of the federal and provincial governments in charging and later remitting taxes charged on sales and services. For example, Staples, the seller of office furniture illustrated on page B4, must remit GST to the CCRA and PST to the Treasurer of Ontario. Notice that even if Staples has not received payment from a customer buying on account before the due date for the remittance, the tax must still be paid to the government authorities. As a registrant, however, Staples will also benefit from claiming input tax credits and recording a reduction in amounts payable from applying GST on sales.

## GST (HST)

When remitting the amount owed to the federal government at the end of a reporting period for GST (or HST), the amount of GST payable is reduced by any amount in the GST Recoverable account. Any difference is remitted, as shown in the following journal entry, using assumed amounts payable and recoverable:

A  =  L  +  OE
−2,500   −6,250
−3,750

Cash flows: −3,750

| | | | |
|---|---|---|---|
| June 30 | GST Payable | 6,250 | |
| | GST Recoverable | | 2,500 |
| | Cash | | 3,750 |
| | To record remittance to CCRA for GST. | | |

The GST (HST) remittance form requires the registrant to report at specified dates, depending on the business's volume of sales. That is, the amount of the sales and other revenue as well as the amount of GST charged on these sales, whether collected or not. The amount of the input tax credits claimed is also entered on the form to reduce the amount owing to CCRA. If the GST recoverable exceeds the GST payable, the remittance form should be sent as soon as possible in order to ask for a refund. The entry to record the cash receipt from a GST refund will be similar to the entry shown above, except that there will be a debit to Cash, instead of a credit.

The above discussion of the remittance of GST explains why all registrants need two general ledger accounts. One account, GST Payable, is used to keep track of all GST charged on sales and revenues. The second account, GST Recoverable, is used to keep track of the GST input tax credits that have been paid on all of the business's purchases. Failure by a business to capture the proper amounts of input tax credits has a significant impact on income and on cash flows.

## PST

The remittance of PST to the Treasurer or Minister of Finance of the applicable province or territory is similar to that of GST except that, since no credit can be claimed, the amount paid at the end of each reporting period is the amount of the balance in the PST Payable account.

Consequently, the entry to record a remittance of PST, using an assumed amount payable, would appear as follows:

A  =  L  +  OE
−7,400   −7,400

Cash flows: −7,400

| | | | |
|---|---|---|---|
| June 30 | PST Payable | 7,400 | |
| | Cash | | 7,400 |
| | To record remittance of PST. | | |

# Conclusion

Be careful when you record the amounts of taxes charged or claimed in the business accounts. Numbers must be rounded carefully. If the amount of the tax calculated is less then half a cent, the amount should be rounded down. If the amount of the tax as calculated comes to more than half a cent, the amount should be rounded up. For example, applying 7% GST on an amount of $44.20 would give you $2.954. The tax amount to be recorded can be rounded down to $2.95. Rounding might seem insignificant, but with many transactions the amounts can add up and the registrant is responsible to the government authorities for any shortfall created in error.

Sales tax law is intricate. It has added a lot of complexity to the accounting for most transactions flowing through today's businesses. Fortunately, computers that are programmed to automatically determine and record the correct sales tax rate for each good or service provided have simplified matters somewhat. Before recording sales tax transactions, however, it is important to understand all of the relevant sales tax regulations. Check the federal and provincial laws in your jurisdiction.

# Brief Exercises

**BEB–1** Journalize the purchase on account of $7,000 of merchandise for resale in the province of Manitoba. The company uses a perpetual inventory system and the purchase is PST exempt.

*Journalize inventory purchase with GST—perpetual inventory system.*

**BEB–2** Journalize the return of $1,000 of the merchandise purchased in BEB–1.

*Journalize purchase return—perpetual inventory system.*

**BEB–3** Journalize the cash purchase of $500 of office supplies in the province of Saskatchewan, where PST is 6%.

*Journalize purchase of supplies with GST and PST.*

**BEB–4** Journalize the purchase on account of a $15,000 delivery truck in the province of Nova Scotia, where HST is 15%.

*Journalize truck purchase with HST.*

**BEB–5** Journalize the purchase on account of $100 of office supplies and $4,000 of merchandise for resale in the province of Ontario. The company uses a perpetual inventory system and the purchase of merchandise is PST exempt. The PST rate is 8%.

*Journalize purchase of supplies and inventory, with GST and PST—perpetual inventory system.*

**BEB–6** Journalize the sale on account, for $1,800, of merchandise costing $1,200 in the province of Prince Edward Island. Assume the company uses a perpetual inventory system. The PST is 10% and the GST is included in the provincial sales tax base.

*Journalize sales with GST and PST—perpetual inventory system.*

**BEB–7** Half of the shipment described in BEB–6 is returned as the incorrect sizes have been shipped. Journalize the credit memorandum of the business selling the goods.

*Journalize sales return, with GST and PST—perpetual inventory system.*

**BEB–8** Journalize the sale in BEB–6 and the credit memorandum in BEB–7 assuming the business uses a periodic inventory system.

*Journalize sales and sales return with GST and PST—periodic inventory system.*

**BEB–9** Journalize the billing for $250 of services by R. R. Dennis, dentist, in the province of British Columbia. Dental services are exempt from GST and PST.

*Journalize exempt services.*

**BEB–10** Journalize the billing of accounting fee revenue of $600 for the preparation of personal income tax returns in the province of Alberta. GST is applicable on this service. Alberta does not charge PST.

*Journalize fees with GST.*

**BEB–11** Journalize two payments: one cheque to the Receiver General for GST and one to the Treasurer of Ontario for PST. The balances in the accounts are as follows: GST Payable $4,450, GST Recoverable $1,900, and PST Payable $4,870.

*Journalize the remittance of GST and PST.*

**BEB–12** Journalize the deposit of a cheque from the Receiver General for a refund of $690 following the filing of an HST return. The balances in the accounts are as follows: HST Payable $2,920 and HST Recoverable $3,610.

*Journalize HST refund.*

# Exercises

**EB–1** Stratton Company is a merchant operating in the province of Ontario where the PST rate is 8%. Stratton uses a perpetual inventory system. Transactions for the business are shown below:

*Journalize sales transactions with sales taxes—perpetual inventory system.*

Interactive Homework

Mar.   1  Paid March rent to the landlord for the rental of a warehouse. The lease calls for monthly payments of $5,500 plus 7% GST.

        3  Sold merchandise on account and shipped merchandise to Marvin Ltd. for $20,000, terms n/30, FOB shipping point. This merchandise cost Stratton $11,000.

Mar.  5 Granted Marvin a sales allowance of $500 for defective merchandise purchased on March 3. No merchandise was returned.

7 Purchased on account from Tiller Ltd. merchandise for resale at a list price of $14,000, plus applicable tax.

12 Made a cash purchase at Home Depot of a desk for the shipping clerk. The price of the desk was $600 before applicable taxes.

31 Paid the monthly remittance of GST to the Receiver General. The balances in the accounts were as follows: GST Payable $4,280 and GST Recoverable $1,917.

*Instructions*

(a) Prepare the journal entries to record these transactions on the books of Stratton Company.
(b) Assume instead that Stratton operates in the province of Alberta, where PST is not applicable. Prepare the journal entries to record these transactions on the books of Stratton.
(c) Assume instead that Stratton operates in the province of Prince Edward Island, where PST is charged on GST at 10%. Prepare the journal entries to record these transactions on the books of Stratton.
(d) Assume instead that Stratton operates in the province of New Brunswick, where HST is 15%. Prepare the journal entries to record these transactions on the books of Stratton.

**EB–2** Using the information for the transactions of Stratton Company in EB–1, assume now that Stratton uses a periodic inventory system.

*Journalize sales transactions with sales taxes—periodic inventory system.*

*Instructions*

(a) Prepare the journal entries to record these transactions on the books of Stratton Company.
(b) Assume now that Stratton operates in the province of Alberta, where PST is not applicable. Prepare the journal entries to record these transactions on the books of Stratton.
(c) Assume now that Stratton operates in the province of Prince Edward Island, where PST is charged on GST at 10%. Prepare the journal entries to record these transactions on the books of Stratton.
(d) Assume now that Stratton operates in the province of New Brunswick, where HST is 15%. Prepare the journal entries to record these transactions on the books of Stratton. Assume that the GST balances on March 31 provided in EB–1 are the balances in the HST accounts.

*Journalize service transactions with sales taxes.*

**EB–3** Tom LeBrun is a sole practitioner providing accounting services in the province of Manitoba. The provincial sales tax rate in Manitoba is 6%, but accounting services are exempt of provincial sales tax. Transactions for the business are shown below:

June  8 Purchased a printer on account at a cost of $1,200. The appropriate sales taxes were added to this purchase price.

10 Purchased toner for the printer for $50 cash from a local stationery store. The store added the appropriate sales taxes to the purchase price.

12 Billed a client for accounting services provided. The fee charged was $750 and GST was added to the fee billed.

15 Collected $107 on account. The original fee was $100 and the GST charged was $7.

30 Paid the monthly remittance of GST to the Receiver General. The balances in the accounts were as follows: GST Payable $1,520.60 and GST Recoverable $820.45.

*Instructions*

Prepare the journal entries to record these transactions on the books of Tom LeBrun's accounting business.

# Problems

*Journalize transactions with sales taxes—perpetual inventory system.*

**PB–1** Mark's Music is a store that buys and sells musical instruments in Ontario, where the provincial sales tax is charged at a rate of 8%. Mark's Music uses a perpetual inventory system. Transactions for the business are shown below:

Nov.  2 Purchased two electric guitars from Fender Supply Limited, on account, at a cost of $700 each.

Nov. 4 Made a cash sale of two keyboards for a total invoice price of $2,200, plus applicable taxes. The cost of each keyboard was $750.

5 Received a credit memorandum from Western Acoustic Inc. for the return of an acoustic guitar which was defective. The original invoice price before taxes was $400 and the guitar had been purchased on account.

7 One of the keyboards from the cash sale of Nov. 4 was returned to the store for a full cash refund because the customer was not satisfied with the instrument.

8 Purchased store supplies from a stationery store. The price of the supplies is $100 before all applicable taxes.

10 Sold one Omega trumpet to the Toronto Regional Band, on account, for an invoice price of $2,700 before applicable taxes. The trumpet had cost Mark's Music $1,420.

13 Purchased two saxophones from Yamaha Canada Inc. on account. The invoice price was $2,100 for each saxophone, excluding applicable taxes.

14 Collected $4,025 on account. The payment included GST of $245 and PST of $280.

16 Returned to Yamaha Canada Inc. one of the saxophones purchased on Nov. 13, as it was the wrong model. Received a credit memorandum from Yamaha for the full purchase price.

20 Made a payment on account for the amount owing to Fender Supply Limited for the purchase of Nov. 2.

30 Paid the monthly remittance of GST to the Receiver General. The balances in the accounts were as follows: GST Payable $5,540 and GST Recoverable $1,860.

30 Paid the monthly remittance of PST to the Treasurer of Ontario. The balance in PST Payable is $5,920.

*Instructions*

Prepare the journal entries to record the Mark's Music transactions.

**PB–2** Transaction data for Mark's Music are available in PB–1. Assume Mark's Music uses a periodic inventory system instead of a perpetual inventory system.

*Journalize transactions with sales taxes—periodic inventory system.*

*Instructions*

Prepare the journal entries to record the Mark's Music transactions.

**PB–3** David Simmons, LL.B., is a lawyer operating as a sole practitioner in Nunavut. Nunavut does not charge provincial sales taxes. Transactions for the business are shown below:

*Journalize service transactions with sales taxes.*

May 1 Signed a two-year lease for the office space and immediately paid the first and last months' rent. The lease calls for the monthly rent of $1,500 plus applicable taxes.

4 Purchased an office suite of furniture, on account, from Leon's at a cost of $3,400. The appropriate sales taxes were added to this purchase price.

5 Returned one chair to Leon's due to a defect. The cost of the chair before taxes was $400.

6 Billed a client for the preparation of a will. The client was very pleased with the product and immediately paid David's invoice for fees of $1,000 plus taxes.

10 Purchased paper for the photocopier for $200 cash from a local stationery store. The store added the appropriate sales taxes to the purchase price.

13 Billed Manson Ltd. for legal services rendered connected with the purchase of land. The fee charged is $900 plus applicable taxes.

18 Paid Leon's for the furniture purchase of May 4, net of returned items.

19 Paid $5 cash to a local grocery store for coffee for the office coffee machine. Groceries are GST exempt.

21 In accordance with the lease agreement with the landlord, David must pay for water supplied by the municipality. The water invoice was received and the services amounted to $100 plus GST.

May 25 Collected a full payment from Manson Ltd. for the May 13 bill.

27 Completed the preparation of a purchase and sale agreement for Edwards Inc. and billed fees of $1,200.

June 20 Deposited a cheque from the Receiver General for a refund of $270 following the filing of the May GST return. The balances in the accounts were as follows: GST Payable $990 and GST Recoverable $1,260.

*Instructions*

Prepare the journal entries to record these transactions on the books of David Simmons' law practice.

# appendix C
# Accounting Systems

In the textbook, we learned how to record accounting transactions in a general journal. Each journal entry was then individually posted to its respective general ledger account. However, such a practice is only useful in a company where the volume of transactions is low. In most companies, it is necessary to use additional journals (called special journals) and ledgers (called subsidiary ledgers) to record transaction data.

We will look at subsidiary ledgers and special journals in the next sections. Both subsidiary ledgers and special journals can be used in either a manual accounting system or a computerized accounting system.

## Subsidiary Ledgers

Imagine a business that has several thousand customers who purchase merchandise from it on account. It records the transactions with these customers in only one general ledger account—Accounts Receivable. It would be virtually impossible to determine the balance owed by an individual customer at any specific time. Similarly, the amount payable to one creditor would be difficult to locate quickly from a single accounts payable account in the general ledger.

Instead, companies use subsidiary ledgers to keep track of individual balances. A **subsidiary ledger** is a group of accounts that share a common characteristic (for example, all accounts receivable). The subsidiary ledger frees the general ledger from the details of individual balances. A subsidiary ledger is an addition to, and an expansion of, the general ledger.

Two common subsidiary ledgers are:

1. The accounts receivable (or customers') ledger, which collects transaction data for individual customers
2. The accounts payable (or creditors') ledger, which collects transaction data for individual creditors

Other subsidiary ledgers include an inventory ledger, which collects transaction data for each inventory item purchased and sold, as was described in Chapter 5. Some companies also use a payroll ledger, detailing individual employee pay records. In each of these subsidiary ledgers, individual accounts are arranged in alphabetical, numerical, or alphanumerical order.

The detailed data from a subsidiary ledger are summarized in a general ledger account. For example, the detailed data from the accounts receivable subsidiary ledger are summarized in Accounts Receivable in the general ledger. The general ledger account that summarizes subsidiary ledger data is called a **control account**.

**Each general ledger control account balance must equal the total balance of the individual accounts in the related subsidiary ledger.** This is an important internal control function.

## Example

An example of an accounts receivable control account and subsidiary ledger is shown in Illustration C-1 for Mercier Enterprises.

**Illustration C-1 ►**

Accounts receivable general ledger control account and subsidiary ledger

**GENERAL LEDGER**

Accounts Receivable is a control account.

Accounts Receivable                                                                 No. 112

| Date | Explanation | Ref. | Debit | Credit | Balance |
|------|-------------|------|-------|--------|---------|
| 2005 | | | | | |
| Jan. 31 | | | 12,000 | | 12,000 |
| 31 | | | | 8,000 | 4,000 |

The subsidiary ledger is separate from the general ledger.

**ACCOUNTS RECEIVABLE SUBSIDIARY LEDGER**

Aaron Co.                                                                 No. 112-172

| Date | Explanation | Ref. | Debit | Credit | Balance |
|------|-------------|------|-------|--------|---------|
| 2005 | | | | | |
| Jan. 11 | Invoice 336 | | 6,000 | | 6,000 |
| 19 | Payment | | | 4,000 | 2,000 |

Branden Inc.                                                                 No. 112-173

| Date | Explanation | Ref. | Debit | Credit | Balance |
|------|-------------|------|-------|--------|---------|
| 2005 | | | | | |
| Jan. 12 | Invoice 337 | | 3,000 | | 3,000 |
| 21 | Payment | | | 3,000 | 0 |

Caron Co.                                                                 No. 112-174

| Date | Explanation | Ref. | Debit | Credit | Balance |
|------|-------------|------|-------|--------|---------|
| 2005 | | | | | |
| Jan. 20 | Invoice 339 | | 3,000 | | 3,000 |
| 29 | Payment | | | 1,000 | 2,000 |

The example is based on the following transactions:

| Credit Sales | | | Collections on Account | | |
|---|---|---|---|---|---|
| Jan. 11 | Aaron Co. | $ 6,000 | Jan. 19 | Aaron Co. | $4,000 |
| 12 | Branden Inc. | 3,000 | 21 | Branden Inc. | 3,000 |
| 20 | Caron Co. | 3,000 | 29 | Caron Co. | 1,000 |
| | | $12,000 | | | $8,000 |

The total debits ($12,000) and credits ($8,000) in Accounts Receivable in the general ledger match the detailed debits and credits in the subsidiary accounts. The balance of $4,000 in the control account agrees with the total of the balances in the individual accounts receivable accounts (Aaron $2,000 + Branden $0 + Caron $2,000) in the subsidiary ledger.

Rather than relying on customer or creditor names in a subsidiary ledger, a computer system expands the account number of the control account. For example, if the general ledger control account Accounts Receivable was numbered 112, the first customer account in the accounts receivable subsidiary ledger might be numbered 112-001, the second 112-002, and so on. Most systems allow inquiries about specific customer accounts in the subsidiary ledger (by account number) or about the control account.

As shown, postings are made monthly to the control account in the general ledger. We will learn, in the next section, how special journals facilitate monthly postings. We will also learn how to fill in the posting references (in the Ref. column) in both the general ledger and subsidiary ledger accounts. Postings to the individual accounts in the subsidiary ledger are made daily. The rationale for posting daily is to ensure that account information is current. This enables Mercier Enterprises to monitor credit limits, send statements to customers, and answer inquiries from customers about their account balances. In a computerized accounting system, transactions are simultaneously recorded in journals and posted to both the general and subsidiary ledgers.

## Advantages of Subsidiary Ledgers

Subsidiary ledgers have several advantages:

1. **They show transactions that affect one customer or one creditor in a single account.** They provide up-to-date information on specific account balances.
2. **They free the general ledger of excessive details.** A trial balance of the general ledger does not contain vast numbers of individual customer account balances.
3. **They help locate errors in individual accounts.** The potential for errors is minimized by reducing the number of accounts in one ledger and by using control accounts.
4. **They make possible a division of labour in posting.** One employee can post to the general ledger while different employees post to the subsidiary ledgers. This strengthens internal control, since one employee verifies the work of the other.

In a computerized accounting system, the last two advantages don't apply. Computerized accounting systems do not make errors such as calculation errors and posting errors. Other errors, such as entry errors, can and do still occur. Internal control must be done using different means in computerized systems since account transactions are posted automatically.

# Special Journals

As mentioned earlier, journalizing transactions in a two-column (debit and credit) general journal is satisfactory only when there are few transactions. To help with the journalizing and posting of multiple transactions, most companies use special journals in addition to the general journal.

A special journal is used to record similar types of transactions. Examples include all sales of merchandise on account, or all cash receipts. The types of special journals used depend largely on the types of transactions that occur frequently. While the form, type, and number of special journals used will vary among organizations, many merchandising companies use the journals shown in Illustration C-2 to record daily transactions. The letters that appear in parentheses following the journal name represent the posting reference used for each journal.

**Illustration C-2 ▶**

Use of special journals and the general journal

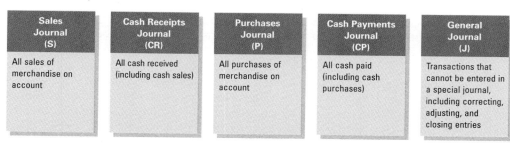

| Sales Journal (S) | Cash Receipts Journal (CR) | Purchases Journal (P) | Cash Payments Journal (CP) | General Journal (J) |
|---|---|---|---|---|
| All sales of merchandise on account | All cash received (including cash sales) | All purchases of merchandise on account | All cash paid (including cash purchases) | Transactions that cannot be entered in a special journal, including correcting, adjusting, and closing entries |

**If a transaction cannot be recorded in a special journal, it is recorded in the general journal.** For example, if you have four special journals as listed in Illustration C-2, sales returns and allowances are recorded in the general journal. Similarly, correcting, adjusting, and closing entries are recorded in the general journal. Other types of special journals may sometimes be used in certain situations. For example, when sales returns and allowances are frequent, an additional special journal may be used to record these transactions. A payroll journal is another example of a special journal. It organizes and summarizes payroll details for companies with many employees.

The use of special journals reduces the time needed for the recording and posting process. In addition, special journals permit greater division of labour because different employees can record entries in different journals. For example, one employee may journalize all cash receipts. Another may journalize credit sales. The division of responsibilities ensures that one person does not have control over all aspects of a transaction. In this instance, recording the sale has been separated from recording the collection of cash from that sale. This may reduce the opportunity for intentional or unintentional error, and is one aspect of a good internal control system.

For a merchandising company, the same special journals are used whether a company uses the periodic or perpetual system to account for its inventory. The only distinction is the number of, and title for, the columns each journal uses. We will use Karns Wholesale Supply to show the use of special journals in the following sections. Karns uses a perpetual inventory system. The variations between the periodic and perpetual inventory systems are highlighted in helpful hints for your information. In addition, special journals under a periodic inventory system are shown more fully at the end of this appendix.

# Sales Journal

The sales journal is used to record sales of merchandise on account. Cash sales of merchandise are entered in the cash receipts journal. Credit sales of assets other than merchandise are entered in the general journal.

## Journalizing Credit Sales

Under the perpetual inventory system, each entry in the sales journal results in one entry at selling price and another entry at cost. The entry at selling price is a debit to Accounts Receivable (a control account supported by a subsidiary ledger) and a credit of an equal amount to Sales. The entry at cost is a debit to Cost of Goods Sold and a credit of an equal amount to Merchandise Inventory. Some companies also set up Merchandise Inventory as a control account supported by a subsidiary ledger.

A sales journal with two amount columns can show a sales transaction recognized at both selling price and cost on only one line. The two-column sales journal of Karns Wholesale Supply is shown in Illustration C-3, using assumed credit sales transactions.

| Date | Account Debited | Invoice No. | Ref. | Accts. Receivable Dr. Sales Cr. | Cost of Goods Sold Dr. Merchandise Inventory Cr. |
|---|---|---|---|---|---|
| **KARNS WHOLESALE SUPPLY** Sales Journal | | | | | S1 |
| 2005 | | | | | |
| May 3 | Abbot Sisters | 101 | | 10,600 | 6,360 |
| 7 | Babson Co. | 102 | | 11,350 | 7,370 |
| 14 | Carson Bros. | 103 | | 7,800 | 5,070 |
| 19 | Deli Co. | 104 | | 9,300 | 6,510 |
| 21 | Abbot Sisters | 105 | | 15,400 | 10,780 |
| 24 | Deli Co. | 106 | | 21,210 | 15,900 |
| 27 | Babson Co. | 107 | | 14,570 | 10,200 |
| | | | | 90,230 | 62,190 |

Illustration C-3 ◄
Sales journal—perpetual inventory system

**Helpful hint** In a periodic inventory system, the sales journal would have only one column to record the sale at selling price (Accounts Receivable Dr., Sales Cr.). The cost of goods sold is not recorded. It is calculated at the end of the period.

The reference (Ref.) column is not used in journalizing. It is used in posting the sales journal, as explained in the next section. Also, note that, unlike in the general journal, an explanation is not required for each entry in a special journal. Finally, note that each invoice is prenumbered to ensure that all invoices are journalized.

If management wishes to record its sales by department, additional columns may be provided in the sales journal. For example, a department store may have columns for home furnishings, sporting goods, shoes, etc. In addition, the federal government, and practically all provinces, require that sales taxes be charged on items sold. If sales taxes are collected, it is necessary to add more credit columns to the sales journal for GST Payable and PST Payable (or HST Payable).

## Posting the Sales Journal

Postings from the sales journal are made **daily to the individual accounts receivable accounts** in the subsidiary ledger. Posting **to the general ledger is done monthly**. Illustration C-4 shows both the daily postings to the accounts receivable subsidiary ledger and the monthly postings to the general ledger accounts. We have assumed that Karns Wholesale Supply does not maintain an inventory subsidiary ledger. However, if it did, the procedure is similar to that illustrated for the accounts receivable subsidiary ledger.

A check mark (√) is inserted in the reference posting column to indicate that the daily posting to the customer's account has been made. A check mark is used when the subsidiary ledger accounts are not individually numbered. If the subsidiary ledger accounts are numbered, the account number is used instead of the check mark in the reference posting column. At the end of the month, the column totals of the sales journal are posted to the general ledger. Here, the column totals are posted as a debit of $90,230 to Accounts Receivable (account no. 112), a credit of $90,230 to Sales (account no. 401), a debit of $62,190 to Cost of Goods Sold (account no. 505), and a credit of $62,190 to Merchandise Inventory (account no. 120). Inserting the account numbers below the column totals indicates that the postings have been made. In both the general ledger and subsidiary ledger accounts, the reference S1 indicates that the posting came from page 1 of the sales journal.

**Illustration C-4 ▶**

Sales journal—perpetual inventory system

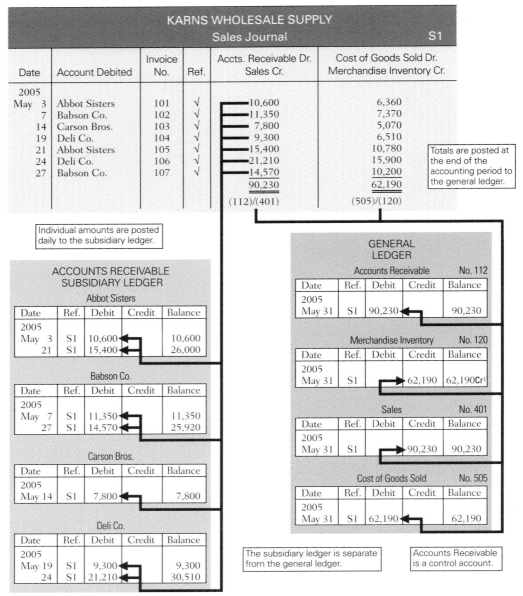

¹ The normal balance for Merchandise Inventory is a debit. But, because of the sequence in which we have posted the special journals, with the sales journal first, the credits to Merchandise Inventory are posted before the debits. This posting sequence explains the credit balance in Merchandise Inventory, which exists only until the other journals are posted.

## Proving the Ledgers

The next step is to "prove" the ledgers. To do so, we must determine two things: (1) The sum of the subsidiary ledger balances must equal the balance in the control account. (2) The total of the general ledger debit balances must equal the total of the general ledger credit balances. The proof of the postings from the sales journal to the general and subsidiary ledgers follows:

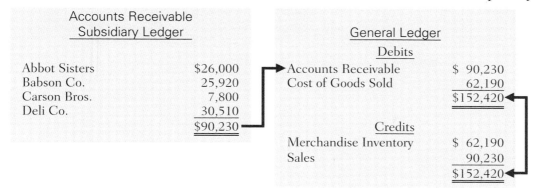

## Advantages of the Sales Journal

The use of a special journal to record sales on account has a number of advantages. First, the one-line–two-column entry for each sales transaction saves time. In the sales journal, it is not necessary to write out the four account titles for the two transactions. Second, only totals, rather than individual entries, are posted to the general ledger. This saves posting time and reduces the possibility of errors in posting. Third, the prenumbering of sales invoices helps to ensure that all sales are recorded and that no sale is recorded more than once. Finally, a division of labour results, because one individual can take responsibility for the sales journal alone. These last two advantages help internal control.

# Cash Receipts Journal

All receipts of cash are recorded in the cash receipts journal. The most common types of cash receipts are cash sales of merchandise and collections of accounts receivable. Many other possibilities exist, such as a receipt of money from a bank loan and cash proceeds from disposals of equipment. A one- or two-column cash receipts journal would not have enough space for all possible cash receipt transactions. A multiple-column cash receipts journal is therefore used.

Generally, a cash receipts journal includes the following columns: a debit column for cash, and credit columns for accounts receivable, sales, and other accounts. The Other Accounts column is used when the cash receipt does not involve a cash sale or a collection of accounts receivable. Under a perpetual inventory system, each sales entry is accompanied by another entry that debits Cost of Goods Sold and credits Merchandise Inventory. A separate column is added for this purpose. A five-column cash receipts journal is shown in Illustration C-5.

Additional credit columns may be used if they significantly reduce postings to a specific account. For example, cash receipts normally include the collection of sales taxes, which are later remitted to the federal and provincial governments. Most cash receipts journals have a separate credit column for sales tax collections. Other examples include the cash receipts of a loan company, such as Household Financial Centre, which cover thousands of collections from customers. These collections are credited to Loans Receivable and Interest Revenue. A significant saving in posting time would result from using separate credit columns for Loans Receivable and Interest Revenue, rather than using the Other Accounts credit column. In contrast, a retailer that has only one interest collection a month would not find it useful to have a separate column for Interest Revenue.

**Illustration C-5 ▶**

Cash receipts journal—
perpetual inventory system

## KARNS WHOLESALE SUPPLY
### Cash Receipts Journal
CR1

| Date | Account Credited | Ref. | Cash Dr. | Accounts Receivable Cr. | Sales Cr. | Cost of Goods Sold Dr. Mdse. Inv. Cr. | Other Accounts Cr. |
|---|---|---|---|---|---|---|---|
| 2005 | | | | | | | |
| May 1 | D. A. Karns, Capital | 301 | 5,000 | | | | 5,000 |
| 7 | | | 1,900 | | 1,900 | 1,240 | |
| 10 | Abbot Sisters | √ | 10,600 | 10,600 | | | |
| 12 | | | 2,600 | | 2,600 | 1,690 | |
| 17 | Babson Co. | √ | 11,350 | 11,350 | | | |
| 22 | Notes Payable | 200 | 6,000 | | | | 6,000 |
| 23 | Carson Bros. | √ | 7,800 | 7,800 | | | |
| 28 | Deli Co. | √ | 9,300 | 9,300 | | | |
| | | | 54,550 | 39,050 | 4,500 | 2,930 | 11,000 |
| | | | (101) | (112) | (401) | (505)/(120) | (X) |

Individual amounts are posted daily to the subsidiary ledger.

Totals are posted at the end of the accounting period to the general ledger.

**Helpful hint** In a periodic inventory system, the Cash Receipts journal would have one column fewer. The Cost of Goods Sold Dr. and Merchandise Inventory Cr. would not be recorded.

### ACCOUNTS RECEIVABLE SUBSIDIARY LEDGER

**Abbot Sisters**

| Date | Ref. | Debit | Credit | Balance |
|---|---|---|---|---|
| 2005 | | | | |
| May 3 | S1 | 10,600 | | 10,600 |
| 10 | CR1 | | 10,600 | 0 |
| 21 | S1 | 15,400 | | 15,400 |

**Babson Co.**

| Date | Ref. | Debit | Credit | Balance |
|---|---|---|---|---|
| 2005 | | | | |
| May 7 | S1 | 11,350 | | 11,350 |
| 17 | CR1 | | 11,350 | 0 |
| 27 | S1 | 14,570 | | 14,570 |

**Carson Bros.**

| Date | Ref. | Debit | Credit | Balance |
|---|---|---|---|---|
| 2005 | | | | |
| May 14 | S1 | 7,800 | | 7,800 |
| 23 | CR1 | | 7,800 | 0 |

**Deli Co.**

| Date | Ref. | Debit | Credit | Balance |
|---|---|---|---|---|
| 2005 | | | | |
| May 19 | S1 | 9,300 | | 9,300 |
| 24 | S1 | 21,210 | | 30,510 |
| 28 | CR1 | | 9,300 | 21,210 |

Accounts Receivable is a control account.

The subsidiary ledger is separate from the general ledger.

### GENERAL LEDGER

**Cash** No. 101

| Date | Ref. | Debit | Credit | Balance |
|---|---|---|---|---|
| 2005 | | | | |
| May 31 | CR1 | 54,550 | | 54,550 |

**Accounts Receivable** No. 112

| Date | Ref. | Debit | Credit | Balance |
|---|---|---|---|---|
| 2005 | | | | |
| May 31 | S1 | 90,230 | | 90,230 |
| 31 | CR1 | | 39,050 | 51,180 |

**Merchandise Inventory** No. 120

| Date | Ref. | Debit | Credit | Balance |
|---|---|---|---|---|
| 2005 | | | | |
| May 31 | S1 | | 62,190 | 62,190Cr. |
| 31 | CR1 | | 2,930 | 65,120Cr. |

**Notes Payable** No. 200

| Date | Ref. | Debit | Credit | Balance |
|---|---|---|---|---|
| 2005 | | | | |
| May 22 | CR1 | | 6,000 | 6,000 |

**D. A. Karns, Capital** No. 301

| Date | Ref. | Debit | Credit | Balance |
|---|---|---|---|---|
| 2005 | | | | |
| May 1 | CR1 | | 5,000 | 5,000 |

**Sales** No. 401

| Date | Ref. | Debit | Credit | Balance |
|---|---|---|---|---|
| 2005 | | | | |
| May 31 | S1 | | 90,230 | 90,230 |
| 31 | CR1 | | 4,500 | 94,730 |

**Cost of Goods Sold** No. 505

| Date | Ref. | Debit | Credit | Balance |
|---|---|---|---|---|
| 2005 | | | | |
| May 31 | S1 | 62,190 | | 62,190 |
| 31 | CR1 | 2,930 | | 65,120 |

## Journalizing Cash Receipts Transactions

To illustrate the journalizing of cash receipts transactions, we will continue with the May transactions of Karns Wholesale Supply. Collections from customers are for the entries recorded in the sales journal in Illustration C-3. The entries in the cash receipts journal are based on the following cash receipts:

May  1  D. A. Karns makes an investment of $5,000 in the business.
     7  Cash receipts for merchandise sales total $1,900. The cost of goods sold is $1,240.
     10  A cheque for $10,600 is received from Abbot Sisters in full payment of invoice No. 101.
     12  Cash receipts for merchandise sales total $2,600. The cost of goods sold is $1,690.
     17  A cheque for $11,350 is received from Babson Co. in full payment of invoice No. 102.
     22  Cash is received by signing a 4% note for $6,000, payable September 22 to the National Bank.
     23  A cheque for $7,800 is received from Carson Bros. in full payment of invoice No. 103.
     28  A cheque for $9,300 is received from Deli Co. in full payment of invoice No. 104.

Further information about the columns in the cash receipts journal follows:

**Debit Columns:**

1. **Cash.** The amount of cash actually received in each transaction is entered in this column. The column total indicates the total cash receipts for the month. The total of this column is posted to the cash account in the general ledger.

2. **Cost of Goods Sold.** The Cost of Goods Sold Dr./Merchandise Inventory Cr. column is used to record the cost of the merchandise sold. (Other columns (e.g., Cash and Sales) record the selling price of the merchandise.) This column is similar to the one found in the sales journal. The amount debited to Cost of Goods Sold is the same amount credited to Merchandise Inventory. One column total is posted to both accounts at the end of the month.

**Credit Columns:**

3. **Accounts Receivable.** The Accounts Receivable column is used to record cash collections on account. The amount entered here is the amount to be credited to the individual customer's account.

4. **Sales.** The Sales column is used to record all cash sales of merchandise. Cash sales of other assets (property, plant, and equipment, for example) are not reported in this column. The total of this column is posted to the account Sales.

5. **Merchandise Inventory.** As noted above, the Cost of Goods Sold Dr./Merchandise Inventory Cr. column is used to record the reduction in the merchandise available for future sale. The amount credited to Merchandise Inventory is the same amount debited to Cost of Goods Sold. One column total is posted to both accounts at the end of the month.

6. **Other Accounts.** The Other Accounts column is used whenever the credit is not to Accounts Receivable, Sales, or Merchandise Inventory. For example, in the first entry, $5,000 is entered as a credit to D. A. Karns, Capital. This column is often referred to as the sundry accounts column.

In a multi-column journal, only one line is generally needed for each entry. In some cases, it is useful to add explanatory information, such as the details of the note payable, or to reference supporting documentation, such as invoice numbers if cash sales are invoiced. Note also that the Account Credited column is used to identify both general ledger and subsidiary ledger account titles. The former is shown in the May 1 entry for Karns' investment. The latter is shown in the May 10 entry for the collection from Abbot Sisters.

Debit and credit amounts for each line must be equal. When the journalizing has been completed, the amount columns are totalled. The totals are then compared to prove the equality of debits and credits in the cash receipts journal. Don't forget that the Cost of Goods Sold Dr./Merchandise Inventory Cr. column total represents both a debit and a credit amount. Totalling the columns of a journal and proving the equality of the totals is called **footing** (adding down) and **cross-footing** (adding across) a journal.

The proof of the equality of Karns' cash receipts journal is as follows:

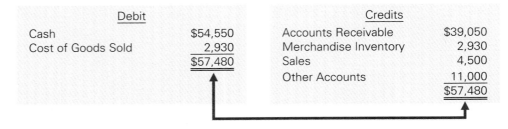

| Debit | | Credits | |
|---|---|---|---|
| Cash | $54,550 | Accounts Receivable | $39,050 |
| Cost of Goods Sold | 2,930 | Merchandise Inventory | 2,930 |
| | $57,480 | Sales | 4,500 |
| | | Other Accounts | 11,000 |
| | | | $57,480 |

## Posting the Cash Receipts Journal

Posting a multi-column journal involves the following steps:

1. All column totals, except for the Other Accounts total, are posted once at the end of the month to the account title specified in the column heading, such as Cash, Accounts Receivable, Sales, Cost of Goods Sold, and Merchandise Inventory. Account numbers are entered below the column totals to show that the amounts have been posted.
2. The total of the Other Accounts column is not posted. Individual amounts that make up the Other Accounts total are posted separately to the general ledger accounts specified in the Account Credited column. See, for example, the credit posting to D. A. Karns, Capital. The symbol X is inserted below the total for this column to indicate that the amount has not been posted.
3. The individual amounts in a column (Accounts Receivable, in this case) are posted daily to the subsidiary ledger account name specified in the Account Credited column. See, for example, the credit posting of $10,600 to Abbot Sisters.

The abbreviation CR is used in both the subsidiary and general ledgers to identify postings from the cash receipts journal.

## Proving the Ledgers

After the posting of the cash receipts journal is completed, it is necessary to prove the ledgers. As shown below, the sum of the subsidiary ledger account balances equals the control account balance. The general ledger totals are also in agreement.

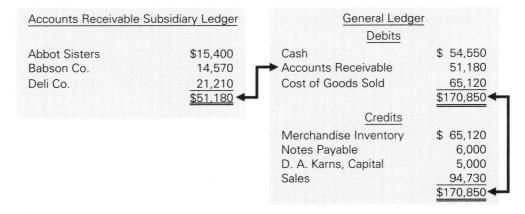

| Accounts Receivable Subsidiary Ledger | | General Ledger | |
|---|---|---|---|
| | | Debits | |
| Abbot Sisters | $15,400 | Cash | $ 54,550 |
| Babson Co. | 14,570 | Accounts Receivable | 51,180 |
| Deli Co. | 21,210 | Cost of Goods Sold | 65,120 |
| | $51,180 | | $170,850 |
| | | Credits | |
| | | Merchandise Inventory | $ 65,120 |
| | | Notes Payable | 6,000 |
| | | D. A. Karns, Capital | 5,000 |
| | | Sales | 94,730 |
| | | | $170,850 |

# Purchases Journal

All purchases of merchandise on account are recorded in the purchases journal. Each entry in this journal results in a debit to Merchandise Inventory and a credit to Accounts Payable. When a one-column purchases journal is used, other types of purchases on account and cash purchases cannot be journalized in it. For example, credit purchases of equipment or supplies must be recorded in the general journal. Likewise, all cash purchases are entered in the cash payments journal. If there are many credit purchases for items other than merchandise, the purchases journal can be expanded to a multi-column format.

The purchases journal for Karns Wholesale Supply is shown in Illustration C-6, with assumed credit purchases.

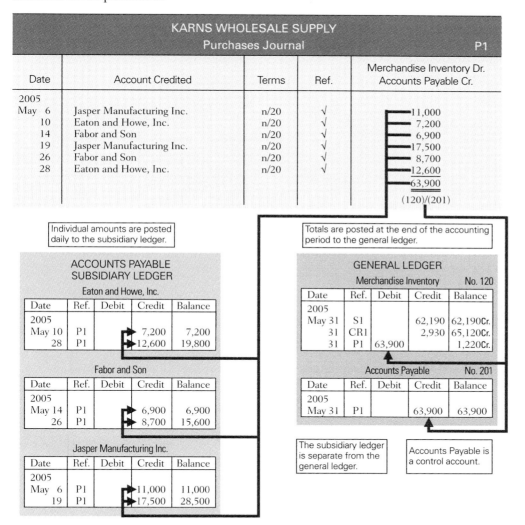

Illustration C-6 ◄

Purchases journal— perpetual inventory system

**Helpful hint** When a periodic inventory system is used, this journal is still known as a purchases journal. The debit to the Merchandise Inventory account is replaced by a debit to the Purchases account.

## Journalizing Credit Purchases of Merchandise

Entries in the purchases journal are made from purchase invoices. The journalizing procedure for the purchases journal is similar to that for the sales journal. In contrast to the sales journal, the purchases journal may not have an invoice number column, because invoices received from different suppliers would not be in numerical sequence.

## Posting the Purchases Journal

The procedures for posting the purchases journal are similar to those for the sales journal. In this case, postings are made **daily** to the accounts payable **subsidiary ledger** accounts and **monthly** to the Merchandise Inventory and Accounts Payable accounts in the **general ledger**. In both ledgers, P1 is used in the reference column to show that the postings are from page 1 of the purchases journal.

Proof of the equality of the postings from the purchases journal to both ledgers is shown by the following:

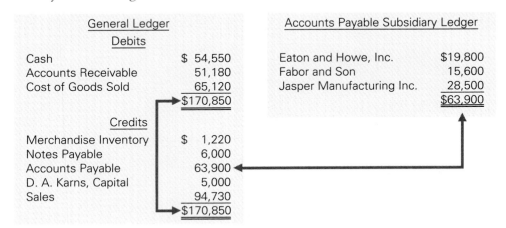

| General Ledger | | Accounts Payable Subsidiary Ledger | |
|---|---:|---|---:|
| **Debits** | | | |
| Cash | $ 54,550 | Eaton and Howe, Inc. | $19,800 |
| Accounts Receivable | 51,180 | Fabor and Son | 15,600 |
| Cost of Goods Sold | 65,120 | Jasper Manufacturing Inc. | 28,500 |
| | $170,850 | | $63,900 |
| **Credits** | | | |
| Merchandise Inventory | $ 1,220 | | |
| Notes Payable | 6,000 | | |
| Accounts Payable | 63,900 | | |
| D. A. Karns, Capital | 5,000 | | |
| Sales | 94,730 | | |
| | $170,850 | | |

Note that not all the general ledger accounts listed above have been included in Illustration C-6. You will have to refer to Illustration C-5 to determine the balances for the accounts Cash, Accounts Receivable, Cost of Goods Sold, Notes Payable, Capital, and Sales.

# Cash Payments Journal

**Alternative terminology**
The cash payments journal is also called the *cash disbursements journal.*

All disbursements of cash are entered in a cash payments journal. Entries are made from prenumbered cheques. Because cash payments are made for various purposes, the cash payments journal has multiple columns. A four-column journal is shown in Illustration C-7.

## Journalizing Cash Payments Transactions

The procedures for journalizing transactions in this journal are similar to those described earlier for the cash receipts journal. Each transaction is entered on one line, and for each line there must be equal debit and credit amounts. It is common practice in the cash payments journal to record the name of the company or individual receiving the cheque (the payee), so that later reference to the cheque is possible by name in addition to cheque number. The entries in the cash payments journal shown in Illustration C-7 are based on the following transactions for Karns Wholesale Supply:

May   3   Cheque No. 101 for $1,200 issued for the annual premium on a fire insurance policy from Corporate General Insurance.

      3   Cheque No. 102 for $100 issued to CANPAR in payment of freight charges on goods purchased.

      7   Cheque No. 103 for $4,400 issued for the cash purchase of merchandise from Zwicker Corp.

   10   Cheque No. 104 for $11,000 sent to Jasper Manufacturing Inc. in full payment of the May 6 invoice.

May 19  Cheque No. 105 for $7,200 mailed to Eaton and Howe, Inc., in full payment of the May 10 invoice.
   24  Cheque No. 106 for $6,900 sent to Fabor and Son in full payment of the May 14 invoice.
   28  Cheque No. 107 for $17,500 sent to Jasper Manufacturing Inc. in full payment of the May 19 invoice.
   31  Cheque No. 108 for $500 issued to D. A. Karns as a cash withdrawal for personal use.

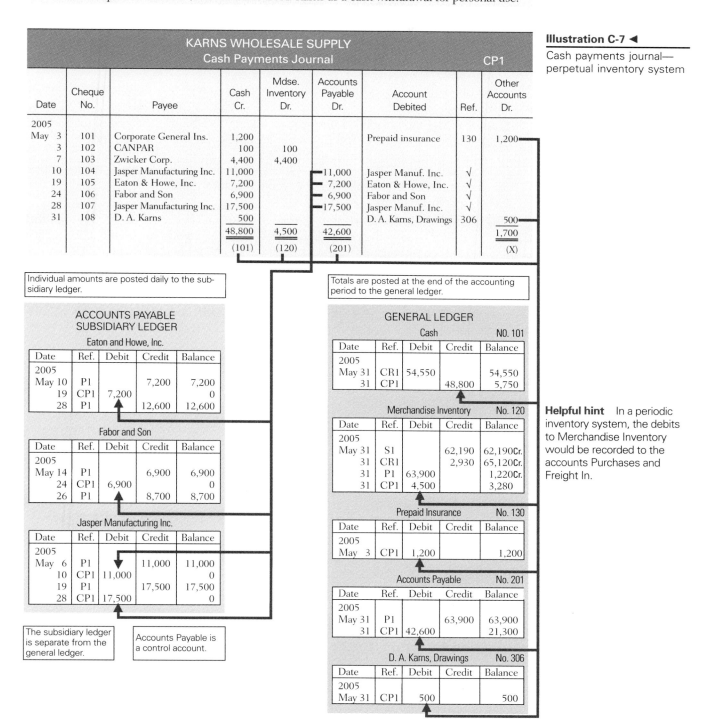

**Illustration C-7 ◄**

Cash payments journal—perpetual inventory system

**Helpful hint**   In a periodic inventory system, the debits to Merchandise Inventory would be recorded to the accounts Purchases and Freight In.

Note that whenever an amount is entered in the Other Accounts column, a specific general ledger account must be identified in the Account Debited column. The entries for cheque numbers 101 and 108 show this situation. Similarly, a subsidiary account must be identified in the Account Debited column whenever an amount is entered in the Accounts Payable column (as, for example, the entry for cheque no. 104).

After the cash payments journal has been journalized, the columns are totalled. The totals are then balanced to prove the equality of debits and credits. Debits ($4,500 + $42,600 + $1,700 = $48,800) do equal credits ($48,800) in this case.

## Posting the Cash Payments Journal

**Helpful hint** If a company has a subsidiary ledger for merchandise inventory, amounts in the merchandise inventory column would be posted daily in the cash payments journal, as well as in the sales, cash receipts, and purchases journals.

The procedures for posting the cash payments journal are similar to those for the cash receipts journal:

1. Cash and Merchandise Inventory are posted only as a total at the end of the month.
2. The amounts recorded in the Accounts Payable column are posted individually to the subsidiary ledger and in total to the general ledger control account.
3. Transactions in the Other Accounts column are posted individually to the appropriate account(s) noted in the Account Debited column. No totals are posted for the Other Accounts column.

The posting of the cash payments journal is shown in Illustration C-7. Note that the abbreviation CP is used as the posting reference. After postings are completed, the equality of the debit and credit balances in the general ledger should be determined. The control account balance should also agree with the subsidiary ledger total balance. The agreement of these balances is shown below. Note that not all the general ledger accounts have been included in Illustration C-7. You will also have to refer to Illustration C-5 to determine the balances for the Accounts Receivable, Cost of Goods Sold, Notes Payable, Capital, and Sales accounts.

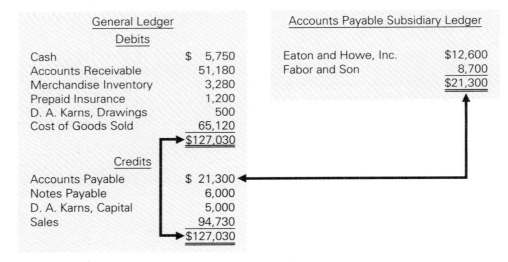

| General Ledger | | Accounts Payable Subsidiary Ledger | |
|---|---|---|---|
| **Debits** | | | |
| Cash | $ 5,750 | Eaton and Howe, Inc. | $12,600 |
| Accounts Receivable | 51,180 | Fabor and Son | 8,700 |
| Merchandise Inventory | 3,280 | | $21,300 |
| Prepaid Insurance | 1,200 | | |
| D. A. Karns, Drawings | 500 | | |
| Cost of Goods Sold | 65,120 | | |
| | $127,030 | | |
| **Credits** | | | |
| Accounts Payable | $ 21,300 | | |
| Notes Payable | 6,000 | | |
| D. A. Karns, Capital | 5,000 | | |
| Sales | 94,730 | | |
| | $127,030 | | |

# Effects of Special Journals on the General Journal

Special journals for sales, purchases, and cash greatly reduce the number of entries that are made in the general journal. **Only transactions that cannot be entered in a special journal are recorded in the general journal.** For example, the general journal may be used to record a transaction granting credit to a customer for a sales return or allowance. It may also be used to record the receipt of a credit from a supplier for purchases returned, the acceptance of a note receivable from a customer, and the purchase of equipment by issuing a note payable. Correcting, adjusting, and closing entries are also made in the general journal.

When control and subsidiary accounts are not used, the procedures for journalizing and posting transactions in the general journal are the same as those described in earlier chapters. When control and subsidiary accounts are used, two modifications of earlier procedures are required:

1. In journalizing, both the control and the subsidiary account must be identified.
2. In posting, there must be a dual posting: once to the control account and once to the subsidiary account.

To illustrate, assume that on May 31 Karns Wholesale Supply returns $500 of merchandise for credit to Fabor and Son. The entry in the general journal and the posting of the entry are shown in Illustration C-8. Note that if cash had been received instead of the credit granted on this return, then the transaction would have been recorded in the cash receipts journal.

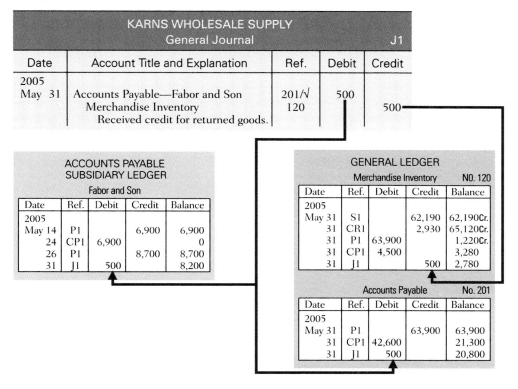

**Illustration C-8 ◄**
General journal

**Helpful hint** In a periodic inventory system, the credit would be to the Purchase Returns and Allowances account rather than to Merchandise Inventory.

Notice that in the general journal two accounts are indicated for the debit (the Accounts Payable control account and the Fabor and Son subsidiary account). Two postings (201/√) are indicated in the reference column. One amount is posted to the control account in the general ledger (no. 201) and the other to the creditor's account in the subsidiary ledger (Fabor and Son).

## Special Journals in a Periodic Inventory System

Recording and posting transactions in special journals is essentially the same whether a perpetual or a periodic inventory system is used. But there are two differences. The first difference relates to the accounts Merchandise Inventory and Cost of Goods Sold in a perpetual inventory system. In this system, an additional column is required to record the cost of each sale in the sales and cash receipts journals, something which is not required in a periodic inventory system.

The second difference concerns the account titles used. In a perpetual inventory system, Merchandise Inventory and Cost of Goods Sold are used to record purchases and the cost of the merchandise sold. In a periodic inventory system, the accounts Purchases and Freight In accumulate the cost of the merchandise purchased until the end of the period. No cost of goods sold is recorded during the period. Cost of goods sold is calculated at the end of the period in a periodic inventory system.

Each of the special journals illustrated in this appendix is shown again here. Using the same transactions, we assume that Karns Wholesale Supply uses a periodic inventory system instead of a perpetual inventory system.

**Illustration C-9 ▶**

Sales journal—periodic inventory system

**Helpful hint** Compare this sales journal to the one presented in Illustration C-4.

| KARNS WHOLESALE SUPPLY Sales Journal | | | | S1 |
|---|---|---|---|---|
| Date | Account Debited | Invoice No. | Ref. | Accts Receivable Dr. Sales Cr. |
| 2005 | | | | |
| May 3 | Abbot Sisters | 101 | √ | 10,600 |
| 7 | Babson Co. | 102 | √ | 11,350 |
| 14 | Carson Bros. | 103 | √ | 7,800 |
| 19 | Deli Co. | 104 | √ | 9,300 |
| 21 | Abbot Sisters | 105 | √ | 15,400 |
| 24 | Deli Co. | 106 | √ | 21,210 |
| 27 | Babson Co. | 107 | √ | 14,570 |
| | | | | 90,230 |

**Illustration C-10 ▶**

Cash receipts journal—periodic inventory system

**Helpful hint** Compare this cash receipts journal to the one presented in Illustration C-5.

| KARNS WHOLESALE SUPPLY Cash Receipts Journal | | | | | | CR1 |
|---|---|---|---|---|---|---|
| Date | Account Credited | Ref. | Cash Dr. | Accounts Receivable Cr. | Sales Cr. | Other Accounts Cr. |
| 2005 | | | | | | |
| May 1 | D. A. Karns, Capital | 301 | 5,000 | | | 5,000 |
| 7 | | | 1,900 | | 1,900 | |
| 10 | Abbot Sisters | √ | 10,600 | 10,600 | | |
| 12 | | | 2,600 | | 2,600 | |
| 17 | Babson Co. | √ | 11,350 | 11,350 | | |
| 22 | Notes Payable | 200 | 6,000 | | | 6,000 |
| 23 | Carson Bros. | √ | 7,800 | 7,800 | | |
| 28 | Deli Co. | √ | 9,300 | 9,300 | | |
| | | | 54,550 | 39,050 | 4,500 | 11,000 |

Illustration C-11 ◄

Purchases journal—periodic inventory system

**Helpful hint** Compare this purchases journal to the one presented in Illustration C-6.

### KARNS WHOLESALE SUPPLY
### Purchases Journal — P1

| Date | Account Credited | Terms | Ref. | Purchases Dr. Accounts Payable Cr. |
|------|------------------|-------|------|-----------------------------------|
| 2005 | | | | |
| May 6 | Jasper Manufacturing Inc. | n/20 | √ | 11,000 |
| 10 | Eaton and Howe, Inc. | n/20 | √ | 7,200 |
| 14 | Fabor and Son | n/20 | √ | 6,900 |
| 19 | Jasper Manufacturing Inc. | n/20 | √ | 17,500 |
| 26 | Fabor and Son | n/20 | √ | 8,700 |
| 28 | Eaton and Howe, Inc. | n/20 | √ | 12,600 |
| | | | | 63,900 |

Illustration C-12 ◄

Cash payments journal—periodic inventory system

**Helpful hint** Compare this cash payments journal to the one presented in Illustration C-7.

### KARNS WHOLESALE SUPPLY
### Cash Payments Journal — CP1

| Date | Cheque No. | Payee | Cash Cr. | Accounts Payable Dr. | Account Debited | Ref. | Other Accounts Dr. |
|------|-----------|-------|----------|----------------------|-----------------|------|---------------------|
| 2005 | | | | | | | |
| May 3 | 101 | Corporate General Ins. | 1,200 | | Prepaid Insurance | 130 | 1,200 |
| 3 | 102 | CANPAR | 100 | | Freight In | 516 | 100 |
| 7 | 103 | Zwicker Corp. | 4,400 | | Purchases | 510 | 4,400 |
| 10 | 104 | Jasper Manufacturing Inc. | 11,000 | 11,000 | Jasper Manuf. Inc. | √ | |
| 19 | 105 | Eaton & Howe, Inc. | 7,200 | 7,200 | Eaton & Howe, Inc. | √ | |
| 24 | 106 | Fabor and Son | 6.900 | 6.900 | Fabor and Son | √ | |
| 28 | 107 | Jasper Manufacturing Inc. | 17,500 | 17,500 | Jasper Manuf. Inc. | √ | |
| 31 | 108 | D. A. Karns | 500 | | D. A. Karns, Drawings | 306 | 500 |
| | | | 48,800 | 42,600 | | | 6,200 |

# Brief Exercises

**BEC–1** Information related to Bryan Company is presented below for its first month of operations. Calculate (a) the balances that appear in the accounts receivable subsidiary ledger for each customer, and (b) the accounts receivable balance that appears in the general ledger at the end of January.

*Calculate subsidiary ledger and control account balances.*

| Credit Sales | | | Cash Collections | | |
|------|------|------|------|------|------|
| Jan. 7 | Duffy Co. | $8,000 | Jan. 17 | Duffy Co. | $7,000 |
| 15 | Hanson Inc. | 6,000 | 24 | Hanson Inc. | 5,000 |
| 23 | Lewis Co. | 9,000 | 29 | Lewis Co. | 9,000 |

**BEC–2** Identify in which ledger (general or subsidiary) each of the following accounts is shown:

*Identify general and subsidiary ledger accounts.*

1. Rent Expense
2. Accounts Receivable—O'Malley
3. Notes Payable
4. Accounts Payable—Kerns
5. Merchandise Inventory
6. Sales

**BEC–3** Chiasson Co. uses special journals and a general journal. Identify the journal in which each of the following transactions is recorded:

*Identify special journals.*

1. Paid cash for equipment purchased on account.
2. Purchased merchandise on credit.
3. Paid utility expense in cash.

4. Sold merchandise on account.
5. Granted a cash refund for a sales return.
6. Received a credit on account for a purchase return.
7. Sold merchandise for cash.
8. Purchased merchandise for cash.

**Identify special journals—perpetual inventory system.**

**BEC–4** Swirsky Company uses the cash receipts and cash payments journals illustrated in this appendix for a perpetual inventory system. In April, the following selected cash transactions occurred:

1. Made a refund to a customer for the return of damaged goods.
2. Received payment from a customer.
3. Purchased merchandise for cash.
4. Paid a creditor.
5. Paid freight on merchandise purchased.
6. Paid cash for office equipment.
7. Received a cash refund from a supplier for merchandise returned.
8. Withdrew cash for personal use of owner.
9. Made cash sales.

*Instructions*

Indicate (a) the journal, and (b) the columns in the journal that should be used in recording each transaction.

**Identify special journals—periodic inventory system.**

**BEC–5** Identify the journal and the specific column title(s) in which each of the following transactions is recorded. Assume the company uses a periodic inventory system.

1. Cash sale
2. Credit sale
3. Sales return on account
4. Cash purchase of merchandise
5. Credit purchase of merchandise
6. Payment of freight on merchandise purchased from a supplier
7. Return of merchandise purchased for cash refund
8. Payment of freight on merchandise delivered to a customer

# Exercises

**Identify special journals.**

**EC–1** Below are some transactions for Dartmouth Company:

1. Payment of creditors on account
2. Return of merchandise sold for credit
3. Collection on account from customers
4. Sale of land for cash
5. Sale of merchandise on account
6. Sale of merchandise for cash
7. Credit received for merchandise returned to a supplier
8. Payment of employee wages
9. Revenues and expenses closed to income summary
10. Amortization on building
11. Purchase of office supplies for cash
12. Purchase of merchandise on account

*Instructions*

For each transaction, indicate whether it would normally be recorded in a cash receipts journal, cash payments journal, sales journal, purchases journal, or general journal.

**EC–2** Sing Tao Company uses special journals and a general journal. The company uses a perpetual inventory system and had the following transactions:

Sept. 2 Sold merchandise on account to T. Mephisto, $520, invoice #101, terms n/30. The cost of the merchandise sold was $360.
3 Purchased office supplies on account from Berko Company, $575.
10 Purchased merchandise on account from Miramichi Company, $800, FOB shipping point, terms n/30. Paid freight of $50 to Apex Shippers.
11 Returned unsatisfactory merchandise to Miramichi Company, $200, for credit on account.
12 Purchased office equipment on account from Wells Company, $8,000.
16 Sold merchandise for cash to L. Maillette, for $800. The cost of the merchandise sold was $480.
18 Purchased merchandise for cash from Miramichi Company, $450, FOB destination.
20 Accepted returned merchandise from customer L. Maillette, $800 (see Sept. 16 transaction). Gave full cash refund. Restored the merchandise to inventory.
24 Paid the correct amount owing for the merchandise purchased from Miramichi earlier in the month.
25 Received payment from T. Mephisto for Sept. 2 sale.
26 Sold merchandise on account to M. Christie, $890, invoice #102, terms n/30, FOB destination. The cost of the merchandise was $520. The appropriate party paid $75 to Freight Co. for shipping charges.
30 Paid September salaries, $3,250.
30 The owner, Mr. Sing Tao, withdrew cash for his personal use, $600.
30 Paid for office supplies purchased on September 3.

*Instructions*

(a) Draw a sales journal and a purchases journal (see Illustrations C-3 and C-6). Use page 1 for each journal.
(b) Record the transaction(s) for September that should be journalized in the sales journal.
(c) Record the transaction(s) for September that should be journalized in the purchases journal.

**EC–3** Refer to the information provided for Sing Tao Company in EC–2.

*Instructions*

(a) Draw cash receipts and cash payments journals (see Illustrations C-5 and C-7) and a general journal. Use page 1 for each journal.
(b) Record the transaction(s) provided in EC–2 that should be journalized in the cash receipts journal.
(c) Record the transaction(s) provided in EC–2 that should be journalized in the cash payments journal.
(d) Record the transaction(s) provided in EC–2 that should be journalized in the general journal.

**EC–4** Argentina Company has the following selected transactions during March:

Mar. 2 Purchased equipment on account, costing $7,400, from Lifetime Company.
5 Received credit memorandum for $300 from Lyden Company for merchandise returned that had been damaged in shipment to Argentina.
7 Issued a credit memorandum for $400 to Marco Presti for merchandise the customer returned. The returned merchandise has a cost of $275 and was restored to inventory.

Argentina Company uses a purchases journal, a sales journal, two cash journals (receipts and payments), and a general journal. Argentina also uses a perpetual inventory system.

*Instructions*

(a) Journalize the appropriate transactions in the general journal.
(b) In a brief memo to the president of Argentina Company, explain the postings to the control and subsidiary accounts.

**EC–5** Maureen Company uses both special journals and a general journal. On June 30, after all monthly postings had been completed, the Accounts Receivable controlling account in the general ledger had a debit balance of $320,000, and the Accounts Payable controlling account had a credit balance of $87,000.

*Record transactions in sales and purchases journals—perpetual inventory system.*

Interactive Homework

*Record transactions in cash receipts, cash payments, and general journals—perpetual inventory system.*

Interactive Homework

*Record transactions in general journal and explain posting.*

*Determine control account balances and explain posting.*

The July transactions recorded in the special journals are summarized below. Maureen Company maintains a perpetual inventory system. No entries that affected accounts receivable and accounts payable were recorded in the general journal for July.

> Sales journal: total sales, $161,400; cost of goods sold, $112,800
> Purchases journal: total purchases, $56,400
> Cash receipts journal: accounts receivable column total, $141,000
> Cash payments journal: accounts payable column total, $47,500

*Instructions*

(a) What is the balance of the Accounts Receivable control account after the monthly postings on July 31?

(b) What is the balance of the Accounts Payable control account after the monthly postings on July 31?

(c) To what accounts are the column totals for total sales of $161,400 and cost of goods sold of $112,800 in the sales journal posted?

(d) To what account(s) is the accounts receivable column total of $141,000 in the cash receipts journal posted?

**Post journals to control and subsidiary accounts.**

Interactive Homework

**EC–6** On September 1, 2005, the balance of the Accounts Receivable control account in the general ledger of Pirie Company was $11,960. The customers' subsidiary ledger contained account balances as follows: Bickford, $4,820; Cavanaugh, $2,060; Jana, $2,440; Kingston, $2,640. At the end of September, the various journals contained the following information:

> Sales journal: Sales to Bickford, $800; to Jana, $1,260; to Iman, $1,030; to Cavanaugh, $1,100. The cost of each sale, respectively, was $480, $810, $620, and $660.
>
> Cash receipts journal: Cash received from Cavanaugh, $1,310; from Bickford, $2,300; from Iman, $380; from Kingston, $1,800; from Jana, $1,240.
>
> General journal: A $220 sales allowance is granted to Bickford, on September 30.

*Instructions*

(a) Set up control and subsidiary accounts, and enter the beginning balances.

(b) Post the various journals to the control and subsidiary accounts. Post the items as individual items or as totals, whichever would be the appropriate procedure. Use page 1 for each journal.

(c) Prepare a list of customers and prove the agreement of the control account with the subsidiary ledger at September 30.

**Record transactions in sales and purchases journals—periodic inventory system.**

**EC–7** Refer to the information provided for Sing Tao Company in EC–2. Complete instructions (a), (b), and (c), assuming that the company uses a periodic inventory system instead of a perpetual inventory system.

**Record transactions in cash receipts, cash payments, and general journals—periodic inventory system.**

**EC–8** Refer to the information provided for Sing Tao Company in EC–3. Complete instructions (a) to (d), assuming that the company uses a periodic inventory system instead of a perpetual inventory system.

# Problems

**Record transactions in special and general journals—perpetual inventory system.**

**PC–1** Selected accounts from the chart of accounts of Genstar Company are shown below:

| | | | |
|---|---|---|---|
| 101 | Cash | 201 | Accounts payable |
| 112 | Accounts receivable | 401 | Sales |
| 120 | Merchandise inventory | 412 | Sales returns and allowances |
| 126 | Supplies | 505 | Cost of goods sold |
| 157 | Equipment | 726 | Salaries expense |

The company uses a perpetual inventory system. The cost of all merchandise sold is 60% of the sales price. During January, Genstar completed the following transactions:

Jan.  3 Purchased merchandise on account from Sun Distributors, $19,800.
      4 Purchased supplies for cash, $280.

Jan.  4 Sold merchandise on account to R. Gilbertson, $8,500, invoice no. 371.
      5 Issued a debit memorandum to Sun Distributors and returned $450 of damaged goods.
      6 Made cash sales for the week totalling $4,650.
      8 Purchased merchandise on account from Irvine Co., $5,400.
      9 Sold merchandise on account to Mays Corp., $5,600, invoice no. 372.
     11 Purchased merchandise on account from Chaparal Co., $4,300.
     13 Paid Sun Distributors account in full.
     13 Made cash sales for the week totalling $5,980.
     15 Received payment from Mays Corp. for invoice no. 372.
     15 Paid semi-monthly salaries of $14,300 to employees.
     17 Received payment from R. Gilbertson for invoice no. 371.
     17 Sold merchandise on account to AMB Co., $1,500, invoice no. 373.
     19 Purchased equipment on account from Johnson Corp., $4,800.
     20 Cash sales for the week totalled $3,400.
     20 Paid Irvine Co. account in full.
     23 Purchased merchandise on account from Sun Distributors, $7,800.
     24 Purchased merchandise on account from Levine Corp., $4,690.
     27 Made cash sales for the week totalling $3,370.
     30 Received payment from AMB Co. for invoice no. 373.
     31 Paid semi-monthly salaries of $13,200 to employees.
     31 Sold merchandise on account to R. Gilbertson, $9,330, invoice no. 374.

Genstar Company uses a sales journal, a purchases journal, a cash receipts journal, a cash payments journal, and a general journal.

### Instructions

(a) Record the January transactions in the appropriate journal.
(b) Foot and cross-foot all special journals.
(c) Show how postings would be made by placing ledger account numbers and check marks as needed in the journals. (Actual posting to ledger accounts is not required.)

**PC–2** Selected accounts from the chart of accounts of Tigau Company are shown below:

| | | | |
|---|---|---|---|
| 101 | Cash | 145 | Buildings |
| 112 | Accounts receivable | 201 | Accounts payable |
| 120 | Merchandise inventory | 401 | Sales |
| 126 | Supplies | 505 | Cost of goods sold |
| 140 | Land | 610 | Advertising expense |

*Journalize transactions in special and general journals—perpetual inventory system.*

The company uses a perpetual inventory system. The cost of all merchandise sold was 65% of the sales price. During October, Tigau Company completed the following transactions:

Oct.  2 Purchased merchandise on account from Madison & Co., $15,800.
      4 Sold merchandise on account to Petroleum Corp., $8,600, invoice no. 204.
      5 Purchased supplies for cash, $315.
      7 Made cash sales for the week that totalled $9,610.
      9 Paid the Madison & Co. account in full.
     10 Purchased merchandise on account from Quinn Corp., $4,900.
     12 Received payment from Petroleum Corp. for invoice no. 204.
     13 Issued a debit memorandum to Quinn Corp. and returned $260 of damaged goods.
     14 Made cash sales for the week that totalled $8,810.
     16 Sold a parcel of land for $25,000 cash, the land's book value.
     17 Sold merchandise on account to Callebaut Co., $5,530, invoice no. 205.
     18 Purchased merchandise for cash, $2,215.
     21 Made cash sales for the week that totalled $8,640.
     23 Paid in full the Quinn Corp. account for the goods kept.
     25 Purchased supplies on account from Frey Co., $260.
     25 Sold merchandise on account to Golden Corp., $5,520, invoice no. 206.
     25 Received payment from Callebaut Co. for invoice no. 205.
     26 Purchased for cash a small parcel of land and a building on the land to use as a storage facility. The total cost of $35,000 was allocated $16,000 to the land and $19,000 to the building.

Oct. 27 Purchased merchandise on account from Schmid Co., $9,000.
    28 Made cash sales for the week that totalled $9,320.
    30 Purchased merchandise on account from Madison & Co., $16,200.
    30 Paid advertising bill for the month from *The Gazette*, $600.
    30 Sold merchandise on account to Callebaut Co., $5,200, invoice no. 207.

Tigau Company uses a sales journal, purchases journal, cash receipts journal, cash payments journal, and general journal.

*Instructions*

(a) Record the October transactions in the appropriate journals.
(b) Foot and cross-foot all special journals.
(c) Show how postings would be made by placing ledger account numbers and check marks as needed in the journals. (Actual posting to ledger accounts is not required.)

Record transactions in special and general journals, post, and prepare trial balance—perpetual inventory system.

**PC–3** The post-closing trial balance for Gibbs Music Co. follows:

**GIBBS MUSIC CO.**
**Post-Closing Trial Balance**
**December 31, 2004**

|     |                                      | Debit     | Credit    |
|-----|--------------------------------------|-----------|-----------|
| 101 | Cash                                 | $ 49,500  |           |
| 112 | Accounts receivable                  | 15,000    |           |
| 115 | Notes receivable—S. Lava             | 45,000    |           |
| 120 | Merchandise inventory                | 22,000    |           |
| 140 | Land                                 | 25,000    |           |
| 145 | Building                             | 75,000    |           |
| 146 | Accumulated amortization—building    |           | $ 18,000  |
| 157 | Equipment                            | 6,450     |           |
| 158 | Accumulated amortization—equipment   |           | 1,500     |
| 200 | Notes payable                        |           | –         |
| 201 | Accounts payable                     |           | 42,000    |
| 275 | Mortgage payable                     |           | 82,000    |
| 301 | M. Gibbs, capital                    |           | 94,450    |
| 310 | M. Gibbs, drawings                   | –         |           |
| 401 | Sales                                |           | –         |
| 410 | Sales returns and allowances         | –         |           |
| 505 | Cost of goods sold                   | –         |           |
| 725 | Salaries expense                     | –         |           |
| 810 | Interest revenue                     |           | –         |
| 920 | Loss—damaged inventory               | –         |           |
|     |                                      | $237,950  | $237,950  |

The subsidiary ledgers contain the following information:

1. Accounts Receivable—S. Armstrong, $4,500; R. Christof, $3,000; B. Hibberd, $7,500
2. Accounts Payable—Fieldstone Corp., $9,000; Harms Distributors, $16,000; Watson & Co., $17,000

Gibbs Music Co. uses a perpetual inventory system. The transactions for January 2005 are as follows:

Jan.  3 Sold merchandise to B. Rohl, $1,000. The cost of goods sold was $400.
     5 Purchased merchandise from Warren Parts Co., $2,400.
     7 Received a cheque from S. Armstrong, $3,000, in partial payment of its account.
    11 Paid freight on merchandise purchased, $350.
    13 Received payment of account in full from B. Rohl.
    14 Issued a credit memo to acknowledge receipt of $600 of damaged merchandise returned by R. Christof. The cost of the returned merchandise was $250. (*Hint*: Debit Loss—Damaged Inventory instead of Merchandise Inventory.)
    15 Sent Harms Distributors a cheque in full payment of account.
    17 Purchased merchandise from Lapeska Co., $1,900.
    18 Paid salaries of $4,400.
    20 Gave Watson & Co. a 2-month, 6% note for $17,000 in full payment of account payable.

Jan. 23 Total cash sales amounted to $9,600. The cost of goods sold was $3,840.
  24 Sold merchandise on account to B. Hibberd, $7,800. The cost of goods sold was $3,300.
  27 Sent Warren Parts Co. a cheque for $950 in partial payment of the account.
  29 Received partial payment on a note of $35,000 in addition to $175 interest, from S. Lava.
  30 Returned merchandise costing $600 to Lapeska Co. for credit.
  31 Withdrew $800 cash for personal use.

*Instructions*

(a) Open general and subsidiary ledger accounts and record December 31, 2004, balances.
(b) Record the January transactions in a sales journal, a purchases journal, a cash receipts journal, a cash payments journal, and a general journal, as illustrated in this appendix.
(c) Post the appropriate amounts to the subsidiary and general ledger accounts.
(d) Prepare a trial balance at January 31, 2005.
(e) Prepare a listing to show that the subsidiary ledgers agree with control accounts in the general ledger.

**PC–4** The post-closing trial balance for Scholz Co. follows:

*Record transactions in special and general journals, post, and prepare trial balance—perpetual inventory system.*

**SCHOLZ CO.**
**Post-Closing Trial Balance**
**April 30, 2005**

| | | Debit | Credit |
|---|---|---|---|
| 101 | Cash | $ 36,700 | |
| 112 | Accounts receivable | 15,400 | |
| 115 | Notes receivable—Cole Company | 48,000 | |
| 120 | Merchandise inventory | 22,000 | |
| 157 | Equipment | 8,200 | |
| 158 | Accumulated amortization—equipment | | $ 1,800 |
| 200 | Notes payable | | – |
| 201 | Accounts payable | | 43,400 |
| 301 | C. Scholz, capital | | 85,100 |
| 310 | C. Scholz, drawings | – | |
| 401 | Sales | | – |
| 410 | Sales returns and allowances | – | |
| 505 | Cost of goods sold | – | |
| 725 | Salaries expense | – | |
| 730 | Rent expense | – | |
| 810 | Interest revenue | | – |
| | | $130,300 | $130,300 |

The subsidiary ledgers contain the following information:

1. Accounts Receivable—L. Cellars, $7,400; W. Karasch, $3,250; G. Parrish, $4,750
2. Accounts Payable—Buttercup Distributors, $17,400; Elite Sports, $15,500; Winterware Corp., $10,500

Scholz uses a perpetual inventory system. The transactions for May 2005 are as follows:

May 3 Sold merchandise to B. Simone, $2,400. The cost of the goods sold was $1,050.
  5 Purchased merchandise from Werner Widgits, $2,600, on account.
  7 Received a cheque from G. Parrish, $2,800, in partial payment of account.
  11 Paid freight on merchandise purchased, $318.
  12 Paid rent of $1,500 for May.
  13 Received payment in full from B. Simone.
  14 Issued a credit memo to acknowledge $750 of merchandise returned by W. Karasch. The merchandise (original cost, $325) was restored to inventory.
  15 Sent Buttercup Distributors a cheque in full payment of account.
  17 Purchased merchandise from Lancio Co., $2,100, on account.
  18 Paid salaries of $4,700.
  20 Gave Elite Sports a two-month, 10% note for $15,500 in full payment of account payable.
  20 Returned merchandise costing $510 to Lancio for credit.
  23 Total cash sales amounted to $9,500. The cost of goods sold was $4,450.
  27 Sent Werner Widgits a cheque for $1,000, in partial payment of account.
  29 Received partial payment on a note of $40,000 in addition to $1,600 interest from Cole Company.
  31 Withdrew $1,000 cash for personal use.

*Instructions*

(a) Open general and subsidiary ledger accounts and record April 30, 2005, balances.
(b) Record the May transactions in a sales journal, a purchases journal, a cash receipts journal, a cash payments journal, and a general journal, as illustrated in this chapter.
(c) Post the appropriate amounts to the subsidiary and general ledger accounts.
(d) Prepare a trial balance at May 31, 2005.
(e) Determine whether the subsidiary ledgers agree with the control accounts in the general ledger.

**Record transactions in special and general journals—periodic inventory system.**

**PC–5** Selected accounts from the chart of accounts on Weir Company are shown below:

| | | | |
|---|---|---|---|
| 101 | Cash | 401 | Sales |
| 112 | Accounts receivable | 412 | Sales returns and allowances |
| 126 | Supplies | 510 | Purchases |
| 157 | Equipment | 512 | Purchase returns and allowances |
| 201 | Accounts payable | 726 | Salaries expense |

During February, Weir completed the following transactions:

Feb.  3 Purchased merchandise on account from Zears Co., $9,200.
       4 Purchased supplies for cash, $290.
       4 Sold merchandise on account to Gilles Co., $7,220, invoice no. 371.
       5 Issued a debit memorandum to Zears Co. and returned $450 worth of goods.
       6 Made cash sales for the week totalling $3,950.
       8 Purchased merchandise on account from Fell Electronics, $5,200,
       9 Sold merchandise on account to Mawani Corp., $7,050, invoice no. 372.
      11 Purchased merchandise on account from Thomas Co., $3,100.
      13 Paid Zears Co. account in full.
      13 Made cash sales for the week totalling $4,850.
      15 Received payment from Mawani Corp. for invoice no. 372.
      15 Paid semi-monthly salaries of $14,700 to employees.
      17 Received payment from Gilles Co. for invoice no. 371.
      17 Sold merchandise on account to Lumber Co., $1,600, invoice no. 373.
      19 Purchased equipment on account from Brown Corp., $6,400.
      20 Cash sales for the week totalled $4,900.
      20 Paid Fell Electronics account in full.
      23 Purchased merchandise on account from Zears Co., $8,800.
      24 Purchased merchandise on account from Lewis Co., $5,130.
      27 Made cash sales for the week totalling $3,560.
      28 Received payment from Lumber Co. for invoice no. 373.
      28 Paid semi-monthly salaries of $14,900 to employees.
      28 Sold merchandise on account to Gilles Co., $9,810, invoice no. 374.

Weir Company uses a sales journal, purchases journal, cash receipts journal, cash payments journal, and general journal. Weir uses a periodic inventory system.

*Instructions*

(a) Record the February transactions in the appropriate journal.
(b) Foot and cross-foot all special journals.
(c) Show how postings would be made by placing ledger account numbers and check marks as needed in the journals. (Actual posting to ledger accounts is not required.)

# Cumulative Coverage—Chapters 2 to 6 and Appendix C

Kassam Company has the following opening account balances in its general and subsidiary ledgers on January 1. All accounts have normal debit and credit balances. Kassam uses a perpetual inventory system. The cost of all merchandise sold was 40% of the sales price.

## GENERAL LEDGER

| Account No. | Account Title | January 1 Opening Balance |
|---|---|---|
| 101 | Cash | $ 35,050 |
| 112 | Accounts receivable | 14,000 |
| 115 | Notes receivable | 39,000 |
| 120 | Merchandise inventory | 20,000 |
| 125 | Office supplies | 1,000 |
| 130 | Prepaid insurance | 2,000 |
| 140 | Land | 50,000 |
| 145 | Building | 100,000 |
| 146 | Accumulated amortization—building | 25,000 |
| 157 | Equipment | 6,450 |
| 158 | Accumulated amortization | 1,500 |
| 201 | Accounts payable | 36,000 |
| 275 | Mortgage payable | 125,000 |
| 301 | A. Kassam, capital | 80,000 |

| Accounts Receivable Subsidiary Ledger | | | Accounts Payable Subsidiary Ledger | |
|---|---|---|---|---|
| Customer | January 1 Opening Balance | | Creditor | January 1 Opening Balance |
| R. Draves | $1,500 | | Liazuk Co. | $10,000 |
| B. Jacovetti | 7,500 | | Mikush Bros. | 15,000 |
| S. Kysely | 5,000 | | Nguyen & Son | 11,000 |

Kassam's January transactions follow:

Jan.  3 Sold merchandise on credit to B. Soto $3,100, invoice no. 510, and J. Ebel $1,800, invoice no. 511.

   5 Purchased merchandise from Welz Wares for $3,000 and Laux Supplies for $2,700.

   7 Received cheques for $5,000 from S. Kysely and $2,000 from B. Jacovetti on accounts.

   8 Paid freight on merchandise purchased, $180.

   9 Sent cheques to Liazuk Co. for $10,000 and Nguyen & Son for $11,000 in full payment of accounts.

   9 Issued credit memo for $400 to J. Ebel for merchandise returned. The merchandise was restored to inventory.

  10 Summary cash sales totalled $16,500.

  11 Sold merchandise on credit to R. Draves for $1,900, invoice no. 512, and to S. Kysely for $900, invoice no. 513.

  15 Withdrew $2,000 cash for A. Kassam's personal use.

  16 Purchased merchandise from Nguyen & Son for $15,000, from Liazuk Co. for $13,900, and from Welz Wares for $1,500.

  17 Paid $400 cash for office supplies.

  18 Returned $500 of merchandise to Liazuk and received credit.

  20 Summary cash sales totalled $17,500.

  21 Issued $15,000 note to Mikush Bros. in payment of balance due. The note bears an interest rate of 10% and is due in three months.

Jan.  21  Received payment in full from S. Kysely.
      22  Sold merchandise on credit to B. Soto for $1,700, invoice no. 514, and to R. Draves for
          $800, invoice no. 515.
      23  Sent cheques to Nguyen & Son and Liazuk Co. in full payment of accounts.
      25  Sold merchandise on credit to B. Jacovetti for $3,500, invoice no. 516, and to J. Ebel
          for $6,100, invoice no. 517.
      27  Purchased merchandise from Nguyen & Son for $14,500, from Laux Supplies for
          $1,200, and from Welz Wares for $2,800.
      28  Paid $800 cash for office supplies.
      31  Summary cash sales totalled $19,920.
      31  Paid salaries of $6,900.
      31  Received payment in full from B. Soto and J. Ebel on account.

*Instructions*

(a) Record the January transactions in the appropriate journal—sales, purchases, cash receipts,
    cash payments, and general.
(b) Post the journals to the general and subsidiary ledgers. New accounts should be added and
    numbered in an orderly fashion as needed.
(c) Prepare an unadjusted trial balance at January 31, 2005. Determine whether the subsidiary
    ledgers agree with the control accounts in the general ledger.
(d) Prepare adjusting journal entries. Prepare an adjusted trial balance, using the following
    additional information:

    1. Office supplies at January 31 total $700.
    2. Insurance coverage expires on September 30, 2005.
    3. Annual amortization on the building is $6,000 and on the equipment is $1,500.
    4. Interest of $45 has accrued on the note payable.
    5. A physical count of merchandise inventory has found $44,850 of goods on hand.

(e) Prepare a multiple-step income statement and a statement of owner's equity for January,
    and a classified balance sheet at the end of January.
(f) Prepare and post the closing entries.
(g) Prepare a post-closing trial balance.

# Company Index

A cumulative index appears at the end of each Part.

# Subject Index

A cumulative index appears at the end of each Part.

# Photo Credits

All images copyright © 2001 Photodisc Inc., unless otherwise noted.
Logos are registered trademarks of the respective companies and are reprinted with permission.

Chapter 1
OPENER: The Forzani Group Ltd. Page 5: © Taxi/Getty Images. Page 23: © Photodisc/Getty Images. Page 44: Corel Corporation logo is a trademark of Corel Corporation Limited.

Chapter 2
OPENER: Sweet Factory/Monsieur Félix & Mr. Norton. Page 57: Toronto Blue Jays Baseball Club. Page 65: The Goodyear Tire & Rubber Co.

Chapter 3
OPENER: Seneca College of Applied Arts & Technology. Page 117: © Corbis Digital Stock.

Chapter 4
OPENER: Moulé. Page 166: © Corbis Digital Stock.

Chapter 5
OPENER: Mountain Equipment Co-op. Page 235: © Photodisc/Getty Images.

Chapter 6
OPENER: College of the North Atlantic.

Chapter 7
OPENER: Lori Kays photograph courtesy of Barrett & MacKay Photography Inc. Page 346: Bank of Montreal. Page 348: Scotiabank.